Lecture Notes in Computer Science 4158

Commenced Publication in 1973
Founding and Former Series Editors:
Gerhard Goos, Juris Hartmanis, and Jan van Leeuwen

T0180662

Laurence T. Yang   Hai Jin
Jianhua Ma   Theo Ungerer (Eds.)

Autonomic and Trusted Computing

Third International Conference, ATC 2006
Wuhan, China, September 3-6, 2006
Proceedings

 Springer

Volume Editors

Laurence T. Yang
St. Francis Xavier University, Department of Computer Science
Antigonish, NS, B2G 2W5, Canada
E-mail: lyang@stfx.ca

Hai Jin
Huazhong University of Science and Technology
School of Computer Science and Technology
Wuhan, 430074, China
E-mail: hjin@hust.edu.cn

Jianhua Ma
Hosei University, Faculty of Computer and Information Sciences
3-7-2, Kajino-cho, Koganei-shi, Tokyo 184-8584, Japan
E-mail: jianhua@k.hosei.ac.jp

Theo Ungerer
University of Augsburg, Institute of Informatics
Eichleitnerstr. 30, 86159 Augsburg, Germany
E-mail: Theo.Ungerer@informatik.uni-augsburg.de

Library of Congress Control Number: 2006931402

CR Subject Classification (1998): D.2, C.2, D.1.3, D.4, E.3, H.4, K.6

LNCS Sublibrary: SL 2 – Programming and Software Engineering

ISSN	0302-9743
ISBN-10	3-540-38619-X Springer Berlin Heidelberg New York
ISBN-13	978-3-540-38619-3 Springer Berlin Heidelberg New York

Springer is a part of Springer Science+Business Media

springer.com

© Springer-Verlag Berlin Heidelberg 2006
Printed in Germany

Typesetting: Camera-ready by author, data conversion by Scientific Publishing Services, Chennai, India
Printed on acid-free paper   SPIN: 11839569   06/3142   5 4 3 2 1 0

Preface

Welcome to the proceedings of the Third International Conference on Autonomic and Trusted Computing (ATC 2006) which was held in Wuhan and Three Gorges, China, September 3-6, 2006.

Computing systems including hardware, software, communication and networks are growing with ever increasing scale and heterogeneity, and becoming overly complex. The complexity is getting more critical along with ubiquitous permeation of embedded devices and other pervasive systems. To cope with the growing and ubiquitous complexity, autonomic computing focuses on self-manageable computing and communication systems that perform self-awareness, self-configuration, self-optimization, self-healing, self-protection and other self-ware operations to the maximum extent possible without human intervention or guidance.

Any autonomic system must be trustworthy to avoid the risk of losing control and to retain confidence that the system will not fail. Trust and/or distrust relationships in the Internet and pervasive infrastructure-based global computing exist universally in the course of dynamic interaction and cooperation of various users, systems and services. Trusted computing targets computing and communication systems as well as services that are available, predictable, traceable, controllable, assessable, sustainable, dependable, persist-able, security/privacy protect-able, etc. A series of grand challenges exist to achieve practical self-manageable autonomic systems with truly trustworthy services.

The ATC 2006 conference provided a forum for engineers and scientists in academia, industry, and government to address the most innovative research and development including technical challenges and social, legal, political, and economic issues, and to present and discuss their ideas, results, work in progress and experience on all aspects of autonomic and trusted computing and communications. ATC 2006 as a conference came from the First International Workshop on Trusted and Autonomic Ubiquitous and Embedded Systems (TAUES 2005) held in Japan, December, 2005, and the International Workshop on Trusted and Autonomic Computing Systems (TACS 2006) held in Austria, April, 2006.

There was a very large number of paper submissions (208), representing 18 countries and regions, not only from Asia and the Pacific, but also from Europe, and North and South America. All submissions were reviewed by at least three Program or Technical Committee members or external reviewers. It was extremely difficult to select the presentations for the conference because there were so many excellent and interesting submissions. In order to allocate as many papers as possible and keep the high quality of the conference, we finally decided to accept 57 papers for presentations, reflecting a 27% acceptance rate. We believe that all of these papers and topics not only provided novel ideas, new results, work in progress and state-of-the-art techniques in this field, but also stimulated the future research activities in the area of autonomic and trusted computing and communications.

The exciting program for this conference was the result of the hard and excellent work of many others, such as Program Vice-Chairs, external reviewers, Program and Technical Committee members, and Publication Chairs under a very tight schedule. We are also grateful to the members of the Local Organizing Committee for supporting us in handling so many organizational tasks, and to the keynote speakers for accepting to come to the conference with enthusiasm. Last but not least, we hope you enjoy the conference program, and the beautiful attractions of Three Gorges, China.

Laurence T. Yang, Hai Jin, Jianhua Ma
Theo Ungerer, David Ogle
Manish Parashar, Kouichi Sakurai
ATC 2006 Steering, General and Program Chairs

Organization

ATC 2006 was organized and sponsored by Huazhong University of Science & Technology (HUST), co-sponsored by the National Science Foundation of China, 863, ChinaGrid, and International Federation for Information Processing (IFIP). It was held in cooperation with the IEEE Computer Society and *Lecture Notes in Computer Science* (LNCS) of Springer.

Executive Committee

Honorary Chairs:	Yunhe Pan, Zhejiang University, China
	Kishor S. Trivedi, Duke University, USA
General Chairs:	Hai Jin, Huazhong University of Science & Technology, China
	Theo Ungerer, University of Augsburg, Germany
	David Ogle, IBM, USA
Program Chairs:	Laurence T. Yang, St. Francis Xavier University, Canada
	Manish Parashar, Rutgers University, USA
	Kouichi Sakurai, Kyushu University, Japan
International Advisory Committee:	Chin-Chen Chang, Feng Chia University, Taiwan
	Zhong Chen, Peking University, China
	Petre Dini, Cisco Systems, USA
	Tadashi Dohi, Hiroshima University, Japan
	Minyi Guo, The University of Aizu, Japan
	Salim Hariri, University of Arizona, USA
	Janusz Kacprzyk, Polish Academy of Sciences, Poland
	Sy-Yen Kuo, National Taiwan University, Taiwan
	Franz J. Rammig, University of Paderborn, Germany
	A Min Tjoa, Vienna University of Technology, Austria
	Xinmei Wang, Xidian University, China
	Stephen S. Yau, Arizona State University, USA
Steering Chairs:	Jianhua Ma, Hosei University, Japan
	Laurence T. Yang, St. Francis Xavier University, Canada

Program Vice-Chairs: Xiaolin (Andy) Li, Oklahoma State University,
                        USA
                        Michael Smirnov, Fraunhofer Institute FOKUS,
                        Germany
                        Bin Xiao, Hong Kong Polytechnic University,
                        China

Publicity Chairs: Emmanuelle Anceaume, IRISA, France
                        Silvia Giordano, University of Applied Science,
                        Switzerland
                        Xiaobo Zhou, University of Colorado at
                        Colorado Springs, USA

International
Liaison Chairs: Leonard Barolli, Fukuoka Institute of Technology,
                        Japan
                        Andrzej Goscinski, Deakin University, Australia
                        Indrakshi Ray, Colorado State University,
                        USA

Publication Chairs: Tony Li Xu, St. Francis Xavier University,
                        Canada
                        Yuanshun Dai, Indiana University-Purdue
                        University, USA
                        Maria S. P.-Hernandez, University Politecnica de
                        Madrid, Spain
                        Deqing Zou, Huazhong University of Science &
                        Technology, China

Award Chairs: Jingde Cheng, Saitama University, Japan
                        Antonino Mazzeo, Second University of Naples,
                        Italy
                        Mazin Yousif, Intel Corporation, USA

Panel Chair: Roy Sterritt, University of Ulster at Jordanstown,
                        UK

Financial Chair: Xia Xie, Huazhong University of Science &
                        Technology, China

Web Chairs: Deqing Zou, Huazhong University of Science &
                        Technology, China
                        Tony Li Xu, St. Francis Xavier University,
                        Canada

Local Organizing Chair: Xia Xie, Huazhong University of Science &
                        Technology, China

Program/Technical Committee

Jemal Abawajy   Deakin University, Australia
Kemal Bicakci   Vrije University, The Netherlands

Raouf Boutaba   University of Waterloo, Canada
Fabian E. Bustamante   Northwestern University, USA
Roy Campbell   University of Illinois at Urbana-Champaign,
                                    USA
Xiaowen Chu   Hong Kong Baptist University, China
Falko Dressler   University of Erlangen, Germany
Schahram Dustdar   Vienna University of Technology, Austria
Torsten Eymann   University of Bayreuth, Germany
Pascal Felber   University of Neuchatel, Switzerland
Noria Foukia   University of Otago, New Zealand
Roy Friedman   Technion - Israel Institute of Technology,
                                    Israel
Sachin Garg   Avaya Labs, USA
Swapna Gokhale   University of Connecticut, USA
Kathleen Greenaway   Queen's University, Canada
Johann Groszschaedl   Graz University of Technology, Austria
Dong-Guk Han   Korea University, Korea
Naohiro Hayashibara   Tokyo Denki University, Japan
Yanxiang He   Wuhan University, China
Valerie Issarny   INRIA, France
Hiroaki Kikuchi   Tokai University, Japan
Dan Jong Kim   Michigan State University, USA
Seungjoo Kim   Sungkyunkwan University, Korea
Sandeep Kulkarni   Michigan State University, USA
Fang-Yie Leu   Tunghai University, Taiwan
Kuan-Ching Li   Providence University, Taiwan
Zhitang Li   Huazhong University of Science &
                                    Technology, China
Alex Zhaoyu Liu   University of North Carolina at
                                    Charlotte, USA
Zakaria Maamar   Zayed University, UAE
Mark Manulis   Ruhr University of Bochum, Germany
Wenbo Mao   HP Laboratories, China
Jean-Philippe Martin-Flatin   Université du Québec à Montréal, Canada
Rodrigo de Mello   University of Sao Paulo, Brazil
Refik Molva   EURECOM, France
Alberto Montresor   University of Bologna, Italy
Yi Mu   University of Wollongong, Australia
Christian Muller-Schloer   University of Hannover, Germany
Maurice Mulvenna   University of Ulster, UK
Dimitris Nikolopoulos   College of William and Mary, USA
Huw Oliver   Ericsson, Ireland
Jeong-Hyun Park   ETRI, Korea
Joon S. Park   Syracuse University, USA
Gerard Parr   University of Ulster, Northern Ireland
Fernando Pedone   University of Lugano (USI), Switzerland

Additional Reviewers

Table of Contents

Keynote Speech

Track 1: Autonomic/Organic Computing and Communications

Track 2: Trust Models and Trustworthy Systems/Services

Track 3: Cryptography, Security and Privacy

Track 4: Reliability, Fault Tolerance and Dependable Systems

Emergence in Organic Computing Systems: Discussion of a Controversial Concept

Christian Müller-Schloer[1] and Bernhard Sick[2]

[1] Institute for Systems Engineering – System and Computer Architecture
University of Hannover, Appelstrasse 4, 30167 Hannover, Germany
cms@sra.uni-hannover.de
[2] Faculty of Computer Science and Mathematics – Institute of Computer Architectures
University of Passau, Innstrasse 33, 94032 Passau, Germany
bernhard.sick@uni-passau.de

Abstract. Philosophy of mind has investigated the emergent behavior of complex systems for more than a century. However, terms such as "weak" or "strong" emergence are hardly applicable to intelligent technical systems. Organic Computing has the goal to utilize concepts such as emergence and self-organization to build complex technical systems. At first glance this seems to be a contradiction, but: These systems must be reliable and trustworthy! In order to measure, to control, and even to design emergence, a new notion or definition of emergence is needed. This article first describes the definition of emergence as used in philosophy of mind because this definition is often misunderstood or misinterpreted. Then, some very recent approaches for definitions of emergence in more or less technical contexts are discussed from the viewpoint of Organic Computing. The article concludes with some new thoughts that may help to come to a unifying notion of emergence in intelligent technical systems.

1 Introduction

Organic Computing (OC) has emerged recently as a challenging vision for future information processing systems, based on the insight that we will soon be surrounded by systems with massive numbers of processing elements, sensors, and actuators, many of which will be autonomous. Due to the complexity of these systems it will be infeasible to monitor and control them entirely from external observations; instead they must monitor, control, and adapt themselves. To do so, these systems must be aware of themselves and their environment, communicate, and organize themselves in order to perform the actions and services required. The presence of networks of intelligent systems in our environment opens up fascinating application areas but, at the same time, bears the problem of their controllability. Hence, we have to construct these systems – which we increasingly depend on – as robust, safe, flexible, and trustworthy as possible. In particular, a strong orientation towards human needs as opposed to a pure implementation of the technologically possible seems absolutely central. In order to achieve these goals, our intelligent technical systems must act more independently, flexibly, and autonomously. That is, they must exhibit life-like (organic) properties. Hence, an *Organic Computing System* is a technical system, which adapts dynamically to the current

L.T. Yang et al. (Eds.): ATC 2006, LNCS 4158, pp. 1–16, 2006.
© Springer-Verlag Berlin Heidelberg 2006

conditions of its environment. It will be self-organizing, self-configuring, self-healing, self-protecting, self-explaining, and context-aware. OC goes beyond Autonomic Computing by studying the mechanisms of self-organized emergence in technical systems and finding methods to control and direct it.

The vision of OC and its fundamental concepts arose independently in different research areas such as Neuroscience, Molecular Biology, and Computer Engineering. Self-organizing systems have been studied for quite some time by mathematicians, sociologists, physicists, economists, and computer scientists, but so far almost exclusively based on strongly simplified artificial models. Central aspects of OC systems are inspired by an analysis of information processing in biological systems. Within short time, OC became a major research activity in Germany and worldwide [1][1].

A key issue of OC is the technical utilization of *emergence* and *self-organization* as observed in natural systems. Emergent and self-organizing behavior has been observed in nature, demonstrated in a variety of computer-simulated systems in artificial life research, and also utilized in highly complex technical systems (such as the Internet) where it sometimes has led to unexpected global functionality.

In philosophy of mind, the *emergent* behavior of more or less complex systems has been investigated for more than a hundred years. Today, it turns out that phenomena that are interesting in OC or related fields such as autonomic or proactive computing and phenomena that are interesting in philosophy of mind require very different terms and definitions. For example, a question studied in philosophy of mind is: Why and how does *experience* arise? In organic computing we are interested in self-organization, for instance: How can new and *unexpected behavior* of a team of robots be characterized, measured, and / or controlled?

Certainly, if we want to control emergence, we have to answer some other questions first (cf. [2]), for example:

1. What are the underlying principles of emergence?
2. How can we define emergence within the contect of OC?
3. How can we model emergence?
4. What are pre-conditions for emergence to occur?
5. How can we measure emergence?
6. What are the limits of emergence?

In this article, we begin to answer these questions; the focus will be on various definitions of emergence. Initially, we will take a look at various historical, philosophical definitions or notions of emergence and discuss whether they could be useful for us (Section 2). Then, some very recent definitions of emergence that could be appropriate for OC are analysed in Section 3. We have selected publications (authored by STEPHAN, DE WOLF and HOLVOET, FROMM, ABBOTT, and MNIF and MÜLLER-SCHLOER, the first author of this article) that have a close relationship to intelligent technical systems. They all appeared in 2005 or 2006. We assess all these suggestions and alternatives from the viewpoint of OC and set out some new thoughts that may help to come to a unifying notion of emergence in the field of Organic Computing (Section 4).

---

[1] The URLs of the OC Websites are http://www.organic-computing.de/SPP and http://www.organic-computing.org.

2   Emergentism in Philosophy of Mind

Philosophy of mind provides terms such as "weak emergentism" and "strong emergentism" that well be analysed from the viewpoint of OC in this section (see [3] for a comprehensive and detailed review of emergentism).

2.1   Weak Emergentism

Weak emergentism is based on the following three theses: the thesis of physical monism, the thesis of systemic (collective) properties, and the thesis of synchronous determinism. Weak emergentism is termed to be the basis for higher grades of emergentism – those could be defined by adding new requirements (theses).

The *thesis of physical monism* restricts the type of components of complex systems with emergent properties. Basically, it says: "All systems – including those systems that have emergent properties – consist of physical entities." In particular, it means that there are no supernatural influences. This thesis has certainly some historical importance (cf. the debate vitalism vs. mechanism).

The *thesis of systemic (collective) properties* characterizes the type of properties that are candidates for being termed emergent properties. Essentially, it says: "Emergent properties are collective (systemic), i.e., the system as a whole has this property but single components do not have properties of this type." Often, this sentence is cited this way: "The whole is more than the sum of its parts." But the meaning of these two sentences is significantly different; the former has much stronger requirements.

The *thesis of synchronous determinism* specifies the relation between the "micro-structure" of a system and its emergent properties. It says: "The emergent properties of a system depend on its structure and the properties of its components in a nomological way". In particular, it says that there is no difference in systemic properties without changes in the structure of the system or changes of the properties of the components.

Examples for systems that have emergent properties in (at least) a weak sense are:

- *Artificial Neural Networks*: Combinations of simple nodes and connections can be used for pattern matching problems;
- *Mineralogy*: Carbon atoms build up materials of different hardness – a property that cannot be assigned to a single atom – depending on the type of the crystal lattice (e.g. graphite vs. diamond);
- *Electronics*: Components such as a resistor, an inductor, and a capacitor build a resonant circuit (cf. Figure 1);
- *Artificial Life*: Swarms of artificial animals, e.g. birds (boids) that are able to avoid obstacles;
- *Robotics*: Robots play soccer or build heaps of collected items (cf. Figure 2).

We observe that in many of these examples, terms at the component level are not sufficient to describe properties that arise at the system level, for example: Rules, patterns, classes are terms that are not used at the level of synapses or neurons (artificial or not). Resonant frequency and damping factor are not used at the level of single electrical components. Hardness and temperature are properties which single atoms in isolation

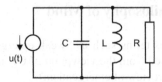

Fig. 1. Resonant circuit as an example for weak emergence: The electrical circuit consists of a resistor (R), an inductor (L), and a capacitor (C). Resonant frequency and damping factor are properties of the overall circuit, they cannot be attributed to any of its components.

(a) Initial configuration (five robots and items)   (b) Clusters of items after 30 minutes

Fig. 2. A team of robots building heaps of items as an example for weak emergence: The robots can have two states – obstacle avoidance or item carrying – depending on values of proximity sensors (images are taken from [4])

do not have. Are there cases where the same terms can be used at the two levels? For example: The weight of a car is the sum of the weights of its components. In this case, however, the thesis of systemic (collective) properties claims that single components do not have properties of the same type as the overall system.

Comment

From the viewpoint of OC, the thesis of physical monism is somehow self-evident – we are always considering artificial systems explainable on the basis of physical laws. The thesis of systemic (collective) properties seems to be a very important, necessary requirement. It is obvious that many intelligent technical systems have such systemic properties. The thesis of synchonous determinism certainly describes a necessary pre-condition. Otherwise, we would admit supernatural influences. Altogether, we can state that from our viewpoint the thesis of systemic properties is definitely most important. We also should state explicitly that the sentence "The whole is more than the sum of its parts." does not define weak emergence – there must be some new property at the system level. From the viewpoint of OC weak emergence is certainly a necessary pre-condition, but not sufficient. There are many intelligent technical systems that are emergent in this weak sense but their emergent properties are not really interesting.

2.2   Strong Emergentism

In philosophy of mind, a notion of emergence that adds very stringent requirements to weak emercenge is called *strong emergence*. Strong emergentism (synchronous emergentism) is based on the so-called thesis of irreducibility and it can be regarded as the "highest" grade of emergentism.

The *thesis of irreducibility* addresses the question why a system has a certain property. A *reductive explanation* aims at explaining properties of a system by using descriptions of components of a system, their properties, their arrangement, etc. Here are two examples where we do not have an emergent behavior in a strong sense because we can explain the behavior: The weight of a car is the sum of the weights of its component parts (trivial; this is not emergent even in a weak sense). The car's drivability in curves can be determined knowing many properties of component parts and their interactions (difficult). The thesis of irreducibility basically says: "A systemic property of a system is irreducible if one of the following conditions hold:

- As a matter of principle, it does not arise from the behavior, the properties, and the structure of components.
- As a matter of principle, it does not arise from the properties that the components show either in isolation or in other configurations."

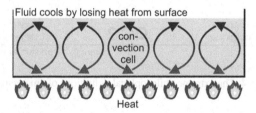

Fig. 3. BÉNARD's experiment as a counter-example for strong emergence: If the temperature at the bottom plane is increased, something dramatic happens in the fluid: convection cells appear. The microscopic random movement becomes ordered at a macroscopic level.

Many systems that OC people call emergent are certainly not emergent in this strong sense. Examples are:

- *Artificial Neural Networks*: Pattern recognition capabilities can be explained knowing a network architecture, weights of connections, etc.;
- *Artificial Life*: Swarm behavior of boids can be explained knowing some simple interaction rules, e.g. "avoid collisions", "adapt your velocity to your neighbors velocity", or "stay in in the neighborhood of other boids";
- *Electronics*: The behavior of a resonant circuit can be explained by means of differential equations;
- *Dissipative structures*: The movement of water in form of rolls (convection cells) is optimal with respect to energy (BÉNARD's experiment, cf. Figure 3).

Comment

From the viewpoint of philosophy of mind, strong emergence may be a necessary definition. From the OC viewpoint there is often simply a so-called *explanatory gap*. Possible reasons are: We do either not have the knowledge to explain expected behavior in advance or we did not specify the components or systems that we investigate in a sufficiently detailed way. As an intermediate result we can state: "The macro behavior of a system can in principal not be explained knowing the micro behavior of components, their interaction rules etc." is strong emergence. From the OC viewpoint this notion of strong emergence does not help because in general, artificial systems are not emergent in a stong sense. We always assume that they follow the laws of nature even when our software shows some completely unexpected behavior, for instance. It is mind-boggling, however, whenever very complex behavior on the system level follows from very simple rules of the components level or the like.

3   Novel Definitions of Emergence

From the viewpoint of OC, traditional, philosophical definitions of emergence are either too weak or too stong. The former means that too many systems are termed emergent, the latter implies that almost no artifical (technical) systems are emergent (cf. Figure 4). However, it makes sense not to neglect historical philosophical approaches.

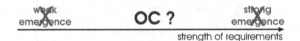

Fig. 4. The extreme philosophical definitions of emergence

We certainly need a new technical-oriented notion of emergence (somehow weak emergence + ε) possibly depending on the type of organic systems we investigate and the type of questions we ask. Again, there have been various attempts in the past which are worth looking at. In the following, we will therefore set out some alternative notions of emergence that may be important from one viewpoint and useless from another.

3.1   Achim Stephan's Definition Alternatives

In his work on emergentism [5], STEPHAN suggests a few alternative definitions of emergence that may be very valuable from the OC viewpoint. They all add some stronger requirements to the notion of weak emergence as described above. The suggestions are partly based on earlier work by CLARK, STEELS, BEDAU, and others.

The first alternative is to see emergence as a consequence of *collective self-organization*. The reason is that in many cases, interesting properties at the system level (e.g. certain communication patterns) are realized by an interaction of identical or very similar (and often simple) components. Examples are systems that behave such as ant colonies or bird swarms.

As a second alternative, STEPHAN suggests to define emergence as a consequence of *non-programmed functionality*. The reason is that many systems, which interact with their environment, show a certain goal-oriented, adaptive behavior that is not a result of dedicated control processes or explicit programming. A typical example is a robot creating heaps of items by following very simple, local rules only addressing the way of movement (e.g., „change direction whenever load is too high").

The third alternative is to see emergence as a consequence of *interactive complexity*. Here is the rationale that many interesting systemic properties, patterns, or processes are the result of a complex (cyclic or not) interaction of components. An example is a dynamic sensor network in which nodes exchange descriptive and / or functional knowledge with automomously chosen partners at any point in time they want in a self-organizing way (see Figure 5).

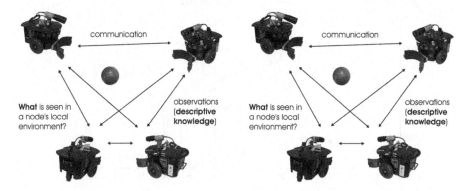

(a) Robots exchange descriptive knowledge that describes what is seen in their local environment

(b) Robots exchange functional knowledge that describes how to interpret these observations and how to react

Fig. 5. Knowledge exchange within a team of robots (or, alternatively, in a sensor network or a multi-agent system) as an example for emergence in the sense of interactive complexity (cf. [6]): Robots decide when, with whom, and what kind of knowledge is exchanged. Therefor, they must be equipped with self-awareness and environment-awareness capabilities.

The fourth alternative describes emergence in the sense of *incompressible development*. The idea is that a system is called emergent if a macrostate of that system with a certain microdynamic can be derived from the microdynamics and the system's external conditions but only by simulation. This definition of emergence is based on an analysis of cellular automata (cf. CONWAY's game of life).

The fifth alternative is to define emergence in the sense of *structure-unpredictability*. There are many systems where the formation of new properties, patterns, or structures follows the laws of *deterministic chaos* and where it is unpredictable in this sense. Examples are certain population models (see Figure 6), recurrent neural networks, or BÉNARD's experiment.

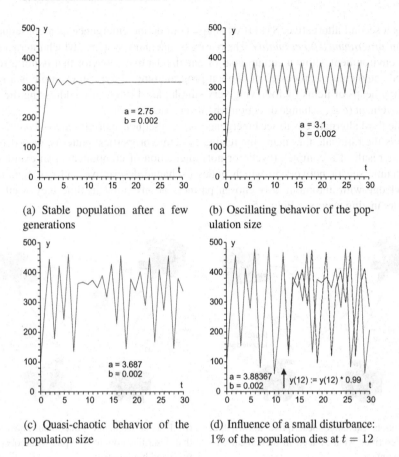

(a) Stable population after a few generations

(b) Oscillating behavior of the population size

(c) Quasi-chaotic behavior of the population size

(d) Influence of a small disturbance: 1% of the population dies at $t = 12$

Fig. 6. Population model as an example for emergence in the sense of unpredictability (cf. [7]): The population size is described by the formula $y(t) := a \cdot y(t-1) - b \cdot a \cdot y(t-1)^2$ with $y(0) := 100$ as starting point

Comment

All these types of emergence actually occur in intelligent technical systems. In particular, emergence due to collective self-organization covers a large class of OC systems. There are also first attempts to measure this kind of emergence (cf. Section 3.5). Emergence as a consequence of interactive complexity is very interesting from the viewpoint of OC when this interaction is adaptive, nonlinear, and temporally asynchronous, when it takes place at multiple levels, or when it is realized with various types of feedback. However, measurement is certainly very difficult in this case. An important observation is that it depends on the type of the posed question which of those definitions of emergence one should use! As an example, consider BÉNARD's experiment again: For example, the notion of emergence in the sense of collective self-organization could be used when one is interested in the fact that the water moves in an ordered way. The notion of emergence in the sense of structure-unpredictability could be more appropriate when one is interested in the direction of the circular movement at a certain point in the vessel. Also, we can state that these various types of emergence are not ordered according to a "degree" of emergence (cf. Section 3.2, for instance). One important question that arises now is whether it is possible to get along with a single definition of emergence that is "sufficient" from the viewpoint of OC.

3.2 Jochen Fromm's Emergence Classes

In [8], FROMM aims at providing a comprehensive classification and universal taxonomy of the key types and forms of emergence in multi-agent systems (see also [2,9]). The ultimate goal is to develop new forms of complex and robust systems. His suggestions are based on a thorough analysis of related work.

Table 1. Major Types of Emergence according to FROMM [8]

Type	Name	Roles	Predictability	System
I	Nominal (intentional or unintentional)	Fixed	Predictable	Closed, with passive components
II	Weak	Flexible	In principle predictable	Open, with active components
III	Multiple	Fluctuating	Not predictable (or chaotic)	Open, with multiple levels
IV	Strong	New world of roles	In principle not predictable	New or many levels

The following (somehow recursive) definition is used as a starting point: "A property of a system is emergent, if it is not a property of any fundamental element, and emergence is the appearance of emergent properties and structures on a higher level of organization or complexity." Explanation, reduction, prediction, and causation are mentioned as key issues to understand emergence. Table 1 shows the major types of emergence according to [8] (additional subtypes are mentioned for the types I, II, and III). The table summarizes the names of those types of emergence, the roles of components involved, the predictability of emergent behavior, and the properties of the system showing this emergence. In some more detail, the four types or classes of emergence (nominal, weak, multiple, and strong) can be described as follows:

1. Class I deals with *nominal emergence* that is either intended or not. An example for the first case is the planned function of a machine which is an emergent property of the machine components. Properties of a (large) number of identical particles or molecules such as pressure or temperature are an example for the second case.
2. Class II comprises systems with top-down feedback that may lead to stable or instable forms of *weak emergence*. Examples are flocks of animals that interact directly (e.g. bird swarms) or animals that interact indirectly (e.g. ants interacting by pheromones). Forms of weak emergence can also be found in purely technical fields, e.g. emergent behavior due to self-organization in open source software projects.

3. Class III includes systems with multiple feedback, e.g. short-term and long-term feedback. An example for *multiple emergence* is the stock market with many feedback mechanisms yielding sometimes oscillating or chaotic behavior. Also, an ecological system with catastrophic events influencing evolution by accelerating adaptation is an example for this type of emergence.
4. Class IV contains systems exhibiting *strong emergence*. Strong emergence is "related to very large jumps in complexity and major evolutionary transitions". Thus, typical examples are the emergence of life on earth or the emergence of culture.

Comment

In contrast to the types of emergence set out by STEPHAN, those defined by FROMM seem to be ordered. The classes II and III may contain intelligent technical systems that are interesting from the viewpoint of OC. FROMM's definition of "weak" and "strong" differs from the definitions used in philosophy of mind. He explicitly states: "The term strong emergence is sometimes used to describe magic, unscientific or supernatural processes. This is apparently a wrong concept which must be modified." According to his definition a system must be termed strongly emergent if the emergent behavior cannot be explained within reasonable time. This reminds of cryptographic methods that are called secure when they cannot be outsmarted with reasonable computational effort. The definition of weak emergence requires a feedback mechanism.

3.3   Tom De Wolf's Relationship of Emergence and Self-organization

DE WOLF and HOLVOET discuss in [10] the meaning and relationship of the terms emergence and self-organization based on a comprehensive analysis of related work. In this article, a historic overview of the use of each concept as well as a working definition, that is compatible with the historic and current meaning of the concepts, is given. They introduce in their definition the term "emergent" (as noun) as a *result* of a process in contrast to the process itself, which leads to a certain macroscopic pattern: "A system exhibits emergence when there are coherent emergents at the macro-level that dynamically arise from the interactions between the parts at the micro-level. Such emergents are novel w.r.t. the individual parts of the system." Emergent are properties, behavior, structure, or patterns, for instance. Self-organization is defined as "... a dynamical and adaptive process where systems acquire and maintain structure themselves, without external control." Structure can be spatial, temporal, or functional.

Self-organization and emergence are seen as emphasizing different characteristics of a system. Both can, according to the authors, exist in isolation or together. A self-organizing system without emergence controls itself without external interference but lacks central properties of an emergent system such as radical novelty, micro-macro effect, flexibility with respect to the entities, and decentralized control. On the other hand, there are also systems exhibiting emergence without self-organization. An example given is "... a gas material that has a certain volume in space. This volume is an emergent property that results from the interactions (i.e. attraction and repulsion) between the individual particles. However, such a gas is in a stationary state. The statistical complexity remains the same over time, i.e. the particles can change place but the amount of structure remains the same. In this case, we have a system whose initial conditions are enough to exhibit emergent properties." But no self-organization capability is attributed to such a system (since it is stationary).

Finally, the authors discuss the combination of emergence and self-organization as a desired effect in order to be able to control complex systems. An example given is a large multi-agent system. They conclude: "Both phenomena can exist in isolation, yet a combination of both phenomena is often present in complex dynamical systems. In such systems, the complexity is huge, which makes it infeasible to impose a structure a priori: the system needs to self-organize. Also, the huge number of individual entities imposes a need for emergence."

Comment

While a separate discussion of the phenomena self-organization and emergence is definitely valuable, it is questionable whether emergence without self-organization is actually a relevant option from the viewpoint of OC. The gas in a stationary state has the system level property "temperature". According to the definitions used in philosophy of mind (cf. Section 2.1), this type of emergence is only weak; according to FROMM it is only nominal (cf. Section 3.2). DE WOLF's attempt to get by with a single definition of emergence that separates emergent from non-emergent behavior does not really help to characterize interesting emergent behavior in intelligent technical systems.

3.4   Russ Abbott's Explanation of Emergence

In his approach to explain emergence [11], ABBOTT defines emergence as a relationship between a phenomenon and a model, where a model is a collection of elements with certain interrelationships.

Central to ABBOTT's definition of emergence is the concept of *epiphenomena*. An epiphenomenon is defined "as a phenomenon that can be described (sometimes formally but sometimes only informally) in terms that do not depend on the underlying phenomena from which it emerges". An example is the BROWNian motion of molecules, a stochastic process which is a result of a collision of molecules. Then, a phenomenon is called emergent over a given model if it is epiphenomenal with respect to that model. That is, "all epiphenomena are emergent, and all emergent phenomena are epiphenomenal" and the two terms can be regarded as synonymous.

ABBOTT also discusses two kinds of emergence: *static emergence* and *dynamic emergence*. An emergent behavior is called static if its implementation does not depend in time. Thus, hardness as a property of a material (and not a property of isolated atoms) or the resonant frequency of a resonant circuit (and not of its components) could be attributed to this variety of emergence. In contrast an emergent behavior is regarded as dynamic if it is defined "in terms of how the model changes (or doesn't change) over some time". Typical examples are multi-agent systems, robotics, or BÉNARD's experiment. Dynamically emergent phenomena can additionally be subdivided into *non-stigmatic* dynamic phemomena and *stigmatic* dynamic phenomena. The former can be defined by means of continuous equations, the latter involves autonomous entities that may assume discrete states and interact with their environments. The example shown in Figure 5 could be assiged to this emergence class.

Comment

ABBOTT's definition is certainly quite broad. It includes all emergent properties that may be important from the viewpoint of OC, but it also includes many properties that may only be called "emergent" in a weak sense (cf. Section 2.1 and Section 3.2). However, the distinction of static and dynamic emergence is very interesting. In particular, stigmatic dynamic emergence is central to many OC systems.

3.5   Christian Müller-Schloer's Quantitative View of Emergence

According to the work of MÜLLER-SCHLOER and MNIF published in [12] it is necessary to to automate the recognition of emergent behavior to build self-organizing, intelligent technical systems. The goal is to build so-called *observer/controller architectures* with emergence detectors. They have the purpose to trigger certain actions within the system in order to avoid (*negative emergence*) or to strengthen (*positive emergence*) certain system behaviors.

It is the objective of their work to make emergent effects quantitatively treatable in a technical environment. Rather than starting from the existing definitions of emergence, the authors propose a notion of emergence based strictly on measurements. They concede that this definition leads to a more narrow definition of emergence excluding stronger requirements such as "principal unpredictability". In order to avoid confusion with already existing terms, this aspect of emergence is called *quantitative emergence*. Quantitative emergence is defined as the formation of order from disorder based on self-organizing processes. The proposed definition builds on SHANNON's information theory, in particular on the information-theoretical entropy. The following is a brief sketch of the idea, for details see [12].

There seem to be certain necessary ingredients for an observed phenomenon to be called "emergent": A large population of interacting elements (e.g. agents) without central control and hence based only on local rules leads to a macroscopic behavior with new properties not existent at the element level. This macroscopic pattern is perceived as structure or order. Although the resulting order is a necessary pre-condition for quantitative emergence, it is not sufficient. The definition requires that this order has developed without external intervention – i.e. in a self-organized way.

The meaning of order as perceived by a human observer is certainly ambiguous. For example, a homogeneous mixture of two liquids can be regarded as "orderly" (Figure 7, right). Applying the concept of thermodynamic entropy, however, will result in lower entropy (i.e. higher order) for the left example of Figure 7. Apparently, the measurement of order depends on the selection of certain attributes by the (human) observer. If we are interested in the spatial structure, we have to base our measurement on the positions of the molecules (Figure 7, left), if we are interested in homogeneity we can use the relative distances between the molecules (Figure 7, right). The emergence definition presented here is based on the statistical definition of entropy (which essentially can be explained as counting events or occurrences).

Fig. 7. Example of order perception: Both pictures of a glass containing a mixture of two liquids could be perceived as high order (left: more structure, right: more homogeneity) depending on the objective of the observer

The computation of the entropy of a system S with N elements e_i is done as follows:

1. Select an attribute A of the elements of S with discrete, enumerable values a_j.
2. Observe all elements e_i and assign a value a_j to each e_i. This step corresponds to a quantization.
3. Transform into a probability distribution (by estimating the probability by means of the relative frequency) over the attribute values a_j (i.e. a histogram) with p_j being the probability of occurrence of attribute a_j in the ensemble of elements e_i.
4. Compute the entropy H_A of attribute A according to SHANNON's definition

$$H_A := - \sum_{j=0}^{N-1} p_j \; \text{ld} \; p_j.$$

If the attribute values are equally distributed (all p_j are equal) the maximum entropy is obtained. Any deviation from the equal distribution will result in lower entropy values (i.e. higher order). In other words: The more structure is present (unequal distribution), the more order is measured. The unit of measurement is bit/element. Thus, the entropy value can be interpreted as the information content necessary to describe the given system S with regard to attribute A. A highly ordered system requires a simpler description than a chaotic one.

Entropy is not the same as emergence. Entropy decreases with increasing order while emergence should increase with order. Emergence is the result of a self-organizing process with an entropy value H_{start} and a lower entropy value H_{end}. Quantitative emergence is the difference H between the entropy at the beginning of this process and at the end: $H := H_{\text{start}} - H_{\text{end}}$. This definition must be refined in several ways. It is desirable to introduce an absolute reference point (chosen to be H_{max} for H_{start}) and to exclude effects of a change of abstraction level (i.e. entropy changes not due to self-organization) from the calculation (for details see [12]).

In [12], the authors also discuss the limitations of their approach: The definitions are not directly applicable if the macro phenomenon is totally different from the micro behaviors as seemingly in the case of the resonance frequency as an emergent property resulting from the interaction of a capacitor and an inductor. The quantitative definition of emergence is based on the assumption that emergent phenomena can be observed in terms of patterns (space and/or time) formed by large ensembles of elements. The resonance frequency of a resonant circuit does not constitute the emergent pattern but is rather a property of such a pattern. Order can also be determined in the time or frequency domain. Therefore, the above emergence definition could be applied to the resonance frequency example if the system behavior is observed after a Fourier analysis.

The authors admit that their model does not cover strong emergence as defined in philosophy of mind, which demands that emergence is a phenomenon principally unexplainable. They claim that "principal unexplainability" is a quite unscientific way of argument. To the contrary, it is proposed that only a quantifiable phenomenon resulting in a (self-organized) increase of order deserves to be accepted as emergence. If this definition is too restrictive, excluding some unexplainable emergent effects, the authors could accept that what is measured with the above method is "quantitative emergence" and constitutes a certain aspect of emergence meaningful in technical systems.

Comment

While the other publications aim at defining emergence from the viewpoint of its origins and mechanisms, MÜLLER-SCHLOER takes a different, very promising way: Emergence is seen from the viewpoint of measurement and analysis. However, the mechanisms of self-organization have certainly to be considered when appropriate attributes have to be defined, selected, and combined. It still must be shown, for example, how the following types of emergence could be quantified: emergence due to interactive complexity (STEPHAN, cf. Figure 5), multiple emergence (FROMM), or stigmatic dynamic emergence (ABBOTT). While this definition might not be satisfactory from the philosophical viewpoint, it seems to be – so far – all that can be practically used in a technical environment such as OC. However, definitions used in philosophy of mind should not be regarded as "unscientific" – it would be better to say that they are not sufficient from the viewpoint of engineering. Basically, the approach could perfectly coexist with the definitions of weak and strong emergence as set out in Section 2.

4   Conclusion

In technical systems, we want to "do" (design or allow) emergence but must, at the same time, keep it under control. This reminds of the following quotation (*The Sorcerer's Apprentice*, JOHANN WOLFGANG VON GOETHE, translation by EDWIN ZEYDEL 1955):

> *Ah, he comes excited.*
> *Sir, my need is sore.*
> *Spirits that I've cited*
> *My commands ignore.*

Is an emergent behavior of organic systems achieved by something that could be termed as a meet-in-the-middle approach?

– We specify systems in a way such that we can expect a certain kind of emergent behavior, e.g. by self-organization.

- Having some assumptions about the type of emergent behavior, we will be able to assess and to control it.

Emergence in intelligent technical systems actually must be "designed" in a certain sense! Consider the example of a robot collecting items (cf. Figure 2): When you investigate this system you expect that heaps of items will emerge. You would be very surprised if these items suddenly would start moving themselves, for instance. That is, the emergent behavior of organic systems must be achieved by a balanced approach where the emergent or creative processes are counteracted and kept within the desired boundaries by certain supervision and control mechanisms. If we specify systems in a way such that they show emergent behavior, we better have a clear understanding of the types and properties of emergence in order to control it safely.

We need a definition of emergence or a taxonomy of varieties of emergence applicable to intelligent technical systems. Weak emergence as defined in philosophy of mind may be the baseline; other requirements must be added. In this article, we have collected and juxtaposed certain recent ideas about types of emergence. We hope that this collection of ideas helps towards an agreeable solution. But we concede that we are not there yet. We can, however, state a few requirements we want to see fulfilled by such a common notion of emergence. This notion of emergence ...

- ... may coexist with the traditional definitions of weak and strong emergence used in philosophy of mind even if these notions are not sufficient for our purpose (too weak or too strong). We should not put them in question and change their well-known definitions. Rather, we have to sharpen the definition to be useful in the technical context.
- ... must be practically usable, i.e. technically realizable. Emergence must become measurable. We want either to distinguish emergent from non-emergent behavior or to determine a "degree" of emergence. Therefore, an analysis-oriented approach is mandatory.
- ... must definitely be objective, i.e. independent from the knowledge of the observer or the observation (measurement) techniques. This does not exclude, however, that different viewpoints of the observer – expressing his purpose of action – might result in different aspects of emergent behavior.
- ... should consider that emergence in technical systems is related to self-organization and hence to temporal development or processes (dynamic emergence in the sense of ABBOTT).

Certain types of emergence such as nominal emergence (FROMM) or static emergence (ABBOTT) are not interesting from the viewpoint of OC. In contrast, other types such as emergence due to interactive complexity (STEPHAN), multiple emergence (FROMM), or stigmatic dynamic emergence (ABBOTT) must be covered by an OC-related definition.

Certainly, we must avoid coming up with a fresh definition of emergence for each and every case. We observe that in the past the phenomenon of emergence has been discussed from a variety of viewpoints without converging to a generally accepted definition. We expect that the objective of a utilization of emergent effects in engineering will enforce such a solution. For this purpose, we suggest that

1. the candidate phenomena termed to be emergent are described in more detail, and
2. existing methods for the measurement of emergence are checked for their applicability, and if not appropriate new ones are developed.

The analysis of emergent phenomena must be based on scientific methods (i.e. well described and reproducible experiments). We must answer questions such as: What emerges (structure, properties etc.)? What influences the emergent behavior? At which time scale does it take place?

We expect that there will exist a variety of measures for different emergent phenomena and different system objectives, resulting in a collection of emergence "detectors". For each application we must determine the appropriate attributes that characterize emergence, e.g. measures for order, complexity, correlation, information flow.

Acknowledgements

We wish to thank Alcherio Martinoli for the permission to use the images of Figure 2.

References

1. Müller-Schloer, C.: Organic computing – on the feasibility of controlled emergence. In: IEEE/ACM/IFIP International Conference on Hardware/Software Codesign and System Synthesis (CODES+ISSS 2004), Stockholm. (2004) 2 – 5
2. Fromm, J.:   Ten questions about emergence (2005) (Technical Report; online: http://arxiv.org/abs/nlin.AO/0509049).
3. Stephan, A.: Emergenz: Von der Unvorhersagbarkeit zur Selbstorganisation. 2 edn. Mentis, Paderborn (2005)
4. Martinoli, A., Mondada, F.: Collective and cooperative group behaviors: Biologically inspired experiments in robotics. In Khatib, O., Salisbury, J.K., eds.: Experimental Robotics IV, The 4th International Symposium. Volume 223 of Lecture Notes in Control and Information Sciences. Springer (1997) 1 – 10
5. Stephan, A.: Zur Rolle des Emergenzbegriffs in der Philosophie des Geistes und in der Kognitionswissenschaft. In Sturma, D., ed.: Philosophie und Neurowissenschaften. Number 1770 in Taschenbuch Wissenschaft. Suhrkamp, Frankfurt am Main (2006) 146 – 166
6. Buchtala, O., Sick, B.: Techniques for the fusion of symbolic rules in distributed organic systems. In: Proceedings of the IEEE Mountain Workshop on Adaptive and Learning Systems (SMCals/06), Logan. (2006) 85 – 90
7. Cruse, H., Dean, J., Ritter, H.: Die Entdeckung der Intelligenz oder Können Ameisen denken? Deutscher Taschenbuch Verlag, München (2001)
8. Fromm, J.:   Types and forms of emergence (2005) (Technical Report; online: http://arxiv.org/abs/nlin.AO/0506028).
9. Fromm, J.: The Emergence of Complexity. Kassel University Press (2004)
10. De Wolf, T., Holvoet, T.: Emergence versus self-organisation: Different concepts but promising when combined. In Brueckner, S., Di Marzo Serugendo, G., Karageorgos, A., Nagpal, R., eds.: Engineering Self-Organising Systems, Methodologies and Applications. Number 3464 in Lecture Notes in Computer Science. Suhrkamp, Frankfurt am Main (2005) 1 – 15
11. Abbott, R.: Emergence explained: Getting epiphenomena to do real work (2005) (Technical Report; online: http://cs.calstatela.edu/abbott/).
12. Mnif, M., Müller-Schloer, C.: Quantitative emergence. In: Proceedings of the IEEE Mountain Workshop on Adaptive and Learning Systems (SMCals/06), Logan. (2006) 78 – 84

Managing Trust in Distributed Agent Systems

Stephen S. Yau

Department of Computer Science and Engineering
Arizona State University
Tempe, AZ 85287-8809, USA
yau@asu.edu

Abstract. Software agent technology has attracted much attention for developing various distributed systems, composed of autonomous agents interacting with one another using particular mechanisms and protocols. Such systems provide high-level reconfigurability, flexibility and robustness in dynamic environments, and have applications in many areas. However, the great advantages of distributed agent systems are often overshadowed by the challenges of providing flexible and consistent security management for agent interactions in the dynamic and heterogeneous computing environments. Trust, which is the belief of an agent that the other agent will act or intend to act beneficially, is a basis for secure distributed agent systems. In this paper, various major research issues of managing trust among various entities are identified, and the approaches in dealing with them are discussed. A framework for managing trust among various entities in distributed agent systems is presented.

Keywords: Distributed agent systems, trust, trust management, security, situation-awareness.

1 Introduction

With the rapid development of various types of open infrastructures, including Internet, Grid and wireless networks, distributed computing systems with a range of quality of service (QoS) requirements are widely built and deployed by integrating individual components or services over various networks. The recent directions of distributed computing systems, such as ubiquitous computing and situation-awareness [38,39], will enable us to interact with an intelligent environment at home/office, in shopping malls or while traveling in order to support commerce, entertainment or monitoring and even controlling your health.

Recently software agent technology [5,24,30,33] has attracted much attention for developing distributed intelligent systems, which are composed of autonomous agents interacting with one another using particular mechanisms and protocols. These autonomous agents act on behalf of their users and may migrate code and data from one host machine to another to perform tasks. Such distributed agent systems (DAS) provide high levels of concurrency, reconfigurability and flexibility and reduced communication costs in the dynamic distributed computing environments. They have applications in many areas, including collaborative research and development, healthcare, electronic commerce, disaster management and homeland security. However,

L.T. Yang et al. (Eds.): ATC 2006, LNCS 4158, pp. 17–25, 2006.
© Springer-Verlag Berlin Heidelberg 2006

the great advantages of distributed agent systems are often overshadowed by difficulties in ensuring flexible and consistent security in agent interactions in the dynamic and heterogeneous computing environments [22,35].

Existing "hard security" mechanisms, such as cryptographic algorithms and firewalls, assume complete certainty, and can only allow complete access or no access at all. Trust, as a particular level of belief of an agent that the other agent will act or intend to act beneficially, precludes uncertainty. Therefore, managing trust to ensure security to an acceptable level becomes an important and widely used 'soft' approach to tackling the security issues in distributed systems [1]. However, it is a challenging task to manage trust among various entities in the agent systems to contain the risk of damages from malicious agents or execution environments because we still have little knowledge on how to represent and evaluate trust value in agent systems, and trust values may be continuously changing. For example, a trustor may interact with a trustee which may totally unknown to the trustor at the beginning. As time goes on, the trustor's trust in the trustee is changing based on its knowledge of the trustee. Therefore, approaches to managing trust in distributed agent systems should be able to adapt to the dynamic and heterogeneous computing environments.

In this paper, the properties of trust and major research issues of managing trust in distributed agent systems will be first identified. The existing approaches to dealing with these issues will be discussed. Then, a framework for managing trust in distributed agent systems will be presented.

2   Trust in Distributed Agent Systems

As one of the fundamental challenges for the success of open distributed systems, trust has been studied in various contexts, such as decentralized access control [6,7,10,19], public key certification [9], and reputation systems for P2P networks [12,23,37]. However the notion of trust remains very vague and there is no consensus in the literature on what trust is and what constitutes trust management [16,29,36], although many researchers recognize the importance of trust [11,13,14]. In general, trust is a subjective and elusive concept relating to the belief in the honesty, truthfulness, competence, reliability, etc., of the trusted person or software agent. Based on the definitions of trust in distributed agent systems [11,14,31], we define *trust* as *a particular level of belief of an agent that the other agent will act or intend to act beneficially*. We call the former agent *trustor*, and the latter agent *trustee*. Therefore, the level of trust is affected by the actions performed or will be performed by the trustee and depended on how these actions affect the trustor's own actions. Thus, trust forms the basis for agents to make decisions on what to interact with, when to interact with, and how to interact with. [4,21,27,31].

A trust relationship between two agents is often not absolute and not symmetric [21]. A trustor only trusts a trustee with respect to specific actions within a specific context. An agent will never trust another agent to do any actions because it may choose to satisfy its selfish interests. Moreover, agent A's trust in agent B regarding the performance of an action is not usually the same as B's trust in A. The level of trust may be discrete or continuous. Discrete values, such as *high*, *medium* or *low*, may be sufficient for some simple systems, while other systems may need numeric qualifications for trust.

Managing trust in distributed agent systems involves the following two categories of trust relationships [16,31]:

1) *Managing trust relationships among agent execution environments and agents.* As an agent may roam on multiple machines, the trust relationship between the agent and each of the hosting machines needs to be established and managed such that the agent will not do something bad to the hosting machine, and at the same time the hosting machine will not modifying and stealing information contained in the agent.

2) *Managing trust relationships in the agent-to-agent interactions.* When multiple agents need to collaborate to complete a task, the problems of what, when and how the agents trust each other need to be solved.

Managing these trust relationships in distributed agent systems have the following major research issues:

a) *Evidence management.* What data to collect as trust evidences and how to efficiently store this data are related to the trust model of the system and have direct impact on the security, scalability and usability of the entire system. A flexible framework is needed to for uniformly specifying various forms of evidences.

b) *Lightweight trust decision making.* Techniques for analyzing trust evidences and making trust decisions should be efficient but general enough to cover the two different trust relationships.

c) *Secure interoperation in different domains.* An agent may roam in different security domains with different security policies and infrastructures. The system needs to manage trust relationships among agents from heterogeneous security domains.

d) *Usability.* Usability often represents a central requirement of trust management to be accepted by the public.

3   Current State of the Art on Trust Management

Existing approaches to managing trust can be classified in two categories: *credential-based trust management* [6,7,10,19,26] and *reputation-based trust management* [9,23,37]. These two categories of approaches have been developed in different environments with different assumptions, but address the same problem - establishing trust among interacting parties in distributed and decentralized systems. The credential-based approaches are for structured organizational environments and use certificate authorities as the source of trust. On the other hand, the reputation-based approaches address the unstructured user community, such as peer-to-peer systems, and use community opinions as the course of trust. Consequently, they employ different mechanisms to managing trust. We will discuss these in more detail in the following subsections:

3.1 Credential-Based Trust Management

As trust is a basis for access control, Blaze *et al.* defined the term *trust management*, as "a unified approach to specifying and interpreting security policies, credentials, and relationships that allow direct authorization of security-critical actions" [6]. The research focus of such credential-based approaches is on employing different policy languages and engines for specifying and reasoning the rules for trust establishment. The goal is to determine whether an agent can be trusted based on a set of credentials and a set of policies.

Several credential-based trust management systems, including PolicyMaker [6], KeyNote [7], and REFEREE [10], are developed based on the above concept. PolicyMaker directly specifies what a public key is authorized to do, and hence binds access rights to a public key in a single step instead of two steps as in the traditional certificate frameworks, such as X.509 [38] and GPG [15]. PolicyMaker [6] is essentially a query engine that checks whether a requested action and the credentials presented by the requestors comply with the local security policies. Security policies and credentials are written in an assertion language, selected by users. Keynote [7], the successor to PolicyMaker, uses the same design principles of assertions and queries, but includes some improvements, such as signature verification in query engine and the predefined assertion language, for ease of integration with applications. Both systems only address authorization based on public keys, instead of covering the comprehensive trust problem [16]. Based on PolicyMaker, REFEREE [10] is a trust management system for making access control decisions relating to Web documents. These three systems do not provide mechanisms to automatically collect missing certificates and do not support negative rules preventing access. Herzberg, Mass and Mihaeli [19] developed a trust management system based on an extended role-based access control model. This system "allows a business to define a policy to map accessed users to roles based on the certificates received from the user and collected automatically by the system". This system is similar to PolicyMaker, but permits negative rules.

Credential-based trust management systems are used to manage a static form of trust through "hard security" mechanisms, such as digital certificates and trusted certificate authorities for control the access of users to resources. Moreover, the trust decision is usually based on policies or credentials with well defined semantics providing strong verification and analysis support, such as the logical policy specification languages [18,20,25,26,34]. Hence, these approaches cannot overcome the limitations of "hard security" mechanisms, and can hardly address the problem of dynamic trust adapting to the changing situations in which the trust decision is made.

3.2 Reputation-Based Trust Management

Reputation-based trust management approaches have been proposed for managing trust in public key certificates [15], in P2P systems [9,23,37], and in Semantic Web [32]. These approaches rely on a "soft" approach to mitigating risks involved in interacting and collaborating with unknown and potentially malicious parties. In these approaches, the trust is typically decided based on the trustee's reputation. A reputation is an expectation about an agent's behavior based on information about or observations of its past behavior, such as local interaction experiences with the trustee and the recommendations given by other agents in the community (e.g., agents who have interaction experiences with the trustee). Therefore, the trust decision can be dynamically changed when the behavior history of the agents changes.

The major research issues for reputation-based trust management approaches are: 1) the trust metric [12,27] - how to model and evaluate the trust, and 2) the management of reputation data [3,37] - how to securely and efficiently retrieve and store the data required by the trust decision making process

As one of the early attempts at formalizing the trust, simple trust metrics based on linear equations are used in [28]. An extension of this work was presented by Abdul-Rahman and Hailes [2] to model the trust in virtual communities. In these approaches, simple formal constructs of the form T(a,b), which means "a trusts b", are used as the basis to model trust [2,28]. Based on this primitive construct, the features, such as temporal constraints and predicate arguments, are incorporated. Given these primitives, classical or modal logic connectives, trust rules are expressed in logic formulas. Properties of trust relationships, such as transitivity, can be defined and analyzed. Most of the existing reputation-based trust management approaches for P2P systems [9,23,37] followed the similar trust and reputation models.

Currently, the model for evaluating trust, which is based on the behavior history and/or recommendations is often application-specific and developed in an ad hoc manner. The level of expertise required to evaluating dynamic trust among agents for various applications are beyond the ability and resources available to the average system developers and security managers of distributed agent systems.

3.3 Integration of Credential-Based and Reputation-Based Trust Management Approaches

Trust management is broader than authorization or reputation management. As defined in [17], "trust management is the activity of collecting, encoding, analyzing and presenting evidence relating to competence, honesty, security or dependability with the purpose of making assessments and decisions regarding trust relationships". Both credentials and reputations are evidences related to competence, honesty, security or dependability of a trustee. Both credential-based and reputation-based trust management approaches have certain advantages and limitations when they are applied in various applications environments. A hybrid trust management approach [8] is motivated to combine credential-based trust with numerical trust estimates based on a large number of sources (e.g., agent community). Such a hybrid approach provides versatile trust management involving both structured organizational environments and unstructured user communities.

In distributed agent systems, a hybrid framework seems to be promising for managing different types of trust relationships. Such a framework should be able to specify security policies and requirements of trust evidence collection, collect trust evidence information, and make dynamic trust decisions in various situations. We define a *situation* as a set of contexts over a period of time that is relevant to future security-related actions. A *context* is any instantaneous, detectable, and relevant property of the environment, the system, or users, such as time, location, available bandwidth and a user's schedule [39,40].

4   A Framework to Managing Trust in Distributed Agent Systems

In this section, we will present an overview of our framework for managing dynamic trust in distributed agent systems. This framework will integrate reputation-based and credential-based trust management, and utilize our research results of situation-aware computing [39,40,42] to monitor and analyze evidences for making trust decisions. To improve the efficiency of trust decision making, security agents and situation-aware agents are generated for trust computation.

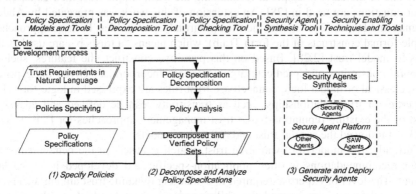

Fig. 1. Overview of our approach to managing trust among agents

As shown in Figure 1, the approach consists of the following three iterative steps:

1) *Specify trust policies.* This step generates policy specifications, including security policy specifications [41, 42] formally representing various security requirements of the systems and situation-awareness specifications [39, 40] for the trust decision making process.

2) *Decompose and analyze policy specifications.* In this step, a policy specification is first decomposed into multiple security agent and situation-aware agent specifications [43, 44]. Then, the properties of each security agent or situation-aware agent specification are verified, such as consistency and redundancy, to ensure that each agent specification can be correctly synthesized in a security agent or a situation-aware agent.

3) *Generate and deploy security agents.* Finally, security agents and situation-aware agents for making trust decisions are synthesized directly from the verified security agent specifications [43, 44]. Security agents are capable of making a trust decision based on the situational information collected from situation-aware agents and the security policies.

It is noted that the above three steps are iterated when security policy analysis detects errors or the security requirements have been changed.

These steps needs the following tool supports as identified in the dashed boxes in Figure 1. In Step (1), situation awareness [38, 39] and security policy specification models and tools are needed to facilitate the formalization of trust requirements. A set of trust reasoning rules is also needed for security agents [42] to make the trust decision based on the specified policies and their knowledge learned from other agents.

In Step (2), a distributed agent system can involve a large number of agents and very complex agent interactions, and hence may include many situation-aware security policies regarding the security of complex agent interactions over the network. To distribute the task of making trust decisions, and to achieve better manageability of the system, policies need to be decomposed into multiple small sets of policies. A *policy specification decomposition tool* is needed for facilitating the decomposition process. Moreover, a *policy checking tool* is provided for checking the properties of each security agent or situation-aware agent.

In Step (3), a *logic proof engine* is provided for synthesizing security agents and situation-aware agents from policy specifications in the form of logical formula [42]. *Enabling security techniques and tools*, such as encryption algorithms and mechanisms for generating credentials, will provide basic security functions needed in trust management. To collect system situational information required for security agents to make trust decisions, situation-awareness agents are also generated and deployed to collect context data and analyze situations.

Overall, using a logic-based and automated security and situation-awareness agent generation technique, this framework should provide an easy-to-use approach to managing trust in distributed agent systems.

5 Concluding Remarks

Trust is a fundamental concern in all interactions among the agents that have to operate in uncertain and dynamic environments. We have defined the trust in distributed agent systems, and discussed the existing approaches to managing trust in distributed systems. Most of these approaches are simplistic and not rigorous or complete enough to model distributed-agent systems. We have discussed a framework for generating security agents and situation-aware agents to efficiently establish and manage trust relationships in distributed agent systems.

Acknowledgment

The work presented here was partially supported by National Science Foundation, Grant No. IIS-0430565. The author would like to thank Yisheng Yao for numerous stimulating discussions during the preparation of this paper.

References

1. A. Abdul-Rahman and S. Hailes, "A distributed trust model," *Proc. 1997 workshop on New Security Paradigms*, 1997, pp. 48-60.
2. A. Abdul-Rahman and S. Hailes, "*Supporting Trust in Virtual Communities*," *Proc 33rd Annual Hawaii Int'l Conf. on System Sciences*, 2000, pp. 1-9.
3. K. Aberer and Z. Despotovic, "Managing trust in a peer-2-peer information system," *Proc. 10th Int'l Conf on Information and Knowledge Management*, 2001, pp. 310-317.
4. E. Amoroso *et al.*, "Toward an Approach to Measuring Software Trust," *IEEE Computer Society Symp. Research in Security and Privacy*, 1991, pp. 198-218.

5. J. Baumann, F. Hohl, K. Rothermel and M. Straber, "Mole– Concepts of a mobile agent system", *World Wide Web J.*, vol.1(3),1998, pp. 123-137.
6. M. Blaze, *et al.*, "The KeyNote Trust Management System (version 2)," *RFC2704*, 1999
7. M. Blaze, J. Feigenbaum, and M. Strauss, "Compliance Checking in the PolicyMaker Trust Management System," *Proc. 2nd Int'l Conf. of Financial Cryptography*, 1998, pp. 254-274.
8. P. Bonatti, C. Duma, D. Olmedilla, N. Shahmehri, "An Integration of Reputation-based and Policy-based Trust Management", *Semantic Web and Policy Workshop*, 2005, Available at http://cs.na.infn.it/rewerse/pubs/swpw05-rep.pdf
9. G. Caronni, "Walking the Web of Trust," *Proc IEEE 9th Int'l Workshops on Enabling Technologies: Infrastructure for Collaborative Enterprises (WET ICE'00)*, 2000, pp. 153-158.
10. Y. Chu, et al., "REFEREE: Trust Management for Web Applications." *World Wide Web Jour*, vol 2(3), 1997, pp. 127-139.
11. P. Dasgupta, "Trust as a commodity," In Gambetta, D. (ed.), *Trust: Making and Breaking Cooperative Relations*, Blackwell, pp. 49-72.
12. C. Duma, N. Shahmehri, and G. Caronni, "Dynamic trust metrics for peer-to-peer systems," *Proc. 2nd IEEE Workshop on P2P Data Management, Security and Trust*, 2005, pp.776-781.
13. N. M. Frank and L. Peters, "Building Trust: the importance of both task and social precursors," *Int'l Conf. on Engineering and Technology Management: Pioneering New Technologies - Management Issues and Challenges in the Third Millennium*, 1998, pp. 322-327.
14. D. Gambetta, "Can We Trust Trust?," In *Trust: Making and Breaking Cooperative Relations*, D. Gambetta (ed.). Basil Blackwell. Oxford, 1990, pp. 213-237.
15. S. Garfinkel, "PGP: Pretty Good Privacy," O'Reilly & Associates Inc., 1995.
16. T. Grandison and M. Sloman, "A survey of trust in internet applications," *IEEE Communications Society, Surveys and Tutorials*, vol. 3(4), 2000, pp. 2-16.
17. T. Grandison, *"Trust Management for Internet Applications,"* PhD thesis, Imperial College London, 2003.
18. J. Y. Halpern and V. Weissman, "Using first-order logic to reason about policies," *Proc. Computer Security Foundations Workshop*, 2003, pp. 187-201.
19. A. Herzberg, Y. Mass, and J. Mihaeli, "Access control meets public key infrastructure, or: Assigning roles to strangers," *Proc. IEEE Symp. on Security and Privacy*, 2000, pp. 2-14.
20. S. Jajodia, P. Samarati and V.S. Subrahmanian., "A logical language for expressing authorizations," *Proc. IEEE Symp$_o$ on Security and Privacy*, 1997, pp. 31-42.
21. A. Jøsang and S. J. Knapskog, "A Metric for Trusted Systems," *21st National Security Conf.*, 1998, http://www.idt.ntnuno/~ajos/papers.html
22. N. Karnik and A. Tripathi, "Security in the Ajanta mobile agent system," *Software -- Practice & Experience*, vol.31(4), 2001, pp. 301-329.
23. S. D. Kamvar, M. T. Schlosser, and H. Garcia-Molina, "Eigenrep: Reputation management in p2p networks," *Proc. 12th Int'l WWW Conference*, 2003, pp. 640–651.
24. D. Kotz and B. Gray, "Mobile agents and the future of the internet," *ACM Operating Systems Review*, vol. 33(3), 1999, pp. 7-13.
25. N. Li, B. N. Grosof, and J. Feigenbaum, "Delegation Logic: A logic-based approach to distributed authorization," *ACM Trans on Information and System Security (TISSEC)*, vol. 6(1), 2003, pp.128-171.
26. N. Li and J. Mitchell, "RT: A Role-Based Trust Management Framework," Proc. 3rd DARPA Info. Survivability Conf. and Exposition, 2003, pp. 201-212.
27. D. W. Manchala, "Trust Metrics, Models and Protocols for Electronic Commerce Transactions," *18th Int'l. Conf. Distributed Computing Systems*, 1998, pp. 312-321.
28. S. P. Marsh, "Formalising Trust as a Computational Concept," in *Computing Science and Mathematics*, University of Stirling, 1994, p. 170.

29. D.H. McKnight and N.L Chervany.: The Meanings of Trust. *Trust in Cyber-Societies - Lecture Notes in Artificial Intelligence*. Vol. 2246, 2001, pp. 27–54.
30. Object Management Group, "Mobile Agent Facility (MAF) Specification, Version 1.0", 2000, URL: http://www.omg.org/cgi-bin/doc?formal/2000-01-02
31. S. Ramchurn, D. Huynh, and N. R. Jennings, *"Trust in multiagent systems,"* Knowledge *Engineering Review*, vol. 19, 2004, pp.1-25.
32. M. Richardson, R. Agrawal and Pedro Domingos, "Trust Management for the Semantic Web," *Proc. 2nd Int'l Semantic Web Conference*, 2003, pp. 351-368.
33. Thomas, R.J.; Mount, T.D., "Using software agents to test electric markets and systems," *IEEE Power Engineering Society General Meeting, 2005*, 2005, pp. 2808- 2812
34. A. Uszok, et al, "KAoS policy and domain services: toward a description-logic approach to policy representation, deconfliction, and enforcement," *Proc. IEEE 4th Int'l Workshop on Policies for Distributed Systems and Networks (POLICY 2003)*, 2003, pp. 93-96.
35. U. G. Wilhelm, L. Butty`an, and S. Staamann, "On the problem of trust in mobile agent systems," *Symp. on Network and Distributed System Security*, 1998, pp. 114-124.
36. D. Xiu and Z. Liu, "A Formal Definition for Trust in Distributed Systems," *Lecture Notes in Computer Science*, Vol. 3650, 2005, pp. 482 - 489.
37. L. Xiong and L. Liu, "PeerTrust: Supporting Reputation-Based Trust for Peer-to-Peer Electronic Communities," *IEEE Trans. Knowl. Data Eng.* Vol. 16(7), 2004, pp.843-857.
38. The Public-Key Infrastructure (X.509) (pkix) Working Group of the Internet Engineering Task Force, http://www.ietf.org/html.charters/pkix-charter.html, accessed on June 1, 2006.
39. S. S. Yau, Y. Wang and F. Karim, "Development of Situation-Aware Application Software for Ubiquitous Computing Environments", *Proc. 26th IEEE Int'l Computer Software and Applications Conf*, 2002, pp. 233-238.
40. S. S. Yau, *at el*, "Reconfigurable Context-Sensitive Middleware for Pervasive Computing," *IEEE Pervasive Computing*, Vol. 1, No. 3, 2002, pp. 33-40.
41. S. S. Yau, Y. Yao and V. Banga, "Situation-Aware Access Control for Service-Oriented Autonomous Decentralized Systems", *Proc. 7th Int'l Symp. on Autonomous Decentralized Systems*, 2005, pp. 17-24.
42. S. S. Yau, D. Huang, H. Gong and Y. Yao, "Support for Situation-Awareness in Trustworthy Ubiquitous Computing Application Software", *Jour. Software: Practice and Engineering,* to appear.
43. S. S. Yau, *at el* "Automated Agent Synthesis for Situation-Aware Service Coordination in Service-based Systems", *Technical Report,* Arizona State University, August, 2005.
44. S. S. Yau and Y. Yao, "An Adaptable Distributed Trust Management Framework for Development of Secure Service-based Systems", *Jour. Autonomic and Trusted Computing (JoATC),* to appear.

Towards a Standards-Based Autonomic Context Management System*

Jadwiga Indulska, Karen Henricksen, and Peizhao Hu

School of Information Technology and Electrical Engineering,
The University of Queensland
and
National ICT Australia (NICTA)
{jaga, peizhao}@itee.uq.edu.au, Karen.Henricksen@nicta.com.au

Abstract. Pervasive computing applications must be sufficiently autonomous to adapt their behaviour to changes in computing resources and user requirements. This capability is known as context-awareness. In some cases, context-aware applications must be implemented as autonomic systems which are capable of dynamically discovering and replacing context sources (sensors) at run-time. Unlike other types of application autonomy, this kind of dynamic reconfiguration has not been sufficiently investigated yet by the research community. However, application-level context models are becoming common, in order to ease programming of context-aware applications and support evolution by decoupling applications from context sources. We can leverage these context models to develop general (i.e., application-independent) solutions for dynamic, run-time discovery of context sources (i.e., context management). This paper presents a model and architecture for a reconfigurable context management system that supports interoperability by building on emerging standards for sensor description and classification.

1   Introduction

There is a growing body of research on the use of context-awareness as a technique for developing applications that are flexible, adaptable, and capable of acting autonomously on behalf of users. This research addresses context modelling, management of context information, techniques for describing and implementing adaptive behaviour, and architectural issues. However, further research is needed before context-aware applications can be said to be truly autonomic.

The research so far focuses mostly on one aspect of autonomy: evaluation of context information by context-aware applications to make decisions about necessary adaptations to the current user context/situations. While numerous architectures and context management systems exist that define how sensor data

---

* National ICT Australia is funded by the Australian Government's Department of Communications, Information Technology, and the Arts; the Australian Research Council through Backing Australia's Ability and the ICT Research Centre of Excellence programs; and the Queensland Government.

L.T. Yang et al. (Eds.): ATC 2006, LNCS 4158, pp. 26–37, 2006.

used in context-aware applications can be gathered, processed and evaluated, the solutions developed so far address a reasonably static environment. In particular, they assume that a context-aware application is supported by a pre-defined set of information sources, which typically take the form of physical and logical sensors. They do not consider the types of autonomic behaviour required to (i) support mobile users who move between environments or administrative domains, or (ii) overcome problems such as sensor failures or disconnections.

Compelling examples of applications that require a high degree of autonomic behaviour include vehicles that need to fuse data from on-board sensors with sensors encountered in the environment (e.g., military unmanned vehicles and intelligent wheelchairs able to discover sensors in the infrastructure to adapt their path), and emergency response software that opportunistically gathers information from sensors located in the vicinity of an emergency. In this paper, we address the challenges of highly autonomic context-aware applications by proposing a model for autonomic, run-time reconfiguration of context management systems. To support both dynamic discovery of context information and interoperability between different context management domains, our model incorporates newly emerging standards for sensor description and classification.

The structure of the paper is as follows. Section 2 presents two application scenarios that motivate the work presented in this paper. Section 3 presents a context model for one of the scenarios, which we use in our discussions and examples in the remainder of the paper. Section 4 reviews existing approaches to context management as well as emerging standards for sensor description and classification. Section 5 describes our standards-based model for sensor description, while Section 6 presents the architecture of our reconfigurable context management system and illustrates the roles of context models and sensor descriptions in supporting dynamic discovery of sensors. Section 7 illustrates how sensor observations can be mapped into application-level context models, and Section 8 summarises the contributions of the paper.

2   Scenarios

Context-aware applications rely on evaluation of context information to make decisions about necessary adaptations to the current context/situations. This information is most commonly gathered from sensors; therefore, numerous architectures and context management systems have been developed to support the gathering, processing and evaluation of sensor data. However, these are unsuitable for applications that require a high degree of autonomic behaviour because these applications (i) operate in frequently changing environments with dynamically changing context sources and (ii) cannot rely on explicit setup or re-configuration of context sources by humans (either users or administrators). In this section, we present two scenarios that illustrate such applications and their requirements with respect to the sensing infrastructure.

Emergency Services Scenario. A context-aware application providing surveillance of critical infrastructure is supported by a network of sensors, including cameras, audio sensors, temperature and light sensors, and weather stations (detecting fog, rain, and so on). The surveillance application provides sophisticated processing of sensor information including face, scene and number plate recognition for detection of abnormal events. Part of the sensor network is destroyed in a physical attack. Emergency services arrive in vehicles equipped with cameras, audio sensors and temperature sensors. Based on the application context model, which describes the types of context information required by the application, a discovery protocol identifies new vehicle-based sensors that can be used by the surveillance application in place of the lost sensors (taking into account sensor types, capabilities and locations). The application is dynamically reconfigured to use the newly discovered sensors.

Mobile Phone Scenario. A next-generation mobile phone adapts its configuration according to the user's context. In order to support this behaviour without on-board sensors, a small context gathering utility is installed on the phone to collect relevant context information from sensors encountered within the environment. The phone is capable of determining its location (within a few metres accuracy) using triangulation, and it uses this knowledge to support discovery of information supplied by nearby sensors. The phone takes advantage of information from a wide variety of sensor types, including the lighting level (to appropriately adjust backlight settings) and noise level (to ensure that the ring volume is audible). In addition, it fuses the information from all of the available sensors to infer the user's current activity: for example, it infers that the user is probably sleeping when the lights are off and there is no sound or movement, and switches automatically to silent mode.

3   Context Modelling Approach

Context-aware applications have traditionally been developed using one of the following three approaches:

1. each application directly queries sensors and processes the sensor data to make decisions about how to adapt (*no application-level context model*);
2. applications are built using shared context processing infrastructure/toolkits that assist with gathering and processing data (*implicit context model*); or
3. applications have their own well-defined context models and use a shared context management infrastructure to populate the models at run-time using sensors and other context sources (*explicit context model*).

The third approach is the most appropriate for applications that require highly autonomic context management. Although a variety of context models have been proposed for context-aware systems [1], some are more suitable than others. The most appropriate models for autonomic context management are those that define not only the types of information required by the application, but also metadata that can be used in binding the model to suitable sensors (for example, quality metadata and classification of information types into sensed and

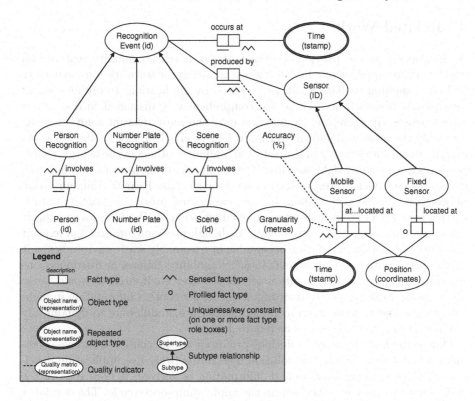

Fig. 1. Context model for an emergency response application

non-sensed types). Our previously developed fact-based context modelling approach [2,3] meets this requirement, and is therefore used as the basis for the work presented in this paper. However, it should be noted that our solution for autonomic context management can be used with any fact-based model.

To illustrate our context modelling notation, we present an example context model in Fig. 1 for the emergency services scenario described in Section 2. The context model describes three types of events that can be recognised by various types of sensors: face recognition events, number plate recognition events and scene recognition events. Face recognition events are associated with a person ID derived by matching to a database of known people. Similarly, number plate recognition events are associated with plate numbers, and scene recognition events with scene identifiers.

Each recognition event is associated with a timestamp and one or more sensors. Sensors in turn have locations (a single location value in the case of fixed sensors, and multiple location readings with associated timestamps in the case of mobile sensors). Each event-sensor pair (represented by the "produced by" fact type) can also have an accuracy measure, showing the rate at which the sensor correctly detects events of the given type. Similarly, location readings can be associated with both accuracy and granularity measures.

4   Related Work

As mentioned in the previous sections, the research community working on context-aware applications has developed a variety of software infrastructures and programming toolkits which can be used by applications to obtain context information from sensors. These are comprehensively discussed in one of our recent papers [4]; therefore, we mention only the most relevant solutions here. Arguably the most well known solution is Dey et al.'s Context Toolkit [5]. However, a crucial shortcoming of this solution (and most others in the field) is that it produces a reasonably tight coupling between applications, sensors, and intermediaries responsible for interpreting low-level sensor data. Remote communication between the components responsible for sensing and processing context data is carried over HTTP, which requires pre-configuration of IP addresses or explicit discovery using *discoverer* components. Although pre-configuration and explicit discovery of components may be acceptable in reasonably static environments, it is not appropriate for environments in which mobility, failures or disconnections are common. A preferable solution for these latter environments would be to allow applications to specify their requirements for context information in high-level terms, and to leave it up to the infrastructure/middleware to dynamically re-discover and re-bind sensors as required.

One of the most advanced solutions produced by the context-awareness community is Solar [6]. While this solution does not entirely free application developers from specifying how context information is derived, it does remove the task of discovering components from the application source code. The developer specifies the derivation of context information in the form of operator graphs, which include sources, sinks and channels. In this model, sensors are represented as sources, and application components as sinks. Intermediate components responsible for interpreting or otherwise processing the data act as both sources and sinks. At run-time, operator graphs are instantiated and managed by the Solar platform. The platform is capable of handling both mobility and component failures. However, it still requires the sensor configuration to be well specified in advance in the operator graph, rather than allowing for truly dynamic discovery and reconfiguration. It is not possible to substitute previously unknown types or configurations of sensors that are capable of providing the required information.

The sensor network community has addressed dynamic discovery and reconfiguration to a greater extent than the context-awareness community. However, this community predominantly focuses on low-level issues, such as networking protocols for wireless ad-hoc sensor networks [7] and protocols that provide low power [8] or energy-aware [9] operation. Similarly, the discovery protocols and query languages developed by the sensor network community are low-level, rather than application-focused. That is, they address problems such as finding neighbouring sensors and supporting database-like queries over sensor networks [10], rather than enabling high-level requests that specify only the nature of the required context information and desired information quality, without reference to particular sensors or sensor types.

Separate work is currently underway to develop standards for producing comprehensive descriptions of sensors. The results of this work include the Sensor Model Language (SensorML)[1], which is being developed as part of the Sensor Web Enablement (SWE) initiative with the goal of enabling sensors to become accessible via the Web, and the IEEE 1451 family of standards[2], which describes transducer (i.e., sensor or actuator) interfaces to enable interoperability. The goals of these two standards efforts are quite different: the SWE initiative is mainly concerned with describing sensor capabilities and observations (including geolocation of observations), while IEEE 1451 concentrates on the static characteristics of the sensor hardware. However, both families of standards can be used to help support dynamic discovery of sensors and/or observations. In particular, the SWE recommendations enable metadata-based discovery using standard semantic Web search tools and methods. To date, however, very little work has been done on sensor discovery and management using these standards (although work on sensor and observation discovery using Sensor Registries is planned by members of the SWE initiative). In this paper, we consider these issues in light of the requirements of autonomic context-aware systems that are based on well defined context models. In particular, we look at how SWE and IEEE 1451 descriptions can be combined and augmented to support autonomic discovery and management of sensors. The following section addresses sensor description using the two families of standards in more detail.

5   Sensor Descriptions

To support both wide adoption and interoperability, the sensor descriptions that support dynamic sensor discovery, identification and configuration should be based, to the extent possible, on standard descriptions and classifications of sensors. This is the main reason that our approach for describing sensors is based on the two families of emerging standards which are briefly discussed in this section.

IEEE 1451 Family of Standards. IEEE 1451 comprises a family of open standards defining common interfaces for transducers (sensors and actuators) to communicate with other components. Three standards from the family, 1451.0, 1451.2 and 1451.4, specify TEDS (Transducer Electronic Data Sheet), which contains detailed information that can be used for sensor identification and self-configuration, ranging from the sensor model number to sensing capabilities.

IEEE P1451.0 is a preliminary (with prefix "P") standard, which aims to define a set of common commands, common operations and TEDS for IEEE 1451 smart transducers. IEEE 1451.2 offers network independence by introducing Network Capable Applications Processors (NCAP), together with an extensive set of stand-alone TEDS for a wide range of transducers. IEEE 1451.4 defines the Mixed-Mode Interface to enable analog and digital signals to share the same

---

[1] http://vast.uah.edu/SensorML/

[2] http://ieee1451.nist.gov/

wires, and redefines a subset of 1451.2 TEDS to minimise the size of non-volatile memory used by TEDS. Limited configuration information is encoded according to assigned templates, and stored either in Electronic Erasable Programmable ROM or in a Virtual TEDS[3] file that is accessible through the Internet.

We base our approach on IEEE 1451.4 as it provides a flexible, memory-lean TEDS model to suit transducers with varying capabilities, including small devices such as microphones, thermocouples and accelerometers.

Open Geospatial Consortium Recommendations. The Sensor Web Enablement initiative is an ongoing activity carried out by the Open Geospatial Consortium (OGC)[4] with the aim of allowing sensors and sensor data to become discoverable and accessible in real time over the Web. Two of the main products of the initiative so far have been the SensorML and Observations & Measurements (O&M) recommendations. These deal with the representation of sensor descriptions and observations, respectively.

SensorML and O&M can each be used to support aspects of autonomic context management, as we show in the remainder of this paper. SensorML descriptions can be used for discovery of context sensors (as discussed in Sections 5 and 6), while O&M can be used to support the mapping of sensor observations into application-level context models (as discussed in Section 7).

SensorML models sensors as processes with inputs, outputs, parameters and methods. SensorML processes can be composed into process chains in order to model composite sensor systems. Four properties of sensors in the model that are relevant for reconfiguration are *sml:identification*, *sml:classification*, *sml:capabilities*, and *sml:characteristics*. In a similar way to the IEEE 1451 TEDS, *sml:identification* and *sml:classification* are used to assist sensor discovery and "plug-n-play" functionality: *sml:identification* provides information such as the manufacturer ID, model number and serial number, while *sml:classification* provides information concerning sensor types, applications, and supported sensing phenomena. *sml:capabilities* and *sml:characteristics* provide detailed technical specifications which can be used for autonomic sensor reconfiguration.

The O&M model defines a number of terms used for describing sensed observations and relationships between them. An observation is modelled as an event with a timestamp and a value describing the sensed phenomenon. The *locator* property is utilised to define the location of the observation, while a *procedure* described using SensorML defines the sensor or instrument used to capture the observations. Finally, related observations (such as a sequence of observations taken at regular intervals) can be grouped using observation arrays. An example observation for a "FaceRecognition" phenomenon is shown later in Section 7.

Hybrid Sensor Description Model. We envisage that in the future, most sensors will provide either embedded or virtual TEDS descriptions; therefore, we describe sensors by integrating SensorML and TEDS. That is, we base the part of the SensorML sensor description related to sensor identification, classification, reconfiguration and calibration on the IEEE 1451 standard. The advantage of

---

[3] http://www.ni.com/teds
[4] http://www.opengeospatial.org

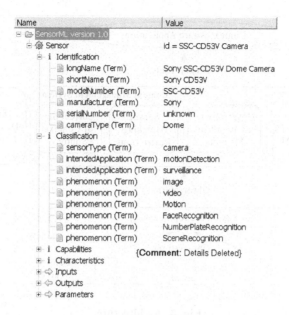

Name	Value
⊟ 🗁 SensorML version 1.0	
⊟ ⚙ Sensor	id = SSC-CD53V Camera
⊟ i Identification	
📄 longName (Term)	Sony SSC-CD53V Dome Camera
📄 shortName (Term)	Sony CD53V
📄 modelNumber (Term)	SSC-CD53V
📄 manufacturer (Term)	Sony
📄 serialNumber (Term)	unknown
📄 cameraType (Term)	Dome
⊟ i Classification	
📄 sensorType (Term)	camera
📄 intendedApplication (Term)	motionDetection
📄 intendedApplication (Term)	surveillance
📄 phenomenon (Term)	image
📄 phenomenon (Term)	video
📄 phenomenon (Term)	Motion
📄 phenomenon (Term)	FaceRecognition
📄 phenomenon (Term)	NumberPlateRecognition
📄 phenomenon (Term)	SceneRecognition
⊞ i Capabilities	{Comment: Details Deleted}
⊞ i Characteristics	
⊞ ⇨ Inputs	
⊞ ⇦ Outputs	
⊞ ⇨ Parameters	

Fig. 2. Camera SensorML example (shown as a screenshot from the SensorML editor from http://vast.uah.edu/SensorML/, rather than an XML document, for brevity)

this approach is that this part of the SensorML description can be generated automatically from the TEDS description.

Sensors can be either physical (e.g., temperature sensors, GPS devices) or logical, which are often physical sensors enhanced with additional software to support more sophisticated types of sensing phenomena than the physical sensor alone. An example of a logical sensor is the camera described in Fig. 2. The camera as a physical sensor provides a stream of images, whereas the smart camera required in our emergency services scenario is augmented with face, scene and number plate recognition software. This is indicated in the camera description in Fig. 2 by the list of sensing phenomena this particular sensor/device provides.

6   Reconfiguration of Context Sources

The role of context management systems is to acquire and store context information, typically in the form of context facts, and to disseminate this information to applications through querying and/or notification based on subscriptions.

Figure 3 illustrates a simplified architecture of a context-aware system, in which only the context management system is shown at the middleware level. The left side of the figure (Context Model and Context Facts) represents information stored in most current context management systems, including our own previously developed system [4]. However, we argue that in order to allow run-time discovery and replacement of context sources, some additional information and functionality is required in context management systems. This includes:

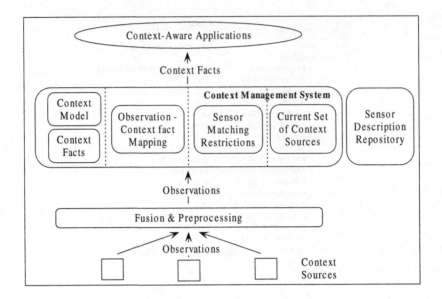

Fig. 3. Architecture

1. *Sensor Description Repositories*, to support discovery of sensors. As we have already shown in Section 5, sensor descriptions can be based on standards to support interoperability in pervasive systems. We use a combination of TEDS and SensorML, as TEDS supports dynamic discovery and identification of sensor instances, while SensorML can describe additional information needed in sensor matching and management.
2. *Current Set of Context Sources*, to support run-time replacement of sensors. The context management system requires knowledge of current sensor bindings in order to facilitate their replacement in the case of sensor failures or user mobility.
3. *Observation - Context Fact Mapping*, to support the integration of sensor observations from arbitrary sensors into the application-level context model, which represents context information in terms of facts. This mapping can be specified by the designer of the context model in terms of metadata that extends the model. We propose an approach in which the mapping assumes that inputs are in the observation format specified by the OGC's O&M recommendation, in order to facilitate interoperability across sensor types and context management systems.
4. *Sensor Matching Restrictions*, to support discovery of new sensors based on context fact types defined for the application. As shown in Fig. 4, the restrictions should be created by the application designer based on the *Observation - Context Fact Mapping*. The restrictions should stipulate the required sensing phenomena (e.g., "FaceRecognition"), as well as application-dependent restrictions (e.g., sensors must be within a well-defined geographical region or in close proximity to a given object).

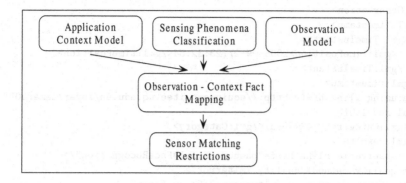

Fig. 4. Design process

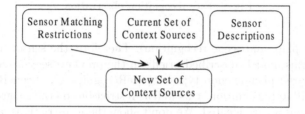

Fig. 5. Re-organisation

Context management systems that provide these features can support dynamic re-organisation as follows: based on both the description of the current sources (including the sources that must be replaced) and the sensor matching restrictions, the sensor description repository can be searched for appropriate sensors. This is shown in Fig. 5.

7 Mapping Observations to a Context Model

As discussed in the previous section, reconfigurable context management systems not only need to be able to dynamically discover appropriate sensors with which to populate application-level context models, but also to map observations reported by the chosen sensors to the representations used by the models (in our case, context facts). The mapping from sensor observations to high-level context information can be specified at design-time in terms of mapping descriptions that extend the context model. Although the mapping can potentially be expressed in any format, basing it on standards promotes interoperability. Therefore, we base our mapping on the O&M recommendation.

In the remainder of this section, we illustrate an example mapping related to the emergency services scenario and the context model shown in Fig. 1. As discussed in Section 3, the context model captures three types of recognition events

```
<gml:Observation>
  <gml:timestamp>
    <gml:TimeInstant>
      <gml:timePosition>2005-09-27T23:32:54</gml:timePosition>
    </gml:TimeInstant>
  </gml:timestamp>
  <om:using xlink:href="http://equipment.itee.uq.edu.au/foyer/camera03" />
  <gml:resultOf>
    <gml:Category>P343989961</gml:Category>
  </gml:resultOf>
  <om:observable xlink:href="phenomena.xml#FaceRecognition"/>
  <om:quality method="quality.xml#error">
    <om:Error uom="units.xml#percent">5</om:Error>
  </om:quality>
</gml:Observation>
```

Fig. 6. Face recognition observation

(face, number plate and scene recognition). Therefore, the sensor matching restrictions for this model (described briefly in the previous section), should stipulate the required phenomenon types ("FaceRecognition", "SceneRecognition" and "NumberPlateRecognition"), as well as restrictions on the geographical area in which the sensors are located. We don't show these restrictions, as they vary from one emergency to another and therefore need to be generated at run-time.

Each of the three observation types requires its own mapping to one or more facts. We focus on the mapping of observations for the "FaceRecognition" phenomenon by way of example. Figure 6 shows a face recognition observation specified using O&M. The observation, produced by a camera described by the SensorML document located at "http://equipment.itee.uq.edu.au/foyer/camera03", represents an event in which the camera recognises a person with ID P343989961 with a 5% likelihood of error. This observation can be mapped to the following facts, where fact types are shown in brackets:

- "23434 involves P343989961" [PersonRecognition involves Person]
- "23434 occurs at 2005-09-27T23:32:54" [RecognitionEvent occurs at Time]
- "23434 produced by http://equipment.itee.uq.edu.au/foyer/camera03", accuracy = 0.95 [RecognitionEvent produced by Sensor]

The mapping of the observation values to the above facts is performed on the basis of fact templates that select values from observations using the XML Query language (XQuery)[5], and then carry out any necessary transformations.

8   Conclusions

In this paper we presented a model and architecture for autonomic context management systems which can discover and replace sources of context information

---

[5] http://www.w3.org/XML/Query/

at run-time. This work extends our previous context management system, developed as part of our infrastructure for context-aware applications [4].

The proposed reconfigurable context management system is a general solution suitable for highly autonomic, context-aware applications that use context models specified in terms of high-level facts. To create sensor descriptions that support dynamic sensor discovery we combined SensorML and IEEE 1451. In addition, to support the integration of observations from arbitrary sensors into application-level context models at run-time, we developed a mapping technique based on the OGC's O&M recommendation for representing sensor observations. The use of emerging standards in our solution leverages the fact that future sensors will provide standard descriptions, and promotes interoperability between context management systems.

References

1. Strang, T., Linnhoff-Popien, C.: A context modeling survey. In: UbiComp 1st International Workshop on Advanced Context Modelling, Reasoning and Management, Nottingham (2004)
2. Henricksen, K., Indulska, J., Rakotonirainy, A.: Modeling context information in pervasive computing systems. In: 1st International Conference on Pervasive Computing (Pervasive). Volume 2414 of Lecture Notes in Computer Science., Springer (2002) 167–180
3. Henricksen, K., Indulska, J.: Developing context-aware pervasive computing applications: Models and approach. Journal of Pervasive and Mobile Computing **2** (2006) 37–64
4. Henricksen, K., Indulska, J., McFadden, T., Balasubramaniam, S.: Middleware for distributed context-aware systems. In: International Symposium on Distributed Objects and Applications (DOA). Volume 3760 of Lecture Notes in Computer Science., Springer (2005) 846–863
5. Dey, A.K., Salber, D., Abowd, G.D.: A conceptual framework and a toolkit for supporting the rapid prototyping of context-aware applications. Human-Computer Interaction **16** (2001) 97–166
6. Chen, G., Li, M., Kotz, D.: Design and implementation of a large-scale context fusion network. In: 1st Annual International Conference on Mobile and Ubiquitous Systems (MobiQuitous), IEEE Computer Society (2004) 246–255
7. Lim, A.: Distributed services for information dissemination in self-organizing sensor networks. Journal of the Franklin Institute **338** (2001) 707–727
8. Polastre, J., Hill, J., Culler, D.: Versatile low power media access for wireless sensor networks. In: 2nd International Conference on Embedded Networked Sensor Systems, Baltimore (2004) 95–107
9. Shah, R.C., Rabaey, J.M.: Energy aware routing for low energy ad hoc sensor networks. In: Wireless Communications and Networking Conference (WCNC). Volume 1. (2002) 350–355
10. Yao, Y., Gehrke, J.: Query processing for sensor networks. In: 1st Biennial Conference on Innovative Data Systems Research (CIDR), Asilomar (2003)

Formal Modeling and Verification of Systems with Self-x Properties*

Matthias Güdemann, Frank Ortmeier, and Wolfgang Reif

Lehrstuhl für Softwaretechnik und Programmiersprachen,
Universität Augsburg, D-86135 Augsburg
{guedemann, ortmeier, reif}@informatik.uni-augsburg.de

Abstract. In this paper we present a case study in formal modeling and
verification of systems with self-x properties. The example is a flexible
robot production cell reacting to system failures and changing goals.
The self-x mechanisms make the system more flexible and robust but
endanger its functional correctness or other quality guarantees. We show
how to verify such adaptive systems with a "restore-invariant" approach.

1 Introduction

Still today, many technical systems are tailored very rigidly to the originally
intended behaviour and the specific environment they will work in. This sometimes causes problems when unexpected things happen. A possible way to make
such systems more dependable and failure tolerant is to build redundancy in
many components. Another approach is to design systems from the beginning
in such a way, that they can dynamically self-adapt to their environment. The
benefit of these adaptive systems is that they can be much more dependable
than conventional systems, without increasing system complexity too much, as
not every scenario must be modeled explicitly.

From the point of view of formal methods, these systems are more difficult to
describe as their structure may change with the adaption. This can lead to problems when functional correctness of such a system is to be proven. Nevertheless,
in many safety critical fields like production automation, avionics, automotive
etc., functional correctness and quality guarantees are crucial. We show how an
adaptive system can be modeled with formal methods and its functional correctness be proven under adaption. We illustrate this technique with a case study
from production automation.

2 Case Study

The case study describes an automated production cell which is self-organizing
in case of failures and adapts to changing goals. It consists of three robots, which
are connected with autonomous transportation units.

* This research is partly sponsored by the priority program "organic computing" (SPP
OC 1183) of the German research foundation (DFG).

L.T. Yang et al. (Eds.): ATC 2006, LNCS 4158, pp. 38–47, 2006.

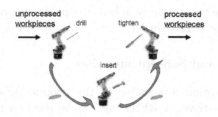

Fig. 1. Valid configuration of robot cell

2.1 Description

In the production cell every robot can accomplish three tasks: drilling a hole in a workpiece, inserting a screw into a drilled hole and tightening an inserted screw. These tasks are done with three different tools that can be switched. Every workpiece must be processed by all three tools in the given order (drill, insert, tighten = DIT). Workpieces are transported from and to the robots by autonomous carts. Changing the tool of a robot is assumed to require some time. Therefore the standard configuration of the system is to spread out the three tasks between the three robots, and the carts transfer workpieces accordingly. This situation is shown in fig. 1.

2.2 Self-organization

The first interesting new situation occurs when one or more tools break and the current configuration allows no more correct DIT processing of the incoming workpieces. In fig. 2 the drill of one robot broke and DIT processing is not possible, as no other robot is configured to drill.

As the robots can switch tools it should be possible for the adaptive system to detect this situation and reconfigure itself in such a way, that DIT processing is possible again.

This can be resolved as shown in fig. 3. Now the left robot drills, the right robot tightens the screws and the middle robot is left unchanged. For this error resolution, not only the assignment of the tasks to the robots must be changed, but also the routes of the carts and the direction of the incoming and outgoing

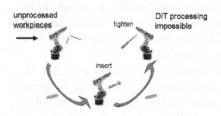

Fig. 2. Hazard due to broken drill

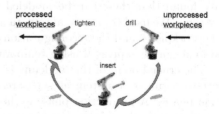

Fig. 3. Reconfigured robot cell

workpieces. If only the tools were switched, the processing of all tasks would be possible, but not in the correct order.

2.3   Self-adaption and Self-optimization

Another form of adaption is possible in the production cell when partially processed workpieces arrive. A RFID tag can be used on the workpieces that indicates whether they have already a drilled hole. Those that have the hole drilled do not have to be processed by the robot assigned the drill task. If there is an additional transport cart available, then it can bring the partially processed workpieces directly to the robot that inserts the screws.

When this has happened, the robot that has been assigned the task to insert the screws might become the bottleneck in the system. If an additional robot and cart are available, they can be integrated to self-optimize the throughput of the production cell.

Again, self-x properties are only possible because of internal redundancy in the system. This includes redundant tools that can be switched and redundant robots or transport carts. The difference to traditional redundant systems is that they are dynamically configured and may be used for other tasks if not needed at the moment.

The production cell is also capable to self-adapt using *graceful degradation* to fulfill at least parts of its functions as long as possible. In this example this could be drilling holes in a workpiece and inserting screws but not tighten them. Yet another form would be to use one robot to accomplish more than one task. This is also a case of *graceful degradation* because it preserves the functionality but diminishes the throughput of the production cell considerably.

Although small, the example exhibits several aspects of self-x properties and especially self-adaption. Nevertheless, several interesting questions arise: How does the dynamically changing organization of the production cell affect functional correctness? What happens while a reconfiguration takes place? Does the system produce correctly after a reconfiguration?

3   Formal Model

When trying to build a formal model for an adaptive system, the question arises how to represent the dynamically changing characteristics of such a system. We found that these can be modeled with techniques similar to conventional systems. We used transition automata as representation for the robots, the carts, the workpieces and the reconfiguration control. The functional properties of the system can be expressed using temporal logic formulas.

The crucial point of the modeling is the treatment of the reconfiguration. We regard a run of a system as separated in production phases and reconfiguration phases. A production phase is characterized by the invariant "The system configuration allows for processing a workpiece in DIT order". The end of a production phase is marked by the violation of this invariant. The purpose of the reconfiguration phase is the restoration of the invariant. When this is achieved, the reconfiguration phase is over and a new production phase starts. We use the term "restore-invariant" for this approach.

We did not implement a specific reconfiguration algorithm in the model but only specified it in a "top-down" way, as restoration of a functional invariant. This technique can also be applied to the other mentioned self-x properties. The crucial point here is that the algorithm must be able to decide whether these invariants hold and restore them if not. Seeing reconfiguration in this abstract way gives us the advantage that it is sufficient to prove that an algorithm can restore the invariant to show that the algorithm provides correct reconfiguration, thus modularizing our model.

We implemented the formal model of the adaptive production cell as transition system in the SMV model checker [7]. This formalization allows specification of functional correctness in CTL (computational tree logic) and LTL (linear time logic), or their semantics see[3].

3.1   Transition Systems

Due to space restrictions not all transition systems are shown for the automata. The respective transition preconditions are explained in the text. Dashed lines indicate the effect of an interrupting reconfiguration. If used, this confines reconfiguration from normal functioning.

Control Transition System. The Control performs the reconfiguration of the production cell. Its transition system is shown in fig. 4. It waits in state *Reconf* until all robots and carts are in their respective reconfiguration states. Then it enters the state *Initialize*. After this, one of the states of the *Robot1Conf* multi-state is entered, then one of the *Robot2Conf* states and finally one of the *Robot3Conf* states. Which one of the states is entered, decides which task is assigned to the corresponding robot. The assignment of the routes to the carts is done analogously in the *Cart1Conf* and *Cart2Conf* multi-states. Which task is assigned is chosen indeterministically. Correct assignment for processing workpieces is assured by the specification of the reconfiguration algorithm explained in Sect. 3.3.

Robot Transition Systems. The initial state *Reconf* is left when the Control assigns a new task to the corresponding robot. The succeeding states are either *readyD*, *readyI* or *readyT* for the respective tasks.

When the robot is in *readyD* state it waits for a new workpiece to arrive. When this happens it enters state *busyD*. If the workpiece has already been processed with the tool the robot uses, it enters directly *doneD*, simulating passing through of the already processed workpiece. After *busyD* the *doneD* state is entered indicating that the workpiece processing is complete and the robot waits for a cart that fetches the workpiece. When this happens, the robot enters *readyD* again. The same holds for the other possible tasks. When a reconfiguration is initiated by the Control, then the robot leaves its current state and reenters *Reconf*.

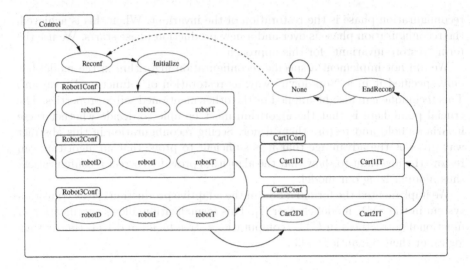

Fig. 4. Control transition system

Workpiece Transition Systems. The workpieces are defined via two automata. The first one is WP_i^{pos}. It describes the position of the workpiece i in the production cell.

The initial state is *Before* if the cell is configured, then the next state is *infrontD* as the workpieces are delivered to the driller not with the aid of carts but with a conveyor that is not modeled. When the robot that has been assigned the drill task is ready, then WP_i^{pos} enters the state *inD*. When the task is done, it enters *behindD*. When the workpiece is fetched, it enters either the state *Cart1* or *Cart2*, depending on which cart arrived. After the respective cart arrives at either the *infrontI* or *infontT* position, the WP_i^{pos} enters the state corresponding to this position. The other tasks are modelled in a similar way, the only difference is, that after *behindT*, the WP_i^{pos} enters the state *Before* again, instead of being put on a cart.

The second transition system for the workpiece is WP_i^{state}. It indicates which tasks have already been completed on the workpiece. It consists of an 3-bit array, each bit corresponds to one of the possible tasks and has the value 1 if the task has been done and 0 otherwise. When the workpiece leaves the production cell, then WP_i^{state} is reset to its initial state and it is reintroduced into the production cell. When a reconfiguration takes place, the workpieces that are in the production cell are brought to the *Before* state again, but their completed tasks are preserved.

Cart Transition System. The carts are represented as the product automaton of three different automata. The first one is C_i^{conf}, see fig. 5. Its initial state is *Reconf*. The succeeding state is either *DI* or *IT*, depending on the configuration that the Control automaton assigns. If $C_i^{conf} = DI$ then the corresponding

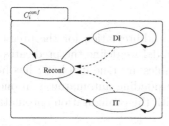

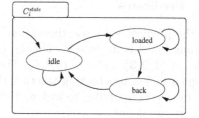

Fig. 5. Cart configuration   **Fig. 6.** Cart state

cart is assigned the route between the drilling and the screw-inserting robot, $C_i^{conf} = IT$ is then the route between the screw-inserting robot and the screw-tightening one. When a reconfiguration starts, then C_i^{conf} enters *Reconf* again, to get a new configuration.

The second automaton for describing a cart is C_i^{state}, see fig. 6. The initial state is *idle* and indicates that the cart is waiting behind a robot and waiting for a workpiece processed by this robot. The state *loaded* is entered when a workpiece has been processed by the robot the cart waits behind, and is to be transported on the assigned route. When the cart arrives at the next robot and the workpiece is fetched, then the state *back* is entered. The *idle* state is reentered when the position of the cart is again behind the robot.

The third automaton for the description of the carts is C_i^{pos}. It represents the position the cart is at. The positions correspond to the possible positions of the workpieces. The initial state is *Undefined*. Its route is abstracted to three states, behind a robot, between two robots and in front of the next robot. Depending on the assigned configuration these are either the drilling and inserting or the inserting and tightening robot.

Failure Automata. For the modeling of failures we use failure automata. These can be either *transient* or *persistent* see fig. 7. The initial state of a failure automaton is *no*, i.e. there is no error at the moment. The automaton can indeterministically enter state *yes*, indicating that an error has occurred. A *transient* failure can disappear, again in an indeterministic way.

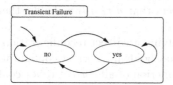

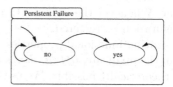

Fig. 7. Failure automata for transient and persistent failures

3.2   Predicates

For the predicates we use the notion $A = s$ as abbreviation for the predicate "automaton A is in state s". For the formal model we define the predicates R_i^a with $i \in \{1, 2, 3\}$ and $a \in \{d, i, t\}$. These variables are true if robot i has been assigned task a by checking whether the corresponding automaton is in one of the states corresponding to task a. Together with the configuration automata of the carts we define:

$$robotConf := (R_1^d \vee R_1^i \vee R_1^t) \wedge (R_2^d \vee R_2^i \vee R_2^t) \wedge (R_3^d \vee R_3^i \vee R_3^t)$$

$$cartConf := (C_1^{conf} \neq Reconf) \wedge (C_2^{conf} \neq Reconf)$$

$$conf := robotConf \wedge cartConf$$

$$ditCapable := \bigwedge_{a \in \{d,i,t\}} (\bigvee_{j \in \{1,2,3\}} R_j^a \wedge (\bigwedge_{k \in \{1,2,3\} \setminus j} \neg R_k^a))$$

$$cartCapable := (C_1^{conf} \neq C_2^{conf}) \wedge (C_1^{conf} \neq Reconf) \wedge (C_2^{conf} \neq Reconf)$$

This means that $robotConf$ holds when all robots have a task assigned. The same holds for the carts with $cartConf$. The variable $ditCapable$ is true when the assignment of tasks to robots includes all three tasks. As the variables R_i^a are defined via the states of the robot automata, the formula $R_i^a \rightarrow \bigwedge_{b \in \{d,i,t\} \setminus a} \neg R_i^b$ always holds.

To model broken tools as failures in the model of the production cell we define transient failure automata as explained in Sect.3.1 for all tools of all robots. A complete list of possible failure modes can be found with techniques like failure-sensitive specification [8] or HazOp [5]. These failure automata are called $fails_i^a$ with $i \in \{1, 2, 3\}$ and $a \in \{d, i, t\}$. Using these automata we define additional boolean variables:

$$ditFailure_j := \bigvee_{a \in \{d,i,t\}} (R_j^a \wedge (fails_j^a = yes))$$

$$ditFailure := \bigvee_{j \in \{1,2,3\}} ditFailure_j$$

This means that $ditFailure_j$ holds if robot j has been assigned a task it cannot perform as the corresponding tool is broken and $ditFailure$ indicates that one or more robots have been assigned a task that is impossible at the moment. Whenever the external Control detects that $ditFailure$ holds, then a reconfiguration is triggered.

For proving functional properties and specifying a correct reconfiguration algorithm the predicate $ditPossible$ is needed that holds if a correct configuration is still theoretically possible. We used the disjunction of all correct robot configurations for this. It is important to mention, that this is not needed in the model itself but only to specify the reconfiguration algorithm and to prove functional correctness. That means that $ditPossible$ may also be defined in another way, e.g. to model *graceful degradation* adaption.

3.3   Specification of Reconfiguration

For this specification of the reconfiguration we used LTL. SMV allows LTL formulas in assumed properties. The two specifications are as follows:

$$conf DIT := \mathbf{G}\left((robotConf \wedge cartConf) \rightarrow ditCapable \wedge cartCapable\right)$$
$$confCorrect := \mathbf{G}\left((Control = EndReconf) \rightarrow\right.$$
$$\mathbf{X}\left(ditPossible \rightarrow \neg ditFailure\right))$$

That is, $conf DIT$ specifies that every reconfiguration results in a sensible configuration of the production cell. Every tool must be available and the carts have distinct routes assigned. The property $confCorrect$ specifies that whenever a reconfiguration has just been finished, $ditFailure$ is false as long as correct configuration is still possible. All functional properties in the next section are proven under the assumption that $conf DIT$ and $confCorrect$ hold.

4   Verification

We see a run of the system divided in phases of production and reconfiguration. In a production phase, workpieces are processed in a straightforward way. When a tool breaks, then a reconfiguration takes place that changes the organization of the cell. The propositions we want to prove are the same as in a conventional system, i.e. that processing of the workpieces is done in correct DIT order and on all workpieces that enter the production cell.

Proposition 1 assures that as long as $ditPossible$ holds every workpiece will finally be processed by all tools. Therefore, as long as processing is theoretically possible, all tasks are executed on all the workpieces.

$$\mathbf{AG}\left(ditPossible \rightarrow \left(\mathbf{AF}\, WP_i^{state} = [1,1,1]\right)\right) \tag{1}$$

This does not yet guarantee that processing is done in the correct DIT order. For this property we prove the following:

$$\mathbf{AG}\, WP_i^{state} = [0,0,0] \vee$$
$$\mathbf{A}\left[WP_i^{state} = [0,0,0]\,\mathbf{until}\, WP_i^{state} = [1,0,0] \vee\right.$$
$$\left(\mathbf{A}\left[WP_i^{state} = [1,0,0]\,\mathbf{until}\, WP_i^{state} = [1,1,0] \vee\right.\right.$$
$$\left.\left.\left(\mathbf{A}\left[WP_i^{state} = [1,1,0]\,\mathbf{until}\, WP_i^{state} = [1,1,1]\right]\right)\right]\right)\right] \tag{2}$$

Proposition 2 proves that processing is never done in a wrong order. Together with proposition 1 we know that as long as processing is possible, processing with all three tools is done.

The next propositions show that the modeling of our cell is sensible Proposition 3 shows that workpieces never occupy the same position "in" a robot.

Proposition 4 shows that carts are never at the same position. Their position is not tracked in a reconfiguration phase. Proposition 5 shows that if for a cart is loaded, then it carries a workpiece, i.e. a workpiece has the same position as the cart.

$$\mathbf{AG}\,(WP_i^{pos} = WP_j^{pos} \rightarrow WP_i^{pos} \notin \{inD, inI, inT\}) \tag{3}$$

$$\mathbf{AG}\,((C_i^{conf} \neq Reconf \wedge C_j^{conf} \neq Reconf) \rightarrow (C_i^{pos} \neq C_j^{pos})) \tag{4}$$

$$\mathbf{AG}\,(configured \rightarrow (C_i^{state} = loaded \rightarrow \exists j : WP_j^{pos} = C_i^{pos})) \tag{5}$$

These proposition show that the modeling of the production cell is correct according to the requirement that failures can occur and processing is correctly adapted to these failures as long as possible. Furthermore we provided several propositions that showed that the cell is modeled in a sensible way beyond the adaption capabilities.

5 Related Work

Much of the available work on adaptive systems and verification thereof is based on agent-oriented programming. These mentioned papers have no similar concept to our "restore-invariant" technique for top-down design for systems with self-x properties.

Bussman et al. [1] define several functional requirements and software engineering requirements that an agent-oriented system must fulfill in order to be qualified for industrial control problems. Both functional and software engineering requirements are met by our model of the production cell, although it was not designed having agent-orientation in mind.

In [2] Bussmann et al. describe an adaptive production system based on agent-technology. An auction based approach is taken where agents bid for tasks and a self-organization of material flow takes place. They prove that their approach is free of deadlocks and give good reasons and empirical observations for increased productivity. This differs from our approach as it is more directed to increasing throughput and not to make the system more dependable to failure of components.

Kiriakidis and Gordon-Spears describe in [4] an approach to restore supervision and assure specified behaviour of robot teams. It it based on transition automata and a language that is expressed by these automata. This language is changed by learning algorithms triggered by unforeseen events. This approach is directed more to team composition instead of robot functionality as in our example.

Another approach is taken by Cornejo et al. in [6]. A dynamic reconfiguration protocol is specified and verified using the LOTOS language. It consists of a configurator agent and application agents that communicate over a software bus. Its asynchronous communication would be an interesting way to implement a reconfguration algorithm that fulfills the mentioned invariant.

6   Conclusion

We presented a case study in formal modeling and verification of self-adaptive systems. The example production cell exhibits several self-x properties, particularly self-organization.

We have shown a way how to guarantee functional correctness under the presence of failures and reconfiguration. The idea is to impose invariants to be maintained by the system. In case of failures, the invariant is violated and the task of the reconfiguration or the adaption is to restore these invariants. This leads to a "top-down" design approach for self-adaptive systems, separating specifications from their implementations. We call this approach "restore-invariant".

In the example we focused on functional correctness but the invariants could also express other goals like throughput performance, load-balancing or graceful degradation.

The next step is to look at the additional self-x properties of the production cell mentioned in Sect. 2.3. Other interesting topics are overcoming the limitations of finite state spaces and measuring the benefit of adaptive systems. Of course we will also generalize the concepts from this case study to make this approach applicable to general forms of self-adaptive systems.

References

[1] S. Bussmann. Agent-oriented programming of manufacturing control tasks, 1998.
[2] S. Bussmann and K. Schild. Self-organizing manufacturing control: An industrial application of agent technology, 2000.
[3] Doron A. Peled Edmund M. Clarke Jr., Orna Grumberg. *Model Checking*. The MIT Press, 1999.
[4] K. Kiriakidis and D. F. Gordon-Spears. Formal modeling and supervisory control of reconfigurable robot teams. In *FAABS*, pages 92–102, 2002.
[5] T. A. Kletz. Hazop and HAZAN notes on the identification and assessment of hazards. Technical report, Inst. of Chemical Engineers, Rugby, England, 1986.
[6] R. Mateescu M. A. Cornejo, H. Garavel and N. De Palma. Specification and verification of a dynamic reconfiguration protocol for agent-based applications. In *Proc. of the IFIP TC6*, pages 229–244, Deventer, The Netherlands, The Netherlands, 2001. Kluwer, B.V.
[7] K. L. McMillan. *Symbolic Model Checking*. Kluwer Academic Publishers, 1990.
[8] F. Ortmeier and W. Reif. Failure-sensitive specification: A formal method for finding failure modes. Technical Report 3, Institut für Informatik, Universität Augsburg, 2004.

A Novel Autonomic Rapid Application Composition Scheme for Ubiquitous Systems

Junaid Ahsenali Chaudhry and Seungkyu Park

Graduate School of Information and Communications,
Ajou University, South Korea
{junaid, sparky}@ajou.ac.kr

Abstract. In this paper we present an autonomic rapid application composition scheme for ubiquitous systems. The main contribution of this paper is to provide a mode through which a mobile user can receive transparent service environment during his mobility period using the benefits of service composition paradigms. We propose a novel service selection matrix that enables the selection of the services similar to the ones that user was previously using. We observed that the user context is not the only key to improve the service selection rather some selection heuristics are also needed. Those search heuristics are provided through the degree of adaptive similarity. Our over all objective is to achieve high levels of service consistency and quality of service at higher layers.

1 Introduction

Trends are changing fast in ubiquitous world. With the growing popularity of ubiquitous systems [1], the importance of enabling technologies and enabling methods is also increasing. Based on Service Oriented Architecture (SOA) the OSGi [2] is one of the biggest candidates for ubiquitous middleware standard. But it is more network-centric and more prone to point of failure bottle neck, service inconsistency; irregular service lifecycle, end to end update notification etc are the prime examples of problems in OSGi. Services are the building blocks of ubiquitous applications and service composition a good tool to put these blocks together [3]. One of the reasons why different services are composed for a mobile user is that a service or a set of that a user enjoys during his connectivity with a gateway may not be the same or even present at the new gateway [4]. In 3G mobile networks, it's the handoff procedures that transfer the user context from one base station to the other but in 4G, to accurately compose a target application, it is not only the specification of the previous user session but user, device and environmental preferences [5].

There are many shopping emporiums around that offer electrical appliances from various vendors and brands under one roof. Consider a scenario where a prospective buyer is looking e.g., for a digital camera within a specified price range and technical specifications. A service discovery mechanism that selects services i.e. a service to compose specifications and shortlist the shops, a map service guiding the user and intelligently selecting the shops on a parameter say price, some finance and bank account management service etc, would be needed in an order to assist user in a meaningful way.

L.T. Yang et al. (Eds.): ATC 2006, LNCS 4158, pp. 48–56, 2006.

In this paper we propose an autonomic rapid application composition scheme that identifies the target service on multifaceted criterion and composes applications for consistent smart space experiences. The exchange of some metadata i.e. selection algorithms consisting of searching criteria with search heuristics, access level policies, obligation policies, at configuration level brings back the same application environment for the user which he enjoyed at the last gateway.

The discussion in the remainder of this paper is arranged as follows. Related work is presented in section 2. In section 3 we present the proposed scheme. Section 4 contains simulation results. In section 5 we conclude this paper.

2   Related Work

The most renowned industrial component models (CCM, EJB, .NET) are ill-suited for sensor based applications development. The main reason is that they are resource consumers and gateways can be resource constrained systems. They can be systems similar to embedded systems. In this section we discuss some related projects of component models and projects of embedded mobile systems.

Service Synthesizer on the Net (STONE) project [1] explores new possibilities for users to accomplish their tasks seamlessly and ubiquitously. The project focuses on the development of context-aware services in which applications are able to change their functionality depending on the dynamically changing user context. In STONE project the service discovery is considered as one of the general resources on internet. This linear resource needs application pipelining and remote service delivery which is certainly not the theme of the scheme proposed in this paper. We believe that service delivery distance plays a great role in increasing the QoS and decreases the load on the network. We categorize service pool into Local Service Pool (LSP), and Virtual Service Pool (VSP). The services with high payload are processed in LSP and the services with low payload can be accessed and used remotely. We maintain the user context at his local device so that when he leaves the gateway the application context goes with him. Service synthesis and service mobility are significant components for achieving a consistent service delivery. It can be achieved by collecting necessary functions and combining them dynamically in response to changes in time and place. We consider backtracking and finding the candidate services to replace the 'out-of service' services in future work. The STONE project also considers these issues as key issues.

In [6] applications are built using context-aware architectures, meaning that context (e.g., location, environment, and user task) is used as a filter to determine which building blocks are relevant to the application at any given time. The main concept underlying this vision is dynamically available building blocks, i.e., building blocks that can appear or disappear at any time. The authors of [6] propose that only limited amount of context can select the right services but we argue that its the search heuristics along with the context that are needed to select the right services. Moreover the solution proposed in gravity can not be called scalable as in the presence of many services at service gateway, many services may have similar context so it would be more or less the same problems of service selection.

The Robust Self-Configuring Embedded Systems (RoSES) [7] is a project that is exploring graceful degradation as a means to achieve dependable systems. But only reconfiguration can not solve the complicated service selection problems. The scalability of this system is confined to a local area network. With the increasing size of network the scalability comes down drastically. The heterogeneity levels at large MANET scale may cause the system to lose its self configuring value as the increasing type of devices makes the scenario very complex. Unlike the scheme proposed, ROSES doesn't perform any offline learning function. Moreover it doesn't give any functional assurance. RoSES reboots after reconfiguring the software. In MANET environments, the reboot procedure is avoided. The Amaranth QoS Project [8] is a Quality of Service project that emphasizes admission policies. The key idea is to have tasks with at least two levels of services: baseline and optimized. A system could thus be operated to guarantee critical baseline functionality via static system sizing, with idle resources employed to provide optimized performance on an opportunistic per-task basis. Although this project doesn't have drastic scalability issues, it can not handle heterogeneity of high levels. The system doesn't have total system awareness rather it considers active recourses only. Amaranth QoS project unlike RoSES doesn't reboots the system rather it eliminates the unnecessary tasks.

3 The Proposed Scheme

In this section, we present the architecture, the component, and their functionality. Figure.1. shows the service architecture of our scheme.

3.1 System Model

In this section we will discuss about the architecture of the system proposed. The figure 1(a) shows that it is considerably usual that a mobile user leaves the one space and enters into the premises of another. Now he demands the same application environment as it was in the previous smart space. Se we either need to pipeline the application that the user was using at the old gateway or make a new one, very similar to the previous one. In order to do the later, the new gateway would require some application context from the user. Since the application made on top of OSGi are supposed to be highly volatile, we can not guarantee to have the application context from the old gateway if requested. In figure 1(b), the layered architecture of the scheme proposed is shown. After system software the gateway software is the embedded software. There are two types of service pools.1) Local service Pool and 2) virtual service pool. Those services which are not present locally reside in the Virtual Service Pool (VSP). The Context Manager arranges the context received in profiles. The context assimilation later embeds the context in service composition process. The application pool contains the applications that are generated and with the changes in the context they are updated i.e. services are either added or removed from the application string. It is a difficult job to find the right services but the most important and basic thing is how to arrange them. There can be two kinds of service pools in a smart service oriented environment: the service pools which contain services that are dependent on each other and the service pool which contains totally independent services. The complexity of each software system depends upon its functionality. We assume the software we are considering in the following mathematical model, comprises of atomic functions with occasional iterations in it. It is the responsibility of the link manager to prepare and transfer the meta-level description of the services present in both local and virtual service pool. The meta-level description includes (1) Main purpose of application and other related information, (2) Model, view, and controller elements information, (3) Application running environments and requirements such as device capability, (4) Events definition between each application entity for transmission of data, (5) Data description for saving data of the application, (6) Migration policy which describe the restriction of migration.

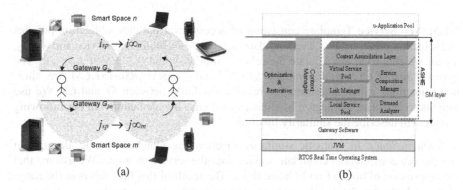

Fig. 1. The Proposed Architecture

The optimization and restoration parts are adaptive self management parts of scheme. In this research we are using them for exception handling but in future we plan to use them for real time system and network management.

3.2 Mathematical Model

In this section we discuss the mathematical model and the steps of the proposed scheme. The total Service composition process consists of the following parts.

- Service Selection
  - Syntactic Similarity
  - Functional Similarity
  - Contextual Similarity
- Instantiation and Binding
  - Reserve Request
  - Reserve Confirmation
- Policy Formation and Application Generation

Service Selection: The dynamic selection of suitable services involves the matching of service requirements with service compatibility rather than simple search keywords. Several solutions for service discovery problem have been used, e.g. LDAP [9], MDS [10], and Universal Description Discovery and Integration (UDDI).

The UDDI 2 lacks a rich query model and is not well equipped to handle environments that contain resource providers with unpredictable availability because of its limited support for the expiration of stale data [9]. So we plan to use the service bundle of Lightweight Directory Access Protocol (LDAP) provided in embedded builder, a bundle development software, to test our scheme. We use the following algorithm for service searching.

$$MS(ST,CS) = \left[\frac{\begin{array}{l} w_1 \times SyntacticSim(ST,CS) + \\ w_2 \times FunctionalSim(ST,CS) + \\ w_3 \times ContextualSim(ST,CS) \end{array}}{w_1 + w_2 + w_3} \right] \in [0..1] \tag{1}$$

Where ST= Service Template consisting of access level policies, obligation policies and selection preferences, CT= Candidate Service, MS= Matching Service and w_1, w_2, w_3 are weights used to calculate the relative similarity and $0 \leq MS(ST,CS) \geq 1$. The $SyntacticSim(ST,CT)$, $FunctionalSim(ST,CS)$, and $ContextualSim(ST,CS)$ are similarity functions which determine the relative similarity between ST and CS. We use weights to calculate the degree of similarity for ease in calculations. In the following text we will describe the similarity functions.

SyntacticSim(): In syntactic similarity function, we match the name, description and the sub constructs in candidate service with the service template. We assume that the description of both ST and CS are finite. The result of this function is in the range of 0 and 1. As per desired different Quality of Service requirements, we can opt for strict matching and make the higher values of *SyntacticSim()* as standards or keep it low and expect the errors. The details of the function are represented through the following equation.

$$\begin{aligned} & SyntacticSim(ST,CS) \\ &= \left[\frac{w_4 * NameMatch(ST,CS)}{\begin{array}{l} + \dfrac{w_5 * DescrMatch(ST,CS)}{} \\ + \dfrac{w_6 * ParsesubsMatch(ST,CS)}{w_4 + w_5 + w_6} \end{array}} \atop Descr[ST] \neq \phi, Descr[CS] \neq \phi, Parsesubs(ST,CS) \neq \phi \right] \in [0..1] \end{aligned} \tag{2}$$

Name similarity can be calculated through string matching algorithms and description similarity can be calculated through *n-gram* algorithm however for sub constructs, we use the algorithm below.

```
Fetch sub_constructs1 [n];

Fetch sub_constructs2 [m];

for (i=0; i++; i<=n) for (j=0;j++;j<=m)

parsesubsmatch(execute (sub_constructs1[i],result1),
execute (sub_constructs1[j],result2);

if (result1==result2)save sub_construct1 $$
sub_construct2 $$ result2 -> matchfile.log;
```

The above mentioned algorithm executes and matches the out puts of the code segments. Using this functionality gives us the syntactic level similarity values.

FunctionalSim (): It is not only the semantic similarity of the service which needs to be considered but also the input and output matching of *CS* and *ST*. In the previous section we matched the output of the code segments. It is highly likely that when code segments combine together, they give different output e.g. use of global functions can change values considerably. The following formula describes the functioning of *Functionalism ()*.

$$FS = \frac{\sum_{i=0}^{n} fs_i}{n} \in [0..1] \qquad (3)$$

where,

fs_i= best functional similarity of an operation of *ST*
n= number of operation of *ST*

$$getFM\left(OP_{ST}, OP_{CS}\right) = best\left(getfm\left(OP_{ST}, OP_{CS}\right)\right) \qquad (4)$$

Where, OP_{CS} represents individual operation of *CS* and *getfm()*'s specifications are in the following formula.

$$fs = getfm(OP_{ST}, OP_{CS})$$
$$= \left[\frac{\begin{array}{l} w_7 \times SysSim(OP_{ST}, OP_{CS}) + \\ w_8 \times ConceptSim(OP_{ST}, OP_{CS}) + \\ w_9 \times IOSim(OP_{ST}, OP_{CS}) \end{array}}{w_7 + w_8 + w_9} \right] \in [0..1] \qquad (5)$$

Where *SynSim()* is the similarity of names and descriptions, *ConceptSim()* is the ontological similarity. The similarity of the input and output operations are not calculated in this work. We need to develop a testing oracle that can provide the correct parameters to a service in order to generate the results so that they can be matched with the results of the other service. We intend to do this task in future work.

Contextual Sim (): As shown in figure 1(a) that one service provider can provide service to many service gateways. We have indexed the gateways managed by one service provider with i and the other with j. Now when a user leaves the nth gateway managed by the service provider i, and enters into m^{th} gateway managed by the service provider j, we can represent it via the following equation.

$$\eta i_n \cong w(ServiceSimilarity)\eta j_m \qquad (6)$$

Where, η = Coefficient of Service Consistency

The condition holds if and only if the weights of service similarity are within the user defined tolerance range. At this stage our work is confined to differentiating between the service provider and the gateway parameters. We plan to add more parameters such as environmental entities and functional relation of the user with those entities.

Instantiation and Binding: The inconsistencies in OSGi framework have increased the importance of root composite controllers and binding controllers. These entities have helped in eliminating the inconsistencies at the service discovery, service substitution and service coordination level. The following is one of the examples binding tables maintained at the gateway level. It shows the current service in execution, service in pipeline, the parameters to pass them and Time to Live (TTL). In the binding table given below different source services have various services preceding which creates a sting of services. The TTL is calculated from the binding time plus 3000 milliseconds. Calculation of TTL reserves one service and the service clash are eliminated through it.

Table 1. The Binding Table

SID*	TSID`	Parameters	TTL
C001455D	C001456D	$r_1,s_1,w\{w_1,w_{n-1}\}$	001589GHJ+3000
C001456D	C001457D	$T_1,T_2,s_2, w\{w_1,w_n\}$	001589GHJ+3000
C001457D	C001458D	$T_2,T_3,s_3, w\{w_1,w_n\}$	001589GHJ+3000
C001458D	C001459D	$T_3,T_4,s_4, w\{w_1,w_n\}$	001589GHJ+3000
C001459D	C001455D	$T_4,T_5,s_5 ,w\{w_1,w_n\}$	001589GHJ+3000
C001455D	C001456D	$T_5,T_6,s_6, w\{w_1,w_n\}$	001590GHJ+3000

*SID= Service ID, `TSID= Target Service ID, w=weights as par.

In mPRM the services can be accessed from a remote location. That is why we have a virtual service pool hosting the services that are used from a remote location. The Virtual Service Pool (VSP) is activated and LDAP search is performed when no suitable service is found at the Local Service Pool (LSP).

4 Simulation Results

To simulate the scenario, we made a service pool and registered a number of services in it. Then we run the service composition scheme proposed in this research. The first experiment is done at a local personal computer. The simulation results in 2(a) shows that an application is developed and after about 300 milliseconds it is decomposed. That is where our service composition scheme activates and again after about 340 milliseconds the application is restored and it is up and running again. But that solution is not really long lasting and application faces faults again. This time our scheme takes 280 milliseconds to reconvert the application at downgraded environment (less resources then before). In 2(b) the simulation results show the life time of three different applications on the gateway. Mainly because of the internal resilience of transportation protocols, in distributed environment, the applications survive for longer and more up time is gained. There are three applications in action and we observe different times of failure which can be because of many reasons which are out of scope of this context. We have used the Virtual Service Pool (VSP) for application binding. We have used TCP/IP suit and have done socket programming to access the services present in different servers. When the service number 1 has finished binding with remote services, it gives way to application 2 (since application generation requests are placed in a queue). After remote binding and processing the application 3 begins processing.

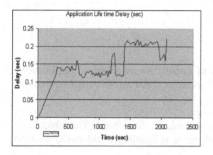
(a) Application generation from LSP

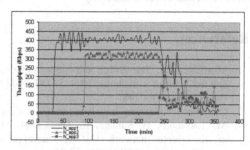
(b) Distributed App. Binding Using VS

Fig. 2. Simulated Modules of the Composition Scheme

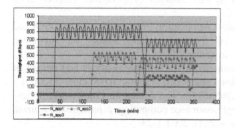
(a) Distributed App. Binding Using VSP (Higher Throughput)

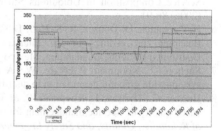
(b) Different Connection Schemes

Fig. 3. Simulated Modules of the Composition Scheme

The Service Composition Manager serves as a service gateway in the middle of the client application and the services present on the different servers. The results are shown in figure 3(a). Figure 3(a) shows the same scheme as shown in figure 3 but with the higher throughput. Figure 3(b) shows the comparison between UDP and TCP. We observe that there is not much difference in the two approaches rather TCP performs better in regards to time.

5 Conclusion

This paper described a service portability scheme that selects the services for service composition when a user leaves one gateway and enters into another. In order to receive the same application environment at the new gateway he had in previous gateway, the service composition must be done in exactly the same way as it was done previously. Our paper placed emphasis on the service selection process and presented some parameters on which the services can be selected. The user transfers the application context in the form of metadata to the new gateway and on the bases of the user preferences, the services are selected. The simulation results obtained show a promising picture and we aim to work on not only improving on the presented parameters but to try to discover more. We also aim to work on contextual and on environmental context matching.

References

1. Morikawa, H.: The design and implementation of context-aware services. Applications and the Internet workshops, 2004. *SAINT 2004 Workshops. 2004 International symposium on*; 1(2004) 293 – 298
2. Open service Gateway Initiative, http://www.osgi.org.
3. M. Takemoto, H. Sunaga, K. Tanaka, H. Matsumura, E. Shinohara: The ubiquitous service-oriented network (USON) – an approach for a ubiquitous world based on P2P technology. *Proc. P2P (2002)*, 17-21
4. M. Yu, A. Taleb Bendiab, D. Reilly, W. Omar: Ubiquitous service interoperation through polyarchical middleware. *Proc. IEEE/WIC' 03*, (2003) 662-665
5. Junaid Ahsenali Chowdary, Seung-Kyu Park and Suk-Kyo Hong: On Recipe Based Service Composition in Ubiquitous Smart Spaces. *Journal of Computer Science* 2(1): (2006) 86-91
6. H. Cervantes, D. Donsez, R. S. Hall: Dynamic Application Frameworks Using OSGi and Beanome, proceedings of the International Symposium and School on Advanced Distributed Systems, Guadalajara, Mexico, November 2002
7. Shelton, C., Koopman, P.&Nace, W.: A framework for scalable analysis and design of system-wide graceful degradation in distributed embedded systems. *WORDS03, 3* (2003)
8. Hoover, C., Hansen, J., Koopman, P. & Tamboli, S.: The Amaranth Framework: policy-based quality of service management for high-assurance computing. *International Journal of Reliability, Quality, and Safety Engineering*, 8(4), 2001 1-28
9. W. Yeong, T. Howes, S. Kille, Lightweight Directory Access Protocol. Request for Comments: 1777. ISODE Consortium, March 1995.
10. K. Czajkowski, S. Fitzgerald, I. Foster, C. Kesselman. Grid Information Services for Distributed Resource Sharing. Proceedings of the Tenth IEEE International Symposium on High-Performance Distributed Computing (HPDC-10), IEEE Press, August 2001.

Autonomic Interference Avoidance with Extended Shortest Path Algorithm[*]

Yong Cui[1], Hao Che[2], Constantino Lagoa[3], and ZhiMei Zheng[1]

[1] Department of Computer Science and Technology, Tsinghua University,
Beijing 100084, China
{cy, zzm}@csnet1.cs.tsinghua.edu.cn
[2] Department of Computer Science and Engineering, University of Texas
at Arlington, 76019
hche@cse.uta.edu
[3] Department of Electrical Engineering, Pennsylvania State University,
PA, USA
lagoa@engr.psu.edu

Abstract. The self-optimization of network resource utilization is one of the important goals for Internet Traffic Engineering. To achieve this goal, many label switched path selection solutions are proposed. However, there are two drawbacks in these solutions. First, they are computationally expensive because they identify the critical links based on the maxflow algorithm. Second, they do not consider the self-demand of the current request when trying to avoid the interference. In this paper, we propose a novel Autonomic Interference Avoidance (AIA) algorithm, which autonomically selects the path with the least interference with the future requests, to overcome these shortcomings. First, AIA identifies the critical links in the shortest paths found by the Shortest Path First (SPF) algorithm, instead of the computationally expensive maxflow algorithm. Second, we introduce the competitive principle to take into account the self-demand of the current request as well as the network status. Therefore, AIA achieves both high resource efficiency and low computation complexity.

Keywords: MPLS, LSP, interference, critical link.

1 Introduction

Although the Internet continually evolves towards larger scale and higher capacity, the rapid growth in network traffic and type of services result in ever increasing network congestion. Traffic engineering (TE) [1] is an effective network engineering technology that optimizes network resources by distributing the network traffic to various paths. Multi-Protocol Label Switching (MPLS) [2]

[*] Supported by: (1) The National Natural Science Foundation of China (No. 60403035); (2) The National Major Basic Research Program of China (No. 2003CB314801); (3) The National Science Foundation under grants ANI-0125653 and NeTS-NBD 0519999.

L.T. Yang et al. (Eds.): ATC 2006, LNCS 4158, pp. 57–66, 2006.

plays an important role in TE. It supports the explicit label switched path (LSP) [3,4], which is an ordered node list that the traffic flows pass along, computed by border nodes (Label Edge Router or LER) according to the requests of the traffic and the status of network resources [5]. Due to the more and more widespread and complex deployment of Internet, it is necessary to seek autonomic LSP selection schemes/algorithms to perform self-optimization of the network resource utilization.

In order to achieve the balanced network load and minimize the resource consumption, the shortest widest path algorithm (SWP) and the widest shortest path algorithm (WSP) extend the SPF [6]. However, the above algorithms are so greedy that they do not consider the interference between the current request and the future demands for links. Since the exact interference avoidance between every pair is a NP-hard problem, so many studies adopt heuristics and defer loading the interfered links (also called critical links) [7,8,9]. The minimum interference routing algorithm (MIRA) [7] identifies the critical links based on maxflow mincuts. However, solely avoiding using critical links for a LSP setup may not lead to desired performance. A new algorithm called Lexicographic MIRA (LMIRA) [8] uses a generalized definition of a critical link, called Δ-critical link. But both MIRA and LMIRA concentrate only on reducing the interference caused by granting an LSP demand for one single ingress-egress pair, so they do not take into account the effect of placing an LSP demand on links that are critical to other ingress-egress pairs. Wang et al. proposed WSC [9] which identifies the critical links for multiple ingress-egress pairs. All these algorithms rely on maxflow algorithm for the identification of critical links, which, however, is computationally expensive.

The VFD [10] algorithm by Capone makes use of the statistical information between pairs. However, VFD increases the complexity because it performs path selection for multiple flows, instead of for the original single flow. The PBR [11] algorithm also makes use of the statistical information, predicts the upcoming requests in a certain interval and applies the multi-flow approach to obtain the optimal solution. However, when there are wide gaps between the predicted statistics and the practical requests, high rejection ratio appears in PBR. To maintain low computational complexity for on-line routing, Szeto and Kumar et al. propose two algorithms, i.e., Dynamic Online Routing Algorithm (DORA[12]) and Max-Min Weighted Additional Flow (MMWAF[13]). They are both two-stage routing algorithms with an offline stage and an online stage. Although DORA and MMWAF reduce the online computation complexity, the execution time in the offline stage can be prohibitively long. Several other algorithms are reported, including the Least Interference Optimization Algorithm (LIOA) [14], Hybrid Routing Approach (HYBR) [15], Simple MIRA (SMIRA) [16], and Light Minimum Interference Routing (LMIR) [17]. LIOA and HYBR reduce the interference among the LSP requests by balancing the number of LSPs carried by the links. However, they do not do well when the bandwidth demand variation of LSP requests is large. SMIRA and LMIR obtain the set of critical links by computing the K-priority paths for all I-E pairs. However,

SMIRA, LMIR, and MIRA etc. don't care current request self-demand of links or paths in the network.

All of the algorithms above contribute the MPLS traffic engineering LSP routing to a certain extent at one time, but at the same time they have limitations. Therefore, this paper aims to develop an autonomic LSP selection algorithm, i.e., the Autonomic Interference Avoidance (AIA) algorithm, with low complexity, high performance. It is able to autonomically figure out paths with the least interferences among the dynamically changing LSP set-up requests. There are two major contributions of this algorithm. First, AIA promises to spurn the computationally expensive maxflow algorithm while identifying the critical links. Instead, it identifies the critical links in the shortest paths found by the Shortest Path First (SPF) algorithm. Second, we introduce the competitive principle to take into account the self-demand of the current requests as well as the network status. Therefore, AIA obtains both lower complexity and higher performance than previous algorithms, such as MIRA, WSC, etc.

The rest of this paper is organized as follows. The system model and the ideas of AIA are introduced in Section 2. In Section 3, we describe the approach and implementation of AIA. Performance evaluation is reported in Section 4. Finally in Section 5, we conclude this paper.

2   System Model and Basic Ideas

We consider a uni-directed graph $G(V, E, C)$, where V denotes the set of nodes in G; E represents the set of directed edges (links) in G; and C is the set of link bandwidths. Let $v \in V$ be a node in G, $n =\mid V \mid$ be the number of nodes in G. Further let $(u, v) \in E$ be an edge of G and $m =\mid E \mid$ be the number of edges in G. Also let $c(u, v) \in C$ be the bandwidth of link (u, v). We further define C_r as the set of link residual capacities and $c_r(u, v) \in C_r$ the residual capacity of link (u, v). Also define P as the set of ingress-egress node pairs between which LSPs can be set up. Let $(s, d) \in P$ denote the ingress-egress pair and $p =\mid P \mid$ the number of ingress-egress pairs in G. A request for an LSP can then be defined as a triplet (s, d, bw) , representing the ingress node, the egress node, and the amount of bandwidth requested, respectively.

Definition 1 (interfere). *If the current request selects a LSP which includes link a, but link a is also included in the LSPs of the future requests of other ingress-egress pairs. Thus we say those requests will interfere on link a.*

Definition 2 (critical link). *If the current request interferes with the future requests of other ingress-egress pairs on link a, we say link a is a critical link.*

Definition 3 (minimum interference path). *The minimum interference path of (s, d, bw) is the path of s to d which has the lowest interference with other ingress-egress pairs among all the paths which satisfy the bandwidth constraint.*

The key idea of interference avoidance is to take into account the interference between the current request and the future request of any other I-E pair. That is

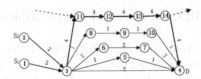

Fig. 1. Competitive Principle

to say, the current request LSP must follow a route that does not "interfere too much" with a route that may be critical to satisfy the future demand. Therefore, we should avoid using the critical links in the network as possible as we can.

There are two potential ingress-egress pairs (S_1, D), (S_2, D) in Fig. 1. The residual bandwidth of each link is shown on it. $(S_1, D, 2)$ is the current request. $(S_2, D, 2)$ is the future potential request. If we just consider the interference avoidance of these I-E pairs, $(S_1, D, 2)$ will be routed along the longest path 1-3-11-12-13-14-4. When the request $(S_1, D, 2)$ arrives the network, it should select the longest path also by applying the interference avoidance idea. This choice needs more network resources and potentially leads to the received bandwidth decreasing.

Now we consider the self-demand of links or paths of the current request, i.e. introducing the competitive principle: when a link belongs to the critical link of both the current request and a future request, it should be used by the first one. Link $(3, 4)$ is the critical link of $(S_1, D, 2)$ and $(S_2, D, 2)$ in Fig. 1, so we should select path 1-3-4 for $(S_1, D, 2)$. When $(S_2, D, 2)$ arrives, it can select path 2-3-6-7-3.

3   AIA Description

3.1   Identify Critical Links

First, AIA assigns the link init-weight as:

$$w_0(u, v) = \frac{\varphi(C_r)}{c_r(u, v)} \tag{1}$$

where $c_r(u, v)$ is the residual capacity of link (u, v), C_r is the set of links residual capacity, $\varphi(C_r)$ is a certain function of C_r, for instance, we can design $\varphi(C_r)$ as the max of all links residual capacity.

Then, AIA applies Dijkstra algorithm K times based on the link weight assigned according to (Eq.1), and obtains K critical paths for each I-E pair. The algorithm starts with selecting the first critical path between a pair (s', d') applying Dijkstra algorithm. Before selecting the next critical path, one of the max weight links should be removed from the network. This procedure is repeated until either K critical paths are found or no more paths are available, whichever occurs first. The critical link set is composed of all the links included in the critical paths of all the I-E pairs. We use $K_{s',d'}$ to indicate the real number of

CP between pair (s', d'). The critical link set C_{sd} is composed of the links on all the critical paths of all the I-E pairs.

3.2 Assign Link Weight

To defer loading the critical link, we should increase the link weight after identifying the critical links. Thus, we define the interference degree as follows:

$$w_1(u, v) = \sum_{(s',d') \in P} \sum_{i=1}^{K_{s'd'}} \lambda \alpha_{s'd'}^i, \quad (u, v) \in CP_{s'd'}^i \qquad (2)$$

where $CP_{s'd'}^i$ is the i-th critical path of the ingress-egress pair (s', d'). $\alpha_{s'd'}^i$ denotes the importance of $CP_{s'd'}^i$. λ is the competition seed. If (s', d') is just the current request, $\lambda = -1$, otherwise $\lambda = 1$.

Then AIA assigns the final link weight as:

$$u(u, v) = w_0(u, v) + \alpha w_1(u, v)$$

$$= \frac{\varphi(C_r)}{c_r(u, v)} + \alpha \sum_{(s',d') \in P} \sum_{\substack{i=1 \\ (u,v) \in CP_{s'd'}^i}}^{K_{s'd'}} \lambda \alpha_{s'd'}^i, \quad (u, v) \in C_{sd}, \alpha > 0 \ (3)$$

where $w_0(u, v)$ as (Eq. 1) reflects the contribution of the link residual capacity to the link weight. $w_1(u, v)$ as (Eq. 2) describes the contribution of the interference of all I-E pairs to link weight. α is a nonnegative const, used to adjust the contribution of the interference to the link weight. $\alpha \alpha_{s'd'}^j$ is the weight increment of the link which belongs to $CP_{s'd'}^i$. The final weight of non-critical link is still $w_0(u, v)$.

We could see that in (Eq. 3) AIA assigns link weights composed of its residual capacity, the interference and competition on that link. λ (competition seed) reflects the integration of interference avoidance and competitive principle. To actualize the purpose of interference avoidance, we think that the request of a certain I-E pair should be routed on those links which other I-E pairs have reserved for it. So the link weights will be increased when it is in the critical path of other I-E pairs, the current request LSP should try its best to avoid selecting this link. But its weight will be decreased when a link is in the critical path of its own I-E pairs. So this link have the priority to be selected while routing the current request. So AIA applies competitive principle while avoiding interference, and guarantees the resource utilization efficiency in MPLS network.

3.3 AIA Description

The chart of Least Minimum Path algorithm which identifies the critical links based on the K shortest paths of each I-E pairs is illustrated in Fig. 2. Given a certain network $G(V, E, C_r)$, when a traffic request $r(s, d, bw)$ arrives at node s, AIA sets up a bandwidth guaranteed LSP if it is reachable and there is sufficient capacity between s and d. The variable w_0 and w denote the link weights when the interference is or not taken into account, respectively. The variable i denotes

INPUT: A residual graph $G(V, E, C_r)$, and a request $r(s, d, bw)$, and K
OUTPUT: A LSP with bw bandwidth units between (s,d)

AIA-Online-Routing:
1) $\varphi(C_r) = \max c_r(u, v)$, $(u, v) \in E$
2)   **FOR EACH** $(u, v) \in E$
3) $w_0(u, v) = \frac{\varphi(C_r)}{c_r(u,v)}$
4) $w(u, v) = w_0(u, v)$
5)   **FOR EACH** $(s', d') \in P$ /*Search each pair's K Critical Paths */
6)   **FOR**$(i = 0; i < K; i + +)$
7)   Dijkstra(G, w_0) /*Search current $CP^i_{s'd'}$ for (s', d')*/
8)   **IF** there is a $CP^i_{s'd'}$ be found
9)   **FOR EACH** $(u, v) \in CP^i_{s'd'}$
10)   **IF** $(s', d') \neq (s, d)$
11) $w(u, v) + = \alpha \cdot \alpha^i_{s'd'}$
12)   **ELSE**
13) $w(u, v) - = \alpha \cdot \alpha^i_{s'd'}$
14) $W = \max w(u, v)$, $(u, v) \in CP^i_{s'd'}$
15)   Eliminate one of the link along $CP^i_{s'd'}$ whose weight is W
16)   **ELSE**
17)   **break**
18)   Recover the eliminated links by line 15
19)   **FOR EACH** $(u, v) \in E$
20)   **IF** $c_r(u, v) < bw$
21)   Delete (u, v) from G
22)   Dijkstra(G, w) /*Search the LSP for $r(s, d, bw)$*/
23)   **IF** there is a LSP be found
24)   **FOR EACH** $(u, v) \in CP^i_{s'd'}$
25) $c_r(u, v) - = bw$
26)   Recover the deleted links by line 19-21

Fig. 2. The chart of Least Minimum Path algorithm

the number of critical paths found for a certain I-E pair. $\alpha^j_{s'd'}$ represents the importance of the i-th critical path of (s', d') pair. $\alpha \cdot \alpha^j_{s'd'}$ is the weight increment of the link which belongs the i-th path of (s', d').

Now we analyze the computational complexity of AIA. It needs to traverse all the links of the network while searching the maximum residual capacity of all the links in line 1. This part has m procedure steps. Assigning weight w_0 and w for all the links in lines 2-4 expends $2m$ procedure steps. There are $K \cdot |P|$ critical paths found for $|P|$ I-E pairs in lines 5-18 by applying Dijkstra. The computational complexity of Dijkstra is $O(n^2)$. So this part executes about $K \cdot |P| \cdot n^2$ steps. The total number of steps of link weight assignment of the $K \cdot |P|$ critical paths is $K \cdot |P| \cdot (n - 1)$, since the longest length of a critical path is $n - 1$. Lines 19-21 needs to traverse all the links of the network again, which also needs m steps. In line 22 executing Dijkstra algorithm once needs n^2 steps. The maximum number of steps in lines 23-25 are $n - 1$. Traversing all the links of the network in line 26 needs m steps again. To sum up all the steps above, there are about $5m+(K\cdot|P|+1)\cdot(n^2+n-1)$ steps in AIA procedure. Thus, AIA's complexity is of order $O(m+K\cdot|P|\cdot n^2)$ expressed as asymptotic time complexity. If the network is on a large scale, thus both K and $|P|$ are absolutely smaller than n, then AIA's complexity is of order $O(m+n^2)$. Therefore, AIA has lower complexity than MIRA and WSC which need maxflow computation and the complexity is of order $O(m^2+n^2\sqrt{m})$.

4   Parameter Regulation and Performance Evaluation

The topology we use in simulations is as shown in Fig. 3. There are 15 nodes and 28 bi-directed edges in this topology. The capacities of the thick edges, which represent OC-48 links, are 4800 units, while those of the thin edges, representing OC-12 links, are 1200 units. There are 5 I-E pairs in Fig. 3. In our simulations, all requests are randomly generated among these I-E pairs and the bandwidth request for each pair is randomly ranged in [1,4]. Given any $(s',d')\in P$ and i, we let $\alpha^j_{s'd'}=1$ and let $\varphi(C_r)$ be the maximum residual capacity in the network.

Definition 4 (rejection ratio). *Given a fixed number of requests, the ratio of the rejected bandwidth by the network to the total requested bandwidth is called rejection ratio.*

4.1   Competitive Principle

We perform three groups of parameter setups, i.e., AIA1 ($K=5,\alpha=1.6$), AIA2 ($K=6,\alpha=2.0$), AIA3 ($K=7,\alpha=2.6$), and for each group of parameters we set $\lambda=-1$ and $\lambda=0$ for the current node ($\lambda=-1$ for other nodes), respectively. The simulation results are displayed in Fig. 4 ("-1" or "0" in parentheses represents the values of λ). It can be found in Fig. 4 that, for each group of parameters lower rejection ratio is obtained when $\lambda=-1$. Therefore, the competitive principle obviously improves AIA in terms of rejection ratio.

4.2   Fixing on the Number of Critical Paths K

From Fig. 5, when K is relatively small, the rejection ratio decreases as K increases. On the contrary, when K is relatively big, the rejection ratio increases as K increases for most of cases. This part of simulations indicates that there exists an appropriate value for K that makes AIA behave the best performance. If K is selected too small, the corresponding critical paths contain too less critical links to be able to reflect the actual interferences between all I-E pairs, while if K is too big, there are too many critical links in K critical paths and they are not able to represent the significance of every link.

4.3   Regulation of α

In Fig. 6, $K=6$ and the competitive principle is considered. It depicts different performance of AIA in terms of rejection ratio when $\alpha=0,1,2,4$, respectively

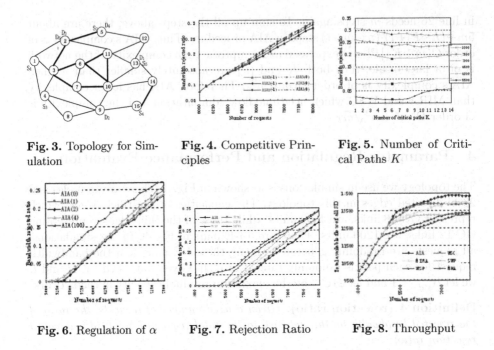

Fig. 3. Topology for Simulation

Fig. 4. Competitive Principles

Fig. 5. Number of Critical Paths K

Fig. 6. Regulation of α

Fig. 7. Rejection Ratio

Fig. 8. Throughput

(the number in parentheses represents the value of α). $\alpha = 0$ shows that link weights are set without regard to the interferences between I-E pairs. The bigger α is, the more important the interference is considered. From Fig. 6, AIA obtains the highest rejection ratio when $\alpha = 100$. Furthermore, if the number of requests is small, the rejection ratio is high when $\alpha = 0$ or 4 and low when $\alpha = 1$ or 2. If the number of requests is large, AIA obtains the highest rejection ratio when $\alpha = 0$ and secondly when $\alpha = 1$ and again $\alpha = 4$. When $\alpha = 2$, it gets the lowest rejection ratio. Therefore, on the whole, AIA behaves the worst when $\alpha = 100$ and the second worst when $\alpha = 0$ but AIA gets the best results when $\alpha = 2$.

It is indicated by this part of simulation results that if only residual capacity is considered, the results are not good, e.g., $\alpha = 0$, while too high or low estimate for the interference is not able to lead to the best performance, as well. In fact, there exist some refined relationship between the effect of interferences upon link weights and the effect of residual capacities upon link weights.

4.4   Performance Evaluation

After the regulation of each parameter through the simulations above, we determine that $K = 6$, $\alpha = 2.0$ and the competitive principle is considered. In Fig. 7, AIA is compared with WSC, MIRA, SWP, WSP and MHA in terms of rejection ratio. It can be found that even at the first simulation point, MHA starts to reject some requests. As more requests arrive, WSP, SWP, MIRA and WSC start to reject requests one after the other. Note that AIA keeps the lowest reject ratio all the time. In Fig. 8, AIA is compared with other algorithms in terms of throughput. When only a small number of requests arrive, the throughput of each algorithm climbs rather rapidly due to low reject ratio. As more and more requests arrive, each algorithm starts to reject requests to some different extent and the throughput ascends slowly. When the number of requests exceeds a certain value, the network becomes saturated and the throughput levels off. Note that in the whole process of simulations, AIA outperforms other algorithms, especially in the case of heavy load.

5   Conclusion

The LSP path selection is the key problem in MPLS traffic engineering. In this paper we propose an AIA algorithm to perform LSP selection. The proposed AIA aims to autonomically solve some problems in MPLS traffic engineering, including high complexity of the least interference path selection and lack of consideration towards the self-demand for links of the current request, etc.

When LSP paths are selected for some traffic, AIA assigns the initial weight of each link as a function reverse to its residual capacity and computes K shortest paths of all I-E pairs according to this weight to identify critical links. To defer loading them, AIA re-assigns the link weight by considering the interference between pairs and introduces the competitive principle based on the interference avoidance. Extensive simulations are performed in this paper and the optimal parameters of AIA are fixed on. Simulation results also show that AIA is able to achieve high throughput and utilization of resources and remarkably outperforms the existing algorithms, e.g., MHA, MIRA, WSC, etc, in terms of rejection ratio and throughput.

References

1. D. Awduche, A. Chiu, A. Elwalid, I. Widjaja, X. Xiao, Overview and Principles of Internet Traffic Engineering, RFC3272, May 2002
2. D. Awduche, J. Malcolm, J.Agogbua, M. O'Dell, and J. McManus. Requirements for Traffic Engineering Over MPLS. RFC2702, Sep. 1999.
3. Swallow, G.; MPLS advantages for traffic engineering. IEEE Communications Magazine, Volume 37, Issue 12, Dec. 1999 Page(s): 54 C 57
4. Anupam Gupta, Amit Kumar, Mikkel Thorup; Routing II: Tree based MPLS routing. Proceedings of the fifteenth annual ACM symposium on Parallel algorithms and architecturesJune 2003
5. Constraint-Based LSP Setup using LDP, rfc3212,January 2002.
6. G. Apostolopoulos, S. Kama, D. Williams, R. Guerin, A. Orda, T. Przygienda. QoS Routing Mechanisms and OSPF Extensions. RFC 2676, August 1999
7. M. Kodialam and T. V. Lakshman, Minimum Interference Routing with Applications to MPLS Traffic Engineering, in INFOCOM 2000, vol.2, pp. 884C893.
8. K. Kar, M. Kodialam, and T. V. Lakshman, MPLS traffic engineering using enhanced minimum interference routing: An approach based on lexicographic maxflow. Proceedings of Eighth International Workshop on Quality of Service (IWQoS), Pittsburgh, USA, June 2000. Page(s): 105-114

9. X. S. B. Wang and C. Chen, A New Bandwidth Guaranteed Routing Algorithm for MPLS Traffic Engineering, IEEE International Conference on Communications, 2002, Vol.2 pp. 1001C1005.
10. A. Capone, L. Fratta, and F. Martignon, Virtual Flow Deviation: Dynamic routing of bandwidth guaranteed connections, QoS-IP 2003, pp. 592-605.
11. S. Suri, M. Waldvogel, D. Bauer, and P. R. Warkhede, Profile-based routing and traffic engineering, Computer Communications, vol. 26, pp. 351C365, 2003.
12. W. Szeto, R. Boutaba, and Y. Iraqi, Dynamic Online Routing Algorithm for MPLS Traffic Engineering, E. Gregori et al. (Eds.): NETWORKING 2002, LNCS 2345, pp. 936C946, 2002.
13. Deepak Kumar, Joy Kuri and Anurag Kumar, Routing Guaranteed Bandwidth Virtual Paths with Simultaneous Maximization of Additional Flows, IEEE International Conference on Communications, 2003, vol.3,pp. 1759-1764.
14. Bagula, A.B.; Botha, M.; Krzesinski, A.E. Online traffic engineering: the least interference optimization algorithm Communications(ICC), IEEE International Conference on Vol.2, Date 20-24 June 2004 Page(s):1232 - 1236
15. Stellenbosch, Western Cape, South Africa ; Hybrid traffic engineering:the least path interference algorithm. ACM International Conference Proceeding Series 2004,Vol. 75 Pages: 89 C 96
16. Ilias Iliadis and Daniel Bauer; A new class of online minimum interference routing algorithms. NETWORKING 2002, LNCS 2345, pp. 959-971, 2002.
17. B. Figueiredo, L. S. da Fonseca, and A. S Monteiro, A Minimum Interference Routing Algorithm, In: Communications(ICC),2004 IEEE International Conference on Date20-24 Volume 4, Page(s):1942 - 1947,

Multi-level Model-Based Self-diagnosis of Distributed Object-Oriented Systems

A.R. Haydarlou*, B.J. Overeinder, M.A. Oey, and F.M.T. Brazier

Vrije Universiteit Amsterdam, De Boelelaan 1081a,
1081 HV Amsterdam, The Netherlands
{rezahay, bjo, michel, frances}@cs.vu.nl

Abstract. Self-healing relies on correct diagnosis of system malfunctioning. This paper presents a use-case based approach to self-diagnosis. Both a static and a dynamic model of a managed-system are distinguished with explicit functional, implementational, and operational knowledge of specific use-cases. This knowledge is used to define sensors to detect and localise anomalies at the same three levels, providing the input needed to perform informed diagnosis. The models presented can be used to automatically instrument existing distributed legacy systems.

1 Introduction

Autonomic computing and self-management have emerged as promising approaches to the management complexity of networked, distributed systems [1]. Self-healing, one of the important aspects of self-management, mandates effective diagnosis of system malfunctioning. Self-diagnosis of anomalies in physically distributed systems for which relations between the different information sources are not always clearly defined, is a challenge.

This paper presents an approach to self-diagnosis within the context of a self-healing framework. Characteristics of this framework are that it (1) can be applied to existing distributed object-oriented applications[1], including legacy applications, (2) distinguishes different use-case based views and levels within an existing distributed system (system-level, component-level, class-level), and (3) provides a structure to support application model construction. The application models needed to achieve use-case based self-diagnosis are the specific focus of this paper.

Sections 2 and 3 present the approach to self-healing in more detail. Section 4 describes the two models: a static and dynamic use-case based model of a system. Section 5 describes the instrumentation of sensors following the same three levels distinguished in both models. Section 6 illustrates the approach for a specific use-case in the domain of financial trading. Section 7 positions the approach in the context of related research.

---

* This research is supported by the NLnet Foundation, http://www.nlnet.nl, and Fortis Bank Netherlands, http://www.fortisbank.nl.

[1] The terms *system* and *application* will be used interchangeably.

L.T. Yang et al. (Eds.): ATC 2006, LNCS 4158, pp. 67–77, 2006.

2   Self-healing Design Rationale

Software engineering involves many different parties each with their own roles and responsibilities, including functional analysts, developers, and system administrators. Each of these parties is interested in the internal working (behaviour) of a system, but have their own view of the system: a *functional, implementational,* or *operational* view, respectively[2]. These views are related to *system use-cases,* which describe the behaviour of a system by specifying the response of a system to a given request. These use-case specifications are acquired in the requirements acquisition phase of a software development process. The views are defined as follows:

Functional View - This view describes the high level functionality of different parts of an application and how these parts are combined to realise a use-case specification. Sequences of actions (*functional steps*) specify what needs to be done by an application to attain the expected functionality. This knowledge can be used to roughly locate the malfunctioning part of an application.

Implementational View - This view describes the low level code of an application and describes how a use-case specification has been implemented as a chain of methods (functions) at code level. Pre- and post conditions of a method are specified as are sequences of important code statements (*implementational steps*) in a method body. This knowledge can be used to localise and address the root-cause of application malfunctioning.

Operational View - This view describes the runtime processes and lightweight threads of control executing within an application and describes how they should be synchronised in order to realise a use-case specification. The structure of interacting processes and lightweight threads are specified as are sequences of process-to-process or thread-to-thread communication (*operational steps*). This knowledge can be used to discover partial system shutdowns and process-oriented application malfunctioning.

Our approach to self-diagnosis is based on these three views. Information from all three views is used to locate the malfunctioning part of a system at the corresponding level as indicated above.

3   Self-healing Architecture

This section presents an overview of a complete self-healing architecture (Fig. 1(a)). At the highest level two modules are distinguished: a managed-system and an autonomic-manager. The *managed-system* can be any existing distributed object-oriented application that has been extended with sensors and effectors. *Sensors* (see Sect. 5) provide runtime information from the running application to the autonomic-manager and *effectors* provide adaptation instructions from the autonomic-manager to the running application.

---

[2] The views are somewhat similar to the logical, implementational, and process views used in Unified Modeling Language (UML) [2].

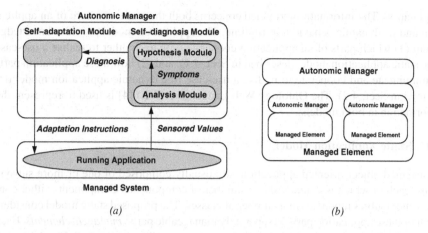

Fig. 1. Self-healing architecture. (a) Interaction between an Autonomic Manager and the Managed System. (b) Each Managed Element has its own separate Autonomic Manager.

The *autonomic-manager* itself has two modules: (1) a self-diagnosis module, and (2) a self-adaptation module. The *self-diagnosis module* continuously checks whether the running application shows any abnormal behaviour by monitoring the values it receives from the sensors placed in the application. If so, the self-diagnosis module determines a diagnosis and passes it to the *self-adaptation module*. This latter module is responsible for planning actions that must be taken to resolve the abnormal behaviour and uses the effectors to do so.

The self-diagnosis module contains the analysis module and the hypothesis module. The *analysis module* is responsible for identifying abnormal behaviour (*symptom*) of a running application based on values received by the sensors and the information available in its application model (see Sect. 4) and its analysis knowledge-base. The *hypothesis module* determines the root-cause of a given abnormal behaviour using the knowledge available in its *hypothesis knowledge-base*.

The *analysis knowledge-base* contains constraint rules (SWRL rules [3]) and meta-knowledge about the constraint rules. Constraint rules define whether observed values coming from different sensors are consistent with a certain symptom associated with a job. Depending on the type of job, symptoms can be functional, implementational, or operational. The meta-knowledge in the analysis module contains strategic rules regarding success or failure of constraint rules.

This paper focuses only on the self-diagnosis module, and in particular on the models and sensors used by the analysis module.

4   Application Model Design

The main goal of designing a model of a running application is to provide useful diagnostic information about the application to the autonomic-manager. Based on the application model and diagnosis information, the autonomic-manager can coordinate its operations for self-configuration, self-healing, and self-optimisation of the managed-application. The information provided concerns both the static structure of an application and its dynamic behaviour at runtime. The application model provides knowledge about (1) which parts of an application cooperate with each other to realise a use-case (the static application model described in Sect. 4.1), and (2) how these application parts communicate and cooperate to realise a use-case (the dynamic application model described in Sect. 4.2). The Ontology Web Language (OWL) [4] is used to represent the information in both models.

4.1 Static Application Model

Distributed object-oriented applications are usually composed of one or more subsystems, each of which is composed of a number of components. Components either contain other (sub)components or a number of classes. The proposed static model considers each of these application parts as separately manageable parts: *managed-elements*. Each managed-element is associated with a separate autonomic-manager (see Fig. 1(b)).

Dividing a system into multiple, smaller managed-elements, each with an associated autonomic-manager has some advantages: (1) it simplifies the description of dynamic behaviour of structurally complex applications, (2) it simplifies and reduces the required self-healing knowledge, and (3) it facilitates the distribution, migration, and reuse of the application elements by equipping each element with its own specific self-healing knowledge. Consequently, in order to coordinate the self-healing actions, the autonomic-managers should communicate with each other as they are divided over multiple elements.

There are different types of managed-elements in a static system model. The ManagedElement is an abstract entity that contains the common properties of all managed-elements. Each ManagedElement is associated with an AutonomicManager and has a list of Connectors that bind the ManagedElement to other ManagedElements. A Connector has a Protocol that is used by ManagedElements to communicate with each other. Furthermore, each ManagedElement and Connector has a list of States and Events.

A State models a data item (of the ManagedElement or Connector) whose value may change during application lifetime and that is important enough to monitor. A State can be either an AtomicState or a CompositeState. A CompositeState consists of one or more states and corresponds to composite data items. An Event models unexpected happenings during execution of the application.

There are four different types of managed-elements: ManagedSystem, Managed-Runnable, ManagedComponent, and ManagedClass. The ManagedSystem is used to describe and manage the collective behaviour of a number of related subsystems. It is composed of a number of ManagedRunnables.

A ManagedRunnable models a part of an application that is runnable, that can be started/stopped. Examples of a ManagedRunnable are a subsystem or an execution thread. When a running application is observed from the operational point of view, the application is monitored at the level of ManagedRunnables. In other words, the ManagedRunnable is the diagnosis unit. From the operational viewpoint, the list of States associated with a ManagedRunnable describes the status of a process or thread. A State within a ManagedRunnable is called a ManagedRunnableState. Events correspond with events such as startup and shutdown of the ManagedRunnable.

A ManagedRunnable is composed of one or more other ManagedRunnables or is composed of a number of ManagedComponents, each of which models a software component or a library that implements a specific functionality (such as a logging component, an object-relational mapping component, or an XML parser component). Usually, the ManagedComponents are the diagnosis units when the running application is observed from the functional point of view. From this viewpoint, the list of States associated with a ManagedComponent describes the status of a component. A State within a ManagedComponent is called a ManagedComponentState. Events correspond with exceptions thrown from the component, or user-defined events associated with the modeled component.

A ManagedComponent is either composed of one or more other ManagedComponents or composed of a number of ManagedClasses. The ManagedClass is an atomic managed-element that corresponds with a coding-level class and models the static properties of that class (such as, class name, class file, and file location). From the implementational point of view, the application malfunctioning can be detected at the ManagedClass level. From this viewpoint, the list of States associated with a ManagedClass describes the set of class and instance (object) variables declared in the modeled class. A State within a ManagedClass is called a ManagedClassState. Events correspond with exceptions raised at coding level.

A Connector binds two ManagedElements together. More precisely, they model the fact that two ManagedElements can interact with each other. For example, a method within one ManagedClass can call a method of another ManagedClass or one ManagedRunnable can send information to another ManagedRunnable over a network via some protocol. The list of States associated with a Connector describes the state of the connection itself, such as whether the connection is up or down. A State within a Connector is called a ConnectorState. Events correspond with exceptions such as a network time-out.

4.2 Dynamic Application Model

Conceptually, the dynamic behaviour of an application can be modeled as a sequence of the following three steps: (1) the application receives a request together with corresponding *input-data* (parameter) to perform some *job*, (2) the application internally goes into a *job execution channel*, and finally, (3) the application returns some *output-data* (result).

Within a job execution channel (Fig. 2), a job is realised by sequentially (or in parallel, but the current assumption is that tasks are sequential) executing a number of *tasks*. Tasks, in general, read some input, manipulate data, and produce some output. The data that they manipulate originates from the job input-data, the shared state of the ManagedElement that executes the job, and/or an external data source (e.g., database, user interface, or queue).

The functional analyst, developer, and system administrator, from their own point of view, can use this simple abstraction of the application's runtime behaviour to describe the internal working of the application. The proposed dynamic system model is based on this abstraction.

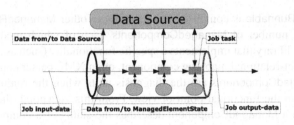

Fig. 2. Dynamic application model

The dynamic application model of an application consists of the specification of a collection of Jobs, Tasks, States, Events, and Sensors. A Job has a name, zero or more inputs, one optional output, a number of tasks, and one or more managed-elements that cooperate to realise the job execution. Depending on which view one takes when modeling the dynamic behaviour of an application, each job corresponds to a single functional behaviour, implementational use-case realisation, or operational use-case realisation. The three types of jobs are called: FunctionalJobs which are associated with ManagedComponents, OperationalJobs which are associated with ManagedRunnables, and ImplementationalJobs which are associated with ManagedClasses.

Each Task within a job corresponds to one or more functional, implementational, or operational steps, depending on the type of job. A specification of a task consists of the task's name, its input and output states, and the name of the ManagedElement that executes this task and whose states can be modified by this task.

Tasks are the basic unit of the dynamic application model and are used to reason about the health status of an application. To detect runtime failures, the execution of a job is monitored. The correct behaviour of a job can be defined in terms of the correct job input-data, the correct job output-data, and the correct changes the job makes to the data it manipulates. Any abnormal, and therefore undesirable, behaviour of a job is described as one or more Symptoms. A Symptom has a name which is associated with a rule (*constraint*). Rules are logical combinations of comparison operators over sensored values. During execution of a job, the autonomic-manager continuously checks to see whether any of these constraints are violated.

Tasks have the common property that they are able to interrupt the normal execution process of their job and cause *exceptional* behaviours. Autonomic-managers can monitor these exceptional behaviours and react accordingly, based on the reaction policy specified in the model.

Tasks are classified as AbstractTask, StateManipulation, JobForker, PeerInvocation, JobInputChecker, and JobOutputChecker. This classification can be extended in the future, if necessary. For the sake of space, only the StateManipulation is described below.

StateManipulation Task - The most frequently occurring tasks within a job are State-Manipulation tasks, which manipulate some type of State. These tasks are used to monitor the manipulation of all incoming and outgoing data items during execution of a job. StateManipulation tasks are further categorised based on the type of State they manipulate. For example, a ManagedElementStateManipulation task manipulates the state of a managed-element, and a DataSourceStateManipulation task manipulates a state coming from an external data source, such as a user interface, persistent storage, or an asynchronous queue).

5 Model Sensors and Observation Points

To perform a diagnosis, an autonomic-manger must monitor the behaviour of the application. To this end, an application is instrumented with *model sensors*, or simply *sensors*, which send runtime information to the autonomic-manager. The values provided by these sensors enable the autonomic-manager to monitor when, and determine why an application does not behave as expected. The application model described in Sect. 4 indicates where to place sensors.

The behaviour of an application is determined by its jobs, more precisely, by its tasks defined in the dynamic model. Monitoring the execution of a task consists of monitoring all data (states) that the task reads and/or writes, and also monitoring whether an event, such as an exception, has occurred during the execution of the task. Sensors are used to monitor these tasks.

The proposed framework distinguishes between two types of Sensors: StateSensors and EventSensors. A StateSensor is used to monitor specific input or output data of a task, or to monitor any data item that is read or written by the task. The data item is part of the ManagedElement associated with the task or comes from an external data source (see Sect. 4.2). Additionally, if the associated ManagedElement of the task also uses a Connector to communicate with another ManagedElement (see static model in Sect. 4.1), the ConnectorState can also be monitored by this type of sensor. The EventSensor is used to monitor any event that occurs during the execution of a task, such as an Exception.

The information supplied by these Sensors to the autonomic-manager include: (1) the value of a data item or the information regarding an event, and (2) the task that has manipulated this data item or the task that has caused the event. With this information the autonomic-manager can determine whether the constraint associated with a Symptom of the corresponding job has been violated. If so, the application has shown abnormal behaviour and the root-cause can be identified since it is known with which task the Symptom has been associated. Subsequently, actions should be taken to remedy the abnormal behaviour.

The problem of where to place a Sensor is now easily solved. As each task is executed by one specific ManagedElement (defined in the static model), the physical place for the corresponding Sensor in the application code is known.

EventSensors form a general mechanism to notify the autonomic-manager of any event that may be of interest. These events can be defined by a user of the framework in the static model (see Sect. 4.1). Examples of such events are: (1) Exception event: an exception has occurred, (2) TimerExpiration event: a timer expires, or (3) TaskExecution event: a specific task (one of the tasks mentioned in Sect. 4.2) starts executing.

States, Tasks, and Sensors are closely related: a specific state-type is manipulated by the corresponding task-type and is monitored by the corresponding sensor-type. For example, a DataSourceState is manipulated by a DataSourceStateManipulation task and is monitored by a DataSourceStateSensor. The framework enforces this relation during the construction of application models.

Each Sensor monitors the value (observedValue) of some item (monitoredItem), which could be a state or an event. Furthermore, each sensor has a corresponding sensorTrigger. The SensorTrigger represents the Task or ManagedElement that defines the context in which the data item or event is monitored.

Sensors are provided either by the self-healing framework or by users. The proposed self-healing framework uses Aspect Oriented Programming (AOP) [5] to instrument sensors at the specified observation points in the compiled code of an existing application. The framework also defines a *SensorInterface* which can be implemented by users to provide information from the running application.

6   Practical Scenario

The scenario described in this section is borrowed from Fortis Bank Netherlands' distributed trading application. The complete application is very complex and consists of a considerable number of subsystems and a large number of components and classes. In this paper, the proposed self-healing model is applied to a simplified version of payments in the trading application.

6.1   Trading Application Static Model

The static model of the simplified trading application consists of a ManagedSystem that contains five ManagedRunnables: a browser, a web application, a legacy backend (mainframe application), a mediator, and a database manager.

Each of these runnables has a large number of ManagedComponents. In this scenario, only the following components are considered: payment component, data access (Hibernate [6]), web interface (Struts [7]), and web service. Each of these components, in turn, consists of a large number of ManagedClasses (Java classes). The ManagedRunnables have four Connectors: (1) a HttpProtocol connector between the browser and the Web application, (2) a SOAPProtocol connector between the Web application and the mediator, (3) a MessageOrientedProtocol connector between the mediator and the legacy backend, and (4) a JDBCProtocol connector between the Web application and the database manager.

6.2   Trading Application Dynamic Model

As stated above, this scenario focuses on the payment use-case. Authorised Fortis employees inspect a trade submitted by an authorised employee of a fund company, and send a payment request to the legacy backend.

Specification 1 shows the specification of states that concern the payment job. Note that, only states that are of importance to the use-case are specified. These states are abstractions of the corresponding objects in the trading application. As the OWL representation has not been introduced in this paper, the model elements are presented in textual format.

```
Fund: CompositeState {
  memberStates:
        (1) fund_name: AtomicState          (2) fund_group: AtomicState
}
Trade: CompositeState {
  memberStates:
        (1) payment_amount: AtomicState     (4) trade_fund: Fund
        (2) account_nr: AtomicState         (5) trade_id: AtomicState
        (3) trade_status: AtomicState
}
```

Specification 1. Example state specifications

For each view, the jobs and sensors used in our scenario are specified below. The functional and operational jobs cover the complete payment use-case. The implementational view is limited to the payment status change.

Functional Job Specifications - Specification 2 shows the specification of the functional payment job with its input, output, tasks, associated managed-elements, and abnormal functional behaviours. The input needed to determine whether a symptom occurs is provided by one or more sensors of which an example is also specified in Specification 2. For example, symptom (1) occurs if the value of Trade.payment_amount, retrieved from a web form after executing task (1), is negative.

```
FPayment: FunctionalJob {
  input:  Trade (without payment status)
  output: Trade (with payment status)
  tasks: (1) Obtain payment command from user    (4) Change trade status in the database
         (2) Send payment to backend             (5) Show updated trade to the user
         (3) Obtain payment status from backend
  managedElements:
         (1) web interface                       (3) web service
         (2) payment component                   (4) data access
  symptoms:
         (1) Trade.payment_amount < 0            (3) not_authorised_exception occurred
         (2) Trade.account_nr == 'unknown'
}

PaymentAmountSensor: WebFormStateSensor {
  monitoredItem: Trade.payment_amount
  observedValue: StateValue,
  sensorTrigger: Task (1)
}
```

Specification 2. Functional job and sensor specifications

Operational Job Specifications - Specification 3 shows the operational payment job related to the payment use-case from the operational point of view and clarifies which processes (or threads) cooperate during realisation of the payment use-case. *Operational symptoms* indicate infrastructural malfunctioning detected by one or more sensors of which an example is also specified in Specification 3. For example, symptom (3) occurs if, during a periodic check, the database manager does not respond.

Implementational Job Specifications - Specification 4 shows the implementational job specification corresponding to the method *changeTradeStatus* defined in the Java class *TradePersistency*. *Implementational symptoms* indicate code malfunctioning detected by one or more sensors of which an example is also specified in Specification 4.

```
OPayment: OperationalJob {
  input:   Trade (without payment status)
  output:  Trade (with payment status)
  tasks:  (1) Send payment command via HTTP request  (6) Send payment status to web application
          (2) Receive HTTP request                    (7) Send trade status change to database
          (3) Send payment to mediator via SOAP           manager via JDBC
          (4) Send payment to backend via MQSeries    (8) Send transaction confirmation
          (5) Send payment status to mediator         (9) Send updated trade to browser via HTTP
  managedElements:
          (1) browser                                 (4) backend
          (2) web application                         (5) database manager
          (3) mediator
  symptoms:
          (1) mediator's max_connections reached      (3) database manager does not respond
          (2) backend does not listen to port x
}

DatabaseManagerSensor: ManagedRunnableStateSensor {
  monitoredItem: ManagedRunnableState
  observedValue: StateValue
  sensorTrigger: TimerExpiration
}
```

Specification 3. Operational job and sensor specifications

```
IChangeTradeStatus: ImplementationalJob {
  input:   trade_id_param, trade_status_param
  output: Trade (with changed status)
  tasks:  (1) Start database session              (4) Write trade to database
          (2) Read trade from database            (5) End database session
          (3) Change trade status                 (6) Return the trade
  managedElements:
          (1) TradePersistency
  symptoms:
          (1) trade_status_param == 'unknown'     (3) non_existing_trade_exception occurred
          (2) Trade.trade_status != trade_status_param
}

TradeStatusParamSensor: TaskInputSensor {
  monitoredItem: trade_status_param
  observedValue: StateValue
  sensorTrigger: Task (3)
}
```

Specification 4. Implementational job and sensor specifications

For example, symptom (1) occurs if the value of Trade.trade_status_param, just before executing task (3), is unknown.

7 Discussion

Self-diagnosis of complex systems is a challenge: especially when existing legacy systems are the target. This paper is based on the concept of a model-based framework for self-diagnosis in which three views of a complex system are defined and related: the functional view, the operational view, and the implementational view. Self-diagnosis is based on both a static and a dynamic model of a complex system in which these views are mapped onto levels of system model specification. Sensors are explicitly related to the levels: sensor types are defined for each of the levels. A system administrator is provided the structure to specify sensors which can be placed automatically.

This research can be seen to extend the Robinson's work [8] in this area. The three views of system requirements is new, as is the explicit distinction between a static and a dynamic model of a system. Symptom specification is comparable with the specification of high-level requirements expressed in a formal language. The autonomic-manager capable of reasoning about a running complex system at the three levels distinguished above, can be viewed as an extension of the *monitor program* proposed by [8].

Dowling and Cahill [9] introduce *K-Component* model as a programming model and architecture for building self-adaptive component software. In the K-Component model, which is an extension of CORBA component model, components are the units of computation. Therefore, this model does not support self-management within the internal structure of components (for example, Java classes if the components are written in Java). The *feedback states* and *feedback events* are comparable with the notion of State and Event.

Baresi and Guinea [10] propose external *monitoring rules* (specified in *WS-COL*) to monitor the execution of WS-BPEL process. A monitoring rule consists of *monitoring location*, *monitoring parameters*, and *monitoring expression*. In our framework, a Sensor contains the same information as the monitoring location and monitoring parameters, and SWRL rules are comparable with monitoring expressions.

Currently, an implementation of the proposed framework is being developed, and the research focuses on extending the framework. For example, meta-knowledge rules in the analysis module will be formulated, and support for parallel execution of tasks within a job execution channel will be designed. Additionally, the proposed framework will be applied in the field of service-oriented computing.

References

1. Kephart, J., Chess, D.: The vision of autonomic computing. Computer **36** (2003) 41–50
2. Rumbaugh, J., Jacobson, I., Booch, G.: The Unified Modeling Language Reference Manual. 2rd edn. Addison-Wesley Professional, Reading, MA (2004)
3. Horrocks, I., Patel-Schneider, P.F., Boley, H., Tabet, S., Grosof, B., Dean, M.: SWRL: A semantic web rule language combining OWL and RuleML. http://www.w3.org/Submission/2004/SUBM-SWRL-20040521/ (2004)
4. Bechhofer, S., Harmelen, F., Hendler, J.A., Horrocks, I., McGuinness, D.L., Patel-Schneider, P.F., Stein, L.A.: Owl web ontology language reference. http://www.w3.org/TR/owl-ref (2004)
5. Elrad, T., Filman, R.E., Bader, A.: Aspect-oriented programming: Introduction. Communications of the ACM **44** (2001) 29–32
6. JBoss Federation: Hibernate framework. http://www.hibernate.org (2006)
7. Apache Software Foundation: Struts framework. http://struts.apache.org (2006)
8. Robinson, W.: Monitoring software requirements using instrumented code. In: HICSS '02: Proceedings of the 35th Annual Hawaii International Conference on System Sciences (HICSS'02)-Volume 9, Washington, DC, USA, IEEE Computer Society (2002) 276.2
9. Dowling, J., Cahill, V.: The k-component architecture meta-model for self-adaptive software. In: REFLECTION '01: Proceedings of the Third Int. Conference on Metalevel Architectures and Separation of Crosscutting Concerns, London, UK, Springer-Verlag (2001) 81–88
10. Baresi, L., Guinea, S.: Towards dynamic monitoring of ws-bpel processes. In: ICSOC: Proceedings of the 3rd Int. Conference on Service Oriented Computing. (2005) 269–282

From Components to Autonomic Elements Using Negotiable Contracts

Hervé Chang[1], Philippe Collet[1], Alain Ozanne[2], and Nicolas Rivierre[2]

[1] University of Nice Sophia Antipolis, I3S Laboratory
Sophia Antipolis, France
[2] France Telecom R&D Division, MAPS/AMS Laboratory
Issy les Moulineaux, France

Abstract. Autonomic computing aims at producing software systems that can manage themselves. As component-based development also partly addresses the complexity of large applications, we propose to combine the benefits of both approaches by using components equipped with negotiable contracts. These contracts specify the correct behavior of the components and play a central role in feedback control loops to enforce some autonomic features on components. In this paper, we present *ConFract*, a contract-based framework for hierarchical components in which contracts are runtime objects that are dynamically built from specifications, and automatically updated according to dynamic reconfigurations. Moreover, contracts clearly define the responsibilities (guarantor, beneficiaries) between their participating components which are exploited by some negotiations to automatically adapt components and contracts, and revalidate the system. The generic negotiation mechanism and an associated concession-based policy are presented.

1 Introduction

The massive growth of distributed information systems and ubiquitous applications breaks classic approaches of software engineering as development, configuration and maintenance phases have reached unmanageable complexity and cost levels. To tackle these problems, a new paradigm, Autonomic Computing, has emerged, inspired from the autonomic capabilities of biological systems [1,2]. The main objective is to produce software systems that can manage themselves, thus providing some self-management properties [3] mainly *self-configuring, self-healing, self-optimising* and *self-protecting*. This has led researchers to propose significant works in different areas, considering a form of cooperation among computing elements organized around a feedback control loop. Although this makes possible to support reasoning and decision with minimal human intervention, a challenge remains to organize relevant information and integrate autonomic features, as seamlessly as possible, into complex software systems.

In our opinion, the autonomic viewpoint needs to combine with other approaches that aim at mastering software complexity. Among programming paradigms, the component-based paradigm has also received much attention from both industry and academia. This approach enables developers to manage some complexities of software development, in particular by separating interface from implementation and by explicitly describing the architecture of the application. Advanced hierarchical component

L.T. Yang et al. (Eds.): ATC 2006, LNCS 4158, pp. 78–89, 2006.

models also allow developers to have a uniform view of applications at various levels of abstraction, and some component platforms provide reflective capabilities and support dynamic reconfigurations of components [4]. Besides, basic *software contracts* are usually used to validate component assembly, but rich forms of contracts are needed, as contracts should also finely address functional properties as well as extra-functional requirements that concern both the assembly and the execution of components. We argue that these contracts can be seen as some relevant and up-to-date knowledge to support some autonomic features during the four stages (monitor, analyze, plan and execute) of control loops [1]. Contract enforcement clearly corresponds to a form of self-monitoring. Moreover, as contracts can be frequently challenged and violated by the fluctuation of extra-functional properties, mechanisms to manage these violations are needed. Contract negotiation, based on the analysis stage then represents a natural means to organize the planning stage and to setup some contracts between parties. Finally, the planning and execution stages of control loops should also rely on fine-grained information on contracts.

To meet these requirements, we propose *ConFract*, a contracting system for hierarchical components that supports self-healing, and a form of self-configuration and self-protection, by making contracts play a central role in our feedback control loops. Contracts in *ConFract* system are runtime objects that are dynamically built from specifications, and automatically updated according to dynamic reconfigurations. They clearly define some responsibilities between the participating components and are also negotiable. Our negotiation model can restore the validity of contracts by adapting components and contracts themselves at assembly and run times. An *atomic negotiation* is activated for each violated provision of a contract, and it relies on the fine-grained information contained in each provision. Different negotiation policies are intended to be integrated, and we describe here a concession-based negotiation policy.

The rest of the paper is organized as follows. In the next section, an overview of the *ConFract* system is given through a running example. In section 3, the main negotiation model is described and the use of contracts in control loops is discussed. Section 4 illustrates the negotiation model by describing a concession-based policy using our example. In section 5, related work are discussed and finally section 6 concludes this paper with some indications on future work.

2 The ConFract System

ConFract [5] is a contracting system for *Fractal* [4], a general component model with the following main features[1]: composite components (to have a uniform view of applications at various levels of abstraction), shared components (to model resources and resource sharing while maintaining component encapsulation), reflective capabilities (introspection capabilities to monitor a running system and re-configuration capabilities to deploy and dynamically configure a system) and openness (in the model, almost everything is optional and can be extended). Moreover, technical aspects of components such as life cycle, bindings and content (depicted as LC, BC and CC in figure 1), can be managed by *controllers*, following the principle of separation of concerns. As the *Fractal* model is very general [4], our contributions are possibly applicable to other component models.

---

[1] The reader can find more details at http://fractal.objectweb.org.

2.1 Contracts

Using the *ConFract* system, one can specify and verify, on hierarchical software components, properties that go beyond interface signatures. The *ConFract* system [5] dynamically builds contracts from specifications at assembly time and updates them according
to dynamic reconfigurations of components. A contract is thus a first class entity, always
up-to-date regarding the architecture and which also refers to components needed for its
evaluation. *ConFract* distinguishes several types of contracts according to the specifications given by the designers. *Interface contracts* are established on the binding between
a client and a server interface, only retaining specifications on the interface scope. They
are similar to object contracts [6]. *External composition contracts* are located on the
external side of each component. They consist of specifications which refer only to external interfaces of the component. They thus express the usage and external behavior
rules of the component. *Internal composition contracts* are located on the internal side
of a composite component. In the same way, they consist of specifications which refer
only to internal interfaces of the component and to external interfaces of its subcomponents. They express the assembly and internal behavior rules of the implementation of
the composite component.

In the *ConFract* system, the various contracts are managed by *contract controllers*
(named CTC in figure 1) which are located on the membrane of every component. They
drive the construction and the verification of contracts when appropriate events occur. In
each contract, well-defined responsibilities are also assigned to involved components.
It uses a metamodel that describes responsibility patterns for each category of specifications (e.g a precondition of an external composition contract). These responsibilities
can be either *(i) guarantor* which acts to ensure the provision and must be notified in
case of violation of the provision, *(ii) beneficiaries* which can rely on the provision or
(iii) possible *contributors* which are needed to check the provision. As shown in [5]
different responsibilities are assigned depending on the contract types.

Currently in *ConFract*, specifications are written using an executable assertion language, named *CCL-J (Component Constraint Language for Java)*, which is inspired by
OCL and enhanced to be adapted to the *Fractal* model. It supports classic constructs
such as preconditions, postconditions and invariants, but the scope of specifications can
be on a component or on an interface. Other specification languages are also intended
to be integrated into ConFract [7].

2.2 A Running Example

We use, as a working example, a basic multimedia streaming application, developed
with the Sun Java Media Framework API, which provides control capabilities over
multimedia data and standard RTP/RTCP protocol support for multimedia streaming.
The application is composed of two main parts: the client is responsible for receiving
multimedia streams and the server keeps the information about accessible multimedia resources and sends multimedia streams according to end-user request for video
transmission. The architecture of the video player is shown on figure 1, with a
FractalMultimedia component containing two main subcomponents: Multimed-
iaClient which represents the client side and MultimediaServer on which we

essentially focus on. The `MultimediaServer` is formed out of four subcomponents: `RTPTransmitterManager` which configures and creates the RTP stream to be sent, `Processor` which processes and controls multimedia data (the `start` method begins the video transmission) and manages some of its functioning parameters through attributes, `ApplicationManager` which controls some services provided by the multimedia server (the `expectedCPUUsage` method evaluates the CPU usage of the video streaming service considering the video frame rate) and finally `Logger` which manages a history of played videos (the `lastUrl` method allows one to get the url of the most recently played video).

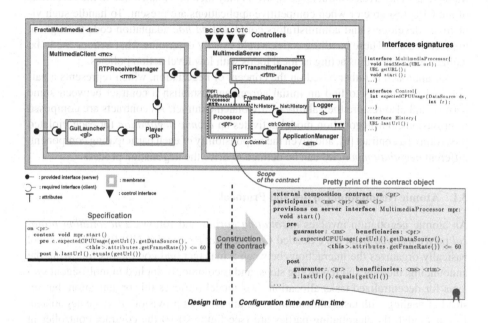

Fig. 1. A composition contract on the Fractal Multimedia System

As for contracts, the specification referring to the component `<pr>` (lower left part of figure 1) will be added to the external composition contract of `<pr>`. This specification defines a precondition for the `start` method of the *Fractal* interface named `mpr`. The precondition refers to another external interface of `<pr>`, the required interface named `c` of type `Control`, to express acceptable server performance in terms of the CPU usage threshold that the video streaming must not exceed. In this specification, 60% has been defined as the upper threshold. As for the postcondition, it refers to the required interface named `h` of type `History` and specifies that the last entry of the history matches the played video. Illustrations of the other types of contracts can be found in [5]. In the remainder of the paper, we refer to this external composition contract to illustrate our contributions. Responsibilities associated to this contract are for example explained and reused in section 3.1.

3   From Contract Negotiation to Autonomy

As shown in the previous section, contracts in *ConFract* are first class entities that follow the life cycle of components, and can be used at different levels of abstraction to report localized failures of the system. As extra-functional properties (Quality of Service, etc.) are often fluctuating, contracts may be frequently challenged and violated. In our example, the component `ApplicationManager` evaluates, through the `expectedCPUUsage` method, the CPU usage to be taken up by the `Processor` for the streaming service, considering different parameters (video encoding complexity and frame rate). The given contract (see figure 1) may then be violated due to the variations of the CPU resource or when competitive applications are present. To handle such violations, developers and administrators could add *ad hoc* adaptation code throughout the architecture. These handling codes would exactly determine what actions are to be realized and when, thus acting as local loops with low level action policies.

Our approach is rather based on the concept of negotiation, which represents a natural and rich means to find an initial agreement, establish a contract between some parties, and also restore the validity of a violated contract. As contracts are composed of provisions, our negotiation model activates an *atomic negotiation* for each violated provision of a contract [8], and given the responsibility of each participating component, different *negotiation policies* can be defined to drive the negotiation process.

3.1   Atomic Negotiation Parties and Protocol

An atomic negotiation involves *negotiating parties* and follows a *negotiation protocol* partly inspired from the extended *Contract-Net Protocol* (CNP) [9]. This protocol basically organizes the interactions between a manager and contractors following the announcing, bidding and rewarding steps, and is commonly applied in multi-agent systems for decentralized tasks allocation. Our model retrieves this organization, but instead of dealing with tasks allocation, these are contract provisions that are negotiated. In our model, the negotiating parties are (see figure 2) *(i)* the contract controller in the role of the negotiation initiator, which controls the negotiation process, as it manages contracts, and *(ii)* several participants, which are composed of the participants of the provision, and of an *external contributor* which helps representing interests from a 'third party' with deeper decision and analysis capabilities. Currently, the role of this external contributor is open and it can be the system administrator willing to embody some policies in the negotiation model to manage its behavior. For example, such policies could be high-level policies specifying objectives of the negotiation process, or lower-level actions intended either to configure the negotiation process (the negotiability of the provision[2], negotiation timeout) or to guide its development (propagation of an atomic negotiation to lower hierarchy levels, correlation of some information issued by various atomic negotiations).

In our example that refers to the external composition contract, the negotiating parties of the precondition on the `start` method are the contract controller of <ms> as initiator, <ms> itself as guarantor and <pr> as beneficiary. For the postcondition, the

---

[2] A provision is *negotiable* if the negotiating parties agree to negotiate it (see section 4.2).

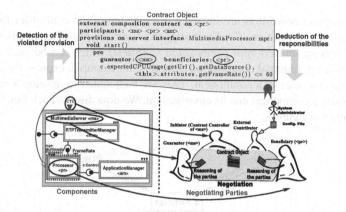

Fig. 2. Negotiating parties for the precondition of the external composition contract

parties are the contract controller of <ms> as initiator, <pr> as guarantor, and <ms> and <rtm> as beneficiaries.

As for the negotiation protocol, the interactions are organized as follows: The initiator first *requests proposals* from the negotiating parties to restore the validity of the violated provision and those parties *propose modifications*. Afterward, the initiator performs the proposed modifications and checks the provision validity. Those steps are iterated over all participants proposals. If a satisfactory solution is found, the negotiation process is finalized and terminates. Otherwise, if none of the proposals restore the validity of the provision or if the negotiation timeout is reached, the negotiation fails. To complete our negotiation model, it is also necessary to define policies. In section 4, a first negotiation policy describes a complete negotiation behavior.

3.2   Contracts in the Feedback Control Loop

The overall structure of the contract-based system management in *ConFract* takes the form of a feedback control loop. We first discuss the role of contracts and then describe each function of the loop.

In our system, contracts play a central role (see figure 3) to increase the autonomy of applications. They specify collaboration properties between parts of the system, they are monitored all along the life cycle of the system and updated according to architectural changes, and they provide a support on which the negotiation model relies to activate and finalize each atomic negotiation. In fact, contracts serve as knowledge and analysis tools to identify, in a fine-grained way, the part of the system to be monitored, the responsible components for each violated provision, and whether the proposed modifications revalidate the contract.

As contracts are managed by contract controllers in *ConFract* (see section 2), each contract controller provides support for instrumenting contracted components it is in charge of and monitoring them both at assembly and execution times. Then it checks the provisions, detects architectural or behavioral contract violations, and finally drives the negotiation activity according to the negotiation rules and policy (see next section).

Therefore contract controllers are involved in each step of the control feedback loop. At any level of composition, *ConFract* supports several types of contracts (*interface contracts, internal and external composition contracts*) which can be used in a feedback control loop. External composition contracts, for example, express the usage and external behavior rules of a component. They are well suited to develop a negotiation policy between a component and its environment. We now discuss each function of the loop, as shown in figure 3.

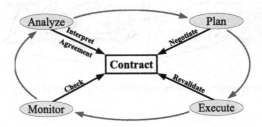

Fig. 3. Contract-based autonomic cycle

- **Monitor.** Contracts define the spatial domains of the system that are visible, that is a component scope, and the temporal context under which provisions have to be checked. The provisions of a contract mainly describe where the observation occur in terms of parts of the system (external or internal side of components, interfaces), when to operate the checking rules, the values to capture, and the verifications to be made. The *CCL-J* language currently supported in *ConFract* and based on executable assertions (see section 2), allows one to easily perform sanity checks and detect contract violations by testing the validity of the input and output values of components. For example, the contract described in the figure 1, in the scope of the component <pr>, defines the entry and exit of the method start of the interface mpr as two positions of the execution to be monitored.
- **Analyze.** Contracts represent a source of knowledge and can be exploited to shift towards finer understanding and analysis of the problems that occur in the system. They can be used to obtain various information that concern the locations of the system where the violations appear and the responsibilities of the impacted components. Each provision of a contract precisely identifies, among the set of participating components, the responsible components in terms of guarantor, beneficiary or contributor of the provision (see section 2.1). For instance, in the external composition contract on the component <pr> of figure 1, the provision constraining the entry of the start method of the mpr interface specifies that the component <ms> is its guarantor, whereas <pr> is its beneficiary.
- **Plan.** To adjust the system in reaction against contract violations, atomic negotiations are activated and they organize the recovery process through a collaborative activity between the negotiating parties (see section 3.1). Atomic negotiations are themselves organized through various *negotiation policies*. Such negotiation policies rely on the role of the participating components and define a complete negotiation behavior. To demonstrate this, a concession-based negotiation policy is

described in the next section. In any negotiation, the responsible components are endowed with a higher degree of autonomy and interact one with another to restore the validity of violated contracts. Moreover, in the negotiation process, the initiator and the other parties have clearly separate abilities. The contract controller drives the whole process by analyzing the violation context and retrieving the responsible components but without knowing the possible appropriate adaptive actions. On the contrary, negotiating parties only have the knowledge about their capabilities in regard to the violated provision, and without knowing the violation. Therefore, the negotiation protocol can be seen as a planning activity between the initiator and the negotiating parties to achieve the recovery process.

– **Execute.** The negotiation aims at restoring the validity of contracts. To achieve this, the actions to execute depend on the negotiation policy and on the own capabilities of the negotiating parties. These actions span from basic re-configurations — through attributes — of components involved in the negotiation to more sophisticated modifications of the contract themselves, as well as advanced architectural changes. The next section will illustrate some of these recovery actions. Finally, it should be noted that contracts are checked to validate the negotiation, so that they participate in ensuring the correctness of the adaptive actions of the feedback control loop.

During negotiations, components can be seen as configuring themselves when they try to (re-)establish valid contracts. A form of self-configuration is thus supported, although our proposal does not deal with automatically finding components [10]. Negotiable contracts are intrinsically acting for the robustness of the overall system by helping each component to deal with detected failures. As shown in the next section, different healing scenarios can be configured and the properties of self-healing and self-monitoring are clearly provided. One aspect of self-protection also appears as the proposed solution offers a protection against undesirable system behaviors by detecting and trying to repair cascading failures. Besides, protections against malicious attacks and self-optimization are not considered in our work.

4   Illustration

4.1   Concession-Based Policy Principles

To illustrate the whole negotiation behavior, we present a concession-based policy in which the negotiation initiator and beneficiaries interacts by a process of concession making. The negotiation initiator requests concessions from the beneficiaries by asking them either to rely on an under-constrained provision or to reconfigure some of their functioning parameters. In this way, such concession proposal can lead to: *(i) change the provision* in the current execution context, or *(ii)* to *reconfigure parameters* by changing some key attributes of beneficiary components, while retaining the same provision.

4.2   Negotiation Process

When the verification of a provision fails, the concession-based negotiation process is decomposed into three steps, as described in figure 4.

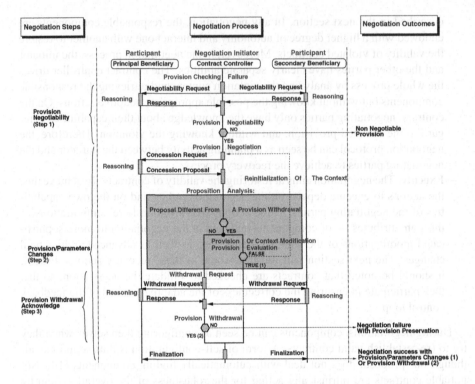

Fig. 4. Concession-based negotiation process

1. The initiator requests the negotiability of the violated provision from the beneficiaries and it evaluates the overall negotiability by computing a weighted linear
   additive scoring function.
2. If the provision is negotiable, the initiator requests concession proposals from principal beneficiaries and for each proposal, it performs changes on the provision or
   on parameters and re-checks the provision. If a proposal revalidates the provision,
   the atomic negotiation is successfully completed and changes are committed.
3. If proposed changes are not satisfactory or the withdrawal of the provision has been
   issued[3], the initiator asks to principal and secondary beneficiaries for permission to
   withdraw the provision.

These steps spread over two stages of the control loop: the planning stage is performed in the three steps as the initiator clearly organizes the negotiation process, and
the execution stage corresponds to the part of step 2 that commits changes.

4.3   Reasoning of the Beneficiaries

To successfully act during the negotiation process, the decision model of the principal beneficiaries is based on sets of alternatives which express their preferences. This

---

[3] A proposal can consist in the *withdrawal of a provision* to suggest to completely remove the
provision.

is closely related to work from Balogh et al. [11] in multi-agent systems. Thus, a component named C may define the following set of alternatives $\mathcal{A}_{\#p,C} := \{ A^1_{\#p,C}, A^2_{\#p,C}, ..., A^n_{\#p,C}, \text{STOP or RELEASE} \}$ to negotiate the provision identified as $\#p$. For every concession proposal requested by the initiator, the component C will successively propose its preferred alternative among this set. In this policy, an alternative $A^i_{\#p,C}$ corresponds either to provision or parameters changes, and STOP or RELEASE are used to notify the end of the concession process while retaining the provision or withdrawing it.

In our example, if the verification of the precondition related to the streaming performance fails, the concession-based negotiation process would involve the contract controller of <ms> as initiator and <pr> as the unique and principal beneficiary. The negotiation outcomes may first lead to progressively adjust the video frame rate of the content stream in order to lower the CPU load. In this scenario, <pr>'s successive concessions may be driven by the following set of alternatives $\mathcal{A}_{pre,<pr>} := \{ (\text{framerate} \leftarrow \frac{\text{framerate}}{2}), \text{STOP} \}$. Using this set, <pr> initially proposes to adjust its FrameRate parameter downwards. The initiator performs the change and checks the provision to revalidate the contract. If the verification succeeds, the negotiation outcome is successful, otherwise if the change is not satisfactory the initiator cancels it, and requests for a new concession. <pr> responds by proposing the termination of the concession process with the STOP alternative, as lowering the frame rate may affect smooth video streaming. The negotiation process finally terminates and fails while retaining the provision. Outside the negotiation process, further actions to be considered can consist in the replacement or the withdrawal of the provision, and the replacement of components.

5 Related Work

Since the *Eiffel* language [6], numerous works focused on contracts with executable assertions in object-oriented languages. The composition contracts provided by *ConFract* can be compared to collaboration contracts on objects proposed by Helm and Holland [12]. The notion of views in the collaboration is similar to the roles of the participants in our contracts. However, in the *ConFract* system, the composition contracts are carried by components — which allows one to distribute them in the hierarchy — and are automatically generated and updated according to the actions of assembly and connection.

The relevance of the quality of systems and other extra-functional aspects has motivated numerous works. To specify the Quality of Service (QoS) of systems, several works use *QML* [13] (*QoS Modeling Language*) or its extensions [14] by specifying expected quality levels. They are expressed through high-level constraints with no explicit representation at runtime and their management during the execution then remains limited. In component-based systems, other related works have focused on the management of QoS properties and resources variations in distributed systems and multimedia applications. At run time, several mechanisms handle fluctuations in the available resources using a monitoring system combined with basic adaptation rules which perform component re-parameterization or structural modifications [15]. Our model leans on contracts and separates the property which leads to the adaptation process (a violated contract provision) from recovery actions. Our recovery process is more flexible as it is organized through a collaborative runtime activity between components with higher degree of autonomy. Some other negotiation-based techniques also consist in selecting other implementations or QoS profiles that fulfill the specification [16], or in trying statically defined alternate services requiring lower quality levels [14].

Some component-based frameworks for autonomic system development have also been proposed. Accord [17] focuses on Grid environments and enables component behaviors and interactions to be managed by rules and an agent infrastructure. Although our solution is not as flexible as a rule-based system, it ensures some correctness properties on feedbacks, whereas in Accord, users are responsible for the correctness of the rules. In [10], the authors propose an architecture for autonomic computing. They define components as basic autonomic elements and describe other desirable elements. Our negotiable contracts align with some of these concepts, even if high-level policies and their mapping to lower levels are not developed yet in *ConFract*. In [18], QoS requirements of computer systems are satisfied using dynamic performance adjustment approach based on control frameworks. Our approach differs as it is based on contracts which aim at specifying various kinds of properties.

6   Conclusion and Future Work

In this paper, we described an architecture to support some autonomic features on component-based systems using negotiable contracts. The proposed *ConFract* system relies on a general hierarchical component model. At any level of composition, *ConFract* supports several types of contracts (*interface contracts, internal and external composition contracts*) which can be used in a feedback control loop. They serve as knowledge and analysis tools to identify, in a fine-grained way, the part of the system to be monitored and the responsible components for each violated contract. Moreover, through their negotiation, modifications can be dynamically proposed and checked against the violated contract. Negotiable contracts thus play a central role to increase the autonomy of applications and result in self-monitoring, self-healing and self-configuration properties. It should also be noted that as contracts are checked to validate a negotiation, they also ensure the correctness of the feedback loop itself.

Nevertheless as modifications made through negotiations are not restricted, it is not possible to check *a priori* whether they are not going to challenge other contracts afterwards. But these problems are still open and they arise commonly in approaches which aim at adapting components in the more general way.

ConFract relies on the hierarchical component model *Fractal*, which is available with its reference implementation under the LGPL. A first version of the *ConFract* system is already functional and should be released soon. Several small applications have been developed for its validation. A larger application, using web services to manage instant messaging communities with automatic grouping and application sharing, is developed to validate the different negotiation mechanisms currently integrated. As future work, we plan to extend and generalize this negotiation model by developing other negotiation policies and designing further recovery actions to address contracts violations. We are currently working on an *effort-based* policy in which the negotiation initiator turns towards the guarantor component and contributors to ask them to make an *effort*.

Acknowledgements. This work is supported by France Telecom under the collaboration contracts number 422721832-I3S, 46132097-I3S and 46133723-I3S.

References

1. IBM: An Architectural Blueprint for Autonomic Computing (2003)
2. Parashar, M., Hariri, S.: Autonomic Computing: An Overview. In: UPP 2004. LNCS 3566, France, Springer Verlag (2004)
3. Sterritt, R., Parashar, M., Tianfield, H., Unland, R.: A Concise Introduction to Autonomic Computing. Advanced Engineering Informatics **19** (2005) 181–187
4. Bruneton, E., Coupaye, T., Leclercq, M., Quéma, V., Stefani, J.B.: An Open Component Model and Its Support in Java. In: CBSE 2004. LNCS 3054, UK, Springer Verlag (2004)
5. Collet, P., Rousseau, R., Coupaye, T., Rivierre, N.: A Contracting System for Hierarchical Components. In: CBSE 2005. LNCS 3489, US, Springer Verlag (2005)
6. Meyer, B.: Applying "Design by contract". IEEE Computer **25** (1992) 40–51
7. Collet, P., Ozanne, A., Rivierre, N.:   Enforcing Different Contracts in Hierarchical Component-Based Systems. In: SC 2006. LNCS 4089, Austria, Springer Verlag (2006)
8. Chang, H., Collet, P.: Fine-grained Contract Negotiation for Hierarchical Software Components. In: EUROMICRO-SEAA 2005, Portugal, IEEE Computer Society (2005)
9. Smith, R.G.: The Contract Net Protocol: High-Level Communication and Control in a Distributed Problem Solver. IEEE Transactions on Computers **29** (1980) 1104–1113
10. White, S.R., Hanson, J.E., Whalley, I., Chess, D.M., Kephart, J.O.: An Architectural Approach to Autonomic Computing. In: ICAC 2004, USA, IEEE Computer Society (2004)
11. Balogh, Z., Laclavík, M., Hluchý, L.: Model of Negotiation and Decision Support for Goods and Services. In: ASIS 2000, Czech Republic (2000)
12. Helm, R., Holland, I.M., Gangopadhyay, D.: Contracts: Specifying Behavioral compositions in Object-Oriented Systems. In: OOPSLA/ECOOP 1990, Canada (1990)
13. Frølund, S., Koistinen, J.: QML: A Language for Quality of Service Specification. Technical Report HPL-98-10, HP Lab (1998)
14. Loques, O., Sztajnberg, A.: Customizing Component-Based Architectures by Contract. In: CD 2004. LNCS 3083, UK, Springer-Verlag (2004)
15. David, P.C., Ledoux, T.: Towards a Framework for Self-Adaptive Component-Based Applications. In: DAIS 2003. LNCS 2893, France, Springer Verlag (2003)
16. Göbel, S., Pohl, C., Aigner, R., Pohlack, M., Röttger, S., Zschaler, S.: The COMQUAD Component Container Architecture and Contract Negotiation. Technical report, Univ. Dresden (2004)
17. Liu, H., Parashar, M., Hariri, S.: A Component-Based Programming Model for Autonomic Applications. In: ICAC 2004, USA, IEEE Computer Society (2004)
18. Bennani, M.N., Menascé, D.A.: Assessing the Robustness of Self-Managing Computer Systems under Highly Variable Workloads. In: ICAC 2004, USA, IEEE Computer Society (2004)

Self-configuration Via Cooperative Social Behavior

Wolfgang Trumler, Robert Klaus, and Theo Ungerer

Institute of Computer Science
University of Augsburg
86195 Augsburg, Germany
{Trumler, Ungerer}@informatik.uni-augsburg.de

Abstract. The way computer systems are built dramatically changed over time. Starting from huge monolithic systems for many users up to ubiquitous computer environments with a lot of distributed and embedded computing power. Also the way these systems are configured has changed. The *Autonomic* and *Organic Computing* initiatives try to solve the upcoming management of complexity problems by utilizing biologically or sociologically inspired methods. One of the demands to the systems is self-configuration.

This paper proposes a self-configuration process for the networked nodes of the AMUN middleware based on a social behavior. Aim of the self-configuration is to find a good distribution of services by calculating a quality of service based on the given resources and the required resources of the services. A configuration specification is provided and flooded into the network to start the cooperative job assignment algorithm. A terminal verification step guarantees the correctness of the found configuration. Evaluations of the completely distributed self-configuration process are provided.

1   Introduction

We are currently at the beginning of the third age of computer systems, the so-called ubiquitous computing. Mark Weiser envisioned this evolution in computer science long ago [1]. Just a decade later the complexity level of computer systems have been raised such that Paul Horn of IBM postulated a new paradigm for future computer systems, the *Autonomic Computing* [2]. About the same time the *Organic Computing* initiative [3] defined the requirements for the next generation of computer systems. Both have in common that they describe the need for new systems to adopt life-like attributes, like self-configuration, self-optimization, self-healing, and self-organisation, to overcome the rapidly growing complexity.

This paper focuses on self-configuration as a mechanism to distribute services in the Autonomic Middleware for Ubiquitous Environments (AMUN) [4] to equally load the nodes of the network, regarding the given resources of the nodes and the required resources of the services. The proposed self-configuration technique can easily be adopted to other autonomic systems.

L.T. Yang et al. (Eds.): ATC 2006, LNCS 4158, pp. 90–99, 2006.

The mechanism of the self-configuration is based on the observation of a social behavior of cooperative groups which have to solve a common problem. If people meet to discuss a problem to find a solution in a constructive way the normal behavior is that one person talks while the others listen. The participants only talk if they have new input or could further improve a already given suggestion.

The advantage of our proposed self-configuration is the distributed approach which can be applied from small to large networks. Another point is the simple metrics and algorithm needed for the calculation of the quality of service.

The remainder of this paper is structured as follows. Section 2 gives an example to illustrate the self-configuration process. In section 3 the configuration specification and the metrics for the calculation of the quality of service are described and in section 4 the self-configuration process is explained. The results of the evaluations are shown in section 5 and related work is presented in section 6. The paper closes with a conclusion and future work in section 7.

2   A Social Behavior for Self-configuration

The following example of a cooperative solution finding process will help to illustrate the way our self-configuration mechanism works.

A company receives an order from a customer. The project that should be done has already been split in different jobs. The project manager invites all the employees to a meeting. The employees have different skills and some of them can do more than one of the jobs while others are experts in programming and should concentrate on the programming part.

Now the challenge is to assign the employees to the jobs such that the overall quality of service is as high as possible. When the meeting starts the project manager hands the list of jobs to all employees. Every employee starts to rate the jobs with a quality how good he can do a job and sorts them in descending order. Than the first employee starts to shout out which job he will do and with what kind of quality he can do it. All other employees mark this job as assigned and write down the quality for this service assignment. Than the next employee announces the job he will do. This continues until all jobs are assigned.

If an employee hears an assignment for a job he can do better, which means that his quality of service for this job is higher, he calls out that he will do the job and announces his higher quality of service. All the other employees who have already assigned the job to the first employee overwrite the job assignment. An employee will call out a reassignment only if he can provide a job with a higher quality of service. Otherwise he silently accepts the previous job assignment.

After all jobs have been assigned the project manager repeats the list with the assigned jobs and asks: "Any further questions?". This is a kind of verification step because it assures that every employee has the same list of assigned jobs. If all jobs have been assigned and all employees have a consistent assignment list the employees start to work.

3   Configuration and Quality of Service

3.1   Configuration Specification

An application is composed of services and monitors. The configuration specification describes the needed services and monitors of the application. The aim of the self-configuration is to find a good distribution of the services for the given configuration specification such that all nodes are loaded equally. The configuration specification is given in XML and consists of different parts needed for the self-configuration process. The definitions of a service, a monitor and a constraint are given below.

```
<service id="2" amount="2" name="DataBase"          <constraints>
        class="de.uau.SqliteBinding" >                <forall>
  <resource name="RAM">                                 <having>
    <value name="size" unit="MB">256</value>              <resource name="IR Sensor" >
  </resource>                                               <value name="range" unit="m">2
  <resource name="CPU">                                     </value>
    <value name="frequency" unit="Mhz">1450</value>       </resource>
  </resource>                                           </having>
</service>                                               <provide>
                                                          <monitor id="656" amount="1"
<monitor id="1" amount="1"                                    name="IR Monitoring Service"
        name="Surveillance System"                            class="de.uau.IrService">
        class="de.uau.SrvMonitor">                        </monitor>
  <resource name="IR SENSOR">                           </provide>
    <value name="range" unit="m">5</value>            </forall>
  </resource>                                         </constraints>
</monitor>
```

Service and **Monitor**: The two main elements are the service and the monitor entries as shown in the parts of a configuration above. The services and monitors are summarized as jobs later on. Both entries have an **id** to uniquely identify them throughout the complete configuration. The attribute **amount** specifies the amount of services or monitors to start. If the amount is higher than one more instances of the service must be assigned. The **name** attribute can be used to give a name or a short description and the **class** attribute is used to specify the class of the service or monitor.

Resource: Resources are defined by symbolic names. Currently the names are predefined and every node, service, and monitor have to use these predefined names to describe its resources and resource requirements, respectively.

Constraints: Constraints are used to describe cases when a service or monitor should be hosted depending on a specific hardware. The definition is derived from the mathematical $\forall$ quantifier and also used in the Object Constraint Language (OCL) [5]. The element **forall** is included in a **constraints** element. The **having** element contains the resource or resources needed to fulfill the quantifier. The **provide** element enumerates the services and monitors to be started if the quantifier evaluates to true. The constraints are evaluated prior to the rest of the assignment process and those nodes who provide the services or monitors defined by the constraints must take the resource consumption into account for the later calculation of the quality of service.

3.2 Metrics for the Quality of Service

During the second step of the self-configuration process the assignment of the jobs is done after all constraints are checked. Every node has to calculate a quality of service for each job (service or monitor) in the configuration. The calculation of the quality of service is important for the self-configuration process as it directly influences the overall quality of the service assignments and thus the quality of the self-configuration. To simplify the calculation of the quality of service the remaining capacity of the resources are calcuated to give an estimation of a node's load.

Let r_i be a resource required by a service, rr_i the remainder of the same resource, and R_i the total amount of the resource provided by a node, then the quality of service (qos_i) regarding resource i is calculated as follows:

$$qos_i = 1 - \frac{rr_i - r_i}{R_i} \qquad (1)$$

and the mean quality of service (qos) for more than one resource is

$$qos = \frac{1}{n} \sum_{i=1}^{n} qos_i \qquad (2)$$

After a service has been assigned to a node the node subtracts the consumed values from the resources and starts to calculate the new quality of service for the remaining jobs. This might lead to a negative value for rr_i the remainder of resource R_i which means, that the node would be loaded beyond its capacity. In the case of negative resource the qos_i of resource i is calculated as follows:

$$qos_i = 1 - \frac{|rr_i| + R_i}{r_i} \qquad (3)$$

Equation 3 results in much lower values for negative rr_i which is intended, as heavily loaded nodes should be rated worse than slightly loaded nodes with a positive value for rr_i. The resulting mean quality of service (qos) is calculated with equation 2 while using equation 1 for positive values for rr_i and equation 3 for negative values.

4 Self-configuration Process

4.1 Distribution of the Configuration Specification

The first step of the self-configuration is to flood the configuration specification into the network to all nodes. Therefore all nodes are listening at the beginning, waiting for an incoming configuration. The administrator loads the configuration specification at an arbitrary node. This node parses the XML file and creates a configuration object containing all constraints and jobs. This configuration object is sent to all other nodes with a broadcast message.

4.2   Cooperative Job Assignment

After every node received the configuration object the constraints are checked against the node. If a constraint is fulfilled the jobs are marked and the available resources are reduced by the amount of the required resources of the jobs. Afterwards two lists are created. One with the jobs the node can provide (job list) and an another with all jobs that cannot be provided by this node due to missing resources. The Quality of Service is calculated for every job that can be provided and the list ist sorted in descending order.

During the assignment process every node switches between an active and an inactive state. Normally the node is in the inactive state while it listens for incoming assignment messages. If the node switches to the active state it processes the received messages and decides how to continue.

All assignments of the received messages are marked in the job list. As long as there are jobs in the job list the next job is taken from the list. If the job is allready assigned and the local QoS is less or equal to the given QoS the job is skipped and the next one is taken. As services are assigned to the local node the available resources change and thus the quality of service must be recalculated to reflect the current state of the node.

4.3   Conflict Resolution

The nodes do not know when the other nodes send their service assignment. This might lead to conflicts in the list of assigned jobs if two nodes want to provide the same job and the assignment messages chronologically overlap. To avoid additional messages a conflict resolution mechanism is used which does not need any further messages. The conflict resolution mechanism has five stages that might be used in consecutive order if the quality of service of a job assignment is equal for at least two nodes.

1. **Load of a node**
   The job is assigned to the node with the least load.
2. **Amount of assigned jobs**
   The node with the least amount of already assigned jobs will get the job, assuming that a lower amount of jobs will produce less load (e.g. process or thread switching will produce additional load).
3. **Length of the list of jobs that can be provided**
   The node with the least amount of jobs that can be provided will get the job because the other nodes have higher possibility to provide another job.
4. **Random number**
   This randomizes the assignment of the jobs in case of quasi equal nodes and to avoid the next step if possible.
5. **Node ID**
   In the unlikely case that two nodes generated the same random number the id of the node is used to decide which node gets the job.

It is obvious that not all information needed to make the decisions is available at any node. So the required data are sent with the job assignment message. The additional information is four integer values: the load of the node, the amount of assigned jobs, the length of the list with the jobs to provide and a random number.

4.4 Configuration Verification

The assignment process stops after all jobs have been marked as assigned. To ensure that all nodes have the same resulting configuration one node sends a broadcast message with its complete configuration after a defined timeout. The timeout is needed because of assignment messages which could possibly overwrite one of the last job assignments.

The best and normal case is that all nodes have the same configuration and thus silently accept the sent configuration. If a receiving node has lower quality of service in its configuration it can replace it with the better assignment without sending a message. This case emerges if a node receives a "configuration completed" message prior to an assignment message or if assignment messages are lost. If the receiver of a configuration message has better assignments for at least one job the node broadcasts its configuration to tell the other nodes that a better configuration exists.

If no message arrives in response to the configuration message after a predefined timeout, the nodes assume the configuration as accomplished and can begin to start the assigned services. In the best case only one additional broadcast message is needed to verify the configuration and to complete the self-configuration process.

4.5 Unrealizable Configuration

A configuration can be unrealizable if a resource is required which none of the nodes can offer. In this case there will be some jobs in the *undoableJobs* list which are not assigned to any node. If no new assignment message arrives within a predefined timeout the node with unassigned jobs sends a request to the other nodes asking about the provider of the unassigned job.

If there is no provider for the unassigned service, no answer would be generated and the sender of the request will send a "ping" message to assure that the communication isn't broken. Any node receiving the "ping" message would answer. If the node gets an answer to the "ping" the configuration can be assumed to be unrealizable because no provider exists for at least one of the jobs. The nodes that receive the "ping" conclude the same and all nodes know that the configuration is unrealizable and that external help is needed (e.g. by an administrator).

5 Evaluation

To evaluate the quality of the self-configuration process we count the amount of messages needed to complete the job assignments. The amount of messages notionally depends only on the amount of jobs to be assigned and not on the amount of nodes in the network. But the evaluations show that the amount of nodes do have an impact on the amount of messages sent during the self-configuration. For a network with a higher amount of nodes the probability of reassignments rises.

5.1 Evaluation Methodology

We distinguish between two cases. The optimal case for the amount of messages needed to assign all jobs is when no reassignments are necessary and only one message for the distribution of the configuration specification and one "configuration completed" message is sent. This is the case if all nodes received all messages and the configuration does not suffer from any conflicts. If j jobs are assigned to n nodes the amount of messages for the optimal case is $m_{best} = j + 2$.

In the suboptimal case we assume one additional message for every node of the network, either a reassignment message or an optimization during the verification of a previously received "configuration completed" message. One additional message is used for configuration specification. The amount of messages is $m_{worst} = j + n + 1$. The diagrams will show these two values as reference points for the effectively counted amount of messages.

To evaluate the self-configuration we use a configuration generator to create varying configurations for different simulation runs. This ensures that the self-configuration is tested with different configurations to prevent very good or bad results from one single configuration.

5.2 Evaluation Results

The most impressive point about the self-configuration mechanism is that all of the accomplishable configurations have been accomplished and all unaccomplishable configuration have been detected. Every parameter setting was simulated 100 times to evaluate the self-configuration mechanism under a wide variety of different starting conditions.

Varying resource consumption: Figure 1 shows the evaluation results for 10, 25, 50, and 100 nodes with three resources and resource consumptions starting from 20% up to 100% for homogeneous and heterogeneous hardware. The optimal and the suboptimal cases are shown as references.

The left chart shows the results with homogeneous hardware which means that all nodes have the same resources and the same amount of available resources. Such a setting can be found in homogeneous networks (e.g. sensor networks) with equal hardware for every node. The chart shows, that independent of the amount of nodes the mean number of messages needed to accomplish a configuration is always between the optimal and the suboptimal case. For 100% resource consumption the self-configuration needs less messages than for lower resource consumptions. The right chart of figure 1 shows the messages needed to accomplish the configurations for heterogeneous nodes with different quantities of available resources.

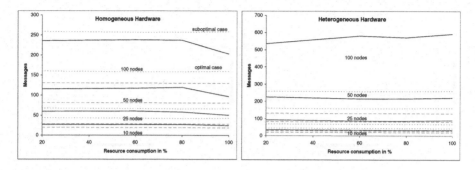

Fig. 1. Resource consumptions with homogeneous and heterogeneous hardware

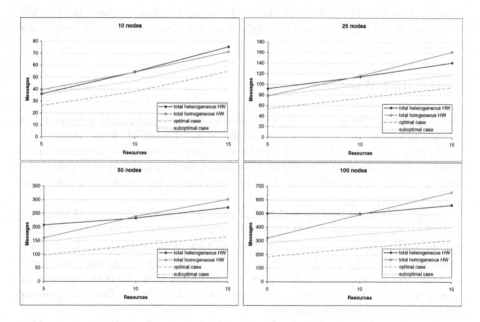

Fig. 2. Different amount of resources

Varying amount of resources: The impact of different amounts of resources is shown in the charts of figure 2. For all amounts of resources greater than three more reassignments are produced due to the higher variability of resource consumptions. The self-configuration performs better for a higher amount of resources and heterogeneous hardware than with homogeneous hardware.

Mean number of messages: Regarding the amount of jobs of a configuration and the number of messages needed to accomplish the configuration the mean number of messages per job can be calculated. Figure 3 shows that the mean values slightly vary depending on the announced resource consumption and the

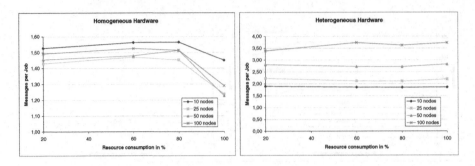

Fig. 3. Messages per job for homogeneous and heterogeneous hardware

amount of nodes. The left chart shows the mean number of messages per job for homogeneous hardware and the right chart for heterogeneous hardware each with three resources.

6   Related Work

The cooperative character of the nodes during the self-configuration process has strong similarities with Multi-Agent-Systems [6]. The IEEE foundation FIPA [7] promotes standards for agent-based technology to foster the interoperability with other technologies. The Agent Technology Roadmap [8] also describes the usage of agents as a possible way to solve the complexity problems of self-* and autonomic computing systems.

An approach to solve the problem of task allocation within an MAS is described by the Contract Net Protocol [9]. The agents bid for an annonced task and the best agent is selected to provide the task. This results in at least three messages per task. In a real system there will be much more than three messages per task because more than one agent will bid for a task. Thus the amount of messages used to allocate the tasks is up to three times higher than the amount needed by the self-configuration.

Another problem of MAS is the calcuation of the QoS. If an agents bids for more than one task, the calculated QoS might either be too optimistic, if the currently available ressources are used without regarding the allready made bids, which might lead to less performance if all the bids of an agent are granted. Otherwise, if the agent calculates the QoS regarding all his open bids, his QoS might be too bad to be selected. This problem does not arise in the proposed self-configuration because the time of the job assignment is not relevant.

SELFCON [10] describes an architecture that uses the directory service to implement self-configuration of networks which can respond dynamically to changes in the configuration policies. It has the drawback that it is a server based approach.

7   Conclusions and Future Work

In this paper we presented a self-configuration mechanism based on a well known social behavior. Every node calculates a quality of service for the jobs to decide which job is assigned to which node during the cooperative assignment process. Constraints can be used to assign jobs to nodes based on defined hardware requirements. Assigned jobs can be reassigned due to a higher quality of service. The verification step at the end of the self-configuration assures that every node has the same list of assignments. In the case of conflicting assignments a conflict resolution mechanism is used to solve the conflict without any further message.

The self-configuration mechanism has been evaluated and shows that about 1.4 messages per job suffice to yield an assignment independent of the amount of nodes and jobs.

Future work will be to include the mechanism into the AMUN middleware and to evaluate the self-configuration in the middleware.

References

1. Weiser, M.: The computer for the twenty-first century. Scientific American (1991) 94–110
2. Horn, P.: Autonomic Computing: IBM's Perspective on the State of Information Technology. http://www.research.ibm.com/autonomic/ (2001)
3. VDE/ITG/GI: Organic Computing: Computer- und Systemarchitektur im Jahr 2010. http://www.gi-ev.de/download/VDE-ITG-GI-Positionspapier Organic Computing.pdf (2003)
4. Trumler, W., Bagci, F., Petzold, J., Ungerer, T.: AMUN - autonomic middleware for ubiquitous environments applied to the smart doorplate. ELSEVIER Advanced Engineering Informatics 19 (2005) 243–252
5. OMG: Object Constraint Language. available online: www.omg.org/docs/ptc/03-10-14.pdf (2003)
6. Wooldridge, M.: An Introduction to Multiagent Systems. John Wiley & Sons (Chichester, England) (2002)
7. IEEE Foundation for Intelligent Physical Agents: Standard FIPA specifications. available online: http://www.fipa.org/repository/standardspecs.html (2006)
8. Luck, M., McBurney, P., Shehory, O., Willmott, S.: Agent Technology Roadmap. available online: http://www.agentlink.org/roadmap/al3rm.pdf (2006)
9. Smith, R.G.: The contract net protocol: High-level communication and control in a distributed problem solver. IEEE Transaction on Computers 29 (1980) 1104–1113
10. Boutaba, R., Omari, S., Singh, A.: Selfcon: An architecture for self-configuration of networks. International Journal of Communications and Networks (special issue on Management of New Networking Infrastructure and Services) 3 (2001) 317–323
11. Dutta, P.S., Jennings, N.R., Moreau, L.: Adaptive distributed resource allocation and diagnostics using cooperative information sharing strategies. In: Proc. 5th Int. Conf. on Autonomous Agents and Multi-Agent Systems, Hakodate, Japan (2006)

Towards Ontology-Based Embedded Services

G. Mahmoudi and C. Müller-Schloer

Institute of Systems Engineering – System and Computer Architecture, Appelstraße 4,
30167 Hannover, Germany
{mahmoudi, cms}@sra.uni-hannover.de

Abstract. Current approaches adopting principles of Organic Computing in embedded environments, like the automotive industry, suffer from different weaknesses regarding mainly the description methodology and the intelligence of the system. This paper shows that an ontology-based description, combined with methods of MultiCriteria Decision-Making (MCDM) opens the way for practical employment of organic computing principles in technical applications. The paper presents the current implementation of our approach and indicates steps towards a complete realization of the presented principles.

1 Introduction

The ever-increasing complexity of automotive systems represents a real challenge for the designers and can be considered as the main source of unexpected failures. New research projects, like the EvoArch project of DaimlerChrysler [2], try to put more value on the autonomy of the different parts of the automobile transforming the automobile to an Organic System. Organic Computing addresses the fact that the requirements of today's technical systems can be fulfilled in analogy with organic systems in the nature. Therefore, it pleads for the adoption of organic behavior to realize self-x-properties in technical systems like: self-organizing, self-configuring, self-healing, self-protecting, and self-explaining [1]. Organic Computing goes beyond Autonomic Computing by studying the mechanisms of self-organized emergence in technical systems and finding methods to control and direct it.

In this paper we present a solution to the shortcomings of the EvoArch approach. We utilize ideas known from Web Services and ontologies and apply them to embedded systems. The objective is an embedded market-place mechanism like in EvoArch, which avoids the rather inflexible description of the configuration alternatives with taxonomies. We call our approach "Ontology-based Embedded Services" (ObES). Considering every electrical or mechatronical part of an automobile as a service implemented on an embedded system, new and interdisciplinary solutions are suggested in ObES to provide facilities for a practical application of Organic Computing. On the basis of EvoArch, ObES encompasses an ontological knowledge representation and methods of Multicriteria Decision-Making (MCDM) as a selection and assessment mechanism. Tools of ontology development, the inference capability, the assessment of the resulting configuration, and the development methodologies presented in our approach are expected to support automobile developers to take advantage of the principles of Organic Computing.

L.T. Yang et al. (Eds.): ATC 2006, LNCS 4158, pp. 100–112, 2006.

This paper is organized as follows: Section 2 presents a survey of related work. Section 3 explains our vision for ObES, its advantages in comparison to EvoArch and the new matching process. ObES-ontologies and ObES-rules are depicted in Section 4. The ObES-Implementation and the presently adopted marketing-scenario are described in section 5. Section 6 discusses MCDM for matching in ObES. Section 7 presents the results of the current ObES-implementation and discusses its limitations. Section 8 draws conclusions.

2   Related Work

In the field of Autonomic Computing Stojanovic et al. [4] emphasized the need for ontologies and developed an ontology-based correlation engine with self-management capabilities (self-healing, self-protecting, self-optimizing and self-configuring). Benefits of defining a machine-processable shared-knowledge extend the design-time advantages of ontologies (like reusability, extendibility, verification, visualization, etc.) to new benefits in run-time, like justification (how a result has been inferred), gap analysis (why a result could not be retrieved), and ranking of the results (according to the breadth and depth of the derivation tree).

For automobile industry the ontology-supported system AVx was presented in [5]. The aim of AVx is to optimize development time, especially the process of building a test-car, in order to enable multiple and successive tests in short time. This ontology was written in F-Logic to answer a restricted collection of questions and to suggest an optimal process chain according to special rules. In 2003 the example ontology was limited to the exhaust system. A complete ontology was expected to be ready to use in 2005. While we suggest building an ontology to enable autonomy in run-time, AVx tries to improve the process of automobile development. But we observe a common belief in benefits expected from ontologically expressed human expertise for the future of automobile industry.

In [3] a skill manager has been introduced. It aims to help the companies to choose the best available employee/applicant for a defined job. This turns out to be a problem of matching between profiles of employees/applicants and a set of requirements. The skill manager makes use of a domain ontology, applies rules to infer knowledge about employees, and improves the matching process through Multiple Attribute Decision Making (MADM) methods. The strict separation made between compensatory and not-compensatory methods of MADM is valid as a way of thinking, but it ignores situations, wherein both methods are simultaneously needed in order to reach a better matching capability. Besides, the skill manager doesn't explain how to set the weights of the criteria and how to evaluate the skills of the employees/applicants. The last points exemplify a deep gap between an excellent theoretical solution and its practicability.

3   ObES: Design Principles

3.1   From EvoArch to ObES

Motivated by the complexity of modern automobile systems, EvoArch [2] aims at giving technical systems the capability of self-organization. For this purpose EvoArch proposes autonomous units gathered around an information space (called arena) to exchange offers and enquiries as in a marketplace (Fig. 1).

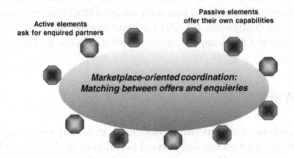

Fig. 1. The marketplace (Arena) of EvoArch

The main ideas behind EvoArch can be described as follows: An automobile consists of autonomous units. The autonomous units are intelligent. They have properties and aims. The properties of the autonomous units are ordered in a taxonomy, according to different aspects. Autonomous units can be active or passive. Active units look for partners to enhance their own functionality, while passive units offer their own capability purposing to be accepted as a partner. If there are many available offers for one enquiry, one offer has to be selected. After the selection of a partner a contract has to be concluded.

In EvoArch some open questions and shortcomings can be registered (some of them are mentioned by the authors of [2]).

1. It is not clear how to build the taxonomy of the autonomous units and/or of their properties. No tools are named to this aim.
2. The granularity of description is not clearly defined. Too precise descriptions lead to a small success when searching for a partner, while too coarse descriptions lead to a big number of candidate partners.
3. Defining roles as "active" or "passive" restricts the ability to build a hierarchical system. In EvoArch the system may consist of up to two layers.
4. Although EvoArch tries to define a kind of priority to estimate the importance of each contract, it doesn't say how to determine these priority values, or how to assess the whole configuration.

ObES addresses the above questions and presents new corresponding solutions. A central idea is to abstract the description problem to a knowledge representation problem. The knowledge of human engineers has to be given to the autonomous units in a machine-processable way. We suggest for this reason the adoption of an ontology-based solution. The semantic dimension guarantees an intelligent matching of high reliability and effectiveness, overcoming the results reached by only syntactical matching.

Additionally, to solve the problem of granularity we define a formal way to include the wishes of active autonomous units, taking into account the balance between a precise and a flexible description.

Also, we allow an additional role to be played by the autonomous units: the "active-passive" role, in order to enable ObES to build a hierarchical system of more than two layers.

To support ObES with a reliable and practical selection capability, and to enable it to assess the resulting system configuration, we redefine the selection process as a Multicriteria Decision making (MCDM) process and suggest the employment of its known methods or adapted forms of them.

3.2 ObES: Matching process

In ObES an intelligent matching process between enquiries and offers is of vital importance. Originally this process was carried out by human developers. Autonomous units should be able to accept this challenge. Analyzing the human way of thinking, we can recognize two steps of making a decision about selecting one offer from a collection of alternatives (Fig. 2).

The **first step** is to understand the own requirements (the enquiry) and the available candidate offers. This covers a semantic evaluation of the words and terms used to describe the offers, and making connections between them and those used to describe the enquiry. Hence we find out that a machine-readable and processable common understanding of the application domain is essential. Features indicated in the last sentence constitute the definition of "ontologies", usually known in the field of Semantic Web [11].

To this point, the matching process regards the individual attributes of the enquiries and offers. Recalling, that enquiries and offers combine many attributes, a decision about the best offer can be made after considering all these attributes. Therefore, the **second step** is to select a possible solution under multi criteria conditions (a choice problematic), aiming to choose the optimal offer available. According to this vision of the matching process, developers of automotives are requested to pour their knowledge in the autonomous units in two forms: an ontological form (concepts, relations, attributes, instances) and a form adequate to MCDM (utility functions, weights of attributes, aggregation functions). We consider these two forms to be a main condition for a feasible and trustworthy autonomy.

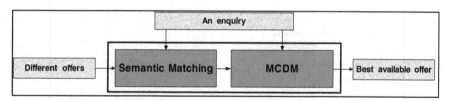

Fig. 2. ObES supports a 2-ary matching process

4 Ontology-based Description

The word ontology stems from philosophy, but we focus on its technical meaning as "a formal and explicit specification of a conceptualization" [9][10]. Terms and relations between them build a conceptualization, i.e. a view of the world, that goes with our purposes. Therefore it depends essentially on the kind of application (application domain) and on the community that shares and commits it. Explicit specification means that the terms and the relations are explicitly given names and definitions. A formal specification has the advantage of being machine processable. With the help of ontologies we explicitly define knowledge in a formal way to make this knowledge available for our "intelligent machines".

The ontology of ObES consists of two parts: the kernel ontology and the application ontology. The former embodies our model of an autonomous unit, while the latter represents the domain ontology of the application under consideration. The next sections present a detailed explanation of these ontologies.

4.1 Kernel Ontology

One of the main goals of our approach is to provide a clear and easy-to-use interface between the human knowledge and the machine-processable knowledge. The kernel ontology of ObES constitutes this interface. According to the principle of autonomy with a marketplace-oriented behavior, we have designed the kernel ontology to take the following points into account:

1. The *role* played by an autonomous unit at any point in time falls into one of two types: active (shopper) or passive (supplier). Some autonomous units are able to change their role from active to passive, named active-passive. These units try at first actively to find partners (passive units), and when they have found them (or a minimum group of partners) they try to offer themselves as passive units. This means that they are able to build a subsystem, and they will offer this subsystem as a passive unit. In this manner a hierarchical system is built. The jump from one role to another is determined by special rules (as explained in section 4.3).

2. An autonomous unit has a *"UnitDescription"*, Fig. 3. A *"UnitDescription"* explains the capabilities and the attributes of the autonomous unit. These are expressed by *"SelfProperties"*. Passive units offer exactly this *"UnitDescription"* to the active units.

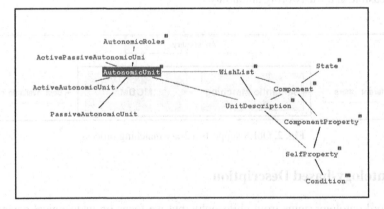

Fig. 3. The kernel ontology constitutes a model of an autonomous unit

3. Every active unit has a *"WishList"* of looked-for components, Fig. 3. A looked-for component is defined as a description of an autonomous unit, so it consists of *"ComponentProperties"*, and it has a *"State"* describing its availability. We can distinguish between two kinds of components: needed components and desired components. In the absence of any one of the needed components the active unit will be unable to achieve its expected functionality. On the other hand, the presence of more desired components will enhance this functionality.

4. Similarly, every looked-for component in the wish list is described through unconditional properties and preferable properties. The former has to be fulfilled unconditionally, while the latter are to be fulfilled preferably. With this approach we provide the user (the designers of automobiles) with the ability to define a minimum of needed components, which satisfy a collection of properties unconditionally. The autonomy of the units may not violate these clearly defined minimum boundaries in order to guarantee a "correct behavior" of the system under all circumstances. At the same time we want to allow our autonomous system reasonable freedom (or latitude) to take advantage of its autonomy. Fig. 4 shows the principle of the wish list. The dark shaded parts exhibit the properties of the needed components to be fulfilled unconditionally, the light shaded parts the unconditionally fulfilled properties of the desired components, and the white parts the preferably fulfilled properties of both types of components.

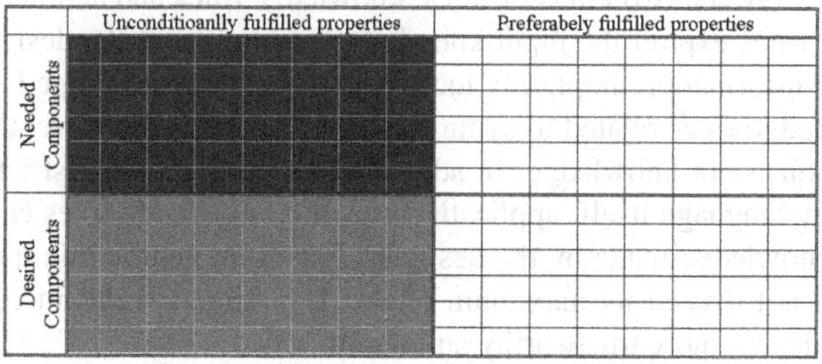

Fig. 4. The wish list

5. The concept "Condition" represents a port for connecting the kernel ontology to arbitrary domain ontologies defined by the designer. Concepts of the domain ontology (or any part of it) must simply be defined as a subconcept of the "condition" concept. Then they can be used to specify properties for the components.

6. "Conditions" may possess values measured with a known measurement unit (see section). The designer can choose a measurement unit or define a new one. In addition, values can be defined as a range of values. For example, "inside a specified range", "out of a specific range", "greater than a specific value", etc.

4.2 Application Ontology (Ontology of Automobile Industry)

The application ontology is strongly dependent on the application domain, and it is up to the designer to define it, to import it, or to extract it from domain specific databases or documents. Our example application ontology (Fig. 5) is from the branch of automobile industry.

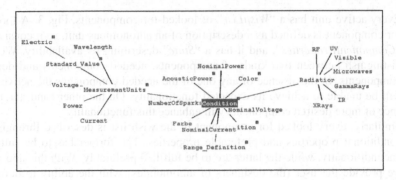

Fig. 5. A simplified view of our application ontology for automobile industry (Instances are not shown)

It includes, among others, concepts like: *"Coordinations"*, *"Colors"*, *"MeasurementUnits"* (*"Voltage"*, *"Ampere"*, *"Watt"*, etc.), *"Radiator"*, etc. The concept *"Condition"* is the central concept, as explained above.

4.3 Rules in ObES

We distinguish between two kinds of rules: knowledge rules and action rules.

Knowledge rules exploit the input knowledge coming from the designer to get the most complete information, implicitly located in the given knowledge (ontology). Beside the knowledge rules related to symmetry, transitivity and inverse, the restrictions guarantees a consistent knowledge. In addition to the rules (and restrictions) defined by the ontology language itself, application-specific knowledge rules can help to verify the input knowledge made by the designer. For example, the minimum value of a condition may not exceed its maximum value. This kind of rules increases the reliability and leads to a more trustworthy autonomy.

Additionally, there is a special group of knowledge rules, which is responsible for semantic matching between different ontologies (or occasionally within one ontology). One rule of this group decides about the comparability between two concepts: two concepts are comparable to each other when their values posses a common measurement unit.

Other semantic matching rules try to infer more information about autonomous units, taking advantage of facts, which state relations to specific standards: Anything designed according to a known standard is expected to fulfill all its requirements.

Moreover, we have defined a group of semantic matching rules depending on the value range of the conditions belonging to offers and enquiries. This group of rules applies to the numeric values of the conditions and can be fired just after a successful semantic matching between the concepts under consideration.

Action rules can be used to trigger special actions in special situations. One of these rules is responsible for changing the role of the autonomous unit from active to passive. The change takes place when all needed components are available.

5 ObES-Arena

5.1 Policy of Marketing

On the marketplace, a deal takes place between active and passive autonomous units. Different scenarios are possible to exchange enquiries and offers. We chose and implemented a scenario, which allocates the matching steps as follows: active units are responsible for accepting or not accepting the coming offers (ontological matching), and a central broker selects the best offer available for every enquiry (MCDM). This decision making process starts after the expiry of a wait time specified for each enquiry. Fig. 6 shows the implemented scenario as a sequence diagram.

While this scenario is selected because of its clarity and its direct correspondence to the principles of ObES, other scenarios still are subject of theoretical and practical comparisons.

Before the autonomous units can start to act as described above, they have to register themselves with the central broker and get a unique ID to be addressed with. This process is not shown in Fig. 6.

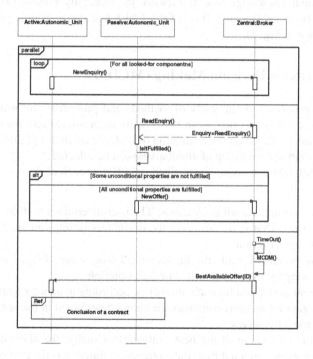

Fig. 6. Implemented scenario in ObES

5.2 ObES Implementation

The whole model has been implemented in Java. We use "Jena" [6] to provide the autonomous unit with inference capabilities. Jena is an open source Java framework for building semantic web applications. It includes a generic rule-based inference engine, besides an OWL API, and query languages (other inference engines and APIs are also supported). The broker is implemented as a common memory space, based originally on Jada [7], a Linda implementation. Jada is a package for Java that allows distributed Java applications to access a shared object space for coordination and data sharing purposes. But in our implementation, Jada can be considered just as a common memory space, because its associative addressing capabilities are not more extensively exploited than as a matching mechanism. Its existence is due to the historical development of the ObES model.

With the ObES GUI, developers can import defined ontologies (as OWL files), enable or disable the autonomous units imported, add new autonomous units to the list, initialize autonomous unit objects (inference), start the ObES arena, and then stop it to show the resulting configuration (in the form of a tree in the bottom part of the GUI). Future versions of ObES-GUI will support MCDM, a way to save and compare the resulting configurations.

For the development of ObES ontologies we use Protégé, a free, open source ontology editor and knowledge-base framework [8] (specially Protégé-OWL, with its plug-ins like: Instance Tree and TGVizTab). ObES has also a specific graphical user interface (shown in Fig. 7).

6 Multi Criteria Decision Making (MCDM)

MCDM can be defined as the study of methods and procedures by which concerns about multiple conflicting criteria can be formally incorporated into the management planning process []. Based on the evaluation of multiple attributes of different alternatives, one alternative (or a group of alternatives) can be selected.

A generic MCDM procedure is described in [13]. For each of the 4 steps many solutions can be found:

1. Determine utilities for all evaluations: The user determines a utility function for each criterion. That is he estimates the usefulness (utility) attained by different values of each criterion.
2. Determine weights for all criteria: As not all criteria are of equal importance to the user, weights are to be attached to each criterion.
3. Compute an evaluation for each alternative according to an aggregation function: An aggregation functions combines the values determined in the last two steps to evaluate the alternatives.
4. Choose the alternative of the best evaluation: Usually, the alternative with the maximum value extracted from the aggregation function is the best one.

6.1 MCDM in ObES

In ObES we can consider the attributes of the enquiries as criteria, and the offers as alternatives (decisions) with different outcomes (attributes). For choosing the most adequate method for each of the 4 steps above, the following recommendations, originating from ObES specifications, have to be considered:

- The alternatives are not known at the development time: this means that the developers are not able to make a comparison between the available alternatives, as the alternatives will be found later at run-time. Therefore, carefully chosen utility functions are very important.
- According to the wish list, the aggregation function along its horizontal dimension can be considered as a mixed function of a weighted product (representing the unconditionally fulfilled properties) and of a weighted sum (representing the preferably fulfilled properties).
- Inconsistent weighting of the criteria is unavoidable and has to be eliminated by the MCDM weighting method.

7 First Results

This section contains an example extracted from the present ObES implementation. The example shows the benefits of applying the inference mechanism on an ontology-based description, as well as the role of the description sharpness on the resulting configuration.

As a demonstration of the capabilities of ObES we present the configuration of the blinker system of an arbitrary automobile. The blinker system is defined through the active unit "blinker_manager" which is looking for two lamps (passive units). Four passive units are defined as follows: one yellow lamp on each of the left and the right side; and one red lamp on the left and the right side. Fig. 7 shows the output configuration with a failed matching because of semantic differences in the ontologies used to describe the active unit (Colors are instances of the concept "Color") and the passive units (Colors are instances of the concept "Farbe").

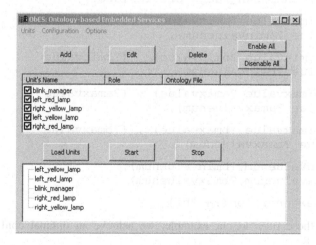

Fig. 7. No match because of sematic differences

In ObES we can define matching rules as a solution. For this example two matching rules are used. The first rule has the form (in the syntax of Jena general purpose rule engine):

```
[comparabilitycheck:

(?a rdf:type pre:Condition) (?b rdf:type pre:Condition)

...

(?atype ?relation ?arestr) (?arestr rdf:type
owl:Restriction) (?arestr owl:allValuesFrom ?something)

(?btype ?relation ?brestr) (?brestr rdf:type
owl:Restriction) (?brestr owl:allValuesFrom ?something)

->(?a pre:comparable ?b) ]
```

This rule discovers that two concepts are comparable to each other when they are subconcepts of "Condition" and their values are restricted to values of a common concept (a common measurement unit). This is valid for the concepts *"Color"* and *"Farbe"*.

The second rule discovers that a condition is applicable to an autonomous unit when its values are inside the range of another condition applicable for the autonomous unit, both conditions define an acceptance range between two values, and the two conditions are comparable to each other:

```
[insideofrulewithcompatibilitytest:

(?a rdf:type pre:Condition), (?b rdf:type
pre:Condition) ,

notEqual(?a,?b), (?a pre:comparable ?b),

(?a pre:condition_range pre:insideof) ,

(?b pre:condition_range pre:insideof),

(?a pre:minvalue ?aminvalue) , (?aminvalue
pre:value ?aminvaluenum),

(?b pre:minvalue ?bminvalue) , (?bminvalue
pre:value ?bminvaluenum),

(?a pre:maxvalue ?amaxvalue) , (?amaxvalue
pre:value ?amaxvaluenum),

(?b pre:maxvalue ?bmaxvalue) , (?bmaxvalue
pre:value ?bmaxvaluenum),

le(?aminvaluenum,?bminvaluenum),
ge(?amaxvaluenum,?bmaxvaluenum)

-> addnewcondition(?a,?b)]
```

Applying these rules to our example, we achieve an optimal configuration as shown in Fig. 8.

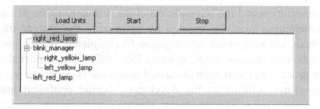

Fig. 8. Optimal configuration (all properties are defined as unconditionally fulfilled)

So far all properties of the looked-for lamps were defined as unconditionally fulfilled properties. Therefore the red lamps had no chance of being partners of the *"blinker_manager"*. We can change this situation if we define the color property of the looked-for lamps as *preferably* fulfilled properties. Fig. 9 shows a possible configuration according to the new wish list. In the absence of MCDM there is for ObES no big difference between a red lamp and a yellow lamp, and there is a probability of choosing the red one. Once ObES will be MCDM-enabled this situation may not arise again.

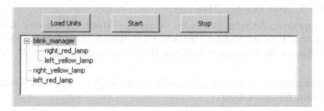

Fig. 9. The color property of the looked for *right_yellow_lamp* is defined as a preferably fulfilled property

One implementation problem is constituted through the high memory demand of the ontology (we use the in-memory ontology model of Jena). As each autonomous unit (a Java object) has its own ontology model, the problem is aggravated with higher numbers of autonomous units. We tend to employ the Jena interface of persistence model processing (through a data base) that decreases the memory demand considerably. Future embedded versions of ObES have to take such solutions into account.

A second aspect of the ObES implementation is the needed inference time. The inference takes place upon system start (initialization) of each autonomous unit with every information retrieval from the ontology, and every time when a rule is fired.

8 Conclusions

In this paper we have presented a new approach towards enabling ontology-based embedded services (ObES). The ObES description methodology and the ObES matching mechanism are based on ontologies, inference on ontologies and MCDM methods. The present implementation shows high success potential by adopting the ontological description and the semantic matching. Limitations faced currently by the ObES implementation must be avoided by optimizing the current implementation. MCDM methods are now under investigation to completely realize our vision about the needed matching process in OC systems like ObES. The expected impact on the development process has also been discussed and some suggestions were made to enable an easy-to-use solution to the developers, beside confident and trustworthy autonomy.

References

1. C. Müller-Schloer: Organic Computing – On the Feasibility of Controlled Emergence. CODES + ISSS 2004 Proceedings, September 8-10, 2004, ACM Press, ISBN 1581139373, pp. 2-5.

2. Peter Hoffmann, Stefan Leboch (Daimler Chrysler AG): Evolutionäre Elektronikarchitektur für Kraftfahrzeuge. Information Technology 47 (2005) 4, Oldenbourg Verlag.

3. York Sure, Alexander Maedche, Steffen Staab: levereging Corporate Skill Knowledge – From ProPer to OntoProPer, In D. Mahling & U. Reimer, Proceedings of the Third International Conference on Practical Aspects of Knowledge Management, Basel, Switzerland, October 30-31, 2000. October 2000.

4. Ljiljana Stojanovic, Juergen Schneider, Alexander Maedche, Susanne Libischer, Rudi Studer, Thomas Lumpp, Andreas Abecker, Gerd Breiter, John Dinger: The Role of Ontologies in Autonomic Computing Systems. IBM Systems Journal, Vol. 43 (No. 3). August 2004.

5. Horst Stegmueller: Audi erprobt semantische Technologien – Zeit fürs Wesentliche. Digital Engineering Magazin, 4/2003.

6. http://jena.sourceforge.net/

7. http://www.cs.unibo.it/~rossi/jada/

8. http://protege.stanford.edu/

9. Thomas R. Gruber: A translation Approach to Portable Ontology Specifications. *Knowledge Acquisition*, 5(2): 199-220, 1993.

10. Thomas R. Gruber: Toward Principles for the Design of Ontologies Used for Knowledge Sharing. International Journal Human-Computer Studies 43, p.907-928 (1993).

11. D. Fensel, J. Hendler, H. Lieberman, W. Wahlster (eds.), Spinning the Semantic Web, pp. 317-359. MIT Press, Cambridge, MA., 2003.

12. International Society on Multiple Criteria Decision Making: http://project.hkkk.fi/MCDM/intro.html

13. H. A. Eiselt, C.-L. Sandblom: Decision Analysis, Location Models, and Scheduling Problems.

TOBAB: A Trend-Oriented Bandwidth Adaptive Buffering in Peer-to-Peer Streaming System[*]

Sirui Yang, Hai Jin, and Xuping Tu

Cluster and Grid Computing Lab
Huazhong University of Science and Technology, Wuhan, 430074, China
hjin@hust.edu.cn

Abstract. Multimedia streaming application is increasingly popular. P2P mode makes it much more suitable for large-scale users to participate into one single application. However, most effort is spent on issues such as overlay construction and content delivery. As a foundational aspect in P2P-based multimedia systems, buffer management needs more exploration and traditional measures should be refined. In this paper, a bandwidth adaptive buffer exchange strategy is proposed, which is similar to the slow start process in TCP protocol. A novel algorithm is applied in a live media streaming system, called Anysee, and has been proven resilient to the bandwidth fluctuation in P2P networks.

1 Introduction

Streaming applications have become increasingly popular. As the centralization architecture always faces the problems of *single-failure-point* and server deployment cost, the streaming applications gradually appear to be *Peer-to-Peer* (P2P) fashion. Previous studies consider two key components supporting streaming applications in P2P networks: overlay construction and content delivery [1]. Due to the uncertain arrival time of each packet in P2P media streaming systems, designing a dynamic and adaptive buffer management policy is more important than ever before. In multimedia applications, buffer management is a guarantee for better *Quality of Service* (QoS). Due to the fluctuant bandwidth and the induced uncertainty of data packets' arrival, a well designed strategy concerning on buffer management is necessary for a robust multimedia architecture.

As no feasible solutions are able to measure connection metrics among peers, buffering algorithms with parameters such as bandwidth can not be scientifically executed. The dynamic characteristic of P2P network, in large geographic coverage and with peers joining and leaving the network frequently, enlarges the difficulty of getting a comparatively exact bandwidth between peer pairs. Besides, to collect media data required by media players, mesh structure in P2P media streaming systems is proposed and multi-source policy is adopted first in CoolStreaming [12]. Multi-source solution imports a new problem: how to assign requests to neighboring peers with consideration of balance between local demand of media data and bandwidth among several peers.

---

[*] This paper is supported by National Science Foundation of China under grant 60433040, and CNGI projects under grant CNGI-04-12-2A and CNGI-04-12-1D.

L.T. Yang et al. (Eds.): ATC 2006, LNCS 4158, pp. 113–122, 2006.

In this paper, we propose an algorithm resembling the TCP slow-start process, called **TOBAB** (Trend-Oriented Bandwidth Adaptive Buffering). It adjusts the request quantity sent to each source peer. The algorithm does not need the accurate bandwidth value between two peers. However, it sends requests which can be *adaptive* (tread on the heels of the bandwidth trend) and *greedy* (take full advantage of available bandwidth).

The rest of this paper is organized as below: in section 2, related works on buffer management is discussed. In section 3, the TOBAB strategy and buffer management in our application, *Anysee*, are presented. In section 4, performance of the algorithm is analyzed and evaluated. We conclude this paper in the last section.

2   Related Work

2.1   Bandwidth Measure

There has been much work on developing techniques for estimating the capacity and the available bandwidth of network paths based on end-point measurements [3]. Many of the proposed capacity estimation schemes are based on the packet-pair principle [6]. Some mathematical methods like a simple stochastic analysis of the bandwidth estimation in the context of a single congested node with asymptotically accurate bandwidth estimators are proposed. In packet-pair principle, a generic queuing model of an Internet router is developed and the estimation problem assuming renewal cross traffic at the bottleneck link is solved [5]. A link bandwidth measurement method using a deterministic model of packet delay is proposed [11]. It derives both the packet-pair property of FIFO queuing networks and a new technique, called packet tailgating, for actively measuring link bandwidths.

Some tools designed to estimate metrics are fully compared and analyzed [7][8][9][10]. Existing bandwidth estimation tools measure one or more of three related metrics: capacity, available bandwidth, and *bulk transfer capacity* (BTC). These tools implement tactics in previous studies. In summary, IP networks do not provide explicit feedback to end hosts regarding the load or capacity of the network. Instead hosts use active end-to-end measurements in an attempt to estimate the bandwidth characteristics of paths they use [4].

However, these studies do not actually find a method to get the physical bandwidth value in network links. Some of them concern on the capacity of the slowest link of the path, while others mainly discuss the smallest average unused bandwidth among the routers of an end-to-end path. It is hard for application layer to get an accurate and meaningful bandwidth situation for a node in the network.

2.2   Buffer Management Strategy in P2P Streaming

Traditional multimedia applications with prefixed and linear buffer management policy do not adapt to dynamic P2P environment [17]. In structured P2P multimedia streaming systems [13][16], where multicast trees are constructed mostly, peers receive media data from one supplying peer (called *father*), and send the data to one or more consuming peers (called *children*). In first version of [13], the buffer size is set to *40* (be able to store *40*-second data). When half of it is fulfilled, the application starts to transfer the media data to media player [15].

In [12][14], where mesh architecture and multi-source are introduced, buffer design needs to take request assignation and bandwidth cooperation into account. A buffer exchange algorithm for peers is discussed [12] to transmit media data pieces effectively in P2P streaming systems. First, an *80*-bit *Slot Map* (SM) is generated on each peer, with each bit representing corresponding buffer block. A SM-like packet is constructed periodically where each bit denotes the corresponding block is ready or not. By exchanging and comparing SM-like packet, application determines which blocks need to be requested from one peer, and which from another. The algorithm mainly depends on bandwidth and the deadline of a block as it should be sent to media player in time. The algorithm becomes a garnish if bandwidth value is not veracious. It does not consider the conflicts among requests in peers, which possibly makes an urgent block request to a supplying peer with insufficient bandwidth.

3 Bandwidth Adaptive Buffer Management

Bandwidth plays a pivotal role in P2P media streaming systems. It affects packet transmission and most algorithms' execution is influenced by bandwidth. Basically, unfulfilled requests decrease program efficiency and QoS to some extent. Thus, fewer requests for media data should be sent out if current bandwidth is awful, and vice versa. As bandwidth is hard to measure exactly, algorithms should be buffer-adaptive.

3.1 Buffer Value Unnecessary in P2P Streaming

Practically, instant bandwidth value (such as *500Kb/s* at *7:10am*) is not much instructive in P2P environment. In common case, a host may run several P2P applications (or other network programs) at one time. The bandwidth (especially the in-bound bandwidth) is shared by these applications.

In most P2P topologies (like unstructured meshes), a peer connects several "neighbors" [19]. Obviously, neighbors share the bandwidth (generally the out-bound bandwidth) of the peer. To measure an instant bandwidth between two peers is not significant, as it varies frequently.

3.2 Buffer Exchange Algorithm

In *CoolStreaming* [12], the Buffer-Map exchange algorithm works well in fixed-bandwidth environment, or the bandwidth value in peer pairs is assumed foreseen. This is always unreal for most P2P applications. We extend it adaptive to bandwidth fluctuation (not prearrange an assumption value any more) in our research.

In our buffer management, we plot a buffer composed by *slots*. One "slot" represents media content in one second. It is built-up by several "packets". We prescribe this kind of policy because data in one second is superfluous to be packed and transmitted. Each packet is set to be the maximal size of a UDP packet (S_{udp}), unless it is the last packet of a slot, which may be less than S_{udp}. Compared to *CoolStreaming*, the buffer map is replaced by Slot Map. Correspondingly, each bit represents not a packet but a slot. When generating a new packet, the timestamp is checked whether it belongs to a new slot. Therefore, the last generated slot is called "fulfilled" or "ready" with its corresponding buffer-map bit set to "1". Otherwise, the bit is "0", as default.

With preparation done and the time point (for buffer exchange) coming, by checking SM, the program starts to count slots which are not "ready". Then it calculates its neighbors' SM by counting the SM-like packets received from neighbors. According to the result, it sends requests to each neighbor. Before the deadline $T_{deadline}$ elapsed, neighboring peers return the requested data. Buffer manager records the transmission status, with which the bandwidth situation is analyzed.

3.3 TOBAB Algorithm

The exchange algorithm resembles *CoolStreaming* but we adjust the bandwidth part. In brief, as requests are sent and responded, bandwidth situation is recorded according to response status. In the buffer request algorithm, bandwidth is first set to a default value based on the landmark difference of the local and remote peers. A *"linear increase, multiplicative decrease"* standard is used. This standard is chosen because the adaptive and greedy algorithm is expected. However, pure TCP-like protocol does not fit the dynamic environment in P2P networks. It should be further mended to be stable and effective. Linear increment is adopted for "greed" purpose and it causes little jitter. As available bandwidth lessens, the multiplicative decrement starts being applied. Meanwhile we adjust the increment not constant (but still linear) and more effective. The increment is direct proportion of the difference between requested and responded packets.

TOBAB algorithm is represented below. The number of requested data packets is initialized as default (e.g. *20* packets are requested for *N* neighbor peers). When $T_{deadline}$ passes, the program counts the number of completed packets. If all requested packets are brought to success (i.e. *20* packets or more), the bandwidth is considered to be **underestimated**. Thus the bandwidth value is raised linearly (e.g. increasing *2* packets each time). Otherwise, not all requested packets are transferred punctually (e.g. only *12* arrived). The bandwidth, in this case, is assumed to be **overestimated**. The bandwidth is thus reduced partially (e.g. mediacy of the requested and the responded, *16* packets). We also record the finishing time of the process of transmission (T_{tran}). In the condition that T_{tran} is much less than $T_{deadline}$ (e.g. less than $T_{deadline}/2$) we get an approximate conclusion that the bandwidth is *much* underestimate. In this case, we accelerate the increasing pace by a ratio *r*. Thus increased packets is not 2 but $2 \times r$. Compared to the *mild* increasing style above, this incremental way is *sharp*. We use the mild increment because we need the request number not to exceed actual bandwidth ability, which will lead to a failure of satisfying the request and reduce following QoS of applications.

While for the VBR (*Variant Bit-rate*) media streaming, which contains varying size of data packets, packet number may not directly stands for bandwidth unit. To fit for this environment, simply adjusting the packet number to packet size in the algorithm will be effective and suitable.

TOBAB algorithm

> *InitReqNum: Initial number of packets to request.*
> *ReqNum: Number of requested packets.*
> *RespNum: Number of responded packets.*
> *IncreNum: Mild incremental packets.*
> *IncreRt: Ratio of sharp incremental packets.*
> *TranTime: Transmission time of last request.*
> *Deadline: Time of the period allowed for transmission.*
> *ReqNum = InitReqNum;*
> **while** *(buffer manager is running){*
>   *RespNum = getResponsePacketNumber();*
>   **if** *(ReqNum ≥ RespNum)*
>   *ReqNum = (ReqNum + RespNum)/2;*
>   **else**{
>   **if**(*TranTime ≥ Deadline/2*)
>   *ReqNum += IncreNum;*
>   **else**
>   *ReqNum += (RespNum − ReqNum) × IncreRt;*
>   *}*
> *}*

4 Performance Evaluation

We now evaluate the TOBAB algorithm. In all following simulations, we set the parameters as below: Maximal slots of *AbsSet*: *80*; *IncreRt*: *0.4*; *IncreNum*; *2*; *InitReqNum*: *20*.

Figure 1 shows a totally "random situation" that host *H* requests packets according to TOBAB and neighbors respond at random. In this case, bandwidth changes randomly. It can be noticed that the request curve is at response curve's heels (response curve stands for the bandwidth dynamic trend).

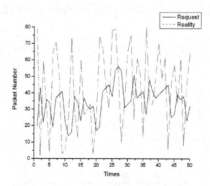

Fig. 1. Random situation (Peer's bandwidth is randomly changing)

In more accordance with real network, peers have their maximal in-bound limits. Figure 2, 3 and 4 simulate the fact that a peer's response sum should not exceed the maximal in-bound bandwidth. In TOBAB, anterior neighbors may be prior to occupy available in-bound bandwidth and complete their transmission, while the posterior may get less available bandwidth. If host H is able to finish all transmissions, it becomes the "random situation" above.

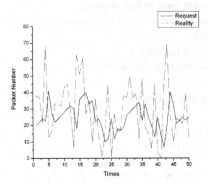

Fig. 2. Peer behavior with downstream limit (Request to 1st neighbor)

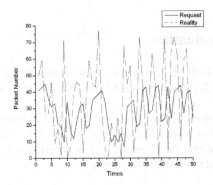

Fig. 3. Peer behavior with downstream limit (Request to 2nd neighbor)

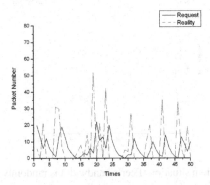

Fig. 4. Peer behavior with downstream limit (Request to 3rd neighbor)

We simulate the real situation whose responses obey both the in-bound bandwidth limit and the neighbors' in-bound limit (i.e. out-bound bandwidth limit of *H*). Here we assume the local peer owns *3* neighbors. The results are in Figure 5, 6 and 7.

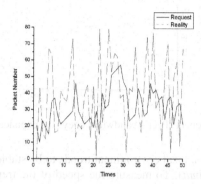

Fig. 5. Live peer's process (Request to 1st neighbor)

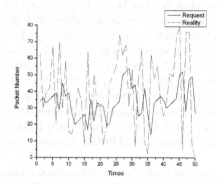

Fig. 6. Live peer's process (Request to 2nd neighbor)

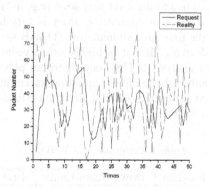

Fig. 7. Live peer's process (Request to 3rd neighbor)

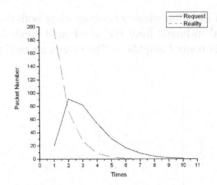

Fig. 8. Reality exponent (Peer's bandwidth obeys the exponential distribution)

In large scale networks, local environment trends to be stable, and the function will sequel to a constant (a *limit*). To measure the speed of the trend to this limit, we assume that the response curve follows the exponential distribution. That means the bandwidth is easily available at the beginning, however, as more active peers joining and other applications running, rest bandwidth becomes much less, until it gets into a vibrancy in a tiny scope. The simulation result is shown in Figure 8. In the simulation, we assume the maximal bandwidth is able to transfer *80* packets in time.

The performance result analysis is listed in Table 1. In the table, the request loop in TOBAB algorithm is executed *50* times, as shown in figures above. *Overestimating* times means the phenomenon that request packets is beyond the bandwidth ability, which means unsatisfactory. *Tendency Speed* is the time used that request is always near the reality, which describes the adaptation (allowing an offset of a 2-packet, i.e. the *IncreNum*). *Accuracy* is the total times that request is near the reality, which can describe the accuracy of the request in TOBAB. *Average* value is the mean value for the four situations.

We simulate four situations while their randomization characteristics decrease one by one. According to the statistics in Table 1, we can find out that, *overestimating* seldom occurs in all simulations except "*Random*". If real bandwidth converges to a limit, TOBAB will be adaptive to the limit very soon (e.g. in "*Exp.*"). The result is in less than *7* steps, i.e. 7 seconds in *Anysee*. *Accuracy* is very high in this simulation (more than *86%*). From the first three simulations, TOBAB will be more exact as the random characteristics decrease. But it is highly effective in regular distributions. According to distribution analysis in [18], our algorithm plays its role very well in real networks. Besides, although the initial requesting packet number is predefined in TOBAB, casually planned parameters will not affect the efficiency much, as the algorithm converges rapidly enough.

Table 1. Performance of TOBAB

	Random	Downstream-Limit	Live	Exp.	Avg.
Overestimating	22	7	17	8	13
Tendency Speed	-	-	-	7	7
Accuracy	0	4	11	43	14

5 Conclusion and Future Work

This paper proposes a bandwidth adaptive data request algorithm, TOBAB. The algorithm fits for different situations of the P2P dynamic environment. TOBAB has been proven resilient to the bandwidth fluctuation in P2P networks. It maximizes the bandwidth utilization through making track for the dynamic available bandwidth. The algorithm is especially useful to avoid the *"exceeding-demand"* problem, i.e. data request is beyond current bandwidth ability, which will lead to service unsatisfactory and a vicious circle.

The efficiency of TOBAB algorithm depends much on the parameters such as *IncreRt*, *IncreNum* and *InitReqNum*. In different topology, different groups of parameters will make the system most effective. Tendency Speed in our evaluation can be lower in detailed environment as algorithm improves. We leave these to our future research work.

References

1. V. Agarwal and R. Rejaie, *Adaptive Multi-Source Streaming in Heterogeneous Peer-to-Peer Networks*, Proceedings of SPIE Conference on Multimedia, Computing and Networking, California, Jan. 2005.
2. J.-I. Namgung, S.-Y. Shin, S.-H. Park, L.-S. Lee, and D. Jeong, *Self-Organizing P2P Overlay Network Applying Dynamic Landmark Mechanism for Contents Delivery Network*, Proceedings of 3rd ACIS International Conference, 2005, pp.317-324.
3. K. Lakshminarayanan, V. N. Padmanabhan, and J. Padhye, *Bandwidth Estimation in Broadband Access Networks*, Technical Report MSRTR-2004-44, May 2004.
4. R. S. Prasad, M. Murray, C. Dovrolis, and K. Claffy, *Bandwidth Estimation: Metrics, Measurement Techniques, and Tools*, IEEE Network, Vol.17, No.6, Nov.-Dec. 2003.
5. S.-R. Kang, X. Liu, M. Dai, and D. Loguinov, *Packet-Pair Bandwidth Estimation: Stochastic Analysis of A Single Congested Node*, Proceedings of the 12th IEEE International Conference on Network Protocols, 2004, pp.316-325.
6. N. Hu and P. Steenkiste, *Estimating Available Bandwidth Using Packet Pair Probing*, Tech. Rep., School of Computer Science, Carnegie Mellon University, CMU-CS-02-166, 2002.
7. C. Dovrolis, P. Ramanathan, and D. Moore, *What Do Packet Dispersion Techniques Measure?* Proceedings of Twentieth Annual Joint Conference of the IEEE Computer and Communications Societies (IEEE INFOCOM), Apr. 2001, pp.905-914.
8. B. Melander, M. Bjorkman, and P. Gunningberg, *A New End-to-End Probing and Analysis Method for Estimating Bandwidth Bottlenecks*, Proceedings of IEEE Global Internet Symposium, 2000.
9. V. Ribeiro, R. Riedi, R. Baraniuk, J. Navratil, and L. Cottrell, *pathChirp: Efficient Available Bandwidth Estimation for Network Paths*, Proceedings of Passive and Active Measurements (PAM) Workshop, Apr. 2003.
10. N. Hu and P. Steenkiste, *Evaluation and Characterization of Available Bandwidth Probing Techniques*, IEEE Journal on Selected Areas in Communications, 2003.
11. K. Lai and M. Baker, *Measuring Link Bandwidths Using a Deterministic Model of Packet Delay*, Proceedings of the ACM SIGCOMM, 2000.

12. X. Zhang, J. Liu, B. Li, and T.-S. P. Yum, *CoolStreaming/DONet: A Data-Driven Overlay Network for Efficient Live Media Streaming*, Proceedings of 24th Annual Joint Conference of the IEEE Computer and Communications Societies (INFOCOM), 2005.
13. *http://www.anysee.net*.
14. X. Liao, H. Jin, Y. Liu, L. M. Ni, and D. Deng, *Anysee: Scalable Live Streaming*, Proceedings of INFOCOM'06, 2006.
15. C. Zhang, H. Jin, D. Deng, S. Yang, Q. Yuan, and Z. Yin, *Anysee: Multicast-based Peer-to-Peer Media Streaming Service System*, Proceedings of Asia-Pacific Conference on Communications 2005, Perth, Western Australia, Oct. 2005.
16. V. N. Padmanabhan, H. J. Wang, P. A. Chou, and K. Sripanidkulchai, *Distributing Streaming Media Content Using Cooperative Networking*, Proceedings of NOSSDAV'02, USA, May 2002.
17. Y. Cai, Z. Chen, and W. Tavanapong, *Video Management in Peer-to-Peer Systems*, Proceedings of the 5th IEEE International Conference on Peer-to-Peer Computing, 2005.
18. M. E. J. Newman, *The Structure and Function of Complex Networks*, SIAM Review, Vol.45, No.2, 2003, pp.167-256.
19. Y. Liu, L. Xiao, X. Liu, L. M. Ni, and X. Zhang, *Location Awareness in Unstructured Peer-to-Peer Systems*, IEEE Transactions on Parallel and Distributed Systems, Vol.16, No.2, 2005, pp.163-174.

Interference-Aware Selfish Routing in Multi-ratio Multi-channel Wireless Mesh Networks

Yanxiang He[1], Jun Xiao[1], N. Xiong[2,1], and Laurence T. Yang[3]

[1] College of Computer,
Wuhan University, Wuhan, 430079, China
yxhe@whu.edu.cn, hugesoftcn@yahoo.com.cn
[2] School of Information Science,
Japan Advanced Institute of Science and Technology (JAIST), Japan
naixue@jaist.ac.jp
[3] Department of Computer Science,
St. Francis Xavier University, Antigonish, B2G 2W5, Canada
lyang@stfx.ca

Abstract. In this paper, we consider the selfish routing problem in non-cooperative wireless mesh networks where the capacity can be improved by transmitting over multiple radios simultaneously using orthogonal channels. The problem is that there are some agents who are in charge of their transmissions and each of them is selfish to minimize its own transmission cost without considering the overall performance of the network. But the embarrassment in wireless mesh networks is that the selfish agents perhaps may cause interference for the non-cooperation. We think that the game theoretic tools are helpful for the selfish agents to make feasible choices. We yield a sufficient condition of the existence of pure strategy Nash equilibrium in our *Strong Transmission Game* and prove it in this paper. Some simulations reveal the feasibility of our game theoretic approach.

1 Introduction

Wireless mesh network (WMN) is a new configuration for wireless broadband networks. It is built on a mix of fixed mesh routers (or access points) and mobile nodes interconnected via wireless links. Raffaele et al. believe that WMN can reduce the installation costs, be deployed on a large scale, increase reliability and provide self-management [1]. Thus some cities in USA, such as Medford, Oregon, Chaska and Minnesota etc, have deployed mesh networks [2].

Unlike traditional, the mesh nodes are rarely mobile and may have sufficient energy supply. Moreover, the topology seldom changes, the node failures are limited. But the capacity reduction due to interference among multiple simultaneous transmissions is still an unsatisfactory trouble. Multi-radio and multi-channel are helpful to alleviate this problem [3,4]. With multi-radio and multi-channel, nodes

L.T. Yang et al. (Eds.): ATC 2006, LNCS 4158, pp. 123–132, 2006.

can transmit simultaneously. It makes the transmission in Fig. 1 can work simultaneously if there are more than 4 distinct channels and more than 4 radios on node C in this network. We use different numbers to represent distinct channels in figures throughout this paper.

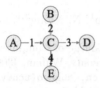

Fig. 1. A wireless Mesh network with 5 nodes

Here, we study selfish routing problem in multi-radio multi-channel wireless mesh networks, where the agents get to choose their paths and make channel assignments in order to minimize the expenses. Unlike most other work on this topic, we assume that the source nodes are owned by different entities and controlled by different agents, who are selfish and rational. Game theory is an appropriate tool to study such a routing. We define a routing game in which the agents need to choose paths from source nodes to sink nodes in the network while at the same time minimizing their costs. We emphasized the collision here is about the probability of the interference that generated by selfish agents for their irrational selfish choices. The network studied here is assumed to be sufficient for any rational agent to choose a relatively low cost route without interfering another's route.

Papadimitriou believed that Game Theory is likely to prove useful tools to model the Internet [5]. We believe that the interactions of the network nodes, especially on the data link layer and the network layer, should be studied as a game. On the data link layer, selfish nodes would like to abuse the protocol for fixing transmission radius and the protocol of assigning channel resources; on the network layer, the emphasis is about saving the energy for the selfish nodes, which is not an important point for wireless mesh networks [6]. In this paper, we will focus on the data link layer and solve the multi-ratio multi-channel selfish routing problem in a distributed manner using game theoretic tools. Throughout this paper, we will use sinks and destinations interchangeably, as well as routes and paths, edges and links. Our contributions are as follows.

- We formulate the selfish routing problem as a *Strong Transmission Game*; this game is a special case, where each source node can transmit flow to corresponding sink node simultaneously.
- We introduce and prove the theorem about the existence of pure strategy Nash equilibria in the *Strong Transmission Game*, which leads to a heuristic search for a pure strategy Nash equilibrium.
- We evaluate the outcome of our game in terms of its price of anarchy [7], and the society cost, etc.

The rest of the paper is structured as follow. we discuss related works in Section 2. This problem is defined in Section 3. We give our algorithms in Section 4. In Section 5, we evaluate our scheme through simulations. Finally, a conclusion is in Section 6.

2   Related Works

Tim Roughgarden and Éva Tardos have widely studied the loss of network performance for the lack of regulation [8]. They found the tight upper bound of linear latency system and the bound is confessed to be $\frac{4}{3}$. T. Boulogne and E. Altman recently extended the competitive routing into multicast communications and some different criteria were applied for this type of game [9]. Adrian Vetta considered the outcome to a submodular system and analyzed the performance of approximation algorithms [10]. The above researches lead to the exploration in wireless networks.

Michel X. Goemans et al. researched the market sharing games in ad-hoc networks [11]. Weizhao Wang, XiangYang Li and Yu Wang researched the truthful multicast routing in selfish wireless networks [12], Luzi Anderegg and Stephan Eidenbenz introduced a game-theoretic setting for routing in a mobile ad hoc network that consists of greedy, selfish agents [13]. Recently, Sheng Zhong, Li (Erran) Li, Yanbin Grace Liu and Yang Richard Yang studied ad-hoc games using game theoretical, cryptographic and incentive-compatible techniques [14]. All these researches induce us to consider the feasibility of using game theory to solve the selfish routing problem in wireless mesh networks. Of course, centralized scheme is still the mainstream in this field. Mansoor Alicherry et al. researched the joint channel assignment problem in multi-radio wireless mesh network with aim to optimize the overall throughput of the system [3]. Richard Draves et al. considered the routing in multi-radio, multi-hop wireless mesh networks [4]. Jian Tang et al. introduced a scheme of QoS Routing in wireless mesh networks [15]. These solutions were always using centralized algorithm and did not take the agent's selfish into account, which may be different to the self-management wireless networks. That is another origin of our scheme.

3   Problem Definition

We use an undirected graph $G(V, E)$ to model the wireless mesh network where V is the set of n wireless stationary nodes and E is the set of m edges. There are a transmission radius $r > 0$ and an interference radius $R = q \times r (q \geq 1)$ associated with every node determined by the transmission power. We let $d(u, v)$ to represent the Euclidean distance between u and v. Then there is an undirected edge $(u, v) \in E$ connecting node u and node v if $d(u, v) \leq r$. The edge (u, v) in G corresponds to a wireless link between node u and node v in the wireless network. Moreover, if there is interference between (u, v) and (u', v'), it is a necessary condition: $d(u, u') < R \bigvee d(u, v') < R \bigvee d(v, u') < R \bigvee d(v, v') < R$.

Transmission may collide in two ways in wireless networks: *primary* and *secondary interference* [16]. *Primary interference* occurs when a node has to transmit and receive simultaneously or transmit/receive more than one packet on the same radio at the same time. *Secondary interference* occurs when a receiver node is just within the range of more then one sender node on the same channel. Half-duplex operation is enforced for each radio to prevent *primary interference*. That means one radio can only transmit or receive at one time. *Secondary interference* is shown as Fig.2 where the two transmissions work simultaneously on the same channel at the same time within the range of interference radius R.

Here we describe the following selfish routing problem in wireless mesh network. There are k source-sink node pairs $\{s_1, t_1\}, \ldots, \{s_k, t_k\}$ in $G(V, E)$, naturally, we denote the agent set $D = \{1, 2, \ldots, k\}$ according to $\{s_1, s_2, \ldots, s_k\}$ and denote the set of $s_i - t_i$ paths as P_i correspondingly. We let $A_i = P_i \bigcup \{\phi\} = \{\phi, p_i^1, p_i^2, \ldots, p_i^{n_i}\}$ to be the set of all action available to agent i, that means the agent i is in charge of choosing a path p_i^j that is from s_i to t_i with feasible channel assignment, and define $P = \prod_i P_i$. A routing flow is a function $f : P \to R^+$; for a fixed flow according to agent i, we denote f_i is a flow from s_i to t_i, and $f = \bigcup_i f_i$. The number of hops with respect to an agent i is $h_i(f)$. We represent the set of orthogonal channels by $OC = \{1, 2, \ldots, K\}, |OC| = K$. The maximum number of radios that per node can use is denoted as Q and the reality number of radios that per node use is a function $\gamma : V \to N$. A function $\zeta : V \to N$ represents the number of channels that are used or interfered by a node.

Strong Transmission Game is a game where each agent can transmit simultaneously through a distinct path with feasible channels assignment without interference among them. It is a hard problem about channel assignment to satisfy the transmission condition to *Strong Transmission Game*. In fact [17] has proved the complexity of a channel assignment problem is NP-hard. So we will build our scheme heuristically.

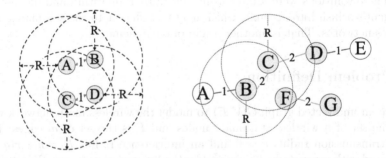

Fig. 2. An interference example   **Fig. 3.** A flow demonstration

In Fig.3, the edge BC interferes with CD and FG. A data package will last for three time slots to flow from node B to D (TDMA mode). In other words, the throughput is reduced to one third to the interference free one. The cost is trebled on the contrary.

We use $IE(e)$ to denote the number of links that interfered with link e on an arbitrary channel and $IE(e, i)$ to denote the number of links that interfered with link e on channel i. Taking the consideration in Fig.3 into account, we define the private cost function to agent i as $c_i(f) = h_i(f) \times \max IE_{e \in p_i}(e)$ and the social cost function $\kappa(f) = \Sigma_i c_i(f)$. As the agents are selfish and rational, they will minimize their private costs and take the interference into account. That means an agent will minimize its $c_i(f)$ subject to $\gamma(v) \leq Q \ \forall v \in p_i^k$ and $\varsigma(v) \leq K \ \forall v \in p_i^k$. What we want here is to know the deteriorative degree that is caused by each agent's selfishness.

We say that action profile $P \in P$ is a pure strategy Nash equilibrium if no agent has an incentive to change its action. That is, for any agent i,

$$c_i(f(P)) \leq c_i(f(P_i'))$$

Here P_i' represents the agent i change its action, which is different from the one in P, to any other one in A_i.

The pure strategy Nash equilibria are important because the agents are unlikely to choose one action amongst many on the basis of probability distribution which is called as a mixed strategy Nash equilibrium. What's more, the strategy space of pure strategy ones is much smaller than the mixed strategy ones. Thus it is important to converge to pure one. Here we will discuss what is sufficient condition for the existence of pure strategy Nash equilibria and how to converge to pure strategy Nash equilibria. By abusing the notation a little bit without confusion, we also use $P \in P$ to denote its corresponding flow f.

Theorem 1. *Take a Strong Transmission Game system (κ, c_i), there is a pure strategy Nash equilibrium.*

Proof. To prove this theorem is just to find a function that can reach a pure strategy Nash equilibrium. Consider a directed graph D, whose node corresponds to one of the possible pure strategy profile which is feasible path and corresponding channel assignment set here. There is an arc from node $P_0 = \{p_i, p_2, \ldots, p_i, \ldots, p_k\}$($p_i$ represents the path and the channel assignment according to agent i) to node $P_1 = \{p_i, p_2, \ldots, p_i', \ldots, p_k\}$ if $c_i(P_1) < c_i(P_0)$ for some agent i. It follows that a node P_N in D corresponds to a pure strategy Nash equilibrium if and only if the node has out-degree zero. So if D is acyclic and there is a node that can satisfy the flow simultaneously, the system has a pure strategy Nash equilibrium. The existing of the flow is satisfied from the *Strong Transmission Game* proposition; we will prove that D is acyclic below.

Suppose D is not acyclic. Then take a directed cycle C in D. Suppose the cycle contains nodes corresponding to the path sets: $P_0 = \{p_1^0, p_2^0, \ldots, p^0\}, P_1 = \{p_1^1, p_2^1, \ldots, p^1\}, \ldots, P_t = \{p_1^t, p_2^t, \ldots, p^t\}$. Here $P_0 = P_t$. It follows that the action profile P_r and P_{r+1} differ in only the path of one agent, say agent i_r. So $p_i^r = p_i^{r+1}$ if $i \neq i_r$ and $c_i(P_{r+1}) < c_i(P_r)$, it must be the case that $\Sigma_{r=0}^{t-1} c_i(P_{r+1}) - c_i(P_r) < 0$. But because in order to avoid interference, if the agent i_r changes its path or adjusts channel assignment then the change will not interfere with the other agents' choices of their paths and channel assignments. That means

$$c_i(\mathbf{P}_{r+1}) - c_i(\mathbf{P}_r) = \kappa_i(\mathbf{P}_{r+1}) - \kappa_i(\mathbf{P}_r)$$

Then, since $\mathbf{P}_0 = \mathbf{P}_t$, we obtain

$$\begin{aligned}
\Sigma_{r=0}^{t-1} c_i(\mathbf{P}_{r+1}) - c_i(\mathbf{P}_r) &= \Sigma_{r=0}^{t-1} \kappa_i(\mathbf{P}_{r+1}) - \kappa_i(\mathbf{P}_r) \\
&= \kappa_i(\mathbf{P}_t) - \kappa_i(\mathbf{P}_0) \\
&= 0
\end{aligned}$$

That is a contradiction to $\Sigma_{r=0}^{t-1} c_i(\mathbf{P}_{r+1}) - c_i(\mathbf{P}_r) < 0$. So D is acyclic. Then Theorem 1 follows.

But it is a well-known open problem to compute Nash equilibria in an arbitrary multi-player game [18]. Then we will give our heuristic algorithm in the next section.

4   Algorithms

We assume the orthogonal channels are more than the source-sink node pairs, i.e. $K \geq k$. Thus the agents can begin their exploration of distinct paths on distinct channels. We assume that each node can use two different radios to receive and send data simultaneously without interference on two different channels, the throughput of the routing will be doubled to the single radio one. Here we assume each node has even radios $(2, 4, 6 \ldots)$. We present an algorithm to find a best path for each agent below.

Algorithm 1. Minimum hop-count path algorithm

Require: Initiate graph $G(V, E)$ and the agents array $D = \{1, 2, \ldots k\}$.

  for each agent $i \in D$ **do**

    Apply Breadth First Search (BFS) algorithm to compute an s-t path p_i in G with minimum hop-count for agent i. Assign all the link $e \in p_i$ with the same spare channel and update the number of spare radios on mediate nodes by subtracting 2 from the foregoing number.

    if path p_i is feasible **then**

      $P = P \bigcup p_i$

    end if

  end for

  if each agent finds a feasible path **then**

    Output P

  end if

Now each agent has got a feasible path and then it will use overall channels to improve its performance next. As the algorithm 2 shows.

Algorithm 2. Channel assignment algorithm

Require: Initialize the paths array P = $\{p_1, p_2, \ldots, p_t\}$, channels set $OC = \{1, 2, \ldots, K\}$ and a number t to represent the current path, a number i to represent the current channel and *channel_flag* = TRUE to control the loop.

  while *channel_flag* **do**
    channel_flag = FALSE
    for each channel $i \in OC$ **do**
      for each path $p_t \in$ P **do**
        Find the link $e \in p_t$ that has the maximum $IE(e)$ and satisfies $IE(e, i) = 1$.
        Assign this edge with channel i and update the interfered link number of
        each affected link in G and let *channel_flag* = TRUE.
      end for
    end for
  end while

We can see from these algorithms, at the end of these two algorithms, we will reach an action profile which is just a point that has out-degree zero. So we can get the following theorem:

Theorem 2. *The outputs of Algorithm 1 and Algorithm 2 are both pure strategy Nash equilibria if they are regarded as two games separately.*

5 Evaluation

In this section we investigate the efficiency of our scheme and evaluate the affection of some factors in a simulated network scenario. We generated a wireless mesh network with 100 nodes as be shown in Fig.4-(a). These nodes are randomly placed in an $800 \times 800m^2$ rectangular region. Each node has 2 radios and $R = r$. We vary the transmission range and the number of $s - t$ pairs, which are generated randomly in each round, to evaluate the affection. On the other hand, the flow for each agent is set to be the same in all these simulations, which will sharpen the competition among the agents. Fig.4-(b) and (c) show the links which indicate that the distance between the two nodes incident with the link is no more than 140m and 190m respectively.

From Fig.4-(d) to (i), we show some examples for our algorithms where the different line colors and styles represent different channels. The $s - t$ node pairs were generated randomly to follow the given requirements. Fig.4-(d), (f) and (h) represent the end of Algorithm 1 where the numbers of $s - t$ node pairs are 2, 5 and 10 respectively. Accordingly, (e), (g) and (i) represent the end of Algorithm 2. The transmission ranges are all 140m in these examples.

The price of anarchy is a main criterion to evaluate the efficiency of the game solution. Here we use a lower bound of the optimal solution instead of the optimal one to compute the price of anarchy. As be shown in Fig.5-(a), the price of anarchy mainly increases as the number of $s - t$ node pairs turns more. That shows more node pairs will sharpen the competition which induce the increase

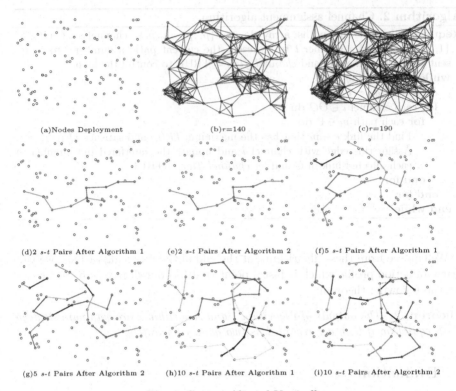

(a)Nodes Deployment   (b)r=140   (c)r=190

(d)2 s-t Pairs After Algorithm 1   (e)2 s-t Pairs After Algorithm 2   (f)5 s-t Pairs After Algorithm 1

(g)5 s-t Pairs After Algorithm 2   (h)10 s-t Pairs After Algorithm 1   (i)10 s-t Pairs After Algorithm 2

Fig. 4. Centers Aligned Vertically

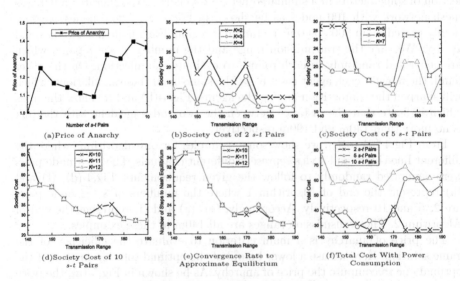

(a)Price of Anarchy   (b)Society Cost of 2 s-t Pairs   (c)Society Cost of 5 s-t Pairs

(d)Society Cost of 10 s-t Pairs   (e)Convergence Rate to Approximate Equilibrium   (f)Total Cost With Power Consumption

Fig. 5. Centers Aligned Vertically

of the price of anarchy. But when the number of $s - t$ node pairs turns from 2 to 6, the price of anarchy decreases. It is because that the increase of the number of $s - t$ node pairs does not affect the existing node pairs for the mediate nodes are sufficient for the agents, nevertheless, it is not always true as the node pairs are too many to be served by the mediate nodes; then the selfishness will be the primary factor and the price turns high.

Some other simulations reveal the relative between the transmission range and society cost with different number of orthogonal channels. As Fig.5-(b), Fig.5-(c) and Fig.5-(d) show, the society cost decreases in a mass as the nodes increase their transmission power lever (transmission range). It is because that the increase of transmission power brings out some new mediate nodes for the agents which may alleviate the competition and decrease the society cost. On the other hand, the number of orthogonal channels is the bottleneck for routing, especially in Fig.5-(b), in wireless mesh network as be shown in these figures where we use K to represent the distinct channel number. When the number of orthogonal channels increases, the society cost decreases dramatically in Fig.5-(b). The reason is that the orthogonal channels are so lacking even for one path. This induces that the research on the orthogonal channels would be a potential breakpoint for the selfish routing in wireless mesh networks.

Another question about our scheme is about the convergence rate to an approximate pure strategy Nash equilibrium. As be shown in Fig.5-(e), we fixed the number of $s - t$ pairs to 10, the numbers of steps to an approximate pure strategy Nash equilibrium decrease as the transmission ranges increase. As more channels bring with more improvements, the number of steps to an approximate pure strategy Nash equilibrium is more than the less channels one.

At last, we considered the question if the agent should pay for the transmission power consumption. Because the power consumption increases super-linearly as the transmission range increases, we use the square of transmission radius, which is divided by a constant, to replace the hop and the results are shown in Fig.5-(f). This figure indicates that the total cost can hardly say to decrease as the transmission range increases. That means each agent should minimize the transmission range to find an approximate pure strategy Nash equilibrium if the power consumption be taken into account.

6 Conclusions

We introduced an attempt to route flow in multi-channel, multi-radio wireless mesh network by using game theoretic tools in this paper; we proved the existence of pure strategy Nash equilibrium in a special game. The evaluation shows the output of our scheme is feasible in some cases.

As we have paid more attention to think this question by a theoretic way, some factors have been ignored such as system bandwidth, the relation between interference radius and transmission radius and so on. We will take all these factors into account in future.

References

1. Raffaele Bruno, Marco Conti and Enrico Gregori.: Mesh Networks: Commodity Mulithop Ad Hoc Networks. *IEEE Communications Magazine* (2005) 123–131
2. Chaska wireless technologies.: http://www.chaska.net/
3. Mansoor Alicherry, Randeep Bhatia and Li (Erran) Li.: Joint Channel Assignment and Routing for Throughput Optimization in Multi-radio Wireless Mesh Networks. In *MOBICOM* (2005) 58–72
4. Richard Draves Jitendra Padhye Brian Zill.: Routing in Multi-Radio, Multi-Hop Wireless Mesh Networks. In *MOBICOM* (2004) 114–128
5. C. Papadimitriou.: Algorithms, games, and the internet. In *STOC* (2001)
6. IEEE 802.16-2004.: Part 16: Air Interface for Fixed Broadband Wireless Access Systems (2004)
7. E. Koutsoupias and C. H. Papadimitriou.: Worst-case Equilibria. In *STACS* (1999) 404–413
8. Tim Roughgarden and Éva Tardos.: How Bad is Selfish Routing?. *JACM* **49** (2002) 236–259
9. T. Boulogue and E. Altman.: Competitive Routing in Multicast. *Networks* **46** (2005) 22–35
10. Adrian Vetta.: Nash Equilibria in Competitive Societies, with Applications to Facility Locations, Traffic Routing and Auctions. In emphFOCS (2002)
11. Michel X. Goemans, Li (Erran) Liy, Vahab S. Mirrokni and Marina Thottan.: Market Sharing Games Applied to Content Distribution in Ad-Hoc Networks. In *MOBIHOC* (2004) 55–66
12. Weizhao Wang, XiangYang Li and Yu Wang.: Truthful Multicast Routing in Selfish Wireless Networks. In *MOBICOM* (2004) 245–259
13. Luzi Anderegg and Stephan Eidenbenz.: Ad hoc-VCG: A Truthful and Cost-Efficient Routing Protocol for Mobile Ad hoc Networks with Selfish Agents. In *MOBICOM* (2003) 245–259
14. Sheng Zhong, Li (Erran) Li, Yanbin Grace Liu and Yang Richard Yang.: On Designing Incentive-Compatible Routing and Forwarding Protocols in Wireless Ad Hoc Networks-An Integrated Approach Using Game Theoretical and Cryptographic Techniques. In *MOBICOM* (2005) 117–131
15. Jian Tang, Guoliang Xue and Weiyi Zhang.: Interference-Aware Topology Control and QoS Routing in Multi-Channel Wireless Mesh Networks. In *MOBIHOC* (2005) 68–77
16. S. Ramanathan and E. L. Lloyd.: Scheduling Algorithms for Multihop Radio Networks. *IEEE/ACM Transactions on Networking* **1** (1993) 166–177
17. Ashish Raniwala, Kartik Gopalan and Tzi-cker Chiueh.: Centralized Channel Assignment and Routing Algorithms for Multi-Channel Wireless Mesh Networks. *ACM Mobile Computing and Communication Review* **8** (2004) 50–65
18. X. Deng, C. H. Papadimitriou and S. Safra.: On the Complexity of Equilibria. In *STOC* (2002) 67–71

Autonomic Group Location Update for Mobile Networks*

Lai Tu, Furong Wang, Fan Zhang, and Jian Zhang

Huazhong University of Science and Technology,
Wuhan, Hubei, P.R. China
tulai@public.wh.hb.cn

Abstract. This paper presents an autonomic group location update
(GLU) scheme for next-generation mobile networks. The GLU scheme
takes account of the cooperative ability of the Mobile Terminals(MTs)
in next-generation mobile networks, thus employs an autonomic group
formation method to report location update in groups. A Leader Mobile
Terminal(LMT) is elected out of all Group Members(GMs) to perform
the location update and administration tasks for the whole group. Not
only the bandwidth is saved for the efficiency of group operation, but
also the whole system energy consumption of location update is significantly reduced in respect that communication range is much shorter in
group than to base station. A leader rotation algorithm based on a variable called *prestige* is also exploited to make it fair. Both analysis and
simulation show that the GLU scheme greatly saves energy for MTs and
with our leader rotation algorithm, fairness can be also achieved.

1 Introduction

Mobile communication has been experiencing tremendous growth over the past
two decades, which drives rapid improvement in wireless communication, network architecture and many other technologies. The major goal of mobile communication is now to provide ubiquitous network accessibility for every user
without regard to location or mobility. The growing density of subscribers and
emergence of micro even pico and nano cellular system underscore the importance of location management [1].

Traditional location management schemes can be divided into statics update
which is most commonly used in current mobile system, and dynamic update
which is composed of three types of update methods: Time based, distance based
and movement based [2]. Taking account of MTs' group mobility characteristics,
several papers have dealt with group location management of mobile networks.
Paper [3] have proposed a group location tracking scheme based on virtual VLR
for transportation system. Paper [4] further discussed group deregistration strategy for PCS networks. Paper [5] presents a spontaneous group management

---

* This work is supported by National Natural Science Foundation of China under
Grant No.60572047

L.T. Yang et al. (Eds.): ATC 2006, LNCS 4158, pp. 133–142, 2006.
© Springer-Verlag Berlin Heidelberg 2006

scheme in mobile Ad Hoc networks. In our previous work, we proposed a prototype of group location update scheme and proved its efficiency in wireless bandwidth cost by analysis [6]. But works in paper [6] are still preliminary. In this paper we exploit an autonomic group management procedure for GLU and estimate energy consumption by both analysis and simulation using a one-dim random waypoint mobility model with group characteristics. Results show our GLU scheme and algorithms have saved energy cost for location update, and with an LMT selection algorithms, every group member fairly shares the energy cost for location update and group organization for the whole system.

The rest of this paper will be arranged as follows: In the second section, we briefly review the GLU scheme in architecture and procedures for location update and call delivery; In section 3, autonomic group management procedures will be presented, including a detailed specification of the LMT Selection algorithm. Section 4 will focus on energy consumption evaluation and comparison of our GLU and traditional individual location update (ILU) scheme, and finally follows the last section which is the conclusion.

2   Group Location Update for Next-Generation Mobile Networks

In 3G and beyond 3G mobile systems, there is a tendency of combination of heterogeneous networks, such as traditional mobile cellular network and Ad Hoc networks [7]. Node to node communications can be achieved and thus used for cooperative applications. Taking account of the group mobility of MTs in some environment, the GLU scheme allows one MT out of the group members to subscribe group update for all to the base station (BS). Group formation can be half autonomic using communication method similar to Ad Hoc with the help of BS.

2.1   Architecture

Typical scenario of this case is a group of large number of MTs cross the border of LAs as shown in Figure 1. Communications in group and between group and BS use different wireless resources. To make it visual, we call in-group communication *horizontal communication*, denote channel for *horizontal communication* as **HC**; call communication between group and BS *vertical communication*, denote channel for *vertical communication* as **VC**.

Therefore, the frequency resources in **VC** for control signaling is greatly saved due to a lot of work have been pushed down to be accomplished on the *horizontal* plane, and the limited frequency resources are used only for *vertical communication*. And as the number of users in the group increases, the advantage of the group update scheme in saving frequency resources improves [6].

The limited energy capacity of mobile computing devices has brought energy conservation to the forefront of concerns for enabling mobile communications.

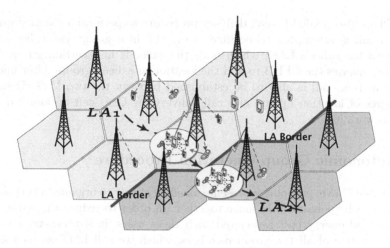

Fig. 1. Typical Scenario of Group Location Update Scheme

The power cost for *horizontal communication* is much lower than *vertical communication* due to the reduction in communication distance, thus the GLU scheme saves battery for mobile phone users, which will be quantitatively discussed in Section 4.

In-group communication will use competition access method like DCF in Ad Hoc when group is forming or no LMT exists in group. After group formation, LMT will periodically broadcast a beacon to its GMs. In-group communication then will be controlled by the LMT using centralized mechanism like PCF in WLAN.

Currently our research only think about using **HC** for in-group cooperation. Downlink paging from BS to MTs and data traffic between BS and MTs are still transferred vertically using traditional way of mobile cellular network for security reasons and technical difficulty in implementation. More detailed group operation procedures will be elaborated in third section of this paper.

In such case, when group has already been established, MTs need not to update by themselves. Instead, LMT will send a group location update message to inform that all members in the group are crossing the border. Location update and call delivery procedures will be different from conventional ILU as follows:

2.2 Location Update and Call Delivery

In the GLU scheme, a Group Location Database (GLDB) is necessary in the network side to accomplish the tasks of group information storing and querying. The GLDB is to some extent similar to a local anchor that records the group location and member registration and deregistration of a group. When a group passes the border of a Location Area (LA), the LMT of the group represents all its member sending a group registration message to the VLR of the new LA, and the VLR sends update message to GLDB to inform group location update and forwards deregistration to former VLR.

GLDB is also needed by call delivery procedure to perform a location query. When a call is attempted to be made to a MT in a group, the caller sends request to the callee's HLR, which finds the callee is in a certain group. The HLR then queries the GLDB to find the location of callee's group. After finding the destination, call is able to be established between the two MTs. Detailed procedures of location update and call delivery for GLU can be found in our previous work [6].

3   Autonomic Group Operation Procedure

As discussed above, grouping represents an efficient way to organize a certain set of users which spontaneously move together. In order to reduce the redundant signaling and energy cost associated with these users, it is necessary to elect a representative of all the group members, which we call LMT as mentioned before. Also, given the dynamic nature of groups, i.e., MTs can join or quit a group at any time, numerous operations are necessary to guarantee the correct behavior of the system. These operations are:

3.1   Group Establishing

The GLU scheme is invoked when a number of mobiles users are spontaneously gathering and near enough. MTs can feel a group is being formed by listening to the HC, therefore they negotiate with each other by exchanging a REQ_ESTABLISH message carrying its *prestige*, a variable represents the MT's remaining energy and the probability to leave. The latter factor is set to 0 at initiation. The MT with largest *prestige* will be regarded as the first LMT and send GROUP_ESTABLISHED message to the BS with group member information, which accomplishes a procedure of group formation.

3.2   Group Leader Selection

Group LMT Selection is performed when group is being established, or when periodical rotation and exceptional reselection is needed, due to energy matter or an unexpected departure or turnoff of former LMT. It is evident to see that LMT takes more responsibility than GMs, which results in higher power consumption of LMT's. As a consequence, Group LMT Selection need to be performed periodically. We call such a procedure *"Regular Rotation"*. Another case of Group LMT Selection being performed is that the former LMT of the group left the group or is turned off, which we call an *"Irregular Selection"*. What's more the Group LMT Selection is also initiated when a new group is establishing. As Group LMT Selection when Group Establishing can be considered as an Irregular Selection as no LMT exists in current group, two different cases can be distinguished:

Regular Rotation. Regular Rotation will be initiated by current LMT, supposed to be LMT_i. A timer will be set at LMT_i when it becomes the LMT of the group by assignment of BS or former LMT. When the timer expired, LMT_i changes its state from *Leader* to *Rotation*, broadcasts a ROTATION_REQ message. GMs in the group receiving the ROTATION_REQ generate their own *prestige*, if non-zero, sends a TAKE_OVER_REQ message containing its identifier and its *prestige* to LMT_i. LMT_i compares all *prestige* values, selects a terminal with the largest, supposed to be T_j, responses it a TAKE_OVER_ACK containing the Group ID G_i. T_j receiving the TAKE_OVER_ACK then changes its role from GM to LMT and broadcasts GROUP_ESTABLISHED message containing its own ID T_j and the Group ID G_i to all GMs in its group. A GROUP_ESTABLISHED beacon is also transmitted periodically to keep group formation. The ex-LMT LMT_i receiving the GROUP_ESTABLISHED message from the new LMT T_j then changes its role from LMT to GM. All other GMs receiving the GROUP_ESTABLISHED message set their LMT ID to T_j. A regular rotation procedure is then completed.

During the LMT Selection process, LMT_i will still take the responsibility of group leader until the new LMT take over it by broadcasting GROUP_ESTABLISHED message.

Irregular Selection. Irregular Selection is performed when former LMT left group or was turned off without notification. When no beacon is heard for a designate time, the GMs will re-negotiate to select a new LMT, as is performed in Group Establishing procedure. MTs negotiate with each other by exchanging a REQ_ESTABLISH message carrying its *prestige*. One difference between Irregular Selection and LMT selection at group formation is that the probability to leave is no longer 0 as the time of group formation passes, and the times of each GMs having been the LMT changes that will also affect the new LMT's election.

Prestige Generation Algorithm. The operation of the GLU scheme is broken into *rounds*, where each *round* begins with a set-up phase, when Group LMT selection procedure is performed, followed by a steady-state phase, when group is formed with a determinate group leader. N *rounds* build up a *cycle*, where N is the mean number of the group members. In order to minimize overhead, the steady-state is long compared to the set-up phase.

Initially, when new LMT is being selected, all group members need to decide whether or not to become a candidate of LMT. To be fair to all MTs, three laws are defined:

Law 1. *No MT shall be reappointed as LMT of one group for two continuous* rounds.

Law 2. *No MT shall have chance to be LMT of a group for 2 times more than the* cycles *it stays in its group.*

Law 3. *Not breaking* Law 1 *and* Law 2, *an MT with highest* prestige, *which is a variable depending on how many the* rounds *an MT has joined the group and its remaining energy, will be selected as LMT.*

The above three laws are supposed to made longer life time of a group and fair power consumption of all members. To decrease the probability of an occurrence of "*Irregular Selection*", MTs with more remaining energy and more likely to stay in group are more possible to be LMT, which is the main purpose of the definition of *Law 3*. No reappointment is allowed to avoid continuous high power consumption of one MT. More energetic MT trends more to be LMT, but it's not its responsibility to do so, which means unfair to it. So *Law 1* and *Law 2* are defined as constraints to keep fair to all MTs while letting energetic MT take a relatively more work.

The decision is made by negotiation or the former LMT comparing each GM's *prestige*. Suppose $p(k)$ is the "*prestige*" of MT_k reported to the former LMT or for negotiation, which depends on its remaining power E_k and the number of *rounds* it passes in the group, denoted as n_k. Before giving the expression of $p(k)$, it is necessary to explain two cumulative density functions (CDF) with respect to the energy consumption and in-group time.

Let $F_E(x)$ be the cumulative density function of the power consumption of a LMT in a group, i.e., the probability of a LMT consuming energy less than x is $F_E(x)$. Let $F_T(x)$ be the cumulative density function of the time that a MT stays in a group, i.e., the probability of a MT being in its group for a time less than x is $F_T(x)$.

Therefore, $p(k)$, the *prestige* of MT_k whose remaining power is E_k and staying in current group for n_k *rounds*, is set as:

$$p(k) = \begin{cases} 0 & MT_k \text{ now is LMT} \\ 0 & L_k > [\frac{n_k}{N}] + 1 \\ F_E(E_k)(1 - F_T(n_k)) & \text{else} \end{cases} \tag{1}$$

Here, L_k stands for the times MT_k has been the LMT of current group since it last joined the group. The non-zero *prestige* in equation 1 then can be interpreted as the probability of the candidate being able to accomplish the task of a LMT in the following *round*.

3.3   Member Join

The LMT of a group, supposed to be LMT_i, shall broadcast a GROUP_ESTABLISHED message containing the group information periodically after group is established. When an MT T_j receives the GROUP_ESTABLISHED message, it measures the received power in order to evaluate the distance d from the LMT. If $d \leqslant d_{Thr}$, where d_{Thr} is the distance threshold for group joining, it generates a GROUP_JOIN_REQ message with its Terminal ID T_j and sends it to LMT_i. Upon receiving GROUP_JOIN_REQ message, LMT_i will response the requesting MT T_j a GROUP_JOIN_CONF message containing its Terminal ID LMT_i and the Group ID G_i and add T_j to its member list. The MT T_j then set its affiliated group to G_i and its group leader to LMT_i after receiving the GROUP_JOIN_CONF message.

A Group Updating procedure will also be invoked by LMT_i transmitting a GROUP_UPDATE message to the BS which contains the new member's ID T_j, the Group ID G_i, and an update type field of *member join*. The BS then adds T_j

to Group G_i's member list and set the T_j's affiliated group to G_i in location database. The location information of T_j will also change to "in group G_i" in HLR database.

Note an MT T_j can receive multiple GROUP_ESTABLIHED messages from different LMTs. It is necessary for it to verify which group to join. MT T_j which receives multiple GROUP_ESTABLISHED messages measures the received power, evaluates the distance d from the different LMTs and then chooses group of the closest LMT to join.

3.4 Member Quit

A group member that leaves from a group employs Group Quitting procedure. It is invoked automatically by an MT T_j transmitting a GROUP_UPDATE message to BS which contains its Terminal ID T_j, its former Group ID G_i and an update type field of *member quit*, when T_j is out of its LMT LMT_i's range, i.e., the distance between T_j and LMT_i, d, which is evaluated by T_j measuring the received power level from LMT_i, is larger than d_{Thr}. Upon received GROUP_UPDATE message, the BS removes T_j from group G_i's member list and sends a GROUP_UPDATE_CONF message with parameter T_j and update type *member quit* to G_i's LMT, LMT_i. LMT_i then removes T_j from its member list. The location information of T_j then will return to its current LA in HLR database.

3.5 Group Update

Group Updating procedure is performed whenever a change occurs to a group, including Group LMT selection, Member joining, Member quitting and location update, which has been already mentioned in previous subsections. To save energy and bandwidth, most of GROUP_UPDATE message is transmitted as a part of LOCATION_UPDATE message or GROUP_ESTABLISHED message. It's not necessary to report update immediately since location update is not such real time service. Reporting when location update occurs or LMT changes will be enough.

4 Power Consumption Analysis and Simulation

One of the main advantages of GLU is that it reduces the location update signalling in the database side significantly as well as the consumption of wireless bandwidth for location update message, which can be found in relevant papers and our previous research. Since the power that an MT uses to transmit a message is on proportion to the square of the distance to the destination [8], the power consumption of the whole system is greatly reduced for the in-group communication range is much shorter than that to communicate with the base station.

Let E be the average power consumption of an MT communicating with the base station and e be the average power consumption between MTs in group. For the communication distance in group is much shorter than to the base station, it is evidence that $E \gg e$.

In traditional ILU scheme, when a group of n GMs crosses one LA to another, every MT sends a location update message to the base station. Therefore the total energy consumption is nE. While in a GLU scheme, MTs form in group and every time the group crosses the border, only one MT is in charge of reporting location update. Despite of relatively tiny power consumption on in-group communication, the whole system only uses E for each crossing. Even we added the cost for member joining, leader selection, leader rotation, the power consumptions are still saved for the whole system.

We use a hybrid mobility model of one-dim random waypoint model and reference point group mobility model for both analysis and simulation. The reference point considered as the group center moves in its trip, individual mobile node randomly chooses a point to join the group, moves with the reference point and randomly chooses another point to leave. This model perfectly illustrates a public transportation system in real life.

Suppose there are totally N MTs in this system, each MT randomly chooses a source-destination pair as its trip in the system. The whole trip of the reference point totally crosses k LAs, at the points x_i $(i = 1, 2, \ldots, k)$. The energy cost expectation of the whole system for ILU scheme and our GLU scheme are denoted as E_I and E_G respectively.

It is easy to get that:

$$E_G = kE + \frac{TE}{\tau} + \frac{Te}{\mu} \tag{2}$$

Here T is the whole time for the trip, τ is the time interval for leader rotation and μ is the time interval for leader beacon.

In ILU scheme, because all MTs independently chooses its waypoints for the whole trip, whether a location update occurs in each border for every MT can be illustrated:

$$L(x_i, x, y) = \begin{cases} 1 & x \leqslant x_i \leqslant y \\ 0 & \text{else} \end{cases} \tag{3}$$

x_i, x, y in equation 3 stand for the point of the ith LA border and where a certain MT joins and leaves the group respectively. As all MTs are same in ILU scheme, we can also get expression for E_I:

$$\begin{aligned} E_I &= NE \sum_{i=1}^{k} \iint_{x \leqslant y} L(x_i, x, y) f(x, y) dx dy \\ &= NE \sum_{i=1}^{k} \frac{2x_i(L - x_i)}{L^2} \end{aligned} \tag{4}$$

In case that LA border points are uniformly distributed over the whole trip, an approximate closed form can be derived:

$$E_I = NE \sum_{i=1}^{k} \frac{2i(k - i)}{k^2} = NE(\frac{k}{3} - \frac{1}{3k}) \approx \frac{kNE}{3} \tag{5}$$

Simulation is done to verify our analysis. We have studied energy consumption of GLU and ILU in various cases of different user number, amount of LA borders, number of discrete stations where MTs join and leave group. Suppose the mean in group range is one tenth of the distance between an MT and the base station, hence approximately $E = 100e$. All energy consumptions are counted in unit in-group communication cost e.

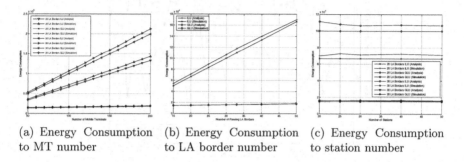

(a) Energy Consumption to MT number   (b) Energy Consumption to LA border number   (c) Energy Consumption to station number

Fig. 2. Energy Consumption Comparison

Figure 2(a) shows energy consumption of different number of MTs in the system increasing from 50 to 200 in pace of 10. 20 LA borders and 30 LA borders are studied respectively. Both analysis and simulation show that energy consumption for whole system increases linearly with the number of MTs in ILU scheme, while stays at a relative low level stably in our GLU scheme. In figure 2(b), different amount of LA borders are considered. Although energy consumption increases both in GLU and ILU scheme, the cost in GLU is much less than in ILU. Increasing amount can be also ignored in GLU compared to in ILU. Figure 2(c) further proofs that the energy costs are independent of the number of the discrete stations, which can be also found in equation 2 and 5.

Fairness of energy consumptions among MTs in group is evaluated by the standard deviation of energy consumption of all MTs. With our leader selection algorithm based on *prestige* prediction, the standard deviation is much lower than that of a randomly selection method without prediction. Simulations are repeated several times. Except one occasional round, this inference is always true in most cases.

5 Conclusions

The GLU scheme uses different communication methods in hybrid networks, as to save energy and the limited bandwidth resource for *vertical communication*. A detailed autonomic in-group operation procedure is studied in this paper. The group leader selection algorithm of the GLU scheme, which plays an important role in GLU as the first step of the formation of a group and each round, is specifically discussed to approach fair energy consumptions of all group members and long lifetime of the group. Analysis and simulation are made to examine the energy costs and fairness of the whole system. Both show that the GLU scheme greatly saves energy for MTs and fairness can also be achieved with our leader selection algorithm based on *prestige* prediction.

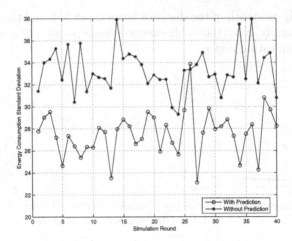

Fig. 3. Energy consumption standard deviation

References

1. I. Han, and D. H. Cho, "Group location management for mobile subscribers on transportation systems in mobile communication networks," *IEEE Trans. Veh. Technol.*, vol. 53, no. 1, pp. 181-191, Jan. 2004.
2. Bar-Noy, et. al., "Mobile Users: To Update or Not to Update?" *ACM-Baltzer J. Wireless Networks*, Vol.1, No.2, July 1995, pp.175-186.
3. I. Han, S. K. Jung, and D. H. Cho, "Distributed group location tracking based on several RIDs and virtual VLRs for transportation systems," in *Proc. IEEE VTC02 Spring.*, vol. 1, pp. 298-302, May 2002.
4. Z. Mao, and C. Douligeris, "Group Deregistration Strategy for PCS Networks," *IEEE Comm. Letter*, vol. 6, no. 4, pp. 141-143, April 2002.
5. L. Galluccio, G. Morabito, and S. Palazzo, "Spontaneous group management in mobile Ad Hoc networks," *Wireless Network*, vol. 10, Issue 4, pp. 423-438, July 2004.
6. F. Wang, L. Tu and et. al., "Group Location Update Scheme and Performance Analysis for Location Management in Mobile Network," to appear in *Proc. IEEE VTC' 05 Spring.*, May-Jun., 2005.
7. I. F. Akyildiz, J. McNair, J. S. M. Ho, H. Uzunalioglu, and W. Wang, "Mobility management in current and future communications networks," *IEEE Network*, vol. 12, pp. 39-49, July/Aug., 1998.
8. M. Mouly and M. B. Pautet, "The GSM system for mobile communications," M. Mouly, Palaiseau, France, Tech. Rep. 1992.

Autonomic and Trusted Computing Paradigms

Xiaolin Li, Hui Kang, Patrick Harrington, and Johnson Thomas

Computer Science Department,
Oklahoma State University, Stillwater, OK 74078
{xiaolin, huk, pharrin, jpt}@cs.okstate.edu

Abstract. The emerging autonomic computing technology has been hailed by world-wide researchers and professionals in academia and industry. Besides four key capabilities, well known as self-CHOP, we propose an additional self-regulating capability to explicitly emphasize the policy-driven self-manageability and dynamic policy derivation and enactment. Essentially, these five capabilities, coined as Self-CHROP, define an autonomic system along with other minor properties. Trusted computing targets guaranteed secured systems. Self-protection alone does not ensure the trustworthiness in autonomic systems. The new trend is to integrate both towards trusted autonomic computing systems. This paper presents a comprehensive survey of the autonomic and trusted computing paradigms and a preliminary conceptual architecture towards trustworthy autonomic grid computing.

1 Introduction

As the proliferation of numerous computing and networking devices and systems, the explosive growth of software applications and services and complicated interactions among software/hardware components, make the management of complex systems a significant challenge. These sophisticated applications and services execute on heterogeneous, dynamic, and fast-evolving hardware platforms. As a result, the increasing complexity, dynamism, heterogeneity, and uncertainty of information systems overwhelm capabilities of system administrators. Inspired by the human autonomic nervous system, autonomic computing has emerged as the only viable solution that addresses these system management issues in a holistic manner [1] [2] [3]. Further, the advent of grid computing environments [4] [5], aimed at integrating geographically distributed computing resources and services for coordinated resource sharing and high performance computing, makes autonomic grid computing systems an urgent need to realize the promises of world-wide grid computing platforms.

The rest of the paper is organized as follows. Sect. 2 presents the autonomic computing paradigm, its functional and architectural concepts, and representative systems. Sect. 3 presents the trusted computing concept and representative solutions. Sect. 4 presents an initial system architecture for trusted autonomic computing. Sect. 5 concludes the paper.

L.T. Yang et al. (Eds.): ATC 2006, LNCS 4158, pp. 143–152, 2006.

2   Autonomic Computing

Autonomic computing is the technology and paradigm aimed at enabling self-managing computing infrastructures in a holistic manner. As shown in Fig. 1, an autonomic computing system, following a goal-oriented approach, starts with the input of high-level requirements. It then goes through the requirement analysis process that analyzes and models the requirement to decompose and formulate policies. The modeling of requirements is a critical component to divide the system requirements or high-level policies into disjoint sub-objectives and ensure that the system follows the desired behavior, which has not been explicitly identified in the past studies. We classify the system aspects into requirement aspects, policy aspects, design aspects, implementation aspects, and operational aspects.

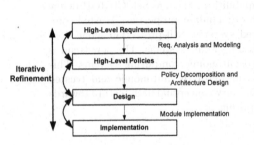

Fig. 1. A Skeleton of Design Lifecycle for Autonomic Systems

Fig. 2. Functional Pillars of Autonomic Systems

2.1   Functional Concepts

As shown in Fig. 2, to meet the high-level requirements, autonomic computing aims to support adaptive functionalities, including following 4 major functional characteristics [3] [6] [7] [8]. *Self-Configuring*: An autonomic system should be able to configure and adaptively reconfigure itself to meet the high-level requirements under varying conditions by following high-level policies. *Self-Healing*: An autonomic system should be able to detect, diagnose, and recover from localized software or hardware problems. *Self-Optimizing*: An autonomic system should be able to monitor system performance, react to dynamics, and proactively optimize itself to improve its performance with minimum overheads. *Self-Protecting*: An autonomic system should be able to defend itself against system-wide malicious attacks and component-level compromise. Trusted computing technologies compensate this functionality by providing explicit policies and criteria. More details will be presented in later sections.

To explicitly emphasize the policy-driven characteristic of an autonomic system [9], we believe that a self-regulating functionality is desired. *Self-Regulating*: An autonomic system should be able to derive policies from high-level policies and requirements at runtime to regulate its self-managing behaviors. Note that the derived policies in this context can not be determined in advance. Further, they may have system-wide effects that may cause adaptations of all functionalities. This capability, enabling dynamic policy creation and enactment, is critical to realize full self-manageability and keep abreast of evolving requirements and technologies. It is also an enabling capability towards trusted autonomic computing as presented in Sect.4. Self-regulating in the autonomic computing context goes well beyond parametric tuning and mainly considers semantic deduction and adaptation to handle uncertainty and emergency under changing environments, evolving requirements, and varying contexts.

Overall, the major functional aspects of autonomic systems include self-Configuring, self-Healing, self-Regulating, self-Optimizing, and self-Protecting, named Self-CHROP. The other 4 minor functional characteristics are self-aware, self-anticipatory, context-aware, and open [6]. These minor functionalities can be used to support major functionalities and meet subsidiary requirements.

2.2   Architectural Concepts

An autonomic system is constructed from a large number of autonomic entities and autonomic managers. Fig. 3 presents an autonomic system architecture. One or more autonomic entities are associated with a managed element, which can be an independent module, a part of executable code, an object, a component, and other building blocks of a computer system. An autonomic entity consists of sensors, actuators, and specialized knowledge-base for particular managed elements. Ashby's ultrastable system architecture has been used to model the global and local feedback control loops in autonomic systems [7] [10]. The local control loop in an autonomic entity typically follows four steps: monitoring through sensors, analyzing and planning according to knowledge bases and policies, then executing through actuators [1] [3] [6]. The local control loop is restricted to handle internal reactions and external interactions with associated managed elements and environments. As shown in the figure, the global control loop involves autonomic managers, autonomic entities, managed elements, and environments. Autonomic managers collaboratively regulate various behaviors using the built-in self-CHROP functionalities and knowledge.

Implementation Paradigms. The following paradigms have been proposed: component-based, recovery-oriented computing, aspect-oriented programming, multi-agent systems, peer-to-peer, and service-oriented computing paradigms. These implementation patterns may have overlapped features.

Component-based paradigm - A natural paradigm to realize the autonomic system architecture is to adopt a component-based implementation. Each component is equipped with self-contained policies and mechanisms [5] [11] [12]. The Accord component-based programming model in the AutoMate project [12] [13] realizes three fundamental separations: 1) a separation of computations from coordination and interactions; 2) a separation of nonfunctional aspects (e.g., resource requirements, performance) from functional aspects; and 3) a separation

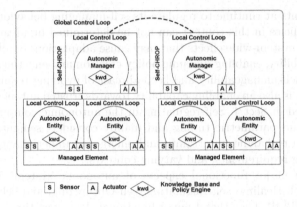

Fig. 3. An Autonomic System Architecture

of policy and mechanism. Smart components [11] can adapt to environmental changes to sustain high performance.

Service-oriented paradigm - Service-oriented architecture gains strong support from academia and industry owing to its open standard and inter-operability [14] [15]. This category covers grid, peer-to-peer, and web service technologies as they are converging in many aspects [5] [14] [16] [17] [18] [19] . Autonomic service architectures have been presented in [18] [20] [21]. The composition and adaptation of autonomic services can be accomplished syntactically by parsing Web Service Description Language (WSDL) representation [22] and semantically by reasoning through Web Ontology Language (OWL) [23].

Recovery-oriented computing paradigm - Recovery-oriented computing (ROC) [24] aims to build highly-dependable Internet services by emphasizing recovery from failure rather than failure-tolerance or failure-avoidance. Primary research areas in ROC include isolation and redundancy, system-wide support for undo, integrated diagnostic support, online verification of recovery mechanisms, design for high modularity, measurability, and restartability, and dependability/availability benchmarking.

Multi-agent paradigm - A rational agent is anything that can perceive its environment through sensors and act upon that environment through actuators [25]. Every single agent has limited functionalities. To collaboratively work towards some objectives, agents are grouped together to form mutli-agent systems (MAS). The MAS model has been used to realize self-organizing systems and support distributed collaborative working environments [26]. It bears some common characteristics with the component-based paradigm.

2.3 Autonomic Systems and Applications

Key research challenges of autonomic computing span many levels, including conceptual, functional, architectural, and application-level challenges [7]. Table 1 lists some representative systems/projects, developed in academia and industry, along with their implementation paradigms, autonomic capabilities, and applications.

3 Trusted Computing

With the advances in programming tools and increasing connected personal computers and devices, malicious software, hacker programs, malware, and corresponding attacks have become a critical security issue in the field of computer science [27]. A malicious program can be easily spread out through the connected network without the awareness of end users. Trusted computing technology aims to protect the computing system by verifying the trustworthy of both third parties and platforms. Although there exist some suspicious and negative opinions due to the potential and controversial obstacles for small companies and open-source software development to deploy their products [28], trusted computing does offer a solution to many applications such as peer-to-peer networks, pervasive computing systems, electronic commerce, and database services [29] [30].

Table 1. Autonomic Systems and Applications

System/Project	Paradigms	Autonomic Capabilities	Applications
Amorphous Computing [31]	Cellular computing	Healing, assembling, re-pairing	Understanding biological systems
Anthill [32]	Peer-to-peer, multi-agent	Configuring, organizing, optimizing, repairing, re-silient	File-sharing Computation-intensive
AutoAdmin [33]		Tuning, administration,	Database administration
AutoMate [13]	Component-based, service-oriented	Configuring, optimizing, protecting	Scientific computing
Autonomia [34]	Mobile-agent	Configuring, healing, optimizing, protecting	Scientific computing Networked applications
Kinesthetics eXtreme [35]	Component-based	Repairing, configuring	Autonomizing legacy systems
OceanStore [36]	Peer-to-peer, service-oriented	Configuring, fault-tolerant	Data storage
OptimalGrid [17]	Component-based	Configuring, Optimizing	Scientific computing GameGrid
Recovery-Oriented Computing [24]	ROC	Healing	Database, online services
SMART [37]		Configuring, Optimizing	Database tuning, self-management

* The prefix self-* is omitted in the column of autonomic capabilities.

Since in autonomic computing systems autonomic elements are tightly interconnected, they could be attacked by malicious software through the network, leading to the degradation or failure of the whole system. The goals described in [38] also emphasize the need for secure authentication protocols between autonomic components and systems.

3.1 Background

Trusted Computing Platform Alliance (TCPA), formed in 1999 by Compaq, Intel, Microsoft, IBM, Hewlett-Packard, etc., aims to improve the trustworthy and security for next century computer systems. Later, they changed the name to Trusted Computing Group (TCG). In consequence, no applications can be run on the future trusted computing platform without the approval from the above companies. Recently, Microsoft started to propose Palladium under the new system, named "Next-Generation Secure Computing Base." Because TCPA is implemented to some extent by additional components in the hardware, we classify it as "hardware based trustworthy protection."

On the other hand, realizing that the traditional approaches, i.e., hardware based methods, are too restrictive, some researchers have focused on developing more flexible architectures, called "model based." The model based trustworthy protection allows the platform to evaluate the credential of an application by some predefined trust models. If the updates does not include any malicious code, it can be run on the platform without the verification of the manufacturer of the platform. From the market view point, this method accommodates third parties to update their products more easily and reduces the work load on hardware.

3.2 Trusted Computing Paradigms

Hardware-based Trustworthy Protection. The typical architecture for TCG is shown in Fig. 4. A new component, trusted platform module (TPM), is integrated into hardware of computers to enable the systems strong configuration management. They assume that all the programs should be validated by some integrity metric [39]; in other words, no unapproved software can be executed on the system. In each TPM, there are at least 16 platform configuration registers (PCRs) which are closely interrelated to the stored measurement log (SML) outside the TPM. The SML records events are represented by the value in PCRs. Based on them, a credential value for a third party is valued by the Privacy CA. If the verification is successful, the program can be run in the system; otherwise fails.

Another aspect of TCG is that it provides the capability of sealing storage data to the third parties and the platforms [40] [41]. An application provided by third parties may contain some data that it does not allow an untrusted platform to access. Therefore they also need to interact with the remote platform to evaluate its credential. If the integrity of platform is certified by the third party, the platform can access the application.

Model-based Trustworthy Protection. Instead of embedding some new components into existing hardware such as CPU and motherboard, "Model-based" method aims to detect the malicious code in a downloaded or new program by some algorithms or trust models [30] [42] [43]. In a distributed computing system, all software components are assumed to be susceptible to attacks and the failure of one node probably affects the performance of whole system. Before any computer run programs sent from remote site, we should check whether the code has been altered maliciously. Unlike the hardware-based trusted computing architecture, cyber attacks and unauthorized program are detected by predefined models. Fig. 5 illustrates a typical flowchart for model-based trusted computing

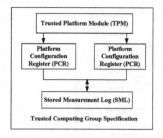

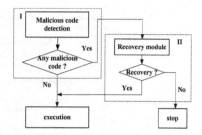

Fig. 4. Architecture of TCG

Fig. 5. Flow chart of model based trusted computing system

scheme. First, the changed program will be sent to the detection module; therein it will use some strategy to decide whether the program is certified as shown in Step I in Fig. 5. For example, in [30] a coding signing technology, called chained-signature binders [44], is added to every components of a program to compare with the original one. Additionally they also remove the malicious code from the program in Step II of Fig. 5 so that the original code can be executed by the systems.

4   Towards Trustworthy Autonomic Computing

This section presents a preliminary architecture towards trustworthy autonomic grid computing (TAGC). As shown in Fig. 6, the proposed architecture is based on the standard grid services specified by open standard protocols OGSA (Open Grid Service Architecture) or WSRF (Web Service Resource Framework) [45][46]. To accommodate dynamic resource availability, a self-organizing overlay network will be built on the top of OGSA/WSRF. The key feature of the TAGC architecture is the separation of mechanisms and policies. As mentioned above, the important feature of self-CHROP to enable trusted computing is the self-regulating capability, which can regulate the autonomic systems by interpreting the trust model and policies and injecting the new policies into the system. According to the classification in Sect. 3, it belongs to the model-based trustworthiness. From the bottom to the top, the policy aspect of TAGC, depicted as a four-layer pillar, consists of an autonomic component design catalog, knowledge base (for the rule-based and case-based reasoning engine), self-managing policy engine, and users' QoS requirement analysis and modeling modules. The mechanisms aspect of TAGC consists of four layers: semantic-based service discovery middleware, decentralized coordination substrate, autonomic runtime manager, and programming models and specifications. On the top of TAGC system layers are autonomic grid applications, such as scientific applications, collaborative information processing in wireless sensor networks, and other commercial applications.

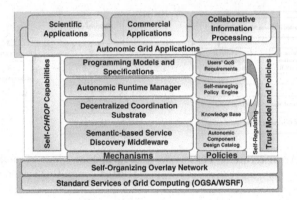

Fig. 6. The Conceptual Architecture of Trustworthy Autonomic Grid Computing (TAGC)

5   Conclusion

This paper presented a comprehensive overview of the forefront research efforts in autonomic and trusted computing. We proposed a self-regulating capability to emphasize the policy-based adaptation and regulation. The autonomic computing concepts are described according to its functional and architectural aspects. A collection of representative autonomic systems and applications is classified and compared. Moreover, we described the trusted computing concepts according to two implementation paradigms: hardware-based and model-based. Further, based on the investigation of the existing solutions and paradigms, a preliminary TAGC architecture towards trustworthy autonomic grid computing is proposed. TAGC features the separation of mechanisms and policies following the multi-layer organization. The trustworthiness is enabled through the self-regulating capability, which accommodates the trust model and policies and dynamically injects the adaptation into the policy engine. Since autonomic and trusted computing are still in their infancy, to realize full-fledged trustworthy autonomic systems, techniques from many disciplines, such as artificial intelligence, control theory, machine learning, human-computer interaction, psychology, neural science, economics, and others, should be integrated synergistically to address the grande challenge.

References

1. Ganek, A.G., Corbi, T.A.: The dawning of the autonomic computing era. IBM Systems Journal **42** (2003)
2. Hariri, S., et al.: The Autonomic Computing Paradigm. Volume 8 of Cluster Computing: The Journal of Networks, Software Tools, and Application. Kluwer Academic Publishers (2006)
3. Kephart, J.O., Chess, D.M.: The vision of autonomic computing. IEEE Computer **36** (2003) 41–50

4. Foster, I., Kesselman, C.: The Grid: Blueprint for a New Computing Infrastructure. 2nd edn. Morgan Kaufmann (2004)
5. Parashar, M., Browne, J.C.: Conceptual and implementation models for the grid. Proceedings of the IEEE, Special Issue on Grid Computin **93** (2005) 653–668
6. Horn, P.: Autonomic computing: Ibm's perspective on the state of information technology. Technical report, IBM Corporation (2001)
7. Parashar, M., Hariri, S.: Autonomic computing: An overview. Volume 3566 of LNCS,in UPP 2004., Mont Saint-Michel, France, Springer Verlag (2005) 247–259
8. Salehie, M., Tahvildari, L.: Autonomic computing: Emerging trends and open problems, St. Louis, Missouri, presented at Workshop on the Design and Evolution of Autonomic Application Software (2005)
9. : (Ibm research, policy technologies) http://www.research.ibm.com/policytechnologies/.
10. Ashby, W.R.: Design for a Brain. Chapman & Hall Ltd (1960)
11. Jann, J., Browning, L.M., Burugula, R.S.: Dynamic reconfiguration: Basic building blocks for autonomic computing on ibm pseries servers. IBM Systems Journal **42** (2003)
12. Liu, H., Parashar, M., Hariri, S.: A component-based programming framework for autonomic applications, New York, presented at The 1st IEEE International Conference on Autonomic Computing (ICAC-04) (2004)
13. Parashar, M., et al.: Automate: Enabling autonomic grid applications. Cluster Computing: The Journal of Networks, Software Tools, and Applications, Special Issue on Autonomic Computing **9** (2003)
14. Hau, J., Lee, W., Newhouse, S.: Autonomic service adaptation using ontological annotation, Phoenix, AZ., presented at The 4th Int. Workshop on Grid Computing (Grid 2003)
15. Booth, D., Hass, H., McCabe, F., Newcomer, E., Champion, M., Ferris, C., Orchard, D.: (Web services architecture.) AmorphousComputinghttp://www.w3.org/TR/ws-arch/.
16. Foster, I., Iamnitchi, A.: On death, taxes, and the convergence of peer-to-peer and grid computing, (presented at 2nd International Workshop on Peer-to-Peer Systems (IPTPS '03))
17. Kaufman, J., Lehman, T.: Optimalgrid: The almaden smartgrid project autonomous optimization of distributed computing on the grid. Newsletter of IEEE Task Force on Cluster Computing **4** (2003)
18. Liu, H., Bhat, V., Parashar, M., Klasky, S.: An autonomic service architecture for self-managing grid applications, Seattle, WA, presented at the 6th IEEE/ACM International Workshop on Grid Computing (Grid 2005) (2005)
19. Pattnaik, P., Ekanadham, K., Jann, J.: Autonomic Computing and Grid. 2003 edn. Grid Computing: Making the Global Infrastructure a Reality. Wiley Press (2003)
20. Adams, B., Brettf, P., Iyer, S., Milojicic, D., Rafaeli, S., Talwar, V.: Scalable management: Techonologies for management of large-scale, distributed systems, Presented at the Second International Conference on Autonomic Computing(ICAC'05) (2005)
21. Gurguis, S., Zeid, A.: Towards autonomic web services: Achieving self-healing using web services, St. Louis, Missouri, presented at 2005 Workshop on Design and Evolution of Autonomic Application Software (2005)
22. : (Web services description language (wsdl)) http://www.w3.org/TR/wsdl.
23. : (Web ontology language (owl)) http://www.w3.org/TR/owl-features/.

24. : (Recovery-oriented computing (roc) project) http://roc.cs.berkeley.edu/.
25. Russell, S., Norvig, P.: Artificial Intelligence: A Modern Approach. 2nd edn. Prentice Hall (2003)
26. Serugendo, G.D.M., Karageorgos, A., Rana, O.F., Zambonelli, F.: Engineering self-organising systems. In: Nature-Inspired Approaches to Software Engineering (Engineering Self-Organising Applications Workshop, ESOA 2003). Volume 2977 of Lecture Notes in Computer Science., Springer (2004)
27. Balthrop, J., Forrest, S., Newman, M.E.J., Williamson, M.M.: Technological networks and the spread of computer virues. Science **304** (2004) 527–529
28. Oppliger, R., Ryze, R.: Does trusted computing remedy computer security problems? Security & Privacy Magazine, IEEE **3** (2005) 16–19
29. Balfe, S., Lakhani, A.D., Paterson, K.G.: Trusted computing: Providing security for peer-to-peer networks, Peer-to-Peer Computing. Fifth IEEE International Conference on (2004) 117–127
30. Park, J.S., Jayaprakash, G.: Component integrity check and recovery against malicious codes, International Workshop on Trusted and Autonomic Computing Systems (TACS06) (2006) to apppear.
31. : (Amorphous computing) http://www.swiss.csail.mit.edu/projects/amorphous/.
32. : (Anthill) http://www.cs.unibo.it/projects/anthill/.
33. : (Autoadmin) http://research.microsoft.com/dmx/autoadmin/default.asp.
34. Dong, X., Hariri, S., Xue, L., Chen, H., Zhang, M., Pavuluri, S., , Rao, S.: Autonomia: an autonomic computing environment, (Presented at the 2003 IEEE International Conference on Performance, Computing, and Communications (IPCC'03))
35. : (Kinestheticsextreme) http://www.psl.cs.columbia.edu/kx/index.html.
36. : (Oceanstore) http://oceanstore.cs.berkeley.edu/.
37. Lohman, G.M., Lightstone, S.S.: Smart: Making db2 (more) autonomic, Hong Kong, China, presented at 28th International Conference on Very Large Data Bases (VLDB 2002) (2002)
38. Chess, D.M., Palmer, C.C., White, S.R.: Security in an autonomic computing environment. IBM Systems Journal **42** (2003)
39. Arbaugh, B.: Improving the tcpa specification. Computer **35** (2002) 77–79
40. Kelly, R.: A survey of trusted computing specifications and related technologies. Technical report, SANS Institute (2003)
41. Reid, J., Nieto, M.G., Dawson, E., Okamoto, E.: Privacy and trusted computing, Database and Expert Systems Applications, 2003. Proceedings. 14th International Workshop on. (2003) 383–388
42. Cahill, V., et al.: Using trust for secure collaboration in uncertain environments. Volume 2., IEEE Pervasive Computing Mobile and Ubiquitous Computing (2003) 52–61
43. Oppenheimer, D.L., Martonosi, M.R.: Performance signatures: A mechanism for intrusion detection, San Diego, CA, Proceedings of the 1997 IEEE Information Survivability Workshop (1997)
44. Part, S.J., Sandhu, R.S.: Binding identities and attributes using digitally signed certificates. Proceedings of 16th Annual Conference on Computer Security Application (2000)
45. Foster, I., Kesselman, C., Nick, J., Tuecke, S.: (The physiology of the grid) http://www.globus.org/alliance/publications/papers/ogsa.pdf.
46. : (The ws-resource framework) http://www.globus.org/wsrf/specs/ws-wsrf.pdf.

Autonomic K-Interleaving Construction Scheme for P2P Overlay Networks

Khaled Ragab[1] and Akinori Yonezawa[2]

[1] Japan Science and Technology Agency, Computer Science Dept., Tokyo University
[2] Computer Science Dept., Tokyo University
{ragab, yonezawa}@yl.is.s.u-tokyo.ac.jp

Abstract. A platform that simultaneously hosts multiple of cooperative services is proposed and called Autonomic Community Computing Infrastructure (*ACCI*). In autonomic and dynamic fashions, it formulates, composes, monitors and manages the services' components. To publish the existence and functionalities of these services, a *Peer-to-Peer* Overlay Network is constructed and denoted by *Rendezvous Overlay Network* (*RvON*). In addition, *RvON* allows end-users to discover the service's advertisement efficiently. Thus, this paper proposes an autonomic *K-interleaving* scheme that organizes *RvON* into *RvON-Clusters*. Each *RvOn-Cluster* is constructed over *K* physical hops and there is no two rendezvous nodes stored the same advertisement. As results, users accessing from different areas are able to efficiently discover service's advertisement within a constant *K* physical hops.

Keywords: Autonomic Computing, Peer-to-Peer, Overlay Networks.

1 Introduction

The peer-to-peer overlay network has drawn increasing attention nowadays. It is best suited depends on the application and its required functionalities and performance metrics such as scalability, network routing performance, file sharing, location service, content distribution, and so on. Several of these schemes have been applied to the sharing of music, replication of electronic address books, multi-player games, provisioning of mobile location or ad-hoc services, and distribution of workloads of mirrored websites. However, there is no P2P overlay network enable the service providers to outsource their services to the end-users with the required QoS except the proposed *Autonomic Community Computing Infrastructure* (*ACCI*) [17]. Outsourcing offers an opportunity for the smaller/medium retailers to provide their services regardless they have no/shortage of resources. Moreover, outsourcing reduces the management system cost reaches 80% of the IT [3], [1]. The *ACCI* allows SPs to outsource their services by exploiting the resources (e.g. processor, memory, storage, etc.) of the end-users. It simultaneously hosts multiple of autonomic cooperative information services [17]. *Autonomic Cooperative Services* are self-contained (well described) services (*Web-services*) that should autonomously cooperate to manage and adapt their behaviors to fit to the user's requirements and the *Quality of Service* (QoS). *ACCI* runs the web services at the end-users' nodes not at the service providers' nodes and allocates/reallocates community resources of end-users from a shared pool among cooperative services to assure their QoS efficiently in the face of

L.T. Yang et al. (Eds.): ATC 2006, LNCS 4158, pp. 153–162, 2006.

dynamically changing global requirements with minimal resources utilization. *ACCI* organized the nodes of the end-users into an *Autonomic Community Overlay Network* (ACON) [17]. It is a self-organized logical topology as shown in figure 1. Every resource in the ACON (node, node's resources, group, pipe, service, etc.) is described and published using advertisements. ACCI introduces two different types of nodes *Edge Nodes (EN)* and *Rendezvous Nodes (RN)*. Each *EN* offers a computing power and storage area for hosting web-services and publishing the associated advertisements. Each *RN* offers a storage area for advertisements that have been published by edge nodes.

ACON is divided into two types of overlay networks. First, *Rendezvous Overlay Network (RvON)* is a self-organized logical topology of rendezvous nodes. *Service Group Overlay Network (SGON)* is made up of several end-users nodes that host and provide same service. This paper focuses on the construction of the *RvON* for efficient discovery by efficiently publishing the advertisements of the services. It autonomously organizes *RvON* into *RvON-Clusters*. Each *RvON-Cluster* is constructed over K physical number of hops. In *RvON-Cluster* there are no two rendezvous nodes stored the same advertisement. To satisfy this property, each *RvON-Cluster* is colored with C_t different colors associated with C_t advertisements at instance of time t. There are no two RN nodes belongs to a *RvON-Cluster* having same color. Thus, within a constant K physical number of hops end-users accessing from different areas are able to discover services' advertisements.

A significant amount of research on P2P overlay networks has focused on the services replications and services discovery schemes such as *Chord* [6], *CAN* [18] and *Pastry* [24]. *Distributed Hash Tables (DHTs)* constitute a primary mechanism to build highly structured P2P networks [6]. For example, *Chord* performs service discovery over a *DHT*. The lookup delay in N nodes over *Chord* is $O(log(N))$ while the lookup delay over the proposed *RvON* is $O(K)$ where K is number of physical hops, $K<log(N)$ for large N. To our knowledge, there is no article manipulate K-interleaving scheme to cluster the overlay network for efficient service replication and discovery.

The rest of this paper is organized as follows. Section 2 briefly introduces the Autonomic Community Computing concept and system architecture. Section 3 explores 2-tier architecture of the *RvON* and the *K-interleaving* construction scheme. Section 4 evaluates the performance through simulation. Finally, a conclusion is drawn in section 5.

2 Autonomic Community Computing: Concept and Architecture

Grid [9], Web services [10], etc are emerging distributed applications and computing environments. They have reached a level of complexity, heterogeneity, and dynamism for which current programming environments and infrastructure are becoming unmanageable, brittle and insecure. Two approaches, *Autonomous Decentralized System* (ADS) concept [2] and *Autonomic Computing* [4], [7] induced from the strategies operated by the biological systems to deal with complexity, heterogeneity and uncertainty are loomed ahead. An autonomic computing system is one that has the capabilities of being self-defining, self-healing, self-configuring, self-optimizing, self-protecting, contextually aware, and open [8]. Inspired from ADS and *Autonomic Computing* and cooperation in the social communities, an *Autonomic Community*

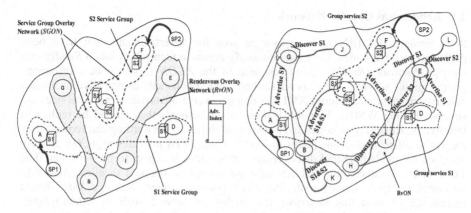

Fig. 1-a. *ACON*   **Fig. 1-b.** Service Discovery and Publish

Computing Infrastructure (*ACCI*) is proposed [17]. *ACCI* autonomously manages and monitors the pool of the resources that are owned by some service providers and end-users nodes as well. *ACCI* relaxes the relationship between end-users and SPs to a cooperative model. In this model, end-users provide their resources to SPs, while SPs provide their information services to end-users for free.

The *ACCI* architecture is made up of set of entities (end-user and/or SP nodes) as shown in figure 1. They organized in an *Autonomic Community Overlay Network* (*ACON*). We employ *JXTA* [11] that provides a set of protocols for forming *ACON* on top of current existing Internet and non-IP based networks. *ACON* is a self-organized logical topology as follows. *ACON* is a set of end-user and SP nodes (*community node simply node*) with considering the non-hierarchy, and the existence of loops. Each node is an execution platform that is in charge of autonomous membership management and services discovery, composition, execution and migration to deliver the service while guarantees the QoS. In *ACON* each node keeps track of its immediate neighbors in a table contains their identifiers as shown in figure 1. *JXTA* [11] identified nodes by *ID*, a logical address independent of the location of the node in the physical network. Two types of nodes participate in *ACON*, *edge nodes* (e.g. *C, D*, etc. as shown in figure 1-a) and *rendezvous nodes* (e.g. *B, E*, etc. as shown in figure 1-a). In *ACON,* lines are the logical links (e.g. *Pipe* in *JXTA* [11]) among the nodes. Pipes are virtual communication channels used to send and receive messages. The communication among nodes based upon *JXTA* protocols [11] and *SOAP* (*Simple Object Access Protocol*) [12], [13]. In *ACCI* to expose the service functionalities and interfaces the *WSDL* (Web Services Definition Language) [12] is used. The web services used a meta-service called *UDDI* [16] for locating web services. Unlike in the Web services, in ACCI there is no centralized discovery mechanism to locate services. Instead a peer-peer approach is used for locating services' advertisements and then follows up the associated services. In *ACCI*, each node autonomously recognizes member and non-member of the *ACON*. Moreover, it communicates with other nodes to monitor the resource consumption of the system cooperatively to adapt the changes to assure the required QoS.

ACON is organized into two types of overlay Networks, *Rendezvous Overlay Network* (*RvON*) and *Service Group Overlay Network* (*SGON*) as follows.

2.1 Rendezvous Overlay Network

Rendezvous nodes (RN) offer a storage area for advertisements that have been published by edge nodes. They autonomously organize themselves into a *Rendezvous Overlay Network* (*RvON*). Every resource in the *ACON* (node, node's resources, group, pipe, service, etc.) is described and published using advertisements. Advertisements are structured XML documents except advertisements of services are structured using WSDL. To publish these advertisements they should be replicated into *RvON*. Rendezvous nodes have the extra ability of forwarding the request they receive to other rendezvous nodes in *RvON*. Thus, *JXTA* provides to *ACON* an easy interface for publishing and discovering web services in a peer to peer manner. The *JXTA* discovery query and publish message should be updated to allow *ACON* to guarantee the QoS. For example, the *JXTA* discovery query message *XML* should include an element that describes the quality of service such as *<qualityInfo> <availability> 0.9 </availability> </qualityInfo>*. Section 3 describes the K-interleaving scheme that divides *RvON* into *RvON-Clusters* for providing an implicit scoping mechanism for restricting the propagation of discovery and search requests. Thus, the service discovery delay is improved as manifested in section *4* through the simulation results.

2.2 Service Group Overlay Network

Edge nodes are able to communicate with other nodes in *ACON*. They store the index file of the resources' advertisements they discovered in the network. *Service Group Overlay Network* (*SGON*) is made up of several end-users edge nodes providing same service. For example, figure 1 shows an example of *ACON* that consists of two *SGON S1* and *S2*. The main motivation of creating *SGON* is to tolerate the node failure/leave within the group. *SGON* serves to subdivide *ACON* into regions, providing an implicit scoping mechanism for restricting the propagation of discovery and search requests. In addition, the *SGON* autonomously adapts the dynamic network changes by outstretching (adding more replica nodes) or shrinking (removing some replica nodes) to guarantee the QoS delivered to consumer with minimum resource utilization. End-user node can be a member of one or several service groups such as node *C* in figure 1-a. Node *C* provides both services and monitors its resources utilization (e.g. load, bandwidth, etc.) to guarantee their QoS; otherwise it should leave one of these service groups. Indeed, fairness among members in *SGON* is significant to encourage end-users to join it. Constructing *SGON* is out the scope of this paper.

2.3 Services Advertisement and Discovery

Any SP can outsource its service as follows first bootstraps into *ACON*, joins the root peer group *NetPeerGroup* of *ACON* and then replicates its service into *ACON*. For example, as shown in figure 1-b node *SP1* joins *ACON* and then forms *SGON S1* containing nodes *A, C, D*. Then each replica initiates and then sends an advertisement of *S1* to rendezvous nodes. Similarly, any customer wishing to utilize a service replicated in *ACON* need to first bootstrap into *ACON*, join it, advertise its resources, discover the service advertisements and then follow the service's advertisement to open a *JXTA* output pipe. The output pipe allows the node to send a query to service discovery module. In addition, it opens *JXTA* input pipe to wait for the query result.

For non-member customers, the *ACON* can not send a service query or utilize it. *JXTA* provides an entry-level trust model [19] that can assure the *ACCI* security. It allows the node to store local information under the protection of its password phrase. When a node contacts another node in *ACON*, the former node can be authenticated by the latter using the *TLS* (*Transport Layer Security*) [20] handshake's certificate request/response and certificate verification. Further security issues are not the scope of this paper. However, we believed that *ACCI* must handle the security problems in the future.

3 K-Interleaving RvON Construction Scheme

We formed and engaged *RvON* to publish and discover service's advertisement efficiently. This section focuses on the construction of *RvON* along with preserving a specific property called '*K-interleaving*' for efficient service discovery as follows.

3.1 K-Interleaving *RvON*

Figure 2-a shows the 2-tiers architecture of the *RvON*. It is composed of multiple *RvON-Clusters* RC_j; $j=1, ..., \beta$ in level 1. Each RC_j has a *landmark* rendezvous node (Seed RN) called L_j. The distance between any $u \in RC_j$ and L_j is $\delta(u, L_j) \leq r$; $K=2r$ as shown in figure 2-a. In level 2 a seed rendezvous cluster containing all landmark rendezvous nodes is constructed and called *Seed-Cluster* as shown in figure 2-a. The size of the Seed-Cluster is denoted by β and equaled to the number of *RvON-Clusters*. All advertisements had published in *RvON* must be stored in each *RvON*-Cluster.

Definition 1 (*K-Interleaving*): Given a graph $G = (V, E)$, where each edge $e \in E$ is associated with a positive number $l(e)$ called its *length*, $|V| = N$ and each vertex $v \in V$ is associated with a non-negative integer $\alpha(v)$ it is the number of color slots the node v has. Each node $v \in V$ is colored by $\alpha(v)$ different colors. The graph G and K an integer, construct a coloring of G so that no connected sub-graph with diameter K contains two vertices colored the same, where K is the *interleaving parameter*.

The history of the work on interleaving schemes is rather brief. Blaum et al. [21] introduced interleaving schemes and analyzed them on two- and three-dimensional arrays. The follow-up paper [22] generalized interleaving schemes to those with repetitions, where in any connected cluster of size $|S|$ any label is repeated at most ρ times. Asymptotically optimal constructions on *2D* arrays were presented for the case $\rho = 2$. In this paper we extend interleaving schemes beyond. This paper organizes *RvON* into *K*-interleaving *RvON-Clusters*. Each *RvON*-Cluster is a self-organized cluster that maintains the *K*-interleaving property with $\rho = 1$ as shown in the following subsections. Each *RvON-Cluster* is constructed over *K* physical hops. There are no two RN nodes belongs to a *RvON*-Cluster stored same advertisement. The intersection between any two *RvON* clusters is empty.

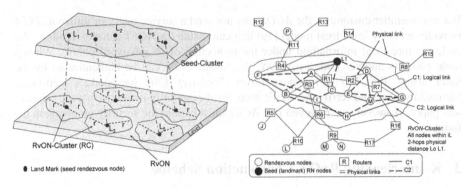

Fig. 2-a. *RvON* Architecture   **Fig. 2-b.** *RvON-Cluster* Architecture

Each *RvON*-Cluster stores all advertisements published in *RvON*. Similar to *Gnutella* [15], each *RvON*-Cluster utilizes flooding of the discovery query locally within the cluster to lookup the service's advertisement. Each advertisement is hashed into a *24*-bit RGB color number. Each RN node belongs to *RvON*-Cluster is colored by $\alpha(v)$ color slots associated with the advertisements it stored. Thus, the overhead of any discovery request for any advertisement is $O(K)$ bounded by the K physical hops. *Chord* performs service discovery over a *DHT*. Lookup delay over *Chord* is $O(log(N))$ [6] in contrast it is $O(K)$ in *RvON-Cluster* where K is a constant number of physical hops, $K<log(N)$ for large N (total number of *RN*). The lookup delay of most of discovery algorithms is function of N, while it is constant in *RvON*.

3.2 *RvON* Cluster

RvON is organized into multiple of *RvON-Clusters*. Each *RvON*-Cluster (*RC*) is constructed as a *2d-regular* graph composed of d independent edge-disjoint *Hamilton Cycles* (*HC*) [23]. Each node has *2d* neighbors (node connectivity). Those neighbors are labeled as $g_p^{(1)}$, $g_s^{(1)}$, $g_p^{(2)}$, $g_s^{(2)}$, ..., $g_p^{(d)}$, $g_s^{(d)}$. For each i, $g_p^{(i)}$ denotes the neighbor node's predecessor and $g_s^{(i)}$ denotes the neighbor node's successor on the *i-th HC*. For example, figure 2-b shows a *RvON*-Cluster consists of two *Hamilton* cycles over the underlying network. The distance between the landmark *L1* and any RN node is less than or equal two ($K = 2$) backbone physical hops between their routers. This paper constructs *RC* as *regular-graph* for three arguments as follows. First, regular graphs are chosen because it is required that all nodes having the same degree. Second, we construct the *RC* as an intermediate of a completely ordered regular network and a fully random network for achieving two interesting features: high clustering i.e., there is a high density of connections between nearby nodes, which is a characteristic of the regular topologies, and short network diameter. Finally, the *RC* composed of *HC* having the advantage that joining or leaving processes will require only local changes and resilience to dynamic RN nodes behaviors [5].

Definition 2 (*Coloring RvON-Cluster*): Assume $\left|RC_j\right|_t$ is the number of rendezvous nodes in the RC_j at instance of time t $\left|RC_j\right|_t < N$ and Adv_t is the number of advertisements at t. If $Adv_t \leq |RC_j|_t$ $\forall$ RC_j; $j=1, ..., \beta$, then each RN node stores one advertisement and colored by an associated color. Otherwise, each RN node stores different advertisements and the associated $\omega(v)$ different colors slots are filled.

The adjacent RN nodes in $RvON$-$Cluster$ are colored with different colors. The non-colored rendezvous node that did not store any advertisement is called *Standby Rendezvous Node (SRN)*. The number of advertisements Adv_t at an instance of time t is equal to the number of different colors C_t. Periodically, each seed (landmark) rendezvous node L_j counts both $|RC_j|_t$ and C_t by flooding counting request to all RN nodes in RC_j.

3.3 Step-Step *RvON* Construction Algorithm

When an end-user node X is stable and has enough capabilities to be a rendezvous node then it calls *Join_RvON()* process that runs the following steps.

1. X looks up for a seed rendezvous node (landmark RN) by using random walk or physical IP multicast and then finds L_j.
2. If $(|RC_j|_t > C_t \wedge \delta(X, L_j) \leq r;$ $K=2r)$ then the rendezvous node X calls *Join_RONCluster(RC_j)* process to join the $RvON$-$Cluster$ RC_j. This process chooses d random rendezvous nodes $u_i \in RC_j; i (= 1,..., d)$ and then inserts node X between each node u_i and its successor node $(u_i \rightarrow successor)$ in the i-th HC similar to our previous work in [5]. Finally, X becomes a standby rendezvous node SRN and doesn't store any advertisement.
3. If $(|RC_j|_t \leq C_t \wedge \delta(X, L_j) \leq r;$ $K=2r)$ then the rendezvous node X similarly calls *Join_RONCluster(RC_j)* and then picks up some colors slots form the existing RN nodes in RC_j (for Load balance) and stores their associated advertisements.
4. Otherwise $(\delta(X, L_j) > r)$, the seed node L_j broadcasts a join request message in the *Seed-Cluster* and then waits *time-out* τ period for a reply from the seed rendezvous nodes in the Seed-Cluster. There are two cases:
   a) No response is received within the time-out interval τ, then node X creates its own new *RvON-Cluster* and becomes a seed rendezvous node $L_{\beta+1}$ (land mark) (increases number of seed nodes $\beta+1$). This new *RvON-Cluster* operated as a standby cluster (i.e. all its RN nodes are standby) until having enough number of RN nodes to maintain K-interleaving property.
   b) If L_j receives multiple of replies then it selects the L_r with the smallest distance to X where $\delta(X, L_r) \leq K$ and the minimum $|RC_r|_t$. Then node X calls *Join_RONCluster(RC_r)* process to join the $RvON$-$Cluster$ RC_r.

The K-interleaving construction scheme organizes $RvON$ into $RvON$-$Clusters$. The number of messages required to join $RvON$ is $O(log(\beta))$. Each $RvON$-$Cluster$ contains all the participated services' advertisements in $RvON$. Any new advertisement will be published to all $RvON$-$Clusters$ with overhead $O(log(\beta))$ number of messages. In addition, end-users accessing from different areas are able to efficiently discover the service's advertisement within a K constant number of Physical hops.

4 Performance Evaluation

This section describes the simulations to demonstrate that *K-interleaving* step-step construction scheme of the *Rendezvous Overlay Network*. To evaluate the effectiveness of the proposed *K-interleaving* step-step construction scheme of *RvON* on the discovery of service's advertisement overhead, we use the following metrics.

- **Service Discovery Delay (SDD).** It measures the communication delay to discover a service's advertisement within a *RvON-Cluster*. It defines the communication delay of the shortest path from a requester *RN* to the *RN* that stores the required service's advertisement. Moreover, the worst discovery communication delay is denoted by **Maximum Service Discovery Delay (MSDD).**

- *Average Service Discovery Delay (ASDD).* It defines the average of the *SDD* for all *RvON-Clusters*. The simulation randomly selects a RN belongs to each *RvON-Cluster* that sends a discovery request and then determines the required *SDD* to discover the required service's advertisement in each one. Finally, it calculates the *ASDD*.

- **Average Maximum Service Discovery Delay (AMSDD).** It defines the average of the *MSDD* for all *RvON-Clusters*. Similarly, the simulation determines the *MSDD* in each *RvON-Cluster*. Finally, it calculates the *AMSDD*.

4.1 Simulation Setup

The simulation consists of *100-1000* backbone routers linked by core links over two underlying topology models, *transit-stub* model and *Waxman* model. The *Georigia Tech* [31] random graph generator is used to create both network models. Random link delay of *4-12*ms was assigned to each core link. The *Rendezvous nodes (RN)* were randomly assigned to routers in the core with uniform probability. Each *RN* was directly attached by a LAN link to its assigned router. The delay of each LAN link was set to be *1*ms. The *transit-stub* network model consists of three stub domains per transit node, with no extra transit-stub or stub-stub edges. The edge probability between each pair of nodes within each stub domain is *0.42, 0.6, 1.0* respectively. However, the edge probability the simulation used to generate the *Waxman* network model is *0.03*. The simulation ran with different number of rendezvous nodes ranged from *100 - 10,000*. It did not take into consideration the required queuing time for the advertisement discovery requests. Only one replica of each advertisement is replicated into each *RvON-Cluster* (i.e $\rho = 1$).

4.2 Simulation Results

Figure 3-a plots the variations of the *AMSDD* along with the number of routers over hierarchy (*transit-stub*) and non-hierarchy (*Waxman*) network models. It shows that the *AMSDD* in the transit-stub network model lies within the range 22-24ms with standard deviation $\sigma = 0.92$ and while it lies within the range 30-34ms with standard deviation $\sigma = 1.29$ in Waxman network model. Similarly, figure 3-b shows the variations of the *ASDD* along with the number of routers. It shows that the *ASDD* in the transit-stub network model lies within the range 12-14ms with standard deviation $\sigma = 0.44$ while it lies within the range 17-21ms with standard deviation $\sigma = 1.014$ in Waxman network model. Clearly the *ASDD* and *AMSDD* values are oscillated in

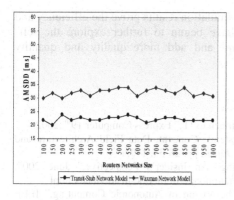

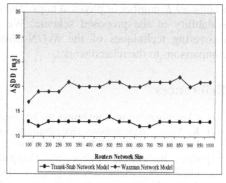

Fig. 3-a.   **Fig. 3-b.**

small interval while the number of routers is increased. This proves that the proposed *K*-interleaving scheme constructs *RvON* that enables efficient and scalable service discovery. Moreover, both *ASDD* and *AMSDD* over Waxman topology are larger than over transit-stub topology. That is to be expected because of the small edge probability that is used by the simulation to generate the Waxman topology. Figure 3-c represents the variations of the *AMSDD* over two topology along with the radius of the *RvON-Cluster* r; K=2r. We note that by increasing r, the *AMSDD* over transit-stub topology proportionally increases. That is to be expected because of the delay of the hierarchical of the transit-stub model. Finally, we noticed that the variant of the number of *RN* nodes did not affect the performance metrics.

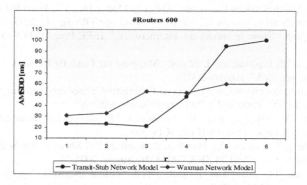

Fig. 3-c.

5 Conclusion

The *RvON* is constructed that allows the *ACCI* to advertise and discovery services efficiently. This paper focuses on the proposition of a novel Autonomic K-interleaving construction scheme for organizing *RvON* into sub-clusters. *RvON* is self-organized overlay network for publishing the advertisements and discovering the services associated with these advertisements efficiently. *RvON* enables end-users accessing from different areas to efficiently discover services' advertisements within a constant K number of physical hops. The simulation results prove the efficiency and scalability of the proposed scheme. We have begun to further explore the self-recovering techniques of the *RvON-Cluster* and add more quality and quantity comparisons to the related works.

References

[1] "Autonomic computing brings the healing touch to IT," Express Computer 19th ,2002.
[2] K. Mori, "Autonomous Decentralized Systems: Concept, Data Field Architecture and Future Trends," IEEE Proc. of ISADS'93, Japan, pp. 28-34, 1993.
[3] Peter Brittenham, "Autonomic Computing: An insider's Perspective," June 2005, http://www-128.ibm.com/developer works/autonomic/library/ac-inside/index.html.
[4] Jeffrey O. Kephart, Divad M. Chess, "The Vision of Autonomic Computing," IEEE Computer, PP. 41-50, 2003.
[5] K. Ragab, Et. al. "Autonomous Decentralized Community Communication for Information Dissemination," IEEE Internet Computing Magazine, Vol. 8 No. 3, pp. 29-36, May/June 2004.
[6] I. Sotica, R. Morris, D. Karager, F. Kasshoek, H. Balakrishnan, "Chord: A scalable peer-to-peer lookup service for Internet Applications," ACM SIGCOMM'01, August 2001.
[7] Bantz, D.F., Et. al. "Autonomic personal computation," *IBM Systems Journal*, vol. 42, no.1, 2003, pp. 165-176
[8] "An architectural blueprint for Autonomic Computing," White page, 3rd edition June 2005.
[9] Ian Foster, Carl Kesselman, "The Grid 2: Blueprint for a New Computing Infrastructure," Morgan Kaufmann Publishers; 2nd edition, November, 2003.
[10] Kenneth P. Birman, "Reliable Distributed Systems Technologies, Web Services and Applications," Springer 2005.
[11] Brendon J. Wilson, "*JXTA*", New Riders Publishing 1st edition June, 2002.
[12] E. Cerami, "Web Services Essentials," O'Reilly Media, Inc.; 1st edition February, 2002.
[13] "SOAP Specification version 1.2," http://www.w3.org/TR/soap12 , 2003.
[14] E. W. Zegura, "How to model an Internetwork," IEEE-Proc. INFOCOM, 1996, San Francisco.
[15] A. Iamnitchi M, Ripeanu and I. Foster. "Mapping the Gnutella Network," IEEE Internet Computing, pp. 50-57, January 2002
[16] OASIS standards consortium, "Universal Description, Discovery and Integration of Web Services (UDDI)," Version 2.0, 2002, http://www.uddi.org/
[17] K. Ragab, Y. Oyama, and A. Yonezawa "K-interleaving Rendezvous Overlay Construction Schem," Proc. Of IEEE, ICIS 2006.
[18] S. Rantasamy, P. Francis. M. Handley, R. Karp and S. Shenker, "A Scalable Content-Addressable Network," ACM SIGCOMM'01, August 2001.
[19] B. Traversat, Et. Al, "The Project JXTA Virtual Network," www.jxta.org/docs/ JXTAprotocols.pdf, May 2001.
[20] T. Dierks and C. Allen, "The TLS Protocol," IETF RFC2246, Jan. 1999.
[21] M. Blaum, J. Bruck, and A. Vardy. Interleaving schemes for multidimensional cluster errors. IEEE Transactions on Information Theory, 44(2):730–743, 1998.
[22] M. Blaum, J. Bruck and P.G. Farell, "Two-dimensional Interleaving Schemes with repetitions," IBM Research Report RJ 10047, Oct. 1996.
[23] B. Jackson and H. Li, "Hamilton Cycles in 2-Connected k-regular Bipartite Graphs," Comb. Theory Series A, 44 (2): 177-186, 1998.
[24] A. Rowstron and P. Druschel, "Pastry: Scalable, decentralized object location and routing for large-scale peer-to-peer systems", 18th IFIP/ACM Middleware 2001, Germany, November 2001

Self Awareness and Adaptive Traffic Signal Control System for Smart World

Lawrence Y. Deng[1] and Dong-liang Lee[2]

[1] Dept. of Computer Science and Information Engineering, St. John's University, 499, Sec. 4, Tam King Road Tamsui, Taipei, Taiwan
[2] Dept. of Information Management, St. John's University, 499, Sec. 4, Tam King Road Tamsui, Taipei, Taiwan
{[1]lawrence, [2]lianglee}@mail.sju.edu.tw

Abstract. The most city dwellers are concerned with the urban traffic issues very much. To provide a self awareness and adaptive facilities in traffic signal control system is become more and more urgent. In this paper, we improved the video surveillance and self-adaptive urban traffic signal control system to achieve the development trend in intelligent transportation system (ITS). A self awareness and adaptive urban traffic signal control (TSC) system that could provide both the video surveillance and the traffic surveillance as smart hyperspace. We investigated the vision-based surveillance and to keep sight of the unpredictable and hardly measurable disturbances may perturb the traffic flow. We integrated and performed the vision-based methodologies that include the object segmentation, classify and tracking methodologies to know well the real time measurements in urban road. According to the real time traffic measurement, we derived a grid Agent Communication and the Adaptive Traffic Signal Control strategy to adapt the traffic signal time automatically. By comparing the experimental result obtained by traditional traffic signal control system which improved the traffic queuing situation, we confirmed the efficiency of our vision based smart TSC approach.

1 Introduction

A smart world is created on both cyberspaces and real spaces. As Jianhua Ma [1][2] discussed that the computing devices are becoming smaller and smaller, and can be embedded or blended to many things in the daily life. Therefore, the computing/communicating, connecting and/or being connected to each other, and behaving and acting rationally with some smartness or intelligence are occurring spontaneously. Current and potential applications of intelligent networks may include: military sensing, physical security, air traffic control, traffic surveillance, video surveillance, industrial and manufacturing automation, distributed robotics, environment monitoring, and building and structures monitoring. The smart objects in these applications may be small or large, and the networks may be wired or wireless. However, ubiquitous wireless networks of various sensors probably offer the most potential in changing the world of sensing [3, 4].

L.T. Yang et al. (Eds.): ATC 2006, LNCS 4158, pp. 163–172, 2006.

In this paper, we improved the grid Agent Communication Network (or ACN) and video surveillance for urban traffic surveillance. ACN is dynamic [5]. It involves as agent communication proceeds. Agents communicate with each other since they can help each other. For instance, agents share the traffic information and should be able to pass traffic signal control messages to each other so that the redundant manual processes can be avoided. A grid Agent Communication Network (ACN) then serves this purpose. Each node in an ACN (as shown in figure 1) represents a client agent on a computer network node and the grid server agent is served/ integrated as a Business Process Grids. The scope of Business Process Grids covers business process provisioning, outsourcing, integration, collaboration, monitoring, and management infrastructure [6]. The business process grid is an emerging area, and it's clear that significant research and development will be necessary to make it a reality. When the research results mature, the proposed grid Agent Communication Network for Smart TCS System may primarily cover business process integration and how to bridge the gap between business goals and IT implementations. For this grid, it is necessary to develop a flow technology capable of adapting to the dynamic grid environment and the changing requirements of grid applications.

Since client agent of the same goal wants to pass and to receive local traffic information to the adjacent agents and the grid server agent. Each client agent maintains the local and adjacent traffic information by a client agent active record. The client agent active record comprises four fields: CAID, adjacent agents, number of cars, and signal time messages. 'CAID' is the client agent ID that signifies the critical traffic zone number, direction, road number, and section number. The 'adjacent agents' field takes down the CAIDs these related with adjacent agents by a road junction (i.e. both to serve the possible cars coming and going). The 'number of cars' filed minutes the section's number of cars by a vision-based surveillance technology dynamically (i.e. current number of cars/maximums capacity of cars). Signal time field records the Signal time field records the go-straight, turn-right, and turn-left signal times.

As a result of the growing rapidly of urbanization, the traffic congestion occurs when too many vehicles attempt to use a common urban road with limited capacity. The efficient, safe, and less polluting transportation of persons and goods calls for an optimal utilization of the available infrastructure via suitable application of a variety of traffic control measures and Mech. Traffic control directly depends on the efficiency and relevance of the employed control methodologies [6]. Recently, more and more researcher investigated the real time vision based transportation surveillance system [7] [8] [9]. They deliberate to analysis and detect the objects first then measuring the number of cars after that they could extrapolate the transportation information of the main urban road. There are three essential methodologies to detect the vehicles: the Temporal Differencing [10][11][12], the Optical flow[13], and the Background subtraction [14] [15]. The Temporal Differencing and the Optical flow methods provide the abilities for processing successive images and detecting the moving objects. But they are not suit for motionless or slow motioning objects. Therefore, these methods don't fit the very busy urban road situation. The method of Background Subtraction could deal with the motionless or slow motion objects by way of comparing the preparative background and the current image. This method could make use of the very busy urban road situation.

SCII-2 [16] proposed a transportation expert system with adaptive traffic control mechanism. It set out and tune up the cycle time, phase and split in every 20 min. situation. [17] figured out the different traffic control strategies for influencing traffic conditions. Adaptive control degraded the conventional "fixed-time Control" queuing phenomena (and corresponding delays) while the infrastructure capacity is fully utilized. The main drawback of fixed-time strategies is that their settings are based on historical rather than real-time data. This may be a crude simplification for the following reasons [6][18][19]. (1) Demands are not constant, even within a time-of-day. (2) Demands may vary at different days, e.g., due to special events. (3) Demands change in the long term leading to "aging" of the optimized settings. (4) Turning movements are also changing in the same ways as demands; in addition, turning movements may change due to the drivers' response to the new optimized signal settings, whereby they try to minimize their individual travel times. (5) Incidents and farther disturbances may perturb traffic conditions in an unpredictable way.

In this paper, we integrated the grid agent technologies and image processing technology to analysis current traffic situation form receiving video, and then send a signal to control traffic light's scope to improve to the higher class the traffic condition. This integrated technology, more reliable wire/wireless communication, and low-cost manufacturing have resulted in small, inexpensive, and vision-based imager with embedded processing and wireless networking capability. Such smart communication networks can be used in many new applications, ranging from environmental monitoring to industrial sensing, as well as TCS applications.

The background subtraction issues by a client agent, and the object segmentation model is presented in section 2. The preliminary experimental evaluation by self awareness and adaptive traffic signal control system are discussed in section 3 and, finally, the conclusion is given in Section 4.

2   Vision-Based Supervision with Self Awareness

In order to measure the very busy urban road situation and then deal with the motionless or slow motion objects. We compared the preparative background and the current image firstly. With combined average and inpaint method, we built the background for separated foreground object.

Average Method: Computing the average value of pixel value in background bitmap (the pixel value at (x,y) in jth iteration background bitmap) and current image (the pixel value at (x,y) in jth image) at same position.

Inpaint Method: Computing two continuous images and to find each pixel's lightness difference whether it belongs to background or not. If the difference is lower than the threshold value (set by user), filled it in background bitmap at same position.

Building Background steps: (1) Get two continuous images. (2) Compute the difference of each pixel value. Determine whether the difference is lower than the threshold value or not. (3) Ignoring the lower one, and take it as a background and fill in background bitmap at same position. (4) Repeat the step 1 to step 3 until the complete background bitmap is built.

(a) current image   (b) updating background

Fig. 1. Building the background image with combining the Average and the Inpaint methods

Figure 1 shows the successive current image and the updating background images. We used median filter and morphological operations to eliminate noise and then to merge the object's fragment.

(a) After Median filter and segmentation   (d) after classify each objects

Fig. 2. The object classification

Rearranging all the pixels value (with gray-level) with a N*N mask in a sequential order and the medium value is the center pixel value. For example, if we got the set {104, 255, 136, 25, 38, 206, 178, 193, 236}, rearranging it to {25, 38, 104, 136, 178, 193, 206, 236, 255}. The medium value: 178 is the center pixel's value. Then compare the background and the difference of lightness in each pixel respectively. If the difference is larger than the threshold, this point will be taken as a part of object.

We removing the isolation point and smoothing the current image by using the Median filter, then adopt the morphological operations closing (Perform the dilation followed by erosion operation) to eliminate the noise spikes, filling in the small anomalies (like holes) and merging the object's fragment. We got more precisely object's number. Figure 2 illustrated the object classification processes. According to the number of cars information, we could decide whether if the traffic signal should be adapted to increase or decreased the period of red/green light.

3   Adaptive Traffic Signal Control and Preliminary Experimental Results

Once traffic lights exist, they may lead to more or less efficient network operations, therefore there must keep an adaptive control strategy leading to minimize the total time spent by all vehicles in the network. Server agents (to serve a critical traffic zone) play the leading role as rendezvous and supervision service center. They receive the traffic information from active client agents with the same zone number.

Grid Server agent verifies the CAID firstly, and then record to the database (as Table 1 shown). CAID is composed by three numbers. For example, CAID = 01.001.02 means: this client agent is located in zone 01, road number is 001 (if the lower two bit is odd that express this road is same with the longitude direction and if the first bit 0 means it only monitors from north to south traffic, 1 means it only monitor from south to north; if the lower two bit is even that express this road is same with the latitude direction and if the first bit 0 means it only monitors from east to west traffic, 1 means it only monitors from west to east traffic). The third number 02 is the section number of road 01. Number of cars field records the current number of cards and the maximum capacity cars of this section. Signal time field records the go-straight, turn-right, and turn-left signal times.

Table 1. ATSC database maintained by grid server agent

CAID	Adjacent Agents	Number of cars	Signal time
...			
01.001.02	01.001.01, 01.102.01, 01.002.02,	80/250, 95/200, 34/200,	90.90.30
	01.001.03, 01.004.01, 01.104.02,	90/250, 41/200, 35/200,	
01.101.02	01.101.03, 01.004.02, 01.104.01,	65/250, 55/250, 47/200,	90.90.30
	01.101.01, 01.102.02, 01.002.01,	58/200, 39/200, 35/200,	
...			

With grid strategy, server agent could compute the traffic load with percentage. Server agent takes the statistical inference and then decrease/increase the signal time with specific sections of roads.

The factors of traffic jam contains: Uniform Arrivals period, Random Arrivals period, and Platoon Arrivals period. The uniform arrivals period was proposed by May [21] :

$$D = \frac{r^2}{2C\left(1 - \dfrac{q}{s}\right)}$$

(1)

Where,

D: average delay(sec/car);

C: cycle(sec);

r: time of red light;

q: arrival rate of adjacet road(%);

s: saturation rate of adjacet road(%)。

Webster [22] and HCM [23] had considered both Random Arrivals period, and Platoon Arrivals period :

$$d_t = 0.9[UD + RD] = 0.9\left[\frac{C\left(1 - \dfrac{g}{C}\right)^2}{2\left(1 - \left(\dfrac{g}{C}\right)X\right)} + \frac{X^2}{2q(1-X)}\right]$$

(2)

Where,

d_t : average delay (sec/car);

C : cycle(sec);

g : period of green light(sec);

X : saturation(%);

q : flow(car/sec);

So, then get the uniform dely(UD)

$$d_u = \frac{C[1 - (g/C)]^2}{2[1 - (g/C)X]} ,$$

(3)

the random dely (RD) :

$$d_r = \frac{X^2}{2q(1-X)} ,$$

(4)

the adjustment:

$$d_e = -0.65(C/q^2)^{1/3} X^{2+5(g/C)}$$

(5)

is got from the real world measurements (about 5%~15% of the d_t).

The delay estimation by HCM:

$$d = d_1(PF) + d_2 + d_3$$

(6)

where,

$$d_1 = \frac{0.5\left(1 - \dfrac{g}{C}\right)^2}{1 - \left[\min(1, X)\dfrac{g}{C}\right]}$$

(7)

$$d_2 = 900T\left[(X-1) + \sqrt{(X-1)^2 + \frac{8klX}{cT}} \right]$$

(8)

Where,

d : average delay (sec/car);

d_1 : uniform delay(sec/car);

d_2 : incremental delay(sec/car);

d_3 : initial queue delay(sec/car);

C : average delay (sec/car);

X : saturation(%);

c : capacity(number of car);

T : duration of analysis period(h);

k : increasing adjustment factor;

l : decreasing adjustment factor;

PF : progression adjustment factor)

$$PF = \frac{(1-P)f_{PA}}{\left(1-\dfrac{g}{C}\right)}$$

(9)

Where,

P : arrivals rate;

f_{PA} : Platoon Arrivals factor;

In order to prove our approaches, we recorded the video at the very busy crossroad of MinQuan W. Rd. and ChenDer Rd. Taipei in morning business hours. We installed four cameras in each intersection with a bird's-eye view and capture the video simultaneously. By the way of image processing methods as we mentioned above, we measure the traffic condition for individual intersection (such as queuing length, average vehicle speed, and the number of vehicle...etc.).

Figure 3 shows the experimental results of queuing vehicles in four directions. After six times random testing, we proved our system can downgrade 20% the queuing situation approximately. If we make a conversion the queuing vehicles into time cost with estimating speed 10 km/hr, by any means , we may save about 15~20 second a car. As you know, the traffic congestion results in excess delays, reduced safety, and increased environmental pollution. So, we will investigate the more efficient and practicable adaptive TSC system as our future-proof.

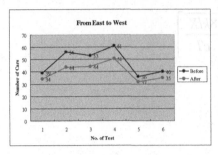
(a) Queuing vehicles form east to west

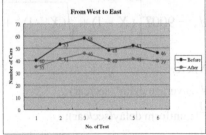
(b) Queuing vehicles form west to east

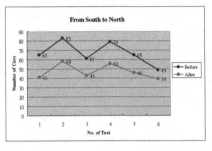
(c) Queuing vehicles form south to north

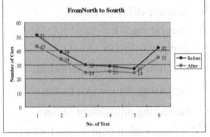
(d) Queuing vehicles form north to south

Fig. 3. An experimental result of Agent monitoring the queuing vehicles in four directions

4 Conclusion

In this paper, a vision-based adaptive traffic signal control system with grid Agent Technology for smart world has been presented. We performed the real-time traffic surveillance and to solve the unpredictable and hardly measurable disturbances (such as incidents, illegal parking, pedestrian crossings, intersection blocking, etc.) may perturb the traffic flow. We investigated the self awareness and adaptive Agent technologies, vision-based object classification (as well as segmentation and tracking) methodologies to know well the real time measurements in urban road. According to the real time traffic information, we derived the adaptive traffic signal control with grid server agent centralized stratagem to settle the red–green switching time of traffic lights. In our experiment results, they diminished approximately 20% the degradation of infrastructure capacities. In fact, the applications are only limited by our imagination. The ubiquitous intelligence indeed can make our living more convenient and comfortable but also take us to some potential dangerous environments with the possibility of sacrificing privacy and the risk of out of control. Therefore, the potential applications of underlying ubiquitous intelligence would at first go to those environments where the privacy may not be a serious or sensitive issue to users or can be well under control. Benefiting from the intelligence evolution, human life and working style are evolving towards more convenient, comfortable, and efficient.

References

1. Jianhua Ma, Laurence T. Yang, Bernady O. Apduhan, Runhe Huang, Leonard Barolli and Makoto Takizawa: Towards a Smart World and Ubiquitous Intelligence: A Walkthrough from Smart Things to Smart Hyperspaces and UbicKids, in Journal of Pervasive Computing and Communication vol. 1, (2005) 53–68
2. Jianhua Ma: Ubiquitous Intelligence - The Intelligence Revolution, ID People Magazine, (2005)
3. CHEE-YEE CHONG, AND SRIKANTA P. KUMAR: Sensor Networks: Evolution, Opportunities, and Challenges, PROCEEDINGS OF THE IEEE, VOL 91, NO 8, (2003) 1248–1256
4. 10 emerging technologies that will change the world, Technol. Rev., vol. 106, no. 1,(2003) 33–49
5. Lawrence Y. Deng, Timothy K. Shih, Teh-Sheng Huang, Chun-Hung Huang, Ruei-Xi Chen and Yang-Long Chang: Universal Access for Roaming User via Mobile Agent Technology, in the International Journal of Tamkang Journal of Science and Engineering, Vol. 5, No. 3, (2002) 175–186
6. Liang-Jie Zhang; Haifei Li; Lam, H.: Toward a business process grid for utility computing, IT Professional Volume 6, Issue 5, (2004) 62–64
7. Markos Papageoggius, Christina Diakaki, Vaya Dinopoulou, Apoatolos Kotsialos, and Yibing Wang: Review of Road Traffic Control Strategies, PROCEEDINGS OF THE IEEE, VOL. 91, NO. 12 (2003).
8. Giusto, D.D., Massidda, F., Perra, C.: A fast algorithm for video segmentation and object tracking, Digital Signal Processing, 2002. DSP 2002. 2002 14th International Conference on , Volume: 2 , (2002) 697–700.
9. Haritaoglu, I., Harwood, D., Davis, L.S.: W4: real-time surveillance of people and their activities, Pattern Analysis and Machine Intelligence, IEEE Transactions on , Volume: 22 , Issue: 8 , (2000) 809–830.
10. Hsu, W.L.; Liao, H.Y.M.; Jeng, B.S.; Fan: Real-time vehicle tracking on highway, The Proceedings of the 2003 IEEE International Conference on Intelligent Transportation Systems, (2003) 909–914.
11. D. J. Dailey, L. Li: An algorithm to estimate vehicle speed using uncalibrated cameras, Proceedings of IEEE/IEEJ/JSAI International Conference on Intelligent Transportation System, (1999) 441–446.
12. M,-P. Dubuisson, A.K. Jain: Object Contour Extraction Using Color And Motion, Proceedings of IEEE Computer society Conference on Computer Vision and Pattern Recognition, (1993) 471–476.
13. T. Nakamishi, K. Ishii: Automatic vehicle image extraction based on spatio-temporal image analysis, Proceedings of 11th IAPR International Conference on Pattern Recognition. Vol.1. Conference A: Computer Vision and Applications, (1992) 500–504.
14. Y. Mae, Y. Shirai, J. Miura, Y.Kuno: Object tracking in cluttered baced on optical flow and edges, Proceedings of the 13th International Conference on Pattern Recognition Volume: I, (1996) 196–200.
15. D. Koller, J. Weber, and J. Malik: Robust Multiple Car Tracking with Occlusion Reasoning, Technical Report UCB/CSD-93-780, University of Calibornia at Berkely (1993).
16. Y. Matsushita, S. Kamijo, K. Ikeuchi and M. Sakauchi: Image Processing Based Incident Detection at Intersections, Proceedings of the Fourth Asian Conference on Computer Vision 2000, (2000) 520–527.

17. May, Adolf D.: Traffic Flow Fundamentals, Premtice Hall, Englewood Cliffs New Jersey (1990).
18. Reports of urban traffic signal control in the Taiwan, the Transportation Institute of the Ministry of Communications (2001).
19. T. Van Vuren: Signal control and traffic assignment, in Concise Encyclopedia of Traffic and Transportation Systems, Papageorgiou, Ed, Oxford, U.K.: Pergamon (1991) 468–473.
20. U.S. Department of Transportation/ FWHA, Traffic Control System Handbook (1985).
21. May, Adolf D.: Traffic Flow Fundamentals, Prentice Hall, Englewood Cliffs New Jersey (1990).
22. Webster, F.V.: Traffic signal settings, Road Research Technical Paper No. 39, Road Research Laboratory, Her Majesty's Stationery Office, London, U.K. (1958).
23. Special Report 209: Highway capacity manual, Transportation Research Board, National Research Council, Washington, D. C. (2000).

Development and Runtime Support for Situation-Aware Security in Autonomic Computing

Stephen S. Yau, Yisheng Yao, and Min Yan

Department of Computer Science and Engineering
Arizona State University
Tempe, AZ 85287-8809, USA
{yau, yisheng.yao, min.yan}@asu.edu

Abstract. To overcome increasing complexity and dynamic nature of distributed computing system, such as ubiquitous computing systems, it is critical to have computing systems that can manage themselves according to their users' goals. Such systems are called *autonomic computing systems*. It is essential that such systems, especially those for critical applications, have the capability of self-protection from attacks under various situations without much human intervention or guidance. To achieve this goal, situation-aware security (SAS) needs to be considered in the development process. In this paper, a model-driven development framework for SAS in autonomic computing systems is presented. The runtime support for SAS is provided by a situation-aware middleware. The advantages of using the development framework and the situation-aware middleware to build autonomic computing systems with SAS are discussed and illustrated.

Keywords: Autonomic computing, security, security policy, ubiquitous computing, model-driven development framework, situation-aware middleware.

1 Introduction

Ubiquitous computing (ubicomp) provides transparent information access and computing resources for users any time and anywhere. Due to the complex, decentralized and dynamic nature of ubiquitous computing, we may encounter various issues, such as information overload, increased uncertainty and risks of using services provided by unknown or adverse parties, and high burden of system management. Therefore, autonomic computing [1], which focuses on building self-managing computing systems, is critical to avoid the risk of losing control of such ubiquitous complexity, to retain users' confidence in their trustworthiness, and to realize the benefits of ubiquitous computing and information resources. It is essential that such systems, especially those for critical applications, have the capability of situation-aware security (SAS), i.e. self-protection from attacks under various situations without much human intervention or guidance. We define a situation as a set of contexts over a period of time that is relevant to future security-related actions. A context is any instantaneous, detectable, and relevant property of the environment, the system, or users, such as time,

L.T. Yang et al. (Eds.): ATC 2006, LNCS 4158, pp. 173–182, 2006.

location, available bandwidth and a user's schedule [2, 3]. To achieve SAS, the system needs to be carefully engineered throughout its life cycle [1]. However, current software development approaches often neglect security in all the development levels, and suffer from lack of tools for incorporating security in development as well as developers' experience with dealing with security during development.

In this paper, we will present a model-driven development framework to provide development support for SAS in autonomic computing systems. A model-driven approach enables developers to separate models of security requirements and technical details of security implementation, and hence simplifies security management. The framework includes a model for specifying, managing and analyzing security policies in autonomic computing systems. A situation-aware middleware is used for providing runtime support for *situation-aware security*, i.e. the capability of being aware of situations and adapting system's security behavior based on situation changes.

2   Challenges of SAS in Autonomic Computing

Security in autonomic computing includes two major concerns: (i) *How can a set of autonomic services interact through an untrustworthy network infrastructure to achieve the security goals without human guidance?* (ii) *How can a system protect itself against potential attacks under various situations and maintaining acceptable performance?* In order to address these concerns, various security mechanisms, such as authentication, access control, secure communication, and auditing, should be implemented effectively. However, even if the necessary security mechanisms for protecting autonomic computing systems are available, it is still difficult for the systems to protect themselves against malicious tasks because developers may not be able to apply these security mechanisms properly. To provide security in autonomic computing, the following challenges need to be addressed by the system development approach and system runtime support:

C1) *Heterogeneity and Interoperability.* Devices in autonomic computing may vary from powerful servers to small embedded devices. Hence, applications of different platforms need to communicate with each other for collaboration on situation evaluation and security management across organizational boundaries.

C2) *Usability.* Usability represents a central requirement of security engineering for a secure system. For example, if the specification and management of security policies is too complex and difficult to implement or enforce, errors will inevitably occur, or system developers simply ignore parts of the security requirement.

C3) *Extensibility.* The system should be easily extended for new QoS features, such as real-time and fault-tolerance, required in various applications.

C4) *Scalability and Efficiency.* Autonomic systems may involve a large number of entities, including user, service, process, etc. Interactions among these entities are complex. The developed systems must be efficient with a large number of entities.

C5) *Decentralized and Distributed.* Information needed for making security decisions are usually distributed on multiple systems. Hence, the security solution for autonomic computing should support decentralized architecture.

C6) *Flexibility*. The system must determine the access right for any subjects with respect to any actions on services under any situation. As situation changes, the security requirements of the system are often continuously evolving.

3 Current State of Art

The Model-Driven Architecture (MDA) [4], together with UML, provides an approach to improving the quality of complex software systems by creating high-level system models and automatically generating system architectures from the models. The MDA paradigm has been specialized in the model driven security [5 -8] as a methodology for developing secure systems. Using this methodology, a developer can build the system models along with security requirements, and automatically generate a configured security enforcement infrastructure from these models.

Recently, UML has been extended for representing security requirement models [9-12]. Epstein and Sandhu [9] utilized UML as a language to represent role-based access control (RBAC) models. Shin, et al [10] presented an alternative technique to utilize UML to describe RBAC models. Some UML extensions [11-12] accommodate security requirements in software requirement modeling and development. However, existing research on this aspect does not support situation aware security.

On security requirement specification, industrial standards, such as Security Assertion Markup Language (SAML) [13], eXtensible Access Control Markup Language (XACML) [14], WS-Security [15] and WS-SecurityPolicy [16] have been established. These XML-based security policy specification languages provide fine granularity of security policy specification. These languages need additional formal semantics for formal analysis on security policies, such as the semantics for WS-SecurityPolicy [17]. Logic-based security policy specification languages have attracted much attention for their unambiguous semantics, flexible expression formats and various types of reasoning support [18-20]. However, to address the above challenges, formal approaches to policy composition and transformation are needed for these logic-based security policy specification languages.

4 Development Support for SAS in Autonomic Computing

4.1 Our Development Framework

Our development framework is based on the model-driven architecture (MDA) perspective [4]. The system requirements are first modeled using Platform-Independent Models (PIM), such as PIM-Business and PIM-Security Policy. A PIM exhibits a specific degree of platform independence, and hence it is suitable for use with a number of different platforms of similar types. The PIM is then transformed into Platform Specific Models (PSM) in order to specify how the system can use a specific type of platform.

As shown in Figure 1, the functional requirements of the system are modeled and transformed to PSM following the standard model-driven development process. Similarly, using a security enhanced UML (seUML), the security requirements are modeled as a PIM-Security Policy, which is then mapped to PSM- executable security policies in a process calculus, such as the AS^3 calculus [21]. Similar to SecureUML [11], seUML is an improved UML. But, seUML has facilities to model situation constraints based on our situation-aware access control (SA-AC) model [22]. As shown in Figure 2, SA-AC extends the basic RBAC model by including the constraints in user-role and role-permission assignments as situations. The system situation information can represent the security condition of the system. With situation constraints in security policies, security decisions can be self-adapted to current system situations. An example of using seUML will be presented in Section 6.

Various decomposition rules and transformation rules are needed in the mapping process. The *decomposition rules* represent the domain knowledge on how to efficiently enforce security policies in the system. The *transformation rules* represent the domain knowledge on how to transform high-level security policies to executable security policies. High-level security policies specify the security goals without detail information on underlying system implementation. For example, *"the communication among collaborators should be protected"* is a high-level security policy, whereas *"the communication among the applications should be encrypted using AES-128"* is an executable security policy.

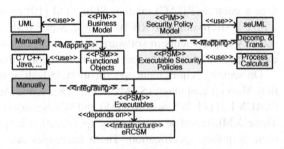

Fig. 1. Our development framework for SAS

Functional objects and executable security policies are integrated in PSMs, which can be run on specific computing platforms. We have extended our previous situation-aware middleware in ubicomp [2, 3, 22], to provide runtime support for SAS. This extension will be presented in Section 5.

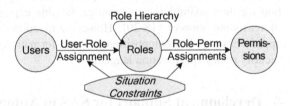

Fig. 2. An overview of our SA-AC model

4.2 Challenges Addressed by Our Development Framework

Our development framework addresses the challenges C1-C3 of SAS in autonomic computing discussed in Section 2 as follows:

- To address C1, our development framework provides support for rapid MDD of SAS in autonomic computing systems. The computing system is first depicted in PIM, which can easily be transformed to PSM executables on different platforms.

- To address C2, our framework automates many tasks in security management by encapsulating the complexity of security policy management and situation-awareness (SAW) processing in the middleware platform. The seUML provides a powerful tool for security administrators to specify high-level security policies without the need of knowing how it is implemented. Therefore, the security administrators of computing systems can concentrate on setting the security policy, and the framework will figure the implementation details of specified security policies by model transformation.
- To address C3, our framework can be easily extended to include new QoS properties based on the extensible MDA architecture and the extensible seUML.

5 Runtime Support for SAS in Autonomic Computing

5.1 Major Components for Providing Runtime Support

Our previous RCSM [2, 3] has a CORBA compliant architecture, providing the support of situation-awareness, distributed object invocation and situation-aware communication. We have extended our previous RCSM to eRCSM to support SAS in autonomic computing systems. The architecture of our eRCSM is shown in Figure 3 and consists of the following four major components:

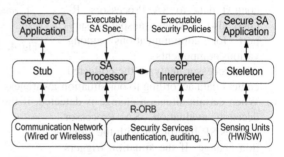

Fig. 3. The architecture of our eRCSM for providing SAS runtime support

1) *Secure SA Application* (sSAA), which is developed by modeling security and functional requirements in PIMs, transforming PIMs into PSM executables, as shown in Figure 1. In this development process, sSAA skeletons/stubs, as well as the corresponding executable security policies, are also generated.
2) *Security Policy Interpreter (SP Interpreter)*, which makes security decisions on an object invocation request based on the enforceable security policies, current security context and system situation.
3) *SA Processor*, which manages SA requirement specification, maintains the context and action history, detects situation based on context and action history, and updates the security policy interpreter on the current system situation.
4) *RCSM Object Request Broker (R-ORB)*, which provides interfaces for context discovery, collection and propagation. It also discovers and invokes the appropriate object implementation for the requests from sSAA's. For security, upon receiving an object invocation request, R-ORB enforces the security decisions made by the SP Interpreter.

5.2   The Execution Model of Our eRCSM for Providing SAS

The execution model of our eRCSM for providing SAS includes SAW processing model and security decision evaluation and enforcement model.

A) Situation-awareness processing
The flowchart for SAW processing is shown in Figure 4, and includes the following steps:

1) When an sSAA starts on eRCSM, it registers SAW requirements with SA Processor.
2) SA Processor sends requests for the contexts needed for processing the registered SAW requirements.
3) The hardware/software sensing units collect the necessary contexts, including some security-related data.
4) R-ORB propagates the collected context data to SA Processors. R-ORB also provides transparent support for communications among various components.
5) SA Processor analyzes the collected context data according to our situation-awareness model [24].

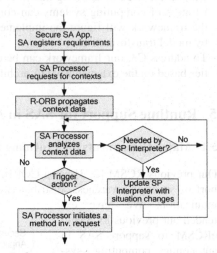

Fig. 4. The flowchart for SAW processing

6) When certain situation change is detected, if this situation is needed for security decision evaluation, SA Processor updates SP Interpreter with the situation change. If the situation triggers certain action, SA Processor will initiate action requests to related sSAA.

B) Security enforcement
The flowchart for security decision evaluation and enforcement is shown in Figure 5 and includes the following steps:
1) An sSAA or an SA Processor initiates a method invocation.
2) R-ORB locates a remote sSAA.
3) R-ORB receives the request and consults the SP Interpreter for checking security.
4) The SP Interpreter evaluates the request initiated by the sSAA or SA Processor. Decisions on whether to trust the request are made according

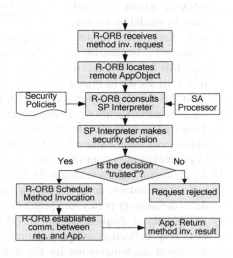

Fig. 5. The flowchart for security decision evaluation and enforcement

to executable security policies and current system situations. Various underlying security services may be invoked through a standard interface of R-ORB for decision evaluation.

5) If the security decision is 'trusted', R-ORB schedules the method invocation.

6) R-ORB establishes a channel between the requesting sSAA and the remote sSAA. After processing the request, the remote sSAA returns the output data back to the requesting sSAA.

5.3 Challenges Addressed in eRCSM

Our eRCSM can address challenges C4-C6 of SAS in autonomic computing discussed in Section 2 as follows:

– To address C4, a number of SA Processors and SP Interpreters will be deployed. Each responsible for processing different SAW requirements and security policies. Moreover, the publication/subscription style of situation updates between SA Processors and SP Interpreters reduces the overhead of situation constraint computation.

– To address C5, SA Processors and SP Interpreters can be deployed over the network for managing the security policies and SAW requirements.

– To address C6, situation awareness is incorporated into security decision evaluation. SAS security policies can be specified, based on which security decision on a request may be changed when the situation changes. Moreover, new emerging security mechanisms can be plugged in the system as underlying security services. When security requirements change, new security policies can be specified and transformed to executable security policies, and activated by SP Interpreters immediately.

6 An Example

Let us consider a situation-aware net meeting system (SANM) with the following functionalities for users to easily have a net meeting: A meeting organizer can organize a net meeting by inputting desired meeting date and time duration, indicating attendees and specifying security policies. To arrange the meeting time, the system queries the calendar service on the computing devices of the expected attendees, and gets approval from them. The system will automatically distribute meeting notice to all expected attendees. An attendee's device of SANM can join the meeting session, when the specified meeting situations are detected. Documents will be delivered to related attendees during (or before) the meeting, as needed.

By implementing an sSAA object oMeeting with a set of situations and roles, SANM can self-manage the security of the system. Meeting attendees can join the meeting session M and send secure message by calling either method msg256 (with strong encryption) or method msg64 (with fast encryption) of oMeeting. Likewise, an organizer can securely distribute documents using either doc256 or doc64. The kickout method is triggered to remove an untrusted attendee from M.

To provide security in this system, the administrator of SANM may set the following high level security policies for M:

a) To protect privacy, attendees should not be in public places, such as shopping mall.
b) Confidentiality of the messages and documents sent over the network must be ensured. To keep good performance of the meeting, the protection can be flexible. If the system detects that the response of a user's mobile device is too slow when using 256-bit encryption, the system can establish a new security context to use 64-bit fast encryption.
c) When a device is reported to be stolen, the device cannot continue the meeting.

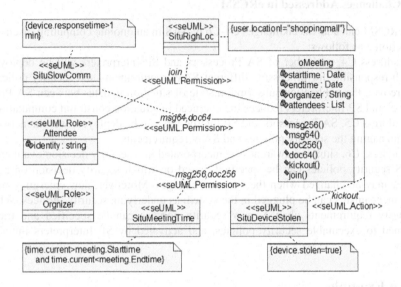

Fig. 6. seUML specification for Policies a)-c)

These policies show that the system should self-reconfigured for security purpose when the situation changes. Using our framework, this can be achieved as follows:

A) Security policy specification using seUML
Following our SA-AC model, system administrators can specify the above security policies in seUML, as partially shown in Figure 6. Permissions, such as "join", "msg256,doc256", "msg64,doc64", and "kickout" are specified as the associations among roles and objects. For Policy a), SituRightLoc (*Attendee is located in an appropriate meeting environment*) is needed. SituMeetingTime (*The meeting is ongoing*) is needed for Policy b). For Policy c), we need SituDeviceStolen (*Device of an attendee is reported stolen*) and SituSlowComm (*Device response time is more than 1 minute when processing 256-bit encryption*).

B) Security policy decomposition, transformation and enforcement
B1) Decomposition. Security policies in seUML can be exported to XML-based specifications, and can be further decomposed to different sets according to their entities. In this example, if the policy decomposition rule is "*attendees' access and*

system actions should be controlled by two separate sets of security policies", these policies can be decomposed to multiple policy sets as follows:

- *Policy Set A)*:
  a) An attendee can enter join the meeting if
     SituRightLoc is true.
  b-1) When **SituMeetingTime** is true, attendee can send message
       or documents using msg256 or doc256.
  b-2) When **SituSlowComm** is true, attendee can send message or
       documents using msg64 or doc64.

- *Policy Set B)*:
  c) When **SituStolen** is true, oMeeting can remove the related
     attendee using kickout.

   B2) Transformation. Each set of security policies is transformed to platform-dependent executable security policies. A fragment of executable security policies in AS^3 calculus [21] for policy set A) is shown below.

```
Fix G = (principal, permission) || (SituSituRightLoc)          //process G implemets Policy set A)
              || (SituMeetingTime) || (SituSlowComm) .    //get security request and situations
    if ( (hasAuthenticate(principal) == 'true') and
        ((permission=='join' and SituRightLoc == 'true') or
        (permission=='msg256,doc256' and SituMeetingTime == 'true') or
        (permission=='msg64,doc64' and SituSlowComm == 'true'))  //check permissions and situa-
tions
        ) then <"trusted">.G                              //output security decisions
    else <"denied">.G
```

B3) Enforcement. The executable security policies will be deployed on eRCSM. At runtime, upon an access request from a principal, the SP Interpreter on eRCSM will execute related executable security policies. Security decisions are made according to executable security policies and current situation values

7 Conclusion and Future Work

In this paper, we have presented a model driven development framework and a middleware-based runtime support for SAS in autonomic computing systems. We have discussed how our framework and middleware-based runtime support address the challenges to support SAS in autonomic computing systems. As illustrated by the example, the above support can greatly simplify the development effort and facilitate the autonomic execution and reconfiguration of security in dynamic and complex systems, such as ubiquitous computing systems. Future work includes analysis of the expressiveness of seUML, and development and runtime support for satisfying more QoS requirements, such as real-time, fault-tolerance, survivability.

Acknowledgment

This work was supported by National Science Foundation under grant number CNS-0524736. We would like to thank Dazhi Huang for many helpful discussions.

182   S.S. Yau, Y. Yao, and M. Yan

References

1. J. O. Kephart and D. M. Chess, "The vision of autonomic computing," *IEEE Computer*, vol. 36, no.1, 2003, pp.41-50.
2. S. S. Yau, Y. Wang and F. Karim, "Development of Situation-Aware Application Software for Ubiquitous Computing Environments", *Proc. 26th IEEE Int'l Computer Software and Applications Conf*, 2002, pp. 233-238.
3. S. S. Yau, *at el*, "Reconfigurable Context-Sensitive Middleware for Pervasive Computing," *IEEE Pervasive Computing*, Vol. 1, No. 3, 2002, pp. 33-40.
4. OMG, "MDA Guide Version 1.01", URL: http://www.omg.org/, accessed on 03/18/2006.
5. C.C. Burt, *et al*, "Model driven security: unification of authorization models for fine-grain access control," *Proc. 7th IEEE Int'l Enterprise Distributed Object Computing Conf.*, 2003. pp. 159- 171.
6. D. Basin, J. r. Doser, and T. Lodderstedt, "Model driven security for process-oriented systems," *Proc. 8th ACM Symp. Access Control Models and Tech.*, 2003, pp. 100-109.
7. J. Jürjens., "Model-Based Security Engineering with UML," *Lecture Notes in Computer Science*, Volume 3655, 2005, pp. 42 - 77.
8. Y. Nakamura, *et al*, "Model-Driven Security Based on a Web Services Security Architecture," *Proc. 2005 IEEE Int'l Conf. on Services Computing*, 2005, pp.7-15.
9. P. Epstein and R. Sandhu, "Towards a UML based approach to role engineering," *Proc. 4th ACM Workshop on Role-Based Access Control*, 1999, pp. 135-143.
10. M. E. Shin and G.-J. Ahn, "UML-Based Representation of Role-Based Access Control," *Proc. 9th IEEE Int'l Workshops on Enabling Technologies: Infrastructure for Collaborative Enterprises*, 2000 pp. 195-200.
11. T. Lodderstedt, D. A. Basin, and J. Doser, "SecureUML: A UML-Based Modeling Language for Model-Driven Security," *Proc. 5th Int' l Conf. on the Unified Modeling Language*, 2002, pp.426-441.
12. T. Doan, *et al*, "MAC and UML for secure software design," *Proc. ACM Workshop on Formal Methods in Security Eng.*, 2004, pp. 75-85.
13. OASIS, "Security Assertion Markup Language (SAML) Version 2.0," URL: http://www.oasis-open.org/, accessed on 03/18/2006.
14. OASIS, "eXtensible Access Control Markup Language (XACML) version 2.0," URL: http://docs.oasis-open.org/xacml/, accessed on 03/18/2006.
15. WS-Security, URL: http://www.ibm.com/developerworks/, accessed on 03/18/2006.
16. WS Security Policy, URL: http://www.ibm.com/developerworks/, accessed on 03/18/2006.
17. K. Bhargavan, C. Fournet, and A.D. Gordon, "A semantics for web services authentication," *Proc. 31st ACM Symp. on Principles of Programming Languages*, 2004, pp.198-209.
18. E. Bertino, *et al*, "Temporal Authorization Bases: From Specification to Integration," *Jour. Computer Security*, vol. 8(4), 2000, pp. 309-354.
19. S. Jajodia, *et al*, "Flexible Supporting for Multiple Access Control Policies," *ACM Trans. on Database Systems*, vol. 26(2), 2001, pp.214-260.
20. A. Uszok, *et al*, "KAoS policy and domain services: toward a description-logic approach to policy representation, deconfliction, and enforcement," *Proc. IEEE 4th Int'l Workshop on Policies for Distributed Systems and Networks*, 2003, pp. 93-96.
21. S. S. Yau, *at el* "Automated Agent Synthesis for Situation-Aware Service Coordination in Service-based Systems", *Technical Report*, Arizona State University, August, 2005.
22. S. S. Yau, Y. Yao and V. Banga, "Situation-Aware Access Control for Service-Oriented Autonomous Decentralized Systems", *Proc. 7th Int'l Symp. on Autonomous Decentralized Systems*, 2005, pp. 17-24.

A Social Network-Based Trust Model for the Semantic Web

Yu Zhang, Huajun Chen, and Zhaohui Wu

Grid Computing Lab, College of Computer Science,
Zhejiang University, Hangzhou 310027, Zhejiang, China
{yzh, huajunsir, wzh}@zju.edu.cn

Abstract. Trust is very essential to secure and high quality interactions on the Semantic Web. In this paper, we introduce a trust model, which incorporates pairwise trust ratings and reliable factors of acquaintances and constructs an edge-weighted graph to calculate trust values. We interpret trust in two dimensions to better deal with it. We apply the theory in social network field to calculate trust and simulate the trust relationships between humans. We also take advantage of formulas in probability and statistics to analyze the similarities between agents. The algorithm of the trust model aims to be simple, efficient and flexible.

1   Introduction

In our common life, we place our trust in people and the services those people provide. We judge how to act based upon the trust we have in others. Without trust, our life would rapidly descend in to chaos or inactivity. We face even worse situation when dealing with trust issues on the web as the potential cost of making a wrong trust decision is drastically higher than the cost of not offering trust. With the development of Internet technology, e-commerce, e-bank and e-learning enter into common people's lives. Therefore, it is very essential to guarantee secure and high quality interactions on the web.

The Semantic Web [17] in the future can be viewed as a collection of intelligent agents. With the introduction of ontology and RDF (Resource Description Framework) [13], meta-data of the distributed web is machine-understandable which makes trust information can be processed by machine with few human's effort. By its nature, resources are semantically connected by predicates. For example, aspirin can cure headache effectively. We can use the triple (x, P, y) as a logical formula $P(x, y)$ [3], where the predicate P relates the object x to the object y. This simple statement can be interpreted by RDF terms as follows:

1. The *subject* is the word "aspirin".
2. The *predicate* is the verb "cure".
3. The *object* is the name of the disease "headache".

There is a relationship named "cure" which connects two concepts "aspirin" and "headache". Therefore, the two resources are born to related with each other.

L.T. Yang et al. (Eds.): ATC 2006, LNCS 4158, pp. 183–192, 2006.

In this paper, we follow Jennifer Golbeck et al.'s method to explore trust management on the Semantic Web [9]. Although our model bears some similarities with Golbeck's, the contribution of this paper is multifold: *(i)* it extends the framework [9] based on social network analysis by adding several mechanisms to increase efficiency: trust report mechanism, push mode and pull mode, honor roll and blacklist. *(ii)* it evaluates trust from two dimensions: trust rating and reliable factor. Agents use trust rating as the criteria of choosing interaction partners while use reliable factor to decide whether to believe the trust news from their acquaintances. *(iii)* it exploits formulas in probability and statistics to analyze similarities between agents, which helps them to acquire more appropriate recommendations. *(iv)* it provides an algorithm which allows each path to compute trust values simultaneously. If two paths do not intersect, then they are independent from each other. When there is an update happened on a single path, the trust ratings from other paths remain the same and wait at the sink to be merged.

2   Related Work

There is a wealth of research into social networks in a wide range of disciplines [11]. The most famous one is commonly known as "Small World". The main idea of "Small World" is that any two people in the world can be connected to each other through short chains of intermediate acquaintances (theorized to be six) [12]. Since Milgram conducted a series of striking experiments in the 1960s, it has grown into a significant area of study in the social sciences and also has been applied to the analysis of the hyperlink graph of the World Wide Web as well. Lada A. Adamic made an intensive study in "Small World" phenomenon and demonstrated that World Wide Web is also a small world, in the sense that sites are highly clustered yet the path length between them is small [2].

The web of trust also has been studied from non computer science perspective. Jason Rutter focuses on the importance of trust in business-to-consumer e-commerce and suggests a number of nontechnical ways in which successful e-commerce retailers can build trust [14]. In [10], Teck H and Weigelt investigated trust in a laboratory setting using a novel multi-stage trust game where social gains are achieved if players trust each other in each stage. Results shows that subjects are more trustworthy if they are certain of the trustee's intention and are more trusting and trustworthy when the stake size increased.

eBay [5] is a centralized reputation application which provides a simple strategy to manage trust and reputation. A rating from a unique member only affects once to another member's score. Satisfaction increases the feedback score by 1, neutrality doesn't affect the score, and dissatisfaction decreases by 1. Depending on centralized agency to manage trust can greatly reduce the workload of interactions, however, due to the sheer magnitude and diversity of information sources, it is virtually infeasible for the Semantic Web to manage trust in a centralized fashion.

In [9], approaches are developed in the field of social network analysis. By introducing ontological trust specifications base on the Friend of a Friend(FOAF) [16], the model takes the first step to add the semantic ingredients to trust management. FilmTrust is a web site that uses trust in web-based social networks to create predictive movie recommendations [7]. It combines social networks with movie ratings and maintain lists of friends and personalizes the information based on the friends.

Users can annotate their analysis of information sources and express credibility and reliability of the sources explicitly or implicitly by using THELLIS [6]. The shortcoming of THELLIS is that the values of trustworthiness are not personalized and it requires users to reach an agreement on the credibility of the sources.

EigenTrust [15] algorithm computes a global trust value similar to PageRank in a peer-to-peer network. EigenTrust emphasizes on security problems such as betrayal and lie between peers, but it does not support personalized trust calculation either.

3 Trust Model

The Semantic Web can be viewed as a group of intelligent agents. The trust network composed by these agents in essence reflects the social network of humans. Trust, by its nature, is a sociology issue, therefore, the research fruits from social network field should be considered. We follow method in [9] [8] to extend FOAF project [1] that allows users to specify who they know and build a web of acquaintances. FOAF project is about creating a Web of machine-readable homepages of people and the things they do. Technically, FOAF is an RDF/XML Semantic Web vocabulary, therefore, FOAF data is easy to process and merge by machines.

A graph representing the information about the relations among resources can be an very efficient way of describing a social structure. Viewing the Semantic Web as a directed graph G, resources as vertices V and predicates as edges E, we can write $G = (V, E)$. In order to present the trust model, we first introduce some basic definitions.

3.1 Basic Definitions

Definition 1. *Trust Rating:* *If $v_1, v_2 \in V$ and $(v_1, v_2) \in E$, then trust rating $T_{v_1 \rightarrow v_2}$ denotes $v_1's$ belief in $v_2's$ competence to fulfill a task or provide a service.*

Definition 2. *Reliable Factor:* *If $v_1, v_2 \in V$ and $(v_1, v_2) \in E$, then reliable factor $R_{v_1 \rightarrow v_2}$ denotes to which degree v_1 believes in $v_2's$ words or opinions.*

The ranges of trust rating and reliable factor are the same: $[0,1]$, however, they have different meanings. Trust rating denotes that to which degree a consumer's evaluation about a provider's ability. Agents use trust rating as the criteria of choosing interaction partners. Reliable factor denotes to which degree that a

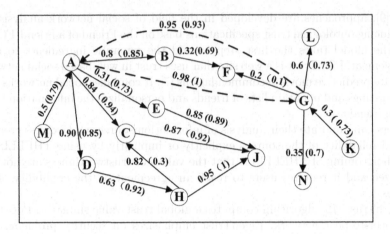

Fig. 1. *Neighbor and Friends.* On each edge, the number inside the parenthesis denotes *reliable factor* and the number outside the parenthesis denotes *trust rating.*

consumer agent believes the trust information from its acquaintances. Agents use reliable factor as the criteria of adopting whose recommendations during trust information propagation.

Definition 3. *Neighbor:* *If $v_1, v_2 \in V$ and $(v_1, v_2) \in E$, then v_2 is $v_1's$ neighbor, note as $v_1 \mapsto v_2$.*

Definition 4. *Friend:* *If $v_1, v_2 \in V$ and $(v_1, v_2) \in E$ and $R_{v_1 \rightarrow v_2} > 0.9 \cup R_{v_2 \rightarrow v_1} > 0.9$, then v_1 and v_2 are friends, denote as $v_1 \Leftrightarrow v_2$.*

As shown above (See Fig. 1), B, C, D and E are $A's$ neighbors while A and G are friends to each other. Two broken direct edges that connect A and G indicate the friends' relationship. Friends are reachable from one to the other. The friends relationships in the graph are shortcuts for agents to obtain useful information and find qualified providers. The consumer agent can rely on its friend's recommendation to choose providers instead of expanding out the network to gather trust information.

4   Basic Mechanisms

4.1   Local Database Storage

Generally speaking, an agent has more neighbors than friends. In order to make full use of memory, we exploit linked list to store information of each agent. Each agent can maintain a list of friends and neighbors.

For example, the profile of node A is as follows:

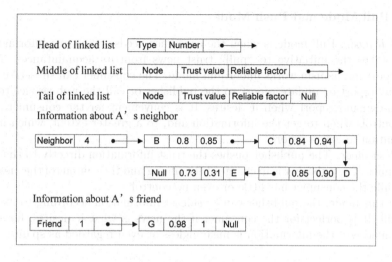

Fig. 2. Information about node $A's$ friends and neighbors

4.2 Trust Report Mechanism

A key feature of the Semantic Web is openness. A resource can come and go at any time and the services provided by agents may change dramatically within a short period. Therefore, it is very hard to know whether our past experience is valuable or meaningless. In this section, we introduce trust report mechanism to solve this problem.

We define three types of trust report: routine report, update report and on-demand report.

1. *Routine Report*: An agent can subscribe news to another agent which is regarded as a publisher according to its individual requirements. When the publisher accepts the subscription, it will report the corresponding trust news to the subscriber regularly no matter whether the news is changed or not. This kind of trust report is called routine report. Different subscribers may have different cycles of gathering information, therefore, the different time intervals of trust report are base on subscribers' personal requirements.

2. *Update Report*: The publisher reports to the subscribers as soon as it gets update of the trust news. In this case, the subscriber cares about the changes of the information. For example, many web sites provide downloading of files. A previous fast web site suddenly can not be accessed. Consumer agent A gets the news from its publisher M as soon as the change happens, therefore, agent A will refer to other downloading web sites instead.

3. *On-demand Report*: The publisher reports the trust news when the agent requires to. This kind of information is usually collected for immediate use, so it has a higher privilege. When the network is busy, the routine report should give way to on-demand report.

4.3   Pull Mode and Push Mode

1. *Pull mode*: Pull mode is when the consumer needs some trust information, it takes the initiative to "pull" trust news from its acquaintances. Trust report mechanism works under pull mode. The consumer can subscribe routine report or update report to the publisher or call the web service to get on-demand report when it desires. It is convenient for the consumer, who controls when to get the information and, to a greater extent, which information to get or ignore.
2. *Push mode*: The publisher pushes the trust information directly to the consumer. The publisher is in charge of the timing and the content of the message while the consumer has little or even no control.
   In this mode, the publisher can broadcast information according to its own will. It is perfect for the consumer if the news is what it desires, however, sometimes, the information is meaningless or even regarded as spam.

4.4   Honor Roll and Blacklist

It consumes much time to calculate trust values and transfer information. In order to speed up the process, the concept of honor roll and blacklist are introduced in this paper. The information of honor roll and blacklist is also stored in a linked list in the local database.

The agents who behave well and steadily in a certain period of time are placed on the honor roll while those who always behave badly are in the blacklist. When a consumer wants to get services from a provider, it can check whether the provider is on its honor roll. If the answer is yes, then it omits the investigation and interacts with the provider directly. Or else, it needs to pull trust information from its friends or neighbors. If the potential partner is on the blacklist, it will be killed without further query.

Honor roll and blacklist also need to be updated. After interactions, when the consumer is dissatisfied with the service provider, it can move the provider from honor roll to common agents' group or even to blacklist. For a provider who is on the blacklist, if there is news from consumers' acquaintances shows that its service has been improved, then the consumer may have a try and rejudge the provider's trust level. If the trust value exceeds 0.5 during the interaction, the previous notorious provider can return to common agents' group.

4.5   The Algorithm of the Trust Model

Due to the sheer magnitude and diversity of information sources on the Semantic Web, our algorithm of trust calculation has the following features:

1. *Easy-to-compute*: the Semantic Web itself is a huge system and still expanding. Therefore, if the algorithm is complicated, the overhead incurred by the calculation is tremendous and the clients cannot wait to see the trust recommendations.

2. *Parallel arithmetic*: The search takes breadth-first strategy and expands out from the source to sink through the trust network. All the paths can compute trust values simultaneously and the time complexity is only determined by the longest path. When the longest path finishes calculation, the final trust value can be worked out immediately after addition.

3. *Two dimensions*: Trust is evaluated from two dimensions: trust rating and reliable factor. Agents use trust rating as the criteria of choosing interaction partners while use reliable factor as the criteria of adopting whose opinions during trust information propagation. In this way, the trust issue is evaluated in a more specific way.

N denotes the number of paths from P to Q. D_i denotes the number of steps between P and Q on the i_{th} path. We call the set of $Q's$ friends or neighbors as M. M_i denotes $Q's$ immediate friend or neighbor on the i_{th} path. w_i denotes weight of the i_{th} path. The weight of each path is calculated as follows:

$$w_i = \frac{\dfrac{1}{D_i}}{\sum\limits_{i=1}^{n} \dfrac{1}{D_i}} \tag{1}$$

If $P \mapsto Q$ or $P \leftrightarrow Q$, then $T_{P \to Q}$ can be got directly from the edges, or else $T_{P \to Q}$ can be calculated as follows:

$$T_{P \to Q} = \sum_{i=1}^{n} \frac{T_{m_i \to Q} \times \prod\limits_{i \mapsto j \cup i \leftrightarrow j} R_{i \to j} \times \frac{1}{D_i}}{\sum\limits_{i=1}^{n} \dfrac{1}{D_i}} \tag{2}$$

The search expands out through the trust network simultaneously. Meanwhile the number of steps on each path is counted in pace with searching. The longest path L from source to sink determines the time complexity of the calculation. The other short paths will wait for L at the sink for trust combining. As soon as L finishes searching, the trust rating can be calculated at once.

4.6   Similarity of Preferences

In real life, a person tends to trust people that are significantly more similar to him than arbitrary users [4]. In this section, we will focus on how to measure the similarity of agents in a network based on their ratings to the same group of providers(See Fig. 3 and Table 1). We exploit mathematical methods in probability and statistics theory to calculate the proximity of the agents. Under normal conditions, two agents may give different trust ratings to the same information provider. For each common provider they rate, the closer of each pair of trust ratings, the more similar of the two agents. Therefore we first get the difference of each pair of trust ratings for the same provider, which is one of the criterions to evaluate similarity.

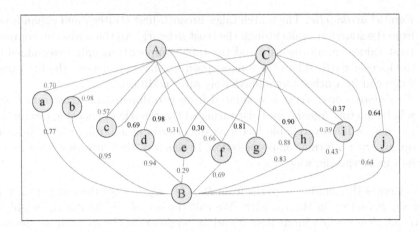

Fig. 3. Trust ratings of information Providers

Table 1. Trust ratings of information providers A, B, C

Information Consumer	Trust rating of information Provider									
Agent	a	b	c	d	e	f	g	h	i	j
A	0.70	0.98	0.57	–	0.31	0.66	0.1	0.88	0.39	0.1
B	0.77	0.95	0.1	0.94	0.29	0.69	0.1	0.83	0.43	0.64
C	0.1	0.1	0.69	0.98	0.30	0.81	0.90	0.37	0.64	0.1

In the trust network, the trust rating varies from time to time, so the difference of each pair of trust ratings can be regarded as a random variable x. We investigate similarities in two aspects: firstly, we calculate mathematical expectation $E(x)$ — the average of all the differences. Similar agents are expected to have a $E(x)$ around 0. If two agents have a very big $E(x)$, it shows that they are divergent at least in some aspects. It is not enough to distinguish two agents' similarities only base on $E(x)$, therefore, we use standard deviation $S(x)$ to evaluate the degree of deviation from $E(x)$. If $S(x)$ is small, it means that x doesn't fluctuate very much. The smaller of $S(x)$, the more similar of the two agents. In this paper, we define that if $|E(x)| < 0.3$ and $S(x) < 0.1$, then the two agents are regarded as similar agents. For example , B and C are $A's$ neighbors and they give different trust ratings to the group of other agents in the community(See Table 2 and Table 3).

Table 2. Trust ratings given by A, B for the same group of providers

Information Consumer	Trust rating of information Provider					
Agent	a	b	e	f	h	i
A	0.70	0.98	0.31	0.66	0.88	0.39
B	0.77	0.95	0.29	0.69	0.83	0.43
$x = T_{A \to i} - T_{B \to i}$	-0.07	0.03	0.02	-0.03	0.05	-0.04

Table 3. Trust ratings given by A, C for the same group of providers

Information Consumer	Trust rating of information Provider				
Agent	c	e	f	h	i
A	0.57	0.68	0.66	0.68	0.36
C	0.69	0.63	0.81	0.94	0.31
$x = T_{A \to i} - T_{B \to i}$	0.12	0.01	0.15	0.02	0.02

$$E_{A \to B}(x) = \frac{(-0.07) + 0.03 + 0.02 + (-0.03) + 0.05 + (-0.04)}{6} = -0.0067$$

$$S_{A \to B}(x) = \sqrt{E\left([x - E_{A \to B}(x)]^2\right)} = 0.043$$

From the above calculation, we can see that $|E_{A \to B}(x)| = 0.0067 < 0.1$, $S_{A \to B}(x) = 0.0043 < 0.1$, therefore agent A and B are similar according to our predefined rule.

$$E_{A \to C} = \frac{(-0.12) + 0.05 + (-0.15) + (-0.02) + 0.02}{6} = -0.086$$

$$S_{A \to C}(x) = \sqrt{E([x - E_{A \to C}(x)]^2)} = 0.12$$

We can see that $|E_{A \to C}(x)| = 0.086 < 0.1$ but $S_{A \to B}(x) = 0.12 > 0.1$; therefore agent A and agent C are not similar. Statistically speaking, $B's$ trust evaluation is more useful to A, therefore, when different recommendations are obtained from both B and C, A will adopt $B's$. By analyzing the similarity between agents, the trust model can let the agents to decide the friends' relationships, which can greatly improve the accuracy of trust evaluation. Friend relationship can be regarded as a shortcut for recommendation and reference.

5   Conclusion

In this paper, we introduce a trust model, which incorporates pairwise trust ratings and reliable factors of acquaintances and constructs an edge-weighted graph to calculate trust values. The trust model interprets trust in two dimensions: trust rating and reliable factor to better deal with the trust issue. We apply the theory in social network field to calculate trust and simulate the trust relationships between humans. We also take advantage of formulas in probability and statistics to analyze the similarities between agents. The trust network grouped by similar agents tends to provide more accurate trust recommendations and the algorithm of the model is simple, efficient and flexible. Trust calculation can be worked out simultaneously through the chain of the trust network and update on one path can be adjusted quickly without interfering with other paths.

At the moment, our trust model does not provide a mechanism to deal with lying or betrayal of agents. In order to make the model more robust and ready to be used in real open environment, we plan to incorporate reasoning and learning abilities. In the future, we will focus on the above aspects and try to improve the model.

Acknowledgement

The research was supported by China NSF program (NO.NSFC60503018), subprogram of China 973 project (NO.2003CB317006), the Science and Technique Foundation Programs (NO.NCET-04-0545). and also a grant from Zhejiang Provincial Natural Science Foundation of China (NO.Y105463).

References

1. The foaf project. http://www.foaf-project.org/.
2. Lada A. Adamic. The small world web. In *Proc. of ECDL*, pages 443–452, september 1999.
3. Grigoris Antoniou and Frank van Harmelen. *A Semantic Web Primer*. The MIT Press, 2004.
4. Cai-Nicolas Ziegler and Jennifer Golbeck . Investigating correlations of trust and interest similarity - do birds of a feather really flock together? to appear in Decision Support Systems, 2005.
5. eBay Web Site. http://www.ebay.com.
6. Y. Gil and V. Ratnakar. Trusting information sources one citizen at a time. In *Proc. of the first International Semantic Web Conference*, pages 162–176, Sardinia, Italy, 2000.
7. Jennifer Golbeck. Generating predictive movie recommendations from trust in social networks. In *Proceedings of the Fourth International Conference on Trust Management*, Pisa, Italy, May 2006.
8. Jennifer Golbeck and James Hendler. Inferring reputation on the semantic web. In *Proceeding of the Thirteenth International World Wide Web Conference*, New York, May 17-22 2004.
9. Jennifer Golbeck, Bijan Parsia, and James Hendler. Trust networks on the semantic web. In *Proc. of Cooperative Intelligent Agents*, 2003.
10. Teck H. Ho and Keith Weigelt. Trust among strangers. In *Experimental Social Science Laboratory (Xlab)*, August 1 2004.
11. Kieron O'Hara, Harith Alani, Nigel Shadbolt, and Yannis Kalfoglou Trust strategies for the semantic web. In *Proceedings of Workshop on Trust, Security, and Reputation on the Semantic Web, 3rd International (ISWC'04)*, Hiroshima, Japan, 2004.
12. Stanley Milgram. The small world problem. *Psychology Today*, pages 60–67, 1967.
13. RDF Primer. http://www.w3.org/TR/rdf-primer/.
14. Jason Rutter. From the sociology of trust towards a sociology of 'e-trust'. *International Journal of New Product Development & Innovation Management*, 2001.
15. M.T. Schlosser S.D. Kamvar and H. Garcia-Molina. The eigentrust algorithm for reputation management in p2p networks. In *Proc. of the Twelfth International World Wide Web Conference*, Budapest, Hungary, 2003.
16. FOAF Vocabulary Specification. http://xmlns.com/foaf/0.1/.
17. Tim Berners-Lee, James Hendler, and Ora Lassila. The semantic web. *Scientific American*, May 2001.

Fuzzy Model Tuning for Intrusion Detection Systems

Zhenwei Yu and Jeffrey J.P. Tsai

Department of Computer Science
851 S. Morgan Street
University of Illinois, Chicago, IL 60607
tsai@cs.uic.edu

Abstract. Intrusion Detection System (IDS) detects ongoing intrusive activities in information systems. However, an IDS usually suffers high false alarm especially in a dynamically changing environment, which forces continuous tuning on its detection model to maintain sufficient performance. Currently, the manually tuning work greatly depends on the user to work out and integrate the tuning solution. We have developed an automatically tuning intrusion detection system (ATIDS). The experimental results show that when tuning is not delayed too long, the system can achieve about 20% improvement compared with the system without model tuner. But the user can only control whether the tuning should be performed by sending/blocking feedbacks. To give the user more powerful but intuitive control on the tuning, we develop a fuzzy model tuner, through which the user can tune the model fuzzily but yield much appropriate tuning. The results show the system can achieve about 23% improvement.

1 Introduction

Intrusion Detection (ID) is a process to identify abnormal activities in a computer system. Traditional intrusion detection relies on extensive knowledge of security experts. To reduce this dependence, varied data mining and machine learning methods have been applied in some Intrusion Detection System (IDS) research projects [1-8]. However, Julish pointed out that data mining based IDS usually relies on unrealistic assumptions on the availability and quality of the training data [9], which makes the detection models built on such training data loose the efficiency gradually on detecting intrusion as the real-time environment undergoes continuous change. In intrusion detection, it is difficult to collect high quality training data. New attacks leveraging newly discovered security weakness emerge quickly and frequently. It is impossible to collect complete related data on those new attacks to train a detection model before those attacks are detected and understood. In addition, due to new hardware and software deployed in the system, system and user behaviors will keep changing, which causes detection models to degrade in performance. As a consequence, a fixed detection model is not suitable for an intrusion detection system for long time. Instead, after an IDS is deployed, its detection model has to be tuned continually. For commercial products (mainly signature based IDS), the main tuning method is to filter out signatures to avoid noise [10] and/or add new signatures. In data mining-based system, some parameters are adjusted to balance the detection rate and the false rate. Such tuning is coarse and the procedure and must be performed

L.T. Yang et al. (Eds.): ATC 2006, LNCS 4158, pp. 193–204, 2006.

manually by the user. Other proposed methods rely on "plugging in" a dedicated sub-model [11] or superseding the current model by dynamically mined new models [12-14]. However, a dedicated model requires the user to build high quality training data. Mining a new model from real-time unverified data incurs the risk that the model could be trained by an experienced attacker to accept abnormal data.

We have developed an Automatically Tuning Intrusion Detection System (ATIDS). ATIDS takes advantage of the analysis of alarms by the user. The detection model is tuned on the fly with so verified data, yet the burden on the user is minimized. The experimental results on KDDCUP'99 ID dataset show that when the tuning is delayed a short time, the system could reduce about 20% of Total Misclassification Cost (TMC) compared with a system lacking the model tuner. But the user can only control whether the tuning should be performed by sending or blocking feedbacks on the false predictions. Further, the tuning in ATIDS is automatically done with the same tuning degree, which is lake of refinement. To give the user more powerful but intuitive control on tuning the model, we develop a fuzzy model tuner, so the user can tune the model fuzzily but yield much appropriate tuning by defining the fuzzy knowledge base through intuitive graphical user interface and/or familiar nature language. The results under the same experiment setting show the system can achieve about 23% improvement.

We present the system architecture and its core component in section 2. Then the basic knowledge of fuzzy logic and our fuzzy controller is presented in section 3. Our experiments and results on the KDDCUP'99 intrusion detection dataset are shown in section 4.

2 System Architecture

Intrusion detection system is a monitor system, which reports alarms to the system user whenever it infers that abnormal conditions exist. The system user must verify the correctness of the reported alarms and execute defensive actions against an intruder. We believe that verified results provide useful information to further improve the IDS. In the system architecture, we include system user to show the interaction between the user and the system. The detection model is created in training stage. The prediction engine analyzes and evaluates each obtained data record according to the detection model. The prediction results are reported to the system user who verifies the results and marks false predictions and feeds back to the fuzzy model tuner. The fuzzy model tuner automatically tunes the model according to the feedback and its fuzzy knowledge base. The system user could control the tuning by updating the fuzzy knowledge base through nature language or graphical interface.

2.1 Detection Model and Prediction Engine

Different model representations have been used in detection models presented in the literature, among them rules (signatures) [1, 5], statistical model [6, 8], Petri-net [15], decision tree [16] and neural network [17]. In order to allow tuning part of model easily and precisely without affecting the rest of the model, we choose rules to represent the prediction model. In an earlier study, this model has demonstrated good performance [18]. Our model consists of a set of binary classifiers learned from the training dataset by SLIPPER [19], is a general-purpose rule-learning system based on confidence-rated boosting [20]. A weak learner is boosted to find a single weak hypothesis (an IF-THEN rule), and then the training data are re-weighted for next round of boosting. Unlike other conventional rule learners, data covered by learned rules are not removed from the training set. Such data are given lower weights in subsequent boosting rounds. All weak hypotheses from each round of boosting are compressed and simplified, and then combined into a strong hypothesis, constituting a binary classifier. Each rule starts with a predictive label, followed by two parameters used to calculate the confidence in predictions made by this rule.

In SLIPPER [19], a rule R is forced to abstain on all data records not covered by R, and predicts with the same confidence C_R on every data record x covered by R,

$$C_R = \begin{cases} \dfrac{1}{2} ln\left(\dfrac{W_+}{W_-}\right) & if\, x \in R \\ 0 & if\, x \notin R \end{cases} \qquad (1)$$

W_+ and W_- represent the total weights of the positive and negative data records, respectively, covered by rule R in the round of boosting when the rule was built in. Although the data are re-weighted for each round of boosting in training phase, the confidence value with a rule will remain unchanged once the rule has been included into the final rule set.

In SLIPPER, an objective function (Equation (6) in [19]), is used to search for a good rule with positive confidence in each round of boosting. The selected rule with positive confidence is compared with a default rule with negative confidence to determine the result of the boosting. A default rule covers all data records and thus do not have conditions. All default rules are compressed into a single final default rule.

SLIPPER can only build binary classifier. For intrusion detection, the minimal requirement is to alarm in case of intrusive activity is detected. Beyond alarms, operators expect that the IDS will report more details regarding possible attacks, at least the attack type. Usually, attacks could be grouped into four categories, denial-of-service (dos), probing (probe), remote-to-local (r2l), and user-to-root (u2r). Correspondingly, we constructed five binary classifiers from the training dataset. The prediction engine in our system consists of five binary prediction engines together with a final arbiter. We refer to this Multi-Classifier version of SLIPPER as MC-SLIPPER [18]. Each binary prediction engine generates a prediction result on the same input data and the final arbiter determines and reports the final result to the user.

The binary prediction engine is the same as the final hypothesis in SLIPPER [19], which is:

$$H(x) = sign\left(\sum_{R_t:x\in R_t} C_{R_t}\right) \qquad (2)$$

In other word, the binary prediction engine sums up the confidence values of all rules that cover the input data. A positive sum represents a positive prediction. The magnitude of the sum represents the prediction confidence in the prediction.

Obviously, conflicts may arise between the results of the different binary prediction engines. For instance, there might be more than one positive prediction on a single input data record, or there may be no positive prediction. We implemented three arbitration strategies to solve such conflicts in [18]. In our ATIDS, we selected the second arbitration strategy ("by confidence ratio"), compares the prediction confidence ratio (*PCR*), to balance the computing burden and performance:

$$i = \{ j \mid PCR_j = MAX \{ PCR_1, PCR_2 ..... PCR_n \} \} \qquad (3)$$

$PCR_j = PC_j / MAX\{ PC_j^1, PC_j^2, ..., PC_j^m \}$ where PC_j is the prediction confidence of prediction engine j on the data in test dataset while PC_j^m is the prediction confidence of prediction engine j on the mth example in its training dataset. The result i indicates the ith class representing the final result.

2.2 Basic Model Tuner

The classifier in SLIPPER is a set of rules. Only those rules that cover a data record have their contributions (Equation (2)) to the final prediction on this data record. This property ensures that if we change a rule, except for those data which satisfy the rule, the prediction on other data will not be affected. Currently, we don't change the rules (new rules can be learned using some other methods if they are necessary, such as incremental learning techniques.). We change the associated confidence to adjust the contribution of each rule for the binary prediction. Thus, our tuning ensures that if a data record is covered by some rules in the original model, then it will be covered by those exactly same rules in the tuned model and vice versa. To limit the possible side effect, we only change the associated confidences of those positive rules because a default rule covers every data record.

When a binary classifier is used to predict a new data record, there will generate two different types of false predictions according to the sum of confidences of all rules that cover a data record. When the sum is positive, the binary classifier will predict the data record to be in positive class, if this prediction is false, we call it false positive prediction and notate it as "P". When the sum is negative, the binary classifier will predict the data record to be in negative class, if this prediction is false, we call it false negative prediction and notate it as "N". We use notation "T" for true prediction, then the sequence of prediction results could be written in notation as: ...$\{P\}^l\{N\}^i\{T\}^j$... where $l > 0$, $i, j >= 0$ and $i + j > 0$. Obviously, after the classifier makes a false positive prediction, the confidences of those positive rules should be decreased to avoid the false positive prediction made by those same rules on the successive data. After the classifier makes a false negative prediction, the confidences of those positive rules should be increased to avoid the false negative predictions made by those same rules on the successive data. All rules except the default rule have positive confidences in SLIPPER. We choose to multiple a pair of values (tuning degree factor p and q) to the original confidence to adjust the confidence because the new confidence will keep positive although it might be very small when the adjustment procedure repeats many times in one direction. Formally,

$$C_R' = \begin{cases} p \cdot C_R & \text{if } R \propto P \\ q \cdot C_R & \text{if } R \propto N \end{cases} \qquad (4)$$

Where $p < 1$, $q > 1$ and R $\propto$ P implies that positive rule R contributes on the false positive prediction.

When a false positive prediction occurs on a data record, in the training viewpoint, this data is a negative data record for those rules that cover the data but misclassified as a positive data record. Therefore, we can move some weights from W_+ to W_- while keeping the sum of weights unchanged as following (the confidence is "smoothed" to avoid extreme confidence value by adding ε):

$$C_R' = \frac{1}{2} ln \left(\frac{W_+' + \varepsilon}{W_-' + \varepsilon}\right) = p \times C_R = p \times \frac{1}{2} ln \left(\frac{W_+ + \varepsilon}{W_- + \varepsilon}\right) \tag{5}$$

$$W_+' + W_-' = W_+ + W_-$$

Solve Equation (5) we get,

$$W_+' = \frac{(W_+ + \varepsilon)^p}{(W_+ + \varepsilon)^p + (W_- + \varepsilon)^p} \times (W_+ + \varepsilon + W_- + \varepsilon) - \varepsilon$$

$$W_-' = \frac{(W_- + \varepsilon)^p}{(W_+ + \varepsilon)^p + (W_- + \varepsilon)^p} \times (W_+ + \varepsilon + W_- + \varepsilon) - \varepsilon \tag{6}$$

Similarly, if a false negative prediction occurs on a data record, this data is a positive data record for those rules that cover it but misclassified as a negative data record in the training viewpoint, we can move some weights from W_- to W_+ while keeping the sum of weights unchanged.

3 Fuzzy Model Tuner

3.1 Preliminary of Fuzzy Logic

Fuzzy logic theory is a theory to deal with fuzziness [21]. There exists fuzziness everywhere in our daily life. For example, we might say, "it is a good cake." However, it depends on individuals whether the cake is actually good or not. Someone may think it is sweet enough to be a good cake, but other may think that it is too sweet to be a good cake. Fuzzy set theory is the fundament of fuzzy logic theory, which is an extension of conventional crisp set theory. Given a crisp set, say a set of students in computer science department, every student either is in this set or not depending on student's major. However, sometimes it is difficult to express a set in binary logic, for example, a set of good students B. Suppose we just use the GPA as the metric and define a characteristic function in Equation (7).

$$f_B(x) = \begin{cases} 1 & \textit{if } x.GPA \in [4.0, 5.0] \\ 0 & \textit{if } x.GPA \notin [4.0, 5.0] \end{cases} \tag{7}$$

Here we assume the maximal GPA is 5.0. Obviously, those students whose GPA is just little lower than 4.0 will complain this function. Also we will feel some guilty that we do not classify those students whose GPA is 3.99 into the set, but treat students whose GPA is 4.0 as good students. Although we can decrease the minimal GPA to make more students happy, complaints may come from some other students.

For such a case, it is better to define a fuzzy set other than a crisp set. Formally, a fuzzy set A on the universe X is defined by a membership function $M_A(x)$, where

$M_A(x)$ is a real value bounded from 0 to 1. The membership value $M_A(x)$ represents the degree of x belonging to the fuzzy set A. We can define the membership function of the fuzzy set B of good students as following:

$$M_B(x) = \begin{cases} 1 & \textit{if } x.GPA \in [4.0, 5.0] \\ x.GPA\Big/5.0 & \textit{if } x.GPA \notin [4.0, 5.0] \end{cases} \tag{8}$$

Now, all of students are happy, there are good students in some degree depending on their GPAs as long as the GPA is not equal to zero. We also feel comfortable because now it is much fair.

Fuzzy control is the first successful application of fuzzy theory where fuzzy rules are applied to control a system. Fuzzy rules are described in nature language using fuzzy sets in IF-THEN form. For example, "IF a student's GPA, x, is high (A_i) THEN the student, y, is good (B_j)", where A could be a fuzzy set with three elements {low, middle, high} on GPA, and B could be another fuzzy set with three elements {weak, fine, good} on student. The fuzzy controller can get a fuzzy output from fuzzy rules given inputs through fuzzy reason. However, if the fuzzy controller will not be like to accept the fuzzy output as an actual control signal, a defuzzifier is needed to translate the fuzzy output to actual precise control signal.

3.2   Input Variables of Fuzzy Controller

As we discussed the basic model tuner in subsection 2.2, the updating of the confidences is done after the user identified a false prediction. In this case, the tuned classifier will not be used to predict the data again when the original classifier just makes false prediction. So it depends on the subsequent data whether tuning could reduce falser predictions. Given any tuning degree factor, p and q where $p < 1$, $q > 1$, since the confidence of default rule is unchanged, trivially, there exists a number n, after updating the confidences n times continuously, the sign of the sum of confidences of all rules (positive rules and default rule) will be changed. That means the tuned classifier could make true prediction on the data that the original classifier makes false prediction on. Formally, $\exists n$, $(\{P\}^{n+1})_o => (P)_o(\{P\}^{n-1}T)_t$, $\exists m$, $(\{N\}^{m+1})_o => (N)_o(\{N\}^{m-1}T)_t$ where $(..)_o$ represents the sequence of prediction results of original classifier and $(..)_t$ stands for the sequence of prediction results of tuned classifier. Obviously, for a long sequence of subsequent false predictions, the lower p or greater q is, the smaller n and m will be, and the more false predictions the tuning could reduce. Of course, if the next data is such data that the original classifier makes true prediction, the tuning triggered by the last false prediction might be negative that the tuned classifier makes false prediction on the data, i.e., $(PT)_o => (P)_o(N)_t$, or $(NT)_o => (N)_o(P)_t$. In this case, the lower p or greater q is, the higher risk of negative tuning there exists. Unfortunately, the subsequent data are unknown future data to the model tuner. Thus it is almost impossible to work out the best p and q to reduce the false predictions as much as possible. But the prediction confidence of the false prediction is known to the model tuner. In general, if the magnitude of prediction confidence is high, p could be low or q could be high to reduce more false predictions meanwhile trying to lower the risk of negative tuning. Correspondingly, if the magnitude of prediction confidence is low, p could be high or q could be small.

In the discussion above, the tuned classifier is assumed to be available immediately to predict subsequent data. Even though the time to calculate the new confidence by computer can be ignored, the time to identify a false prediction manually by the user can't be ignored compared to the interval of coming data. If the user takes t intervals of coming data to identify the false prediction, these t subsequent data will be still predicted by the original classifier. It is possible that the original classifiers make false predictions on all of those t subsequent data. But it is also possible that the original classifiers could make true predictions on some of those t subsequent data. Obviously, if the original classifier could make true predictions on all t subsequent data, then it is not necessary to tune the classifier, or p should be high or q should be small to lower the risk of negative tuning. On the other hand, if the original classifier could make no or few true predictions on those t subsequent data, then p could be low or q could be high to reduce false predictions more. Unfortunately, it is impractical to know how many true predictions the original classifiers could made on those t subsequent data when the model tuner tunes the model, because the user just finishes verifying one false prediction. However it is easier for the prediction engine to record coverage patterns at least for data in a slide window and share those pattern records with the model tuner. A coverage pattern for an input data records whether each rule covers the data or not. Further, the rate of the coverage pattern can be calculated from those shared pattern records. In our system, the binary classifiers consist of up to 52 rules. We use a 64-bit union to save the coverage pattern for each data and map the rule number in a classifier to the bit position in the union. If a rule covers the data, then the corresponding bit in the union is set. For example, if only rule 2, 9, 20, 36, 51 in the rule set of a classifier cover a data, the coverage pattern for this data is 0x0004000800080102. If the false prediction on this data is identified, the tuner model will search 0x0004000800080102 in the shared pattern records and calculate the rate. The high rate implies that those rules are active to make false prediction together, so tuning degree factor p could be low or q could be high when tuning those rules to avoid making more false predictions. Correspondingly, if the rate is low, p could be high or q could be small to lower the risk of negative tuning.

3.3 Fuzzy Controller

Fuzzy controller applies fuzzy rules to control a system through the reasoning of rules in the fuzzy set. So the core of constructing a fuzzy controller is to define fuzzy sets and fuzzy rules, which are referred as fuzzy knowledge base. Fuzzy sets can be defined by membership functions. The membership function could be any function as long as its range is between 0 and 1, but usually they are triangular, trapezoidal or Gaussian function [22]. In our fuzzy controller, all fuzzy sets are defined by a trapezoidal membership function shown in Equation (9):

$$M(x) = \begin{cases} 0 & if \quad x \notin [X1, X4] \\ \dfrac{x - X1}{X2 - X1} & if \quad x \in [X1, X2) \\ 1 & if \quad x \in [X2, X3] \\ \dfrac{X4 - x}{X4 - X3} & if \quad x \in (X3, X4] \end{cases} \tag{9}$$

As we discussed in subsection 3.2, the two fuzzy input variables are defined as: *PC* for prediction confidence and CR for coverage rate. Four fuzzy sets "Low Confidences" (*LC*), "Average Confidences" (*AC*), "High Confidences" (*HC*) and "Extreme high Confidences" (*EC*) are defined for the input variable prediction confidence *PC* on the crisp variable *c*. Four fuzzy sets "Low Rates" (*LR*), "Average Rates" (*AR*), "High Rates" (*HR*) and "Extreme high Rates" (*ER*) are defined for the input variable coverage rate *CR* on the crisp variable *r*. Three fuzzy sets "Slight Tuning" (*ST*), "Moderate Tuning" (*MT*) and "Aggressive Tuning" (*AT*) are defined for a fuzzy output variable *TD* for tuning degree on the crisp variable *d*. As an example, the membership function for fuzzy set "High Confidence" is given in the notation as $M_{HC}(c)$ and is defined by a quad (4,6,7,9) along with Equation (9).

Since there are 16 different combinations of these two fuzzy inputs, correspondingly, total 16 fuzzy rules are defined in our fuzzy knowledge base. Some examples of fuzzy rules are shown in the following:

---

(1) If prediction confidence (*PC*) is *low* (*LC*) and coverage rate (*CR*) is *low* (*LR*), and then tuning degree (*TD*) should be *slight* (*ST*).

(2) If prediction confidence (*PC*) is *low* (*LC*) and coverage rate (*CR*) is *extreme high* (*ER*), and then tuning degree (*TD*) should be *moderate* (*MT*).

(3) If prediction confidence (*PC*) is *high* (*HC*) and coverage rate (*CR*) is *low* (*LR*), and then tuning degree (*TD*) should be *moderate* (*MT*).

(4) If prediction confidence (*PC*) is *extreme high* (*EC*) and coverage rate (*CR*) is average (*AR*), and then tuning degree (*TD*) should be *aggressive* (*AT*).

In the fuzzy reasoning procedure, the "PRODUCT-SUM" method [22] is used in our fuzzy controller. The output membership function for each rule is scaled (product) by the rule premise's degree of truth computed from the actual crisp input variables. The combined fuzzy output membership function is the sum of the output membership function from each rule.

$$M_{TD}(d) = \sum_{i=1}^{16} (\alpha_i \times M_{TD(i)}(d))$$ (10)

Where the $M_{TD(i)}(d)$ is the membership function for tuning degree in fuzzy rule *i*. For example, for fuzzy rule 1 (*i* =1), it is $M_{ST}(d)$. The α_i is the rule's premise's degree of truth, which is computed by:

$$\alpha_i = MIN (M_{PC(i)}(c), M_{CR(i)}(r))$$ (11)

Again, for fuzzy rule 1 (*i* =1), $\alpha_1 = MIN (M_{LC}(c), M_{LR}(r))$.

In our fuzzy model tuner, the fuzzy set defined by fuzzy output membership function in equation (10) should be converted into the crisp value p or q in Equation (4) to update the confidence precisely. We apply "CENTROID" defuzzification method [22] to finish this conversion, where the crisp value of the output variable is computed by finding the variable value of the center of gravity of the membership function for the fuzzy value. The center of gravity of the output membership function (the crisp value of tuning degree d) defined in Equation (10) with respect to x is computed by:

$$d = \frac{\int_0^1 x \times M_{TD}(x) \, dx}{\int_0^1 M_{TD}(x) \, dx} = \frac{\sum_{i=1}^{16} (\alpha_i \times \int_0^1 x \times M_{TD(i)}(x) \, dx)}{\sum_{i=1}^{16} (\alpha_i \times \int_0^1 M_{TD(i)}(x) \, dx)} \tag{12}$$

We set p to d and q to $1/d$ in equation (4).

4   Experiments and Results

We performed our experiments on the KDDCUP'99 ID dataset, which was built on DARPA'98 dataset prepared and managed by MIT Lincoln Labs. Lincoln Labs set up an environment to acquire nine weeks of raw TCP dump data for a local-area network (LAN) simulating a typical U.S. Air Force LAN. They operated the LAN as if it were a true Air Force environment, but peppered it with lots of different types of attacks. The raw training data was about four gigabytes of compressed binary TCP dump data from the first seven weeks of network traffic. This was processed into about five million connection records. The test data was constructed from the network traffic in the last two weeks, which yielded around two million connection records. Only 22 out of 39 types of attacks in test data were present in the training data, which reflected a dynamic changing environment with respect to the training dataset. Our MC-SLIPPER was evaluated on KDDCUP'99 ID dataset. The total misclassification cost (TMC) dropped to 72494, 70177, and 68490 with three final arbitral strategies respectively [18]. All of them are better than the KDDCUP'99 contest winner, whose TMC is 72500 [23].

To access the detection model exclusively, the prediction engine and model tuner in ATIDS were implemented in the same thread as shown below. The member variable *Type* of the object *Data* indicates whether it is the input data to be predicted or the feedback data from the user. The member variable *EnableFuzzyTuner* of the thread controls whether the fuzzy controller will be used to calculate the tuning degree for every tuning. The member function TunerModel of the object *myDetectionModel* implemented Equation (6) to update the associated weights on related rules. A verification thread was implemented to simulate the users who verify the prediction results. The goal of the verification thread is put some randomly delay before the model tuner gets the feedback on false predictions from the user. In our experiments, the random delay is limited between 0.5 and 3 minutes.

Pseudo Code for Prediction/Tuning Thread

```
LOOP
ReceiveNewData(&Data);
if ( Data.Type == input_data )
FinalResult =
        myDetectionModel.PredictData(Data);
SendPredictionResult(Data, FinalResult);
else     /* Data.Type == feedback_data */
if ( EnableFuzzyTuner == TRUE ) /*fuzzy model
tuner is enabled*/
c = Data.PredicitonConfidence;
r = GetPatternCoverageRate(Data);
d = myFuzzyController.GetOutput(c, r);
else d = 0.5;     /*fixed tuning degree, basic
model tuner, */
myDetectionModel.TuneModel(Data,d);
End
```

We report our experimental results in a similar form used in KDDCUP'99 contest [24]. The results demonstrate that the fuzzy controller in our ATIDS could improve the overall accuracy while decreasing the total misclassification cost. If we compare ATIDS with MC-SLIPPER, the basic model tuner can reduce 20% total misclassification cost, while the fuzzy model tuner can reduce 23% total misclassification cost. The burden on the user is light, and only 129 (about 0.73%) false predictions are used by the basic model tuner while only 138 false predictions are used by the fuzzy model tuner.

5 Conclusions

A fixed detection model in intrusion detection system looses the efficiency gradually as the real-time environment undergoes continuous change. In this paper, we presented our research work on how to tune an intrusion detection system. Based on our previous work on automatically tuning, we proposed and implemented a fuzzy controller to provide a powerful but yet intuitive tuning method. The tuning degree on the detection model is computed individually in a real-time fashion. The user can tune the model fuzzily but yield much appropriate tuning. Our experimental results on KDDCUP'99 ID dataset show the fuzzy model tuner works better than the basic model tuner does.

Acknowledgements

This work is supported in part by Motorola.

References

1. D. Brbara, el at., "ADAM: Detecting Intrusions by Data Mining," *Proceedings of the 2001 IEEE Workshop on Information Assurance and Security,* June 2001.
2. L. Ertoz, el at., "The MINDS - Minnesota Intrusion Detection System," *Next Generation Data Mining,* MIT Press, 2004.
3. W. Lee, and S. Stolfo, "Data Mining Approaches for Intrusion Detection," *Proceedings of the 7th USENIX Security Symposium (SECURITY'98),* January 1998.
4. W. Lee, S. Stolfo, and K. Mok, "A Data Mining Framework for Building Intrusion Detection Models," *Proceedings of the IEEE Symposium on Security and Privacy,* 1999.
5. W. Lee and S. Stolfo, "A Framework for Constructing Features and Models for Intrusion Detection Systems," *ACM Transactions on Information and System Security,* Vol. 3, No. 4, November 2000.
6. N. Ye, el at., "Statistical Process Control for Computer Intrusion Detection," *Proceedings of DARPA Information Survivability Conference and Exposition (DISCEX II),* Vol.1, June 2001.
7. N. Ye, "Multivariate Statistical Analysis of Audit Trails for Host-Based Intrusion Detection," *IEEE Transactions on Computers,* Vol. 51, No.7, July 2002.
8. N. Ye, S. Vilbert, and Q. Chen, "Computer Intrusion Detection through EWMA for Auto correlated and Uncorrelated Data," *IEEE Transactions on Reliability,* Vol. 52, Issue 1, March 2003.
9. K. Julish, "Data Mining for Intrusion Detection: A Critical Review," *IBM Research Report* (#93450), Feb. 2002.
10. I. Dubrawsky, and R. Saville, "SAFE: IDS Deployment, Tuning, and Logging in Depth," *CISCO SAFE White paper,* http://www.cisco.com/go/safe.
11. K. Lee, S. Stolfo, and P. Chan, "Real Time Data Mining-Based Intrusion Detection," *Proceedings of the DARPA Information Survivability Conference and Exposition (DISCEX II),* Anaheim, CA: June 12-14 2001.
12. E. Eskin, el at., "Adaptive Model Generation for Intrusion Detection Systems," *Proceedings of the Workshop on Intrusion Detection and Prevention, 7th ACM Conference on Computer Security,* November 2000.
13. A. Honig, el at., "Adaptive Model Generation: An Architecture for the Deployment of Data Mining-based Intrusion Detection Systems," *Data Mining for Security Application,* 2002.
14. M. Hossian, and S. Bridges, "A Framework for an Adaptive Intrusion Detection System with Data Mining," *Proceedings of the 13th annual Canadian Information Technology Security Symposium,* June 2001.
15. S. Kumar, and E. Spafford, "A Pattern Matching Model for Misuse Intrusion Detection," *Proceedings of the 17th National Computer Security Conference,* 1994.
16. X. Li, and N. Ye, "Decision Tree Classifiers for Computer Intrusion Detection," *Journal of Parallel and Distributed Computing Practices,* Vol. 4, No. 2, 2003.
17. J. Ryan, M.J. Lin, and R. Miikkulainen, "Intrusion Detection with Neural Network," *Advances in Neural Information Processing Systems,* pp. 943-949, Cambridge, MA: MIT Press, 1998.
18. Z. Yu, and J. Tsai, "A Multi-Class SLIPPER System for Intrusion Detection," *Proceedings of the 28th IEEE Annual International Computer Software and Applications Conference,* September 2004.
19. W.W. Cohen, and Y. Singer, "A Simple, Fast, and Effective Rule Learner," *Proceedings of Annual Conference of American Association for Artificial Intelligence,* 1999.

20. S. Robert, and S. Yoram, "Improved Boosting Algorithms using Confidence-rated Predictions," *Machine Learning,* Vol. 37, No. 3, pp. 297-336, 1999.
21. M. Mukaidono, *Fuzzy Logic for Beginners*, World Scientific Publishing Co., Ltd. 2001.
22. L.X. Wang, *A Course in Fuzzy Systems and Control,* Prentice Hall, 1st edition 1996.
23. B. Pfahringer, "Winning the KDD99 Classification Cup: Bagged Boosting," *ACM SIGKDD Explorations*, Vol.1, No. 2, pp.65-66.
24. C. Elkan, "Results of the KDD'99 Classifier Learning," *ACM SIGKDD Explorations*, Jan 2000.

PATROL-F - A Comprehensive Reputation-Based Trust Model with Fuzzy Subsystems

Ayman Tajeddine, Ayman Kayssi, Ali Chehab, and Hassan Artail

Department of Electrical and Computer Engineering
American University of Beirut
Beirut 1107 2020, Lebanon
{ast03, ayman, chehab, hartail}@aub.edu.lb

Abstract. In this paper, we present PATROL-F, a comprehensive model for reputation-based trust incorporating fuzzy subsystems to protect interacting hosts in distributed systems. PATROL-F is the fuzzy version of our previous model PATROL, and aims at achieving a truly unique model incorporating various concepts that are important for the calculation of reputation values and the corresponding trust decisions. Among the incorporated concepts are direct experiences and reputation values, the credibility of a host to give recommend-dations, the decay of information with time based on a dynamic decay factor, first impressions, and a hierarchy of host systems. The model also implements the concepts of similarity, popularity, activity, and cooperation among hosts. In addition, PATROL-F includes fuzzy subsystems to account for humanistic and subjective concepts such as the importance of a transaction, the decision in the uncertainty region, and setting the value of result of interaction. We present simulations of PATROL-F and show its correctness and reliability.

1 Introduction

One of the most critical issues in distributed systems is security. For an entity to interact with another, it should trust the other entity to ensure the correctness and credibility of its responses. The ideal solution to this concern is to have an environment that is fully trusted by all its entities. However, because such a solution cannot be achieved, research has focused on trust and reputation as means to secure distributed systems.

Our proposed approach requires that an entity inquires about the reputation of a target entity that it wants to interact with. It calculates a reputation value based on its previous experiences and the gathered reputation values from other entities, and then it decides whether to interact with the target or not. The initiator also evaluates the credibility of entities providing reputation values by estimating the similarity, the activity, the popularity, and the cooperation of the queried entity. Moreover, the initiator will use fuzzy subsystems to evaluate humanistic and subjective concepts such as the importance of a transaction, setting the results of interactions, and deciding whether to interact or not when the decision is not obvious. The entities use different dynamic decay factors depending on the consistency of the interaction results with other entities.

L.T. Yang et al. (Eds.): ATC 2006, LNCS 4158, pp. 205–216, 2006.
© Springer-Verlag Berlin Heidelberg 2006

The rest of the paper is organized as follows: Section 2 surveys the previous work in the area of trust and reputation using fuzzy subsystems. Section 3 presents our proposed trust model, PATROL-F, with the fuzzy subsystems. The simulation results are presented in Section 4. Section 5 shows the system overhead. Finally, Section 6 presents some conclusions and directions for future work.

2 Previous Work

In this section, we review recent work done in reputation-based trust. Several research groups have been focusing on fuzzy logic to propose effective trust models.

Ramchurn et al. develop in [1] a reputation and confidence based trust model using fuzzy logic to assess previous interactions. The two methods of evaluating trustworthiness are through confidence, which is derived from direct interactions, and reputation, which is derived from information gathered from the community. Both confidence and reputation are modeled using fuzzy sets.

Shuqin et al. propose in [2] a method for building trust and reputation based on observations and recommendations. In their model, they used fuzzy logic in order to judge issues related to trust.

Castelfranchi et al. develop in [3] and [4] a socio-cognitive trust model using fuzzy cognitive maps. Their model differentiates between internal and external attributes. In the model, trust is derived from trust beliefs, credibility, which is derived from the reliability, number, and convergence of the sources. The model considers four kinds of belief sources: direct experiences, categorization, reasoning, and reputation. Their implementation allows for changing components depending on different situations and personalities.

Rubeira et al. in [5] ascertain that trust information, which is basically how services are provided and whether they suit each host's expectation, should be subjective and dynamic because past behaviors do not infer anything about future ones. The model is implemented using Fril, a prolog-like logic programming language, which incorporates probabilistic and fuzzy uncertainty.

Song et al. in [6] propose a trust model based on fuzzy logic for securing Grid resources. The model secures the Grid by updating and propagating trust values across different sites. The fuzzy trust is incorporated into their model to reduce the vulnerability of platforms and to defend the different sites. In addition, they develop a scheduler to optimize computing power while assuring security under restricted budgets.

In another work, Song et al. in [7] propose a trust model that uses fuzzy logic inferences to handle the uncertainties and the incomplete information gathered from peers. The authors proved the robustness and effectiveness of their model, FuzzyTrust, using simulations over transaction data obtained from eBay and verified that FuzzyTrust is more effective and efficient than the EigenTrust algorithm. In addition, with FuzzyTrust, peers experience lower message overhead.

Ramchurn et al. in [8] develop a trust model based on reputation and confidence for autonomous agents in open environments. Their model uses fuzzy sets to allow agents to evaluate previous interactions and create new contacts.

In [9], Manchala describes trust metrics, variables, and models and uses fuzzy logic to verify transactions. He states that trust propagation should be used in a network of entities, and he develops protocols based on cryptography to reduce breaches.

The TRUMMAR model was developed for mobile agents, and is presented in [10]. PATROL-F is the fuzzy version of our previous model, PATROL described in [11], which itself is an extension of TRUMMAR.

3 PATROL-F

In this section, we present PATROL-F (comPrehensive reputAtion-based TRust mOdeL with Fuzzy subsystems), as an improvement over PATROL that incorporates fuzzy subsystems to set subjective concepts and perform humanistic decisions. PATROL-F is a truly unique and comprehensive model that incorporates most essential humanistic concepts to allow for trust-based decision making.

3.1 The Fuzzy Approach

Fuzzy logic is conceptually easy to understand, flexible and tolerant of imprecise data. In addition, fuzzy logic is based on natural language. In PATROL-F, there are three areas that will benefit greatly from the introduction of fuzzy logic.

First, a fuzzy subsystem is used to set the importance factor and related decisions. To decide and choose which data is critical or indispensable, or which data is needed more quickly, is a highly humanistic concept that fuzzy logic can model.

Moreover, there is the region of uncertainty where an entity is not sure whether to trust or not. In this region, the reputation value is between the thresholds of absolute trust and absolute mistrust. It is in this region where the fuzzy techniques are effectively applied.

Finally, for the result of interaction (RI) value, fuzzy logic can be used to capture the subjective and humanistic concept of a "good" or "better" and "bad" or "worse" interaction. RI becomes the result of several concepts effectively combined to produce a more representative value.

3.2 The Full Model Flow

In this section, we explain the flow of events in PATROL-F. When host X wants to interact with host Y, X will first calculate the importance of the interaction with Y using the Importance subsystem. Then, as in PATROL, X will calculate the time since its last inquiry of reputation vectors. If this time was found to be greater than a pre-defined time interval T_A, X will decide on the number of hosts to query about reputation values. This number is upper-bounded in order not to overflow the network by asking a very large number of hosts.

Afterwards, host X will query other hosts, whose cooperation value is greater than the cooperation threshold, about their reputation vectors. The queried hosts will decay their saved reputation values and send them along with their reputation vectors to host X, which will in turn, calculate the Similarity (Sim) values, the Activity (Act) values, the Popularity (Pop) values, and the Cooperation (Co) values of the queried hosts. Host X will then decay its old reputation values and incorporate all this information to calculate the reputation value of host Y. Note that if the time calculated at the beginning by X does not exceed T_A, X will directly decay its old reputation values, skipping all the steps in between.

After the reputation of Y is calculated, a choice has to be made by host X: if the reputation of Y is less than the absolute mistrust level (ϕ), Y will not be trusted and no interaction will take place; otherwise, if the reputation of Y is greater than the absolute trust level (θ), host X will trust and interact with host Y. However, if the reputation of host Y is between ϕ and θ, host X uses the Decision fuzzy subsystem to decide whether to trust host Y or not.

After the interaction takes place, in case it does, X calculates the result of interaction (*RI*), which is an indicator about how good or bad Y performed in its interaction. This *RI* value is calculated based on the third fuzzy subsystem (the RI subsystem.)

Finally, host X calculates the new decay factor (τ) for host Y based on the difference in host Y values of RIs between successive interactions.

3.3 Importance

In PATROL-F, we set a maximum limit on the number of queried hosts. As this number increases, the waiting time to collect reputation information increases and the size of the exchanged inquiries and reputation information also increases. Thus, as this threshold increases, the time of an interaction and the bandwidth consumption are affected negatively.

For every interaction, there is an importance level that specifies how critical or essential the interaction is. This concept determines other thresholds in the model as follows.

If the interaction is very critical and indispensable, the initiator host will have to spend more time to make sure that the target host it wants to interact with is trusted. Therefore, it will ask a relatively large number of hosts by inquiring about the reputation of that target, and it will be more paranoid, and will have smaller first impression (FI) values. On the other hand, when an interaction is not critical yet it is needed quickly, the host will be more trusting, and thus will increase the FI values, and decrease the number of hosts to ask about the target's reputation. This means that there is a security-time trade-off that the initiator host will have to make based on the importance of the interaction.

When the host decides to ask only a portion of the hosts, the question of which hosts to ask comes up. The initiator host in this case compares the products $B\alpha$, $C\beta$, and $D\delta$ of its neighbors, its friends, and the strangers respectively (see [10] for an explanation of these parameters.) It will then interact with the hosts with the highest products. This will allow for a dynamic hierarchy of hosts, i.e. a friend host may be more trusted to give advice than a neighbor host if it has a higher α (or β or δ) value. This way, we will account for the case when a stranger is better than a friend or a neighbor, or when a friend is better than a neighbor, without losing the initial fixed hierarchy that gives higher multiplicative factors to neighbors, then friends, and finally strangers.

The Importance concept is affected by three main factors. The first factor is the monetary value of the transaction. This factor will affect the Importance value in the following manner: When the monetary value is high, the transaction is considered to be crucial and important and thus its results should not be altered. However, when the monetary value is low, the transaction is less important from the transaction value point of view.

The second factor is the criticality of the results of the transaction. As the criticality level is raised, the results are more crucial and essential; thus less risk can be tolerated, and a higher importance factor is given to the interaction. With low criticality, on the other hand, a lower importance level is given to the transaction.

The third and final factor affecting the Importance level of a transaction is the time in which the results are needed. The total interaction time is the primary issue, and thus it will negatively affect the importance level. If the results are needed very quickly, fewer hosts can be queried about the reputation value of the target host, and thus the transaction will get a lower importance value. On the other hand, when the time is not critical and the results are not hurriedly needed, a higher importance value may be given based on the other factors.

In the fuzzy subsystem for Importance, the monetary value and the criticality of the result factors are divided into three intervals: low, medium, and high; whereas the time factor is divided into two: quickly and unhurriedly. The Importance level is divided into three levels: low, medium, and high.

3.4 The Uncertainty Region

A second fuzzy subsystem is needed for the decision of whether or not to trust in the region where the reputation value is between the absolute trust level and the absolute mistrust level. To address this issue, we introduce a fuzzy subsystem to decide when to interact or not.

In PATROL-F, if the reputation value of a target host is between the two thresholds ϕ and θ, the host can be considered as either trustworthy or not. In this so called grey region, the decision of interaction is a very subjective and humanistic one, where one host may decide to interact, while another may decide not to, based on several issues that are described below.

The fuzzy decision in the uncertainty region is affected by three factors. The first factor is the personality of the source host. As the source host becomes more trusting, it will be more biased towards interacting with the target host even if its reputation value is not that high. However, as the source host becomes more paranoid, it will tend not to interact unless it is a guaranteed good interaction and the target host is believed to have good intentions.

The second factor is the previously-defined fuzzy concept of Importance. The Importance concept will act here as a factor affecting the fuzzy trust decision. As the interaction becomes more important, i.e. the data is more critical or the monetary value is high, the decision will be biased towards not interacting before guaranteeing good results. However, as the importance of the interaction is decreased, i.e. the results are needed very quickly or the criticality and monetary value of the transaction are low, the decision will tend to be to interact without much success guarantees.

The final factor affecting the decision is the reputation value of the target host. This factor is the most important because as the reputation value approaches θ, the target host is more likely to be a good host than a host with a reputation value approaching ϕ. The decision to trust or not is therefore biased by how close the reputation value is to θ or ϕ, respectively.

These three factors combine to evaluate the fuzzy decision whether to interact or not. Notice that the personality of the host can be considered as either trusting or paranoid, while the Importance and the fuzzified reputation values are considered as high, medium, or low.

3.5 RI Calculation

The third fuzzy subsystem in PATROL-F is introduced to set the value of result of interaction (RI.) This value is also subjective: when does a host consider an interaction to be good or bad, and to what degree is it satisfactory?

The RI value is the result of interaction as perceived by the initiator host. This value indicates the degree to which the target host was good or bad in the current interaction. This degree is quite subjective, since one host may decide that an interaction is good while another may decide that it is bad. However, the decision of one host will influence the whole system, as it will affect the reputation value of the target host. Thus, a fuzzy subsystem is introduced here to unify the humanistic criteria upon which an interaction is considered good or bad, while keeping the subjective reasoning of each host.

The RI value depends on three factors. The first factor is the correctness of the result. This factor is decided by the source host after every interaction, by evaluating how correct the results are compared to its expectations. When this correctness value is high, the result is considered to be good and the RI value will tend to be high. However, when an interaction is considered to have given a bad result, a low RI value is assigned.

The second factor is the time of the interaction as compared to the expected time by the source host. If the interaction takes more time than expected, a lower RI value is given. However when the interaction time tends to be equal or smaller than the expected time, the RI value will tend to be higher.

The final factor affecting the RI value is the monetary value of the interaction. This value is the same factor that affects Importance. Interactions that have a high monetary value are considered as valuable services, and thus have a higher RI. However, when the monetary value is low, the RI value is usually lower.

Notice that the result can be considered as good or bad, the interaction time can be fast, equal, or slow as compared to the expected time, and the monetary value, as previously defined, can be high, medium, or low.

4 Experimental Results

4.1 Simulation Setup

In order to evaluate our trust model and prove its effectiveness and reliability in distributed computing, we have simulated a network of ten randomly interacting hosts (two hosts at a time) using Microsoft Visual C++. Only one interaction can occur during any one "cycle". The reputation value can range from 0 to $k = 5$, with values below $\phi = 1$ considered as bad interactions and values above $\theta = 4$ considered as good interactions. For reputation values falling in the region between ϕ and θ, the choice is based on the fuzzy Decision subsystem. Note that in Section 4.2 below (the no-fuzzy case), the trust decision is biased on how close the reputation value is to θ or ϕ. Hosts X and Y are set as bad hosts, thus giving results of interactions randomly distributed between 0 and ϕ, while all other hosts in the system are good hosts giving good results of interactions between θ and k. The constants of the simulation model are shown in Table 1.

The fuzzy subsystems for Importance, Decision, and RI were designed and implemented using the fuzzy toolbox in MATLAB, and incorporated in the C++ code.

Table 1. Constant values in the simulation

A	B	θ	ϕ	FI	ξ	a	b	c	τ_0	τ_{min}	τ_{max}
0.55	0.45	4	1	2.5	0.2	0.4	0.4	0.2	5000	1000	10000

4.2 No-Fuzzy Simulation

In order to assess the improvement introduced by the fuzzy subsystems, we simulate the network first without any fuzzy subsystem. We then introduce the fuzzy subsystems and compare the results to the "no-fuzzy" case. The top plot in Figure 1 shows that the reputation value of a good host O in host M directly increases and settles in the absolute trust region, with only one attempt considered as not trustworthy. This first attempt occurs in the region with a reputation value of 3.8, based upon which M decides probabilistically not to interact with O. In this simulation, M considers the good host O as trustworthy 34 times, and as not trustworthy only once, thus interacting with the good host O 97.14 % of the total attempts. The bottom plot in Figure 1 shows that the reputation value of a bad host X in host M decreases to the absolute mistrust region. In this simulation, M considers X as not trustworthy 35 times and does not interact with it. However, on 7 occasions, as the reputation value of host X returns to the uncertainty region, M decides to give X a chance and to interact with it. In general, host M interacts 20% of the attempts with all of the bad hosts, which are X and Y in the simulated system.

In the simulation, host M had 364 attempts to interact with other hosts. Before each interaction it queries all the other 9 hosts about reputation values, thus sending 3276 inquiries about reputation values throughout the simulation.

4.3 The Importance Effect

In this section, we study the results of adding the Importance fuzzy subsystem on the simulation results: we notice similar results to the "no-fuzzy" case. However, by introducing the Importance concept, we save in network bandwidth. In this simulation host M attempted 367 times to interact with other hosts, resulting in only 1431 inquiries about reputation values. Therefore, on average host M is asking around 4 hosts every time it attempts to interact with any other host. This indicates that with the introduction of the Importance fuzzy subsystem, we save almost 56% on the network bandwidth as compared to the "no-fuzzy" case.

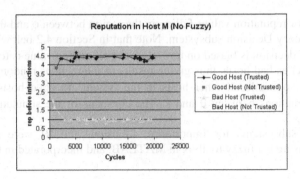

Fig. 1. Behavior of the hosts reputations

4.4 The Uncertainty Region Decision Effect

In this section, we study the effect of the Decision fuzzy subsystem. For this simulation, we have to categorize hosts as trusting or paranoid: every host is given a trusting level between 0 and 10, with 10 being most trusting and 0 being most paranoid. As for the other two inputs of the Decision subsystem, the importance value is generated randomly for every interaction (because the Importance fuzzy subsystem is disabled in this simulation), and the reputation value is calculated.

For a trusting host M, the reputation value of a good host O directly increases to settle in the absolute trust region with interaction on every attempt (33 out of 33 times). This is due to the fact that host O has always maintained a good reputation and due to the trusting nature of host M. For the bad host X, the reputation value at M decreases to the absolute mistrust region. However, due to the trusting nature of host M, M interacts 35.7% (15 out of 42) of the total attempts with host X and 27% (24 out of 87) of the attempts with bad hosts X and Y.

At the paranoid host Q, the reputation values of a good host O also directly increase to the absolute trust region. Similar to M, Q interacts with O on every attempt. This is due to the fact that host O has always maintained an excellent reputation that is considered trustworthy even for a paranoid host.

As for the bad host X, host Q decides to give X a chance only for the first time where the reputation value is 2.2 but the importance of the transaction is very low. Afterwards, even when X's reputation is in the uncertainty region, Q is too afraid to interact with it.

In this simulation, Q considers X as trustworthy only 2% of the time (1 out of 44) and considers both bad hosts X and Y as trustworthy only 2.7% of the attempts (2 out of 71). The total number of inquiries asked by hosts M and Q throughout this simulation is similar to the "no-fuzzy" case, i.e. inquiring all 9 hosts before every attempt to interact with other hosts.

4.5 The RI Calculation Effect

In this section, we study the effect of the RI fuzzy subsystem alone. For the inputs of this fuzzy subsystem, the result (correctness) is calculated after every interaction, and the other two inputs, namely the time (compared to expected time) and the monetary value are randomly generated for every interaction.

In this simulation, we notice a change in the reputation behavior of a good host O, for it increases but remains mostly in the uncertainty region. We have to take into consideration in this case the new concepts that the RI subsystem introduces. The good host O is always giving good interactions; however this will account for the result (correctness) input of the fuzzy subsystem. Since the other two inputs are randomly generated, the RI values of O are not above θ anymore. Host O is no longer considered a very good host, because it is deficient in the interaction times and in the importance of the interactions, or services, it is offering. Consequently, the reputation of host O stays in the uncertainty region most of the simulation run, and consequently, host M interacts with it only 78% (32 out of 41) of the total attempts.

For the bad host X, the reputation value of X decreases and settles in the absolute mistrust region. This result shows that the RI subsystem gives a high weight to the correctness of the result. It is enough, therefore, to produce an incorrect result to consider an interaction as being a bad one.

4.6   A Full Comprehensive Case

In this section, we show the results of the simulation with all three fuzzy subsystems incorporated. Each host has a certain degree as to how trusting it is. We randomly generate the monetary value, results, and time needed for the Importance subsystem. The inputs of the Decision subsystem are available, i.e. trusting/paranoid is a host characteristic, the Importance is taken from the first subsystem, and the reputation is calculated by the model. As for the RI subsystem, the result is calculated after every interaction and the time (with respect to expected time) is randomly generated. The monetary value has the same value as that generated for the Importance of the interaction. In addition, we restrict the hosts in the system not to query more than once every 1000 simulation cycles and not to ask hosts with a cooperation value under two. We also set host O to be an all-good host and host X as an all-bad host.

For a trusting host M, as shown in Figure 2, we notice that the reputation of an all-good host O rises directly and settles in the absolute trust region. Host M interacts with host O 100% of the attempts. As for the all-bad host X, its reputation decreases to the absolute mistrust region. Host M considers X as trustworthy only 17.5% of the attempts.

For a paranoid host Q, as shown in Figure 3, we notice that the reputation of an all-good host O increases after 5 interactions to the trust region. Q considers O as trustworthy 90% (46 out of 51) of the attempts. As for the reputation behavior of the all-bad host X, the reputation value decreases directly to the absolute mistrust region. Host Q considers X as trusted only 2% (1 out of 47) of the attempts. Note that this one trusted time, the reputation of X is 2.5 and the importance of the interaction is low.

In this simulation, we notice the really low number of inquiries sent by the hosts. In 354 attempts to interact, host M sent only 91 inquiries, that is around 0.25 hosts asked per interaction attempt. As for host Q, in 392 attempts to interact, the number of inquiries was 77, i.e. almost 0.2 hosts are asked per interaction attempt. The very low number of hosts inquired per interaction attempt does not affect the robustness of the system in generating the correct trust decision.

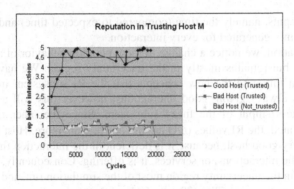

Fig. 2. Host reputations in a trusting host

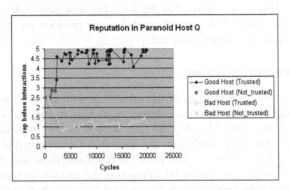

Fig. 3. Host reputations in a paranoid host

5 System Overhead

In order to estimate the communication overhead of the system, we evaluate the number of inquiries asked by all the hosts in the system, to estimate the amount of network traffic needed to exchange the reputation information.

In PATROL, each host queries all the other hosts before every attempt to interact. Each host will therefore ask 9 hosts in our simulation setup before every interaction.

In PATROL-F, on the other hand, the Importance subsystem limits the number of hosts to be queried based on the importance of the interaction. In the simulation, the three inputs of this subsystem are randomly generated per interaction, producing uniformly distributed importance values, and thus uniformly distributed number of hosts to be queried.

We repeat the simulation with different time intervals T_A and evaluate the number of hosts queried before every interaction attempt. As shown in Figure 4, with $T_A = 0$, each host asks almost 4 other hosts (44% of the other hosts) before every attempt to interact. As T_A increases, the number of hosts per attempt decreases quickly until each host is basically working alone without any queries about reputation vectors.

Each reputation vector contains the host identifier (an IP address), the reputation values, and the number of interactions with and from a host during a certain time

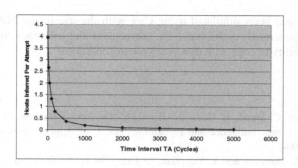

Fig. 4. Number of hosts queried per attempt

interval, summing up to nine bytes. However, with the overhead of packet headers, a total vector size of around 64 bytes is needed.

Considering that we are in a system where the interactions are of random importance, that is each host will inquire about 45% of the other hosts on average, and that every host wants to query about all the other reputation vectors every T_A seconds, which is a worst case scenario, the minimum allowed T_A for an overhead bandwidth utilization of 100 kbps and 1 Mbps are as shown in Table 2.

Table 2. Allowed T_A for a given overhead

Number of hosts	T_A (overhead =100Kbps)	T_A (overhead =1 Mbps)
10	0.21 sec	0.02 sec
20	0.88 sec	0.1 sec
50	5.6 sec	0.56 sec
100	22.8 sec	2.28 sec

The minimum T_A needed, without the fuzzy importance, decreases to less than half the values shown in Table 2, and thus the system is able to keep more up-to-date reputation information without affecting the network bandwidth. These gains change when the average importance of interactions in the network changes: if the importance of the interactions is always very high, the T_A values will remain unchanged. However, with very unimportant interactions, we will get much lower T_A values than those of Table 2.

6 Conclusion

We presented in this paper PATROL-F, a new comprehensive model for reputation-based trust incorporating fuzzy subsystems that can be used in any distributed system. The model is unique in integrating various concepts that are important to the calculation of reputation values and the corresponding decisions of whether to trust or not. PATROL-F incorporates fuzzy subsystems to account for humanistic and subjective concepts.

PATROL-F has been simulated using C++ with the use of the MATLAB Fuzzy Toolbox. The generated results prove the correctness and robustness of PATROL-F, as well as its ability to cope with dynamic system conditions.

References

1. S. Ramchurn, C. Sierra, L. Godo, N. Jennings, "Devising a trust model for multi-agent interactions using confidence and reputation," Int. J. of Applied Artificial Intelligence, 18(9-10), 2004.
2. Z. Shuqin, L. Dongxin, and Y. Yongtian, "A Fuzzy Set Based Trust and Reputation Model in P2P Networks," IDEAL 2004, LNCS 3177, pp. 211–217, 2004.
3. C. Castelfranchi, R. Falcone, and G. Pezzulo, "Trust in Information Sources as a Source for Trust: A Fuzzy Approach," AAMAS'03, July 14-18, 2003.
4. R. Falcone, G. Pezzulo, and C. Castelfranchi, "Quantifying Belief Credibility for Trust-based Decision," AAMAS'02, 2002.
5. J. Rubeira, J. Lopez, and J. Muro, "A Fuzzy Model of Reputation in Multi-Agent Systems," AGENTS'01, May 28-June 1, 2001.
6. S. Song, K. Hwang, and M. Macwan, "Fuzzy Trust Integration for Security Enforcement in Grid Computing," IFIP International Symposium on Network and Parallel Computing (NPC-2004), October 18-22, 2004.
7. S. Song, K. Hwang, R. Zhou, and Y. Kwok, "Trusted P2P Transactions with Fuzzy Reputation Aggregation," IEEE Internet Computing, Nov-Dec 2005.
8. S. Ramchurn, C. Sierra, L. Godo, and N. Jennings, "A Computational Trust Model for Multi-Agent Interactions based on Confidence and Reputation," Workshop on Trust, Privacy, Deception and Fraud in Agent Societies, AAMAS'03, 2003.
9. D. Manchala, "Trust Metrics, Models and Protocols for Electronic Commerce Transactions," Proceedings of the 18th International Conference on Distributed Computing Systems, 1998.
10. G. Derbas, A. Kayssi, H. Artail, and A. Chehab, "TRUMMAR - A Trust Model for Mobile Agent Systems Based on Reputation," ACS/IEEE International Conference on Pervasive Computing (ICPS 2004), July 19-23, 2004.
11. Ayman Tajeddine, PATROL-F – A COMPREHENSIVE REPUTATION-BASED TRUST MODEL WITH FUZZY SUBSYSTEMS, ME Thesis, American University of Beirut (AUB), Beirut, Lebanon, December 2005.

An Integration Framework for Trustworthy Transactions

Yonghwan Lee and Dugki Min[*]

School of Computer Science and Engineering, Konkuk University,
Hwayang-dong, Kwangjin-gu, Seoul, 133-701, Korea
{yhlee, dkmin}@konkuk.ac.kr

Abstract. I/O-driven integration applications, such as EAI, B2Bi, home gateways, and heterogeneous devices integration, need a trustworthy integration framework to process a large volume of I/O-driven transactions with high performance and reliability. This paper proposes an integration framework for trustworthy transactions. This framework employs a design pattern, so-called, the Worker-Linker pattern, that is used for performance stability. According to our experimental results, the pattern helps the integration framework to control the heavy load after the saturation point. Moreover, this framework supports a number of mechanisms for trustworthy integration transactions. In this paper, we describe the mechanisms.

1 Introduction

The evolution of the Internet has brought a new way for enterprises to interact with their partners. Many infrastructures and enterprise information systems have been developed to extend business and value-added services on the Internet. Since markets are rapidly changing, business collaborations tend to be dynamic and require a large volume of integrated transactions. Moreover, heavy workload makes a system unstable in a short time. Therefore, integration systems should provide flexible and trustworthy software architectures and also be afford to process a large volume of transactions stably.

A B2B integration system requires process integration for B2B collaborations [1]. In general, a protocol of B2B collaboration includes a description of message exchange formats, transport binding protocols, business processes, and so on [2, 11]. In ubiquitous environment, I/O-driven integration applications, such as EAI, B2Bi, home gateways, and heterogeneous devices integration, need a trustworthy integration framework to process a large volume of I/O-driven transactions with high performance and reliability. Patterns for efficient I/O-driven distributed applications (i.e., Connector-Acceptor, Reactor, and Proactor patterns) have been proposed to process large volume of transactions [3]. However, how to use the patterns affects the stability of performance and reliability.

In this paper, we propose an integration framework for I/O-driven applications integration. The proposed integration framework copes with a number of software

---

[*] Corresponding author. This paper was supported by Konkuk University in 2006.

L.T. Yang et al. (Eds.): ATC 2006, LNCS 4158, pp. 217–226, 2006.

architectural qualities in various aspects. For performance stability, the framework designs its I/O-related modules using a design pattern, called 'Worker-Linker', for processing a large volume of transactions. The Worker-Linker pattern is based on the Worker pattern [4] that is generally used for I/O efficiency. The Worker-Linker pattern adds a PPC (Peak Point Control) mechanism to the Worker pattern so that it can control the instability of performance caused by request congestion. For the flexibility and reusability of business integration logics, the Worker-Linker pattern implements business logics as UTL-based components and executes them by a command pattern. The UTL (Unified Transaction Language) is a XML-based language for describing data formats of transactions.

In addition to the Woker-Likner pattern for performance stability, the framework employs several other mechanisms for trustworthy integration transactions: processes-based fault tolerance and load balance, automatic process scheduling, separation of service processes from management processes, communication simulation of unavailable communication partners, and testcall checker for automatic self-detecting connection fails.

This paper is structured as follows. Related work is in the next section. Section 3 presents the overall software architecture of the proposed integration framework. Section 4 explains the design aspects of the framework. Section 5 draws a conclusion.

2   Related Works

Some B2B protocols are developed to support B2B e-commerce: ebXML [5], RosettaNet [6], and e-Service [8]. To support multiple B2B protocols, a B2B engine masters the communication between trading partners [7]. Those B2B applications mostly focus more on application level or business level and less on system level like I/O efficiency and performance stability [9].

An Acceptor-Connector pattern has been proposed for improving I/O efficiency [14]. The Acceptor-Connector pattern can be classified into a Reactor pattern and a Proactor pattern by methods of multiplicity for processing I/O events. The Reactor pattern processes events synchronously but the Proactor pattern asynchronously. Accordingly, the Proactor pattern can achieve higher performance than the Reactor pattern. However, the Proactor pattern should provide synchronization for shared resources. In asynchronous I/O, a pair of event and a reference to an event handler puts into a queue. When an event happens, the event handler processes it.

Even though the Acceptor-Connector pattern can achieve efficiency of I/O, if request congestion happens at certain points, the Acceptor-Connector pattern may have the tendency of performance instability. Performance stability is important to e-business integration and device integration or convergence in many ubiquitous environments [10]. To solve these problems in ubiquitous environments, this paper provides the Worker-Linker pattern-based integration framework for improving efficiency of I/O and stability of performance.

3 Software Architecture of Integration Framework

The proposed integration system is an integration communication middleware providing stabile and trustworthy integration transactions between source systems and target systems. The integration system has the responsibility of processing trustworthy integration transactions between source systems and target systems. It is largely comprised of the Admin Console, the System Management, the Gateway, the UTL Processor, and UTL Server. The Admin Console supports the development and management toolkits for coders and system managers. The System Management is in charge of monitoring and managing system-related resources and the Gateway has the responsibility of core functionality, such as network-related details, protocol conversion, message routing. The UTL Processor and the UTL Server is in charge of creating, caching, deploying, and executing UTL components for processing integration business logics. Figure 1 shows the software architecture of the integration system.

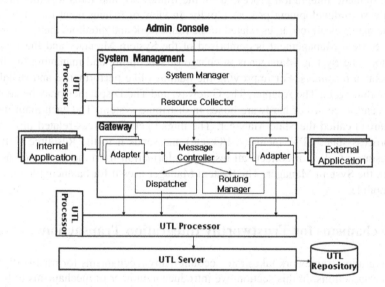

Fig. 1. Software Architecture of the Integration System

The Gateway is comprised of the Adapter, the Message Controller, the Dispatcher, and the Routing Manager. The Adapter is in charge of processing communication-related details of sources systems or target systems, such as connection, listening, and conversion of protocols. The Message Controller has the responsibility of controlling flow of messages. If the Message Controller receives messages from the source adapters or target adapters, it decides the next destination of those messages based on configurations for each task in the Admin Console. If business logics (i.e., data format transformation, data validation, etc) are configured for a specific task, the Message Controller invokes the Dispatcher to perform the business logics before or after communication with the target systems. To process business logic, the Dispatcher gets a UTL component from the UTL Processor and executes it. The UTL Processor is in charge of creating and caching UTL components. If a UTL component does not exist in the UTL Processor, the UTL Processor gets the related information for creating UTL components from the UTL Server and then creates UTL components.

An UTL is an xml-based language for defining data formats of header, request, and response block in a message. The header, request and response element defines data formats of header, request, and response block respectively. An UTL file is saved to the UTL Repository by the UTL Server. The UTL component is generated from the framework after a developer develops an UTL class according to the hook methods defined by the framework for processing business logics.

The Admin Console has a development and a management tool. In view of a development tool, the Admin Console is in charge of managing source codes and various parameters according to the concerned task unit. In other word, the Admin Console categories tasks in a tree form, provides the related source code (i.e., UTL Code) to the task, edits them, compiles them, packages them, distributes them, and tests them via a tool. Also the Admin Console manages setting information which is necessary for each task. Systematic integration processed by the framework and tools together takes the overall system development process rapidly. In view of management tool, the Admin Console manages all resources related to the framework and monitors them.

The System Management is comprised of the System Manager and the Resource Collector. The System Manager is in charge of scheduling and managing the framework-related resources. For improving the qualities like performance and scalability, main modules (i.e., The Adapter, The Gateway, and The Dispatcher) may be deployed to different processes or hardware boxes in distribute system. The each main module has a thread called the State Manager. The thread gets resources-related information (i.e., process state, CPU, memory, I/O, etc) and sends it to the Resource Collector. The Resource Collector collects all resource information from the main modules and sends to the System Manager. The System Manager uses it for balancing load of each main module.

4 Mechanisms for Trustworthy Integration Transactions

Our integration framework takes into account many mechanisms for trustworthy integration transactions. In this section, we introduce a number of mechanisms to be used for trustworthy integration transactions.

4.1 Worker-Linker Pattern for Performance Stability

To process a large volume of transactions in performance stability, the integration framework designs many I/O-related modules (i.e., the Adapter, the Message Controller, the Dispatcher, etc) by the Worker-Linker pattern proposed by this paper. Figure 2 shows a sequence diagram of the Worker-Linker pattern. The Linker is similar to the Connector of the Acceptor-Connector pattern. After the Acceptor receives messages from the Linker, it puts them a queue and wake up a waiting Worker thread. The Worker thread gets them from the queue and gets the delay time from the WorkerManager. After the Worker thread sleeps for the delay time calculated by the

WorkerManager, the Worker thread executes business logics by using a command pattern. Finally, the Worker increments the number of transactions processed by the Worker threads.

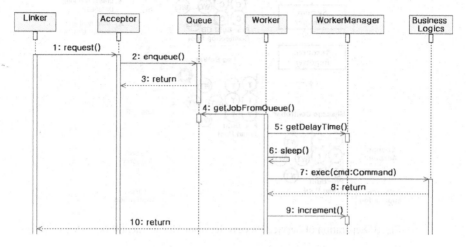

Fig. 2. Sequence Diagram of the Worker-Linker Pattern

The Worker-Linker pattern is the pattern reconstructed with existing patterns, such as the Worker, Command, and Accepter-Connector Pattern. The Worker pattern is similar to the Consumer-Producer pattern in that the Acceptor puts a message into a buffer and the Worker gets the message from the buffer. A Worker pattern is generally used for I/O efficiency. The Worker-Linker pattern adds a PPC (Peak Point Control) mechanism to the Worker pattern [14] so that it can control the instability of performance caused by request congestion. The Worker-Linker Pattern also uses UTL-based components for improving flexibility and reusability of business integration logics. To execute business integration logics, the Worker-Linker pattern uses a command pattern. In other words, UTL components are implemented as command objects. Accordingly, the integration framework can easily add new business logics by implementing just command objects.

4.2 Separation of Service Process Set from Management Process Set

To achieve reliability and high performance, the integration system separates service process set from management process set. Figure 3 shows the separation of service process set from management process set.

The service process set means the processes required for processing online transactions. The management process set means the processes for managing the integration system. In Figure 3, the integrated system may create separate management process for each management-related module, such as the System Manager, Resource Reporter, Log Dispatcher, and Log Server. Separation of service process set from management process set prevents the integration system from stopping service

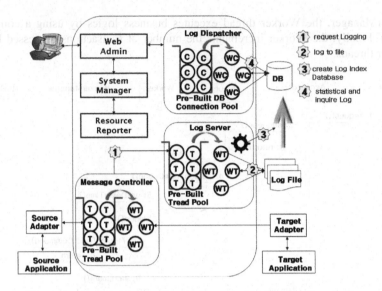

Fig. 3. Separation of Service Process Set from Management Process Set

processes due to the failure of a management process. In other words, a service process can support online transaction service regardless of the failure of a management process.

4.3 Multiple Processes-Based Fault Tolerance and Load Balance

To support large volume of transactions and session failover, the integration framework supports the following mechanisms: multi-thread, connection pooling, multiple processes based-session failover and load balance. In Figure 4, the Source Adapter

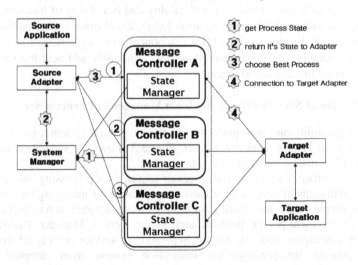

Fig. 4. Multiple Processes-Based Session Failover and Load Balance

can distribute a request to the Message Controller A, B or C by specific scheduling algorithms (i.e., Round Robin, FIFO, etc). Moreover, if the state of the Message Controller process A is fail, the Source Adapter can invoke another process B or C. All processes in the Gateway process have a thread called the State Manager. The thread gets the process-related resource information and sends them to the Resource Collector. The Resource Collector collects all resource information from all related processes and sends them to the System Manager. The Source Adapter uses them for fault tolerance and load balance.

4.4 Automatic Process Management by Scheduling Mechanism

The integration framework supports a web-based Admin Console for automatic process management by a scheduling mechanism. In view of management, the Admin Console classifies nodes and categories process in each node in a tree form, provide the statistics of all resources related with each process, stop and start the processes. In view of integration business logics, The Admin Console categories tasks in a tree form, provides the related source codes (i.e., Java code in UTL script) to the task, edits them, compiles them, packages them, distributes them, and tests them via a tool. Also the Admin Console manages setting information which is necessary for each task. Figure 5 is the steps for starting and stopping processes by a scheduling mechanism. A system manager inputs schedule information to the Admin Console and starts scheduling. Concurrently, the System Manager collects the status information of all processes. The status information of all processes is used for process management and balancing load of processes. When it is the time configured in the schedule, the System Scheduler sends start or stop request to the System Manager. The System

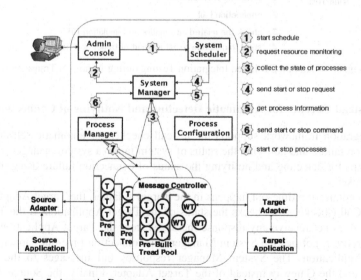

Fig. 5. Automatic Processes Management by Scheduling Mechanism

Manager gets information of processes (i.e., IP, Port, etc) from the Process Configuration and sends start or stop command to each process.

4.5 Communication Simulation for Unavailable Communication Partners

As integration systems have the characteristics of performing integration testing with other partners. The status of other partners should be considered. If some partners are not available for integration testing, the delay caused by unavailable partners may increases project risk. For this purpose, the proposed integration framework provides the communication simulation for supporting integration testing with unavailable partners. While on-line transactions are processed, the Target Adapter saves the processed data to the simulation DB for late usage. Figure 6 is the steps for performing simulation jobs. When the Target Adapter detects connection failure, it gets integration test-related data from the simulation DB and responses instead of the Target Application.

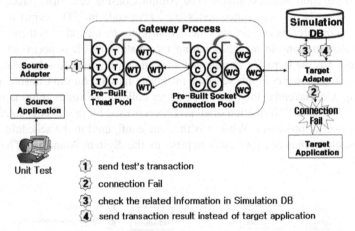

    ① send test's transaction
    ② connection Fail
    ③ check the related Information in Simulation DB
    ④ send transaction result instead of target application

Fig. 6. Simulation DB-based Integration Testing during Abnormal Transaction

4.6 Testcall Checker for Automatic Detecting and Notifying of Connection Fail

The integration framework supports the testcall checker for automatic self-detecting connection failure and notifying the status of system fail to a system manager. Figure 7 is the steps for detecting and notifying the status of connection failure using the Test-Call Checker.

When connection time-out happens in the Target Adapter, the Target Adapter calls the TestCall Checker that checks the status of the Target Application. If the TestCall Checker does not receive any response messages from the Target Application during 3 times retry, it notifies the System Manager that connection time-out happens in the Target Application. The System Manager responses fail messages to the Source Adapter and the Gateway instead of the Target Adapter. Finally, the Source Adapter sends SMS messages to a system manager.

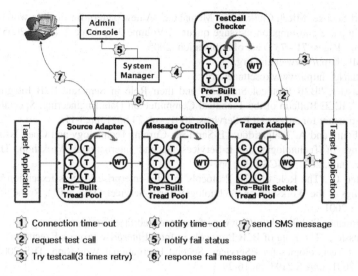

 1 Connection time-out   4 notify time-out   7 send SMS message
 2 request test call   5 notify fail status
 3 Try testcall(3 times retry)   6 response fail message

Fig. 7. Self-Detecting and Notifying Connection Fail Using Testcall Checker

5 Conclusions

I/O-driven integration applications, such as EAI, B2Bi, home gateways, and heterogeneous devices integration, need a trustworthy integration framework to process a
large volume of I/O-driven transactions with high performance and reliability. This
paper describes architecture of the integration framework and the Worker-Linker
pattern for a large volume of transactions. The Worker-Linker pattern adds PPC (Peak
Point Control) mechanism to an existing Worker pattern with I/O efficiency so that it
can control the instability of performance caused by request congestion. In addition to
the Woker-Likner pattern for performance stability, the integration framework employs several other mechanisms to achieve trustworthy integration transactions: processes-based fault tolerance and load balance, automatic process scheduling, separation
of service processes from management processes, communication simulation of unavailable communication partners, and testcall checker for automatic self-detecting
connection fails.

References

1. C. Bussler, "The Role of B2B Protocols in Inter-Enterprise Process Execution", Proceedings of Technologies for EServices, Second International Workshop, TES 2001, Rome, Italy, 2001, LNCS 2193, pp.16-29.
2. C. Bussler, "B2B Protocol Standards and their Role in Semantic B2B Integration Engines", EEE Bulletin of the Technical Committee on Data Engineering, Special Issue on
   Infrastructure for Advanced E-Services, 2001, vol. 24 no. 1, pp.3-11.
3. Douglas C. Schmidt, Michael Stal, Hans Rohert, and Frank Buschmann, Pattern-Oriented
   Software Architecture: Concurrent and Networked Objects, John Wiley and Sons, 2000.

4. Robert Steinke, Micah Clark, Elihu Mcmahon, "A new pattern for flexible worker threads with in-place consumption message queues", Volume 39 , Issue 2 (April 2005) table of contents Pages: 71 - 73 Year of Publication: 2005.
5. ebXML. http://www.ebxml.org.
6. RosettaNet. http://www.rosettanet.org.
7. C. Bussler, "B2B Protocol Standards and their Role in Semantic B2B Integration Engines", IEEE Bulletin of the Technical Committee on Data Engineering, Special Issue on Infrastructure for Advanced E-Services, 2001, vol. 24 no. 1, pp.3-11.
8. T. Pilioura and A. Tsalgatidou, "E-Services: Current Technology and Open Issues", Proceedings of Technologies for E-Services, Second International Workshop, TES 2001, Rome, Italy, 2001, LNCS 2193, pp1-15.
9. Bussler, C, "The Role of B2B Protocols in Inter-enterprise Process Execution", In: Proceedings of the Workshop on Technologies for E-Services (TES 2001), Rome, Italy, September 2001.
10. Performance Stability. http://www.performance-stability.com/
11. C. Bussler, "The Role of B2B Protocols in Inter-Enterprise Process Execution", Proceedings of Technologies for EServices, Second International Workshop, TES 2001, Rome, Italy, 2001, LNCS 2193, pp.16-29.
12. Mercury RoadRunner. http://www.mercury.com/us/products/performance-center/ loadrunner/
13. SNA. http://www.cisco.com/univercd/cc/td/doc/cisintwk/ito_doc/ibmsna.htm
14. Doug Lea, Concurrent Programming in Java, Second Edition, Addison-Wesley, November, 1999.

Daonity: An Experience on Enhancing Grid Security by Trusted Computing Technology*

Fei Yan[1], Weizhong Qiang[2], Zhidong Shen[1], Chunrun Chen[2], Huanguo Zhang[1], and Deqing Zou[2]

[1] Computer School,Wuhan University, Wuhan 430072, China
yfpostbox@yahoo.com.cn
[2] College of Computer Science and Technology, Huazhong University of Science and Technology, Wuhan 430074, China

Abstract. A critical problem for grid security is how to gain secure solution for Grid virtual organization (VO). In Grid practice at present, issues of VO security rely on non-distributed policy management and related PKI mechanism. A practical but difficult solution is to enforce fine granularity policy over distributed sites. The emerging Trusted Computing (TC) technologies offer great potential to improve this situation. In our Project Daonity, Trusted Platform Module (TPM), as a tamper-resistance module, is shared as a strong secure resource among platforms of grid users. Based on the sharing mechanism, a TC-enabled architecture is proposed to improve Grid Security Infrastructure, especially authorization protection and single sign on are enhanced to demonstrate how to gain enhanced and distributed security in grid environment.

1 Introduction

As an information infrastructure, Grid Computing aims at aggregating ensembles of shared, heterogeneous, and distributed resources (potentially controlled by separate organizations), such as high-performance computer and storage devices, to provide transparent computational "power" to applications.

Grid security is an important component in Grid computing. The current Grid security solution, Grid Security Infrastructure (GSI)[1] for Globus Toolkit (GT), offers comprehensive security services by applying PKI technology. Although GSI has provides security services for distributed computing, there is much room to improve GSI on security of VO.

Trusted computing is a new trend in security fields, which is a further development for current security requirements. Because of tamper-resistance property, trusted hardware can be applied in grid computing environment, which can confine the users including the owner of a computing platform to act as expected behavior, for the software systems running on the platform.

* Sponsored by HP Labs China, supported by the National Natural Science Foundations of China under Grant No.60373087, 60473023, 60503040 and 90104005, and supported by the Open Foundation of Key Laboratory of Computer Networks and Information Security (Xidian University), Ministry of Education.

L.T. Yang et al. (Eds.): ATC 2006, LNCS 4158, pp. 227–235, 2006.

In this paper, we describe the architecture for Daonity and identify its functional components. Project Daonity is a research project managed by Trusted Computing Research Group (TC-RG), a charter of the SEC Standard Area of Global Grid Forum (GGF). A non-trivial result from the Daonity team's investigation is that, a TPM, even sparsely deployed, can be a shared security resource to enable strong and advanced Grid security mechanism. Therefore, with TPM as a shared resource, we have been conducting a system development work to design and implement a TC-enabled GSI system. Our current goal in this paper is to explain our TPM-enhanced security.

The rest of paper presents details of our Project Daonity. Section 2 presents key technologies used to in design of Daonity and reviews security requirements in grid computing. Section 3 describes Daonity's architecture. Then we detail the implementation of our goal in Section 4. In Section 5 we discuss the security analysis and performance of our design. Finally, we present future work.

2   Background

Daonity provides a TPM-enhanced grid security. Given an available TPM, following unified global policies; a secure authorization would be implemented on different sites in Daonity. Also based on a remote TPM, Daonity will create a shared secure context on non-TC platform for single sign on. To implements these goals, we modify GSI and employ a trusted middleware following TSS specification.

2.1   Trusted Computing Technology

In recent years, increased reliance on computer security and the unfortunate fact of lack of it, particularly in the open-architecture computing platforms, have motivated many efforts made by the computing industry, especially the Trusted Computing Platform Alliance (TCPA, now is Trusted Computing Group, TCG) and many other related researches [3,4,5,6,7]. The motivation of TCG to add trust to open-architecture computing platforms is to integrate to a computer platform a hardware module called Trusted Platform Module (TPM) with tamper protection property and let it play the role of an in-platform trusted third party agent. Their main concept comes from TCB [2]. Difference from TCB, it is intended that such an agent can function to enforce a conformed behavior for software systems running on the platform and the users using the platform. Under the tamper-protection assumption which is likely to hold and in fact practically achievable using various cost-effective hardware design and implementation techniques, a software system or a user, including one which is under the full control of the platform owner (such as a root user in Unix or Administrator in Windows), cannot bypass security policy set by the TPM. This is the so-called *behavior conformation* [12] property of the TC technology.

Following above approaches, TCG have proposed some technical specifications to design TPM [9,10,11]. And a software middleware specification has been also proposed name TCG Software Stack [17].

Inside TPM, in order to guarantee behavior conformation, a realistic method - "integrity check", is proposed. There is a measurable component called Platform Configuration Register (PCR), through which Daonity has accomplished goals.

2.2 GSI and Grid Security Requirements

Similar to security services for distributed computing systems, important security services, which GSI requires [18], includes entity authentication and user authorization.

For entity authentication , GSI includes X.509 certificates for identifying through creating temporary certificates, called a *proxy certificates*, which includes public key and private key for performing single sign-on and delegation.

For authorization, the client delegates its certificates to the resource through MyProxy [13] online servers to enable subsequent resource access without further intervention. By making use of the "Gridmap" file, a presented certificate named Grid DN is associated with a local user account. But this mechanism can not scale to the case where remote administrators need to control access to local resources. A optional solution is Community Authorization Service (CAS) [20]. Since CAS server controls the privileges directly, and with the enlarging of virtual organization's size, the cost of administration will be severe.

The third requirement is security for VO. When sharing resource for a VO, some flexible and ad hoc security policies would be defined for entities. It is desirable that each of entities has strong security means, which can enforce them in the execution of the policy.

For example, a policy is that a resource can become usable by a user only after the user has done some donations. However, in the current GSI practice, security means that a user, who owned cryptographic certificates, has an exclusive entitlement to some resource. Without behavior conformation, it is very difficult for the VO to apply fine granularity control on VO policies.

In [14], M. Lorch et al have proposed an enhanced a credential repository for Grid PKI secured by secure hardware. In [15], J. Marchesini et al have provided a solution named SHEMP, in which cryptographic operations in MyProxy is secured by IBM4758 and credentials in clients have been protected by secure hardware. In [16], a PorKI for PKI's mobility have been proposed by S. Sinclair et al. J. Marchesini et al have done some experiments on boot loader with TPM in [19]. Compared with Daonity, most of researches related with Grid and trusted hardware focus on PKI problem. From Grid standpoint, Daonity has promoted a novel solution for VO security.

3 Daonity Architecture

Project Daonity attempts to solve the Grid security problem we discussed in Section 2 by making use of the behavior conformation security service from the TCG technology. In the first phase of the project we shall only consider to develop a simple middleware systems to use TPM. It is an attempt to treat

TPM as a strong secure mechanism. The detail of our current phase system design (nonofficial) can be found in [8].

Figure 1 depicts the architecture of Daonity, which is a Grid security infrastructure enhanced by the TC technology. The work of Daonity focuses on the gray components in the figure. We notice that because all the work, which is involved in Daonity, is below the GSS API, therefore, Grid applications in the legacy system can run in Daonity without modification.

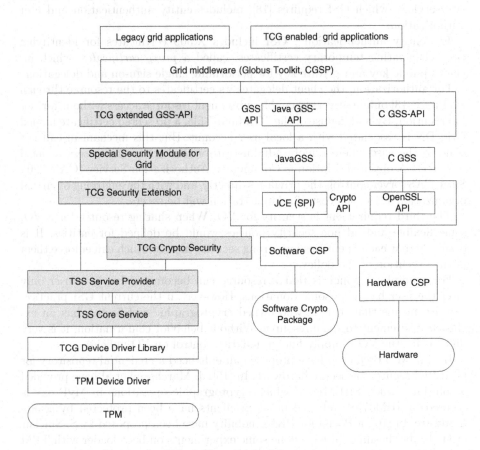

Fig. 1. Daonity Architecture

The work of Daonity can be roughly and vertically divided into two parts: the GSI related and the TSS (TCG Software Stack) related. TSS is a TCG component providing the system developer with a standard means to interact with the TPM hardware and utilize the cryptographic function in the TPM. The work in the GSI related part is to enhance the original GSI functions. The original GSI gets cryptographic services by calling standard Crypto API (SPI in Java, OpenSSL Crypto API in C). Cryptographic service providers (CSP) are the code implementations of crypto algorithms, which can be in either software (running in the general CPU) or hardware (running in, e.g., a smartcard or a USB token). With the same idea, which TCG adopts, CSPs can be implemented in the TPM (with Crypto API calling the TCG Crypto Security Services). The "Special Security Module for Grid" in current Daonity includes authorization protection and TPM shared single sign on.

4   Implementation

In Section 4, we propose the architecture of Daonity. Our goal is to construct a strong secure mechanism to enhance grid security, in which we implement an authorization protection and TPM-shared single sign on.

4.1   Local Policy Enforcement Case: Authorization Protection by TC

Grid service that relates to sensitive resource must be managed correctly. The local authorization over a Globus platform is controlled by the super user of the system. Usually system privileged users have far greater privileges than global grid administrator making local site administrators reluctant to grant such privileges to grid administrators outside their local domain. It is therefore necessary to provide a fine-grain access control for the Grid Map file. In Daonity, the Grid Map-file protection module utilizes the functions provided by PCR in TPM. Figure 2 describes the modules of authorization protection.

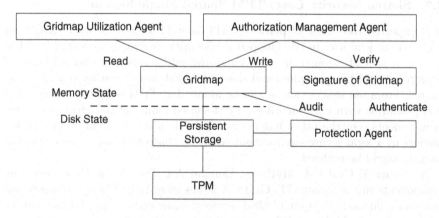

Fig. 2. Gridmap Protection

In Daonity only permits grid administrator who holding proper certificates managing authorization. On one hand, local administrator's authorization privilege delivers back to remote grid administrator. On the other hand, remote grid administrator's behavior is restricted within an audited limit.So only two types entities' behavior is confined. One is authorization administrator and another is authorization requestor. Authorization administrator takes charge of authorization managements while authorization requestor concerns only about the availability of Gridmap file. Because only authorization administrator owing the secret can request TPM to decrypt Gridmap file by proper key, it can resist tampering from a user owning root-privilege. The behavior of two types user is described in Figure 3.

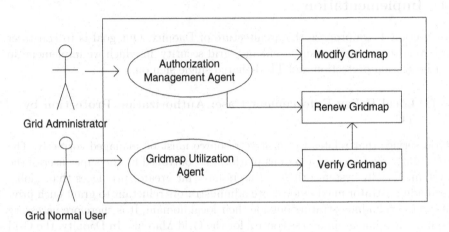

Fig. 3. Behavior of Grid Users

4.2 Shared Security Case: TPM-Shared Single Sign on

It is expected that most of platforms will have TPM, but Daonity should not require each grid user to be equipped so. Security provision supported by TPM acts as a special resource in grid. Following grid's concepts that all kinds of resource should be aggregated and shared for grid users, security is also can be shared. From our description, it can be found that TPM is shared among users and platforms with legal identities. TPM-shared mode satisfies grid-computing requirements. On the other hand, since TPM is a strong security means; behaviors in a legal secure environment could be controlled more easily thus fair sharing would be realized.

In Figure 4, Grid CA, MyProxy, Domain AA, Portal and User Client are components in the legacy GT. Grid CA issues identity certificates of users and resources. Portal is the gate of Grid services; many operations of a user can be performed on it. MyProxy helps users to manage short-lived proxy certificates. Domain AA provides user policy attribute before user access resource.

The domain has two kinds of grid nodes. Client A has not TPM, Client B has TPM. When user Alice is performing on Client A, he may select Client B to act as a proxy agent for her. The proxy agent in Client B is a daemon process for anyone in the same domain, which is upon the TCG software stack. The agent contacts with the Grid portal while User want to submit a job from the Grid portal. After several authentication and authorization, client A would construct

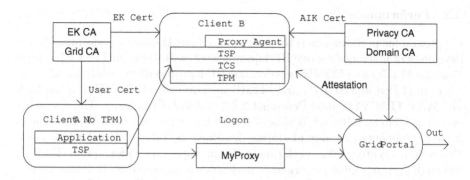

Fig. 4. TPM-shared Single Sign On

a secure context. There are three new components to be added to TCG-enabled GSI. They are: (1) EK (Endorsement key) CA, (2) Privacy CA, and (3) Proxy Agent. (1) And (2) are components from TCG. (3) is our add-on for Daonity.

5 Discussion

Current prototype of Daonity is under the process of writing codes. We have complete system design and detailed design of Daonity. And system design has delivered to GGF 16 in Feb.2006, which can be found in [8]. We have been following the stipulation of the TC-RG Charter and Milestones, and have been conducting a system development work to implement a TCG enabled GSI system before GGF17 in May 2006.

Although our prototype doesn't complete, we still should discuss some about Daonity.

5.1 Security

As we discuss above, the goal of Daonity is to demonstrate that security also can be shared as a strong security means in grid computing. We design two cases: TPM-shared SSO and Authorization Protection to show how security is shared.

We have a premise that TPM is a tamper protection module. In TC platform, not super-privilege users of Operating System but TPM users who hold secrete shared with TPM can access its special resource. Daonity will decrease the risk of private key disclosure in a number of ways.

Each legal TPM in Daonity should have an endorsement certificate. This certificate is related with the root of trust in TPM. In TPM, this root of trust is Storage Root Key (SRK), which will never be exported out of TPM. We call this process *seal*. An authorization solution is provided by endorsement certificate, which can identify platform uniquely.

By using TPM as a strong security mechanism, we can define a behavior set that user should obey. Measurement through PCRs can judge user's behavior normal or anomaly. Thus we can enforce a fine granularity policy in platform.

5.2   Performance

Cryptographic performance is the bottleneck of our Daonity's performance. Our development machines are one HP laptop nc6000 with Infineon TPM V1.1, Intel Pentium M 1.7G and 512MB memory; one HP laptop nc6230 with Infineon TPM V1.1, Intel Pentium M 1.7G and 512MB memory; one JETWAY desktop with JETWAY TPM V1.0, Intel Pentium4 2.4G and 512MB memory. The operating system is Ubuntu 5.10 and RedFlag 7.0 with Linux kernel 2.6.15. We have made some experiments over our platforms described as Table 1. For Authorization Protection, cryptographic performance is an important index. From Table 1, although cryptographic performance is slowdown compared with common algorithm in PC, we still think its performance is practical for our development. The reason is that the protected objects in TPM are all small data, such as key pairs, hash values and etc. Thus the system based on Daonity is operational.

Table 1. Cryptographic Performance of Daonity

Test Items	HP laptop nc6000	JETWAY desktop
RSA Key Generation	30 Pairs per min.	25 Pairs per min.
Random Number Generation	400Bps	20Bps
Encryption (Asymmetric)	44.8Bps	40.8Bps
Decryption (Asymmetric)	16Bps	35.8Bps
Reading PCR	500Bps	320Bps
Writing PCR	240Bps	160Bps

Another factor of performance is the protocol. In our current phase, we implement our TPM-shared Mode Security over TCP layer. For secure communication, we just choose 3-DES to encrypt our packets. From Section 5, our protocol will accomplish in a constant complexity. So in current Daonity, network performance is not a serious problem. In further phase of Daonity, we will consider protocol security as provable security, which means we will meet more complex protocols.

6   Conclusion

We have discussed the system design of Daonity. To satisfy grid security requirements, Daonity implements a security mechanism by TC technology. Through sharing TPM as a strong security means, we have illustrated a TPM-shared single sign on and authorization protection by TC technology. We have been implementing Daonity and would continue our project in the next few years.

As we have discussed in above sections, Daonity needs to be improved in many aspects, such as how to design a high performance secure provable TPM-share protocols, how to design a group secure communication by sharing TPM, and how to design and implement general policy enforcement solutions in platforms.

References

1. Foster, I., et al.: A Security Architecture for Computational Grids. In 5th ACM Conference on Computer and Communications Security. 1998.
2. Department of Defense, Department of Defense Trusted Computer System Evaluation Criteria. DoD 5200.28-STD, December 1985.
3. J. Dyer, M. Lindemann, R. Perez, R. Sailer, S.W. Smith, L.van Doorn, and S. Weingart. Building the IBM 4758 Secure Coprocessor. IEEE Computer, 34:57-66, October 2001.
4. G. Suh, D. Clarke, B. Gassend, M. van Dijk, and S. Devadas. AEGIS: Architecture for Tamper-Evident and Tamper-Resistant processing. In Proceedings of the 17Int'l Conference on Supercomputing, pages 160-171,2003.
5. S.W. Smith. Outbound Authentication for Programmable Secure Coprocessors. International Journal on information Security, 2004.
6. S.W. Smith and S. Weingart. Building a High-Performance, Programmable Secure Coprocessor. Computer Networks, 31:831-860, April 1999.
7. LaGrande Technology Architectural Overview. http://www.intel.com/technology/security/, Sept. 2003.
8. Wenbo Mao, et al. Daonity Specifications Part I Design. https://forge.gridforum.org/projects/tc-rg/, Feb. 2006.
9. TPM Main, Part 1, Design Principles, Specification Version 1.2, Revision 85, Trusted Computing Group, 13 February 2005.
10. TPM Main, Part 2, TPM Structures, Specification Version 1.2, Level 2 Revision 85, Trusted Computing Group, 13 February 2005.
11. TPM Main, Part 3, Commands, Specification Version 1.2, Level 2 Revision 85, Trusted Computing Group, 13 February 2005.
12. TCG Specification, Architecture Overview, Specifications Revision 1.2, 28 April 2004.
13. J. Novotny, S. Tueke, and V. Welch. An Online Credential Repository for the Grid: MyProxy. In Proceedings of the Tenth International Symposium on High Performance Distributed Computing (HPDC-10). IEEE Press, August 2001.
14. M. Lorch, J. Basney, and D. Kafura. A Hardware-secured Credential Repository for Grid PKIs. In 4th IEEE/ACM International Symposium on Cluster Computing and the Grid, April 2004.
15. J. Marchesini, S.W. Smith. SHEMP: Secure Hardware Enhanced MyProxy. In Proceedings of Third Annual Conference on Privacy, Security and Trust. October 2005.
16. S. Sinclair, S. W. Smith. PorKI: Making User PKI Safe on Machines of Heterogeneous Trustworthiness. 21st Annual Computer Security Applications Conference. IEEE Computer Society. December 2005.
17. TCG Software Stack Specification Version 1.1, Trusted Computing Group, August 20, 2003.
18. M. Humphrey, M. Thompson, K. R. Jackson. Security for Grids In Proceedings of the IEEE (Special Issue on Grid Computing), Vol.93, No.3, March 2005.
19. J. Marchesini, S.W. Smith, O. Wild, and R. MacDonald. Experimenting with TCPA/TCG Hardware, Or: How I Learned to Stop Worrying and Love The Bear. Technical Report TR2003-476, Department of Computer Science, Dartmouth College, 2003.
20. L. Pearlman, V. Welch, I. Foster, C. Kesselman, and S. Tuecke, A Community Authorization Service for Group Collaboration, In Proceedings of IEEE 3rd Int. Workshop on Policies for Distributed Systems and Networks, 2002.

Toward Trust Management in Autonomic and Coordination Applications

Yuan Wang, Feng Xu, Ye Tao, Chun Cao, and Jian Lü

State Key Laboratory for Novel Software Technology,
Nanjing University, Nanjing 210093, China
{wangyuan, xf, yt, caochun, lj}@ics.nju.edu.cn

Abstract. Trust management is an efficient approach to ensure the security and reliability in the autonomic and coordination systems. Various trust management systems are proposed from different viewpoints. However, evaluating different trust management approaches is usually more intuitive than formal. This paper presents a role-based formal framework to specify trust management systems. By quantifying two types of trust commonly occurring in the existing trust management systems, the framework proposes a set of elements to express the assertions and recommendation relationships in trust management. Furthermore, some facilities are provided to specify the semantics of trust engines. The framework makes it more convenient to understand, compare, analyze and design trust management systems.

1 Introduction

Trust management (TM) is an efficient approach to ensure the security and reliability in the autonomic and coordination applications, of which the behind idea is to consider the trustworthiness of the cooperators. Trust engines (TE) are the most important components of TM systems. Currently two types of trust evaluation mechanisms exist in TM: credential-based mechanisms (CBM) and reputation-based mechanisms (RBM) [1]. The typical TM systems with CBMs, such as Policymaker [2], Keynote [3], Taos [4], RT [5], and dRBAC [6], do authorizations by reducing credentials based on the deductive logic. While the TM systems with RBMs do authorization by applying principals' reputations as the bases for trust [7,8,9,10]. The RBMs are usually used in systems that involve interactions between distrusting principals, such as the Internet auction site eBay, taobao and various p2p systems.

The CBMs are precise but too strict to suit the open collaborative environments, while the RBMs are more flexible but less precise to suit the situations needing precision rather than flexibility. Consequently, the CBMs and RBMs should be combined to support some particular applications. However, evaluating CBM and RBM is usually more intuitive than systematic or formal. So far, no unified frameworks can be found to specify both kinds of the TM systems. So we need a unified approach to do it. The paper presents a unified framework in 3 steps: (1) Analyzing the information evidence among principals and providing *rich-assertion*s to describe the 2 main evidence: credentials and reputations; (2) providing *assertion-filter-rule*s to reflect the trust in intentions; (3) providing facilities to specify the semantics of TEs. The rest of

L.T. Yang et al. (Eds.): ATC 2006, LNCS 4158, pp. 236–245, 2006.
© Springer-Verlag Berlin Heidelberg 2006

the paper is organized as follows: Section 2 analyzes the evidence in TM systems. Section 3 defines the framework in detail. Section 4 applies the framework to specify three typical TM systems or models to show its abilities. Section 5 analyzes the differences between the two kinds of trust evaluation mechanisms. Finally, we analyze the related work and draw the conclusions.

2 Credentials V.S. Reputations

The credentials and reputations are both kinds of evidence to reflect trust relationships in TM process. They both imply the *beliefs* and the *intentions*.

- *Beliefs*. *Beliefs* are implied when *a* believes *b* is trustworthy in the given contexts. The degree of the *beliefs* in credentials are binary (positive or negative), e.g. "*a* believes that *b* can (not) call service *S*", while the degree of *beliefs* in recommendations are usually expressed by partial order sets [7~10], e.g., "*A*'s reputation of calling service *S* is *v*", where *v* reflects the trust degree. In general, the reputations are collected from multiple entities and combined through some formulas.

- *Intentions*. *Intentions* are implied when *a* is willing to depend on *b*'s belief. One instance of *intentions* in RBM is recommendation relationships between the entities and their recommenders. In CBMs, a principal's *belief* will depend on others' *beliefs*, which is called the delegations. The delegation specifies the trust between the credential issuer and the receiver: The receivers are willing to depend on the credentials that imply the issuers' *beliefs*. The issuers specified by delegations can be viewed as the trusted third parties [2].

The *Beliefs* and *intentions* disclose the two levels of trust. 1) *Trust in beliefs* (TB). TB applies the degree that trusters believe the trustees have particular abilities. In credentials [2,3,6], the TB is binary. While in reputation, the TB is rated. TB can be qualified in [0,1]. The binary TB can be represented by the value 1 or 0, while the rated trust can be represented by arithmetical progression sequences in [0,1]. 2) *Trust in Intentions* (TI). TI suggests the degree that trusters will depend on the trustees' *beliefs*. Typical TIs are recommendation trust relationships (in RBM) and delegations (in CBM). The TI can also be represented by values in [0,1].

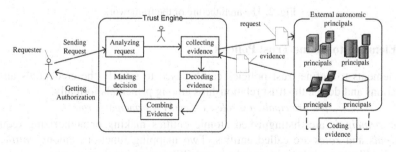

Fig. 1. The processes of trust management

3 The Unified Role Based Framework

To simplify the expression, we think of the standard deployment of a TM system as consisting of a TE coupled together as part of a principal. Fig.1 shows the profile of TM processes including 5 phases: analyzing request, collecting evidence, decoding evidence, combining evidence and making decisions, which should be performed in sequence. Our framework puts focus on providing approaches to express requests, evidence and decisions and specify the behavior of TEs formally in a unified way.

3.1 The Architecture of the Framework

The framework is constructed on the Role Based Access Control (RBAC) model [5,11] suitable for the collaborative environment. The framework applies the roles to express the trust in different context: the assignment of a role to a principal suggests that the assigner trust the principal is able to do the given job in the context relevant with the role. In Fig.2, the framework is divided into two parts: the part under the dotted line shows the elements used to define the trust policies that express evidence and imply the trust relationships among the principals. And the above part shows the facilities to perform trust-related operations, which specify the semantics of TEs. The arrows show the dependences among these elements. *Auth*s are applied to express the authorization statements. The *rich-assertions* and the *assertion-filter-rules* can specify the two kinds of trust (TI and TB) mentioned above. F_C contains the functions that the TEs will invoke in sequence (from bottom to top) to enforce the policies. F_{Engine} consists of F_C and $\leq$ on *Auth*s, expressing the semantics of TEs.

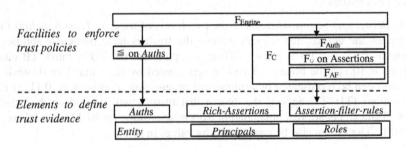

Fig. 2. The architecture of the framework

3.2 Elements to Define Trust Policies

The elements to define trust policies can be used to specify the credentials and the reputations and define the trust relationships among principals formally.

$$p \in principal \,, \; r \in role \,, \; e \in entity = principal \cup role$$

The *principals* are distinguished atomic entities making or authorizing requests. *Principal*s and *role*s are called entities. Two mapping functions among *entities* are defined: *MS* maps a role to its members and *OS* maps a role to its owner.

MS∈Membership	:	Role→ ρ (Principal)	(1)
OS∈Ownership	:	Role→ Principal	(2)

> **Definition** ($\oplus$) $r, r1, r2 \in Role$; $r_1 \leqq r$, $r_2 \leqq r$; when r_1 and r_2 are not exclusive, $\forall r' \in Role$ $r_1 \leqq r'$, $r_2 \leqq r'$, we have $r \leqq r'$. We said r is the least upper bound of r_1 and r_2, $r = \oplus (r_1, r_2)$.

The exclusion of r_1 and r_2 is defined in [5]. We define the " $\leqq$ " relationship as containment which means that if $r_i \leqq r$, and if $p \in MS(r)$, then $p \in MS(r_i)$, where $p \in$ *principal*. The containment of roles implies a containment of permissions. The containing roles always have more permissions than the contained ones. With $\oplus$ and $\leqq$, the set of roles forms a lattice. The *MS*, *OS* and $\oplus$ are all helpful to specify the semantics of actual TEs, which will be explained in section 4.

The *Auth* is a relation between entities and roles to express statements such as "who can do what", which are useful to express the trust statements.

$$a \in Auth : entity \rightarrow role$$

> **Definition** ($\leqslant$ on *auths*) two *auths* a $= e \rightarrow$ r1, a' $= e \rightarrow$ r2, if r1 $\leqslant$ r2 , then a $\leqslant$ a'.

An *Auth* $e \rightarrow r$ means that e can act as the member of role r when e is a principal; when e is a role, it means that the members of e can act as the member of r, which suggests that r is contained by e. We call e the object and r the subject. *Auths* with the same objects can be ordered by $\leqq$ on *auths* and form a lattice based on the role lattice. *Auths* are transferable, reflexive and anti symmetrical.

The *rich-assertions* (RA) can express the *beliefs* that "who *believes* an *auth*". A *RA* made by the trusted third party is an *authorization*. The *RAs* are defined as triples of *principals*, *auths* and *attribute lists* (AL). Credentials, recommendations and reputations can be expressed through it.

$$ra \in Rich - Assertion : principal \times Auth \times attrList$$

A *RA* $<p, a, al>$ means that the principal p believes a; p is the issuer of the *rich-assertions* and al is the AL. The *AL* can be used to express some extra properties important for assertions (e.g. certainties of the statements [10] and valued attributes [6]). The *AL* is composed of *expressions*.

> **<Expression>**::= <Atom expression> | "("<Expression>")" |
>   <Expression>"||" <Expression> | <Expression>"&" <Expression>;
> **<Atom expression>**::= <attribute> <cp><value>; **<cp>**= "<" | ">" | "=" ;

To express TB, an attribute *certainty* is introduced into the AL of the *rich-assertions*. With the *certainty* attribute, the *RAs* can specify credentials, reputations and recommendations. e.g. A *RA* $<p, p' \rightarrow r, ceartainty = x>$, means p said p' can act as a member of r with the certainty x, $x \in [0,1]$. In RBMs, if p is a recommender, *ra* represents a piece of recommendation information; if p is an authorizing principal or unknown entity, *ra* can be viewed as a reputation. While in CBMs, x should be always 1 and *ra* is a credential with p as the issuer. *Rich-assertions* can be ordered according to the relating *Auths* and *certainties*.

> **Definition** (*RAs* order $\leq$) for *RAs* ra=<p, auth, certainty=x>, ra'=<q, auth', certainty=x'>, if $(auth \leq auth') \wedge (x \leq x')$ ', then $ra \leq ra'$

Assertion-filter-rules (*AFR*) are used to specify recommendation relationship and delegations implying the TI. In CBMs, the principal should only trust the credentials whose issuers are specified by the delegation. While in RBMs, a principal will accept recommendations according to its TI on the recommenders. The specified issuers and the recommenders can both be viewed as the trusted third parties that can be specified by the *AFRs* for the particular principals in TM. *AFRs* are applied to assure that *p* will depend on the *belief of p'* according to its TI on *p'*.

$$afr \in Assertion - Filter - Rule : principal \times SR \times ContextSet ,$$

$$sr \in SR : \rho(principal \to tv), tv \in [0,1] , \quad cs \in ContextSet : \rho(Role)$$

An *AFR* <*ap*, *sr*, *cs*>, where $sr = \{ p' \to tv \mid p' \in MS(Rec_{r,ap}), r \in cs \}$, means that *ap* trusts what *p'* said about *cs* with the TI value *tv*. $Rec_{r,ap}$ is a special role whose members are the recommenders of the principal *ap* about the context associated with the role *r*. *ap* represents the authorizing principal. *sr*, an instance of *SR*, specifies the set of recommenders of *ap* about *cs*. For each $p' \to tv$, *p'* is a recommender of *ap* about *cs*. *tv* is the TI value of *ap* on *p'* to represent the recommendation relationship between *ap* and *p'*. The bigger the *tv*, the more *ap* trust *p'*; vice versa. *cs*, a set of roles, is the particular context set.

3.3 Facilities to Enforce Trust Policies

The facilities can specify the semantics of TEs.

$$F_{AF}^{1}: \rho (RA) \times \rho (AFR) \times Principal \to \rho (RA)$$

According to the *AFRs*, F_{AF} filters the *authorizations* or generates some new *authorizations* from the collected *RAs*. The *principal* is the one filtering the assertions.

$$F_{U}: \rho (RA) \times Principal \to RA; \qquad F_{Auth} : Principal \times RA \to_{m} Auth$$

F_U expresses the action of the *principal* to combine the set of *RAs* into a single *RA* that summarize all the *RAs* in the set. Because the two kinds of TM systems explain assertions in different ways, so the framework does not give the precise semantics of F_U. F_U is just an interface in the framework, the specifications are left to the practical TM systems. F_U is one of the most important elements in the framework, which should be specified according to each practical TM system. The essential difference in the behavior of different TM systems is how to specify a proper F_U. Section 4 will give the proper specifications of F_U for each practical systems.

The F_{Auth} function maps one *RA* to an *auth* ($\to_m$ represents monotone). The *principal* parameter represents the principal who makes the mapping operation. When the *certainty* of a *RA* is beyond the threshold the principal sets in advance, the *RA* can be simplified to an *auth* by the principal. The monotone of F_{Auth} ensures that the *auth* granted by F_{Auth} can not bigger than the *auth* of the *RAs*.

The framework uses F_C to specify the sequence to invoke the three functions defined above. It express the action of a TE to get a proper decision made by a given principal from the sets of *RAs* and *AFRs*.

---

[1] The suffix means "assertion-filter".

$$F_C{}^2: \wp\,(RA) \times \wp\,(AFR) \times Principal \rightarrow Auth$$
$$F_C\,(\wp\,(RA))\,(\wp\,(AFR))(p) = F_{Auth}(p)(\,F_{\cup}\,(F_{AF}\,(\wp\,(RA))(\wp\,(AFR))(p))(p))$$

The parameter of *principal* in F_C represents the authorizing principal. Through using F_C and $\leq$, F_{Engine} is defined to specify the semantics of TEs.

$$F_{Engine}: Principal \times Auth \times \wp\,(RA) \times \wp\,(AFR) \rightarrow BOOL$$
$$F_{Engine}(p,\,a,\,\wp\,(RA),\,\wp\,(AFR)) = \;a \leq F_C\,(\wp\,(RA))(\wp\,(AFR))(p)$$

4 Applying the Framework

To show the abilities of the framework, this paper uses it to specify three typical TM systems or models: dRBAC [6], KeyNote [3] and the Abdul-Rahman Model [7].

4.1 Specifying the dRBAC System

dRBAC is a role-based scalable decentralized TM system with the CBM that grants the permissions defined by roles in a transitive fashion.

$$p \in principal\,,\; r \in role\,,\; e \in entity = principal \cup role$$

The proof foundations of dRBAC are delegations. The delegations in the dRBAC have the forms [*subject* $\rightarrow$ *r*] *issuer*, which can be expressed by the *RA*s.

$$ra \in RA :< issuer, subject \rightarrow r, certainty = 1 >$$

In dRBAC, a principal trusts a delegation issued by the trusted third party. The set of trusted third parties can be specified by the *AFR*s. *r* and *r'* is defined in [6].

$$afr - dRBAC \in AFR : \;< ap, \{p \rightarrow 1 \mid p \in OS(r) \cup MS(r')\}, \{r\} >$$

The *afr-dRBAC* implies that the owner of the role *r* and the members of *r'* have the right to grant the permission. The F_{AF} function enforces the *afr-dRBAC* rules and specifies the dRBAC subscription function [6]. dRBAC uses the following reducing rule to reduce *auth*s (delegations).

Reducing Rule (How to get an *auth-chain*) if $(e \rightarrow r \;\wedge\; r \rightarrow r1) \;\rightarrow\; (e \rightarrow r1)$.

According to the rule, we define $F_{\cup 1}$ as follows:

Definition ($F_{\cup 1}$): *p* is the authorizing principal. $A_1 = <p_1,\,d_1,\,certainty=1>$, $A_2 = <p_2,\,d_2,\,certainty=1>$; A_1 and A_2 are both *authorizations*.
0 : d_2= NIL; $F_{\cup 1}(\{A_1,A_2\})(p) = <p,\,d_1,\,certainty=1>$;
1 : $d_1 = e \rightarrow r_1$, $d_2 = e \rightarrow r_2$; $F_{\cup 1}(\{A_1,A_2\})(p) = <p,\,e \rightarrow \oplus\,(r_1,r_2),\,certainty=1>$;
2: $d_1 = e \rightarrow r_1$, $d_2 = r_2 \rightarrow r_3$,
        if $r_2 \leq r_1$ then $F_{\cup 1}(\{A_1,A_2\})(p) = <p,\,e \rightarrow \oplus\,(r_1,r_2,r_3),\,certainty=1>$;
others: $F_{\cup 1}(A_1,A_2) =$ NIL

---

[2] The suffix means "<u>c</u>ombine".

The recursive definition of $F_{\cup n}$ is as follows

> **Definition** ($F_{\cup n}$): $\rho\,(RA) = \{a_1, a_2, \ldots, a_{n+1}\}$, p is the authorizing principal
> $F_{\cup n}(\rho\,(RA)(p) = F_{\cup 1}(a_i, F_{\cup(n-1)}(\rho\,(RA) - \{a_i\})(p))(p)$, where $1 \leqq i \leqq n+1$

$F_C(\rho\,(RA))(\{afr\text{-}dRBAC\})(p) = F_{Auth}(p)(F_{\cup}(\{F_{AF}(ra)(\{afr\text{-}dRBAC\})(p) | ra \in \rho\,(RA)\})(p))$

$F_{Engine}(p, a, \rho\,(RA), \{afr\text{-}dRBAC\}) = a \leqslant F_C(\rho\,(RA))(\{afr\text{-}dRBAC\})(p)$

4.2 Specifying the KeyNote System

KeyNote is a flexible TM system with the CBM. There are no concepts of roles in KeyNote and it uses *action attributes* to represent requests and *value* to represent permissions [3]. To specify KeyNote, firstly we map action attributes to roles.

$$action = \rho(\,action - attribute - set\,)\,,\ r \in role : action \rightarrow value\,,\ p \in principal$$

The *value* is an element of the order set defined by the particular application [3]. We define each clause in the *condition* fields of Keynote assertions as a role. Then the KeyNote assertions are mapped to *auth*s. We define an *auth* for KeyNote as follows, in which p represents the *licensee* in KeyNote assertions.

$$a \in Auth : p \rightarrow r$$

The *RA*s are used to specify the credentials of KeyNote:

$$ra \in Rich - Assertion :< p, a,\ certainty = 1 >$$

In KeyNote, "Policy" is the only principal considered being able to perform any actions. Policy can authorize any roles to any principals and each principal can authorize roles it is authorized to others. We define *CS* as the set of all contexts. The *AFR*s of KeyNote are defined as follows:

$$afr - KeyNote :\ < ap, \{Policy \rightarrow 1\}, CS >,\ < ap, \{< p \rightarrow 1 >| p \in MS(r)\}, \{r\} >$$

In a KeyNote checking process, if the principal p wants to operate as a member of r, the TE should find a trust chain like this: $< Policy, p_1 \rightarrow r >, certainty = 1 >$, $< p_1, p_2 \rightarrow r, certainty = 1 >, \ldots, < p_n, p \rightarrow r, certainty = 1 >$. So $F_{\cup}$ is defined as follows:

$$F_{\cup} : \rho(\,RA\,) \times Policy \rightarrow RA$$

$F_{\cup}$ finds all the trust chains with p in the trails in $\rho\,(RA)$ and generates a new *RA*. p represents the requesting principal and r_i is the trail of each trust chain:

$$< Policy, p \rightarrow r_1 \cup \ldots \cup r_n, certainty = 1 >$$

We define other functions as follows:

$F_C(\rho\,(RA))(\{afr\text{-}KeyNote\})(Policy) =$

$\qquad F_{Auth}(Policy)(F_{\cup}(F_{AF}(\rho\,(RA))(\{afr\text{-}KeyNote\})(Policy))(Policy))$

$F_{Engine}(Policy, a, \rho\,(RA), \{afr\text{-}KeyNote\}) = a \leqslant F_C(\rho\,(RA))(\{afr\text{-}KeyNote\})(Policy)$

4.3 Specifying the Abdul-Rahman Model

The Abdul-Rahman Model is proposed in [7]. Each authorizing principal will have several recommenders with different TI and combine the recommendation information from them to determining a given request. The trust in the model includes the direct trust relationships (TB) and the recommender trust relationships (TI). We introduce two types of entities for the model: *principal* and *role*.

$$p \in principal \, , \ r \in role \, , \ e \in entity = principal \cup role$$

The *RA*s are defined as follows to express TB and reputation information:

$$ra \in RA \ : <p, e \rightarrow r, certainty=x>, x \in [0,1]$$

x can be quantified by the set $S = \{0, 0.5, 0.625, 0.75, 0, 875, 1\}$, which corresponds to the set, {*distrust, ignorance, minimal, average, good, complete*}, defined in [7]. *AFR*s are defined as follows to specify the TI.

$$afr - arm \in AFR :< ap, \{ p \rightarrow tv \mid p \in MS \ (\ Rec_{r,ap}) \}, \{r\} >, tv \in [0,1]$$

tv can be quantified by the set S as same as x.

This model uses aggregation functions to combine all the recommendations into an *auth* to form a reputation.

$$F_{FA} (\{ < p', e \rightarrow r, certainty=x > \})(\{ < p, \{p' \rightarrow tv\}, \{r\} > \}) \ (p)=$$
$$<p, e \rightarrow r, certainty=x*tv >$$

$$F_{\cup}(\{<p_i, e \rightarrow r \, , certainty_i=x_i >| \ 1 \leqslant i \leqslant |MS(Rec_{r,ap})|\})(ap)$$

$$= \begin{cases} <ap, e \rightarrow r, certainty'=x, \ x> \ \varepsilon \\ NIL \qquad , x \leqslant \varepsilon \end{cases}$$

$$\text{Where } Certainty' = \sum_{i=1}^{n} Certainty_i \, / \, n$$

The F_{FA} function is used to process the transferred recommendation information. And the purpose of $F_{\cup}$ is getting a composed assertion from all filtered information to form the reputation of the object. By applying $F_{\cup}$, F_C and F_{Engine} can be easily defined as follows.

$$F_C \ (\ \rho \ (RA)) \ (\ \rho \ (afr\text{-}arm))(p)= F_{Auth}(p)(\ F_{\cup}(F_{AF} \ (\ \rho \ (RA))(\ \rho \ (afr\text{-}arm))(p))(p))$$
$$F_{Engine}(p, a, \ \rho \ (RA), \rho \ (afr\text{-}arm)) = \ a \ \leqslant F_C \ (\ \rho \ (RA))(\ \rho \ (afr\text{-}arm))(p)$$

The framework is also able to specify some other TM models with RBMs, such as TVM[10], the Beth Model[8], the Jøsang Model [9] and so on.

5   The Analysis: Differences Between Two Types Trust Evaluation Mechanisms

Three main differences exist between CBMs and RBMs through the framework.

- Base of $F_{\cup}$. $F_{\cup}$ is the interface to combine several related assertions into a single assertion that summarize the meanings of these assertions. In CBMs, $F_{\cup}$ is implemented to reduce credentials, whose reducing mechanism of TEs is based on the deductive logic [2,3,6]. While in RBMs, assertions are combined through some aggregation functions [7,8,9,10] usually based on some mathematical approaches.
- Approaches to make authorizations. The CBMs make authorizations by finding a trust chain started with the requester and ended with the permission including the request. The absence of any credential will cause the authorizing process fail. While

in the RBMs, no assertions are absolutely necessarily for a particular authorizing. As long as the collected assertions can form a reputation beyond a certain threshold, the authorization can be granted.

• Evidences of authorizing. In the CBMs, the evidences of authorizing are credentials. The fact that all credential can be expressed by *rich-assertions* with *certainty* 1 means that the CBM considers only actions with "probabilities of success" of 1 or 0. While in the RBM, it uses evidences with more value to consider request actions.

6 Related Work and Conclusion

TM is the activity of collecting, codifying, analyzing and presenting evidence relating to competence, honesty, security or dependability with the purpose of making assessments and decisions regarding trust relationships for Internet applications [12]. In 2001, S.Weeks proposed a formal framework to specify the TM systems with CBMs[13]. The framework is build upon the λ -calculusand use the credential lattices to specify the system behavior. But it cannot specify the RBMs without the credentials. In contrast, V.Shmatikov proposed a semi-formal framework for RBMs in [1]. It provides an object-oriented approach to express the reputations and the relevant operations. However, it cannot be able to specify CBMs formally. In [14], M.Nielson presented some challenges in establishing a formal foundation for the notion of trust. He said that TM systems need languages to specify trust and give a method based on lattices to express domain semantics although it is too simple to express practical systems. In 2003, Tyrone Grandison present the SULTAN toolkit for the specification, analysis and monitoring of TM [12]. The toolkit is composed of four components: the specification editor, the analysis tools, the risk services and the monitor services. Although it is a toolkit to specify TM systems, our framework differs from it in two aspects: 1) our framework uses roles instead of "AS" in SULTAN to express the context dependable property of trust and attribute list to replace "L" and "Cs" in SULTAN, which is a more general approach to abstract permissions. 2) Our framework emphasizes particularly on specify the semantics of TEs. It provides a set of facilities to describe the behavior of TEs. While SULTAN puts focus on facilitating the analysis of trust specification for conflicts and enabling information on risk and experience information to be used to help in decision-making.

The proposed framework can specify almost all the existing TM systems. Firstly, it uses quantifying methods to unify trust and express the context dependable attribute of trust through roles. Then it provides some general elements to define trust policies of TM. This framework specifies the recommendation relationships and delegations among the principals by *assertion-filter-rule*s. And trust evidence, like credentials, recommendations and reputations, can be specified by *rich-assertion*s. Finally, based on the elements to define trust policies, the framework provides a set of facilities to specify the semantics of TEs, which describe the behavior of TM systems formally and precisely. The framework puts a focus on providing a unified approach to specify, analyze, compare, and design TM systems.

Acknowledgement

This paper is funded by 973 of China (2002CB312002), 863 Program of China (2005AA113160, 2005AA113030, 2005AA119010), and NSFC (60233010, 60403014).

References

[1] V. Shmatikov, et al. Reputation-Based Trust Management. Accepted to *Journal of Computer Security*, special issue on selected papers of WITS '03 (ed. R. Gorrieri), 2004.

[2] M. Blaze, et al. Decentralized trust Management. In *Proc. Of IEEE Conf. On Privacy and Security, 1996.*

[3] M. Blaze, et al. KeyNote: Trust management for public-key infrastructures. In *Proc. of Security Protocols International Workshop, 1998.*

[4] E. Wobber, et al. Authentication in the Taos operating system. ACM Transactions on Computer Systems, 12(1):3-32, Feb. 1994.

[5] N. Li, et al. *RT: A Role-based Trust-management Framework.* In *Proceedings of The Third DARPA Information Survivability Conference and Exposition (DISCEX III)*, Washington, D.C., April 2003. IEEE Computer Society Press, L.A., California, pp. 201--212.

[6] E. Freudenthal, et al. drbac: Distributed role-based access control for dynamic coalition environments.In *Proceedings of the 22nd International Conference on Distributed Computing Systems(ICDCS'02)*, 2002.

[7] A. Abdul-Rahman, et al. A Distributed Trust Model. In *Proceedings of the 1997 New Security Paradigms Workshop*, pages 48-60, Cumbria, 1997. ACM.

[8] T. Beth, et al. Valuation of Trust In Open Network. In *Proceedings of European Symposium On Research in Security*, pages 3-18, Brighton, 1994. Springer-Verlag.

[9] A. Jøsang, An Algebra for Assessing Trust in Certificate Chains. The Internet Society Symposium on Network and Distributed System Security February 03 - February 05, 1999.San Diego, California.

[10] F. XU, et al. Design of A Trust Valuation Model in Software Service Coordination. Journal of software, 2003,14(6): 1043~1051.

[11] D. Ferraiolo, et al. A Role-Based Access Control Model and Reference Implementation Within a Corporate Intranet. *ACM Transactions on Information and System Security*, Vol. 2, No. 1, February 1999, 34-64.

[12] T. Grandison, et al. Trust Management Tools For Internet Application. Trust Management, First International Conference, Heraklion, Crete, Greece, May 28-30, 2002.

[13] S. Weeks. Understanding Trust Management System. IEEE Symposium on Security and Privacy, May 14 - 16, 2001, Oakland, California.

[14] M. Nielsen, et al. Towards a formal notion of trust. *Proceedings of the 5th ACM SIGPLAN international conference on Principles and practice of declaritive programming* Uppsala, Sweden Pages: 4 - 7 Year of Publication: 2003 ISBN: 1-58113-705-2.

Bayesian Network Based Trust Management

Yong Wang[1,2,*], Vinny Cahill[1], Elizabeth Gray[1],
Colin Harris[1], and Lejian Liao[3]

[1] Distributed Systems Group, Department of Computer Science,
Trinity College Dublin, Dublin 2, Ireland
wangyong@bit.edu.cn,
{vinny.cahill, grayl, colin.harris}@cs.tcd.ie
http://www.dsg.cs.tcd.ie
[2] School of Software, Beijing Institute of Technology, Beijing 100081, China
[3] School of Computer Science and Technology, Beijing Institute of Technology, Beijing 100081,
China
liaolj@bit.edu.cn

Abstract. Trust is an essential component for secure collaboration in uncertain environments. Trust management can be used to reason about future interactions between entities. In reputation-based trust management, an entity's reputation is usually built on ratings from those who have had direct interactions with the entity. In this paper, we propose a Bayesian network based trust management model. In order to infer trust in different aspects of an entity's behavior, we use multi-dimensional application specific trust values and each dimension is evaluated using a single Bayesian network. This makes it easy both to extend the model to involve more dimensions of trust and to combine Bayesian networks to form an opinion about the overall trustworthiness of an entity. Each entity can evaluate his peers according to his own criteria. The dynamic characteristics of criteria and of peer behavior can be captured by updating Bayesian networks. Risk is explicitly combined with trust to help users making decisions. In this paper, we show that our system can make accurate trust inferences and is robust against unfair raters.

1 Introduction

Ubiquitous computing foresees a massively networked infrastructure supporting a large population of diverse but cooperation entities. Entities will be both autonomous and mobile and will have to be able to capable of dealing with unforeseen circumstances ranging from unexpected interactions with other entities to disconnected operation [1]. Trust management is a suitable solution to provide self-protection for these entities by reasoning about another entity's trustworthiness in future interactions according to one's direct interactions with that entity and recommendations (ratings) from other entities.

Trust is a multi-faceted concept. It is subjective and non-symmetric [1]. Each entity makes its own decision to trust or not based on the evidence available for personal evaluation. Even if two entities are presented with the same evidence they may not

* Yong Wang was a visiting scholar in Trinity College Dublin from April 2005 to March 2006. Her study was supported by China Scholarship Council and National Science Foundation of China under grant No. 60373057.

L.T. Yang et al. (Eds.): ATC 2006, LNCS 4158, pp. 246–257, 2006.

necessarily interpret this information in the same way. Trust is also context-specific such that trust in one environment does not directly transfer to another environment. Trust usually changes according to the outcomes of the latest interactions, which means that the dynamic property of trust must be captured. Trust is inherently linked to risk and explicitly involving risk can help users to understand the semantics of trust. In order to provide finer-grained inference of trust in different aspects of an entity's behavior, trust should also be multi-dimensional.

Many existing computational trust models use intuitive and ad hoc hand-crafted formulae to calculate trust values. Some models using probabilistic approaches based on Bayesian theory have also appeared during last few years. However none of these models consider all the characteristics of trust described above. For example, ratings are weighted and then summed to get reputation values in [2][3][6], but the weights are selected in an ad hoc way and remain unchanged over time, which does not reflect the dynamic context. All ratings are treated equally in [2][3], raters' confidence in his level of trust for ratees is not considered. As to the unfair rating problem, [4][8][10] use the difference between the aggregated and individual ideas about an entity to determine the reliability of raters. The subjectivity of trust is not taken into consideration. If the proportion of unfair raters is large, say 40%, this kind of system can not determine which raters are malicious. However, the approach proposed in [5] is not practical in many distributed applications (e.g., E-commerce), since the actual outcomes of interactions between two agents can not be observed by other agents. [2][6] do not consider risk explicitly. [2][3][6][9][10] use a single value or a pair to represent trust in a user, making it difficult to evaluate different dimensions of trust.

The above Bayesian-based trust models simply sum rather than using statistical methods to combine direct observations and weighted ratings from different raters as beta distribution parameters. It is difficult to show whether the aggregated beta distribution is close to the real distribution. Bayesian networks can be used to tackle this issue. There are two trust models based on Bayesian networks. The authors of [6] use Bayesian networks to combine different dimensions of trust and estimate the reliability of raters. But the reputation values are still calculated using hand-crafted formula with fixed weights. Their system with Bayesian networks performs only slightly better than the one without Bayesian networks. In [7], the authors use a polytree (singly connected directed acrylic graph) to revise belief in some knowledge and to update the reputation of information sources. In fact, it uses the aggregated reputation as evidence to determine the reliability of information sources. In addition, the assumption of the probability of unreliable information sources giving correct information reduces the accuracy of inference. In this paper, we describe a probabilistic computational trust model which covers all important characteristics of trust. We use the e-commerce scenario, where buyers evaluate the trustworthiness of sellers, to illustrate the model in the following sections.

2   Bayesian Network Based Trust Model Overview

Our model consists of three components: trust formation, reputation estimation and risk-related decision making.

A trust value is calculated as the expectation value of beta probability density functions as [2][3][9][10], but it is finer-grained in our model to represent more application-specific notions of trust and to allow the definition of trust to be extended flexibly. For example, a buyer can evaluate the trustworthiness of a seller in three dimensions: the probability of shipping goods as described, the probability of shipping lower quality goods and the probability of not shipping any goods.

Only ratings from reliable buyers (raters) are used to estimate the sellers' reputation. First, we compare the ratings of the decision maker and other raters. If the probability of having similar opinions to the decision maker is very small, the rater will be regarded as unfair. Both unfairly positive raters and unfairly negative raters can be identified.

After filtering out unreliable raters, we use a Bayesian Network to estimate reputation values from ratings given by reliable raters.

A reputation value for each dimension of trust is calculated. Since decision makers have different attitudes towards risk and their attitudes can change over time, we should combine reputation values and risk attitudes in order to make subjective and context-specific decisions. A natural way is to use utility functions to model attitudes towards risk and then use the estimated reputation values as parameters to calculate the expected utility, which can be used as the basis of the decision.

3   Bayesian Network Based Trust Management

3.1   Trust Formation

We use beta probability density functions to represent the distribution of trust values according to interaction history as in [2]. The beta-family of distributions is a continuous family of distribution functions indexed by the two parameters and . The beta PDF can be expressed using the gamma function as:

$$\text{beta}(p\,|\alpha,\beta) = \frac{\Gamma(\alpha+\beta)}{\Gamma(\alpha)\Gamma(\beta)} p^{(\alpha-1)}(1-p)^{(\beta-1)}, where\ 0 \le p \le 1,\ \alpha,\beta > 0. \quad (1)$$

The probability expectation value of the beta distribution is given by:

$$E(p) = \frac{\alpha}{\alpha+\beta} \quad (2)$$

Posteriori probabilities of binary events can be represented as beta distributions. Suppose a process has several possible outcomes and one of them is outcome x. Let r be the observed number of outcome x and let s be the number of outcomes other than x. Then the probability density function of observing outcome x in the future can be expressed as a function of past observations by setting:

$$\alpha = r + 1, \beta = s + 1, where\ r, s \ge 0. \quad (3)$$

The authors of [2] only consider two possible outcomes for each interaction. We make more detailed analysis of interactions and extend to multi-dimension application-specific outcomes. The granularity (the number of dimensions) is determined by the complexity of applications and the requirement of users.

In the e-commerce scenario, we use three tuples $(r_G, s_{\overline{G}}), (r_L, s_{\overline{L}}), (r_C, s_{\overline{C}})$ for three dimensions of trust of a seller. G means shipping goods as described and $\overline{G}$ means not shipping goods as described. L means shipping lower quality goods and $\overline{L}$ means not shipping lower quality goods. C means not shipping any goods and $\overline{C}$ means shipping goods. are the numbers of interactions with outcome i, and $r_i (i \in \{G, L, C\})$ is the number of interactions without outcome i. Then the parameters of the beta probability density functions are set as:

$$\alpha_i = r_i + 1, \beta_{\overline{i}} = s_{\overline{i}} + 1, \quad (i \in \{G, L, C\}, \overline{i} \in \{\overline{G}, \overline{L}, \overline{C}\}). \tag{4}$$

$$\tau_i = \frac{\alpha_i}{\alpha_i + \beta_{\overline{i}}}, \quad (i \in \{G, L, C\}, \overline{i} \in \{\overline{G}, \overline{L}, \overline{C}\}). \tag{5}$$

$$\text{Since} \qquad \beta_{\overline{G}} = \alpha_L + \alpha_C - 1, \tag{6}$$

$$\text{then} \qquad \tau_i = \frac{\alpha_i}{\displaystyle\sum_{j \in \{G,L,C\}} \alpha_j - 1} = \frac{r_i + 1}{\displaystyle\sum_{j \in \{G,L,C\}} r_j + 2} (i \in \{G, L, C\}). \tag{7}$$

We then normalize these to get the trust values:

$$P_i = \frac{\tau_i}{\displaystyle\sum_{j \in \{G,L,C\}} \tau_j + 2} (i \in \{G, L, C\}). \tag{8}$$

Where, P_i can be interpreted as the probability of outcome i happening in the future. In our model, we consider buyers' confidence $\gamma_i (i \in \{G, L, C\})$ in calculated trust values, which is a measure of the probability that the actual trust value lies within an acceptable level of error ϵ about the calculated trust value P_i. The confidence factor can be calculated as (9):

$$\gamma_i = \frac{\displaystyle\int_{P_i - \epsilon}^{P_i + \epsilon} \kappa^{\alpha_i - 1}(1 - \kappa)^{\beta_{\overline{i}} - 1} d\kappa}{\displaystyle\int_0^1 \rho^{\alpha_i - 1}(1 - \rho)^{\beta_{\overline{i}} - 1} d\rho} (i \in \{G, L, C\}). \tag{9}$$

Then the buyer can set a threshold θ_γ to determine if he has enough confidence. If the buyer's trust value about a seller fulfills formula (10), then he feels confident to predict the seller's future behavior.

$$\gamma_G > \theta_\gamma, \gamma_L > \theta_\gamma, \gamma_C > \theta_\gamma \tag{10}$$

Since the three tuples have relationships (see formula (6)), we can combine them to save storage space. The formats of trust values and confidence factors for sellers stored by buyers are (P_G, P_L, P_C) and $(\gamma_G, \gamma_L, \gamma_C)$ respectively.

Because sellers may change their behavior over time, we use a fading factor $\lambda_\gamma \in [0, 1]$ to forget old observations as (11).

$$r_{t+1} = \lambda_\gamma r^t + r \qquad s_{t+1} = \lambda_\gamma s^t + s. \tag{11}$$

In which, are the trust parameters for $t+1$ interactions, the outcome of the $t+1$th interaction is (r, s).

3.2 Reputation Estimation

If a buyer is not confident enough in a seller's trustworthiness according to formula
(10) or wants to interact with an unknown seller, he will ask for other buyers' advice
or recommendations (ratings). The ratings are the trust values given to sellers by other
buyers. Then the buyer can estimate the seller's reputation according to the ratings for
the seller as well as the other buyers' reliability as raters. A Bayesian network is constructed to perform the estimation for each dimension of trust (shipping described goods
or shipping lower quality goods or not shipping goods in the E-commence scenario).
All Bayesian networks have the same structure but different parameters. Figure 1 shows
the structure of Bayesian networks. Node B_i represents one dimension of the trust value

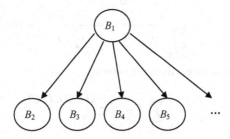

Fig. 1. Bayesian Network for Reputation Estimation

(P_G, P_L, P_C) given by buyer b_i. Since it is buyer b_1 that estimates a sellers' reputation, B_1 is the root node and others are leaf nodes. The trust value is a real number
between 0 and 1. In order to express a trust value using the state of a node, we need
to discretise it by dividing the interval into several subintervals according to the required accuracy denoted as the comparison threshold θ_P^1 set by b_1. The subintervals are
$[k\theta_P^1, (k+1)\theta_P^1)$, $(k = 0, 1, \ldots, \frac{1}{\theta_P^1} - 1)$ and the number of subintervals is $\frac{1}{\theta_P^1}$, which determines the numbers of states for each node. For simplicity, we denote the subintervals
with I_k $(k = 0, 1, \ldots, \frac{1}{\theta_P^1} - 1)$ and denote the states as S_i $(i = 0, 1, \ldots, \frac{1}{\theta_P^1} - 1)$. The conditional probability table (CPT) of node B_1 and node B_i $(i = 2, 3, 4, \ldots)$ are shown in
table 1 and table 2 respectively.

Table 1. The CPT of Node B_1

$B_1 = S_0$	$B_1 = S_1$	$\ldots$	$B_1 = S_{\frac{1}{\theta_P^1} - 1}$
$P(B_1 \in I_0)$	$P(B_1 \in I_1)$	$\ldots$	$P(B_1 \in I_{\frac{1}{\theta_P^1} - 1})$

Table 2. The CPT of Node B_i

B_1	$B_i = S_0$	$B_i = S_1$	...	$B_i = S_{\frac{1}{\theta_P^1}-1}$
S_0	$P(B_i \in I_0 \mid B_1 \in I_0)$	$P(B_i \in I_1 \mid B_1 \in I_0)$	...	$P(B_i \in I_{\frac{1}{\theta_P^1}-1} \mid B_1 \in I_0)$
S_1	$P(B_i \in I_0 \mid B_1 \in I_1)$	$P(B_i \in I_1 \mid B_1 \in I_1)$	...	$P(B_i \in I_{\frac{1}{\theta_P^1}-1} \mid B_1 \in I_1)$
...	...	...	...	...
$S_{\frac{1}{\theta_P^1}-1}$	$P(B_i \in I_0 \mid B_1 \in I_{\frac{1}{\theta_P^1}-1})$	$P(B_i \in I_1 \mid B_1 \in I_{\frac{1}{\theta_P^1}-1})$	...	$P(B_i \in I_{\frac{1}{\theta_P^1}-1} \mid B_1 \in I_{\frac{1}{\theta_P^1}-1})$

Next we use the expectation maximization algorithm [11] to learn probabilities in CPTs from the ratings, which are called cases. Let the rating of shipping described goods for seller s_j given by b_i at time 0 be denoted as $P^j_{i(0)}$, then we can get the cases shown in table 3. In this table, the elements in column "B_1" are the trust values given by b_1 in which he has sufficient confidence according to (10).

Table 3. Cases for CPT Learning

B_1	B_2	...	B_i
$P^1_{1(0)}$	$P^1_{2(0)}$	...	$P^1_{i(0)}$
$P^2_{1(0)}$	$P^2_{2(0)}$	...	$P^2_{i(0)}$
...	...	...	...
$P^1_{1(1)}$	$P^1_{2(1)}$	...	$P^l_{i(l)}$

To reflect the dynamic characteristic of trust, a buyer should update his Bayesian networks regularly by fading old probabilities before taking new cases into consideration. We adopt the method from Netica [11] shown in formula (12) and (13) to update CPTs, in which, $\lambda_\gamma \in [0, 1]$ is the fading factor; P_i $(i \geq 0)$ are the probabilities at time t_i $(i \geq 0)$ is the normalization constant at time i.

$$t_0 = 1; \quad t_{n+1} = \frac{1}{\sum_{j=0}^{\frac{1}{\theta_P^1}-1} (P_n(B_i \in I_j \mid B_1 \in I_k)t_n\lambda_\gamma + 1 - \lambda_\gamma\})} \tag{12}$$

$$P_0(B_i \in I_j \mid B_1 \in I_k) = \frac{1}{\theta_P^1}; \quad P_{n+1}(B_i \in I_j \mid B_1 \in I_k) = \frac{1}{t_{n+1}(P_n(B_i \in I_j \mid B_1 \in I_k)t_n\lambda_\gamma + 1 - \lambda_\gamma)} \tag{13}$$

The reputation of a seller can be estimated easily using Bayes rule. Suppose that the recommendation given to a seller by b_i lies in I_i, then the probability that b_i's rating lies in can be calculated using formula (14). Since all leaf nodes B_i are conditionally independent given B_1, we can deduce formula (15) to formula (16). The value of B_1 can be estimated as the expectation value of its states using formula (16).

$$P(B_1 \in I_{i_1} \mid B_2 \in I_{i_2}, \ldots, B_k \in I_{i_k}) = \frac{P(B_2 \in I_{i_2}, \ldots P(B_k \in I_{i_k} \mid B_1 \in I_{i_1})P(B_1 \in I_{i_1})}{P(B_2 \in I_{i_2}, \ldots, P(B_k \in I_{i_k})}$$

$$(14)$$

$$P(B_1 \in I_{i_1} \mid B_2 \in I_{i_2}, \ldots, B_k \in I_{i_k}) = \frac{P(B_2 \in I_{i_2} \mid B_1 \in I_{i_1}) \ldots P(B_k \in I_{i_k} \mid B_1 \in I_{i_1})P(B_1 \in I_{i_1})}{P(B_2 \in I_{i_2}) \ldots P(B_k \in I_{i_k})}$$

$$(15)$$

$$P = \sum_{i=0}^{i=\frac{1}{\theta_P^l}-1} \frac{(2i+1)\theta_P^l}{2} P(B_1 \in I_i)$$

$$(16)$$

In order to increase the accuracy of estimates and to reduce the computational overhead, we can first select the most reliable buyers as raters and then use only the recommendations from these reliable buyers to infer sellers' reputations. In other words, in the Bayesian network, only the nodes corresponding to reliable buyers are set to specific states according to the ratings, the other nodes are set to an unknown state.

If the trust value calculated by b_i according to his own observations lies in the same or adjacent subintervals as the trust value given by b_1, then b_i has a similar opinion to b_1. From the CPT's point of view, the probabilities on the three diagonals from top left corner to bottom right corner represent situations where bi has similar opinions to b_1. Elements where b_i has similar opinions to b_1 are bolded in Table 2. Then we use the average value of the probabilities on the three diagonals to evaluate b_i's reliability in rating sellers. If no trust value from b_1 lies in I_j, then $P(B_1 \in I_j) = 0$ or close to 0 (different parameter learning algorithms give different estimation), which means b_1 has no idea about sellers whose trust values lie in I_j. So it is not reasonable to consider $P(B_i \in I_k \mid B_1 \in I_j), (k = 0, 1, \ldots, \frac{1}{\theta_P^l})$ when calculating b_i's reliability. Usually, uniform probabilities are given to unknown states, that is $P(B_i \in I_k \mid B_1 \in I_j) = \theta_P^l, (k = 0, 1, \ldots, \frac{1}{\theta_P^l})$. The number of subintervals covered by b_1's interaction experience is denoted as N_1, and then the reliability of b_i can be calculated using formula (17).

$$P(b_i \text{ is reliable}) = \frac{1}{N_1} \Big(\sum_{j=0, P(B_1 \in I_j) \neq 0}^{j=\frac{1}{\theta_P^l}-1} P(B_i \in I_j \mid B_1 \in I_j) + \sum_{j=1, P(B_1 \in I_j) \neq 0}^{j=\frac{1}{\theta_P^l}-1} P(B_i \in I_{j-1} \mid B_1 \in I_j)$$

$$+ \sum_{j=0, P(B_1 \in I_j) \neq 0}^{j=\frac{1}{\theta_P^l}-2} P(B_i \in I_j + 1 \mid B_1 \in I_j) \qquad (17)$$

b_1 then sets a threshold to determine b_i's reliability. If formula (18) is fulfilled, then b_i is reliable enough in providing ratings.

$$P(b_i \text{ is reliable}) \geq \theta_R^l \qquad (18)$$

The probabilities below the three diagonals represent b_i giving lower ratings than b_1. Then the average value of these probabilities can be used to estimate the probability that b_i gives unfairly negative ratings as (19). Similarly, the probabilities above the three lines represent b_i giving higher ratings than b_1. The average value of these probabilities can be used to estimate the probability that b_i gives unfairly positive ratings as (20).

$$P(b_i \text{ is unfairly negative}) = \frac{1}{N_1} \sum_{j=2,P(B_1 \in I_j) \neq 0}^{j=\frac{1}{\theta_P^I}-1} \sum_{k=0}^{k=j-2} P(B_i \in I_k \mid B_1 \in I_j) \qquad (19)$$

$$P(b_i \text{ is unfairly positive}) = \frac{1}{N_1} \sum_{j=0,P(B_1 \in I_j) \neq 0}^{j=\frac{1}{\theta_P^I}-2} \sum_{k=2}^{k=j+2} P(B_i \in I_k \mid B_1 \in I_j) \qquad (20)$$

3.3   Decision Making Based on Reputation and Risk

After obtaining reputation values $(P_G, P_L P_C)$ for a seller, b_1 normalizes them to get $(P'_G, P'_L P'_C)$ which are then used to calculate the utility of dealing with the seller. Buyers can select a utility function according to their attitude to risk. A buyer with risk-tolerant behavior can choose an exponential function for the utility, a risk neutral buyer can choose a linear one and a risk-averse buyer can choose a logarithmic function.

Taking an exponential utility function $U_R(x) = 1 - e^{\frac{-x}{R}}$ as an example, the parameter R, called the risk tolerance, determines how risk-averse the function is. As R becomes smaller, the function becomes more risk-averse. Suppose that the price of an item is q and the intrinsic value of it is v. If the seller ships the item as described, the gain of b_1 is $v - q$. If the seller ships a lower quality item, whose intrinsic value is $v' < v$, the gain of b_1 is $v' - q$. In case the seller does not ship any item, the gain of b_1 is $-q$. The utility function is , thus the expected utility can be calculated as (21). $EU > 0$ means that dealing with the seller is worth the risk, otherwise it is too risky.

$$EU = P'_G \times U_R(v - q) + P'_L \times U_R(v' - q) + +P_{C'} \times U_R(-q) \qquad (21)$$

4   Simulation

To evaluate the effectiveness of our approach in estimating reputation values in different scenarios and filtering unfair ratings, we used simulations. We revised the Trade Network Game (TNG)[12] to simulate an e-commerce environment. TNG is open source software that implements an agent-based computational model for studying the formation and evolution of trade networks in decentralized market economies. We modified the trader behavior sequence generation and partner selection part as described below and added a rating function for buyers.

For the sake of simplicity, each agent in our system plays only one role at a time, either seller or buyer. The behaviors of sellers are determined by behavioral probabilities (the probabilities of shipping described goods, shipping lower quality goods and not shipping goods). Buyers rate sellers differently. They can be honest, unfairly positive or unfairly negative or combined according to some rating behavior patterns. We use the Netica API [11]to implement the Bayesian Networks.

4.1 Simulation Setup

The market consists of 5 sellers and 10 buyers. The simulation is divided into 800 sessions and each session has 10 rounds. In each round, each buyer can buy one item with fixed price from a selected seller who has the maximal expectation utility according to (20), while each seller can interact with as many buyers as its productive capacity allows. We use similar behavior patterns for sellers as [3]. Sellers' original behavioral probabilities B_G, B_L and B_C are 0.85, 0.1 and 0.05 respectively. After each session, sellers change their behavioral probabilities randomly as follows.

$$beta(p \,|\, \alpha, \beta) = \frac{\Gamma(\alpha + \beta)}{\Gamma(\alpha)\Gamma(\beta)} p^{(\alpha-1)}(1 - p)^{(\beta-1)}, where\ 0 \le p \le 1,\ \alpha, \beta > 0. \qquad (22)$$

Buyers exchange ratings for sellers after each session. The exchanged ratings of the first 20 sessions are used to estimate the reliabilities of other buyers. They update their Bayesian networks by fading all the CPTs first, then learning again using the latest case. $\lambda_v = 0.98$; $\lambda_y = 0.99$; $\theta_p^l = 0.05$; $\theta_r^l = 0.8$; $q = 100$, $v = 200$, $v' = 60$; the utility function is $U_{50}(x) = 1 - e^{\frac{-x}{50}}$.

4.2 Simulation Results

The Effect of Unfair Raters. In order to evaluate the accuracy of the estimation, we compare the trust values calculated by a buyer using his own observations and the reputation values estimated using his Bayesian networks.

As buyers only select reliable buyers as raters, it would be expected that the proportion of unfair raters has little effect on the accuracy of estimation. Figure 2 and figure 3 show the reputation values and trust values ($P_G and P_L$) of seller s_4 for 780 sessions when there are no unfair buyers. It can be seen that reputation values follow trust values closely with only little difference. In figure 2, the average difference between reputation values and trust values is 0.024 and the maximal difference is 0.114 (in sessions 530-540). During sessions 530-540, the trust value decreases suddenly to a very low level that never happened before (never appeared in the cases), so the estimate given by the Bayesian network does not concentrate on one or two most possible subintervals but on several neighboring subintervals according to previous case learning. In figure 3, the average difference and maximal difference are 0.016 and 0.086 respectively. Figure 4 and figure 5 show the comparison results when the proportion of unfair raters is 50% (5 fair buyers) and 80% (only one fair buyer other than b_1) respectively. The average difference and maximal difference are 0.023 and 0.103 in figure 4. We can see that the accuracy of estimation in the situation where more than half of the raters are unfair is very similar to that in the situation without unfair raters. In figure 5, the average difference and maximal difference are 0.033 and 0.185. Although the estimation is not as accurate as that of figure 4 because of the presence of fewer reliable raters, the system still gives a reasonable reference for decision makers.

The Effect of Different Rating Criteria. As mentioned in section 1, trust is subjective. Each buyer can give different estimate to the same sellers according to their different

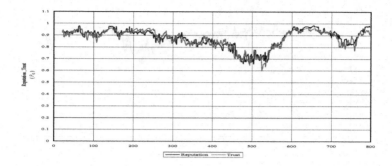

Fig. 2. Reputation Value and Trust Value (P_G) for Seller s_4 by Buyer b_1 without Unfair Buyers

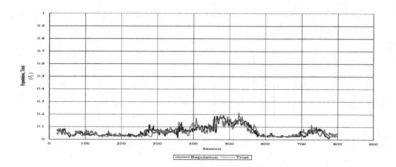

Fig. 3. Reputation Value and Trust Value (P_L) for Seller s_4 by Buyer b_1 without Unfair Buyers

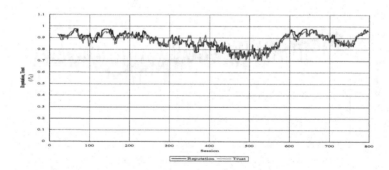

Fig. 4. Reputation Value and Trust Value (P_G) for Seller s_4 by Buyer b_2 with 50% Unfair Buyers

criteria. Suppose there is a kind of unstable buyer, whose behavior changes over time. Sometimes they give neutral ratings as ordinary buyers, sometimes they give harsher ratings because they require that items should be exactly the same as described by sellers, and they can also be tolerant to giving better ratings. Assume they change their

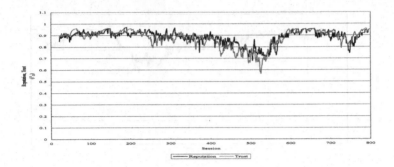

Fig. 5. Reputation Value and Trust Value (P_G) for Seller s_4 by Buyer b_1 with 80% Unfair Buyers

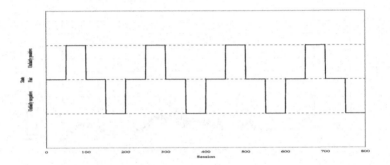

Fig. 6. Sequence of Rating Behavior States of Unstable Buyers

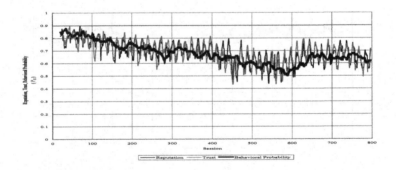

Fig. 7. Reputation Value and Trust Value (P_G) for Seller s_4 by Buyer b_3

behavior according to the state sequence shown in figure 6. Figure 7 shows his estimation based on similar ratings as his own for seller s4. The estimate is still very accurate although it is obviously different from the real behavioral probability.

5   Conclusions

In our trust management model, we use Bayesian networks for both estimating reputation values of other entities and filtering out unfair raters. Simulations show that the estimation follows the decision makers' subjective, dynamic criteria very well. Our model can be easily extended in two directions. On one hand, we can add a Bayesian network for a new dimension of trust or for a new context. On the other hand, we can combine different dimensions of trust or different contexts to get a general opinion using a Bayesian network with some nodes for representing trust dimensions and some nodes for different contexts. Users can select different components according to specific situations. In fact, different context can be represented by different cases. We plan to add this trust management model to the SECURE framework [1] to provide more flexible security mechanisms for collaboration in uncertain environments.

References

1. V. Cahill, E. Gray, J.-M. Seigneur, C. Jensen, Y. Chen, B. Shand, N. Dimmock, A. Twigg, J. Bacon, C. English, W. Wagealla, S. Terzis, P. Nixon, G. Serugendo, C. Bryce, M. Carbone, K. Krukow, and M. Nielsen. Using Trust for Secure Collaboration in Uncertain Environments. In Pervasive Computing Magazine, volume 2, IEEE Computer Society Press, 2003.
2. L. Mui, M. Mohtashemi, C. Ang, P. Szolovits, and A. Halberdtadt. Ratings in Distributed Systems: A Bayesian Approach. 2002.
3. R. Ismail and A. Josang. The beta reputation systems. In Proceedings of the 15th Bled Conference on Electronic Commerce,Slovenia, 2002.
4. A.Whitby, A. Josang, and J.Indulska. Filtering out unfair ratings in bayesian reputation systems. In Proceedings of the Workshop on Trust in Agent Societies, at the 3rd Int. Conf. on Autonomous Agents and Multi Agent Systems, 2004.
5. J. Patel, W.T. Luke Teacy, N. R. Jennings, and M. Luck. A Probabilistic Trust Model for Handling Inaccurate Reputation Sources. In Proceedings of the Third International Conference, iTrust 2005, Paris, France, May 2005.
6. Y. Wang, J. Vassileva. Trust and Reputation Model in Peer-to-Peer Networks. In Proceedings of the Third International Conference on Peer-to-Peer Computing 2003.
7. K. Suzanne Barber, Joonoo Kim. Belief Revision Process Based on Trust: Agents Evaluating Reputation of Information Sources. Trust in Cyber-societies. Lecture Notes in Artificial Intelligence, 2001.
8. C. Dellarocas. Mechanisms for coping with unfair ratings and discriminatory behavior in online reputation reporting systems. In ICIS,2000.
9. S. Ganeriwal, M. B. Srivastava. Reputation-based framework for high integrity sensor networks,?ACM Security for Ad-hoc and Sensor Networks, 2004.
10. Buchegger, S., Boudec, J.Y.L. A robust reputation system for p2p and mobile ad-hoc networks. In: Proceedings of the Second Workshop on the Economics of Peer-to-Peer Systems, 2004.
11. http://www.norsys.com/.
12. http://www.econ.iastate.edu/tesfatsi/tnghome.htm.

An Improved Global Trust Value Computing Method in P2P System[*]

Fajiang Yu[1], Huanguo Zhang[2], Fei Yan[3], and Song Gao[4]

School of Computer, Wuhan University, Wuhan 430072, Hubei, China
[1] qshxyu@126.com, [2] liss@whu.edu.cn, [3] yfpostbox@yahoo.com.cn,
[4] gaosongbox@163.com

Abstract. Building a trust and reputation mechanism in P2P system is very important. This paper gives an improved global trust value computing method of choosing trusted source peers in P2P system. First, we give a basic description of our trust mechanism; then we bring out the global trust value computing method; third, we define trust computing operator; fourth, we introduce other related trust mechanisms; and finally we do some simulations to compare the performance of our method with other trust mechanism.

1 The Introduction of Trust in P2P System

With the rapid development of P2P systems recently, they attract increasing attention from researchers, but they also bring up some problems. Some peers might be buggy and cannot provide services as they advertise. Some might be malicious by providing bad services to get more benefit. Since there are no centralized nodes to serve as an authority to supervise peers' behaviors and punish peers that behave badly, malicious peers can get away with their bad behaviors.

How to distinguish potential benevolent peers from potential buggy or malicious peers is the current research hot spot of P2P system. If these problems were resolved, the P2P system would have more applications greatly. At present the main method of resolving these problems is to build trust and reputation in the system.

The trust and reputation mechanism is derived from human society. Trust is at the core of most relationships between human beings. Take the simple example of purchasing an item from a shop. We may choose to buy a certain brand because we have found it to be trustworthy in the past or it has a reputation for being widely "trusted".

Trust between peers in P2P system begins to mirror those real-world relationships in the society. A very important application of P2P system is electronic commerce. In the electronic markets, trading partners have limited information about each other's reliability or the product quality during the transaction. The

---

[*] Foundation item: Supported by the National Natural Science Foundation of China (90104005, 60373087, 60473023) and Network and Information Security Key Laboratory Program of Ministry of Education of China.

main issue is the information asymmetry between the buyers and sellers. The buyers know about their own trading behavior but do not know the quality of the products. And the sellers know about the quality of the products they are selling but do not know the buyers' trading behavior. Then Trading partners just use each other's reputations to reduce this information asymmetry so as to facilitate trusting trading relationships. Besides electronic markets, trust and reputation also play important roles in other P2P applications.

Because of the importance of trust and reputation, some researches have been done in the field. [1] and [2] both gave a trust model with Beta distribution. This type of trust model only can be used in the case whose interaction has binary results. [3] gave a subjective logic trust mechanism, and [4], [5], [6] gave the trust mechanism by using the Theory of Evidence. The subjective logic is similar to the theory of evidence; both use an uncertain parameter to represent trust. But this uncertainty comes from inadequate conditions of the object, which has something different from trust with fuzzy concept. [7] has done some research in trust by using fuzzy set theory. The current fuzzy math trust model only uses fuzzy set and subject degree definitions to represent trust concept, how to use deep fuzzy math theory to compute trust needs further research. In this paper, we give an improved global trust value computing method of choosing trusted source peers to enhance the trust degree of whole P2P system.

2   The Basic Description of Trust Mechanism

In this section, we give a general basic description of trust mechanism in P2P system.

2.1   Trust Value

There is not a clear line between the trusted peers and distrusted peers. Trust is a fuzzy object in real world. One peer i usually says an 80 percent probability that another peer j is a trusted peer. There also have instances peer i trust peer j than j'. This hints that trust has different levels or degrees. 80 percent or 0.80 represents the trust degree between peer i and j. We use *trust value*, T_{ij}, to represent the trust degree between peer i and j, and $T_{ij} \in [0,1]$. If peer i has got the trust value with peer j, she can predict the future performance of j, and can judge whether j is a good or bad peer. Then peer i can reduce the loss of interactions with peer j because of the unknown to j's next behavior.

2.2   Direct Trust Value, Indirect Trust Value, Reputation Value and Total Trust Value

In order to get the trust value, peer i will analyze its interaction history with j. We call the trust value from peer i's direct experiences *Direct Trust Value*, denoted as DT_{ij}. But i only has limited direct interaction experiences with peer j, a natural way to get more accurate trust value for peer i is to ask its acquaintances about their opinions. We call the trust value from asking its one acquaintance k *Indirect Trust Value*, denoted as IDT_{ikj}. We call the trust value from asking its all acquaintances *Reputation Value*, denoted as Rep_{ij}. Rep_{ij} is equal to the "sum" of all Indirect trust value. Then peer i will combine direct trust value and reputation value to get more accurate trust value. We call this more accurate trust value *Total Trust Value*, denoted as TT_{ij}. The combining way is defined as, $TT_{ij} = \alpha \cdot DT_{ij} + (1 - \alpha)Rep_{ij}$, $\alpha \in [0, 1]$. α is a learning parameter, which represents the importance of peer i's direct experiences.

2.3   Indirect Trust Value Computing

Peer i asks its one acquaintance, k, to get the indirect trust value with j. This is shown in Fig. 1. Peer k has direct interaction experiences with j, the direct trust value between k and j is noted as DT_{kj}. In this instance, there is a recommending ship between k and i. Peer k recommends its direct experiences to i, and then these experiences become indirect experiences of i. But maybe k is not a very familiar friend for peer i, or k has recommend i inaccurate experiences in the past, peer i does not think k's recommendation is completely right. For example, i says a 60 percent probability that k's recommendation is right. Sixty percent or 0.60 shows the degree of k's recommendation for i. We use *Recommendation Value*, $R_{ik} \in [0, 1]$, to represent this degree. Then the indirect trust value computing is defined as, $IDT_{ikj} = R_{ik} \circ DT_{kj}$. Usually, we choose traditional multiplying, '$\times$', in real number field as recommending operating '$\circ$'. Then, $IDT_{ikj} = R_{ik} \times DT_{kj}$. Because $R_{ik} \in [0, 1]$ and $DT_{kj} \in [0, 1]$, then $IDT_{ikj} \in [0, 1]$.

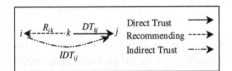

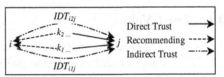

Fig. 1. One Level Recommending   **Fig. 2.** Two Recommending Path

This is a useful way to gain a view of the objective peer that is wider than its own experiences. However, the trust values still only reflect the experience of peer i and his acquaintances. In order to get a wider view, peer i may wish to ask his friends' friends. This two levels indirect trust value computing is defined as, $IDT_{ij} = (R_{ik_1} \otimes R_{k_1k_2}) \circ DT_{k_2j}$. The recommendation value "multiplying" operator will be discussed in Sect. 4.

If peer i continue in this manner, it will get more and more accurate trust value with j. Then multi levels recommending instance will arise. There is a recommending chain or path. The multi levels indirect trust value computing is similar to two levels recommending, $IDT_{ij} = (R_{ik_1} \otimes R_{k_1k_2} \otimes \cdots \otimes R_{k_{(r-1)}k_r}) \circ DT_{k_rj}$.

2.4   Reputation Value Computing

Generally, a peer in the P2P system has not only one acquaintance. It can ask all its acquaintances' options about the object peer, then combines all these indirect trust value to obtain the reputation value. Reputation value equals the "sum" of all indirect trust value. The two acquaintances or two recommending paths instance is shown in Fig. 2. How to combine the indirect trust value into reputation value is defined as, $Rep_{ij} = IDT_{i1j} \oplus IDT_{i2j}$. The indirect trust value "summing" operator will be discussed in Sect. 4. The three or more acquaintances instance is similar to two acquaintances, $Rep_{ij} = IDT_{i1j} \oplus IDT_{i2j} \oplus \cdots \oplus IDT_{isj}$.

3   Global Trust Value Computing Method

In a P2P system, one peer does not know all other peers, and then its all acquaintances are only part of all the peers. Its reputation value from all acquaintances is not all other peers' global options about the objective peer, just is *local trust value*. We can suppose all other peers are peer i's "acquaintances", the recommending value with real acquaintances $R_{ik} \neq 0.5$, $k \in [acquaintances]$, represents good or bad recommendation; the recommending value with pseudo acquaintances or strangers $R_{ik'} = 0.5$, $k' \in [strangers]$, represents no recommendation. On this supposition, peer i can ask all other peers to obtain the *global trust value* about object peer. This global trust value computing instance is illustrated in Fig. 7. We suppose there are n peers in a P2P system; this global trust value computing can be expressed, $IDT_{ij} = \sum_{k=1}^{n} \oplus(R_{ik} \circ DT_{kj})$.

In general P2P application, when peer i want to obtain some service, it always chooses some peers as source providers in the system. If there is not any trust and reputation mechanism, this choosing is absolutely random. In the trust and reputation system, peer i chooses the peers with highest trust value. Then peer i will compute the indirect trust value or reputation value with all other "acquaintances", IDT_{i1}, IDT_{i2}, ..., IDT_{in}. It is clear that this is similar to general vector and array multiplying, we can write this in vector and array manner.

$$(IDT_{i1}, IDT_{i2}, \ldots, IDT_{in}) = (R_{i1}, R_{i2}, \ldots, R_{in}) \circ \begin{pmatrix} DT_{11} & DT_{12} & \ldots & DT_{1n} \\ DT_{21} & DT_{22} & \ldots & DT_{2n} \\ \vdots & \vdots & \vdots & \vdots \\ DT_{n1} & DT_{n2} & \ldots & DT_{nn} \end{pmatrix}$$

We use $\overrightarrow{IDT_i}$ represents the vector IDT_{i1}, IDT_{i2}, ..., IDT_{in}, $\overrightarrow{R_i}$ represents the vector R_{i1}, R_{i2}, ..., R_{in}, $\mathcal{DT}$ represents the matrix (DT_{ij}). Then this vector global trust value computing can be expressed as $\overrightarrow{IDT_i} = \overrightarrow{R_i} \circ \mathcal{DT}$.

But this vector global indirect trust value is only form one level recommending, if peer i wants to get more accurate trust value, it will compute the indirect trust value from two and more levels recommending. We use a superscript represents the recommending level, then the above one level vector global indirect trust value computing expression can be modified as $\overrightarrow{IDT_i}^1 = \overrightarrow{R_i} \circ \mathcal{DT}$. For the express unification, we write the direct trust value in zero recommending level form, $\overrightarrow{IDT_i}^0 = \overrightarrow{DT_i}$. Referring to the two levels recommending, the two levels recommending global trust value is computed as

$$IDT_{ij}^2 = \sum_{l=1}^n \oplus \Big(\sum_{k=1}^n \oplus (R_{ik} \otimes R_{kl}) \circ DT_{lj} \Big) = \sum_{l=1}^n \oplus \Big(\Big(\sum_{k=1}^n \oplus (R_{ik} \otimes R_{kl}) \Big) \circ DT_{lj} \Big)$$

We write this in vector and array multiplying form, $\overrightarrow{IDT_i}^2 = (\overrightarrow{R_i} \otimes \mathcal{R}) \circ \mathcal{DT}$. The three or more levels recommending global indirect trust value computing is similar to the above two levels instance, $\overrightarrow{IDT_i}^3 = (\overrightarrow{R_i} \otimes \mathcal{R}^2) \circ \mathcal{DT}$, /dots, $\overrightarrow{IDT_i}^m = (\overrightarrow{R_i} \otimes \mathcal{R}^{(m-1)}) \circ \mathcal{DT}$.

This computing will stop until $\big| \overrightarrow{IDT_i}^m - \overrightarrow{IDT_i}^{(m-1)} \big| \le \delta$ or $m \ge (n-2)$. δ is a any little number as user defined. We do not need proof $\overrightarrow{IDT_i}^m$ is convergent, because when $m \ge (n-2)$, the recommending path must have same recommending peers, and the loop recommending instance will appear. So we will force to stop the computing at this time, even though $\big| \overrightarrow{IDT_i}^m - \overrightarrow{IDT_i}^{(m-1)} \big| > \delta$.

After the global indirect trust value $\overrightarrow{IDT_i}^m$ computing over, the global reputation value can be computed, $\overrightarrow{Rep_i} = \overrightarrow{IDT_i}^1 + \overrightarrow{IDT_i}^2 + \cdots + \overrightarrow{IDT_i}^m$. Then the global total trust value can be computed, $\overrightarrow{TT_i} = \alpha \cdot \overrightarrow{DT_i} + (1-\alpha)\overrightarrow{Rep_i}$. Peer i will choose the object peers with highest global total trust value TT_{ij} to obtain service, this can avoid great risk from unknown to the opposite peers.

4   Trust Computing Operator Definition

In the trust and reputation mechanism, there are two types of operating, indirect trust value "summing", $IDT_{i1j} \oplus IDT_{i2j}$, and recommendation value "multiplying", $R_{ik_1} \otimes R_{k_1 k_2}$.

In our improved method, we define indirect trust value "summing" as taking the maximal value, and define the recommendation value "multiplying" as taking the minimal value, $IDT_{i1j} \oplus IDT_{i2j} = max(IDT_{i1j}, IDT_{i2j})$, $R_{ik_1} \otimes R_{k_1 k_2} = min(R_{ik_1}, R_{k_1 k_2})$. This definition can avoid repeating recommending direct interaction experiences and looping recommending instances.

In the trust and reputation value computing, there usually appears repeating recommending direct interaction experiences instance, which is illustrated by Fig. 3. In Fig. 3, only P_2 have direct interaction experiences with P_5. But there have two recommending paths to P_1, $Rep_{15} = IDT_{125} + IDT_{1325}$. If the indirect trust value "summing" is defined as general summing in real number field, this can lead repeating recommendations. The direct interaction experiences would be exaggerated, then the malicious peers may be chosen as service providers. But in our definition, $Rep_{15} = max(IDT_{125}, IDT_{1325})$, there never has repeating recommending instance. The risk from direct interaction experiences exaggerated can be avoided.

There also usually have some recommending cycles in the trust and reputation computing, this instance is illustrated in Fig. 4. In the recommending path, P_2 has appeared two times, $IDT_{12325} = (R_{12} \otimes R_{23} \otimes R_{32}) \circ DT_{25}$. If the recommendation value "multiplying" is defined as general multiplying in real number field, because $0 \leq R_{ij} \leq 1$, the interaction experiences would be depressed, then the good peers may be not chosen as service providers.

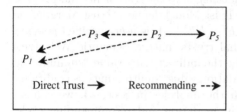

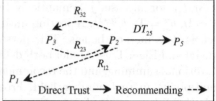

Fig. 3. Repeating Recommending   **Fig. 4.** Recommending Cycle

But in our definition, $IDT_{12325} = min(R_{12}, R_{23}, R_{32}) \circ DT_{25}$. In Fig. 4, there has another recommending path in fact, $IDT_{125} = R_{12} \circ DT_25$. Then the reputation value can be computed

$$Rep_{15} = IDT_{12325} \oplus IDT_{125} = \big((R_{12} \otimes R_{23} \otimes R_{32}) \circ DT_{25}\big) \oplus (R_{12} \circ DT_{25})$$

The recommending operating 'o' has been defined as traditional multiplying '×'. We can easily proof that the recommending operating 'o' is distributive with indirect trust value summing '⊕'. Then

$$Rep_{15} = \big((R_{12} \otimes R_{23} \otimes R_{32}) \oplus R_{12}\big) \circ DT_{25}$$
$$Rep_{15} = max\big(min(R_{12}, R_{23}, R_{32}), R_{12}\big) \circ DT_{25}$$

Because $min(R_{12}, R_{23}, R_{32}) \leq R_{12}$, then $max\big(min(R_{12}, R_{23}, R_{32}), R_{12}\big) = R_{12}$, $Rep_{15} = R_{12} \times DT_{25}$. We can see this has solved recommending cycle problem.

5   Other Related Trust and Reputation Mechanisms

In recent years, trust and reputation has been the research hotspot, and some researchers have given some trust and reputation mechanisms. Among these mechanisms, EigenTrust Model [8] and Semantic Web Trust Model [9] are most similar to the mechanism given in this paper.

EigenTrust Model got a complete view of P2P file sharing network by computing $t = (C^T)^n c_i$ after $n = large$ iterations. C is the matrix (c_{ij}), c_{ij} is the normalized local trust value; c_i is the vector containing the value c_{ij}. t is a global trust vector in this model, its elements, t_j, quantify how much trust the system as a whole places peer j. We can see there is no recommendation conception in EigenTrust Model, which confuses direct trust with recommendation notion. When there are malicious or unfair "direct recommending" or "direct rating" peers in the system, EigenTrust Model will lose the ability to find out these unfair peers.

Semantic Web Trust Model describes the credibility of web statements that are supposed as logical assertions, which has something different from the trust in P2P system. This model defines *personal belief*, b, to the statement; and *personal trust*, t_{ij}, for any user j. Semantic Web Trust Model defines "Trust Merging" as $b^0 = \mathbf{b}$, $b^n = \mathbf{T} \cdot b^{(n-1)}$, repeating until $b^n = b^{(n-1)}$. $\mathbf{b}$ is user specified personal beliefs, b is merged beliefs, $\mathbf{T}$ is personal trusts matrix. Semantic Web Trust Model and EigenTrust Model both define the indirect trust value "summing" as traditional summing, and the recommendation value "multiplying" as traditional multiplying in real number field. From the analyses in Sect. 4, we can see this definition can lead repeating recommendation and recommending cycles instances.

6   Trust Mechanism Simulation

In this section we will do some experiments to assess the performance of our improved method comparing with EigenTrust Model.

6.1   Threat Model

In the P2P system, there are three threat models generally. The first is *Independent Malicious Source Peers Threat Mode* (IMSPTM). In this mode, there are some independent malicious source peers in the P2P system. The malicious peer is always providing unauthenticated service. The second is *Independent Malicious Source and Recommending Peers Threat Mode* (IMSRPTM). There are some malicious source and recommending peers in the P2P system. The malicious peer always provides unauthenticated service, and the malicious recommending peer always gives positive recommendation value. The third is *Collective Malicious Source and Recommending Peers Threat Mode* (CMSRPTM). There are some malicious source and recommending peers in the P2P system. In this mode, the malicious source peers and recommending peers unite to cheat the challenger. The malicious source peer always provides unauthenticated service. The malicious recommending peer gives positive recommendation value only when the object peer is malicious source peer; when the object peer is good source peer, the malicious recommending peer gives right recommendation value normally.

We will do our experiments in CMSRPTM threat mode, because this mode is the most complicated threat mode, which is most difficult for the trust mechanism to find out the malicious source peers and recommending peers.

6.2   Initialization and Basic Rules

In our simulation, there are 60 peers in the whole system. At the beginning, the direct trust value and the recommending value both are 0.50 each other, which means there is not any thing to judge whether the opposite peer is trustworthy or not trustworthy. But the peer always trusts himself, so $R_{ii} = 1.0$, $DT_{ii} = 1.0$. After computing the total trust value over, first we choose 15 highest total trust value peers, and then choose 13 peers from the 15 peers as source peers randomly. This can reduce the load of highest trust value peers at a certain extent.

After having chosen source peers, if the object peer is good, then the direct trust value between the challenger and the object peer will be added with a positive rating 0.02; the recommendation value on the recommending path also will be added with a positive rating 0.02. If the object peer is bad, the direct trust value and recommendation value are will be decreased 0.10. The absolute value of decreasing is higher than increasing, because good impression needs many good interactions, but bad impression needs only one bad interaction.

We call that the process, in which a challenging peer computes the total the trust value, changes the direct the trust value and recommending value based on the property of chosen peers, is a cycle. There are 500 cycles in every experiment. After the simulation system has run some cycles, the challenging peer can pitch on more and more good peers as source peers to get service. When 12 or 13 good peers can be chosen steadily, we can record the number of cycles that the system has run to see the performance of the trust mechanism.

6.3   CMSRPTM Simulation

In the CMRSPTM threat model, the performance of EigenTrust Model and our improved method is illustrated in Fig. 5 and Fig. 6. Fig. 5 shows the cycle number needed when 12 trusted peers have been chosen steadily. Fig. 6 shows the cycle number needed when 13 trusted peers have been chosen steadily. The x-coordinate represents the different number of malicious source peers (MSPN) and malicious recommending peers (MRPN). From the figures we can see the more the P2P system has malicious peers, the more the cycle number is needed to pitch on 12 or 13 trusted peers. And under the condition of same number of malicious peers, pitching on 13 trusted peers need more cycle number than pitching on 12 trusted peers. In the same number of malicious peers and same trusted peers chosen, our improved method needs less cycle number than EigenTrust Model. Our improved method has higher performance of choosing trusted peers.

We also have done some experiments to test how much of the learning parameter α is most suitable in our trust and reputation mechanism, which is illustrated in Fig. 8. Learning parameter α represents the importance of direct experiences. In CMRSPTM experiments for comparing the performance of EigenTrust Model and our improved method, we set $\alpha = 0.7$ as a default value. In fact learning parameter can affect the trust mechanism's performance very much. We set the malicious source peer number as 25, the malicious recommending peer number as 30, α is from 0.4 to 0.8, we record the cycle number needed when 12 or 13

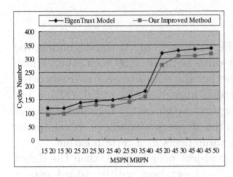

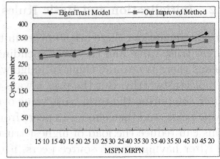

Fig. 5. CMSRPTM 12 Peers Chosen   **Fig. 6.** CMSRPTM 13 Peers Chosen

trusted peers is pitched on steadily. We can see, when $\alpha = 0.65$ the cycle number needed is minimal in pitching on both 12 and 13 trusted peers. $\alpha = 0.65$ is most suitable to our improved global trust value computing mechanism.

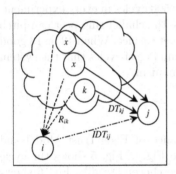

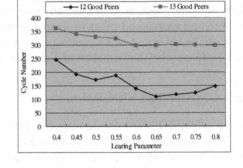

Fig. 7. Global Trust Value   **Fig. 8.** The Effect of Learning Parameter

7   Conclusion and Future Work

From the simulation we can see our improved method of choosing trusted source peers in P2P system has higher performance than other related trust mechanism. We add the recommendation value concept to find out the unfair or malicious ratter or the recommending peer. Many other related trust model could not filter the unfair recommendations well. We also define the indirect trust value summing operator to replace traditional summing, and define the recommendation value multiplying operator to replace traditional multiplying. This way avoids repeating recommending direct experiences and solves the recommending cycle problem.

In the future, we will redefine the indirect trust value summing operator and recommendation value multiplying operator, because the Maximal operating and

Minimal operating lost lots of information in the computing process. We also will use fuzzy relation theory to describe the trust or recommendation relationship. And we will use the way of fuzzy clustering to choose the trusted source peers in P2P system.

References

1. Jigar Patel, W. T. Luke Teacy, Nicholas R. Jennings, and Michael Luck.: A Probabilistic Trust Model for Handling Inaccurate Reputation Sources. The Proceedings of iTrust 2005, Trust Management, Third International Conference, Paris, France (2005)
2. Audun Jøsang, R. Ismail.: The beta reputation system. The Proceedings of the 15th Bled Conference on Electronic Commerce, Bled, Slovenia (2002)
3. Audun Jøsang.: An Algebra for Assessing Trust in Certification Chains. The proceedings of NDSS'99, Network and Distributed System Security Symposium, The Internet Society, San Diego (1999)
4. Zhang Jingmei, Zhang Jingxiang.: Researches on Trust Models of P2P Network Security. Computer Application Research, 2003.3 76–77
5. Zhu Junmao, Yang Shoubao, Fan Jianping, and Chen Mingyu.: A Grid&P2P Trust Model Based on Recommendation Evidence Reasoning. Computer Research and DevelopmentVol.42, 2005.5 797–803
6. Sun Huaijiang.: A Trust Acquisition Method for Trust Management in Open Multiagent System. Computer Engineering and Application, 2004.29 135–138
7. Tang Wen, Chen Zhong.: Research of Subjective Trust Management Model Based on the Fuzzy Set Theory. Journal of Software, 2003.14(8) 1401–1408
8. Sepandar D. Kamvar, Hector Garcia-Molina.: The EigenTrust Algorithm for Reputation Management in P2P Networks. The Proceedings of the Twelfth International World Wide Web Conference, 2003
9. Matthew Richardson, Rakesh Agrawal, Pedro Domingos.: Trust management for the semantic web. The Proceedings of the Second International Semantic Web Conference, Sanibel Island, FL, USA (2003)

Trusted Priority Control Design for Information Networks Based on Sociotechnology

Noriaki Yoshikai

Nihon University
Advanced Research Institute for the Sciences and Humanities,
12-5, 5-bancho, Chiyoda-ku, Tokyo 102-8251 Japan
`yoshikai@arish.nihon-u.ac.jp`

Abstract. In order to achieve the optimum theoretical network values as described in this paper, it is necessary to provide a link between Information Technology (IT) and Social Network (SN) considerations. Since for an SN in an on-line community the characteristics of both individual participants and the group organization can be expressed in the same graph, the SN can be related to the IT design because the organization aspects of the SN are relevant to the network communities formed by the IT network. As an example of an application using both IT and SN aspects, a novel trusted priority control method for VPNs is proposed as a case study and its effectiveness is demonstrated.

1 Introduction

On-line communities on the Internet, using mobile phones, pervasive computing and distributed processing technologies, are growing fast and spreading widely. In addition, some social issues, such as the sharing and utilizing of knowledge in a community, or the trust in a community, are becoming important issues for a variety of organizations for enhancing the activities of communities. Analyzing the relationship between IT (Information Technology) and social issues calls for a sociotechnical research approach, and some research results using this approach have been published [1].

A network consists of a social network plane and an information network plane. Normally these two network planes have been investigated independently. However, in order to implement a network model which can be adopted widely in society, network researchers have to consider both planes simultaneously, because the groups in the social network become the on-line community in the information network.

In this paper, an integrated network architecture based on sociotechnology is first described. Next, it is proposed that the centrality of affiliation networks in the social network plane can be used for the priority control in the information network. Finally, a case study relating to priority control in VPNs is discussed.

2 Integrated Network Architecture Based on Sociotechnology

Pew Inc. has researched the relationship between the Internet and social networks [2]. This report mentions the impact of the existing internet, based on current technology,

L.T. Yang et al. (Eds.): ATC 2006, LNCS 4158, pp. 268–278, 2006.

on social network. There is no report which evaluates the effects of new technologies, such as P2P or ubiquitous computing. There is also no study about the relationship between network value and the social network.

Dr. Reed researched a combination of the influence of the information network and that of the social network, and discovered that the network value in a communication network is dependent upon the number of on-line communities and the size of each community [3]. Since an on-line community can be considered to be a group in a social network, the information network plane can be related to the social network plane by using the number of the groups, as shown in Fig. 1. The network value can be increased by a design which controls not only technological parameters which cover end-to-end traffic performance, error rate, reliability, security and usability, but also movement in the social parameters, which include the social network, so that the number of groups and the size of each group can be increased.

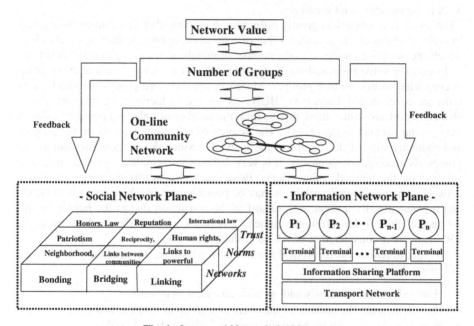

Fig. 1. Integrated Network Architecture

Reed's law applies to on-line communities on the Internet, where all sorts of chat rooms, message boards, blogs and auction markets have added new ways for people to form groups online. This means that the power of a network that enhances social networks on the information networks increases exponentially with the number of different human groups that can use the network increases.

However, this idea is based on the premise that every network participant would be able to find all the members and groups of interest to him/her, to connect to these members, and then to participate in these groups. This premise is not realistic. The scale of group composition, that is the size of each group, should be considered at least. According to Dr. Dunbar, an anthropologist who studied the scale of group behavior of primates and its relation to the size of the relevant part of the brain, natural groups of around 150 persons are likely to be formed in human society, regardless of the function and the purpose of the group [4]. This hypothesis implies that a group composition of more than about 150 persons is unrealizable on account of processing restrictions in the human brain.

Since the group size with the number of the maximum members which constitutes one group is given by the number of combination of group composition, the network value can be expressed as equation 1 [5].

$$Vr = \sum_{K=1}^{m} \frac{N(N-1)\cdots(N-K+1)}{K(K-1)\cdots 1} \tag{1}$$

where K means the number of members in a group and m is the maximum number of K, N is the number of all members.

The value of a network is greatly influenced by the number of members in a group. In order to augment the potential value of a network, it may be seen that technology which encourages an increase in the number of members in a group is very important.

In existing networks based on the Internet, there is no network where every group is connected to every other group. Moreover, as there are groups on which many links are concentrated, known as "HUBs", a layered or hierarchical structure should also be considered. Since these factors limit the number of links, the potential value of the existing network is decreased. The amount of reduction depends on the purpose and characteristics of the groups in the network. Since the average life time of the groups also changes dynamically, it is very difficult to formulate a general analytical solution for the network value. Since these restrictive factors are items relating to network composition or structure, it may be possible to solve these issues technically and organizationally, except with regard to the restriction due to the human brain's processing ability. Therefore, the value of a network which corresponds to groups of 150 members is considered to be a kind of theoretical limit.

In order to realize the theoretical limit of network value, it is necessary to study the following three items:

- How to form groups easily and as wide an extent as possible.
- How to increase the number of members in a group as much as possible.
- How to form connections between groups as effectively as possible.

Many technologies for a network community have been studied and put into practical use. Consequently, many widespread on-line community groups have been realized easily. However, in many cases the subsequent management and operation of the community don't work well. A method of organization management which utilizes the social network is effective in solving this problem. Specifically, a social network is first created by monitoring the behavior of every user in the network. Evaluation parameters including Degree, Vulnerability, Closeness Centrality, Betweenness Centrality, and Information Centrality [6, 7] can be derived from the social network, so that the characteristics of the organization activities of the member between the groups, or in a group, can be described quantitatively. As a result, a member who is at the core of a group, or a link which is a hindrance to activity can be identified. This data is useful in improving the network value, because the number of groups and the link distributions can be changed on the basis of this data. This means that the efficiency of the group activity can be increased by using this data, so improving the information network and the social network. For example, if social network evaluation shows that the position of one person who is expected to be a leader has no centrality in the group, the connections in both the social network and the information network have to be changed so that his/her position is centered in the group. This kind of social data can be also used for the trusted priority control in the information network.

3 Affiliation Network and Priority Control for Information Network Design

3.1 Network Design Based on Social Network Analysis

In conventional network traffic engineering, which aims to enhance the usage ratio of the network and to optimize network performance, the usage of network resources and network performance are measured, and, based on the measured data, traffic control parameters are selected, routing tables are adjusted, network resources are classified, and priority control is applied. The degree of importance of data carried in the network is indicated by the users, and the network is designed and controlled on the basis of this user-indicated data. However, it is not always best to leave the responsibility of prioritization to users in this way.

Take, as an example, the case where a group with its members dispersed in a number of locations is given the responsibility of developing a new product, and the group members communicate with each other over a virtual private network (VPN) within their organization or company. To engineer this network, the estimated volume of data to be generated by the group, and the reliability and security requirements are first collected, and the required functionality is determined. Then, paths are logically dimensioned and the routes for the physical links are determined. Usually, a network configuration so designed will reflect, in one way or another, the social network within the project group, which is characterized by the positions and authorities of individuals in the group. For example, links are usually set up to the project leader, who is in the central position, and the priority control for traffic is designed around the leader. However, a social network is usually built gradually, based on the purpose and activities of the group on the network. It is normal for the structure of the social network to be invisible to the network administrator, or even to users. It is not unusual for there to be both the nominal leader and a real leader in a group, or for users who function as brokers to emerge. It is usually the case that, as group activities proceed, core members emerge. They make practically all the key decisions and take charge of important matters, and most information tends to be directed to these members. Such core members are not necessarily closely associated with official positions within the group. In spite of the fact that the group cannot function well if the roles played by the core members are disregarded, conventional network design has not been based on information about such a social network.

If core members should remain disconnected for some time from the real network, the group would cease to function well. Therefore, it is necessary to provide some redundancy and ensure high reliability for links between core members. To enable a group to function well through communication over the real network, it is necessary to build the real network in a way that the emergence of such key members in the group, and the implications for reliability requirements, are taken into account in the traffic engineering and reliability design, in particular, information management and the information transfer algorithms.

Figure 2 shows the functional diagram of a network design system that takes the analysis of the social network into consideration.

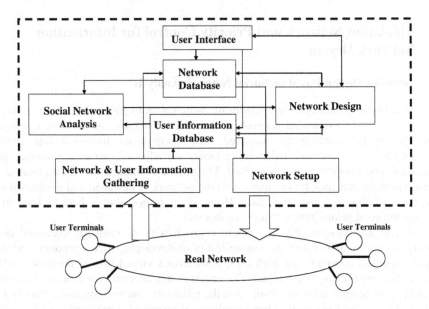

Fig. 2. Network Design Using Social Network Analysis

This system consists of the user interface, a network database, a user information database, and functions for the gathering of network information, network design, network setup, and social network analysis. The system is connected to the real network, to which user terminals are also connected. The network information gathering part gathers the configuration and operational status of devices within the real network, and the operational status of the network itself. It also gathers information about the individuals using the network. Specifically, it gathers the personal number and location information of each user, which are used for user authentication. It then stores these items of information in the network database and the user information database as appropriate.

Specifically, the network information includes the communication capacity of each device within the network, the connection configuration between the devices, the capacity of each of the links (active and standby) connecting the devices, and the volume and distribution of traffic on the real network. The user information includes (1) the information needed for user authentication, such as user ID, password, time stamp, and electronic certificate, (2) information about the group in which the user participates, (3) information about the ranking of the services and groups the user may access in the future, (4) information identifying the user location, such as the terminal being used and the location of that terminal, (5) information about the relationship between signed-in users, and (6) the type and volume of information that has flowed between users.

The user interface accepts requests from the network administrator or users. Specifically, a request includes the service class (quality requirement for the real network), the end-to-end quality of the link to be set up (delay, bandwidth, and reliability), and information about the group to be formed over the real network (member names, the relationship between members, etc.).

The network design part designs the real network based on the requests from the network administrator or users, the network configuration information stored in the network database, and the user information stored in the user information database, and then saves the network design information into the network database and the user information database.

The design sequence is as follows. First, the social network is analyzed based on given user information, which identifies the centrality and vulnerability within each group and between groups. Next, based on this result, the capacity required of each device and each link within the real network as well the required reliability measures, such as the provision of multiple links, are determined.

The network setup part configures the real network based on the design results from the network design part and the network information stored in the network database.

When a user requests a service via a user terminal, the user information is delivered to the user information database via the network information gathering part. The user is authenticated on the basis of the information in the user information database, and, if successful, a use permission is sent to the user terminals that use the authentication result. Finally, a connection is set up to enable the terminals that are the subject of the request to communicate with each other.

The network design part determines whether a request from the network administrator or a user has been satisfied, based on the network operational status information stored in the network database and the analysis result from the social network analysis part. If the request is not satisfied, the network design part determines the changes required in the network configuration, the network operation rules, or the equipment capacities as necessary, stores the changed design data in the network database and the user information database, and causes the network setup part to reconfigure the real network based on the revised design data.

3.2 Centrality in Affiliation Networks

In Sociology, collectives linked through multiple memberships of participants (called actors) are referred to as affiliation networks. An affiliation network consists of two key elements: a set of actors and a collection of subset of actors which is a group in the social network.

By belonging to an organization, individuals gain various possibilities as well as restrictions on their behavior. At the same time, interactions with other individuals both within and outside the organization change both the organizations and individuals. Those individuals who belong to a number of organizations can act as a bond between the different organizations, thereby enhancing their centrality in their organizations. By belonging to a higher-class organization, an individual can gain higher centrality. Moreover, an organization that acquires an individual with higher centrality can gain higher centrality for itself. This duality of person and group can be identified through the analysis of centrality on an affiliation network based on the graph theory. [8]

The definition of centrality and the method of calculating it are described in [8]. For example, "degree centrality" is based on a numerical model in which actors are linked to other adjacent actors. The model can be used to derive the number of other individuals or organizations that are directly linked to the individual or the organization in question. The "betweenness centrality" is a model for the degree of broker activity. If an actor with high centrality is removed, a large number of other actors may suffer disruption to their mutual associations. This means that the organization has high vulnerability. "Flow centrality" is an extension of betweeness centrality, obtained by associating it with a value-associated graph from a network flow viewpoint. Flow centrality permits the attachment of a weight to each link.

Conventionally, the main use to which qualitative information on the centralities of a group active in a social network has been has been put is for group management, such as the evaluation of the activities of each individual and the review of the status or role of each individual. We have chosen to apply this information to the configuration and control of an information network.

3.3 Social Network Analysis and Its Application to Priority Control

Social network analysis, which has been developed as a tool to make activities of an organization visually comprehensible, can be applied to understanding the activities of a community (group) created on a real network, on the basis of exchanges of emails between members and the content of blogs. "Centrality within a social network", which can be derived as one of the analysis results, is an important parameter indicating who is the central figure in the group's activity, and how vulnerable the group is if that individual is removed from the group. The parameter is also useful for the design of a real network. In other words, in a LAN or VPN, which uses user authentication to permit only specific users to access the network, the relationships between users can map onto the links on the real network through IP addresses and the personal information of the users. Therefore, centrality within a network can be used in the design of a trusted priority control of traffic and reliability control on the real network. The method of centrality analysis in a social network is described in detail in [6].

4 Case Study

The application of the analysis of the activity of a group created on the network to the design of a real network is illustrated in the following case study.

Figure 3 illustrates a situation where there are 10 users active on the network and the users belong to 6 different network communities (groups). Since the upper row indicates the individuals and the lower row the groups, this graph is called a bipartite graph. The adjacent matrix of this graph is shown in Fig. 4. Generally, if there are n individuals and m groups, the matrix is an (n+m) x (n+m) square matrix. The matrix consists of the individual part and the group part.

The degree centrality and the betweenness centrality of Fig. 3 can be derived as follows.

4.1 Degree Centrality Model

In a bipartite graph, the centrality of an individual and the centrality of a group can be derived by calculating the matrix diagonal of $X=AA^T$ (where A^T is a transpose of A matrix. In this case, the result is {1,1,3,3,2,2,2,3,1,3,4,3,2,4,4,4} This value represents the centrality derived from the entire picture of the network, including both individuals and groups. Using X, it is also possible to evaluate individuals and groups separately. Specifically, the n-th column of the non-matrix diagonal in X represents the number of groups to which a pair of individuals belongs. Therefore, the sum of a row can be considered to express the degree of the group activity by an individual. Since the sums of the (n+1)-th row to the m-th row of the non-matrix diagonal in X represents the number of members in each group, it can be considered to express the activities of individuals in each group. Let us call the centrality model derived from the entire picture of the network Model 1, and the centrality model in which groups and individuals are evaluated separately Model 2. Table 1 shows the result of calculating centrality for the bipartite graph in Fig. 3. In conventional network design, if several members are at the same rank, priority is given to the members with the largest number of links connected to them. Therefore, users 3, 4, 8 and 10 are given the same priority because they all have 3 links and are at the same rank. However, in terms of the activity in the group, user 10 has the highest activity, followed by users 3 and 4, and by user 8. In other words, in both models 1 and 2, user 10 is most strongly linked to other members, and thus is considered the leader of the group. If we assume that the number of links is proportional to the degree of activity within the group, user 10 is the most active member, and it is desirable to ensure that sufficient bandwidth and adequate links, including some spare bandwidth and links, are allocated for user 10 in the network.

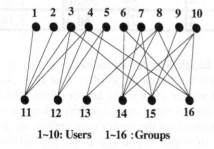

Fig. 3. Example of Bipartite Graph

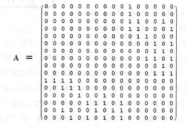

Fig. 4. Adjacent Matrix of Fig.3

4.2 Betweenness Centrality Model

Betweenness centrality can be determined by calculating the number of links that pass through the point in question by using the simulator [9].

The betweenness centralities obtained for the social network shown in Fig. 3 are given in Table 1. User 3 has the highest score from the viewpoints of both the overall network and personal betweenness, and thus plays the highest broker role. Therefore, it is desirable that duplicate or multiple links be provided for user 3 so that the service of user 3 will not be disrupted.

Besides this centrality, it is possible to create a flow-centric model, which represents the weighted network flows of communication traffic. The result of this analysis is a social network model based on the data on the real network, which can be effective for use in priority control and reliability control of the real network.

The network control over a VPN using Multi-Protocol Label Switching (MPLS) takes the social relationship given in Fig. 3 into consideration. A server-client type information delivery system is considered here. An MPLS network consists of edge nodes (label edge routers), which generate labels for incoming data,

Table 1. Centrality data of Fig.3

		Degree		Betweenness	
		Model1	Model2	Model1	Model2
U	1	1	3	0	0
	2	1	3	0	0
	3	3	8	48.93	17.136
s	4	3	8	46.62	14.832
	5	2	3	11.76	0.504
e	6	2	6	3.78	0.504
r	7	2	6	9.03	3.168
	8	3	7	26.46	3.168
	9	1	3	0	0
	10	3	9	23.94	4.68
G	1(11)	4	4	58.17	0
	2(12)	3	5	30.03	1.66
r	3(13)	2	3	10.08	0.66
o	4(14)	4	6	25.41	0.66
u	5(15)	4	5	55.86	1.66
p	6(16)	4	7	50.4	3.34

and core nodes (label switch routers), which handle MPLS packets based on the labels attached to them. The IP priority information written in the header of an IP packet sent from a user terminal is written into the service class in the header of the MPLS label. The MPLS network performs priority control based on this priority information. Since the priority of each user can be determined on the basis of an analysis of the associated social network, it is possible to apply sophisticated priority control involving ranking by using multiple labels.

For the social network shown in Fig. 3, the following design parameters can be derived for use in priority control that takes centrality into consideration. In this particular case, user 10 has the highest number of links to other members, and thus is the most likely to be affected by highly fluctuating traffic of other users. A reverse case also tends to happen.

Therefore, it is desirable to ensure uninterrupted data flow to and from other users by providing a high-capacity link between the server and the terminal of user 10, and a mirror server for the data which user 10 transmits. It is also desirable to provide two alternative routes between the server and user 3, who tends to function as a broker in the group activity.

Let us assume that both user 4 and user 5 who are connected to the same edge node, and that user 5 has a lower activity than user 4. User 4 belongs to groups 11, 12 and 16. The importance of each packet sent by user 4 depends on the rank of the group to which the packet is destined. User 5 belongs to groups 12 and 13. If group 12 is the highest ranking group on the network, it is important to ensure that user 5 can send information to the members of group 12. Therefore, for the edge node to which users 4 and 5 are connected, it is advisable to send low-priority packets from user 4 on a low-speed, low-capacity link while sending high-priority packets from user 5 on a high-speed, high-capacity link.

5 Conclusion

In order to achieve the optimum network value, this paper has proposed a method of network design based on a network architecture that integrates the information network and the social network that share the same groups. As a specific example of application, a method of using the analysis of a social network for the design of an information network has been presented. Using a simple user group model, a possible design of priority control in an MPLS network has been derived. As a result, it has been shown that, by adding the analysis of a social network to the priority control, which has traditionally been based on traffic characteristics and priority information provided by the user, it is possible to implement network design which is better aligned with the activities of the groups on the network.

The author plans to verify the relationship between the analysis of a social network and its group activity on the information network, and to develop an integrated network simulator.

Acknowledgements

The author would like to thank Dr. Jun Kanemitsu for his helpful discussions on the concept of social network and its analysis from the sociological viewpoint.

This work was supported in part by Nihon University Individual Research Grant for 2006 and in part by JSPS (Japan Society for the Promotion of Science).

References

1. Huysman, M. , Wulf, V., "Social Capital and Information Technology", The MIT Press (2004).
2. Horrigan, J., Lee, R., Fox, S.: "Online Communities: Networks that Nurture Long-distance Relationships and Local Ties", Pew Internet and American Life Projects, www.pewinternet.org, (2001).
3. http://www.reed.com/Papers/GFN/reedslaw.html
4. Dunbar, R.: "Grooming, Gossip and the Evolution of Language", Faber and Faber, London (1996)
5. Yoshikai, N. "A Network value model and its application to technology evaluation for the on-line community", APSITT2005, pp.399-404, November 2005.
6. Kanemitsu, J.; "Social Network Analysis", Keisou-shobou, 2003. (in Japanese)
7. Kanemitsu, J., "From Social Capital to Human Capital: Theory and Analysis of Social Capital", Aoyama Management Review, pp.45-52, 2002. (in Japanese)
8. Faust, K. "Centrality in affiliation networks", Social Network vol.19, pp.157-191, 1997.
9. Social Network Analysis Software NetMiner : http://www.netminer.com/NetMiner

Autonomic Trust Management in a Component Based Software System

Zheng Yan and Ronan MacLaverty

Nokia Research Center, Helsinki, Finland
{zheng.z.yan, ronan.maclaverty}@nokia.com

Abstract. Trust plays an important role in a software system, especially when, the system is component based and varied due to component joining and leaving. How to manage trust in such a system is crucial for embedded devices, such as mobile phones. This paper presents a trust management solution that can manage trust adaptively in a component based software (CBS) system. We develop a formal trust model to specify, evaluate and set up trust relationships that exist among system entities. We further present an autonomic trust management architecture that adopts a number of algorithms for trust assessment and maintenance during component execution. These algorithms use recent advances in Subjective Logic to ensure the management of trust within the CBS system.

1 Introduction

The growing importance of software in the domain of mobile systems introduces special requirements on trust. The first requirement is that any software design must support a product-line approach to system development. This normally implies that system software consists of a number of components that are combined to provide user features. Components interact over well defined interfaces; these are exported to applications that can combine and use the components to provide features to consumers. Thus, common components can be effectively shared by applications. A typical feature of mobile devices with CBS is to allow addition of components after deployment, which creates the need for run-time trust management.

From system point of view, trust is the assessment of trustor on how well the observed behavior (quality attributes) of trustee meets trustor's own standards for an intended purpose [1]. From this, the critical characteristics of trust can be summarized, it is: subjective, different for each individual in a certain situation; and dynamic, sensitive to change due to the influence of many factors. Therefore, we need a proper mechanism to support autonomic trust management not only on trust establishment, but also on trust sustaining.

Most trust management systems focus on protocols for establishing trust in a particular context, generally related to security requirements. Others make use of a trust policy language to allow the trustor to specify the criteria for a trustee to be considered trustworthy [2]. Grandison and Sloman studied a number of existing trust management systems in [2]. These systems evaluate a viewpoint of trust that is quite closely tied to systems that implement access control or authentication. In [3],

L.T. Yang et al. (Eds.): ATC 2006, LNCS 4158, pp. 279–292, 2006.
© Springer-Verlag Berlin Heidelberg 2006

SULTAN framework provides the means to specify, and evaluate trust relationships for Internet applications. However, its computational overhead means it is not feasible inside an embedded system, especially in the role of trust monitor and controller.

The evaluation of trust, only when a relationship is set up, does not cater for the evolution of the relationship from its stated initial purpose to accommodate new forms of interaction. Furthermore, the focus of the security aspect of trust tends to assume that the other non-functional aspects of trust, such as availability and reliability, have already been addressed.

At present, there is no common framework to enable trust management in a commercial CBS system, even though there is a pressing need to support a range of new applications. This framework must support autonomic trust management through trust assessment and maintenance over the dynamic CBS system, consisting of different functionalities provided by various disparate companies. We need technologies for the development and validation of the trusted systems based on the integration of multiparty software while at the same time reducing the cost and integration time. The research described in this paper is an initial attempt at addressing some of these needs, which aims to establish trustworthy middleware architecture for the embedded systems with CBS.

This paper introduces an autonomic trust management solution that supports dynamic changes of trustworthiness in the CBS system. The main contributions of this paper are: a formal trust model that specifies the trust relationships for the CBS systems or devices; an autonomic trust management architecture that incorporates the new trust model allowing explicit representing, assessing and ensuring of the trust relationships, and deriving trust decisions in a dynamic environment; and a range of algorithms for incorporating trust into a system, demonstrating the feasibility of the architecture.

The rest of the paper is organized as follows. Section 2 specifies the problems we need to overcome. Section 3 presents a formal trust model we will apply into the autonomic trust management in the CBS systems. Section 4 details the design of trust management framework and develops algorithms for the autonomic trust management. Finally, conclusions and future work are presented in Section 5.

2 Trust in CBS Systems

In mapping trust to the CBS systems we can categorize trust into two aspects: trust in the component, and trust in a composition of components. For the component-centered aspect we must consider trust at several decision points: at download time and during execution. At a component download time, we need to consider whether a software provider can be trusted to offer a component. Furthermore, we need to predict whether the component is trustworthy for installation. More necessarily, when the component is executed, we have to ensure it can cooperate well with other components and the system provides expected performance and quality. The trust relationship changes during the above procedure.

When discussing a CBS system, the execution of components in relation to other entities of the system needs to be taken into account. Even though the component is trustworthy in isolation, the new joined component could cause problems because it will share system resources with others. This influence will impact the trustworthiness of the system. Consequently, the system needs mechanisms to control its performance, and to ensure its trustworthiness even if internal and external environment changes. Additionally, some applications (e.g. a health care service) need special support for trust because they have high priority requirements, whereas game playing applications, while exhibiting similar functionality (e.g. a network connection) will not have the same priority. Therefore, system-level trustworthiness is dependent on the application domain, so the system needs a trust management framework that supports different trust requirements from the same or different components. This paper mainly focuses on the autonomic trust management for CBS at system runtime.

3   A Formal Trust Model

Trust involves two roles: a trustor (tr) and a trustee (te). In a CBS system, a trustor can be a system user or the user's representatives (e.g. a trusted computing platform and its protected trust management framework). A trustee is the entity who holds the essential competence and quality to offer the services the trustor expects. Since trust is subjective, the trust is greatly influenced by a trustor's policy (py). Trust is also dynamic and is related to the context (ct) of the trustor and the trustee, for example, time (t), environment (e) and the intended purpose (p). Most importantly, it is mainly influenced by the trustee's competence, performance and quality. Some quality attributes of a trustee (qa) behave as referents for trust assessment. A referent will be evaluated based on evidence (ev) collected from previous experience of the trustor or other entities (e.g. recommenders). The result of a trust assessment could be a value set (b, d, u) that reflects the trustor's opinion (op) on the trust. This opinion is described as a 3-tuple: belief, disbelief and uncertainty [4].

3.1   Definitions

A CBS system can be represented as a structure (E, R, O), where E represents the set of the system entities, R the set of trust relationships between the entities, O the set of operations for the management of such trust relationships.

1) CBS system entities:
These entities can be any parties that are involved into or related to the CBS system. These entities include a CBS system user, a component consumer, a component provider, a service, a component (composition of components), an application, a subsystem and a system, as well as an operation or a mechanism provided by the system.

An application is a software entity that provides a set of functions to a user. A component is a unit of trading that may contain multiple services. A service is a unit of software instantiation that is contained in a component and conforms to a component model. A system is a combination of a platform, a set of components, a runtime environment (RE) and a set of applications that can provide a user with a set of functions. A platform provides access to the underlying hardware. The relationships among above entities are described in Figure 1.

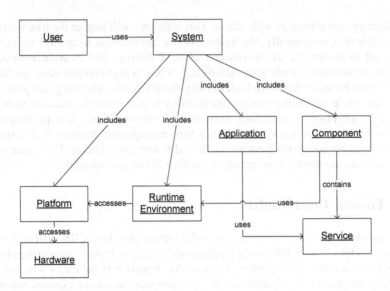

Fig. 1. Relationships of CBS system entities

2) Trust relationship

A trust relationship in a CBS system can be specified as a 6-tuple $TR = \{tr, te, py, ct(t,e,p), ev, op(b,d,u)\}$ which asserts that entity tr trusts entity te with regard to tr's trust policy py in the context $ct(t,e,p)$, based on the evidences of te: ev, and $op(b,d,u)$ indicates the trust valuation.

Where:

- tr and te are subsets of the set of system entities (E).
- py is the subset of the set (PY) of all policies regarding trust management. $PY = \{to, ir, ep, cr\}$, where to is a threshold opinion for trust, $ir = \{ir_{qa\_1}, ir_{qa\_2}, ir_{qa\_3}, ..., ir_{qa\_n}\}$ is the importance rates of different quality attributes qa of the te, and ep is the policy about the evidence used for the trust assessment. cr ($cr = \{tv_{qa\_1}, tv_{qa\_2}, tv_{qa\_3}, ..., tv_{qa\_n}\}$) is the criteria for setting positive or negative points on different quality attributes (refer to section 4.3 for details). It specifies the trusted values or value scope of different factors reflecting the quality attributes of the trustee.
- $ct(t,e,p)$ expresses the context of the trust relationship, in which t is the time constraint during which the relationship is valid, e is the environment of the trust relationship (e.g. system configurations and the domain the system located), and p is the purpose of establishing the trust relationship.
- $ev=(qa, rn)$ denotes the evidences of quality attributes, where rn is a subset of recommendations RN, and qa is the subset of the set

$$QA = \begin{cases} sec urity(\text{confidentiality, integrity, safety}); reputation; usability; \\ dependability(\text{reliability, availability, adaptability, maintainability})... \end{cases}$$. Each qual-

ity attribute has a number of factors that are referents of it. These factors can be quantified and thus monitored. For example, the 'availability' quality attribute can be reflected by uptime and response time. The trust adaptability can be measured as *MTTS/(MTTE+MTTS+MTTB)*, where *MTTB* is the mean time of response regarding trust relationship break, *MTTS* is the mean time of trust sustaining and *MTTE* is the mean time for trust establishment and re-establishment. The *QA* has a tree-like structure, which benefits the reasoning of trust problems.

A recommendation can be expressed as $rn = (rr, re, te, op, ct)$, where it asserts that *rr* recommends *re* that *rr* holds opinion *op* on *te* in the context of *ct*. Note that $rn = (rr, re, te, op, ct)$ is one kind of evidence.

- *op(b,d,u)* is the trust assessment result of this trust relationship. It is probabilities of opinion on *te* regarding belief (*b*), disbelief (*d*) and uncertainty (*u*). Particularly, *b*, *d*, and *u* satisfy: $b + d + u = 1$, and $0 \leq b, d, u \leq 1$. Herein, belief means the probability of the entity *te* can be trusted by the entity *tr*; disbelief means the probability of *te* can not be trusted by *tr*; and uncertainty fills the void in the absence of both belief and disbelief. Particularly, the bigger the value of *b*, *d*, and *u*, the more probability.

4) Trust management operations

The trust management operations compose a set $O = \{T_e, T_m, T_a, T_c\}$, where T_e is the set of operations or mechanisms used for trust establishment and re-establishment, T_m is the set of operations or mechanisms applied for monitoring and collecting the evidences or the factors regarding the quality attributes of the trustee, T_a is the set of operations or mechanisms for trust assessment, and T_c is the set of operations or mechanisms for controlling trust in order to sustain the trust relationship. The operations in T_e and T_c are classified in terms of enhancing different quality attributes. Thus the system knows which operation should be considered in order to ensure or support some quality attribute.

3.2 Trust Model for Components

The trust model for a component, given below, describes the trust specifications of all the operations implemented by services in the component. The trust request level (*trust_level*) indicates the importance of the operation (*impl_opr*). This level is upgraded when an application requests a service. *Resource* and *consumption* specifies the resource requirements that the operation requires in order to provide the performance described by *performance*. In addition, composition rules (*com_rule*) are criteria for composing this model with other trust models. The composition rule could be as simple as selecting the maximum or minimum value, or as complicated as an algorithm based on the relationships of service operations. How to specify a composition rule is beyond the scope of this paper.

m = *TM*,
where *m* is a *Trust Model* and *TM* is a set of *tm* (the trust specification of an operation).

tm = (*impl_opr*, *resource*, *consumption*, *trust_level*, *performance*, *com_rule*), for operation *impl_opr*.

Resource	= $r \in \{memory, cpu, bus, net...\}$.
Consumption	= *claim*, in case *resource* is *cpu*.
Consumption	= (*claim, release*), in case *resource* is *memory*.
Consumption	= (*claim, time*), in case *resource* is *bus*.
Consumption	= (*claim, speed*), in case *resource* is *net*.
Trust_level	= $tl \in TL$, where *TL* is the set of trust level.
Performance	= (*attribute, value*)
	Attribute = attr $\in$ {response time, uptime, mean time of failure, mean time of hazard, mean time of repair,...}: a set of factors that are referents of the quality attributes.
	Value = asserted trust value of the attribute
Com_rule	= *crule $\in$ CRULE*, where *crule* is a composition rule and *CRULE* is a set of *crule* (composition rules for composing with other trust models)
Crule	= (*cr_resource, cr_consumption, cr_trust_level, cr_performance, composition_type*), specifying composition rules for *resource, consumption, trust_level* and *performance*.

The trust model of a component can be composed based on the composition rules. It has several usages. At download time, it can be used to help system trust management framework to predict whether a component may have some trust influence on the system. The system firstly composes all related trust models based on their composition rules, and then investigates if the resource and trust requirements can be satisfied. At execution time, the trust model is used by the system execution framework to arrange resources for the services. In addition, it could help the trust management framework to monitor the performance of the services (e.g. the composed performance could play as the default trust criteria for the trust assessment), thus assess if the component's services and the subsystem containing the component are trusted or not. It could also be used to reason the trust problems at some services in a component.

3.3 Autonomic Trust Management Model

The trust assessment can be expressed as a 6-tuple $TA = (tr, te, ct, ev, py, TM)$, which asserts that *tr* assesses *te*'s trustworthiness in the context *ct*, based on the *tr*'s policy *py* and according to evidence *ev* on the *te*'s quality and the trust model *TM*. The trust assessment result has three possibilities: 1 – trusted; 0 – distrusted; and -1 – unknown. Autonomic trust management can be expressed as a 3-tuple $ATM = (TR, TA, O)$, which asserts that operations *O* are applied for the trust relationship *TR* according to the trust assessment *TA*.

4   An Autonomic Trust Management Architecture

4.1   CBS System Structure

The software architecture of a CBS system has many constraints; most of these are common across a range of industries and products. Therefore, although each product has a different software structure, a general architectural style has emerged that combines component based development with product-line software architectures [5]. The work here is based on the Robocop Component model [6], which embodies this generic style. The style consists of layered development architecture with 3 layers: an application layer that provides features to a user; a component-based middleware layer that provides functionality to applications; and, a platform layer that provides access to lower-level hardware. Using components to construct the middleware layer divided this layer into two developmental layers: a component sub-layer that contains a number of executable components and a runtime environment (RE) sub-layer that supports component development.

The component runtime supporting frameworks also exist at the runtime sub-layer. These provide functionalities for supporting component properties and for managing components. These frameworks also impose constraints on the components, with regard to mandatory interfaces, associated metadata etc. The runtime environment is consists of a component framework that treats DLL-like components. This provides a system-level management of the software configuration inside a device. Each component contains services that are executed and used by applications. The services have interactions with other services; they consume resources; and, they have trust models as described in 3.2 attached.

For some of the frameworks in the runtime environment, they have to be supported with platform functionality. For example, for resource framework, support for resource usage accounting and enforcement is required from the platform layer. In terms of trust management, the platform needs to provide security mechanisms, such as access control, memory protection and encryption/decryption. In this case the security framework offers functionality for the use of security mechanisms, provided by the platform, to develop and maintain a secure system. The platform layer also provides trusted computing support on the upper layers [7, 8].

Placing trust management inside this architecture means linking the trust management framework with other frameworks responsible for the component management (including download), the security management, the system management and the resource management. Figure 2 describes interactions among different functional blocks inside the running environment sub-layer. The trust management framework is responsible for the assessment on trust relationships and trust management operations, system monitoring and autonomic trust managing. The download framework requests the trust framework for trust assessment about components to decide if to download a component and which kind of mechanisms should be applied to this component. When a component service needs cooperation with other components' services, the execution framework will be involved, but the execution framework will firstly request the trust management framework for decision. The system framework takes care of system configurations related to the components. The trust management framework is located at the core of the runtime environment sub-layer. It monitors the system performance and instructs the resource framework to assign suitable resources to different processes. This allows the trust management framework to shutdown any misbehaving component, and to gather evidence on the trustworthiness of a system entity. Similarly, the trust management framework controls the security framework, to ensure that it applies the necessary security mechanisms to maintain a trusted system. So briefly, the trust management framework acts like a critical system manager, ensuring that the system conforms to its trust policies.

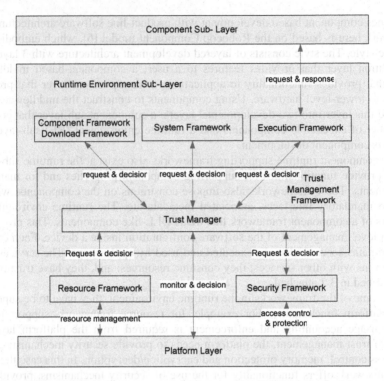

Fig. 2. Relationships among trust framework and other frameworks

4.2 Trust Management Framework

Figure 3 illustrates the structure of the trust management framework. The trust manager is responsible for trust assessment and trust related decision-making, it closely collaborates with the security framework to offer security related management. The trust manager is composed of a number of functional blocks:

- Trust policy base saves the trust policy (*py*) regarding making trust assessment and decision.
- Recommendation base saves various recommendations.
- Experience base saves the evidence *Qa(ev)* collected from the CBS system itself in various contexts;
- Decision/reason engine is used to make trust decision by request. It combines information from experience base, recommendation base and policy base to conduct the trust assessment. It is also used to identify causes of trust problems.
- Mechanism base saves opinions regarding the mechanisms in T_e and T_c that are supported by the system and attached to special context or configurations.
- Selection engine is used to select suitable mechanisms to ensure the system's trust in a special context.

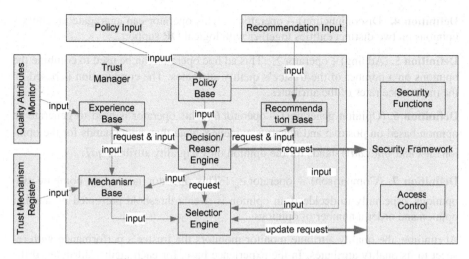

Fig. 3. A structure of trust management framework

In addition, recommendation input is the interface for collecting recommendations. Policy input is the interface for the CBS system entities to input their policies. Trust mechanism register is the interface to register trust mechanisms that can be applied in the system. Quality attributes monitor is the functional block used to monitor the CBS system entities' performance regarding those attributes that may influence the trust. The trust manager cooperates with other frameworks to manage the trust of the whole system.

4.3 Trust Assessment at Runtime

There are several existing mechanisms that can be applied for assessing trust through the evidence. Here subjective logic (SL) [4] has been chosen as the formal base for trust assessment because of its sound mathematical foundation in dealing with evidential beliefs; and the inherent ability to express uncertainty explicitly. Subjective Logic consists of a belief model called opinion and set of operations for aggregating opinions. Herein, we apply a simplified scheme of the Subjective Logic as in [9, 10]. We use seven SL operators to illustrate how to assess trust based on the formal trust model and the trust management framework. (Refer to Appendix for Definition 5-7, and [9, 10] for Definition 1-4.)

Definition 1. (Bayesian Consensus) – operator $\oplus$: This operator can be used to combine opinions of different entities on the same entity together. For example, it can be used to combine different entities' recommendations on the same entity (e.g. a service) together.

Definition 2. (Discounting) – operator $\otimes$: This operator can be used to generate opinion of a recommendation or a chain of recommendations. For example, it can be used by an entity (trustor) to generate an opinion on a recommendation.

Definition 3. (Conjunction) – operator $\wedge$: This operator can aggregate an entity's opinions on two distinct entities together with logical AND support.

Definition 4. (Disconjunction) – operator ∨ : This operator can aggregate an entity's opinions on two distinct entities together with logical OR support.

Definition 5. (Adding) – operator $\sum$: This ad hoc operator can be used to combine the opinions on a number of the trustee's quality attributes. The combination is based on the importance rates of the attributes.

Definition 6. (Opinion generator) – operator θ : This operator is used to generate an opinion based on positive and negative evidence. Note that $op(x)$ stands for the opinion on x and $op(x.qa1)$ stands for the opinion on x's quality attribute $qa1$.

Definition 7. (Comparison) – operator $\geq_{op}$: This operator is used to compare two opinions, especially to decide if an opinion is over a threshold presented by another opinion and order a number of opinions.

At runtime, the quality attribute monitor monitors the trustee's performance with respect to its quality attributes. In the experience base, for each quality attribute, if the monitored performance is better than the criteria (saved in the policy base), the positive point of that attribute is increased by 1. If the monitored result is worse than the criteria, the negative point of that attribute is increased by 1. The opinion of each quality attribute can be generated based on the opinion generator θ. In addition, based on the importance rates of different attributes ir, combined opinion on the trustee can be calculated by applying the operator $\sum$. By comparing to the trust threshold opinion (to), the decision engine can decide if the trustee is still trusted or not. The algorithm for trust assessment at runtime is described as below.

Initialization
    te: the assessed target (a system or subsystem or a service)
    $py(to, ir, ep, cr)$: the policy on te:
    $n_{qa\_i} = p_{qa\_i} = 0$; $r_{qa\_i} = 2$; $(i = 1,...,n)$
    $op(qa\_i) = (0,0,1)$; $op(te) = (0,0,1)$

1. Monitor te's performance regarding te's quality attributes in specified period t.
2. For $\forall qa\_i(i = 1,...,n)$,

    If the monitored result is better than $py.cr.tv_{qa\_i}$, p_{qa_i}++ ;

    Else, n_{qa_i}++
3. For $\forall qa\_i(i = 1,...,n)$, calculate the opinion:

    $op(qa\_i) = \theta(p_{qa\_i}, n_{qa\_i}, r_{qa\_i})$.
4. Based on the importance rates on different attributes, calculate a combined opinion: $op(te) = \sum_{i=1}^{n} \{ir_{qa\_i}, op(qa\_i)\}$.

5. If $op(te) \geq_{op} py.to$, make trust decision; else, make distrust decision.

4.4 Algorithm for Autonomic Trust Management

Autonomic trust management includes several aspects.

- Trust establishment: the process for establishing a trust relationship between a trustor and a trustee. The trust establishment is required when a component or a bundle of components is downloaded and installed at the system.
- Trust monitoring: the trustor or its delegate monitors the performance of the trustee. The monitoring process aims to collect useful evidence for the trust assessment.
- Trust assessment: the process for evaluating the trustworthiness of the trustee by the trustor or its delegate. The trustor assesses the current trust relationship and decides if this relationship is changed or not. If it is changed, the trustor will make decision which measure should be taken.
- Trust control and re-establishment: if the trust relationship will be broken or is broken, the trustor will find reasons and take some measure to control or re-establish the trust.

Trust management operations applied by the system are registered at the mechanism base with its attached context ct. The opinions on all trust management operation are generated at the mechanism base. Based on a trust assessment result, if the result is trusted, increase the positive point of the applied operations by 1. If the result is distrusted, the trust manager reasons the problem based on the structure of QA and finds out the operations that cannot ensure a trust. At the mechanism base, the system increases the negative point of those operations by 1. The opinions on all applied trust management operations can be generated based on the opinion generator θ. If the opinions on some operations are below threshold, or the trust assessment result is not trusted, the operations that raise problems should be upgraded or replaced by better ones. At the selection engine, we select suitable operations based on the following mechanism. For each composition of a set of operations, we generate a common opinion on it through combining the opinion of each operation. If the combined opinion is above the threshold, we save it. By ordering all possible compositions, we can select one composition with the highest opinion belief via applying operator $\geq_{op}$. The algorithm for the trust assessment on the operations and the operation selection is described below.

```
Initialization
    Considering ATM = (TR, TA, AO)
    AO = {ao_i}(i = 1,...n) : the trust management operations applied
    for TR
    n_{ao_i} = p_{ao_i} = 0 ;  r_{ao_i} = 2 ;  (i = 1,...,n)
    op = op(ao_i) = (0,0,1)
    py(to, ir, ep, cr): the policy on AO
    S = ∅ : the set of selected operations
```

At the Mechanism Base, generate opinions on operations

1. Do trust assessment, if $TA = 1$, $p_{ao\_i} ++ (i = 1,...,n)$

    Else, find the operations *po_i* that cause the problems:

    $PO = \{po\_i\}(i = 1,...,k)$ $(PO \subseteq AO)$, $n_{ao\_i} ++ (i = 1,...,k); ao\_i \in PO$

3. For $\forall ao\_i$, $op(ao\_i) = \theta(p_{ao\_i}, n_{ao\_i}, r_{ao\_i})$

4. If $py.to \geq_{op} op(ao\_i)$ or $TA \neq 1$, put ao_i (with opinion below

    threshold) or *po_i* into a set $RO = \{ro\_i\}(i = 1,...,l)$, upgrade

    these operations in *RO* with better ones
    At the Selection Engine, select suitable operations.
    For each composition of a set of upgrading operations CO, do
    4.1 Get existing opinions of new selected operations sup-
        ported by the system *op(co_j)* (j=1,...,m)
    4.2. Aggregate above opinions

    $op = \wedge\{op(co\_j), op(ao\_i)\}(j = 1,...,m)(i = 1,...,n-l)$, $ao\_i \in AO - RO$

    4.3. If $op \geq_{op} py.to$, add *CO* into *S*

    4.4. If $S \neq \phi$, order all opinions of the operation sets in *S*

        using $\geq_{op}$, select operation set with highest opinion be-

        lief from *S*; else raise warning message
5. Go to step 1

5 Conclusions and Future Work

This paper is the first to develop a trust management solution for the CBS system based on the Subjective Logic. We have identified the trust issues in the CBS system. We then developed a formal trust model to specify, evaluate and set up trust relationships amongst system entities. Based on this trust model, we further designed the autonomic trust management architecture to overcome the specified issues. This design is compatible with the CBS system architecture. Thus it can be easily deployed in practice in order to enhance the trustworthiness of the middleware software. Once instantiated this architecture allows explicit trust policies to be defined and managed, thereby it supports human device interaction and provides autonomic trust management with the guideline of the system users. In addition, the proposed trust management architecture will enable the trust for both system users and system internal entities since it supports managing the trust relationship between any two entities inside the CBS system.

Desirable emerging properties can be obtained by applying this proposed trust management architecture to a CBS device. These include enabling the trust assessment at runtime based on the system monitoring on a number of quality attributes of the assessed entity; autonomic trust management on the basis of trust assessment and auto-selection of trust management operations. These emerging properties allow the trust at the system runtime to be better addressed.

For future work, we will further refine the architecture design, improve the algorithms towards context-aware support and study the adaptability of this trust management solution. We are planning to build and test the trust management architecture inside a mobile device, to check its feasibility and to gain experience in the practical use for the protection of the mobile device from both malicious attacks and unforeseen feature interactions. The goal of this is to ensure that users have a positive relationship with their devices.

Acknowledgement

This work is sponsored by EU ITEA Trust4All project. The authors would like to thank Dr. Peng Zhang, Nokia Venture Organization, Dr. Silke Holtmanns, Nokia Research Center, and Dr. Rong Su, Technische Universiteit Eindhoven, for their valuable comments.

References

1. DE Denning, A New Paradigm for Trusted Systems, Proceedings of the IEEE New Paradigms Workshop, 1993.
2. T. Grandison and M. Sloman, A Survey of Trust in Internet Applications, IEEE Communications and Survey, Forth Quarter, 3(4), pp. 2–16, 2000.
3. Tyrone Grandison, Morris Sloman, Trust Management Tools for Internet Applications. In Proceedings of the First International Conference of Trust Management (iTrust 2003), Crete, Greece, May 2003.
4. A. Jøsang, A Logic for Uncertain Probabilities, International Journal of Uncertainty, Fuzziness and Knowledge-Based Systems, 9(3), pp.279–312, June 2001.
5. Van Ommering, R. 2002. Building Product Populations with Software Components. In Proceedings of the 24th International Conference on Software Engineering, ICSE '02, Orlando, Florida, May 19 - 25, 2002, ACM Press, New York, NY, pp. 255-265.
6. Muskens, J. and Chaudron, M. 2004. Integrity Management in Component Based Systems. In Proceedings of the 30th EUROMICRO Conference (Euromicro'04), Volume 00, Washington, DC, August 31 - September 03 2004, pp. 611-619
7. England Paul, Lampson Butler, Manferdelli John, Peinado Marcus, Willman Bryan, A Trusted Open Platform, IEEE Computer Society, July 2003, pp. 55-62.
8. Trusted Computing Group (TCG), TPM Specification, version 1.2, 2003. https:// www. trustedcomputinggroup.org/specs/TPM/
9. Lin, C.; Varadharajan, V.; Wang, Y.; Pruthi, V., Enhancing Grid Security with Trust Management, Proceedings of IEEE International Conference on Services Computing (SCC 2004), 15-18 Sept. 2004, pp. 303 – 310.
10. Twigg, A., A Subjective Approach to Routing in P2P and Ad Hoc Networks. In Proceedings of the First International Conference of Trust Management (iTrust 2003), Crete, Greece, May 2003.

Appendix: Definitions of Additional Subjective Logic Operators

Definition 5 (adding) – Operator $\sum$

Let $QA = \{qa_1, qa_2, \ldots, qa_n\}$ is a set of attributes that may influence an entity's opinion on a proposition. $IR = \{ir_1, ir_2, \ldots ir_n\}$ ($\sum_{i=1}^{n} ir_i = 1$) is a set of importance rates of attributes in QA, which marks the entity's weight of considerations on different attributes. That is ir_i is the importance rate of qa_i. $\Omega = \{\omega_1, \omega_2, \ldots \omega_n\}$ is a set of opinions about quality attributes. $\omega_i = (b_i, d_i, u_i)$ is the entity's opinion on qa_i. Let $\omega_\Sigma = (b_\Sigma, d_\Sigma, u_\Sigma)$ be opinion such that

$$b_\Sigma = \sum_{i=1}^{n} ir_i b_i \;;\; d_\Sigma = \sum_{i=1}^{n} ir_i d_i \;;\; u_\Sigma = \sum_{i=1}^{n} ir_i u_i$$

Then ω_Σ is called the sum of ω_i on a proposition.

Definition 6 (opinion generator) – Operator θ

Let $\omega = (b, d, u)$ be an entity's opinion about a proposition (or its attributes). Where

$$b + d + u = 1$$
$$b = p/(p + n + r)$$
$$d = n/(p + n + r)$$
$$u = r/(p + n + r)$$

and p is the positive points of evidence on the proposition, n is negative points of evidence on the proposition, $r \geq 1$ is a parameter controlling the rate of loss of uncertainty, which can be used to tune the use of uncertainty in the model for the requirements of different scenarios (we often take $r = 2$). Note that other definitions on b, d and u can be also applied.

This operator $\theta(p, n, r)$ can be used for generating an opinion based on positive and negative evidence.

Definition 7 (Comparison) - Operator $\geq_{op}$

Given two opinions $\omega_A(b_A, d_A, u_A)$ and $\omega_B(b_B, d_B, u_B)$, we define $\geq_{op}$ as an opinion comparison operator, whereby $\omega_A \geq_{op} \omega_B$ holds, if $b_A > b_B; d_A < d_B; u_A < u_B$. And we say that opinion $\omega_A(b_A, d_A, u_A)$ is over a threshold presented by $\omega_B(b_B, d_B, u_B)$.

A Risk Assessment Model for Enterprise Network Security*

Fu-Hong Yang, Chi-Hung Chi, and Lin Liu

School of Software, Tsinghua University, Beijing, China 100084
chichihung@mail.tsinghua.edu.cn

Abstract. A formal model of security risk assessment for an enterprise information security is developed. The model, called the Graph Model, is constructed based on the mapping of an enterprise IT infrastructure and networks/systems onto a graph. Components of the model include the nodes which represent hosts in enterprise network and their weights of importance and security, the connections of the nodes, and the safeguards used with their costs and effectiveness. The model can assist to identify inappropriate, insufficient or waste protector resources like safeguards that are relative to the needs of the protected resources, and then reallocates the funds or protector resources to minimize security risk. An example is provided to represent the optimization method and process. The goal of using Graph Model is to help enterprise decision makers decide whether their security investment is consistent with the expected risks and how to allocate the funds or protector resources.

1 Introduction

With the rapid growth of the network technologies and the evolution of enterprise information systems, more and more enterprises and organizations conduct their transactions and services over the Internet nowadays. Businesses via Internet can gain more competitive advantages, but this dependence upon network will lead to lots of security hidden troubles. One of them that should take good consideration is virus. Due to the propagation property of virus, this self-replicating and propagation behaviors can cause the entire network to break down if one host in an enterprise is infected with some special virus or worms. The influence contains enterprise productivity and revenue; even the reputation will be affected.

Customers will engage in Internet transaction only if they are confident that their personal information is secure. So the security and reliability of enterprises network are very important. Although a majority of enterprise have adopted some security technologies, most of them still suffer losses from being attacked by virus. Though the security risk can never be fully eliminated no matter how much money we invest or what countermeasure we take, it can be minimized by effective allocation of funds and resources. Security optimization is a way that spending the right amount of money on the right place to result in the least network security risk on current condition, and let it be more economically and efficiently. In order to have a more precise description and assessment of the effect of enterprise due to virus, this paper

* This research is supported by the funding 2004CB719400 of China.

L.T. Yang et al. (Eds.): ATC 2006, LNCS 4158, pp. 293–301, 2006.

presents a quantitative model and its associated security optimization method to measure and minimize the impact of security risk.

2 Background

One of the earliest used estimators in the computer industry was Annual Loss Expectancy (ALE), a quantitative method for performing risk analysis. It was published in Federal Information Processing Standard (FIPS) by National Bureau of Standards in 1979. Then Cost-Benefit Analysis (CBA) techniques are widely used in the assessment of computer-related risks. Shawn A. Butler [3] puts forward a cost-benefit analysis method called Security Attribute Evaluation Method (SAEM) to compare alternative security designs with the enterprises current selection of security technologies to see if a more cost effective solution is possible. Lately, Kevin J. Soo Hoo [1] provided a Decision-Driven Model which analyzes Net Benefit in order to make decisions. Evan Anderson [4] put forward an Entity-Relationship Model (ERM) for enterprise security which is based on set theory and is represented by an Entity-Relationship diagram. In [2], a quantitative approach which forecast the security risk by measuring the security strength of a system was provided. And Paco Nathan, William Hurley [5] developed a Non-Equilibrium Risk Model (NERM) in enterprise network security which was derived from biology and provided a mathematical method for quantitative analysis for risk aggregation. There are also many different quantitative models [6][7][8] for network security risk, such as a model for risk analysis using Petri Nets [9], using Distributed Coloring Algorithms [10], and using Belief Networks [11]. Most existing models consider each individual in a network separately when analyzing security risk, not as a hole. Most computers in an enterprise are interconnected. They can interact with each other, especially when attacked by virus or worms, because once a host is infected, it may spread to the hole network [12]. So under this newly condition, a model that calculates risks in a holistic way is needed.

3 A Graph Model

3.1 Overview of Graph Model

A graph model which is based on graph theory considers an enterprise network as a hole and assesses its security risk in a holistic form. Through graph optimization [13][14], it can assist to identify inappropriate, insufficient or waste protector resources like safeguards that relative to the needs of protected resources, and then reallocate the constant or limited funds or protector resources to minimize security risk. Given the constant funds, this model can help to find out the best policy, namely optimal allocation of the resources. If enterprise decision-makers want to add certain money, then we can figure out where the added money should be placed to deploy which security technologies. The method can be used as a guide for an optimal deployment of security enhancements.

3.2 Description of Model

In Figure 1, a diagram of Graph Model represents a mapping network topology defined by a set N of n nodes and a set W of relationship of links. For mathematical clarity and facility, the following variable identifiers will be used.

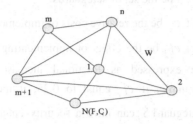

Fig. 1. A Diagram of Graph Model

$N = [N_1, N_2...N_m...N_n]$ Let N be n hosts in an enterprise network. Let $[N_1, N_2...N_m]$ be m mainly important hosts(Data Server, Mail Server, Application Server, File Server etc.), while $[N_{m+1}...N_n]$ are ordinary ones like employee hosts.

$P = [P_1, P_2...P_m...P_n]$ Let P be the importance of the value in hosts in a network.

$Q = [Q_1, Q_2...Q_m...Q_n]$ Let Q be the security or how safe of the hosts.

$$W = \begin{bmatrix} - & w_{1,2} & ...w_{1,n} \\ w_{2,1} & - & ...w_{2,n} \\ ... & ... & \\ w_{n,1} & w_{n,2} & ...- \end{bmatrix}_{n \times n} \qquad w_{i,j} = \begin{cases} 0 & N_i \text{ and } N_j \text{ are not connected} \\ 1 & N_i \text{ and } N_j \text{ are connected} \end{cases}$$

where W describes the connections of the N nodes. In the rest of this section, we will explain the model in great detail.

3.2.1 P: Importance of Value in Hosts

The value of P_i is determined by several significant attributes.

$A = [A_1, A_2...A_r]$ Let A be the attributes that determine the value of P_i, and A_i can be the importance of the data and services' value in a host N_a, can be the impact of the services in other hosts due to the performance degradation or even crash of N_a, it also can be the impact of reputation when N_a breaks down, and so on. Let r be the number of attributes.

$\alpha = [\alpha_1, \alpha_2...\alpha_r]$ Let α be the relative weights of the attributes.

$\vec{v} = [v_1, v_2...v_r]^T$ Let $\vec{v}$ be the relative value or score of the attributes.

Then $P_i = P_i(\vec{v}) = \alpha \cdot \vec{v} = \sum_{j=1}^{r} \alpha_j \cdot v_j$, $i = 1, 2...n$ (1)

3.2.2 Q: Security or How Safe of Hosts

The value of Q_i is determined by the installation or implementing of the safeguards. For example, Firewall, Intrusion Detection System, Anti-Virus Software, Encryption, Central Access Control, Biometric authentication, Smart cards etc.

$S = [S_1, S_2...S_s]$ Let S be the set of safeguards

$c = [c_1, c_2...c_s]$ Let c_j be the relative costs of implementing safeguard S_j.

$ef = [ef_1, ef_2...ef_s]$ Let ef_j be the effect of implementing safeguard S_j which can be expressed as fractional increase in effectiveness. For example, if ef_j equal to 0.25, it means that implementing safeguard S_j can have a security enhancement of 25 percent.

Generally, the value of ef_j can be determined by security managers who rely on experience, judgment, and the best available knowledge. It also can be deduced from the enterprise statistical data or some surveys such as CSI/FBI Computer Crime and Security Survey and Global Information Security Survey etc, because it can be calculated from the value of df_j and cf_j, which mean fractional reduction in frequency of occurrence and fractional reduction in consequences resulting from virus or bad events as a result of implementing safeguard S_j. A simple relationship is:

$$ef_j = \frac{1}{(1-df_j)\cdot(1-cf_j)} -1, \ j = 1, 2...s$$

$$\vec{q} = \begin{bmatrix} q_{1,2} & q_{1,2} & ...q_{1,s} \\ q_{2,1} & q_{2,2} & ...q_{2,s} \\ ... & ... & \\ q_{n,1} & q_{n,2} & ...q_{n,s} \end{bmatrix}_{n\times s} \qquad q_{i,j} = \begin{cases} 0 & not \ implementing \ S_j \ on \ N_i \\ 1 & implementing \ S_j \ on \ N_i \end{cases}$$

Let $\vec{q}$ be the policy of safeguards. Then:

$$Q_i = Q_0 \cdot \prod_{j=1}^{s}(1+ef_j \cdot q_{i,j}), \ i = 1, 2...n \tag{2}$$

Let Q_0 be the initial value of Q_i when enterprise decision-makers haven't implement any safeguards on host i.

$$C = \sum_{i=1}^{n}\sum_{j=1}^{s} c_j \cdot q_{i,j} \tag{3}$$

where C represent the total funds or money spent.

3.2.3 W: Connection of N Nodes

W describes the connection of the N nodes, we can easily get that W is a symmetric matrix:

$$w_{i,j} = w_{j,i} \ , \ i = 1, 2...n \ , j = 1, 2...n \ , i \neq j \tag{4}$$

Each $w_{i,j}$ has an associated weight $e_{i,j}$ which represents the likelihood of the node N_j being infected when the node N_i has been infected by virus. A $e_{i,j}$ is a probability of N_j will be infected if the node N_i has been infected and is infective. For example, $e_{i,j} = 0$, $i \neq j$ it means that the virus can not propagate from N_i to N_j.

Let v_i be the probability of N_i being the first one to be infected in an enterprise network.

3.3 Modeling of Graph Model

We can easily tell that when the value of Q_j increases, the value of $e_{i,j}$ decreases, and vice versa. And also does the relationship between Q_i and v_i.

$$e_{i,j} = w_{i,j} \cdot g(Q_j) \ , \ i = 1, 2...n \ , j = 1, 2...n \ , i \neq j \tag{5}$$

Let function g be the relationship between Q_j and $e_{i,j}$

$$v_i = \varphi(Q_i) \ , \ i = 1, 2...n \tag{6}$$

Let function φ be the relationship between Q_i and v_i

Assumption

1. A network topology structure is unchangeable during a considerable long time.
2. The investment on ordinary hosts is a constant, and the protector resources on them will not be altered or taken into account, and will not affect the security policy.
3. The losses can be determined by calculating the loss of each host including the importance, the probability of being infected and any other factors considered.
4. The same safeguard will be implemented at most 1 times on a host when allocating safeguards. For example, one host can not be implemented the same two safeguards like two firewalls.

We know that the risk level is associated with the losses or damage due to virus, and the losses or impact of the entire enterprise network resulting from N_i being the first one to be infected can be constituted of two parts. One is the losses of N_i: expressed as $\eta \cdot P_i$, and the other is possible losses of the rest hosts: expressed as $\sum_{\substack{j=1 \\ j \neq i}}^{n} \eta \cdot e_{i,j} \cdot P_j$. So the definition of security risk can be:

$$f = \sum_{i=1}^{n} v_i \cdot (\eta \cdot P_i + \sum_{\substack{j=1, \\ j \neq i}}^{n} \eta \cdot e_{i,j} \cdot P_j) \tag{7}$$

Let η be a direct proportional coefficient between the losses and the value of P. Substitute equations (5) and (6) for $e_{i,j}$ and v_i, we get:

$$f = \sum_{i=1}^{n} \varphi(Q_i) \cdot (\eta \cdot P_i + \sum_{\substack{j=1, \\ j \neq i}}^{n} \eta \cdot w_{i,j} \cdot g(Q_j) \cdot P_j) \tag{8}$$

Generally, the protector resources like safeguards in an enterprise are always implementing on the mainly important hosts (Data Server, Mail Server, Application Server, File Server etc.), but not on the ordinary ones like employee hosts. So we suppose that the investment on ordinary ones is a constant, and will not affect the security policy. So the equation (3) can be reduced to (9), the expression of $\vec{q}$ can be reduced to (10). If the ceiling amount funds or money that an enterprise is willing to pay is C_{max}, so C is no more than C_{max}, and we can get the equation (11).

$$C = \sum_{i=1}^{m} \sum_{j=1}^{s} c_j \cdot q_{i,j} \tag{9}$$

$$\vec{q} = \begin{bmatrix} q_{1,2} & q_{1,2} & \cdots q_{1,s} \\ q_{2,1} & q_{2,2} & \cdots q_{2,s} \\ \cdots & \cdots & \\ q_{m,1} & q_{m,2} & \cdots q_{m,s} \end{bmatrix}_{m \times s} \qquad q_{i,j} = \begin{cases} 0 & \text{not implementing } S_j \text{ on } N_i \\ 1 & \text{implementing } S_j \text{ on } N_i \end{cases} \tag{10}$$

$$\sum_{i=1}^{m} \sum_{j=1}^{s} c_j \cdot q_{i,j} \leq C_{max} \tag{11}$$

4 Security Optimization

Though the security risk can never be fully eliminated no matter what countermeasure we take, it can be minimized by effective allocation of funds and resources, because there must be an allocation state that makes the security risk achieve to the bottom level. So security optimization is a process of finding the best policy to minimize the risk. So the mathematical model of optimization is given as follows: (consider equations (2) and (8), than we can get (12))

Goal: $f(\vec{q}^*) = \min f(\vec{q}) =$

$$\min \sum_{i=1}^{n} \varphi(Q_0 \cdot \prod_{k=1}^{s} (1 + ef_k \cdot q_{i,k})) \cdot (\eta \cdot P_i + \sum_{\substack{j=1, \\ j \neq i}}^{n} \eta \cdot w_{i,j} \cdot g(Q_0 \cdot \prod_{k=1}^{s} (1 + ef_k \cdot q_{j,k})) \cdot P_j) \tag{12}$$

Decision Variable:

$$\vec{q} = \begin{bmatrix} q_{1,2} & q_{1,2} & \cdots q_{1,s} \\ q_{2,1} & q_{2,2} & \cdots q_{2,s} \\ \cdots & \cdots & \\ q_{m,1} & q_{m,2} & \cdots q_{m,s} \end{bmatrix}_{m \times s} \qquad q_{i,j} = \begin{cases} 0 & not\ implementing\ S_j\ on\ N_i \\ 1 & implementing\ S_j\ on\ N_i \end{cases} \qquad (10)$$

Constraints: $\displaystyle\sum_{i=1}^{m}\sum_{j=1}^{s} c_j \cdot q_{i,j} \le C_{max}$ (11)

$q_{i,j} = 0\ or\ 1\ ,\ \ i = 1, 2 \ldots m\ ,\ j = 1, 2 \ldots s$ (13)

$ef_k \ge 0\ ,\ \ k = 1, 2 \ldots s$ (14)

$w_{i,j} = 0\ or\ 1\ ,\ \ i = 1, 2 \ldots n\ ,\ j = 1, 2 \ldots n\ ,\ i \ne j$ (15)

The goal is finding a minimum value of f by searching the space of decision variable under the constraints. It is an N-P hard problem that we can hardly enumerate all the probably solution of $\vec{q}$, because $\vec{q}$ can have 2^{ms} possible combinations. To solve a discrete combinatorial optimization problem have several methods at present, as Genetic Algorithm, Particle Swarm Optimization, Ant Colony Optimization, and so on. In this paper we attempt to use Genetic Algorithms (GA) to optimize the goal function f .

4.1   Optimization Using a Genetic Algorithm

To resolve the optimization problem in this paper, we particularize our methods based on genetic algorithm in more detail: First, a matrix of $\vec{q}$ represents a solution, and randomly initialize a population of h solutions or individuals under the constraints.

$$pop = \begin{bmatrix} a_{1,2} & a_{1,2} & \cdots a_{1,m}, & fit1 \\ a_{2,1} & a_{2,2} & \cdots a_{2,m}, & fit2 \\ \cdots & \cdots & \\ a_{h,1} & a_{h,2} & \cdots a_{h,m}, & fith \end{bmatrix}_{h \times m} \qquad ,\ i = 1, 2 \ldots h \qquad (16)$$

For convenience, we transform the format of $\vec{q}^{\ i}$ into $[a_{i,1}, a_{i,2} \ldots a_{i,m}]$, the row $[q_{j,1}\ q_{j,2} \ldots q_{j,s}]$, $j = 1, 2 \ldots m$ in $\vec{q}^{\ i}$ is concatenated to be a string and than transform to a decimal number $a_{i,j}$. So $[a_{i,1}, a_{i,2} \ldots a_{i,m}, fiti]$, $i = 1, 2 \ldots h$ will be an individual, and corresponding to $\vec{q}^{\ i}$ and the fitness of $\vec{q}^{\ i}$. We take the expression of f to calculate fitness directly for convenience. After having initialized the first generation and calculated the fitness of each individual of the population, than we sort the individuals according to their fitness from small to large, and start to perform repeating three operators: selection, crossover, and mutation. In the selection operator, we select several best individuals to replicate to the next generation without performing the rest two operators. In the crossover operator, we select some remnant individuals to perform crossover according to crossover rate p_c. We use Two-point Crossover in this paper. (See Figure 2)

$$A:[a_{i,1},\ a_{i,2},a_{i,3},a_{i,4}\cdots a_{i,m-2},a_{i,m-1},\ a_{i,m}] \rightarrow A':[a_{i,1},a_{i,2},a_{j,3},a_{j,4}\cdots a_{j,m-2},a_{j,m-1},a_{i,m}]$$
$$B:[a_{j,1},a_{j,2},a_{j,3},a_{j,4}\cdots a_{j,m-2},a_{j,m-1},\ a_{j,m}] \rightarrow B':[a_{j,1},a_{j,2},a_{i,3},a_{i,4}\cdots a_{i,m-2},a_{i,m-1},\ a_{j,m}]$$
$$\uparrow \qquad\qquad\qquad \uparrow \qquad\qquad\qquad \uparrow \qquad\qquad\qquad \uparrow$$
$$point1 \qquad\qquad\qquad point2$$
$$i,\ j=1,2...h,\quad point1=0,2...m-1,\quad point2=1,2...m$$

Fig. 2. A Diagram of Two-point Crossover

After having performing crossover operator, we select some individuals to perform mutation according to mutation rate p_m. Randomly choose an individual, then randomly choose an element in that individual, and then randomly generate a new element to replace the former one. All the new individuals generated from crossover operator and mutation operator must be checked up whether they are followed the constraints or not. If not, it must be performed again to generate new ones until meeting the constraints.

5   Conclusions and Future Work

In this paper, we have presented a conceptualization and methodology for the security risk assessment in an enterprise network due to virus. And we attempt to describe the security risk in a holistic way based on graph theory. Beyond its strength as a descriptive model, it can be used to provide recommendations to decision makers to allocate resources by implementing optimization using Genetic algorithms. Extensions of this work are focused on three aspects: First one is the development of a dynamic model using the variables and relationships defined and specified in the Graph Model. A dynamic model is a model that considers the dynamic change of an enterprise network topology which is assumed to be unchangeable during a considerable long time in this paper. Secondly, we aim to present a more complicated virus propagation model for calculating risks. Third, subdivision the effectiveness of safeguards by types, such as virus attack, unauthorized access, denial of service and so on, while we mainly consider the virus attack in this paper. The purposes of the extensions are to search for improvements, rationalize protector resources, optimize security solutions and develop best practices.

References

[1] Kevin J. Soo Hoo, "How Much Is Enough? A Risk-Management Approach to Computer Security," Consortium for Research on Information Security and Policy (CRISP), Stanford University, June 2000

[2] Stuart Edward Schechter, "Computer Security Strength & Risk: A Quantitative Approach,"Doctoral Dissertation, Harvard University, May 2004.

[3] Shawn A. Butler, " Security Attribute Evaluation Method: A Cost-Benefit Approach," Proc. 24th Int'l Conf. Software Eng. (ICSE 02), IEEE CS Press, 2002, pp. 232-240.

[4] Evan Anderson, Joobin Choobineh, and Michael R. Grimaila, "An Enterprise Level Security Requirements Specification Model," HICSS, 2005.

[5] Paco Nathan, William Hurley, "Non-Equilibrium Risk Models in Enterprise Network Security," Symbiot, Inc. P.O. Box 9646 Austin, TX 78766-9646

[6] David Moore, Geoffrey M. Voelker and Stefan Savage, "Quantitative Network Security Analysis," Cooperative Association for Internet Data Analysis (CAIDA), NSF-01-160, 2002.

[7] Stuart E. Schechter, "Toward Econometric Models of the Security Risk from Remote Attacks," In Proceedings of the Third Annual Workshop on the Economics of Information Security, 2004.

[8] Carol A. Siegel, Ty R. Sagalow, Paul Serritella, "Cyber-Risk Management: Technical and Insurance Controls for Enterprise-Level Security," Information Systems Security, Volume 11, Issue 4, 2002.

[9] Peter. R. Stephenson, "A Formal Model for Information Risk Analysis Using Colored Petri Nets," Colored Petri Nets (CPN), 2004.

[10] Adam J. O'Donnell, Harish Sethu, "On Achieving Software Diversity for Improved Network Security using Distributed Coloring Algorithms, " ACM Conference on Computer and Communications Security, Oct 2004, pp. 121-131.

[11] Brenda McCabe, Donald Ford, "Using Belief Networks to Assess Risk," Winter Simulation Conference, 2001, pp. 1541-1546.

[12] Jonghyun Kim, Sridhar Radhakrishnan, Sudarshan K. Dhall, "Measurement and Analysis of Worm Propagation on Internet Network Topology," IEEE ICCCN2004 Technical Program, Oct 2004, pp.495-500.

[13] Ravindra K. Ahuja, James B. Orlin, "Graph and Network Optimization," url = "http://www.ise.ufl.edu/ahuja/PAPERS/Ahuja-ELOSS-Chapter2003.pdf ".

[14] Martin Skutella, "Network Optimization," url="http://www.mathematik.uni-dortmund.de/lsv/lehre/ss2005/opt/LectureNotes.pdf ",2005.

A Security Management Framework with Roaming Coordinator for Pervasive Services*

Minsoo Lee[1], Sehyun Park[1,**], and Sungik Jun[2]

[1] School of Electrical and Electronics Engineering, Chung-Ang University,
221, Heukseok-Dong, Dongjak-Gu, Seoul 156-756, Korea
lemins@wm.cau.ac.kr, shpark@cau.ac.kr
[2] Electronics and Telecommunications Research Institute
161 Gajeong-dong, Yuseong-gu, Daejeon, 305-350, Korea
sijun@etri.re.kr

Abstract. The ubiquitous and autonomic computing environments is open and dynamic providing the universal wireless access through seamless integration of software and system architectures. Therefore the roaming services with the predefined security associations among all of the mobile devices in various networks is especially complex and difficult. Furthermore, there has been little study of security coordination for realistic autonomic system capable of authenticating users with different kinds of user interfaces, efficient context modeling with user profiles on Smart Cards, and providing pervasive access service by setting roaming agreements with a variety of wireless network operators. This paper proposes a Smart Card based security management framework that supports the capability of interoperator roaming with the pervasive security services among the network domains. Our proposed system with Roaming Coordinator is more open, secure, and easy to update for security services throughout the different network domains such as public wireless local area networks (PWLANs), 3G cellular networks and wireless metropolitan area networks (WMANs).

Keywords: 4G, AAA, context management, pervasive computing, roaming, security, smart card, ubiquitous networks.

1 Introduction

Computing and networking devices are being embedded into everyday appliances and become the really common parts of our environment. The need for computing and communication services at anytime, anywhere have urged the researchers to develop ideas for managing secure interworking and end-to-end

---

* This research was supported by the MIC(Ministry of Information and Communication), Korea, under the Chung-Ang University HNRC(Home Network Research Center)-ITRC support program supervised by the IITA(Institute of Information Technology Assessment).
** The corresponding author.

L.T. Yang et al. (Eds.): ATC 2006, LNCS 4158, pp. 302–311, 2006.

Quality of Service (QoS) assurance. Furthermore, there has been increasing demands for autonomous services in daily life. Seamless security, mobility and QoS management are therefore required for mobile users, often equipped with several wireless network technologies, for example, public wireless local area networks (PWLANs), third-generation (3G) cellular networks and wireless metropolitan area networks (WMANs)[1][2]. The open nature of the heterogeneous communication environments raises the security and privacy concerns that need to be addressed in a coherent manner along with the development of the required services and service infrastructures.

In the security services, user authentication tends to rely on at least one of the following 'factors': something you know, something you own, or some personal (biometric)characteristic. Frequently, Smart Cards play a central role in user authentication systems, independent of which factors are used [3]. It is very important to appreciate that a Smart Card provides 'easy-to-use and tamper-resistant security'. If the ease of use was the major criterion then this could be reproduced by simply coding the same functionality in a PC and using the Smart Card for de-icing the car. Since they can store secret identifiers securely and engage in cryptographically protected (challenge-response) protocols, it is generally accepted that Smart Cards currently play a very useful role in secure authentication.

The future usage of Smart Cards will be very application dependent. Perhaps the most interesting challenge to the card format comes from mobile applications and services. There are over 1 billion cellular network subscribers and each of them has a Smart Card based authentication token - called a SIM (Subscriber Identity Module). Among the various mobile operators in the heterogeneous networks, a user might like to re-personalize the SIM quite regularly or perhaps it would be even more convenient to host several operator accounts and always select the best deal. The proper choice of the operators and the best connected networks should be the key functions for seamless secure roaming services in 4G networks.

However, for a normal SIM-based user, there are some obstacles in the initial phase. There are too many gadgets and setups at client side, such as the SIM card/reader, drivers and complex interactions among various elements. Furthermore, there has been little studies of a security coordination for realistic cellular/PWLAN infrastructure construction capable of authenticating users with different kinds of user interfaces, efficient context modeling with user profiles on Smart Cards, and providing pervasive access service by setting roaming agreements with a variety of wireless network operators.

In this paper, we devised a security management framework that takes advantages of the secure authentication of Smart Cards in the interoperator roaming services and applications for mobile networks. We present a novel design of a security architecture that addresses the specific requirements of authentication and trust establishments in roaming services for future mobile networks. We also designed *Roaming Coordinator* that exploits the user profiles [4] in the Smart Card and enables the establishment of dynamic secure association with various network domains. Our architecture solves the problems related to the management of security relationship in roaming services while minimizing the signaling and computational overhead at the mobile nodes(MNs).

The rest of this paper is organized as follow. Section 2 gives related works about security and roaming services in future wireless networks. Section 3 presents our Smart Card based secure roaming management framework with Roaming Coordinators. Section 4 describes the performance analysis through the implementation testbed and application examples. Section 5 concludes this paper.

2   Related Works

Toward seamless security in 4G mobile networks, fundamental features such as smooth roaming and interworking techniques, QoS guarantee, data security, user authentication and authorization are required. For smooth roaming, several studies have been made on a fast handover management in IPv6 Networks [5]. As solutions for integrating 3G and WLAN services some of the studies have focused on a gateway [6], interworking techniques and architectures [7], a roaming and authentication service framework [8]. A feasibility study [9] was also conducted by the 3rd Generation Partnership Project (3GPP). However the study does not deal with context-aware efficient security and roaming management techniques which are indispensable features for the next generation wireless networks. Recently, [10] presents an approach to use PWLANs as a complement to the cellular data network with practical considerations to establishing a mixed authentication(SIM- and Web-based) environment and roaming. However, in the cellular/PWLAN networks the problem of efficient seamless security coordination for the highly dynamic interoperator roaming has not been adequately considered in respect of reducing secure handover signaling as well as satisfying the QoS guarantees. This paper concentrates mainly on the security schemes with Roaming Coordinator and context transfer to enforce security for seamless interworking in 4G systems.

3   USIM-Based Secure Roaming Management Framework

One fundamental aspect of the heterogeneous networks is the ability to dynamically find paths through the network for forwarding information between specific MNs [11]. Connectivity at the physical layer is mandatory, but it does not automatically solve the problem. To support interoperator roaming from pervasive service viewpoint, extra intelligence is required so that the network can find a specific terminal or a proper network entity and switch to the most appropriate one. Primary motivation of our secure roaming management framework with Roaming Coordinators is to quickly re-establish context transfer candidate without requiring the MN to explicitly perform all protocol flows for seamless security services. Our architecture for Roaming Coordinator and the multi-mode MN of the interworking network is shown in Fig. 1. The Fig. 2 shows the proposed

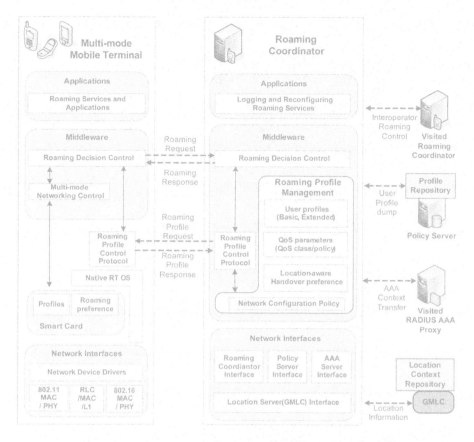

Fig. 1. The Proposed Reference Architecture for Seamless Roaming Services

roaming management framework. Based on interworking aspects listed in 3GPP Technical Specification 22.934 [9] and practical considerations [10], we describe the features implemented in our framework.

*   *Security and Interworking aspects:* We assume that a MN is a triple-mode terminal with three interfaces 3G, WLAN and WMAN. For secure interworking we considered that authentication and key management should be based on the UMTS authentication and key agreement (AKA) and Extensible Authentication Protocol (EAP)-AKA or EAP-SIM for WLAN [12]. On 3G/WLAN interworking, a feasibility study [9] was conducted by the 3GPP with the loosely and tightly coupled solutions. The loose coupling solution allows a customer to access 3G packet-switched (PS) services over WLAN and to change access between 3G and WLAN networks during a service session. Tight Coupling refers to the alignment of WLAN interfaces with the access interfaces of the 3G network. WLAN is connected to Gateway GPRS support node (GGSN) in the 3G network. The principle advantage of this solution is that the mechanisms for security, mobility and QoS in the UMTS core network can be directly reused. We

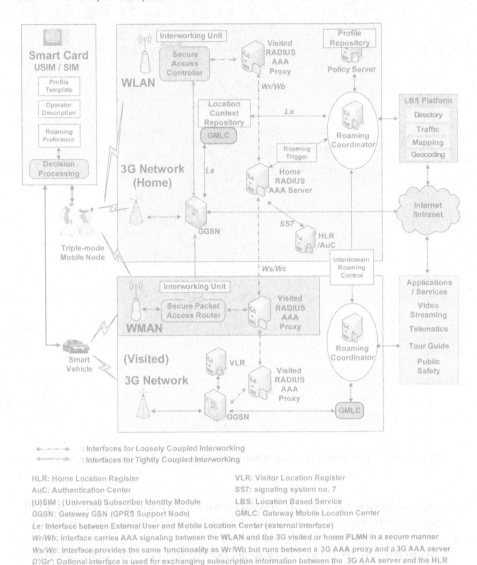

Fig. 2. The Proposed Secure Roaming Management Framework in Mobile Networks

have also considered the interworking of the wireless metropolitan area networks (WMANs) with IEEE 802.16[13]. For several networking interfaces we adopt the notation and functionality specified in [14].

* *Interoperator Roaming aspects:* For scalable management of the interworking architecture, implementation of Roaming Coordinator may be done centrally and in a distributed manner by the cooperation of Roaming Coordinators. Intradomain (micro-mobility) Authentication, Authorization, and Accounting (AAA) are handled together with Roaming Coordinator and AAA server. When a MN moves into a foreign network for interdomain roaming (macro-mobility), Roaming Coordinator, AAA proxies and AAA servers take charge of reauthentication process. To minimize the signaling overhead, AAA context transfer protocol [15] is used for the fast secure roaming between the AAA proxy in visited public land mobile network (PLMN) and the AAA server in home PLMN.

* **Roaming Coordinator Design aspects:** We consider the following abstraction layers of Roaming Coordinator with re-configurable components as addressed in [16]. Middleware platform, typically with a virtual execution environment for distributed processing includes *Roaming Decision Control* interact with that of MNs for the fast secure roaming with pre-authentication. After receiving roaming request Roaming Decision Control evaluates the roaming profile [4] of the MN then triggers AAA context transfer. The network interface module includes several interfaces to perform the cooperation of other Roaming Coordinators, profiling with Policy Servers, and AAA management. The key figures in our approaches are the roaming context interfaces to the lower layers and Roaming Decision Control for identifying the next appropriate network in the interworking network.

* **Mobile Node Design aspects:** The Roaming Control functions have to be included in MNs as well for end-to-end services. Due to resource limitations, *Roaming Control Engine* just collapse to one operating system platform. The middleware layer of the MN are typically quite restricted and with a limited virtual execution environment. Compared to Roaming Coordinator, the Smart Card is a new component.

* **Smart Card based Authentication aspects:** The MN for accessing Roaming Coordinator is installed with a Universal IC Card (UICC) reader (a Smart Card reader implemented as a standard device on the Microsoft Windows platform). The UICC reader interacts with the UMTS SIM card (i.e., the UICC containing the SIM application) to obtain authentication information. The Smart Card which includes subscriber identities and also user's classified profiles [4], can be used ideally for personal services like electronic wallet.

* **USIM based Secure Roaming Protocol:** We designed the intelligent roaming protocol supporting autonomous registration and seamless session delivery. The example in Fig. 3 shows a message sequence diagram for secure roaming in an interdomain case. First, the MN detects new access points and selects its target Access Router (AR). Subsequently, a request from AR1 to AR2 is issued to the current Roaming Coordinator. This Roaming Coordinator must detect that AR2 is located in a different domain. A roaming request is subsequently sent from Roaming Coordinator 1 to Roaming Coordinator 2 in order to request security association(pre-authentication) from the new domain. After the validation of the request message Roaming Coordinator 2 evaluates the roaming profile of the MN and triggers the AAA context transfer between the AAA server and AAA proxy. Depending on the result of the pre-authentication, Roaming Coordinator 2 send the corresponding message back to Roaming Coordinator 1, which in turn informs the MN about the result. If the pre-authentication has succeeded, Roaming Coordinator 2 waits for a roaming confirmation message from the MN.

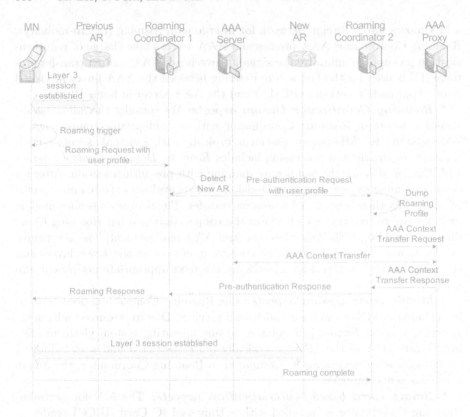

Fig. 3. Our Roaming Protocol Sequences for Interoperator Secure Roaming Services

If this message is not received within a certain time, the pre-authentication is automatically released.

4   Implementation Testbed and Performance Evaluation

We developed the testbed of our secure roaming management with Roaming Coordinator and the secure context transfer in the simulation environment as shown in Fig. 4. Roaming Coordinator, Policy Server and ARs are running on Solaris 8 server machines of Pentium III 933 MHz, 512 MB RAM. AAA Servers and AAA proxies are running on the servers of Pentium III 800 MHz (Linux OS) and the modified FreeRADIUS [17] library for RADIUS functionality. The AP is working on a Pentium III 500MHz machines (Linux OS) with Lucent Orinoco 802.11b WLAN Network Interface Card (NIC). MNs were the 3G-WLAN dual laptops that equips with both the same WLAN NIC and a WCDMA module. The platform of the MNs was Pentium III 800 MHz, 256MB RAM, Windows XP OS platform. As most of USIMs exploit the processor based on ARM7, we used the 441fx board(ARM7TDMI) as a USIM simulation target board with USB

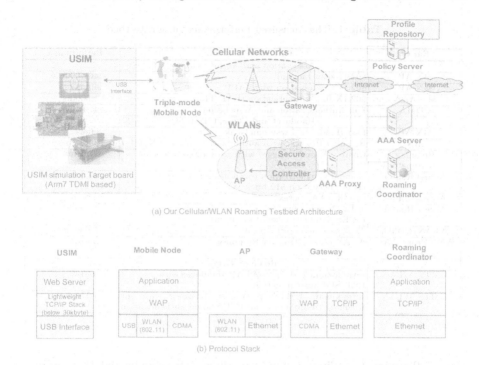

Fig. 4. Testbed for the proposed Secure Roaming Management in Mobile Networks

interface that communicates to obtain the authentication information required in both 3G network and WLAN. Programming language was GNU C(cross compiler), C, C++ compiler and ADS(ARM Developer Suite) v1.2. The cryptographic library was OpenSSL 0.9.7c [18], and data size were 1KB in token verification and 10 KB in context transfer. During our investigation of the roaming issues, we completed the a through performance analysis of the most commonly used security protocols both for the intradomain and interdomain roaming services, namely EAP-TLS, EAP-AKA. The designed lightweight roaming control and TCP/IP module at our USIM target board is compatible with common Smart Cards which use 32-bit processor and its size is about 31.28 Kbyte. Table 1 summarizes our performance experiments on the testbed.

Our roaming method sets up AAA context in advance before the handover events and only performs token verification if the Roaming Coordinator successfully indicates and provides the next roaming network. The right AR for the next handover has the authentication information of users. As the users don't have to gain each authentication from the AAA servers for further handovers, our mechanisms avoid the additional reauthentication delay. Therefore, MN experiences low latency relatively when it uses our secure context-aware handover protocol with the Roaming Coordinator. The strength of our AAA management based on Roaming Coordinator and classified profiles on USIM is given its improved security QoS which is achieved at the expense of increasing resource consump-

Table 1. The Measured Performance of our Testbed

Entity	Operation in scenario	Performance
	Association and Authentication	
MN-AP	802.11 scan (active)	40~300ms
MN-AP	802.11 reassociation with IAPP	40ms
MN-AAA	802.1X full authentication (EAP-TLS)	1,600ms
CDMA	Full Authentication and Association	4,300ms
	Handover and Context Transfer	
MN-AP	Fast Handover(4-way handshake only)	60ms
MN	Roaming Request with authorization token of USIM	30.34 ms
Roaming Coordinator	Context transfer trigger with authorization token	27.4 ms
Access Router	Compute authorization token using parameter (RSA encrypt on 512 bit keys)	31.201 KB/s
Access Router	Install AAA context	200 ms
Access Router	Token Verification (3DES Symmetric key decryption)	1.090 MB/sec
WLAN/CDMA	TCP parameter adjustment	5,000ms
AAA Proxy-AAA Server	AAA Context Transfer Response	25ms
	Roaming Delay	
UMTS/WLAN	Intradomain UMTS to WLAN Handover with EAP-SIM authentication	3,313ms
UMTS/WLAN	Intradomain UMTS to WLAN Handover with our Roaming Coordinator and USIM based authentication	1,153ms

tion of Roaming Coordinator. Our experiments have indicated that, using a roaming context gathering and setup phase of 272.74 ms, the system can have a fast response to network changes. Although our testbed is limited in comparison to the real systems, the results of our work show that the time taken to perform roaming control function is small enough not to impact the mobile transactions in the interworking networks. Therefore the context-aware roaming process in our framework may be no obstacle to its implementation on the modern devices.

5   Conclusion and Future Work

In this paper, we presented the design of a security architecture that addresses the specific requirements of authentication and trust establishment in the interoperator roaming services for future mobile networks. Based on the context management from Roaming Coordinators that exploit the classified profiles in the Smart Card of users, we enable the establishment of dynamic secure association with various network domains in the heterogeneous networks. Our architecture solves the problems associated with the management of security relationship in roaming services while minimizing the signaling and computational overhead at the mobile nodes. The performance and analytical results show that our scheme can be used as an intelligent add-on model to an existing system to obtain performance and service improvement. Our future plan is to integrate the proposed security and mobility mechanisms with the secure Web Services infrastructure [19] the new interworking systems [1] [2].

References

1. Lee, M., Kim, G., Park, S.: Seamless and secure mobility management with location aware service (LAS) broker for future mobile interworking networks. Journal of Communications and Networks **7** (2005) 207–221
2. Lee, M., Kim, G., Park, S., Jun, S., Nah, J., Song, O.: Efficient 3G/WLAN interworking techniques for seamless roaming services with location-aware authentication. In: NETWORKING 2005. Volume 3462 of Lecture Notes in Computer Science., Springer (2005) 370–381
3. Keith Mayes, Konstantinos Markantonakis, F.P.: Smart card based authentication - any future? Computers & Security **24** (2005) 188–191
4. Lee, M., Park, S.: A secure context management for QoS-Aware vertical handovers in 4g networks. In: Communications and Multimedia Security. Volume 3677 of Lecture Notes in Computer Science., Springer (2005) 220–229
5. Nicolas Montavont, e.a.: Handover management for mobile nodes in ipv6 networks. IEEE Commun. Mag. **40** (2002) 38–43
6. Feng, V. W.-S., e.a.: Wgsn: Wlan-based gprs environment support node with push mechanism. The Computer Journal **47** (2004) 405–417
7. Salkintzis, A.K.: Interworking techniques and architectures for wlan/3g integration toward 4g mobile data networks. IEEE Wireless Commun. Mag. **11** (2004) 50–61
8. Minghui Shi, Xuemin Shen, M.J.: Ieee 802.11 roaming and authentication in wireless lan/cellular mobile networks. IEEE Wireless Commun. Mag. **11** (2004) 66–75
9. 3rd Generation Partnership Project (3GPP): Feasibility study on 3GPP system to wireless local area network (WLAN) interworking. Technical Report TR 22.934, 3rd Generation Partnership Project (3GPP) (2003)
10. Jenq-Shiou Leu, Rong-Horng Lai, H.I.L.W.K.S.: Running cellular/pwlan services: practical considerations for cellular/pwlan architecture supporting interoperator roaming. IEEE Commun. Mag. **44** (2006) 111–122
11. Zahariadis, T.B., V.K.T.C.Z.N.N.N.: Global roaming in next-generation networks. IEEE Commun. Mag. **40** (2002) 145–151
12. Koien, G.M., H.T.: Security aspects of 3g-wlan interworking. IEEE Commun. Mag. **41** (2003) 82–88
13. IEEE 802.16-2004: IEEE standard for local and metropolitan area networks part 16: Air interface for fixed broadband wireless access systems (2004)
14. 3rd Generation Partnership Project (3GPP): 3gpp system to wireless local area network (wlan) interworking;system description (release 6). Technical Report TR 23.234, 3rd Generation Partnership Project (3GPP) (2005)
15. Loughney, J.: Context transfer protocol. IETF Draft (1999)
16. Prehofer, C., Wei, Q.: Active networks for 4g mobile communication: Motivation, architecture and application scenarios. In: Proc. IWAN 2002. (2002)
17. FreeRADIUS: (http://www.freeradius.org)
18. OpenSSL: (http://www.openssl.org)
19. Lee, M., Kim, J., Park, S., Lee, J., Lee, S.: A secure web services for location based services in wireless networks. In Mitrou, N., Kontovasilis, K.P., Rouskas, G.N., Iliadis, I., Merakos, L.F., eds.: NETWORKING 2004. Volume 3042 of Lecture Notes in Computer Science., Springer (2004) 332–344

A Dynamic Trust Model Based on Feedback Control Mechanism for P2P Applications*

Chenlin Huang, Huaping Hu, and Zhiying Wang

School of Computer, National University of Defense Technology,
Changsha, 410073, Hunan, P.R. China
clhuang@nudt.edu.cn, hphu@nudt.edu.cn, zywang@nudt.edu.cn

Abstract. Trust is critical in P2P online communities. The traditional trust and reputation mechanisms lack flexibility in modeling the diversity and dynamicity of trust in such environment. In this paper, we try to evaluate trust with the introduction of servomechanism and propose DWTrust: a trust model based on dynamic weights for P2P applications. DWTrust adopts a novel feedback control mechanism to realize the assessment of trust in which a set of subjective weights are set and adjusted in time to reflect the dynamicity of trust environment. Trust assessment is simplified by mapping the factors influencing trust to feedbacks on dynamic weights. A series of experiments are designed to demonstrate the effectiveness, benefit and adaptability of DWTrust.

1 Introduction

P2P communities are often established dynamically with peers that are unrelated and unknown to each other [1]. The management of trust for peers is involved with prior experience, reputation, trust context, time and even emotions. Further, the management scheme may change according to different trust phases.

The requirement of a fully evaluation on dynamic trust in P2P online communities exposes the disadvantages in trust and reputation mechanisms so far. Traditional trust models like [2] [3] [4] focus on the centralized management of trust, do not fit P2P networks well in dealing with the dynamicity and the heterogeneity. Additionally, they become too complex when being used to analyze and model the multi-aspect of trust. Some distributed reputation-based trust mechanisms are also proposed for P2P applications in [5] [6] [7] [8]. Trust is managed in a distributed way in these models. While, only a few aspects of trust property are considered in them which are not sufficient to reflect the diversity and dynamic of trust.

Some efforts have been put forward to analyze and model the multi-aspects of dynamic trust in an efficient way in [5] [9]. In this paper, we try to solve the problem from another view of point and propose DWTrust: a dynamic trust model based on dynamic weights. In DWTrust, a set of weights are defined to describe the multi-aspect of trust. Meanwhile, a feedback control mechanism is designed to finish the task of trust evaluation with the adaptive weights which can reflect the dynamic changes in trust relationships.

---

* Supported by the National Natural Science Foundation of China under Grant No. 60573136.

L.T. Yang et al. (Eds.): ATC 2006, LNCS 4158, pp. 312–321, 2006.

2 Analyzing Dynamic Trust

Dynamic trust management is the dynamic procedure (activity) of collecting, encoding, analyzing and presenting subjective and objective evidence relating to competence, honesty, security or dependability with the purpose of adapting the criteria, schemata and policies in trust assessment and decision-making accordingly to fulfill the task of trust management in Internet applications.

The diversity and dynamicity of trust are emphasized in the definition. First, the establishment of the relationship and the propagation of trust are both dynamic. Second, the relationship itself is under the influence of many factors, such as the knowledge of trustor, the trusted property, the circumstances of trust relationship and the establishment or the revocation of related relationships.

To clarify the notion of dynamic trust management, we assign dynamic trust a life cycle of *trust establishment, trust evolution, trust maturation* and *trust-based decision-making* according to different phases in its relationship over time. The factors effecting trust are also pointed out as shown in Fig. 1.

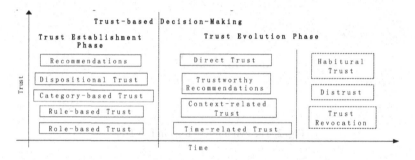

Fig. 1. A framework of dynamic trust model

The subjective and objective factors influencing trust can be viewed as different trust sources that contribute to the dynamic of trust assessment. These sources are reflection of different kinds of evidence. Therefore, the degrees of their effects on trust evaluation and decision-making are differed in different trust phases.

The management of dynamic trust requires a systematic procedure handing many aspects of trust to support decision-making. Meanwhile, the requirements of containing model complexity and improving efficiency are beyond the ability of traditional models. There is a need to develop new trust management mechanism.

3 DWTrust: A Trust Model Based on Dynamic Weights

DWTrust aims to reduce the complexity in modeling and assessing the multi-aspect of dynamic trust. The idea of servomechanism is introduced. The factors effecting trust are mapped into a set of dynamic weights, the modeling of each factor is avoided. Meanwhile, the trust assessment is implemented as a feedback system in which trust values are computed with the incentive of the adjustable weights. The trust based decision making is also part of the feedback system. Since only limited information is used to create feedbacks, the computation cost is greatly reduced.

3.1 The Feedback Control Mechanism in DWTrust

The architecture of feedback control mechanism in DWTrust is shown in Fig. 2. Both trust evolution and decision-making are deeply involved with feedback control mechanism as illustrated. The loop of trust evolution is emphasized within a link of **inputs, trust computation, decision-making** and **feedback control.**

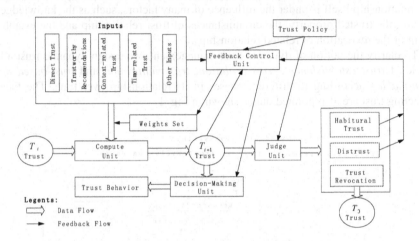

Fig. 2. The evolution of trust in DWTrust

The trust management schema in DWTrust is a dynamic procedure of adapting trust value with a set of weights. The feedback control unit is in charge of adjusting the weights and the thresholds in decision-making to the new trust environment. Judging unit judges the maturation of trust according to trust policy and provides feedbacks to the control unit. The trust computing unit just adds the feedbacks (weights) to the former trust value to update trust state. Finial, whether a trust behavior is triggered is decided by the decision-making unit.

The adoption of feedback control mechanism simplifies the management of dynamic trust. First, the representations of factors relating to trust are simplified. The evidence relating to trust assessment, such as security policy, the current trust level, interacting history (direct trust), recommendation, trust environment (trust context), time, emotions (material trust) etc., are mapped into dynamic weights. DWTrust does not model them separately as most trust models. Their effects are gathered in the feedback control unit and are expressed as contributions to several dynamic weights. The reduction of trust representations decreases the complexity of the whole model regarding dynamic trust. Second, the computation of trust value is simplified. Trust value becomes the sum of different weights and the former value in DWTrust. Consequently, the dependency on statistic data is avoided.

A formalized expression of trust assessment in DWTrust is discussed below.

3.2 Dynamic Trust Assessment

In DWTrust, trust is denoted with time-related opinion [10] as $w_{x,t} \equiv (b_{x,t}, d_{x,t}, u_{x,t}, a_{x,t})$ where $b_{x,t}$, $d_{x,t}$, $u_{x,t}$ and $a_{x,t}$ represent the belief, disbelief, uncertainty and relative atomicity functions on x at time t respectively. The time-related opinion satisfies $b_{x,t} + d_{x,t} + u_{x,t} = 1$ and the expectation of an opinion is calculated with $E_{x,t} = b_{x,t} + a_{x,t}u_{x,t}$. The priority of opinions can be decided according to Def. 10 in [4].

The propagation of trust can be computed with the combination of discounting operation $w_{x,r}^A \equiv w_{B,t}^A \otimes w_{x,s}^B$ (recommendation) and consensus operation $w_{x,r}^{A,B} \equiv w_{x,t}^A \oplus w_{x,s}^B$ (combination) [11].

3.2.1 General Trust Metric

The inputs to the evolution of trust include direct trust, trustworthy recommendations, context-related trust, time-related trust and etc. The design of trust assessment in DWTrust is based on the analysis of these factors.

According to the mapping theory in subjective logic, each kind of inputs can be mapped into evidence space and viewed as a series of binary events which consists of either positive or negative evidence. Then the associated opinion $w_{x,t} \equiv (b_{x,t}, d_{x,t}, u_{x,t}, a_{x,t})$ is computed with Eq. 1 where r and s represent positive evidences and negative evidences respectively [4].

$$b_{x,t} = \frac{r_t}{r_t + s_t + 2}, \; d_{x,t} = \frac{s_t}{r_t + s_t + 2}, u_{x,t} = \frac{2}{r_t + s_t + 2} \quad (1)$$

In dynamic trust model, the effects of these inputs can be transferred to the transaction execution results, time and the importance of transaction in trust assessment. Four dynamic weights are therefore defined in DWTrust to compute the effects of different inputs (evidences) recursively over time using feedbacks from each event in evidence space. The general trust metric in DWTrust is defined below.

Definition 1 (General Trust metric) *Let* $w_{y,i}^x = (b_i, d_i, u_i, a_i)$ *be peer x's opinion on peer y after transaction* i, *and use* α_i, β_i, γ_i *and* λ_i *to represent* **Success Weight, Failure Weight, Time-related Weight** *and* **Importance Weight** *respectively. Let* R_i *be the binary result of transaction i where* $R_i = 1$ *if the transaction is successful, otherwise* $R_i = 0$. *Then the opinion* $w_{y,i}^x$ *can be computed with the Eq. 2:*

$$b_i = \frac{\sum_{k=0}^i \alpha_k \lambda_k R_k \gamma_k}{\sum_{k=0}^i \alpha_k \lambda_k R_k + \sum_{k=0}^i \beta_k \lambda_k (1-R_k) + 1}, d_i = \frac{\sum_{k=0}^i \beta_k \lambda_k (1-R_k)\gamma_k}{\sum_{k=0}^i \alpha_k \lambda_k R_k + \sum_{k=0}^i \beta_k \lambda_k (1-R_k) + 1},$$

$$u_i = \frac{1 + \sum_{k=0}^i (1-\gamma_i)\alpha_k \lambda_k R_k + \sum_{k=0}^i (1-\gamma_i)\beta_k \lambda_k (1-R_k)}{\sum_{k=0}^i \alpha_k \lambda_k R_k + \sum_{k=0}^i \beta_k \lambda_k (1-R_k) + 1}, a_i = a_{i-1} + \Delta a \text{ where}$$

$$(2)$$

$$\begin{cases} \alpha_i = \alpha_{i-1} + \Delta\alpha R_i \\ \beta_i = \beta_{i-1} + \Delta\beta(1-R_i) \\ \gamma_i = \gamma_{i-1} + \Delta\gamma \end{cases} \text{with} \begin{cases} R_0 = 1 \\ a_0 = 0.5 \end{cases}, \begin{cases} \alpha_0 = \beta_0 = 0.5 \\ \gamma_0 = \gamma_1 = 0 \\ \lambda_0 = 0 \\ \alpha_i + \beta_i = 1 \end{cases} \text{and} \begin{cases} \alpha, \beta, \gamma \in [0,1] \\ \lambda \in [0, \infty) \end{cases}.$$

Δa, $\Delta\alpha$, $\Delta\beta$ and $\Delta\gamma$ represent the changes of relative parameters after a transaction.

Success Weight and *Failure Weight* indicate the different degree of influence a transaction has on a peer's opinion with a binary result. They are supposed to reflect both the series of evidence and trustor's trust policy. For optimists, α is assigned a bigger value than β to increase the effect of a successful transaction and to incentive cooperation. For pessimists, $\alpha < \beta$ is adopted to slow down trust behavior. In DWTrust, success weight and fail weight are decided by trust policy, the series of interacting events, the opinions, and the mature trust. Feedback rules are defined in the feedback control unit to change α and β dynamically with $\Delta\alpha$ and $\Delta\beta$.

The context-related trust is treated as an extra factor on direct trust and is defined as *Importance Weight*. The importance weight magnifies the effect of a transaction. Generally $\lambda_i = 1$ is set to treat all transaction equally. But, together with success weight and failure weight, it can also be used to speed up the evolution of direct trust.

Time-related Weight is a dynamically changed small variable simulating the effect of time on trust. It is also a reflection of trust policy and the tendency in direct trust. When $\gamma_i < 1$, the uncertainty in ones opinion will increase over time.

The mature trust has impact on dynamic weights. The probability expectation of an opinion and the sum of its history evidence are adopted as criteria judging mature trust in DWTrust. For *habitual trust*, the effects of the time-related functions could be ignored with $\gamma_i = 1$ and *Fail Weigh* becomes quite low to ensure the stability of habitual trust in the community. On the contrary, the effects of *distrust* equals to putting someone on the blacklist. The *success weight* and *time-related weight* are reset by the feedback control unit to keep a conservative policy.

In conclusion, these dynamic weights are feedbacks from feedback control unit as reflections of the current state of trust in the relationship including trust policy, trust inputs and the evolution phase of a trust relationship. How these weights take effects in DWTrust is explained in the Chapter 3.2.2.

The trust metric defined in DWTrust can be explained with subjective logic.

Theorem 1. *The General Trust Metric defined in DWTrust is consistent with the metric in subjective logic when the dynamic of trust is ignored in trust assessment.*

Proof 1. For opinion $w_{y,i}^x = (b_i, d_i, u_i, a_i)$, b_i, d_i and u_i can be proved separately.

When the dynamic of trust is ignored, only direct trust is considered. According to the mapping theory in [4], the trust metric in subjective logic can be expressed as Eq.1. Meanwhile, the subjective weights in DWTrust can be set as $\alpha_i = \beta_i = 0.5$, $\gamma_i = \lambda_i = 1.0$ with $i \geq 0$; and $\alpha_0 = \beta_0 = 0.5$, $\gamma_0 = 1.0$, $\lambda_0 = 0$, $R_0 = 1$.

Then, the computation of trust function in DWTrust can be expressed as:

$$b_i = \frac{\alpha_0 \lambda_0 R_0 \gamma_0 + \sum_{k=1}^{i} \alpha_k \lambda_k R_k \gamma_k}{\alpha_0 \lambda_0 R_0 + \beta_0 \lambda_0 (1-R_0) + \sum_{k=1}^{i} \alpha_k \lambda_k R_k + \sum_{k=1}^{i} \beta_k \lambda_k (1-R_k) + 1}$$

$$= \frac{\sum_{k=1}^{i} 0.5 R_k}{\sum_{k=1}^{i} 0.5 R_k + \sum_{k=1}^{i} 0.5(1-R_k) + 1} = \frac{\sum_{k=1}^{i} R_k}{\sum_{k=1}^{i} R_k + \sum_{k=1}^{i} (1-R_k) + 2}$$

The positive evidence set and negative evidence set are $r_i = \sum_{k=1}^{i} R_k$ and $s_i = \sum_{k=1}^{i} (1-R_k)$.

Therefore, the metric for trust function in DWTrust is expressed as $b_i = \frac{r_i}{r_i + s_i + 2}$.

Similarly, $d_i = \frac{s_i}{r_i + s_i + 2}$ and $u_i = \frac{2}{r_i + s_i + 2}$ can be proved.

3.2.2 Feedback Control for Dynamic Weights

The feedback control rules for dynamic weights are critical for the effectiveness of trust assessment. As a reflection of subjective trust policy and objective constrains in applications, they can be concluded as two main parts: the range of dynamic weights and the adjusting rules. As an example, the feedback control rules for optimistic policy and pessimistic policy are listed below as a comparison. The assignments of the parameters are according to the results of experiments simulating certain environment.

Table 1. The range of success weight and failure weight for optimist and pessimist

b_i	Optimistic Policy		Pessimistic Policy	
	Successful Transaction	Failure Transaction	Successful Transaction	Failure Transaction
$[0,0.5)$	$\alpha \in [0.5,0.7]$	$\beta \in [0.3,0.5]$	$\alpha \in [0.3,0.5]$	$\beta \in [0.5,0.6]$
$[0.5,0.7)$	$\alpha \in [0.5,0.8]$	$\beta \in [0.2,0.5]$	$\alpha \in [0.5,0.7]$	$\beta \in [0.3,0.5]$
$[0.7,1.0]$	$\alpha \in [0.5,0.7]$	$\beta \in [0.3,0.5]$	$\alpha \in [0.5,0.6]$	$\beta \in [0.4,0.5]$

The feedback control rules limit the values in the adjustment of dynamic weights by the scales in Table. 1. While, the rules in Table. 2 define the timing and the degree of the adjustment of weights. We use T to represent the total number of transactions.

Since time-related weight and importance weight are associated with interactions, we do not discuss them in detail here.

Table 2. The adjusting rules for optimistic policy and pessimistic policy

	Optimistic Policy	Pessimistic Policy
Common Settings	Adjust weights with 4 continued successful transactions or each 2 continued fail transactions	
	$k = 1.0$ if $T \leq 10$; $k = T/10$ if $T > 10$.	
Successful Transactions	$\alpha = \alpha + 0.006 * k$, if α is in the range in Table. 1; else $\alpha = boundary . \beta = 1 - \alpha$.	$\alpha = \alpha + 0.005 * k$, if α is in the range in Table. 1; else $\alpha = boundary . \beta = 1 - \alpha$.
Fail Transactions	$\beta = \beta + 0.01 * k$, if β is in the range in Table. 1; else $\beta = boundary . \alpha = 1 - \beta$.	$\beta = \beta + 0.015 * k$, if β is in the range in Table. 1; else $\beta = boundary . \alpha = 1 - \beta$.

3.3 The Management of Trust Community

DWTrust uses a local trust based community management strategy to reduce the cost of communication. Each peer maintains a small community with dynamic size in which the trustworthy peers are recorded. To make the trust evaluation in small community more reliable, update procedure is designed to gather trust information in the larger society for a peer. With the assumption that the more trustworthy a peer is, the more reliable are its community, we take the community of trustworthy peers as the source of the recommendations. Then, a peer can periodically retrieve trustworthy recommendations to update its community. At the same time, the useless relationships are abandoned in trust revocation. The detailed discussion about the community management in DWTrust can be fount in [12].

3.4 Trust-Based Decision-Making

Trust-based decision-making is the procedure of deciding the trustworthiness of peers in community or making trust-based choice between peers. In DWTrust, the criteria for trust-based decision-making among peers are defined below by priority:

1. The peers with habitual trust should be given highest priority.
2. The peers with distrust relationships should be given lowest priority.
3. The peer with the greatest opinion is the most trustworthy peer.
4. The peer with more interacting events is more trustworthy.

As to a single trust relationship, whether the trust behavior is taken is decided by the thresholds defined in trust policy, which is a reflection of trust evolution and trust policy dynamically.

4 Experimental Evaluation

We perform three sets of experiments to evaluate DWTrust approach and introduce PeerTrust as a comparison in the last two simulations. PeerTrust is a distributed reputation-based trust model proposed in [1] [5] which shares many similar ideas with our DWTrust. We share the same simulation setup as PeerTrust in [1] [5]. The comparison is between two basic trust metrics in both models where the effect of time-related trust and context-related trust are ignored.

In DWTrust, optimistic trust policy is taken and the parameters are set as following: $\gamma_i = 1$, $\lambda_i = 1$, $\Delta a = 0$ and $\Delta \gamma = 0$. The feedback control rules are in Table 1 and Table 2. The trust threshold of trust expectation is set to 0.65 for all peers.

4.1 Optimistic Policy vs. Pessimistic Policy

These sets of experiments are designed to compare the optimistic policy and pessimistic trust policy. To describe the dynamic of peers, the trustee's real ability is assumed to follow two different distributions. In the first experiment, its ability changes from 0.1 to 0.9 gradually. While, in the second experiment the change is from 0.9 to 0.1. Both experiments include 180 transactions for the initialization of trust and 90 transactions in each time unit for simulating interactions. The results of the two simulations are showed in Fig. 3 with subjective logic as a comparison.

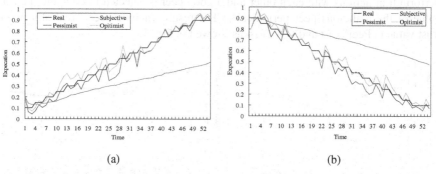

(a)   (b)

Fig. 3. The comparison of the probability expectations among DWTrust with pessimist policy, DWTrust with optimist policy and subjective logic

Both experiments reveal the following two points. First, with the increase of transactions, the adaptability of subjective logic falls. As shown in Fig. 3(b), even the series of fail events do not make much sense in subjective logic. On the contrary, DWTrust adapts well to the changed trust relationship, especially when the evidence set becomes larger. Second, different trust policies indicate different trust behaviors.

The results reveal that DWTrust is able to provide a close perspective about the dynamic of trust with appropriate feedback control rules.

4.2 Benefit of the Trust-Based Peer Selection

This set of experiments demonstrates the benefit of the DWTrust by choosing the peer with highest trust value to interact with. The results in Fig. 4 show that the successful transaction rates in both PeerTrust and DWTrust can reach 100 percent which reveals

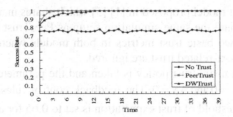

Fig. 4. Transaction successful rate with 25% malicious peers

the fact that trust mechanisms do benefit cooperation in P2P networks with enough trust information and honest peers.

4.3 Effectiveness Against Dynamic Personality of Peers

These experiments show how DWTrust works against the dynamic change of a peer's ability. First, the peer is trying to improve its reputation. Second, the peer oscillates between building and milking reputation. The experiment proceeds as peers randomly perform transactions with each other and a good peer is selected to compute the trust value of the malicious peer periodically. The results include peer's real ability and trust value in PeerTrust and DWTrust as showed in Fig. 5.

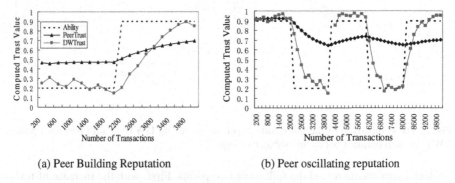

(a) Peer Building Reputation   (b) Peer oscillating reputation

Fig. 5. Effectiveness against dynamic personality and reputation oscillation

Results in Fig. 5 illustrate DWTrust adapts to the change of trustee's ability faster then PeerTrust. First, with PeerTrust basic, the peer is able to take advantage of the transition period by cheating while still maintaining a reasonable reputation. While, DWTrust is able to correct the trust value much sooner by feedbacks on weights. Second, as shown in Fig. 5(b), continued fail transactions decrease trust value fast in DWTrust, and thus the chance to choose a malicious peer to interact is minimized. Third, there is a broken point in Fig. 5(b) which means the target peer is abandoned from the trustor's community for the low trust value. After a while, the target peer rejoins the trustor's community as a recommended peer from trustworthy peers. That is also a proof for the effectiveness of the community management in DWTrust.

5 Conclusion

Compared to the contemporary distributed trust models, there are three features in DWTrust. First, DWTrust adopts a feedback-control mechanism to assess trust dynamically. Second, a direct trust based local trust management scheme is adopted in DWTrust. Compared to trust models with global reputation management scheme like EigenRep and PeerTrust, the communication overload is greatly reduced. Third, DWTrust is designed to model the multiple aspects and dynamicity in trust. There are only a few works suit for modeling dynamic trust, PeerTrust is a prominent one. Compared with PeerTrust, DWTrust is more flexible in representing the multiple aspects of trust with a lower communication overload.

The architecture of DWTrust makes it easily tailed for different distributed applications. We are working on dynamic trust models in ad-hoc and ubiquitous computing based on DWTrust.

References

1. Li Xiong, Ling Liu: PeerTrust: Supporting Reputation-Based Trust for Peer-to-Peer Electronic Communities. IEEE Trans. Knowl. Data Eng. 16(7): 843-857 (2004)
2. T. Beth, M. Borcherding, B. Klein: Valuation of trust in open networks. In Proceedings of the European Symposium on Research in Computer Security. Springer-Verlag, Brighton UK (1994) 3-18
3. Y. Teng, V. Phoha, B. Choi: Design of trust metrics based on dempstershafer theory. http://citeseer.nj.nec.com/461538.html
4. A. Jøsang: A logic for uncertain probabilities. International Journal of Uncertainty. Fuzziness and Knowledge-Based Systems. 9(3): (2001) 279-311
5. L. Xiong and L. Liu: A reputation-based trust model for P2P ecommerce communities. In IEEE Conference on E-Commerce (CEC'03). Newport Beach, California (2003) 275-284
6. Fabrizio Cornelli, Ernesto Damiani, Sabrina De Capitani di Vimercati, Stefano Paraboschi, Pierangela Samarati: Choosing reputable servents in a P2P network. WWW 2002: 376-386
7. Bin Yu, Munindar P. Singh: A Social Mechanism of Reputation Management in Electronic Communities. CIA 2000: 154-165
8. S.D .Kamvar, M.T.Schlosser,EigenRep: Reputation Management in P2P Networks, The Twelfth International World Wide Web Conference. Budapest, Hungary:ACM Press.2003.5,pp.123-134
9. Yu-Ting Caisy Hung, Alan R. Dennis, Lionel Robert: Trust in Virtual Teams: Towards an Integrative Model of Trust Formation. HICSS 2004, 01 05 - 01, (2004)
10. Chenlin Huang, Hu H P, Wang Z Y: Modeling time-related trust. In Proceedings of the third International Conference on Grid and Cooperative Computing. Springer-Verlag, Wuhan, LNCS 3252: (2004) 382-389. SCI IDS Number: BBD88.
11. Chenlin Huang, HP Hu, ZY Wang: The extension of subjective logic for time-related trust. Wuhan University Journal of Natural Sciences, v 10, n 1, January (2005) 56-60.
12. Chenlin Huang, HP Hu, ZY Wang: Community Based Trust Management in P2P Networks. ICOIN 2006. Sandai, Japan (2004). http://www.icoin.org/

Automatic Composition of Secure Workflows

Marc Lelarge[1,*], Zhen Liu[2], and Anton V. Riabov[2]

[1] BCRI University College Cork, Ireland
[2] IBM T.J. Watson Research Center
P.O. Box 704, Yorktown Heights, New York, 10598, USA
lm4@proba.ucc.ie, zhenl@us.ibm.com, riabov@us.ibm.com

Abstract. Automatic goal-driven composition of information processing workflows, or workflow planning, has become an active area of research in recent years. Various workflow planning methods have been proposed for automatic application development in Web services, stream processing and grid computing. Significant progress has been made on the definition of composition rules. The composition rules can be specified based on the schema, interface and semantics-driven compatibility of processes and data. Workflows must also satisfy information flow security constraints. In this paper we introduce and study the problem of workflow planning in MLS systems under Bell-LaPadula (BLP) policy, or a similar lattice-based policy, such as Biba integrity model. Extending results from AI planning literature, we show that under certain simplifying assumptions the workflows satisfying BLP constraints can be constructed in linear time. When the policy allows downgraders for data declassification, the problem is NP-complete; nevertheless, with additional assumptions efficient algorithms do exist.

1 Introduction

Automatic composition of information processing workflows, or workflow planning, has become an active area of research in recent years. Growing need of reliable and efficient application development together with the progress in modular software design and reusable software component frameworks have fueled the interest of researchers in this area. Automatic workflow planning tools can give end users the power to interconnect the components and create new processing workflows for their tasks on demand, based solely on the specification of requirements. Workflow planning systems such as Pegasus [1] and Sekitei [2] can ensure that the workflows use available resources as efficiently as possible. Furthermore, the systems that implement automatic workflow planning are more resilient than those that rely on manual composition: the automatic planning systems can easily adapt to changes by replanning existing workflows under the changed conditions.

The literature on workflow planning is extensive and spans diverse application areas where compositional architectures are used, including Web services [3,4,5], grid computing [6,1], and stream processing [7]. CHAMPS project [8] is an example of successful practical use of planning techniques for composition of change management workflows.

---

* The work was carried out while this author was with IBM T.J. Watson Research Center.

L.T. Yang et al. (Eds.): ATC 2006, LNCS 4158, pp. 322–331, 2006.
© Springer-Verlag Berlin Heidelberg 2006

In previous work on planning, however, the practically important issue of access control constraints on the automatically constructed workflows has not received enough attention. In various business applications security policies place restrictions on the information flow. These restrictions naturally constrain the set of valid workflows that can be executed in the system. The workflow planning methods designed for these environment, in addition to resource, quality, semantic and other constraints, must support access control constraints imposed by the security policies.

In this paper we focus on access constraints defined by lattice-based access control models [9]. One example of lattice-based access control is Bell-LaPadula policy [10] commonly implemented in MLS (multi-level secure) systems. MLS systems can process and store information at a variety of different sensitivity levels without disclosing sensitive information to an unauthorized entity. The MLS model is based on the following principle: 1) clearance is determined for each user; 2) information is marked with a sensitivity label; and 3) access control decisions are made based upon the clearance of the user and the sensitivity of the information. Bell-LaPadula policy requires that no high level information should be allowed to pass to lower level users/processes and that lower level information should be available to higher level users/processes [10]. The latter restriction is often considered too rigid, and can be relaxed. In that case the use of trusted components called downgraders are allowed for declassification of data objects. We discuss the downgraders and associated planning complexity issues in Section 4.

The approaches proposed for automatic workflow composition, including [6,3,1,2,4], use the techniques developed in the area of AI planning. Planning literature describes methods for the composition of series of operations that transform the world of the problem domain from the initial state to the goal state (see survey [11]).

In this paper we show that planning techniques can be used to compose workflows under MLS security policy constraints. The basic planning framework compliant with Bell-LaPadula (BLP) model can be extended to perform automatic workflow composition in systems with other lattice-based models, with trusted downgraders and with Chinese Wall policy (see technical report [12]). The workflows satisfying the BLP constraints can be constructed by the planner very efficiently. The number of operations performed by our algorithm grows linearly in the number of components. And, although the general problem of planning BLP-compliant workflows with the inclusion of downgraders is NP-complete in the worst case, efficient solutions can be given if the system configuration and the security policy have certain structural properties.

The structure of the paper is the following: in Section 2, we formally define the workflow planning problem. In Section 3, we extend the model to include the constraints of the BLP model. In section 4 we show that if trusted downgraders for data declassification are allowed, the problem becomes much harder (NP-complete). In the same section we describe special conditions that enable efficient planning with downgraders. Due to space limitation, we refer to [12] for the technical proofs.

2 Basic Workflow Planning Model

In this section we will formally define the elements of the workflow planning problem studied in this paper. The expressivity of the proposed model is limited so that only the

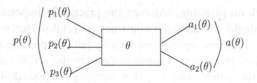

Fig. 1. Operator

workflow composition constraints that are independent of the context can be modeled. This basic model yields a simple solution: as we show below, a feasible workflow (if one exists) can be constructed in time polynomial in the size of the problem. Despite the seeming over-simplicity and even impracticality of the model, it captures a large family of composition constraints arising in practice. More importantly, this model allows us to make a clear distinction between the class of easily solvable planning problems in the absence of access controls, and the corresponding class of NP-complete problems under access control constraints.

To describe the context-independent constraints we will use the concept of data type for expressing the compatibility between the inputs and the outputs of the operators. In particular, we will assume that all data flowing through the system are described by a type or by a set of types. We will further assume that there are a total of n distinct data types used in formulating the problem. In the initial state, before any operators are included into the workflow (i.e, applied), only those types that are produced by the primal sources are available. Each operator has a set of types that must be available at the time when the operator is applied, i.e., the precondition of the operator, and a set of new types that become available after the operator is applied, i.e., the effect of the operator. The workflow planning problem then is to construct a sequence (or a partial ordering) of operators, application of which in that order will make available all types that are included into a given goal set of types.

Throughout the paper we will follow the notation defined below. Let vector $x \in \{0,1\}^n$ be the state vector, describing the set of currently available types. Each non-zero component, i.e. $x_j \neq 0$, of this vector corresponds to a currently available type. For any two vectors x and y, the ordering $x \leq y$ is interpreted componentwise and is thus equivalent to $x_j \leq y_j$ for all $1 \leq j \leq n$.

Each operator $\theta \in O$ is described by a pair of the precondition $p(\theta) \in \{0,1\}^n$ and the effect $a(\theta) \in \{0,1\}^n$, i.e. $\theta := \langle p(\theta), a(\theta) \rangle$, with vector components denoted by $p_i(\theta)$ and $a_i(\theta)$. Let $m := |O|$ be the number of operators. Figure 1 shows a graphical representation of an operator. When the operator θ is applied in state x, it causes the transition to state $\theta(x)$:

$$\theta(x) := \begin{cases} \max(x, a(\theta)), & \text{if } x \geq p(\theta); \\ x, & \text{otherwise;} \end{cases} \tag{1}$$

According to the definition of the state transition above, if the precondition of an operator θ is not satisfied, i.e. if $x \not\geq p(\theta)$, the operator can still be applied (with our way of writing). However, applying such an operator will not change the state.

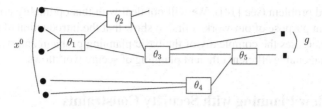

Fig. 2. Plan $\pi = (\theta_1, \theta_2, \theta_3, \theta_4, \theta_5) \in \mathcal{P}(x^0, g)$

A plan π is defined as a sequence of operators. If $\pi = (\theta_1, \ldots, \theta_k)$, we will say that the length of the plan π is k. The effect of the plan π on state x is the result of the application of operator θ_1, then θ_2 and so on.

Given an initial condition $x^0 \in \{0, 1\}^n$ and a goal $g \in \{0, 1\}^n$, we will say that the plan π achieves the goal g with the initial condition x^0 if $\pi(x^0) \geq g$. We will say that π solves (or is a solution of) the planning problem. We denote the set of all planning problem solutions by $\mathcal{P}(x^0, g)$, i.e., $\pi \in \mathcal{P}(x^0, g)$.

The planning problem described above is equivalent to the propositional STRIPS problem with empty delete lists. STRIPS is a well-known planning domain model described, for example, in [13]. We will assume that for all operators the maximum number of nonzeros in the precondition and effect vectors is bounded by a constant $C \geq 1$, which in particular is independent of n and m. Without loss of generality the following inequality can be assumed to hold in all problem instances: $n \leq 2mC$. This bound on n is derived from the fact that there are at most $2C$ nonzeros in the precondition and effect vectors of each operator, and therefore at most $2C$ types are listed in operator description.

Figure 2 shows a graphical representation of a plan. The black dots on the left side represent the data types available in the initial state and the black boxes on the right side represent the goal set of data types. The links between the operator rectangles corresponds to the types required (on the left of the operator) and produced (on the right) by the operator. The figure shows that the plan $\pi = (\theta_1, \theta_2, \theta_3, \theta_4, \theta_5)$ is in $\mathcal{P}(x^0, g)$. Note that the plan $(\theta_4, \theta_1, \theta_2, \theta_3, \theta_5)$ is also a feasible solution, and therefore is in $\mathcal{P}(x^0, g)$.

It is known that STRIPS planning problem without deletion can be solved in polynomial time [14]. In fact, planners can solve this problem in time linear in n and m. The following proposition states this result in our framework.

Proposition 1. *Given a set of m operators satisfying previous conditions, for any initial condition x^0 and a goal g, in $\mathcal{O}(m)$ operations an element of $\mathcal{P}(x^0, g)$ can be found if $\mathcal{P}(x^0, g) \neq \emptyset$. If such an element is not found by this procedure, then necessarily $\mathcal{P}(x^0, g) = \emptyset$.*

We refer to [12] for the description of an algorithm that finds a solution in linear time if it exists.

As shown by Proposition 1, solving the basic planning problem is easy, thanks to the monotonicity property: as long as possible we can produce new types and stop when all operators have been applied. Note that the problem of finding an optimal plan (i.e. a plan with minimal length) in $\mathcal{P}(x^0, g)$ is a much harder task. It has been shown that it is an NP-hard problem (see [14]). We will not deal with this optimality criterium here since the main purpose of our work is first to show that the introduction of the security constraints increases the complexity of the basic planning problem and second to give conditions that enable efficient efficient planning of secure workflows.

3   Workflow Planning with Security Constraints

In this section we add the constraints of the Bell-LaPadula security model to our basic workflow planning model, and describe an efficient algorithm for planning with these constraints. We further show that if the use of trusted downgraders is allowed, finding a feasible plan under security constraints is an NP-complete problem. Due to our general approach to modeling the constraints using a label lattice, the results of this section are applicable not only to the Bell-LaPadula model, but to other lattice-based models, such as the Biba integrity model [15,9].

First, we briefly review the basics of the Bell-LaPadula (BLP) model [10]. BLP is a lattice-based access control model for information flows [16,9]. A lattice $(\mathbb{L}, \prec)$ is a partially ordered set with dominance relation $\prec$, in which an upper bound and a lower bound are defined for each pair of elements. Let $a \vee b$ (resp. $a \wedge b$) denote the upper (respectively, lower) bound of a and b. Under the BLP model, all users (i.e., subjects) and all data (i.e., objects) are assigned security labels, which are elements of the lattice. A particular user is allowed access only to the data with labels that are dominated by the label (i.e., access class) of that user.

The BLP model defines two rules for making access control decisions based on the object label of the data and the access class label of the user. The rules, also called properties, are defined as follows:

- The simple security (ss-)property of the BLP model allows read access to the data, only if the access class label of the user dominates the correspond object label (no read up rule).
- The star (*-)property of the BLP model allows write access to the data only if the corresponding object label dominates the access class label of the user (no write down rule).

3.1   Workflow Planning Model with Bell-LaPadula Security Constraints

Our objective in representing the BLP constraints in the workflow planning model is to define a problem of composing a workflow such that the output, i.e. the goal types, of the workflow can be accessed by a specified access class. Data coming into the system from primal sources, i.e. the types of the initial state, can be labeled with arbitrary object labels, which are provided as input to the planner. In the process of planning, the planner will also assign subject labels to the operators processing the data, as well as object labels to all produced types, and do that such that the BLP policy is satisfied over the entire workflow.

The objects in the basic workflow planning model correspond to the data types, and therefore we extend the model by assigning a security label variable to each data type. As a result, the state space is extended from $\{0, 1\}^n$ in the basic formulation to a subset

S of $\{0,1\}^n \times \mathbb{L}^n$, where $(\mathbb{L}, \prec)$ is a lattice corresponding to the set of security labels. We will denote the state by a pair (x, ℓ). With each type $i \in \{1, \ldots, n\}$ represented by the zero-one indicator x_i, we associate a label $\ell_i \in \mathbb{L}$. If type i is not available in state (x, ℓ), i.e. if $x_i = 0$, then the corresponding label ℓ_i is set to a default value. More precisely, we define the set S as follows

$$S = \{(x, \ell) \in \{0,1\}^n \times \mathbb{L}^n, \text{ if } x_i = 0 \text{ then } \ell_i = \top\}, \tag{2}$$

where $\top \in \mathbb{L}$ is the top element of the lattice, defined as follows: for any $\ell \in \mathbb{L}$, the following holds: $\ell \prec \top$, $\ell \wedge \top = \ell$ and $\ell \vee \top = \top$.

In the extended workflow planning model the operators act on the pair (x, ℓ) and produce another pair $\theta(x, \ell) = (x', \ell')$. The value of x' is determined using (1) as before. We will discuss the computation of ℓ' separately below. We denote $\underline{\theta}(x, \ell) \equiv \underline{\theta}(x) := x'$, where we suppress the ℓ in $\underline{\theta}(x)$ to stress that x' does not depend on the security label ℓ. Similarly, we denote $\overline{\theta}(x, \ell) := \ell'$.

To enforce the *-property we must ensure that when a new type is made available by the operator θ, the label corresponding to this new type dominates all labels of the input types. In practice the upper bound of the input labels is taken and we have formally:

$$\text{if } [x_j = 0 \text{ and } a_j(\theta) = 1] \quad \text{then} \quad \bigvee_{k,\, p_k(\theta)=1} \ell_k = \overline{\theta}(x, \ell)_j = \ell'_j. \tag{3}$$

Note that an operator produces several data types, all with the same security label.

Equation (3) corresponds to the case when an operator produces a new type j. But it may happen that an operator produces a type that is already in x, namely $x_j = 1$ and $a_j(\theta) = 1$. In this case, the same type j can be obtained with two potentially different security labels, namely ℓ_j (already associated with x_j) and ℓ'_j (defined as in equation (3)). If we have $\ell_j \prec \ell'_j$ (or $\ell'_j \prec \ell_j$), it is clear the lowest label ℓ_j (resp. ℓ'_j) should be chosen as the new value of the label.

In workflow planning this corresponds to the case where the same information has been produced by two different methods and has two different security labels. For example one is Top-Secret because the information has been extracted from a Top-Secret document and the other is Public because the information appears in an unclassified document. In this case, the information should clearly be labeled Public, since a user does not need to have a Top-Secret access class to access the same data. We defer further discussion of related issues to the next section.

However, if we do not assume total order on $\mathbb{L}$ (and we refer to Section 4 for the special case of total order), it can happen that none of the two conflicting labels dominates the other. Hence for each type all encountered labels for which domination cannot be determined must be stored. In the example above, we add the new label ℓ'_j to the list: if $x_j = 1$ and, $a_j(\theta) = 1$ then $\overline{\theta}(x, \ell)_j = \{\ell'_j, \ell_j\}$, where ℓ'_j is defined as in equation (3). Consequently, if the data type j is used as a precondition of another operator at a later stage, one of the possible labels from that list must be chosen to be used in new computation (3). Therefore the plan in this extended model must be described as follows:

$$\pi = \left((\theta_1, L_1 = \{\ell_i\}_{i \in P(\theta_1)}), (\theta_2, L_2 = \{\ell_i\}_{i \in P(\theta_2)}) \right), \tag{4}$$

where each L_k contains the choice of labels that are used as input labels by the operator θ_k. For example, suppose that at some stage in the plan the same data type i is produced by operators u and v with two different labels ℓ and ℓ' as shown in Figure 3. We must distinguish between the two different plans that can be constructed with the operator θ taking as input (i, ℓ) or (i, ℓ'). This choice is shown by the double-arrow in the figure. Using our definition of a plan, the security labels produced by θ_k are $\bigvee_{i \in L_k} \ell_i$. We denote by $\{\overline{\pi}(x^0, \ell^0)_{i_j}\}$ the set of security labels obtained for type j by plan π. To summarize, plan π produces data types j if $\underline{\pi}(x^0)_j = 1$ and in this case, the plan may produce different copies of this data with respective security labels $\{\overline{\pi}(x^0, \ell^0)_{1_j}, \overline{\pi}(x^0, \ell^0)_{2_j}, \dots\}$.

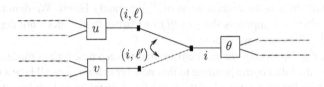

Fig. 3. A conflict between labels ℓ and ℓ' for the same type i

To enforce the ss-property, we must ensure that security level of the user ℓ_{USER} dominates the label of the output data produced by the workflow. The output data corresponds to the data types included in the goal vector g. As we discussed above, each data type may be produced with different security labels and it can be disclosed to the user only if among these security labels, at least one is dominated by ℓ_{USER}. Hence the condition that must be enforced is:

$$\text{if } \underline{\pi}(x^0)_j = g_j = 1 \text{ then, there exists } i_j \text{ such that } \overline{\pi}(x^0, \ell^0)_{i_j} \prec \ell_{USER}. \quad (5)$$

The workflow planning problem is now to find a plan that will achieve the goal g and satisfy equation (5). In other words, the plan π must produce all data types requested in the goal g, i.e. $\pi \in \mathcal{P}(x^0, g)$, and each data type of the result matched to the goal must have a security label less or equal to ℓ_{USER}.

3.2   Planning Algorithm for Workflows with Bell-LaPadula Security Constraints

Despite the seeming complexity of the extended workflow planning model, a minor modification of the planning algorithm for basic model can provide an efficient solution. Note that given Equation (3), the maximum security label of all the types within a plan is the maximum of the input type labels used in the plan. Hence the algorithm to solve the planning problem with security constraints is quite simple. First, we must select all types in x^0 with security labels that are dominated by ℓ_{USER} and remove all other types. Then starting with this new initial state y^0 we must solve the workflow planning problem without the security constraints. In particular, it is no longer required to take into consideration the sets L_k defined in (4) for solving the problem, and the algorithm of Proposition 1 can be used without modification.

Proposition 2. *Finding a solution to the workflow planning problem with the Bell-LaPadula access constraints, or proving that no solutions exists can be done in $\mathcal{O}(m)$ operations.*

This result implies that the problem with Bell-LaPadula constraints is not more difficult than the original workflow planning problem without security constraints. However, the extended workflow planning model with multiple labels for each data type that we developed earlier will come into play in the much more complex case where the use of downgraders is allowed.

4   Secure Workflows with Downgraders

It has been recognized that the *-property can be overly restrictive in practice. Consequently, a class of trusted processes has been included in the model [17]. These processes are trusted not to violate security policy even though they may violate the *-property. More precisely, a trusted process can have simultaneous read access to the objects of classification ℓ_1 and write access to the objects of classification ℓ_2, even if the label ℓ_2 is not dominating the label ℓ_1 in the lattice.

We define new operators to model the trusted processes that we call downgraders. Let ω^i be a map from $\mathbb{L}$ to $\mathbb{L}^n$ defined by: for $\delta \in \mathbb{L}$, we have $\omega^i(\delta) = (\omega^i(\delta)_1, \ldots, \omega^i(\delta)_n)$ with $\omega^i(\delta)_j = \top$ for $j \neq i$ and $\omega^i(\delta)_i = \delta$. Downgrader d^i acts only on the type $i \in \{1, \ldots, n\}$ and is defined as follows:

$$d^i(x, \ell) := \begin{cases} (x, \ell \wedge \omega^i(\delta_i)) & \text{if } x_i = 1 \\ (x, \ell) & \text{otherwise,} \end{cases} \tag{6}$$

where $\delta_i \in \mathbb{L}$ is a constant label associated with the downgrader d^i. By convention, if there is no downgrader that can act on the data of type i, we define $\delta_i := \top$. We consider the vector of downgrader labels $\delta = (\delta_1, \ldots, \delta_n) \in \mathbb{L}^n$ to be a part of the extended planning problem formulation.

Note that in this model there can exist at most one downgrader per type. However this restriction does not limit the generality of the model: if there are defined several downgraders for the same data type, we can consider the composition of all downgraders for this type as a single downgrader for the purpose of our model.

Proposition 3. *The workflow planning problem under the constraints of the Bell-La-Padula policy with the inclusion of trusted processes (downgraders) is NP-complete.*

Although Proposition 3 above shows that in this general formulation the secure workflow planning problem is provably hard, we have discovered several special cases in which the problem can be solved efficiently. We describe these special cases below. The proof of Proposition 3 by reduction to SAT, and the proofs of results for special cases can be found in [12].

Proposition 4. *Under the assumption that the lattice of security labels is totally ordered, a workflow that satisfies Bell-LaPadula access policy with downgraders can be composed in linear time $\mathcal{O}(m)$.*

The corresponding planning algorithm described in [12] has three steps: 1) produce all the possible types (without taking into account the labels); 2) downgrade all the possible labels; 3) produce the optimal labels using regular (non-downgrader) operators. Therefore, given the initial types x^0 and the goal g such that $\mathcal{P}(x^0, g)$ is not empty, there exists a plan which achieves the goal g and which will give the minimal possible label of the final state, and this plan does NOT depend on the initial labels ℓ^0.

The following proposition shows that an ordering of the downgrader labels is sufficient to guarantee the existence of an efficient planning algorithm.

Proposition 5. *If the set of downgrader labels is totally ordered, a workflow that satisfies Bell-LaPadula policy with downgraders can be composed in linear time $\mathcal{O}(m)$.*

For policies where labels can be described by a relatively small number of categories or levels, the following performance bound proven in [12] can be very useful.

Proposition 6. *A workflow satisfying Bell-LaPadula access policy with downgraders can be composed in $\mathcal{O}\left(|\mathbb{L}|^2 m^2\right)$ operations.*

In practice the size of the label set $\mathbb{L}$ is exponential in the number of security categories $\mathcal{C}$ and is linear in the number of levels $\mathcal{H}$. When written in these terms, the complexity of the algorithm described in Proposition 6 is $\mathcal{O}(2^{2|\mathcal{C}|}|\mathcal{H}|^2 m^2)$. Even if the number of categories remains constant, in practical applications of MLS the set of categories is typically large. To avoid the dependence on the size of category set, the complexity bound can be expressed in terms of the number of distinct downgraders:

Proposition 7. *The number of operations required to compose a workflow satisfying Bell-LaPadula access policy with downgraders does not exceed $\mathcal{O}(2^{2^{b+1}}|\mathcal{H}|^2 m^2)$, where b is the cardinality of the set of distinct downgrader labels:*

$$b := |\Delta| = |\{\delta_i, i \in \{1, \ldots, n\}\}|.$$

Proposition 7 implies that a polynomial solution exists if the number of distinct downgrader labels is limited by a constant. Downgraders are often costly in practice due to rigorous verification processes required to certify that the declassification is performed safely on all possible inputs, and hence this assumption will often hold as well.

5 Conclusion

In this paper we have analyzed the computational complexity of problems arising in workflow planning under security constraints. We have shown that in many practical scenarios the planning problem can be solved efficiently. Our analysis framework and a set of basic results can be easily extended for many lattice-based access control policies. In this paper we use the framework to analyze workflow planning problem under the Bell-LaPadula policy. We describe an efficient (linear time) algorithm for planning under these constraints. We also show that if the planning problem becomes much harder (NP-complete) if the use of downgraders is allowed; nevertheless, under certain assumptions planning can be performed efficiently even with downgraders.

The results we present in this paper show that the use of automatic planning techniques within compositional environments with lattice-based access controls constitutes not only an attractive, but also a practically feasible approach.

In this work we have explored only one dimension of context-dependent constraints on workflows. This allowed us to identify and describe the classes of security constraints that correspond to different complexity classes of planning problems. However, in practical systems the security constraints must be used together with other types of context-dependent constraints, such as semantic or resource constraints. All these constraints further increase the complexity. For example, adding simple resource utilization constraints based on an additive resource metric immediately makes the problem NP-hard by reduction to SET COVER. The work in this area currently focuses, and in the near future will continue to focus, on the design of efficient planning algorithms that can support a wide range of composition constraints.

References

1. Gil, Y., Deelman, E., Blythe, J., Kesselman, C., Tangmurarunkit, H.: Artificial intelligence and grids: Workflow planning and beyond. IEEE Intelligent Systems (2004)
2. Kichkaylo, T., Ivan, A., Karamcheti, V.: Constrained component deployment in wide-area networks using AI planning techniques. In: Proceedings of IPDPS-03. (2003)
3. Doshi, P., Goodwin, R., Akkiraju, R., Verma, K.: Dynamic workflow composition using Markov decision processes. In: Proceedings of ICWS-04. (2004)
4. Koehler, J., Srivastava, B.: Web service composition: Current solutions and open problems. In: Proceedings of ICAPS-03, Workshop on Planning for Web Services. (2003) 28–35
5. Pistore, M., Traverso, P., Bertoli, P.: Automated composition of web services by planning in asynchronous domains. In: Proceedings of ICAPS-05. (2005)
6. Blythe, J., Deelman, E., Gil, Y., Kesselman, K., Agarwal, A., Mehta, G., Vahi, K.: The role of planning in grid computing. In: Proceedings of ICAPS-03. (2003)
7. Riabov, A., Liu, Z.: Planning for stream processing systems. In: Proceedings of AAAI-05. (2005)
8. Brown, A., Keller, A., Hellerstein, J.: A model of configuration complexity and its application to a change management system. In: Proceedings IM-05. (2005)
9. Sandhu, R.: Lattice-based access control models. IEEE Computer **26** (1993) 9–19
10. Bell, D., LaPadula, L.: Secure computer system: Unified exposition and Multics interpretation. MTR-2997, MITRE Corp. (1976)
11. Rintanen, J., Hoffmann, J.: An overview of recent algorithms for AI planning. Künstliche Intelligenz (2001) 5–11
12. Lelarge, M., Liu, Z., Riabov, A.: Automatic composition of secure workflows (2006)
13. Fikes, R., Hart, P.E., Nilsson, N.J.: Learning and executing generalized robot plans. Artificial Intelligence **3** (1972) 251–288
14. Bylander, T.: The computational complexity of propositional STRIPS planning. Artificial Intelligence **69** (1994) 165–204
15. Biba, K.: Integrity considerations for secure computer systems. MTR-3153, MITRE Corp. (1977)
16. Denning, D.: A lattice model of secure information flow. Communications of the ACM **19** (1976) 236–243
17. Bell, D.: Secure computer systems: A refinement of the mathematical model. MTR-2547, Vol. III, MITRE Corp. (1974)

TPOD: A Trust-Based Incentive Mechanism for Peer-to-Peer Live Broadcasting

Yun Tang[1], Lifeng Sun[2], Jianguang Luo[1], Shiqiang Yang[1], and Yuzhuo Zhong[2]

[1] Department of Computer Science and Technology,
Tsinghua University, Beijing 100084, P.R. China {tangyun98,
luojg03}@mails.tsinghua.edu.cn
[2] {sunlf, yangshq, zyz-dcs}@mail.tsinghua.edu.cn

Abstract. The prevalence of emerging peer-to-peer (P2P) live broadcasting applications has practically demonstrated that they could scale to reliably support a large population of end users. However, these systems potentially suffer from two major threats: peers generally interact with unfamiliar partners without the benefit of trusted third party or verification authority, resulting in poor service if meeting with *unreliable* upstream nodes, while peers essentially tend to be *selfish* when it comes to the duty rather than the benefits and hence undermine the system performance. The *trust* and *cooperation* issues motivate us to investigate the design of trust-based incentive mechanism which establishes trustful relationship among peers and balances what they take from the system with what they contribute. The proposed **TPOD** mechanism leverages the statistical analysis to the practical service logs of client-server and P2P systems and effectively offers incentive through service differentiation. It goes beyond existing approaches in the following four desirable properties: (1)**T**rust-based; (2)**P**ractical-oriented; (3)**O**bjective metrics about past behaviors and (4)**D**istributed nature upon gossip-based overlay. The experiment results over PlanetLab verify its effectiveness.

1 Introduction

The growing success of peer-to-peer (P2P) networks enlightens a new arena of provisioning data or service to a large population of end users without the need of costly server and network infrastructure support. The concept of P2P exploits the cooperative paradigm for information and data exchange and therefore greatly improve the system scalability with respect to traditional client-server approach. Besides a variety of well-known file sharing and VoIP applications, the prevalence of emerging P2P live broadcasting systems also demonstrated that they could scale to reliably support numerous users across different administrative domains and network boundaries [1,2].

However, all is not rosy. Since "P2P reflects society better than other types of computer architectures" [3], these systems potentially suffer from two major threats: On one hand, peers generally interact with unknown or unfamiliar partners without the benefit of trusted third party or verification authority, resulting in poor service of quality if meeting with unreliable upstream nodes. The

L.T. Yang et al. (Eds.): ATC 2006, LNCS 4158, pp. 332–341, 2006.
© Springer-Verlag Berlin Heidelberg 2006

anonymous, heterogeneous and distributed nature of P2P networks means apparent possibility to disseminate application-specific vulnerabilities, which poses significant risks to the deployment of existing live broadcasting systems. On the other hand, peers essentially tend to optimize towards their self-interests, attempting to exploit services from other nodes without contributing and hence undermine global system performance. Empirical studies show that when those non-cooperative users benefit from so-called "freeriding" on others [4], the "tragedy of the commons" is inevitable [5].

Consequently, many research pioneers had recognized that the trust management and incentive mechanism might be critical to the eventual success of P2P applications and proposed many schemes in file sharing area, comprising token-based, reputation-based and game theoretic approaches [6,7,8,9]. However, P2P live video broadcasting systems are in particular characterized by the stringent playback deadline for video packet delivery and high demanding real-time bandwidth over heterogeneous underlay networks. In this paper we mainly investigate the problem of establishing trustful relationship among peers and encouraging them to balance what they take from the system with what they contribute.

We first make statistical analysis to more than *10 million* service traces from traditional client-server live streaming system in CCTV[1] and service logs from a practical P2P live broadcasting system with concurrent online users about *200,000* for the Spring Festival Evening show in Jan. 2006. The practical-oriented analysis reveals users who had enjoyed video contents for a longer time would be willing to spend more time, regardless of various system architecture. Then the objective metric, namely *online duration*, inherently reflects subjective user behaviors and therefore motivates us to leverage it as one basis of proposed **TPOD** mechanism. Besides, for streaming applications, packets arriving before the playback deadline, termed as *effective traffic*, are of most importance when translating into the visual quality at end users and undoubtedly explored as another basis of TPOD. Intuitively speaking, peers which are active for a longer while and with more contributions are naturally deemed as more trustworthy and we further offer incentive through service differentiation to encourage trustful and cooperative relationship within the community. In this way, faithful peers are rewarded with better quality streaming sessions while freeriders are limited to, if any, poor upstream nodes, resulting in low quality in return. TPOD links the trust and incentive together and has salient properties in terms of (1)**T**rust-based; (2)**P**ractical-oriented; (3)**O**bjective metrics about past behaviors and (4)**D**istributed nature upon gossip-based overlay. The experiments over PlanetLab also verify its effectiveness.

The roadmap of this paper is organized as follows. Section 2 briefly reviews related work. Section 3 presents the statistical analysis to service logs from two practical systems and motivates us to detailedly propose TPOD in Section 4. Section 5 exhibits performance study and experiment results over PlanetLab. We discuss future work and end this paper in Section 6.

---

[1] CCTV: China Central Television Station, http://www.cctv.com

2   Related Work

Trust Management. Previous work on trust management mainly focused on reputation-based approach [7,10,11,12] and they were proposed to discourage maliciousness and motivate trustworthiness in P2P networks. [7] advocated objective criteria to track each peer's contribution and differentiated peers along the dimension of capability and behavior. However, the considerations underlying file sharing pattern make it inapplicable for live broadcasting. By similar reasoning, P2PPrep [10], XPep [11] and EigenRep [12] studied subjective reputation-based approach for file sharing systems, either from binary voting or transitive reputation computation. Our proposed TPOD involves objective metrics to establish trustful relationship and encourage cooperative paradigm within the arena of streaming applications.

Incentive Mechanism. Several incentive mechanisms have been proposed to motivate users to contribute for improving system performance [6,9,13,14]. For the file sharing applications, the Tit-for-Tat and optimistic choking mechanism in the popular BitTorrent worked well for incremental block exchanges [13]. Besides, a natural approach for incentive was to charge users for every download and reward them for every upload through token-based approval of cooperation [6], while some other pioneers advocated the promising game theory to model users' strategies for global outcome equilibrium while retaining individual utility maximization [9]. The recent work [14] might be close to our work due to peer-selection based service differentiation, but TPOD greatly differ from it for the practical-oriented metric and distributed nature upon gossip-based overlay construction.

3   Background: Statistical Analysis for User Behavior

Clearly, the terms "trust" and "cooperation" both exhibit the rational behaviors of end users within P2P community. Therefore, we believe that examining the practical service logs to see what those **real** users will be like is definitely the first step towards the design of an effective trust management and incentive mechanism. Accordingly, we have analyzed more than 10 million traces from traditional client-server service and logs from a practical P2P system with concurrent online users more than 200,000.

3.1   Client-Server Live Broadcasting Service Analysis

We first analyzed more than 10 million traces from Oct. 2004 to Jan. 2005 of client-server video servers at CCTV global websites. Tab.1 lists the basic information of streaming service, comprising the amount of effective traces and average online duration at each channel (CCTV-News, CCTV-4 and CCTV-9).

To understand the intrinsic characteristics within the online duration, we intentionally depict the percentage and cumulative percentage of various online duration distributions, as show in Fig.1. Clearly, although the populations (that

Table 1. Information of service traces

Channel	Effective traces	Average online	Synthesized parameters
1.CCTV-News	8,314,245	772 seconds	$(\mu, \sigma) = (4.421, 1.672)$
2.CCTV-4	2,349,934	542 seconds	$(\mu, \sigma) = (4.037, 1.464)$
3.CCTV-9	676,807	704 seconds	$(\mu, \sigma) = (4.161, 1.438)$
In total	11,340,986	720 seconds	NULL

is, effective traces) vary in different channels, all the three results substantially follow the lognormal distribution. The last column of Tab.1 further provides the synthesized parameters for lognormal distribution in Fig.1(a). The distinctness of each (μ, σ) pair also indicates the differences within each channel, potentially listing from contents, time and program duration, etc.

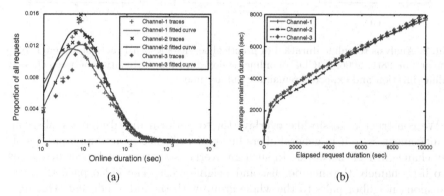

(a)   (b)

Fig. 1. Analysis to online duration of practical service traces: (a)Distribution of online duration and fitted curves; (b)Relation between elapsed online duration and expected remaining online time

However, a characteristic of P2P networks is that peers could change their behaviors and enter or leave the service session frequently and continuously. Thus it is important to get a rough idea about the expected remaining online duration. Fig.1(b) schematically shows the statistical relation between elapsed online duration and expected remaining online time. Observe that users who have enjoyed the service for a longer time would be statistically willing to spend more time. It should be stressed that although this positive correlation is derived from client-server service architecture, it will be helpful to further improve system performance of P2P streaming applications, with the consideration that end users have little knowledge about whether the service is provided via client-server or P2P. In the next subsection, we also statistically analyze service logs from a practical P2P live video broadcasting system to reveal similar characteristics of user behavior.

3.2   P2P Live Broadcasting Service Analysis

We have designed, implemented and deployed a practical P2P live video broadcasting system over global Internet. As a scalable and cost-effective alternative to client-server approach, it was adopted by CCTV to live broadcast Spring Festival Evening show at Feb. 2005 [2] and Jan. 2006. In this section, we first briefly introduce the basic system architecture and then make a statistical analysis to the service logs in P2P context.

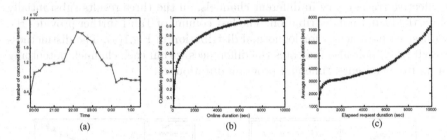

(a)   (b)   (c)

Fig. 2. Analysis to online duration of practical service logs: (a)Practical system evolution at Jan. 28th, 2006; (b)CDF of online session duration; (c)Relation between elapsed online duration and expected remaining online time

We construct a gossip-like overlay [15] to perform distributed membership management since it in general offers inherent resilience to accommodate topology change in P2P networks. In such an overlay structure, each peer maintains two lists, namely the member list and neighbor list. The video packets transmit along neighbor pairs to the whole group with the aid of efficient streaming mechanism [2], while the dynamic membership and neighborship are disseminated within the community in a gossip fashion. For the broadcasting of Spring Festival Evening show over global Internet in Feb. 2005, there were more than 500,000 users from about 66 countries with the maximum number of concurrent users 15,239 at Feb. 8th, 2005. In the second deployment, more than 1,800,000 users from about 70 countries subscribed the service and the maximum concurrent users reached its peak about 200,000 at Jan. 28th, 2006, as shown in Fig.2(a). More details about the system architecture and deployment experiences could be referred to [2].

We analyzed the service logs to reveal user characteristics, specifically with respect to online duration evolution of end users. Fig.2(b) shows the cumulative distribution function of the online session duration. Observe that nearly 50% users spent less than 200 seconds in the community, which indicates that many peers would not stay for a longer while, resulting in extremely high churn rate. However, there are also roughly 20% users would like to keep online for more than 30 minutes. Then we intentionally investigate the relation between elapsed online duration and expected remaining online time in Fig.2(c). It is obvious that peers who had stayed longer would be expected to spend more time to enjoy the service, as similar to previous subsection. The main reason of this positive correlation may reside in the "popularity-driven" access pattern of live video programs.

Towards this end, the practical service traces and logs of client-server and P2P systems described above offer us insightful understandings to statistical characteristics of user online duration. While the result is rather simple, it could be exploited to guide the design of trust management and incentive mechanism in the area of live broadcasting, as discussed in following section.

4 TPOD: A Novel Trust-Based Incentive Mechanism

Recall that most of existing work either sticks on file sharing applications or advocates intuitive criteria for reputation-based trust management and incentive mechanism. Here we aim to link trust management with incentive mechanism, with the benefit of above practical features: by contributing more and staying longer it is quite possible to improve a peer's own trustworthiness and thus the service it obtains in return. The critical questions of this design philosophy come in two steps. One is how to effectively and objectively evaluate the contribution and trust level of a peer in absence of central authority control or trusted third party, while the other is how to provide differentiated service to peers with different levels.

4.1 Design Considerations

Before we go into the details of this mechanism, let's first discuss some critical considerations to identify the fundamental design space for the interplay of trust and cooperation within P2P live broadcasting arena.

Challenges and Requirements. Recognizing the general set of characteristics in P2P networks, when designing a mechanism in the peer community, we are often faced with two challenges, that is, large populations of users and high churn rate of dynamic evolution. The former means that the d mechanism should scale well while the later indicates short life time and few repeated transactions of peers. Besides, specifically with respect to streaming applications, what determines the visual quality of service mainly reside in the packets arriving before the playback deadline rather than the volume of total transferred bytes, and this particular challenge poses a great need on the measurement of effective packet transmission.

Benefits. The experiences of a practical P2P live video broadcasting system significantly benefit us for the design of a trust management and incentive mechanism. On one hand, the gossip-based overlay structure advocates distributed membership management in a gossip fashion and hence is able to be leveraged as the basis of a scalable mechanism. On the other hand, the statistical analysis to the service of client-server and P2P live video broadcasting systems offers us user characteristics in terms of online duration distribution. This objective metric can be adopted to guide the design of subjective issues: trust and cooperation.

4.2   Proposed TPOD Mechanism

The above considerations stimulate us to clearly recognize that only the volume of outgoing traffic measured by their own is far from enough. Therefore, as the basis of trust management and incentive mechanism, we tentatively introduce the *composite trust index*, consisting of two objective metrics, i.e. online duration and effective upstream traffic within the proposed mechanism. The former could be regarded as the measurement of the fidelity of peers, while the "effectiveness" in the later can be evaluated by the downstream partners within the horizon of playback deadline and utilized to encourage mutual cooperation among peers. Roughly speaking, peers are deemed as reputable or trustful when they have been active for a long time and contribute more effective upstream traffic. They are the "fans" of the P2P live broadcasting service and expected to be more stably than other short-lived peers, for instance newcomers. On the other extreme, freeriders, representing those who have exploited quite a lot of others' resources without any contributions, are denoted as lower composite trust index. Formally speaking, we denote δ as the trust factor for each node p, then the composite trust index I_p could be calculated as

$$I_p = \begin{cases} \frac{C_{EBp}}{\gamma C_{Tp}}, \frac{C_{EBp}}{C_{Tp}} < \delta; \\ \gamma_1 C_{EBp} + \gamma_2 C_{Tp}, \frac{C_{EBp}}{C_{Tp}} \geq \delta; \end{cases} \tag{1}$$

where C_{EBp} denotes effective upstream traffic of p, C_{Tp} denotes online duration and $\gamma, \gamma_1, \gamma_2$ are the normalized factors. Note that those who had enjoyed the service for a long time with less effective upstream traffic, in turn low cooperation level, would be perceived by the threshold δ. As each peer subscribing the service is required to synchronize when it joins the community, C_{Tp} could be measured in following equation:

$$C_T = T_{cur} - T_{syn_p} \tag{2}$$

where T_{cur} is current time and T_{syn_p} is the synchronization time of node p. Since node p might be involved in previous transactions, if any, with multiple peers, we could obtain the effective upstream traffic C_{EB} as follows. For each peer i who received effective packets $\{B_{pi}^1, B_{pi}^2, \ldots, B_{pi}^n\}$ in n rounds with p, the effective upstream traffic between i and p could be calculated as:

$$C_{B(p,i)} = \begin{cases} \alpha^n B_{pi}^1 + \alpha^{n-1} B_{pi}^2 + \cdots + \alpha B_{pi}^n, n \neq 0; \\ 0, n = 0; \end{cases} \tag{3}$$

Note that the exponential aggregation ($0 < \alpha < 1$) here is deployed to highlight the most recent upstream traffic. Therefore, the aggregated effective upstream traffic of node p could be objectively calculated as Eq.(4), where m denotes the number of past transaction partners and w_i is the weight of each partner:

$$C_{EBp} = \begin{cases} \sum_{i=1}^{m} w_i * C_{B(p,i)}, m \neq 0; \\ 0, m = 0; \end{cases} \tag{4}$$

In this way, the composite trust index of each peer has been objectively calculated without the need of central control. Now it comes to the question that how to aggregate and distribute this local composite trust index within thousands or millions of peers. Recall that gossip-based overlay structure exchanges a fraction of active members periodically. These composite trust indices could be effectively disseminated and also retrieved in a gossip fashion along with membership maintenance. Although the additional trust information indeed induces a certain number of traffic overhead, we argue that since the chief task of these indices is to identify "fans" as well as "freeriders" and then encourage others to collaborate with partners with more trustworthiness, the volume of traffic overhead could be bounded in a small level (most of composite trust indices for short-lived peers are zero) and is going to be measured in ongoing work.

The proposed mechanism has evaluated the trust level of peers in a distributed and objective manner with practical considerations. For the second question posed at the beginning of this section, we aim to provide service differentiation based on those trust indexes. We borrow the core peer-selection idea in [14] to reward trustful peers with good upstream candidates while impose penalties to those with low trust indexes. The trust-based incentive mechanism, so called TPOD, continues to follow the line of "fans" and freeriders". Peers within the "fans" group have the freedom to choose upstream candidates, resulting in better service quality. "Freeriders" in another group are constrained to few opportunities to select first-rank candidate supplying nodes, certainly resulting in low streaming quality. It should be stressed that these "fans" are also required to randomly foster newcomers to avoid monopolization and overlay division, as similar to optimistic choking scheme in BitTorrent [13].

5   Performance Study and Evaluation

Suppose the node amount of P2P network is N, the number of each node' neighbors is M, and the total amount of live broadcasting segments is Q. We discuss the performance of our algorithm by analyzing the computation complexity of each node and communication overhead of overlay network at first. For the trust level evaluation, the computation burden is to evaluate the trust level of upstream peer when receiving a segment, and hence the computation complexity is $O(Q)$. Note that the computation load on each node is unrelated with the network size N. Similarly, the communication overhead of the evaluation is that each time one peer receives a segment, it updates the contributions of upstream peers and refine the corresponding member list and neighbor list. For the updated information, the communication overhead of the evaluation is $O(Q * N)$.

We further conduct experiments over the Planetlab [16] testbed to evaluate the proposed TPOD mechanism. The prototype in [2] is deployed as the underlying architecture and in total we utilize more than 300 machines as the peers in service community. Tab.2 lists the parameters of experiment setup. Due to page limitation, here we simply refer to the average delivery ratio as the representative metric to exhibit the effectiveness of proposed TPOD mechanism. The delivery ratio of each peer could be calculated as the ratio of packets that arrive before the playback deadline to the total packets, which indicates the visual quality

Table 2. Experiment setup over PlanetLab

Parameter	Value or range
Size of community	300-350
Packet rate	30 packets/sec
Request rate (Poisson arrival)	$\lambda = 1$
Online duration distribution (lognormal distribution)	$(\mu, \sigma) = (4.4, 1.6)$
Request and buffer map interval	1 second

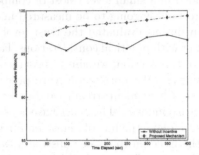

Fig. 3. Comparison of average delivery ration between with and without incentive mechanism

at end users. Fig.3 shows that the average delivery ratio is lower when there is no any trust management and incentive mechanism. With the proposed trust-based incentive mechanism, rational peers are encouraged to stay longer and make more contributions, resulting in better stability of the overlay and more cooperation between peers, and in turn higher average delivery ratio.

6 Conclusion and Future Work

In this paper, we mainly investigate the problem of provisioning trust management and incentive mechanism in P2P live broadcasting system since such applications rely on mutual cooperation between peers. Our contributions come in two-fold. Firstly, we make the statistical analysis to service traces of client-server system and logs of P2P system and then reveal characteristics of user online duration. Secondly, we are motivated to propose TPOD which integrates online duration information with the effective upstream traffic of each peer and thus encourages interactions with trustful peers through service differentiation. More profoundly, the proposed TPOD substantially has following salient features: (1)Trust-based; (2)Practical-oriented; (3)Objective metric about past behaviors and (4)Distributed nature upon gossip-based overlay structure.

Future research could proceed along several arenas. One is to further evaluate the overhead of proposed mechanism and then to deploy it into practical system. It is also interesting to apply scalable coding schemes into for service differentiation.

Acknowledgement

The authors gracefully thank the anonymous reviewers for their comments. This work is supported by the National Natural Science Foundation of China under Grant No.60432030 and No.60503063.

References

1. Xinyan Zhang, Jiangchuan Liu, et al: CoolStreaming/DONet: A Data-Driven Overlay Network for Efficient Live Media Streaming. In: Proceedings of 24th Joint Conference of IEEE Computer and Communications Societies, IEEE IN-FOCOM(2005), 2102-2111
2. Meng Zhang, Li Zhao, Yun Tang, et al: Large-Scale Live Media Streaming over Peer-to-Peer Networks through Global Internet. In: Proceedings of ACM Workshop on Advances in Peer-to-Peer Multimedia Streaming, ACM MM(2005), 21-28
3. David Clark: Face-to-Face with Peer-to-Peer Networking. IEEE Computer 34(2001), 18-21
4. Eytan Adar and B. A. Huberman: Free Riding on Gnutella. First Monday 5(10), October 2000.
5. Garrett Hardin: The Tragedy of the Commons. Science 162(1968), 1243-1248
6. Philippe Golle, Kevin Leyton-Brown, et al: Incentive for Sharing in Peer-to-Peer Networks. In: proceedings of ACM Conference on Electronic Commerce, ACM EC(2001), 264-267
7. Minaxi Gupta, Paul Judge, et al: A Reputation System for Peer-to-Peer Networks. In: Proceedings of 13th International Workshop on Network and Operating Systems Support for Digital Audio and Video, ACM NOSDDAV(2003), 144-152
8. M. Nowak and K. Sigmund: Evolution of Indirect Reciprocity by Image Scoring. Nature 393(1998), 573-577
9. Weihong Wang and Baochun Li: To Play or to Control: A Game-based Control-theoretic Approach to Peer-to-Peer Incentive Engineering. In: Proceedings of 11th International Workshop on Quality of Service, IEEE IWQoS(2003), 174-194
10. F. Cornelli, E.Damiani, et al: Choosing Reputable Servents in a P2P Network. In: Proceedings of 11th International World Wide Web Conference(2002), 376-386
11. E.Damiani, S.D.C.di Vimercati, et al: A Reputation-based Approach for Choosing Reliable Resources in Peer to Peer Networks. In: Proceedings of 9th ACM Conference on Computer and Communication Security(2002), 207-216
12. S.D.Kamvar, M.T. Schlosser and H.Garcia-Molina: The EigenTrust Algorithm for Reputation Management in P2P Networks. In: Proceedings of 12th International World Wide Web Conference, WWW(2003), 640-651
13. Bram Cohen: Incentives Build Robustness in BitTorrent. 1st Workshop on the Economics of Peer-to-Peer Systems(2003), available from http://www.sims. berkeley.edu/research/conferences/p2pecon/program.html
14. Ahsan Habib and John Chuang: Incentive Mechanism for Peer-to-Peer Media Streaming. In: Proceedings of 12th International Workshop on Quality of Service, IEEE IWQoS(2004), 171-180
15. Suman Banerjee, Seungjoon Lee, Bobby Bhattacharjee, et al: Resilient Multicast Using Overlays. In: Proceedings of International Conference on Measurement and Modeling of Computer Systems, ACM SIGMETRICS(2003), 102-113
16. PlanetLab website: http://www.planet-lab.org/

A Group Based Reputation System for P2P Networks*

Huirong Tian, Shihong Zou, Wendong Wang, and Shiduan Cheng

State Key Laboratory of Networking and Switching Technology,
Beijing University of Posts and Telecommunications, Beijing, P.R. China
tianhr@bupt.edu.cn

Abstract. In large scale P2P networks, it is less likely that repeat interactions will occur between same peers for the asymmetric interests between them. So it is difficult to establish the direct trust relationship between peers and the network is vulnerable to malicious peers. A group based reputation system GroupRep for P2P networks is proposed in this paper to solve this problem. In GroupRep, the trust relationship is classified into three tiers: the trust relationship between groups, between groups and peers, and between peers. A peer evaluates the credibility of a given peer by its local trust information or the reference from the group it belonging to. A filtering cluster algorithm is proposed to filter unfair ratings provided by malicious peers. As a result, good peers are distinguished from malicious ones. Choosing the download source based on the trust value of responders can make good peers happy with the high ratio of the success query and the high satisfaction level under malicious collusive attacks with front peers.

1 Introduction

The open accessibility of Peer-to-Peer(P2P) networks attracts users to join the network to offer contents and services for others as well as try to obtain resources from the network. However, it also make the P2P network vulnerable to malicious peers which wishes to poison the network with corrupted data or harmful services for personal or commercial gain [1]. So, ascertaining the validity of the resources or services which peers want to obtain is very important to guarantee their profit.

As determining the validity of resources is a costly operation[1], reputation systems have been presented to solve this problem indirectly. Studies [2][3][4] present mechanisms that enable peers to evaluate the credibility of every file version after they get responses about different file versions. Most reputation systems focus on evaluating the credibility of resource providers. Some of them ([5-8]) calculate a global trust value for every peer. However, in large scale P2P networks, the feasibility and the necessity of establishing global trust for every peer are still doubtful. Others ([1-4], [9, 10]) allow peers to calculate a local trust

* This paper was supported by the National 973 project of China(No.2003CB314806, No2006CB701306), the NSFC (NO.90204003, NO.60472067).

L.T. Yang et al. (Eds.): ATC 2006, LNCS 4158, pp. 342–351, 2006.

value for other peers with shared information. Generally, the shared information is collected by flooding reference trust requests to peers' friends. However, in large scale P2P networks, flooding mechanism is not scalable. In addition, such reputation systems with shared information can't be adopted into the partially decentralized P2P networks where no direct management messages are allowed between peers [8].

Enlightened by the management of companies and the cooperation between them, a group based reputation system GroupRep is proposed in this paper. Peers join in a group and share their ratings by the group reputation management mechanism. The trust relationship in GroupRep can be viewed as three tiers: the trust relationship between groups, between groups and peers and between peers. A peer calculates a given peer's trust value with its local trust information or the group's reference which it belongs to. The probability that repeat interactions occur between the same groups is larger than that occur between the same peers. So in GroupRep it is easy to establish the trust relationship between peers. A cluster filtering algorithm, which is based on personalized similarity of peers and rating importance similarity of peers on providing ratings, is proposed to filter the unfair ratings provided by malicious peers. As a result, GroupRep can distinguish good peers from malicious peers effectively and make them happy with the high ratio of the success query and the high satisfaction level under malicious collusive attacks with front peers.

The rest of this paper is organized as follows: section 2 presents related work. The group based reputation system is defined in section 3. The simulation and analysis of the proposed model is followed. In the final section the conclusion is stated.

2   Related Work

Kamvar S.[5] proposed EigenTrust to calculate a global trust value for every peer based on their behavior history. Dou W.[6] presented a similar trust model where pre-trusted peers are unnecessary while these peers' existence is the basic assumption of EigenTrust. In [7] the direct trust relationship between peers is modeled as the web page link and the global trust value of every peer is calculated by the distributed pagerank algorithm. Mekouar L.[8] proposed a reputation management scheme RMS_PDN for partially decentralized P2P networks to enable every superpeer to maintain the contribution of its leaf peers and calculate their global trust value. Most of the reputation systems enable peers to calculate a local trust value for a given peer with shared information. Marti S.[1] evaluated the performance of P2P networks where peers choose the download source based on the trust value calculated by shared information. Wang Y. [9] proposed a Bayesian network trust model to evaluate a peer's credibility on different aspects according to different scenarios. NICE[10] is distinguished from other reputation systems in the intrinsic incentive that peers are willing to store the ratings which demonstrate themselves credible. PeerTrust[13] differs from other reputation systems in that trust value is computed based on three basic trust parameters and two adaptive factors. PeerTrust is effective against malicious behaviors of peers. The main weakness of PeerTrust is that it doesn't suit highly dynamic environments as it requires peers cooperation for storing the reputation information and it can't distinguish and punish malicious peers.

3   Group Based Reputation System

Enlightened by the management of companies and the cooperation between them, we propose a group based reputation system for P2P networks. The file sharing inside the group seems as peers' providing services for this group while that between the peers which belong to different groups can be viewed as the cooperation between groups.

In GroupRep, the trust relationship is classified into three tiers: the trust relationship between groups, between groups and peers and between peers. Groups establish their direct trust relationship based on the cooperation between them. A group evaluates the credibility of members according to their behavior history of proving services for this group and cooperating with other groups. A peer stores limited local trust information based on the behavior history of other peers. When it calculates the trust value of a given peer, it firstly checks its local trust information. If there is not local trust information of the given peer, it will ask the group which it belongs to to get a reference trust value. On receiving the reference trust request, the group directly gives the trust value if the requested peer is its member; Otherwise, it gets the reference trust value by asking the group which the requested peer belonging to.

In order to clarify the idea easily, we take the P2P network as a file-sharing network, although the proposed reputation system can be adopted by many other P2P service environments.

In this section, the group based reputation system GroupRep is presented at first. Then, we explain the process of trust information updating.

3.1   GroupRep

We assume peers sharing same interests voluntarily construct logic groups. When a peer enters the network, it can use some bootstrap mechanism just as that in Gnutella 0.6[11] to find its interested group. Then it would be accepted as a member by the recommendation of other members in this group. There are one or several group managers in one group. And all the trust information inside and outside the group can be handled correctly. In addition, the communication messages are encrypted to guarantee the integrity and confidentiality.

1. The Trust relationship between groups

Groups and their direct trust relationship form the trust network which is modeled as a directed weighted graph $G_{Trust} = (V, E)$, where $V = \{G_1, ..., G_M |$ $M \in N\}$, $G_i, 1 \leq i \leq M$ is the group in P2P networks; $E = \{e_{G_iG_j} | G_i, G_j \in V\}$, $e_{G_iG_j}$ is the direct trust relationship between G_i and G_j . The weight of $e_{G_iG_j}$ is the trust value $Tr_{G_iG_j}$ of G_i to G_j . We define $Trust_{G_sG_t}^{path} = (e_{G_sG_i}, ..., e_{G_jG_t})$ as the trust reference path from G_s to G_t , which is a path from G_s to G_t in G_{Trust}. Groups calculate the trust value of other groups by the following equation:

$$Tr_{G_iG_j} = \begin{cases} \frac{u_{G_iG_j}-c_{G_iG_j}}{u_{G_iG_j}+c_{G_iG_j}}, & u_{G_iG_j} + c_{G_iG_j} \neq 0 \\ Tr_{G_iG_j}^{reference}, & u_{G_iG_j} + c_{G_iG_j} = 0 \ and \ Trust_{G_iG_j}^{path} \ exists, \\ Tr_{G_iG_{strange}}, & others \end{cases} \quad (1)$$

where $u_{G_iG_j}\geq0$ and $c_{G_iG_j}\geq0$ are the utility and the cost respectively which peers in G_j have brought to peers in G_i . When $u_{G_iG_j} + c_{G_iG_j} = 0$, if $Trust_{G_iG_j}^{path}$ exists, $Tr_{G_iG_j}$ is defined as the reference trust value $Tr_{G_iG_j}^{reference}$ which is calculated based on the strongest path rule. Otherwise, $Tr_{G_iG_j}$ is defined by $Tr_{G_iG_{strange}}$ which is calculated according to the behavior history of strange groups that G_i has had encountered.

The strongest trust reference path. Given a set of trust reference paths from G_i to G_j , the strongest trust reference path is the path along the most credible group. We define the minimal trust value along the trust reference path as the reference trust value of this path. So $Tr_{G_iG_j}^{reference}$ is the reference trust value of the strongest trust reference path. If there are multi strongest trust reference paths, $Tr_{G_iG_j}^{reference}$ is the average of the reference trust values of these paths. As shown in Fig.1, the two strongest trust reference paths from group A to group H are "$A- > D- > C- > H$" and "$A- > F- > G- > H$". And the reference trust value of them is 0.3 and -0.5 respectively. So $Tr_{G_AG_H}^{reference}$ is -0.1.

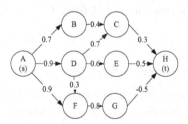

Fig. 1. The strongest trust reference path

Adaptive trust value to strange groups

$$Tr_{G_iG_{strange}} = \begin{cases} \frac{u_{G_iG_{strange}}-c_{G_iG_{strange}}}{u_{G_iG_{strange}}+c_{G_iG_{strange}}}, & u_{G_iG_{strange}} + c_{G_iG_{strange}} \neq 0 \\ 0, & others \end{cases} \quad (2)$$

Where $u_{G_iG_{strange}} \geq 0$ and $c_{G_iG_{strange}} \geq 0$ are the utility and the cost separately which strange groups (groups that have not had transactions with G_i) have brought to G_i .

2. The trust relationship between groups and peers

We define $Tr_i^{G_i}$ as the trust value of group G_i to peer i:

$$Tr_i^{G_i} = \begin{cases} \frac{u_i^{G(i)} - c_i^{G(i)}}{u_i^{G(i)} + c_i^{G(i)}}, & u_i^{G(i)} + c_i^{G(i)} \neq 0 \text{ and } i \in G_i = G(i) \\ Tr_{strange}^{G(i)}, & u_i^{G(i)} + c_i^{G(i)} = 0 \text{ and } i \in G_i = G(i) \\ min\{Tr_{G_iG(i)}, Tr_i^{G(i)}\}, & i \notin G_i \end{cases} \quad (3)$$

$$Tr_{strange}^{G(i)} = \begin{cases} \frac{u_{strange}^{G(i)} - c_{strange}^{G(i)}}{u_{strange}^{G(i)} + c_{strange}^{G(i)}}, & u_{strange}^{G(i)} + c_{strange}^{G(i)} \neq 0 \\ 0, & u_{strange}^{G(i)} + c_{strange}^{G(i)} = 0 \end{cases}, \quad (4)$$

where $G(i)$ is the group that peer i belongs to, $u_i^{G(i)} \geq 0$ and $c_i^{G(i)} \geq 0$ are the utility and the cost separately that i has brought to other peers. $u_{strange}^{G(i)} \geq 0$ and $c_{strange}^{G(i)} \geq 0$ are the utility and the cost separately that peers in $G(i)$ have brought to others when they upload files as the first time. $Tr_{strange}^{G(i)}$ is adapted according to the first uploading behavior of $G(i)$ members against the malicious peers which change ID join the group.

3. The trust relationship between peers

The trust value of peer i to j is defined as follows:

$$Tr_{ij} = \begin{cases} \frac{u_{ij} - c_{ij}}{u_{ij} + c_{ij}}, & u_{ij} + c_{ij} \neq 0 \\ Tr_j^{G(i)}, & u_{ij} + c_{ij} = 0 \end{cases}, \quad (5)$$

where $u_{ij} \geq 0$ and $c_{ij} \geq 0$ are the utility and the cost separately which peer i believes what peer j has brought to it according to its local trust information. If there is no local trust information of j, defines Tr_{ij} as the reference trust value of $G(i)$.

3.2 Trust Information Updating

In GroupRep, a peer keeps limited local trust information which is updated based on its ratings to others. A group would update the trust information of members, familiar groups, strange peer or strange groups weighted by the credibility of ratings it has received.

When peer i has finished a transaction with peer j, it would firstly update its local trust information, then it reports its rating to $G(i)$. If $j \in G(i)$, $G(i)$ updates j's trust information. Otherwise, $G(i)$ updates $G(j)$'s trust information and transfers this rating to $G(j)$ to enable $G(j)$ to update j's trust information. A group would update the trust information of strange peers or strange groups if its members firstly provide service or a strange group firstly provide service to its members. Then the problem is how to determine the credibility of ratings. In order to reduce the effect of unfair ratings, we define a cluster algorithm to filter them. This filtering cluster algorithm is based on the personalized similarity of peers and the rating importance similarity of peers on providing ratings.

The peers which are similar both in personalized similarity and in the rating importance similarity are taken as similar peers. These peers associated by their similar peers within the same group form a cluster. The ratings submitted by the maximum cluster (which is noted as *the rating cluster C_G*) are seemed as credible by the group. Then we define the personalized similarity and the rating importance similarity as following:

1) The personalized similarity of peer i and j: It is measured by the root-mean-square of the ratings which they provide to same peers. It is defined by equation(6)

$$S_{PS}(i,j) = \begin{cases} 1 - \sqrt{\frac{\sum_{k \in ComSet(i,j)} (Tr_{ik} - Tr_{jk})^2}{|ComSet(i,j)|}}, & ComSet(i,j) \neq \emptyset \\ 0, & ComSet(i,j) = \emptyset \end{cases} \quad (6)$$

where $ComSet(i,j)$ denotes the set of peers that have interacted both with peer i and with peer j in the observed period. If $S_{PS}(i,j) > S_{PS}^{threshold}$, peer i and j are personalized similar, where $S_{PS}^{threshold}$ is the threshold to determine whether two peers have the same personalized metric.

2) The rating importance similarity of peer i and j on providing ratings : Given the observation that peers in a malicious collusive group with front peers, front peers give fair ratings outside the group to increase the personalized similarity with these peers, and give high ratings selectively inside group to magnify its partners. The ratings importance similarity of i and j on providing ratings is measured by the relative importance difference of the ratings which they has given to the same peers. It is defined by the following equation:

$$S_{RIS}(i,j) = \begin{cases} 1 - \sqrt{\frac{\sum_{k \in ComSet(i,j)} \frac{|ri_{ik} - ri_{jk}|}{ri_{ik} + ri_{jk}}}{|ComSet(i,j)|}}, & ComSet(i,j) \neq \emptyset \\ 0, & ComSet(i,j) = \emptyset \end{cases} \quad (7)$$

where $ri_{ik} = \frac{T_{ik}}{\sum_{l \in R_j} T_{jl}}$ is the relative importance of the rating which i has given to k to the total ratings which j has given in the observed period, T_{ik}, which can be defined as $u_{ik} + c_{ik}$, is the importance of the rating which i has given to k, and R_j is the set of peers to which j has given ratings in the observed period. Similarly, $ri_{jk} = \frac{T_{jk}}{\sum_{l \in R_i} T_{il}}$]. If $S_{RIS}(i,j) > S_{RIS}^{threshold}$, the ratings given by peer i and j has the same rating importance similarity, where $S_{RIS}^{threshold}$ is the threshold used to determine whether the rating importance is similar.

At the initial stage of P2P systems, there are no enough ratings to get *the rating cluster*. Group $G(i)$ would update the trust information weighted by the trust value of the peers which give the ratings. If $G(i)$ get *the rating cluster $C_{G(i)}$* periodly, it would filter the rating based on $C_{G(i)}$. So $G(i)$ measures the rating credibility given by i by the following equation:

$$Cr_i^{G(i)} = \begin{cases} 1, & C_{G(i)} \neq \emptyset \ and \ i \in C_{G(i)} \\ 0, & C_{G(i)} \neq \emptyset \ and \ i \notin C_{G(i)} \\ 1, & C_{G(i)} = \emptyset \ and \ there \ is \ no \ trust \ information \ in \ the \ group \\ Tr_i^{G(i)}, & others \end{cases}$$

$$(8)$$

and $G(j)(\neq G(i))$ measures the rating credibility given by i by equation (9):

$$Cr_i^{G(j)} = \begin{cases} 1, & there\ is\ no\ trust\ information\ in\ the\ group \\ min\{Cr_i^{G(i)}, Tr_{G(j)G(i)}\}, & others \end{cases}$$

$$(9)$$

If the rating credibility is not larger than 0, the corresponding trust information would not be updated. In addition, each group would discount all the maintained trust information periodly to make a peer's recent behavior always matters and the peer has continuing incentives to behave honestly.

4   Simulation and Analysis

GroupRep is implemented based on Query Cycle Simulator[14]. At the same time, we also implement RMS_PDN and a conventional reputation system with shared information noted as RSSI, where the trust value is calculated by the local trust information or by the reference of friends and friends' friends. We evaluate the effectiveness of GroupRep, RMS_PDN and RSSI against malicious collusive attacks with front peers. The data are collected after the 100th query cycle and the results are averaged over 5 runs.

The efficiency of the network describes how good peers can efficiently get reliable files. They are as follows:

- The Ratio of the Success Query (RSQ): if good peers issue q requests and q_s of them are satisfied with authentic files, then $RSQ = q_s/q$.
- The satisfaction level (Sat): if the size of authentic contents downloaded by i is $authentic_i$, and the size of inauthentic contents downloaded by i is $inauthentic_i$, then $Sat_i = (authentic_i - inauthentic_i)/(authentic_i + inauthentic_i)$. The overall satisfaction level of good peers is $Sat = \frac{\sum_{i \in V_g} Sat_i}{|V_g|}$, where V_g is the set of good peers.

4.1   Simulation Environment

In order to compare with RMS_PDN, the simulated network is partially decentralized with 1000 peers where the fraction of malicious peers f_m is within the range [0.1, 0.5]. Peers are constructed as 20 groups and assigned to groups with the random uniform distribution. In GroupRep, we assume a logic group corresponds with a P2P overlay group constructed with a supernode and its leaf nodes. The reference trust requests between peers in RSSI are forwarded by the manage module of our simulation. In GroupRep and RSSI, the length of the limisted trust information mainted by peers is 10, the TTL of flooded reference trust requests is 3. So in the idea situation, a peer in RSSI can get the trust value of all peers by the reference of its friends and friends' friends. In GroupRep, groups get the rating cluster with $S_{PS}^{threshold} = 0$ and $S_{RIS}^{threshold} = 0.5$ each 5 query cycles and discount all the maintained trust information with factor 0.8 every 3 query cycles.

There are 10000 unique files in the network. Each file is characterized by the content category c and the popularity rank r within this category. c and r both follow the uniform distribution. 20 content categories are hold by 20 groups respectively. Files are distributed with the uniform random distribution based on the content categories that peers are interested in. File sizes are randomly and uniformly between 10MB and 150MB. We assume the files owned by malicious peers are also owned by good peers and all the files can be located successfully. The utility of a success file sharing or the cost of downloading an inauthentic file is equal to the file size.

Peers are always online and issue queries. The peers in the same group share the same interest. Good peers request files randomly in their interested category with the probability 0.8. Malicious peers request files randomly to know other peers. For good peers, the probability of providing inauthentic files is 5%, while malicious peers provide inauthentic files for 80% download requests. On getting the list of file providers, peers choose the most credible provider as the download source based on their trust value.

4.2 Effectiveness Against Malicious Collusive Attacks with Front Peers

Under malicious collusive attacks with front peers, malicious peers act as a collusive group. Most of them upload inauthentic files to good peers while they upload good files to peers within their collusive group. At the same time, in GroupRep and RMS_PDN, they give negative ratings to good peers and give high positive ratings to partners which they have had a transaction with. Others named as front malicious peers act as moles and upload authentic files just as good peers and giving good peers fair ratings. These front malicious peers try to cover other malicious peers behavior by give them high positive ratings. In our simulation, the high positive rating is set as the maximum file size 150. In addition, in GroupRep and RMS_PDN we strength the attack by making malicious peers randomly select another malicious peer to give high positive rating in every query cycle except submitting a rating after a transaction. In RSSI, on receiving reference trust requests, normal malicious peers give reference trust value as 1 if the requested peer is malicious. Otherwise, it would be -1. Front malicious peers would give reference trust value based on their local trust information if the requested peer is not their partners. The peers within this collusive group are noted as CF. In our simulation, the fraction of front malicious peers to the whole malicious peers is 0.2. As the probability that good peers upload authentic files is 0.95, the ratio of the success query is 0.95 and the satisfaction level is 0.9 when there are no malicious peers.

As shown in Fig.2(a), RSQ decreases in GroupRep much more slowly than that does in RMS_PDN and RSSI. This is because in GroupRep the cluster filtering algorithm can filter most unfair ratings and keep still larger than 0.7 when f_m reaches 0.5. In RMS_PDN, the trust information is updated directly, so malicious peers have good reputation by giving highly positive ratings each other. Thus, RSQ of RMS_PDN decrease as f_m increasing quickly. In RSSI, a peer can't evaluate a given peer's trust value exactly. This is more seriously in malicious collusive attacks with front peers as malicious peers always recommends their partners as trusted peers. In addition, if a peer can't calculate the trust value of the given peer by its local information or by trust friends' reference, it has no discernment on good peers and malicious peers. So in RSSI decreases dramatically as f_m increasing. in Fig.2(b), *Sat* always changes with the same trend as *RSQ* does. So it is concluded that GroupRep is more efficient than RMS_PDN and RSSI under malicious collusive attacks with front peers.

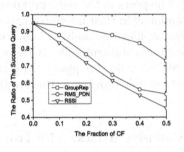
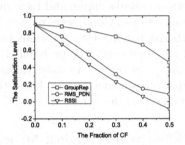

(a) The ratio of the success query   (b) The satisfaction level

Fig. 2. Efficiency

5 Conclusion

Enlightened by the management of companies and the cooperation between them, we propose a group based reputation system GroupRep. The trust relationship in GroupRep is classified into three tiers: the trust relationship between groups, between groups and peers, and between peers. A peer calculates a given peer's trust value based on its local trust information or the reference of the group which it belongs to. So in GroupRep the trust relationship between peers can be established effectively because the probability that repeat transactions occur between same groups is larger than that between same peers. Personalized similarity and rating importance similarity can tell whether two peers are similar on providing ratings. The filtering cluster algorithm based on the similarity between peers can filter unfair ratings given by malicious peers. As a result, good peers can be distinguished from malicious ones. Therefore, choosing the download source based on the trust value of responders makes good peers happy with the high ratio of the success query and the high satisfaction level under malicious collusive attacks with front peers.

References

1. Marti S., and Garcia-Molina H.:Limited Reputation Sharing in P2P Systems. Proceedings of the 5th ACM conference on Electronic commerce, May 17-20, 2004, New York, NY, USA

2. Damiani E., di Vimercati D. C., Paraboschi S., et.al.:A Reputation-Based Approach for Choosing Reliable Resources in Peer-to-Peer Networks. In Proceedings of the 9th ACM conference on Computer and communications security, pages 207-216. ACM Press, 2002

3. Cornelli F., Damiani E., di Vimercati D. C., et.al.: Choosing Reputable Servents in A P2P Network. In: Lassner D, ed. Proc. of the 11th Int'l World Wide Web Conf. Hawaii: ACM Press, 2002. 441 449.

4. Selcuk A.A., Uzun E., and Pariente M.R.: A Reputation-Based Trust Management System for P2P Networks. Cluster Computing and the Grid, 2004. IEEE International Symposium on , April 19-22, 2004 Pages:251 - 258.

5. Kamvar S., and Schlosser M.:The EigenTrust Algorithm for Reputation Management in P2P Networks. WWW, Budapest, Hungary, 2003

6. Dou W., Wang H.M., Jia Y., et.al:A Recommentdation-Based Peer-to-Peer Trust Model. Journal of Software, 2004, 15(4):571 583

7. Yamamoto A., Asahara D., Itao T., et.al.:Distributed Pagerank: A Distributed Reputation Model for Open Peer-to-Peer Networks. Proceedings of the 2004 International Symposium on Applications and the Internet Workshops (SAINTW'04)

8. Mekouar L., Iraqi Y., and Boutaba R.:A Reputation Management and Selection Advisor Schemes for Peer-to-Peer Systems. in 15th IFIP/IEEE International Workshop on Distributed Systems: Operations & Management, CA, USA, 2004

9. Wang Y., and Vassileva J.:Trust and Reputation Model in Peer-to-Peer Networks. Third International Conference on Peer-to-Peer Computing (P2P'03), IEEE, September 01 - 03, 2003

10. Lee S., Sherwood R. and Bhattacharjee B.:Cooperative Peer Groups in NICE. IEEE Infocom, San Francisco, USA, 2003

11. http://rfc-gnutella.sourceforge.net

12. Lai K., Feldman M., Stoica I., et.al:Incentives for Cooperation in Peer-to-Peer Networks. Workshop on economics of p2p systems, June 2003 Berkeley, CA.

13. Xiong L., and Liu L.:PeerTrust: Supporting Reputaion-Based Trust for Peer-to-Peer Electronic Communities. IEEE Transactions on Knowledge and Data Engineering, Vol. 16, No. 7, July 2004.

14. http://p2p.stanford.edu/www/demos.htm

An Approach for Trusted Interoperation in a Multidomain Environment

Yuqing Sun, Peng Pan, and Xiangxu Meng

School of Computer Science & Technology, Shandong University,
250100 Jinan, P.R. China
{sun_yuqing, ppan, mxx}@sdu.edu.cn

Abstract. There are increasing requirements for interoperation among distributed multi-domain systems. The key challenge is how to balance security and collaboration. A novel approach is proposed in this paper to support the trusted interoperation. It introduces the notions of effect scope and life condition into role based access control model to restrict permission to be active only in proper environment. Partial inheritance of role hierarchy is presented to support the finely granular access rights as well as the verification algorithms are proposed to maintain security constraints consistent. As an example, XACML-based platform is provided to combine the existent systems for secure interoperation. Without compromising the collaboration, this approach can effectively enforce a layered security policy and can reduce the complexity of security management.

1 Background

With the development of electronic business, web-based information systems are widely adopted and there is a high degree of interoperation and services sharing among different enterprise systems. It is important to safeguard the resources while providing services to other systems. To support the trusted interoperation, composition of security policies is becoming an important issue for both academic and industry. Many research works have devoted to this topic [1,2,3] and the significant works are introduced here.

From the conceptual level, Gong and Qian [4] presents two important guide rules of autonomy and security: the permitted access in a system should be permitted after composition and the denied access should be denied after composition. The manipulation algebra of access control policies is proposed [5,6], in which policies are interpreted as nondeterministic transformers on permissions set assignments to subjects; operations on policies are interpreted as set theoretical operators on such transformers. But these methods lack of the consistency validation of permission sets combination.

Joachim et al. [7] describe a layered access control model, which exploits the SPKI/SDSI to implement and enforce a policy specification. But it limits to the scenario of existence of a trusted assigner to declare policies. Song et al. [8] propose an aspect-oriented modeling technique that supports verifiable composition of behaviors described in access control aspect models and primary models. Shafiq et al. [9]

L.T. Yang et al. (Eds.): ATC 2006, LNCS 4158, pp. 352–361, 2006.
© Springer-Verlag Berlin Heidelberg 2006

propose a policy integration framework for merging heterogeneous role base access control model (RBAC) policies. It resolves the conflicts arising among the composition by an integer programming based approach. But its complexity is a major problem in dynamic collaborative environment. Literature [10] presents core features of Policy Machine that are capable of configuring, combining and enforcing arbitrary attribute-based policies. Park et al. [11] introduce a composite RBAC approach by separating the organizational and system role structures and by providing the mapping between them. Unfortunately, these work do less on analyses of security constraints and many challenges still exist, mainly including appropriate access restriction to balance common and local objectives; consideration of environment to ensure doing right thing in right time and on right object; extensibility to support multi-level collaborations and flexible policy; reducing down the complexity of management.

Base on RBAC, a novel approach is proposed in this paper to achieve above objectives, which introduces the notions of effect scope and life condition. Life condition restricts permission to be active in proper environment. Effect scope supports layered collaborations and flexible policy. Partial inheritance of role hierarchy is presented to support the fine granular authorization. The verification algorithms are proposed to maintain the security constraints consistent. As an example, this model is applied in a practical system—the Property Right Exchange System (PRES)[12,13] and XACML-based platform is provided to combine the existent application systems. Through analysis, this approach can effectively reduce the management complexity.

The remainder of this paper is organized as follows. In section 2, a practical scenario and basic concepts are given. Section 3 formally describes our proposed model and the verification algorithms. In the following section, the mechanism for secure interoperation is given based on PRES. At last, we draw some conclusions and future wok.

2 Scenarios and Basic Concept

2.1 Application Scenario and Secure Interoperation Requirements

To illustrate our approach effectively, an example of property rights exchange is adopted through the paper. Property Rights Exchange Center (PREC) is a concessionary organization in China for taking on property rights exchange, i.e. enterprise assets exchange, the intangible assets exchange. The government of State-owned Assets Supervision and Administration Commission (SASAC) supervises PREC, consisting of the national council SASAC and many province SASACs. The business relationships together with clients are shown as Fig.1.

From the view of PREC, the interoperation requirements are summarized as five types: interoperation among interior departments of PREC is shown as the double black arrows thin line; interoperation among PRECs is shown as the thick line with double square nodes; interoperation between PREC and SASAC is shown as the thick line with double round nodes; interoperation between the PREC and exchange participants is shown as the thin line with double white arrows. The objective is to ensure security and support interoperation.

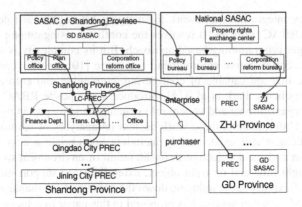

Fig. 1. The organization architecture of PREC and SASAC

2.2 Introduction to RBAC

Recently RBAC model [14] is becoming a natural choice for security administration. The main components are user, role, permission, role hierarchy, constraint, user role assignment (URA) and permission role assignment (PRA) etc. Role is an abstract description of behavior and collaborative relation with others in an organization. Permission is an access authorization to object, which is assigned to roles instead of to individual users. Constraints are principles used to express security policy, like least privilege, cardinality restriction, separation of duties (SOD) etc. Generally, SOD is specified as mutually exclusive roles or permissions, which can be divided into static SOD and dynamic SOD according to the authorization assignments at design or the activation in execution. The notations of U, R, P and O are adopted in our model to apart denote the set of users, roles, permissions and objects.

The motivation of role hierarchy is the observation that individual roles within an organization often have overlapping functions. In the absence of role hierarchies, it is inefficient and administratively cumbersome to specify these general permissions repeatedly for a large number of roles, or assign a large number of users to the general roles. In the presence of role hierarchy, the collection of permissions that compromise a job function can be defined by multiple subordinate roles, each of which may be reused in the sharing of common permissions and formulation of other roles. Due to the length of the article, the other description of the RBAC is omitted. Details can be got in the reference [14].

3 Proposed Model Based on RBAC

The proposed model, shown as Fig.2. There are many domains in a distributed environment; each domain is with the three levels architecture of permission, role and user. To restrict permissions to be active only in proper environment, we introduce effect scope and life condition into permission and divide them into three types of private, territorial and public, denoted as black, bias and white nodes. Role hierarchy

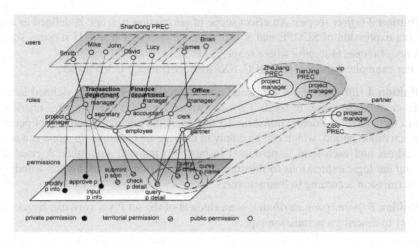

Fig. 2. The proposed model based on RBAC

is supported in the second role level. Different with other models, the inherited permissions of a senior role are partial of juniors' depending on permission type. In user level, users are classified into layered domains that match to the effect scopes of permission, whose authorizations are restricted to be active in the appointed life condition. The formal description of this model is given below.

3.1 Effect Scope and Life Condition

Effect scope is the activation domain of permission and is defined in form of nested multilayer aggregation of subjects or users, like partner and VIP partner. Generally, it corresponds with the organization and relationship of enterprises. Life condition defines the precondition of invoking and withdrawing permission, which reflects the environment restriction like time, address or business restraint etc.

Partial inheritance of role hierarchy is focused on here. Private permission cannot be inherited by senior roles and is used to express the personal or positional jobs, i.e. the right to modify a vend application is restricted to the initiator. Public permission is permitted to inherit by anyone and is used to express common enterprise activity. Territorial permission aims at the collaborative job and is restricted to be active in the appointed effect scope and life condition, i.e. the approval of a plan by a project manager can be only inherited by the same department manager.

Definition 1 (*SCOPE*): A *scope* is a set of subjects, where the subjects are defined according to an enterprise organization. Let SP denotes the set of subjects in the system, *scope* $\subseteq 2^{SP}$. For example: SDPREC={Finance, office, trade1, trade2}; VIPartner={ZJPREC, TJPREC};

Definition 2 (*Scope Operation S_OP*): S_OP is a set of {U,Π,Θ}, where U, Π and Θ denote the union, intersection and difference operations on scope sets. It satisfies the commutative law, associative law and distributive law.

Definition 3 (*effect scope*): An effect scope of permission *p_scope* is defined as a set algebra expression of SCOPE and S_OP, $p\_scope=scope_1 \mid scope_2 \cup scope_3 \mid scope_4 \Pi\ scope_5 \mid scope_6 \Theta\ scope_7$, where $scope_i \subseteq$ SP.

For example: Partner={HBPREC, SXPREC, SHPREC} U VIPartner;

Definition 4 (*life condition*): Life condition of permission *p_cond* is defined as a 4-tuple <*t_cond, ip_cond, b_cond, e_cond*>, where *t_cond* is the temporal restriction and in form of [*date1.time1: date2.time2*] that gives the beginning and end of permission activation period, which can be empty to indicate no restraints. *ip_cond* is a set of IP address and each field is permitted to be * to indicate any value. *b_cond* and *e_cond* are logic expressions to illustrate the precondition of invoking and withdrawing permission according to business rules.

Definition 5 (*permission attribute*): is an element of the set PA = {*private, territorial, public*} to describe a permission type.

Definition 6 (*permission*): A permission *per* is defined as a 5-tupls <*p_act, p_obj, p_attr, p_cond, p_scope* >, where *p_act* is an operation type in the system, *p_obj* is the operated object, p_attr is the permission attribute $p\_attr \in$ PA, *p_cond* and p_scope are the life condition and effect scope of a territorial permission.

Accordingly, the following mapping functions are defined:

LCondcal(*p_cond*)→Boolean: computes the logic value of life condition.

PScope(*per*:P)→SB^2: counts the aggregation of effect scope for the given permission *per*.

Pactive(*per*:P)→Boolean: verifies whether the given permission *per* is active that is in life condition and effect scope.

3.2 Role Hierarchies and Permission Inheritance

Definition 7 (*immediate inheritance*): The immediate inheritance relation of two roles r_1 and r_2 is denoted as $r_1 > r_2$ only if all permissions of r_2 are also permissions of r_1, and all users of r_1 are users of r_2.

Definition 8 (*ancestor inheritance*): The ancestor inheritance relation of two roles r_1 and r_2 is denoted as $r_1 >^* r_2$ only if there exist a series of roles $r_{i1}, r_{i2}, \ldots\ldots r_{ij}$ which $r_1 > r_{i1} > \ldots\ldots > r_{ij} > r_2, j>=1$.

Definition 9 (*role hierarchy*): Role hierarchy RH⊆ R×R is a partial order on R. The inheritance relation is with the properties of antisymmetric and transmissible.

After defining PRA, URA relations and role hierarchies, we can acquire both the set of permissions assigned to a role and the authorized permissions of a user by direct assignments and indirect inheritance via role hierarchy. The following functions are introduced to compute the set.

Rperms(*r*:R)→2^P, enumerates permissions assigned to a role. Rperms(*r*)= {p:p∈ P∩(p,r)∈PRA} ∪ {p:p∈P∩((r>*r')∩(p,r')∈PRA∩(p.attr=Public|Territorial))}.

PRoles(*p*:P)→2^R mapping of a permission onto the assigned role set. PRoles(*p*) = {r: r∈R ∩((p,r)∈PRA ∪ (r' ∈R ∩(r'>*r) ∩ (p.attr=Public | p.attr= Territorial)).

RUsers(r:R)→2^U enumerates the users authorized a role. RUsers(r)= {u: u∈U ∩ ((u,r)∈URA ∪ ((u,r')∈URA ∩ r'∈R ∩(r' >* r))) }

URoles(u:U)→2^R enumerates all roles assigned to a user. URoles(r)= {r: r∈R ∩(u,r)∈URA ∪ (r'∈R ∩(r >*r')) }

Uperms(u:U) →2^P, enumerates the authorized permissions of a user. Uperms(u)= {p: p∈P∩ r∈R∩ r∈URoles(u)∩p∈Rperms(r)∩(p.attr=Public|(p.attr= Territorial ∩ u ∈ PScope(p))) }.

Property1 describes the rule of permission activation.

Property 1. A user u has the authorization of a permission p only if the following four conditions are satisfied. 1) There exist a role r assigned the permission. 2) u is assigned to r directly or inherited by role hierarchy. 3) u is in the effect scope of p. 4) p is in its life condition. Formally, $u∈U$, $p∈P$, authorization(u,p) => $∃r∈R$, ($p∈$ Rperms(r)∩Pactive(p))∩$u∈$Rusers(r) ∩$u∈$PScope(p).

3.3 Consistency Verification of Security Constraints

Security constraints of role cardinality and dynamic SOD are focused on in this paper. Following properties and correlative verification algorithms are introduced to ensure the constraints consistency. Other restraints can be discussed similarly.

Property 2 (*Role cardinality*): Role cardinality restricts the number of authorized users to a role within an appointed boundary. Formally, $r∈R, n∈N$ =>|Rusers(r)|≤ n

Algorithm 1. Consistency verification of role cardinality constraints
INPUT: R, RH, U, P, PRA, URA and role cardinality constraints set CT,
OUTPUT: SUCCESS if all role cardinality constraints are satisfied;
        FAILURE, otherwise.
1. For every *Role cardinality*(*r, n*) in CT, do step 2 to step 4
2. For the *r* of (*r, n*), calculate RUsers (*r*)
3. Check whether the number of RUsers (*r*) is lager than one and not more that *n*. If |RUsers (*r*)| < 1 OR |RUsers (*r*)| > *n* then return FAILURE.
4. Return SUCCESS

Property 3 (*SOD constraint*): Let SD be the set of dynamic SOD constraints. $ps=(n, p_1, p_2,..., p_n)∈$SD. If ps is required for a set of permissions $p_1, p_2,...$and pn, then $p_1, p_2,...$and $_{pn}$ should not be assigned to the same role and further more not assigned to the same user via different roles. Formally: for $1<i<n$

∀ $ps =(n, p_1, p_2,..., p_n)∈$SD, $p_1, p_2,..., p_n∈$P, =>∩ PRoles(p_i) = Ø and

∀ $ps =(n, p_1, p_2,..., p_n)∈$SD, $p_1, p_2,..., p_n∈$P, =>∩Rusers($r∈$PRoles(p_i)) = Ø

Algorithm 2. Consistency verification of SOD constraints

INPUT: SD, R, RH, U, P, PRA and URA
OUTPUT: SUCCESS if all SOD constraints are satisfied; FAILURE, otherwise.
1. For every $ps =(n, p_1, p_2,..., p_n)∈$CT, do step 2 to step 9
2. For each permission p_i in ps do step 3
3. Calculate PRoles (p_i) to set R_i

4. Calculate the intersection set of R_i, to R', $1 \leq i \leq n$
5. If the result is not empty, R'!=ϕ, then return FAULSE
6. For each role r_j in R_i do step 7
7. Calculate RUsers (r_j) to U_{ij}
8. For all i and j Calculate the intersection set of R_{ij} to U'
9. If the result is not empty, U'!=ϕ, then return FAULSE
10. Return TRUE

Suppose n_c and n_s be the number of role cardinality constrains and SOD constrains. Let n_{pr}, n_{ur} and n_{rh} denote the number of PRA set, URA set and role hierarchy set respectively. The worst complexities for algorithm1 and algorithm2 are in polynomial time of $O(n_c*n_{ur}*n_{rh})$ and $O(n_s*n_{pr}*n_{rh}*n_{ur})$. Generally, the PRA and URA number of a concrete role are far less than n_{pr} and n_{ur}. It is similar to role hierarchy. So above algorithms complexity can be greatly reduced down.

4 Secure Interoperation

The comprehensive system architecture is proposed as the thick line blocks in Fig.3. Each block is a domain application system that integrates the proposed model. Five tasks related to security policy are achieved: to define an enterprise organization, role and user set, relationships with others; to describe permission set together with its effect scope and life condition according to the business rule; to define PRA, URA relations and role hierarchies; to specify security constraints and verify their consistency. To generate the security policies for trusted interoperation and stored in the rule database, which used to transform to XACML-based security rules.

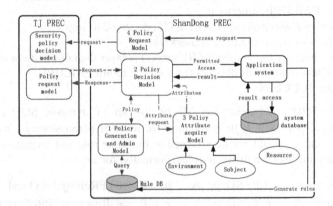

Fig. 3. System architecture

The last task is focused on here due to others having been discussed in last section, which includes four models: policy generation and administration model (PGAM), policy decision model (PDM), policy attributes acquire model (PAM) and policy request model (PRM). These models are responsible for processing and invoking a request of secure interoperation. XACML is adopted, which is the extensible access control marked language and is approved as OASIS Standards in 2005. It is an open general security policy description and decision language. Without remodeling the quondam information system completely, it can achieve the unified administration of different security policies and implement the interoperation among multidomain.

```
- <Policy PolicyId="ProjectPlanAccessPolicy"
        RuleCombiningAlgId="urn:oasis:names:tc:xacml:1.0:rule-combining-algorithm:ordered-permit-
        overrides">
+ <Target>
± <Rule RuleId="1" Effect="Permit">
± <Rule RuleId="2" Effect="Permit">
- <Rule RuleId="3" Effect="Permit">
   - <Target> <Subjects> <Subject>
          -<SubjectMatch MatchId="urn:oasis:names:tc:xacml:1.0:function:string-equal">
          <AttributeValue
              DataType="http://www.w3.org/2001/XMLSchema#string">vip</AttributeValue>
          <SubjectAttributeDesignator AttributeId="type"
              DataType="http://www.w3.org/2001/XMLSchema#string" />   </SubjectMatch>
          </Subject> </Subjects>
      - <Resources> <AnyResource />   </Resources>
      - <Actions> <Action>
          - <ActionMatch MatchId="urn:oasis:names:tc:xacml:1.0:function:string-equal">
          <AttributeValue dataType="http://www.w3.org/2001/XMLSchema#string">detailed query
              </AttributeValue>
          <ActionAttributeDesignator    attributeId="urn:oasis:names:tc:xacml:1.0:action:action-id"
              DataType="http://www.w3.org/2001/XMLSchema#string" />
              </ActionMatch> </Action> </Actions>
      </Target>
      - <Condition FunctionId="urn:oasis:names:tc:xacml:1.0:function:and">
          ±<Condition FunctionId="urn:oasis:names:tc:xacml:1.0:function:string-equal">
          ±<Condition FunctionId="urn:oasis:names:tc:xacml:1.0:function:time-greater-than-or-equal">
          - <Condition FunctionId="urn:oasis:names:tc:xacml:1.0:function:string-equal">
              -<Apply FunctionId="urn:oasis:names:tc:xacml:1.0:function:string-one-and-only">
                  <SubjectAttributeDesignator AttributeId="domain"
                  DataType="http://www.w3.org/2001/XMLSchema#string" />   </Apply>
              <AttributeValue
                  DataType="http://www.w3.org/2001/XMLSchema#string">ZJPREC</AttributeValue>
              </Condition>  </Condition></Rule>
          <Rule RuleId="FinalRule" Effect="Deny" />
  </Policy>
```

Fig. 4. XACML-based access policy

PGAM acquires rules from the rule database and generates the XACML-based security policy to assistant PDM to make decision. In the example of Fig.4, a partner has the right to query the brief information of a trade project and furthermore the VIP partner has the right to access the detailed information of the same project. When the security policy adjusted, the application system exports new rules to database and PGAM will accordingly generate the adjusted XACML-based rules and send to PDM. So it can support the dynamic security management.

PRM generates a XACML-based access request to another web system that includes the subject, the requested resource and action. The example in Fig.5 shows a request of project manager in ZJ-PREC for querying the detailed information of a textile project. Its attribute is VIP partner.

```
- <Request>
  - <Subject SubjectCategory="urn:oasis:names:tc:xacml:1.0:subject-category:access-subject">
    -<Attribute AttributeId="urn:oasis:names:tc:xacml:1.0:subject:subject-id"
          DataType="http://www.w3.org/2001/XMLSchema#string">
      <AttributeValue>partner</AttributeValue>  </Attribute>
    - <Attribute AttributeId="type" DataType="http://www.w3.org/2001/XMLSchema#string">
      <AttributeValue>vip</AttributeValue>  </Attribute>
    - <Attribute AttributeId="domain" DataType="http://www.w3.org/2001/XMLSchema#string">
      <AttributeValue>ZJPREC</AttributeValue>  </Attribute>
    ± <Attribute AttributeId="ip" DataType="http://www.w3.org/2001/XMLSchema#string">
  </Subject>
  - <Resource>-<Attribute AttributeId="urn:oasis:names:tc:xacml:1.0:resource:resource-id"
          DataType="http://www.w3.org/2001/XMLSchema#string">
      <AttributeValue>information of the textile factory project</AttributeValue>  </Attribute>
  </Resource>
  ± <Action>
</Request>
```

Fig. 5. XACML-based access request

PDM is used to acquire the environment attributes, like system time and task state. PDM accepts a XACML-based access request and decides whether it is permitted or denied. If the request matches with the security policy in PDM, it transfers the access to the application system and permits the correspondent operation. Otherwise the request will be rejected. As the above example, ZJ-PREC is a VIP partner of SD-PREC, its subject matches "partner" and "VIP". Then according to the environment attribute of the rule, PDM invokes PAM to get the system time and match it with the rules. If all the comparisons are match, the project manager of ZJ-PREC has the right to access the detailed information of the requested textile project. PDM transfer the access to the information system.

5   Conclusions and Future Work

To support the trusted interoperation among different information systems in multi-domain environments, a novel approach based on RBAC is proposed in this paper. It introduces the notions of effect scope and life condition to restrict permissions to be active only in proper environment. Partial inheritance of role hierarchy is presented to support the finely granular access rights and verification algorithms are also proposed to maintain security constraints consistent. XACML-based platform is provided to combine the existent systems for secure interoperation. As an example, it is applied in a practical system of PRES.

Compared with other models, there exist many advantages of this model. Permission division radically restricts the action on sensitive information. Properties of life condition and effect scope effectively restrict the permission activation in proper environment and support the reuse of policy definition. Partial role inheritance effectively reduces the complexity of security management. Without compromising the collaboration, this approach can enforce a layered security policy. Further work can be done on the algebra operation of effect scope and additional restriction on role hierarchy for stricter security administration.

Acknowledgements

This work was partially supported by the National Nature Science Foundation of China (60373026, 90612021), the ChinaGrid Project (CG03-GF012), Science Development Plan Program of Shandong province of China (2004GG2201131) and the Natural Science Foundation of Shandong Province of China (Y2004G08), SHI Bin and LIU Jia play key roles in the development of the practical system.

References

1. Oh, S. and Park, S.: Task-role-based Access Control Model. J. of Information System, Vol. 28 (2003) 533-562
2. Bertino, E. and Bonatti, P.A.: TRBAC: A Temporal Role-Based Access Control Model. ACM Transaction on Information and System Security, Vol.4, No.3 (2001) 191-223
3. Joshi,J.B.D., Bertino,E., Latif,U., and Ghafoor, A.: Generalized Temporal Role Based Access Control Model (GTRBAC). IEEE Transaction on Knowledge and Data Engineering, Vol.17 (2005) 4-23
4. Gong, L. and Qian, X.: Computational Issues in Secure Interoperation. IEEE Transaction on Software Engineering Vol.22,1 (1996) 43-52
5. Bonatti,P., Di Vimercati,S.D.C. and Samarati,P.:A Modular Approach to Composing Access Control Policies. 7th ACM Conference on Communications and Security (2000) 164-173
6. Wijesekera, D. and Jajodia, S.: A Propositional Policy Algebra for Access Control. ACM Transaction on Information and System Security, Vol.6, No.2 (2003)286-325
7. Biskup, J. and Wortmann S.: Towards a Credential-Based Implementation of Compound Access Control Policies. Proc. of ACM SACMAT'04 (2004) 31-40
8. Song,E., Reddy,R., France,R., Ray,I., GeorgG. and A., R.: Verifiable Composition of Access Control and Application Features. Proc. of SACMAT'05, Stockholm (2005) 120-129,
9. Shafiq, B., Joshi, J.B.D., Bertino, E. and Ghafoor, A.: Secure Interoperation in a Multidomain Environment Employing RBAC Policies. IEEE Transaction on Knowledge and Data Engineering, Vol.17, No.11 (2005) 1557-1577
10. Ferraiolo, D. F., Gavrila, S., Hu, V., Kuhn and D. R.: Composing and Combining Policies under the Policy Machine. Proc. of ACM SACMAT'05, Stockholm (2005) 11-20
11. Park, J.S., Costello, K.P., Neven, T.M. and Diosomito, J.A.: A Composite RBAC Approach for Large, Complex Organization. Proc. of ACM SACMAT'04 (2004) 163-171
12. Sun,Y.Q., Meng, X.X., LIU, S.J. and Pan, P.: Flexible Workflow Incorporated with RBAC. The second volume of LNCS book on CSCW in Design (3865) (2006) 525-534.
13. Sun,Y.Q. and Pan, P.: PRES—A Practical Flexible RBAC Workflow System. Proc. of 7th International Conference on Electronic Commerce (2005) 653-658.
14. Sandhu, R.S., Coyne, E.J., Feinstein, H.L., Youman, C.E.: Rose-Based Access Control Model. IEEE Computer, Vol.29, No.2 (1996) 38-47

Extracting Trust from Domain Analysis: A Case Study on the Wikipedia Project

Pierpaolo Dondio[1], Stephen Barrett[1], Stefan Weber,[1] and Jean Marc Seigneur[2]

[1] School of Computer Science and Statistics, Distributed System Group,
Trinity College Dublin, College Green 2, Dublin
{dondiop, stephen.barrett, stefan.weber} @cs.tcd.ie
[2] University of Geneva, CUI,
24 Rue du Général Dufour, Geneva 4, Switzerland
Jean-Marc.Seigneur@trustcomp.org

Abstract. The problem of identifying trustworthy information on the World Wide Web is becoming increasingly acute as new tools such as wikis and blogs simplify and democratize publications. Wikipedia is the most extraordinary example of this phenomenon and, although a few mechanisms have been put in place to improve contributions quality, trust in Wikipedia content quality has been seriously questioned. We thought that a deeper understanding of what in general defines high-standard and expertise in domains related to Wikipedia – i.e. *content quality* in a *collaborative environment* – mapped onto Wikipedia elements would lead to a complete set of mechanisms to sustain trust in Wikipedia context. Our evaluation, conducted on about 8,000 articles representing 65% of the overall Wikipedia editing activity, shows that the new trust evidence that we extracted from Wikipedia allows us to transparently and automatically compute trust values to isolate articles of great or low quality.

1 Introduction

In the famous 1996 article *Today's WWW, Tomorrow's MMM: The specter of multimedia mediocrity* [1] Cioleck predicted a seriously negative future for online content quality by describing the World Wide Web (WWW) as a nebulous, ever-changing multitude of computer sites that house continually changing chunks of multimedia information, the global sum of the uncoordinated activities of several hundreds of thousands of people who deal with the system as they please. Thus, the WWW may come to be known as the MMM (MultiMedia Mediocrity). Despite this vision, it is not hard to predict that the potential and the growth of the Web as a source of information and knowledge will increase rapidly. The Wikipedia project, started in January 2001, represents one of the most successful and discussed example of such phenomenon, an example of *collective knowledge*, a concept that is often lauded as the next step toward truth in online media.

On one hand, recent exceptional cases have brought to the attention the question of Wikipedia trustworthiness. In an article published on the 29th of November in USA Today [2], Seigenthaler, a former administrative assistant to Robert Kennedy, wrote about his anguish after learning about a false Wikipedia entry that listed him as having been briefly suspected of involvement in the assassinations of both John Kennedy and Robert Kennedy. The 78-year-old Seigenthaler got Wikipedia founder Jimmy

L.T. Yang et al. (Eds.): ATC 2006, LNCS 4158, pp. 362–373, 2006.
© Springer-Verlag Berlin Heidelberg 2006

Wales to delete the defamatory information in October. Unfortunately, that was four months after the original posting. The news was further proof that Wikipedia has no accountability and no place in the world of serious information gathering [2].

On the other hand, Wikipedia is not only being negatively discussed. In December 2005, a detailed analysis carried out by the magazine *Nature* [3] compared the accuracy of Wikipedia against the Encyclopaedia Britannica. Nature identified a set of 42 articles, covering a broad range of scientific disciplines, and sent them to relevant experts for peer review. The results are encouraging: the investigation suggests that Britannica's advantage may not be great, at least when it comes to science entries. The difference in accuracy was not particularly great: the average science entry in Wikipedia contained around four inaccuracies; Britannica, about three. Reviewers also found many factual errors, omissions or misleading statements: 162 and 123 in Wikipedia and Britannica respectively. Moreover, Nature has stated that, among their scientific collaborators, 70% of them had heard of Wikipedia, 17% of those consult it on a weekly basis and about 10% help to update it.

This paper seeks to face the problem of the trustworthiness of Wikipedia by using a computational trust approach: our goal is to set up an automatic and transparent mechanism able to estimate the trustworthiness of Wikipedia articles. The paper is organized as follows: in the next section 2 we review related work on trust and content quality issues; in section 3 we argue that, due to the fast changing nature of articles, it is difficult to apply the trust approaches proposed in related work. In section 4 this discussion will lead us to introduce our approach, that starts from an in-depth analysis of *content quality* and *collaborative editing* domains to give us a better understanding of what can support trust in these two Wikipedia related fields. In section 5 we map conclusions of the previous section onto elements extracted directly from Wikipedia in order to define a new set of sources of trust evidence. In section 6 we present our experiment and evaluation conducted on almost 8,000 Wikipedia articles selected among the most edited and visited, that by themselves represent 65% of the editing activity and 50% of visits of the overall encyclopaedia. Section 7 will collect our conclusions and future work, where we anticipate our intention to organize the method used in this paper into a general trust methodology that can be applied to other application domains.

2 Related Work

There are many definitions of the human notion trust in a wide range of domains from sociology, psychology to political and business science, and these definitions may even change when the application domains change. For example, Romano's recent definition tries to encompass the previous work in all these domains: "trust is a subjective assessment of another's influence in terms of the extent of one's perceptions about the quality and significance of another's impact over one's outcomes in a given situation, such that one's expectation of, openness to, and inclination toward such influence provide a sense of control over the potential outcomes of the situation."[4].

However, the terms trust/trusted/trustworthy, which appear in the traditional computer security literature, are not grounded on social science and often correspond to an implicit element of trust. Blaze et al [5] first introduced "decentralized trust management" to separate trust management from applications. PolicyMaker [6] introduced the fundamental concepts of policy, credential, and trust relationship. Terzis et al. [7] have argued that the model of trust management [5,6] still relies on an implicit notion of trust because it only describes "a way of exploiting established trust relationships for distributed security policy management without determining how these relationships are formed".

Computational trust was first defined by S. Marsh [8], as a new technique able to make agents less vulnerable in their behavior in a computing world that appears to be malicious rather than cooperative, and thus to allow interaction and cooperation where previously there could be none. A computed trust value in an entity may be seen as the digital representation of the trustworthiness or level of trust in the entity under consideration. The EU project SECURE [9] represents an example of a trust engine that uses evidence to compute trust values in entities and corresponds to evidence-based trust management systems. Evidence encompasses outcome observations, recommendations and reputation. Depending on the application domain, a few types of evidence may be more weighted in the computation than other types. When recommendations are used, a social network can be reconstructed. Golbeck [10] studied the problem of propagating trust value in social networks, by proposing an extension of the FOAF vocabulary [11] and algorithms to propagate trust values estimated by users rather than computed based on a clear count of pieces of evidence. Recently, even new types of evidence have been proposed to compute trust values. For example, Ziegler and Golbeck [12] studied interesting correlation between similarity and trust among social network users: there is indication that similarity may be evidence of trust. In SECURE, evidence is used to select which trust profile should be given to an entity. Thus similar evidence should lead to similar profile selection. However, once again, as for human set trust value, it is difficult to clearly estimate people similarity based on a clear count of pieces of evidence. However, the whole SECURE framework may not be generic enough to be used with abstract or complex new types of trust evidence. In fact, in this paper, we extracted a few types of evidence present in Wikipedia (detailed in the next sections) that did not fit well with the SECURE framework and we had to build our own computational engine.

We think that our approach to deeply study the domain of application and then extract the types of trust evidence from the domain is related to the approach done in expert systems where the knowledge engineer interacts with an expert in the domain to acquire the needed knowledge to build the expert system for the application domain. Lerch et al. [13] highlighted the impact of trust in expert systems advices. Ball et al. [14] proposed an expert system that has knowledge about the factors that are important in computing the trust in a certification authority used in a public key infrastructure. It shows that there are different application domains where our approach could be used and may indicate that to formalize a methodology based on our approach may be useful. However, in this paper, we focus on trust computation for content quality and Bucher [15] clearly motivates our contribution in this paper because he argues that on the Internet "we no longer have an expert system to which we can assign management of information quality".

We finish this section by two last computational projects related to content quality in a decentralised publishing system. Huang and Fox in [16] propose a metadata-based approach to determine the origin and validity of information on the Web. They provide a metadata language for expressing judgments on the trustworthiness of a proposition, its author or a specific field. Then, by maintaining information sources and dependencies, it is possible to compute the trustworthiness of a derived proposition based on the trustworthiness of those composed. In this work the key hypothesis is the validity of the basic assertion and their maintenance. Finally, Guha [17] presents a model to integrate user-driven ratings on top of e-services, as it has been done in Epinion, Amazon or Slashdot but not really for Wikipedia. In addition, we could not integrate our new types of trust evidence in Guha's model that merely focuses on recommendations and reputation propagated within the social network formed by the users.

3   The Problem of Wikipedia Articles Trustworthiness

Wikipedia shows intrinsic characteristics that make the utilization of trust solutions challenging. The main feature of Wikipedia, appointed as one of its strongest attribute, is the speed at which it can be updated. The most visited and edited articles reach an average editing rate of 50 modifications per day, while articles related to recent news can reach the number of hundreds of modifications. This aspect affects the validity of several trust techniques.

Human-based trust tools like feedback and recommendation systems require time to work properly, suffering from a well know ramp-up problem [7]. This is a hypothesis that clashes with Wikipedia, where pages change rapidly and recommendations could dramatically lose meaning. Moreover, the growing numbers of articles and their increasing fragmentation require an increasing number of ratings to keep recommendations significant. *Past-evidence trust paradigm* relies on the hypothesis that the trustor entity has enough past interactions with the trustee to collect significant evidence. In Wikipedia the fact that past versions of a page are not relevant for assessing present trustworthiness and the changing nature of articles makes it difficult to compute trust values based on past evidences. In general, user past-experience with a Web site is only at 14th position among the criteria used to assess the quality of a Web site with an incidence of 4.6% [19]. We conclude that a mechanism to evaluate articles trustworthiness relying exclusively on their present state is required. We thought that such a method could be identified by a deeper understanding of the domains involved in Wikipedia, namely, the content quality domain and the collaborative editing domain. After understanding what brings trust in those domains, we mapped these sources of evidence into Wikipedia elements that we previously isolated by defining a detailed model of the application. This resulting new set of pieces of evidence, extracted directly from Wikipedia, allow us to compute trust, since it relies on proven domains' expertise. Through an evaluation phase, we exploited these new sources of evidence to support trust calculation and estimate the trustworthiness of articles.

4   Wikipedia Domain Analysis

We identified two relevant areas involved in Wikipedia: the content quality domain and collaborative working domain, in our case a *collaborative editing*. In this section, we analyse what can bring high quality in these two domains.

The quality of online content is a critical problem faced by many institutions. Alexander [20] underlines how information quality is a slippery subject, but it proposes hallmark of what is consistently good information. He identified three basic requirements: objectivity, completeness and pluralism. The first requirement guarantees that the information is unbiased, the second assesses that the information should not be incomplete, the third stresses the importance of avoiding situations in which information is restricted to a particular viewpoint. University of Berkeley proposes a practical evaluation method [21] that stresses the importance of considering authorship, timeliness, accuracy, permanence and presentation. Authorship stresses the importance of collecting information on the authors of the information, accuracy deals with how the information can be considered good, reviewed, well referenced and if it is comparable to similar other Web content, in order to check if it is compliant to a standard. Timeliness considers how the information has changed during time: its date of creation, its currency and the rate of its update; permanence stresses how the information is transitory or stable. Finally, presentation concerns the layout of the text, the balance among its sections, the presence of images and the quality of the layout. In a study already cited [19], presentation resulted in the most important evaluation criterion with an incidence of 46%.

The Persuasive Technology Lab has been running the Stanford Web Credibility Research since 1997 to identify which are the sources of credibility and expertise in Web content. Among the most well-known results are the ten guidelines for Web credibility [22], compiled to summarize what brings credibility and trust in a Web site. The guidelines confirm what we described so far and again they emphasize the importance of the non anonymity of the authors, the presence of references, the importance of the layout, the constant updating and they underline how typographical errors and broken links, no matter how small they could be, strongly decrease trust and represent evidence of lack of accuracy.

Beside content quality domain, Wikipedia cannot be understood if we do not take into consideration that it is done entirely in a collaborative way. Researches in *collaborative working* [23] help us to define a particular behaviour strongly involved in Wikipedia dynamics, the balance in the editing process. A collaborative environment is more effective when there is a kind of emerging leadership among the group; the leadership is able to give a direction to the editing process and avoid fragmentation of the information provided. Anyway, this leadership should not be represented by one or two single users to avoid the risk of lack of pluralism and the loss of collaborative benefits like merging different expertises and points of view. We summarize our analysis with the prepositions shown in table 1: in the first column are theoretical propositions affecting trust, second column lists the domains from which each preposition was taken.

Preposition 1 covers the authorship problem. Preposition 2 derives from the accuracy issues. Preposition 3, 4 and 5 underline the importance that the article should have a sense of unity, even if written by more than one author. Preposition 7 underlines the fact that a good article is constantly controlled and reviewed by a reasonable high number of authors. Preposition 8 stresses the stability of the article: a stable text means that it is well accepted, it reached a consensus among the authors and its content is almost complete. Preposition 9 emphasizes the risk, especially for historical or

Table 1. A Trust domain-compatible theory. CQ is Content Quality domain and CE is Collaborative Editing domain.

	Prepositions about Trustworthiness of an articles (T). T increases if the article...	Domain
1	was written by expert and identifiable authors	CQ
2	has similar features or it is complaint to a standard in its category	CQ
3	there is a clear leadership/direction in the group directing the editing process and acting like a reference	CE
4	there is no dictatorship effect, which means that most of the editing reflects one person's view.	CQ/ CE
5	the fragmentation of the contributions is limited: there is more cohesion than dissonance among authors	CE
6	has good balance among its sections, the right degree of detail, it contains images if needed, it has a varied sentence structure, rhythm and length	CQ
7	is constantly visited and reviewed by authors	CQ
8	the article is stable	CQ
9	uses a neutral point of view	CQ
10	the article is well referenced	CQ

political issues, that different authors may express personal opinions instead of facts, leading to a subjective article or controversial disputes among users. In order to have meaning, these prepositions need to be considered together with their interrelationships along with some conditions. For example, the length of an article needs to be evaluated in relation to the popularity and importance of its subjects, to understand if the article is too short, superficial or too detailed; the stability of an article has no meaning if the article is rarely edited, since it could be stable because it is not taken in consideration rather than because it is complete.

5 Mapping Domains Theories onto Wikipedia Elements

We first need a model of Wikipedia in order to extract elements useful for our purpose. Wikipedia has been designed so that any past modification, along with information about the editor, is accessible. This transparency, that by itself gives an implicit sense of trust, allows us to collect all the information and elements needed.

Our Wikipedia model is composed of two principal objects (*Wiki Article* and *Wiki User*) and a number of supporting objects, as depicted in fig. 1. Since each user has a personal page, user can be treated as an article with some editing methods like *creating, modifying and deleting article or uploading images*. An article contains the main text page (class *wiki page*) and the *talk page*, where users can add comments and judgments on the article. *Wiki pages* include properties such as its length, a count of the number of sections, images, external links, notes, and references. Each page has a *history page* associated, containing a complete list of all modifications. A modification contains information on User, date and time and article text version.

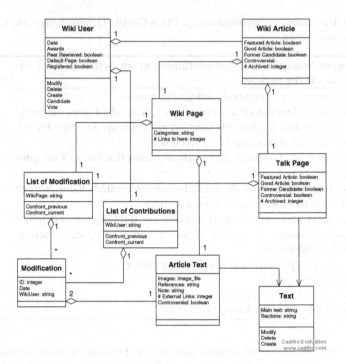

Fig. 1. The Wikipedia UML model

The community of users can modify articles or adding discussion on article's topic (the *talk page* for that article).

We are now ready to map the proposition listed in table 1 onto elements of our Wikipedia model. We outlined 8 macro-areas and we identified about 50 sources of trust evidence. As an example, we described how we model the two macroareas *User's Distribution* and *Stability* (a complete list is available here [24]).

Users' Distribution/Leadership (Propositions 3,5,9)

We model this issue with following formulas. We define $E(u)$ as the number of edits for user u for article w *and* $U(w)$ as the set of all user u that edited the article w. We define:

$$T(w) : w \rightarrow \Im \qquad (1)$$

$$P(n) : [0..1] \rightarrow \Im \ , \ P(n) = \sum_{U_a} E(u) \qquad (2)$$

Where U_a is the set of $n\%$ most active users in $U(w)$. T represent the total number of edits for article w while $P(n)$, given a normalized percentage n, returns the number of edits done by the top $n\%$ most active users among the set $U(w)$. Similar to $P(n)$ is:

$$Pe(n) : \Im \rightarrow \Im \ , \ Pe(n) = \sum_{U_n} E(u) \ , \ U_n = \{u \in U \mid E(u) > n\} \qquad (3)$$

that, given a number of edits n, represent the number of edits done by users with more than n edits. The different between P and Pe is that P considers the most active users in relation to the set of users contributing to the article, while Pe considers the most active users in relation to an absolute number of edit n. Table 3 explains our considerations for each formula:

Table 2. User Distribution Factors

Trust Factors	Comments
Average of E	Average number of edits per user
Standard Deviation of E	Standard deviation of edits
$\dfrac{P(n)}{T}$	Percentage of edits produced by the most active users
$\dfrac{Pe(n)}{T}$	Percentage of edits produced by users with more than n edit for that article
Number of discussions (talk edit)	It represents how much an article is discussed

We explain the meaning of the functions defined: $P(n)/T$ tells us how much of the article has been done by a subset of users. If we pose n equal to 5 and we obtain:

$$\frac{P(5)}{T} = 0.45$$

This means that the 45% of the edits have been done by the top 5% most active users. If the value is low the leadership for that article is low, if it is high it means that a relatively small group of users is responsible for most of the editing process.

We have introduced the function $Pe(n)/T$ to evaluate leadership from a complementary point of view. $Pe(n)/T$ is the percentage of edits done by users that did more than n edits for the article. If we pose n equal to 3 and we obtain:

$$\frac{Pe(3)}{T} = 0.78$$

The above means that 78% of the edits were done by users with more than 3 edits and only 22% by users that did 1, 2 or 3 edits. Thus, $1-Pe(n)/T$ with n small (typically 3) indicates how much of the editing's process was done by occasional users, with a few edits. Thus, it can represent a measurement of the fragmentation of the editing process.

The average and standard deviation of the function $E(u)$ (total edits per user u) reinforces the leadership as well: average close to 1 means high fragmentation, high standard deviation means high leadership. Finally, we model the dictatorship effect (Propositions 3,9) by using the function $P(n)/T$ keeping n very small (<1) to verify if a very small group of users (typically no more than 5) did a great percentage of edits. We also consider the standard deviation of $E(u)$: very high values can represent a strong predominance of few users.

Stability (Proposition 8)

We define the function:

$$N(t): t \rightarrow \mathfrak{I} \tag{4}$$

that gives the number of edits done at time t. Then we define:

$$Et(t) = \sum_{t}^{P} N(t) \tag{5}$$

that, given time t, it returns the number of edits done from time t to the present time P. We then define:

$$Txt(t) : t \rightarrow \Im \tag{6}$$

that gives the number of words that are different between the version at time t and the current one. We remind that T is the total number of edits for an article, i.e. $Et(0)$. We define W as the number of words in the current version.

Table 3. Article's Stability Factors

Trust Factors	Comments
$\dfrac{Et(t)}{T}$	Percentage of edits from time t
$\dfrac{Txt(t)}{W}$	Percentage of text different from current version and version at time t

We evaluate the stability of an article looking at the values of these two functions. If an article is stable it means that Et, from a certain point of time t, should decrease or be almost a constant that means that the number of editing is stable or decreasing: the article is not being to be modified. The meaning of $Txt(t)$ is an estimation of how different was the version at time t compared to the current version. When t is close to the current time point, Txt goes to 0, and it is obviously 0 when t is the current time. An article is stable if Txt, from a certain point of time t not very close to the current time is almost a constant value. This means that the text is almost the same in that period of time. As mentioned above, an article can be stable because it is rarely edited, but this may mean it is not taken in consideration rather than it is complete. To avoid this, the degree of activity of the article and its text quality are used as a logic condition for stability: only active and articles with good text can be considered stable.

6 Evaluation

We selected a case study and developed a working prototype in C able to calculate the trustworthiness of a Wikipedia article. A diagram of the prototype is depicted in figure 2. The system, using the *factors updater* module, is continuously fed by Wikipedia, and it stores data in the *Factors DB*. The Wikipedia database is completely available for download here [25].

When we want to estimate the trustworthiness of an article, the *Data Retrieval module* query the Wikipedia DB (it could retrieve information directly from the web site as well), and it collects the needed data: article page, talk page, modification lists, user's list, article's category and old versions. Then, the *factors calculator module*

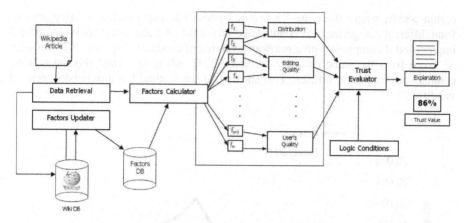

Fig. 2. The Wikipedia Trust Calculator

calculates each of the trust factors, merging them into the macro-areas defined. Using the values contained in the *Factors DB* of pages of the same category or comparable it computes a ranking of the page for each macro-area. Finally, the *trust evaluator module* estimates a numeric trust values and a natural language explanation of the value. The output is achieved by merging the partial trust value of each macro areas using constraints taken from the *Logic Conditions module*. This contains logic conditions that control the meaning of each trust factor in relationship to the others:

- *IF leadership is high AND dictatorship is high THEN warning*
- *IF length is high AND importance is low THEN warning*
- *IF stability is high AND (length is short OR edit is low OR importance is low) THEN warning*

By looking at the page rank in each macro area and considering the warnings coming from the *logic condition module*, explanations and trust values can be provided:

We evaluated our model with an extensive calculation over almost 8,000 articles. The experiment was conducted on the 17th of March 2006 on 7 718 Wikipedia articles. These articles include all 846 featured articles (special articles considered the best of Wikipedia), plus the most visited pages with at least 25 edits. These articles represent the 65% of the editing activity of Wikipedia and the high majority of its access, thus it can be considered a significant set. The results are summarized in figure 3. The graph represents the distribution of the articles on the base of their trust values. We have isolated the featured articles (grey line) from standard articles (black line): if our calculation is valid, featured articles should show higher trust values than standard article. Results obtained are positive and encouraging: the graph clearly shows the difference between standard articles distribution, mainly around a trust value of 45-50%, and the featured articles one, around 75%.

The 77.8% of the featured articles are distributed in the region with trust values > 70%, meaning that they are all considered good articles, while only 13% of standard articles are considered good. Furthermore, 42.3% of standard articles are distributed in the region with trust values < 50%, where there are no featured articles, demonstrating the selection operated by the computation. Only 23 standard articles are in the region >85%, where there are 93 featured ones. The experiment, covering articles from different categories, was conducted on an absolute scale, and it shows a minimal imprecision if compared with a previous experiment conducted on a set of 200 articles all taken from the same category "*nations*" [24], where we could rely on relative comparisons of similar articles. This shows that the method has a promising general validity.

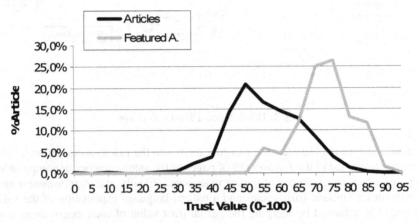

Fig. 3. Articles and Featured Articles distribution by Trust Value

7 Conclusion and Future Work

In this paper we have proposed a transparent, non invasive and automatic method to evaluate the trustworthiness of Wikipedia articles. The method was able to estimate the trustworthiness of articles relying only on their present state, a characteristic needed to cope with the changing nature of Wikipedia. After having analyzed what brings credibility and expertise in the domains composing Wikipedia, i.e. content quality and collaborative working, we identified a set of new trust sources, trust evidence, to support our trust computation. The experimental evidence that we collected from almost 8,000 pages covering the majority of the encyclopaedia activity lead to promising results. This suggests a role for such a method in the identification of trustworthy material on the Web.

Our future work will be focused on the generalization of the scheme proposed in the paper into a formal evidence-based trust methodology called Domain ANalysis/Trust Extraction (DANTE). DANTE will be centered on the idea that in a particular domain humans have developed theories and expertise that have been proved to be effective to guarantee gold-standard and high quality in that domain. We refer to this set of expert-knowledge, proven theories, modus operandi as *domain-related theories*. We trust an entity that can show evidence related to these domain-related theories. The more the entity proves to be associated with such evidence, the more it is trustworthy. Theories define what is trustworthy in that domain, entity evidence related to these theories allow us to compute the degree of trustworthiness.

References

1. Ciolek, T.: M. Today's WWW, Tomorrow's MMM: The specter of multi-media mediocrity, IEEE COMPUTER, January 1996, Vol 29(1) pp. 106-108
2. How much do you trust wikipedia?, article from the website http://news.com.com/2009-1025_3-5984535.html, visited March 2006
3. Gales, J.: Encyclopaedias goes head a head, Nature Magazine, issue N. 438, 15 Decembre 2005
4. Romano, D. M.: The Nature of Trust: Conceptual and Operational Clarification, Louisiana State University. PhD Thesis (2003)
5. Blaze, M., Feigenbaum, J. and Lacy, J.: Decentralized Trust Management,Proceedings of IEEE Conference on Security and Privacy (1996)
6. Chu, Y.: Trust Management for the World Wide Web, Master Thesis, MIT (1997)
7. Terzis, S., W. Wagealla: The SECURE Collaboration Model, SECURE Deliverables D2.1, D.2.2 and D2.3, 2004
8. Marsh, S.: Formalizing Trust as a Computational Concept. PhD thesis, University of Stirling, Department of Computer Science and Mathematics (1994)
9. V. Cahill, et al. Using Trust for Secure Collaboration in Uncertain Environments. IEEE Pervasive Computing Magazine, (July-September 2003)
10. Golbeck, J., Hendler, J., and Parsia, B.: Trust Networks on the Semantic Web,University of Maryland, College Park, (2002)
11. www.foaf-project.com, FOAF project website
12. Ziegler, C., Golbeck, J.: Investigating Correlations of Trust and Interest Similarity - Do Birds of a Feather Really Flock Together?, Decision Support Services, (2005)
13. Lerch, J., M. Prietula & C. Kulik. (1997). The Turing Effect:The nature of trust in expert systems advice. In P. Feltovich,
14. Ball, E., Chadwick, D., Basden, A.: The Implementation of a System for Evaluating Trust in a {PKI} Environment, Trust in the Network Economy, SpringerWein (2003) 263-279.
15. Bucher, H.: Crisis Communication and the Internet: Risk and Trust in a Global Media, First Monday, Volume 7, Number 4 (2002)
16. Huang, J., Fox, S.: Uncertainty in knowledge provenance, Proceedings of the first European Semantic Web Symposium, Heraklio, Greece (May 2004)
17. Guha, R. Open Rating Systems. Technical Report, Stanford University (2003)
18. Burke, R. Knowledge-based Recommender Systems. In Encyclopedia of Library and Information Systems.Vol. 69, Supplement 32, New York (2000)
19. Fogg, B. J.: How Do Users Evaluate The Credibility of Web Sites? In Proceedings of the 2003 conference on Designing for user experiences, ACM Press, NY, USA (2003)
20. Alexander, J., Tate, M.: Web Wisdom: How to Evaluate and Create Information Quality on the Web, Lawrence Eribaum Associates Inc, New Jersey, USA (1999)
21. Cassel. R.: Selection Criteria for Internet Resources, College and Research Library News, N. 56, pag. 92-93, (February 1995)
22. Standford Web Credibility Guidelines web site, http://credibility.stanford.edu/guidelines
23. Roberts, T.: Onine Collaborative Learning, Theory and Practice, Idea Group Pub, USA (2004)
24. Dondio, P., Barrett, S., Weber, S.: Calculating the Trustworthiness of a Wikipedia Article Using Dante Methodology, IADIS eSociety conference, Dublin, Ireland (2006)
25. http://download.wikimedia.org, download site of the Wikipedia project

MTrust: A Reputation-Based Trust Model for a Mobile Agent System

Suphithat Songsiri

Department of Communication Systems
Universität str. 11, D-58084, FernUniversity Hagen, Germany
suphithat.songsiri@fernuni-hagen.de

Abstract. This research promotes MTrust a reputation-based trust model that will ensure cooperative interactions amongst mobile agents and visited hosts in a mobile agent system. MTrust is composed of a reputation system and a trust formation system. A reputation system relies on two components; a truthful feedback submission algorithm and a set of distributed feedback information storages. A trust formation system enables a truster to compute a trustee's trustworthiness. It has two components namely; a feedback aggregation module (*FAM*) and a trust computing module (*TCM*). A *FAM* calculates a trust value from feedback information when there is a lack of direct experiences using Beta distribution. A *TCM* calculates a trust value using Bayesian Network (BN).

1 Introduction

The security of a mobile agent paradigm emphasizes on protecting and preventing a mobile agent from malicious hosts' attacks by applying cryptographic functions. Unfortunately these countermeasures alone are not enough to protect mobile agents from malicious hosts. We summarize that by deciding to visit a trustworthy host, the probability of a mobile agent being attacked can be reduced. MTrust aims to promote cooperative behavior between mobile agents and visited hosts by using trust as a qualitative measurement. A mobile agent utilizes a combination of a host selection scheme (i.e. a method of choosing a visited host based on some criteria such as queue length) and a calculated trust value to decide whether it will migrate and perform tasks on that visited host or not. By integrating a trust model into a mobile agent system will absolutely increase cooperative behavior and cast malicious hosts away from the system. MTrust provides a new truthful feedback submission algorithm using incentive-based timely feedback submission and a fair punishment scheme, a *FAM* for deriving a trust value from feedback information and a BN for a trust computing from direct experiences. The rest of this paper is organized as follows: Section 2 presents definition of trust and reputation. Section 3 explains MTrust architecture. Section 4 demonstrates a truthful feedback system. Section 5 describes a trust formation system. Section 6 summarizes this paper.

2 Definition of Trust and Reputation

In this paper, we define trust as a subjective quantified predictor of the expected future behavior of a trustee according to a specific agreement elicited from the

L.T. Yang et al. (Eds.): ATC 2006, LNCS 4158, pp. 374–385, 2006.

outcomes of the previous interactions, both from direct experiences and indirect experiences; also known as feedbacks. Reputation of an individual refers to certain characteristics related to its trustworthiness ascribed by its interactants. Reputation can be obtained from a set of interaction feedbacks, in a mobile agent system, where mobile agents describe a visited host's performance in fulfilling its obligations.

3 MTrust Architecture

MTrust is composed of a reputation system and a trust formation system as depicted in figure 1.

Fig. 1. MTrust Architecture

We use a scenario of data retrieval mobile agents. An owner, denoted by O_i when i=1, 2,..., n, implements a feedback aggregation module and a trust computing module for calculating the list of trustworthy hosts. O_i generates a set of mobile agents (i.e. $A^{O_i} = \{ ma_1^{O_i},..., ma_j^{O_i} \}$). Each $ma_j^{O_i}$ represents a unique mobile agent's name, which allows visited hosts to trace the agent's owner. Each mobile agent is provided a list of visitable trustworthy hosts obtained from FAM and TCM computation by its owner and will select the visited hosts using the host selection scheme. A visited host vh_I , when I=1, 2,.., m, provides files requested by the mobile agent. Each visited host is assigned a single feedback storage server Fh^{vhI} , which maintains all feedbacks related to this visited host. The objectives of assigning each visited host a feedback storage server are to avoid the problem of long period feedback information searching and to ensure originality of feedback information. Each visited host grants services to a mobile agent according to its reputation. Once a transaction is completed, both $ma_j^{O_i}$ and vh_I must submit their feedbacks. A public key infrastructure is assumed to be available. The notations used throughout this paper are as follows:

- O_i^T (O_i^R): a truster (a rater). ENC_{O_i} is an encryption using a public key of O_i and Sig_{O_i} is a signature using a private key of O_i . $H(m)$ is a hash of message m.

- Reputation: A visited host has two types of reputation, namely; a good service provider and an honest rater. In contrary to a visited host, each mobile agent belonging to the same owner possesses a single (group) reputation, as an honest rater.

- Trust: $T^M_{O^T_i \to vh_I} \in [0,1]$: is a trust value computed using a method from set M, where M $\in$ {Predefined Trust value (PT), General Trust value (GT), Feedback Aggregation method for inexperienced truster (FA_{IN}), Feedback Aggregation method for experienced truster (FA_{EX}), Bayesian Network (BN), A combination of FA_{EX} and BN(CO)}.

- Feedback: It is an evaluation of its partner's obligation. A feedback is either 0 (i.e. dissatisfied) or 1 (i.e. satisfied). $\tilde{F}^{t_n,id}_{vh_I \to ma^{O_i}_j}$ denotes a feedback submitted by vh_I at time t_n for service number "id" containing the services provided to $ma^{O_i}_j$. $F^{t_n,id}_{ma^{O_i}_j \to vh_I}$ indicates a feedback from $ma^{O_i}_j$ comprising of $ma^{O_i}_j$'s feedback on vh_I 's quality of service (i.e. a mobile agent compares what has been agreed with what it actually receives from a visited host).

4 Reputation System

A reputation system [1] represents a promising method for fostering trust among complete strangers and for helping each individual to adjust or update its degree of trust towards its corresponding interaction partner. The fundamental idea of our reputation system is to use an algorithm to encourage transaction participants to evaluate on each others' performances on the previously concurred commitment engagements, by submitting truthful feedbacks. In our scenario, the service host is committed to cater service requested by the mobile agent and to submit feedback, whereas the mobile agent is obliged to submit feedback. In general, threats found in a reputation system are presented as follows:

- Strategic rater: In [2], a single or a collusive group of raters strategically provide a set of unfair feedbacks aiming to destroy (boost) a peer's (its partner's) reputation.
- Strategically malicious visited host: A host can manage its reputation according to its goal. For instance, it fluctuates its performance by cooperating or defecting its partners unevenly in an acceptable range so that it can still engage itself in future interactions.
- Whitewasher: In [3], entities that purposely leave or join the system with a new identity in an attempt to conceal any bad reputations under their previous identity.

To repress strategic raters (i.e. to destroy a peer's reputation), we apply an incentive-based timely feedback submission and a fair punishment scheme. In case of strategically malicious host, we implement BN. To control strategic raters (i.e. to boost their partners' reputation), we apply feedback aggregation algorithms. The prevention of whitewashers will not be discussed in this paper.

4.1 Truthful Feedbacks Submission

This subsection presents an algorithm, which inspires each participant in each transaction to faithfully provide its truthful feedback. Whitby et.al. [1] pointed out that elimination of unfair feedbacks can be achieved by increasing the cost of doing or decreasing the incentive to lie. To avert unfair feedbacks, three relevant approaches could be implemented, namely; detecting-based methods [2, 4-8], incentive-based methods [10-13, 15] and punishment-based methods [10]. The first method attempts to detect or exclude unfair feedbacks using filtering concepts. The second method introduces incentives to motivate (or even benefit) truthful feedback submission. The last approach induces punishment like temporary transaction cessation for any unfair feedback submission found. This paper incorporates incentive-based timely feedback submission method and a fair punishment scheme. The argument for not implementing detection-based method is simply to avoid high cost accruement from constant observation and exclusion of unfair feedbacks. Our algorithm is explained in detailed in the following sub-sections.

4.1.1 Evident of Legitimate Transaction

Prior to any transaction engagement, an agent and vh_I have to agree upon the services vh_I is to provide an agent. This step is to ensure non-repudiated transactions. The presence of ELT does not annihilate the possibility of strategic raters, instead serves only as a tracking mechanism to the number of transactions performed between any mobile agent and vh_I. ELT can be acquired as follows:

- Service Request: A, an agent belonging to O_i, currently residing at host vh_I, requests vh_{I+1} for services.

$$A \xrightarrow{\text{M1}} vh_{I+1} : ENC_{vh_{I+1}} [Sig_{vh_I} (\text{service request})] \tag{1}$$

- Service Offer: vh_{I+1} replies A with types of services and quality of services it will offer.

$$vh_{I+1} \xrightarrow{\text{M2}} A : ENC_{vh_I} [Sig_{vh_{I+1}} (\text{service offer,service id\#})] \tag{2}$$

- Service Agreement: In case A agrees on vh_{I+1}'s services, it sends an acknowledgement for the service agreement to vh_{I+1} and $Fh^{vh_{I+1}}$. vh_{I+1}'s status indicates whether or not vh_{I+1} is under probation period resulted from a recent pair of contradictive feedbacks containing in $Fh^{vh_{I+1}}$'s database.

$$A \underset{\text{M4}}{\overset{\text{M3}}{\rightleftarrows}} vh_{I+1} : \begin{cases} M3 = ENC_{vh_{I+1}} [Sig_{vh_I} (H(M2))] & (3.1) \\ M4 = ENC_{vh_I} [Sig_{vh_{I+1}} (H(M3))] & (3.2) \end{cases}$$

$$A \underset{\text{M6}}{\overset{\text{M5}}{\rightleftarrows}} Fh^{vh_{I+1}} : \begin{cases} M5 = ENC_{Fh^{vh_{I+1}}} [Sig_{vh_I} (Sig_{vh_{I+1}} (\text{service offer,service id\#}))] & (4.1) \\ M6 = ENC_{vh_I} [Sig_{Fh^{vh_{I+1}}} (vh_{I+1}\text{'s status})] & (4.2) \end{cases}$$

- Service Acknowledgement (S_ack): After receiving message M3, vh_{I+1} sends a service agreement M3 and M4 to $Fh^{vh_{I+1}}$.

$$vh_{I+1} \underset{\text{M8}}{\overset{\text{M7}}{\rightleftarrows}} Fh^{vh_{I+1}} : \begin{cases} M7 = ENC_{Fh^{vh_{I+1}}} [Sig_{vh_{I+1}} (H(M3 \| M4)] & (5.1) \\ M8 = ENC_{vh_{I+1}} [Sig_{Fh^{vh_{I+1}}} (H(M7))] & (5.2) \end{cases}$$

After ETL has been completed, A migrates to vh_{I+1} to perform tasks for its owner.

4.1.2 Incentive-Based Algorithm

Once vh_{I+1} has performed its obligations for A, both of them are liable to submit feedbacks. Jurca et al. [12] pointed out that an incentive-compatible scheme for truthful feedback submission ensures that it is for the best interests of a rational rater to actually report truthful feedbacks. From [11], the first issue to be considered is the choice of appropriate incentive, which effectively stimulates truthful feedback submission behaviour. Wu et al. [13] summarized choices of incentives used in Ad-hoc networks to be reputation-based and price-based. This work classifies feedbacks from two raters as follows.

• A pair of consistent feedbacks: Both raters provide feedbacks in the same direction (i.e. either satisfied or dissatisfied). It can be interpreted that both raters are honest or collusive. Klein et al. [14] pointed out the high occurrence tendency of feedback reciprocity. In contrast, feedback retaliations are relative rare.

• A pair of contradictive feedbacks: It is occurred when one rater contributes a feedback, which is opposite to another rater's feedback. This means that one participant is dishonest.

The elimination of feedback reciprocity and retaliation can eventuate if both raters are unaware of each other's feedbacks prior to their feedback submission demonstrated in section 4.1.3. By integrating a fair punishment scheme, the number of contradictive feedback pairs can be reduced. It will be discussed in section 4.1.4.

4.1.3 Timely Feedback Submission Algorithm

The concepts of a timely feedback submission rely strongly on an invisibility of feedback submission and a continuity of future transactions. After a transaction is done, vh_{I+1} submits its feedback to Fh^{vhI+1}. However, A submits its feedback to its owner to be used as direct experience and Fh^{vhI+1} to be compared with vh_{I+1}'s feedback, only after migrating to the next host vh_{I+2}. This is to prevent vh_{I+1} from snooping on A's feedback. If any participant fails to submit its feedback, it will be banned from engaging itself in any future transaction. Both vh_{I+1} and A's feedbacks will be legally obtainable from Fh^{vhI+1} only, once Fh^{vhI+1} has received them. Fh^{vhI+1} will then compare the feedbacks for consistency or contradiction. For contradictive feedbacks, a fair punishment scheme must be exercised.

4.1.4 A Fair Punishment Scheme

The common punishment scheme prohibits both participants from engaging in new transactions for a period of time. This scheme will discourage a 'victim' host or mobile agent from making any future transactions with those specific raters. In addition to the common punishment scheme, the fair punishment scheme exerts the following:

• On mobile agent: temporary transaction cessation for *all* mobile agents belonging to O_i. Upon receiving contradictive feedbacks, Fh^{vhI+1} immediately notifies O_i about its mobile agent and vh_{I+1} participating in the contradictive feedback and broadcasts to all service providers and their storage servers that all O_i's mobile agents are under probation, which implies that no services from any visited host should be provided to them. The reason of punishing all mobile agents belonging to O_i is that O_i, if it is a malicious owner, might produce a set of malicious mobile agents attempting to provide contradictive feedbacks after interacting with target visited hosts.

• On service host: From eq.(4.2) , $Fh^{vh_{I+1}}$ reveals vh_{I+1}'s probation status, thus discouraging all mobile agents from transaction with vh_{I+1}.

Furthermore, the probation status engenders impairment of the continuity of future transaction prospects especially for both all of O_i's mobile agents and vh_{I+1}, as they would most probably evade any future transactions with each other. The scheme is further enhanced if all service hosts collaborate in declining transaction engagements requested by O_i's mobile agents under probation. The fair punishment scheme also introduces collaboration incentive for service hosts, which deny transactions with mobile agents under probation. The incentive is chosen to be reputation. Engaging a transaction with an agent under probation will not improve their reputation, as the feedback submitted to their dedicated storage server will be ignored. A probation period is a function of the number of contradictive feedback pairs that both raters have implicated together.

$$PrP_{A^{O_i},vh_I}(k) = \alpha^k \qquad (6)$$

k is the number of contradictive feedback pairs between both raters and α is any appropriate integer.

5   Trust Formation System

A reputation-based trust value can be computed using many methods [16]. To calculate a trustee's trust value, the types of a truster and status of a trustee towards a truster should be considered. A truster can be categorized into an inexperienced truster; i.e. a truster who is new to the system or an experienced truster; i.e. a truster who has had some transactions with some trustees. Status of a trustee towards a truster can be explained as a newcomer to the system (type1), never transacts with a truster but not new to the system (type2), or has committed some transactions with a truster (type3). The set of methods used by a truster according to a combination of types of a truster and status of a trustee is summarized in the following table 1 and 2.

Table 1. Methods for an inexperienced truster   **Table 2.** Methods for an experienced truster

Truster \ Trustee	Type1	Type2
Inexperienced Truster	PT	FA_{IN}

Truster \ Trustee	Type1	Type2	Type3
Experienced Truster	GT	FA_{Ex}	CO

5.1   Predefined Trust Value(PT)

A predefined trust value is the one most difficult to calculate, because there is no information about a trustee for a truster to consider. Actually, a predefined trust value is a trust value deduced from a truster's behavior.

5.2 General Trust Value (GT)

A general trust value is a trust value concluded from each trust value a truster assigns to each trustee. A general trust value is computed from an averaging of all trustees' trust values.

5.3 Bayesian Network Method (BN)

In [17], Pearl stated that Bayesian methods provide reasoning about partial beliefs under conditions of uncertainty. The heart of Bayesian techniques lies in this formula.

$$p(H \mid e) = \frac{p(e \mid H) * p(H)}{p(e)} \tag{7}$$

An advantage of using BN to compute trust is that it can infer trust in various aspects from the corresponding conditional probabilities. Every owner develops a simple BN model as described in figure 2. Root node T has two stages; satisfying and unsatisfying, denoted by 1 and 0 respectively. The leaf nodes Q, ST and FS each have two stages; "good" and "bad", "fast" and "slow" and "honest" and "biased", which are represented by 1 and 0 respectively.

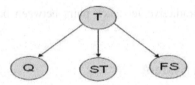

Fig. 2. Bayesian Network

Evidence cannot pass between all the children of T only if the state of T is known. A feedback contains an evaluation (i.e. satisfying or unsatisfying) given the result of interaction shown in eq. (8).

$$F^{tn,id}_{ma_j^{O_i} \to vh_I} = \{1 \text{ or } 0 \mid \text{result of interaction}\} \tag{8}$$

A satisfying evaluation is obtained when $Q + ST + FS \geq 2$. The value of FS is initially assumed to be 1, conferring to truthful feedback submission. An owner updates its BN once a feedback is received. In case of contradictive feedback occurrence broadcast from Fh^{vhI}, the owner re-evaluates the feedback with FS=0, and updates its BN again. BN trust computing allows computation of various conditional probabilities For instance, p(T=1|Q=1,FS=1) is a probability that a trustee is trustworthy in providing good file quality and being an honest rater. To conform to the trust defined in section 2, a trustee's trust value equals the specific conditional probability computed by a truster akin to its interests, as demonstrated in the following equation.

$$T^{BN}_{O_i^T \to vh_I} = p(T=1 \mid \text{specific interest}) \tag{9}$$

The following experiments have been conducted to demonstrate the calculation of trust values using BN. Figures 3.1 and 3.2 illustrate the simulation of a trustee's trust value whose transaction feedbacks are evaluated to be "satisfying" even though it provides a set of fluctuating services. Figure 3.1 demonstrates that if a trustee always commits satisfying transactions (T=1) with good file quality (Q=1), its trust value will increase. However, if a trustee commits satisfying transactions (T=1) with bad file quality (Q=0), its trust value (i.e. p(T=1|Q=1)) generally remains the same as the previous ones. Figure 3.2 presents a trustee who always satisfies transactions with bad file quality, its trust value is equal to its initial trust value.

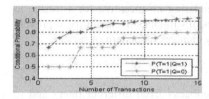

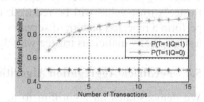

Fig. 3.1.   Fig. 3.2.

From the experiments conducted, it is obvious that if a trustee can manipulate its performance such that the evaluation result always comes out to be satisfying, then its trust value would increase with good file quality or remains equal with bad file quality. To evade such exploitations, both p(T=1|Q=1) and p(T=1|Q=0) must be considered when assigning trust value. A trust value is acquired according to the following equation

$$T^{BN}_{O^T_i \to vh_i} = p_{current}(T = 1 \mid Q = 1) - \Delta p(T = 1 \mid Q = 0)$$ (10)

The second term denotes the difference between the latest and previous values of p(T=1|Q=0). By applying eq. (10), a trustee's trust value will not remain unchanged; instead will vary with the quality of service provided to a truster.

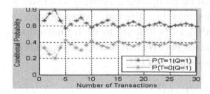

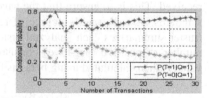

Fig. 3.3.   Fig. 3.4.

Figure 3.3 and 3.4 elucidate the cause for the deterioration of trust value and how a strategically malicious trustee manipulates its trust value. In this scenario, each agent either evaluates each result of transaction to be 1 or 0 with good file quality. Deterioration in trust value eventuates when a mobile agent declares a result of evaluation to be dissatisfying when file quality was good. Figure 3.3 exhibits a pattern of service evaluations such that a trustee is voted to be satisfying for three consecutive transactions and dissatisfying for two consecutive transactions. If a trustee maintains this pattern, its trust value will slightly decrease. A strategically malicious trustee can also boost its trust value by appending a pattern of service, which contained a higher number of satisfying transactions and a lower number of unsatisfying transactions, as shown in figure 3.4 with pattern (4,1). To handle a strategically malicious trustee, a truster must take an observation on trustee's file quality. The assignment of trust value to a strategically malicious trustee is performed as follows:

$$T_{O_i^T \to vh_I}^{BN} = \frac{P_{current}(T=1|Q=1)}{N_R}$$ (11)

Where N_R is the number of repeated patterns. This way, a strategically malicious trustee's trust value will be reduced, thereby rendering no incentive for a trustee to perform a repeated pattern of services. This protocol still lacks in capability to prevent a strategically malicious trustee who dynamically changes its pattern of service.

5.4   Feedback Aggregation Algorithm

We demonstrates an algorithm to aggregate feedbacks from different raters and to form a single trust value representing trustworthiness of a trustee based on the trustee's reputation. In [18], Shi et al. present an average algorithm. They argue that averaging feedbacks simplifies the algorithm design and provides low cost in running the system. From [19], Wang suggests that averaging should be used with feedbacks from unknown sources and weighing should be used from known sources. Xiong et al. [20] propose weighing feedbacks by using personalized similarity between rater and source of feedbacks. Yu et al. [21] only use feedbacks from witnesses who have interacted with a target peer. From [22], the authors use beta distribution model to calculate a trust value. Our algorithm is described as follows;

- **FA$_{IN}$:** It is applied to a scenario where a trust value is computed from received sets of unknown raters' history of feedbacks about a trustee. Firstly; a truster requests sets of history of feedbacks about vh_I from Fh^{vh_I}. With the histories in hand, a truster computes a trust value of vh_I. Firstly, a truster analyzes each history of feedbacks received. This is to ensure that the trust value will be computed according to truster's standards, as each rater's degree of requirements may be different. Subsequently, a truster summarizes each analyzed history of feedbacks belonging to each rater into a number of positive (negative) consistent feedbacks N_P (N_N). A trustee's reputation value is then calculated using beta distribution shown in eq.(12).

$$f(b|\alpha,\beta) = \frac{\Gamma(\alpha+\beta)}{\Gamma(\alpha)\Gamma(\beta)} b^{\alpha-1}(1-b)^{\beta-1}$$ (12)

for $0 \leq b \leq 1$, where b is trustee's behavior (i.e. trustworthy or untrustworthy) towards rater and $\alpha,\beta > 0$. A truster computes each trustee's reputation perceived by each rater as an expectation of beta distribution shown in eq. (13).

$$Rep_{O_i^R \to vh_I} = E[b|\alpha,\beta] = \frac{\alpha}{\alpha+\beta}$$ (13)

where $\alpha = N_P + 1$ and $\beta = N_N + 1$. To determine the accuracy of reputation values, which share the same values, variance is applied (i.e. shown in eq.(14))

$$\sigma^2 = \frac{\alpha\beta}{(\alpha+\beta)^2(\alpha+\beta+1)} \tag{14}$$

Then, a graph of mean (y-axis) versus variance (x-axis); where x-axis is divided into N (integer) equal ranges to represent the groups of least accuracy deviating reputation values, is plotted. Finally, a trustee's trust value is calculated as a summation of a normalized reputation from each raters group. A general form of a trustee's trust value is presented in eq.(15).

$$T^{FA_{In}}_{O^T_i \to vh_I} = \sum_{k=1}^{Num} w_k \overline{rep_k} \quad and \quad \overline{rep_k} = \frac{\sum_{i=1}^{N_k} Re\,p_{O^R_i \to vh_I}}{N_k} \tag{15}$$

where Num is the number of ranges, w_k is the weight for range k, $\overline{rep_k}$ is the average reputation represented by range k and N_k is the number of raters in range k. w_k is a function of the average variance and the number of raters in the range k. By multiplying rep_k with w_k, the average trustee's reputation derived from a range containing a large number of raters with a small value of average variance is more reliable than a range containing a less number of raters with a larger value of average variance. w_k is derived as follows:

$$w_k = f(\overline{\sigma^2}, N_k) = \frac{w'_k}{\sum_{k=1}^{Num} w'_k} \quad and \quad w'_k = \frac{N_k}{N_{total} \overline{\sigma^2}} \tag{16}$$

Where N_{total} is the total number of raters, and the number of raters dedicated to each range is N_k. For the purpose of simulation, a set of histories of feedbacks containing 19 pairs of positive and negative feedbacks from different raters have been used.

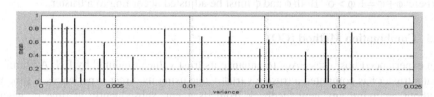

Fig. 4. A graph of mean versus variance

From figure 4, calculation of reputation from range 1 (variance between 0 and 0.005) results in the following: $N_{total}=19$, Num=5, $N_1=8$, $\overline{rep_k} = 0.681$, $\overline{\sigma^2} = 0.000253$, $w_1 = 0.92$. The trust value results in $T^{FA_{In}}_{O^T_i \to vh_I} = 0.63$.

- **FA$_{EX}$:** It is applied to a scenario where a truster receives a set of known and unknown raters' history of feedbacks about a trustee. FA$_{EX}$ is designed to assist a truster in giving each history of feedbacks from different rater a weight factor (w_f) which represents the certainty of each history of feedbacks. Certainty means reliability of history of feedbacks in predicting a trustee's future behaviour. The assignment of a weight factor to each history of feedbacks requires consideration of types of rater (known and unknown). Initially, each unknown rater possesses a weight factor of 1. After an interaction with a trustee, a truster updates all weight factors. The weight factor can be updated such that if a derived reputation value from a rater implies a trustworthy trustee but the result of transaction is dissatisfying, then a truster decreases a weight factor, otherwise it increases it. We assign a weight factor as an average of correctness in predicting all trustees' future behaviour.

$$w_f^{O_i^R} = \sum_{j=1}^{M} p_j \Big/ M \tag{17}$$

where M is the total number of histories of feedbacks that a truster has considered so far from a rater O_i^R and p_j is the percentage of having successful transactions from total transactions with a trustee "j". Each p_j must be updated once a transaction with trustee "j" has been completed. The weight factor is then multiplied with a reputation of trustee calculated from a rater's history of feedbacks, shown in eq. (13), to form a weighted reputation of the trustee. To use FA_{EX}, there are three situations a truster must consider. The first, if all raters are unknown, then the truster applies FA_{IN} with a weight factor of 1 for each rater. The second, if all raters are known, FA_{IN} is utilized with weighted reputation value. The third, if the raters consist of a combination of known and unknown raters, then a truster separates raters into an unknown and a known group, and applies the appropriate methods as described previously. Subsequently, a truster combines trust values from both groups as shown in eq.(18).

$$T_{O_i^T \to vh_I}^{FA_{EX}} = \phi T_{unknown} + \varphi T_{known} \tag{18}$$

Where $\phi + \varphi = 1, \varphi > \phi$. Both ϕ and φ must be adjusted according to a truster.

5.5 Combination Method (CO)

An experienced host uses FA_{EX} to enhance its trust value computed by BN. Assuming that a truster has computed a trustee's trust value using its direct experiences at time t_x without receiving any new feedback from its agent, subsequently at time t_y, when $t_x < t_y$, a truster requires to calculate this trustee's trust value again. A truster retrieves only histories of feedbacks, which have been committed between its latest feedback with a trustee at time $t_z (t_z < t_x)$ and the last feedback of another rater with a trustee before the requesting time $t_v (t_x < t_v < t_y)$. A retrieved history of feedbacks will be used to compute a risk using FA_{EX} algorithm. A truster concludes a trustee's trust value a s eq. (19).

$$T_{O_i^T \to vh_I}^{CO} = \xi T_{O_i^T \to vh_I}^{FA_{EX}} + \zeta T_{O_i^T \to vh_I}^{BT}, \quad \xi + \zeta = 1 \tag{19}$$

where $\zeta = e^{\frac{t_z - t_v}{\theta}}$ and θ is the largest time interval between two consecutive feedbacks from its mobile agents about this trustee.

6 Conclusion

This paper proposes a reputation-based trust model for a mobile agent system. It contains a new incentive-based timely feedback submission algorithm and a fair punishment scheme, which enforce truthful feedback submissions. We present a Bayesian Network based trust computing, its vulnerabilities and propose two algorithms for strategically malicious trustee prevention.

References

1. A. Whitby, A.Jøsang, J. Indulka. "Filtering out unfair Ratings in Bayesian Reputation Systems".The Icfain Journal of Management Research, 4(2), pp.48-64, February 2005
2. W.T. Luke Teacy, J. Patel, N. R. Jennings, M. Luck. "Coping with Inaccurate reputation Sources: Experimental Analysis of A Probabilistic Trust Model". AAMAS 2005
3. S. Marti, H. Garcia-Molina. "Taxonomy of Trust: Categorizing P2P reputation system" March 2005
4. T.D. Huynh,N.R. Jenning, N.R. Shadbolt. "On Handling Inaccurate Witness Report" Proc. 8th International Workshop on Trust in Agent Societies.
5. C. Dellarocas. "Mechanism for Coping with Unfair Ratings and Discriminatory behavior in Online Reputation Reporting systems". Int Conference on Information Systems 2000
6. M. Srivatsa, L. Xiong, L. Liu."TrustGuard: Countering Vulnerabilities in Reputation management for Decntralized Overlay Networks". WWW2005.
7. S. Buchegger, J.Y. Le Boudec. "The Effect of Rumor Sprading In Reputation Systems for Mobile Ad-hoc Networks". Wiopt 2003.
8. R. Jurca, B. Faltings. " Eliciting Truthful Feedback for Binary Reputation Mechanism" IEEE/WIC/ACM International Conference on Web Intelligence (WI'04).
9. Th. Dariotaki, A. Delis. " Detecting Reputation Variation in P2P Networks" The 6th Workshop on Distributed Data and Structures (WDAS'2004)
10. A. Fernandes,E. Kotsovinos, S. Ostring, B. Dragovic."Pinocchio: Incentives for honest participationin distributed trust management".itrust04
11. P. Obreiter, B. König-Ries, G. Papadopoulos." Engineering Incentive Schemes for Ad Hoc Networks". Proceedings of the EDBT Workshop on Pervasive Information Management, Heraklion, Greece, 18. March 2004
12. R. Jurca, B. Faltings. "An Incentive Compatible Reputation Mechanism". (CEC'03).
13. Q. He, D. Wu, P Khosla. "SORI A secure and Objective Reputation-based Incentive Scheme for Ad-hoc Networks". WCNC04.
14. T. J. Klein, C. Lambertz, G. Spagnolo, K. O. Stahl. " Last Minute Feedback". Discussion paper 2005. SFB/TR 15.
15. P. Obreitrt, J. Nimis.A Taxonomy Of Incentive Patterns- the Design Space of Incentives for Cooperation. Technical Repost Nr. 2003-9 University of Karlruhe
16. A. Jøsang, R. Ismail, and C. Boyd. A Survey of Trust and Reputation Systems for Online Service Provision (to appear). Decision Support Systems, 2006.
17. J. Pearl. " Probabilistic Reasoning in Intelligent system"
18. Z.Liang and W. Shi, "PET: A PErsonalized Trust Model with Reputation and Risk Evaluation for P2P Resource Sharing" HICSS05.
19. Y. Wang. "Bayesian Network –Based Trust Model in Peer-to Peer Networks". WI03.
20. L. Xiong, L. Liu. " PeerTrust: Supporting Reputation-Based Trust for Peer-to-Peer Electronic Community. IEEE Transaction on Knowledge and Data Engineering july 2004
21. B. Yu, M. P. Singh, k. Sycara. "Developing Trust in Large Scale Peer-to-Peer Systems".MASS04.
22. Patel, J., Teacy, W. T. L., Jennings, N. R. and Luck, M. (2005) "A Probabilistic Trust Model for Handling Inaccurate Reputation Sources". itrust05 pp. 193-209

Ubisafe Computing: Vision and Challenges (I)

Jianhua Ma[1], Qiangfu Zhao[2], Vipin Chaudhary[3], Jingde Cheng[4],
Laurence T. Yang[5], Runhe Huang[1], and Qun Jin[6]

[1] Hosei University, Tokyo 184-8584, Japan
[2] The University of Aizu, Fukushima 965-8580, Japan
[3] Wayne State University, MI - 48202, USA
[4] Saitama University, Saitama 338-8570, Japan
[5] St. Francis Xavier University, NS, B2G 2W5, Canada
[6] Waseda University, Saitama 359-1192, Japan
ubisafe@googlegroups.com

Abstract. In recent years, a variety of new computing paradigms have been proposed for various purposes. It is true that many of them intend to and really can gratify some of the people sometime, somewhere; a few of them can even gratify some of the people anytime, anywhere. However, at present, none of the computing paradigms intend to gratify all the people anytime, anywhere. With the rapid advance of information technology and the spread of information services, the IT disparity in age, social standing, and race of the people has been expanding and has become a critical social problem of the 21st century. Thus, we have a fundamental question: Can we construct, in a unified methodology, a computing environment that can gratify all the people in all situations, all places and all the time? We propose a novel and inclusive computing paradigm, named *ubisafe computing*, for studying and providing possible solutions to the above problem. The ultimate goal of ubisafe computing is to build a computing environment in which all people and organizations can benefit from ubiquitous services anytime anywhere with assured and desired satisfaction without worrying or thinking about safety. That is, the ubisafe computing vision emphasizes two basic aspects: ubiquitous safety and ubiquitous satisfaction to all people in all situations. This paper presents the motivations for the ubisafe computing vision but focuses on one basic aspect of ubiquitous safety that covers reliability, security, privacy, persistency, trust, risk, out of control, and other watchfulness while considering novel, essential ubicomp or percomp features of unobtrusive computers, diverse users/people and life-like systems.

1 Introduction

Computers are becoming available anytime and anywhere in many different forms. They are distributed ubiquitously, pervasively and unobtrusively throughout the every-day environments in forms of small or large, visible or invisible, attached or embedded or blended, simple or complex, and so on. Wired or wireless networks connect these computers locally or globally, coordinated or ad hoc, continuously or intermittently, etc. Ubiquitous computing and networking has created tremendous opportunities to provide numerous novel services and applications that are built in both real world and cyber spaces. We are working, learning, traveling, entertaining,

L.T. Yang et al. (Eds.): ATC 2006, LNCS 4158, pp. 386–397, 2006.

and doing almost everything with the help of computers. Increasingly, all of us will live in a real-cyber integrated world in which countless physical objects including human bodies will be armed with computers and networks.

Due to the excitement for this new real-cyber integrated world, ubicomp has recently received wide attention from researchers worldwide. Inspired by Weiser's ubicomp vision [1], many new computing paradigms have been proposed, such as pervasive [2], AmI [3], universal, embedded, wearable, invisible, hidden, context-aware [4], context-sensitive [5], sentient [6], proactive [7], autonomic [8], amorphous [9], spray [10], organic [11], persistent [12], or "whatever it is called" computing. Indeed, these new computing paradigms have pushed ubicomp research further by identifying some specific problems and emphasizing some special aspects in the ubiquitous computing world. Although the computing paradigms are for varying purposes with different focuses and approaches, they share a common *any-oriented* vision, i.e., ubiquitous computers as well as services anytime, anywhere and by any means.

Besides the any-oriented service vision, what else are commonly shared or lacked in these computing paradigms? It is apparent that they certainly share safety problems that are severe due to the ubiquitous presence of computers. Also, they share a general goal to offer novel services with some level of satisfaction to their users. Eventually ubiquitous computing will be extended to everyone, which, as a whole, has not been addressed thus far by these computing paradigms. The IT disparity in age, social standing, and race of the people has been expanding and has become a critical social problem of the 21st century. Ubicomp as well as the above computing paradigms address the provision of novel services by arming the computers with a variety of real objects and environments in the real world that is intrinsically rich, changing and uncertain. However, the complexity of various real situations has not been fully realized and studied [13].

Thus, we have a fundamental question: Can we construct, in a unified methodology, an any-oriented computing environment that can gratify all the people in all situations with (almost) perfect safety and satisfaction? To study and provide possible solutions to the above question, we propose a novel and inclusive computing paradigm, named *ubisafe computing,* based on the visions of *ubiquitous safety* and *ubiquitous satisfaction* to diverse people in complex situations. The ultimate goal of ubisafe computing is to build a computing environment in which all people and organizations can benefit from the any-oriented ubiquitous services with assured and desired satisfaction without worrying or thinking about safety.

Due to the broad applicability of ubisafe computing, this paper is focused primarily on one aspect of ubisafe vision: ubiquitous safety. Although computer and network safety has been studied for several decades, we still have several basic questions to answer: (1) Do we really understand all kinds of new risks in using novel computers/networks that are attached, embedded or blended into real objects and environments? (2) Do we really have efficient and effective solutions to precisely predict and further prevent the risks under various situations in the complex computing environment? (3) Can we create risk-less computing environments in which all people can really enjoy ubiquitous services without any anxiety about safety problems covering reliability, security, privacy, persistency, trust, disaster, out of control, and so on? A series of challenges exist to make ubiquitous safe artifacts, systems, and environments so as to let everyone benefit from ubiquitous services, and simultaneously guarantee their desired safety.

The rest of this article is organized as follows. The next section defines some basic concepts and terminologies used in this paper. In Section 3, we briefly review the state-of-art of safe/safety related computing technologies as well as corresponding fundamental characteristics, then discuss some essential changes and brand new features brought from the ubiquitous or pervasive computing trends, which necessarily call for broader vision for next generation safe computing. Section 4 presents several representative visions/scenarios for ubisafe computing in terms of safety and from different viewpoints. Section 5 further clarifies the safety related ubisafe concepts, and discusses the research challenges and issues towards the ubisafe vision. We conclude the paper in Section 6 with some final thoughts.

2 Definitions of Terminologies

To discuss the safe/safety problem in a unified way, we need a common language. In this section, we define some terminologies that will be used throughout this paper. The vocabulary given here is more safety related and by no means complete. It will be updated with the progress of ubisafe technology.

Since we are talking about ubiquitous computing environment(s), we first define the concept of *u-objects* (or *u-things*). Anything in a ubiquitous computing environment is a u-object, whether it is a human user, a computer, a computer network, a cell phone, a car navigation system, a sensor, or an RFID tag. We can classify the u-objects hierarchically. An un-decomposable u-object is called a *u-atom*, and a u-object made up from many u-atoms or smaller u-objects is called a *u-complex*. A u-complex can be used to build a larger u-complex.

The u-objects can be also categorized based on their functions. For example, a basic computing element is called a *u-element* or *u-artifact*, a computing system consisting of the basic elements is called a *u-system*, and the computing environment containing all u-elements, u-systems, and other related u-objects is called the *u-environment*. Note that these definitions are relative, because a u-system can be a u-element in a larger u-system. A u-environment can also be a u-system in a larger u-environment. A u-system or u-environment is a u-complex. A u-element may be a u-atom or a u-complex.

Since the human beings play an important and special role in a u-environment, we call a person involved in a u-environment/u-complex a *u-person*. Since a u-person cannot be decomposed, he/she is a u-atom, although he/she can be much larger in size than a cell-phone, which may be seen as a u-system/u-complex consisting of many smaller processors. Note that a u-person can be an ordinary user, a programmer, a system manager, or someone else. We say a u-person is *non-negative* if he/she does not attack other u-objects (include u-persons and u-systems). We can also define (although not absolutely necessary) strictly *positive u-persons* as those who never even think about attacking other u-objects and may probably be able to help others. In our common sense, non-negative u-persons are good persons. Similarly, *negative u-persons* are those who (sometimes, often or always) try to attack other u-objects. We can also define positive, non-negative and negative u-objects in a similar way.

A u-complex can be defined as a directed graph. Each node is a u-atom or a smaller u-complex. The nodes are related or connected by edges. The relation between two nodes can be passive (follow others' instruction) or active (take own action), positive (help) or negative (attack), steady (fixed) or dynamic (changed), and so on. Normally, all nodes in a u-complex should be non-negative or cooperative and there should be no negative relation between the nodes. In practice, however, we cannot expect that all nodes are reliable or trustable, especially when some nodes are u-persons or *life-like* agents as well as smart/intelligent u-things.

We say a u-object is *absolutely safe* if it does not have negative relation with any other u-objects in the same u-complex, or if it does not have any relation with any negative u-objects. For example, an absolutely safe u-person does not get attacked directly by any u-object. This u-person is surrounded by some kind of firewall, and all kinds of attacks/dangers are blocked and invisible. In practice, however, it is difficult to keep a u-object away from all kinds of attacks. We say a u-object is *relatively safe* or simply *safe* if it functions well even if there are some negative u-objects (or related to negative u-objects). A relatively safe u-object should have the ability to detect various attacks. When an attack is detected, this u-object can call some other anti-attack u-object(s) for help. An anti-attack u-object can be embedded into other u-objects, and can be used when needed.

Note that negative relation or negative u-objects is not the only source of risk. In many (or most) cases, the attack/dangers may come from the failure, mistake or trouble of a positive or non-negative u-object. This is why we must study reliability when we talk about safety since the two are closely related. We say a u-object is *reliable* if the quality of service provided by this u-object is acceptable to related u-objects in the same u-complex. A u-object is reliable only if it is safe. If it is not safe, it can be a troublemaker even if it is positive or non-negative. In fact, a u-object can be harmed or even damaged by its positively related u-objects. This can happen when the non-negative u-objects make some mistakes or have some trouble themselves. Thus, if a u-object strongly depends on some other non-negative u-objects, it is safe only if all these non-negative u-objects are reliable. We may say a reliable u-object is *trustable* to other u-objects only if it is non-negative and reliable. In this sense, most u-persons are not trustable. This is not because u-persons are negative, but because they often make mistakes, and thus they are not reliable in many situations.

In a u-environment, a reliable u-object should be able to provide services with high enough quality to other u-objects, anytime within the lifetime of the u-environment and anywhere in physical or virtual space spanned by the u-environment. For this purpose, a reliable u-object should not stop working during the lifetime of the u-environment. This is obviously too strong a requirement. In practice, we may just employ many u-objects to provide the same kind of services. These u-objects can work together in an asynchronous mode. Some can work, some can sleep, and some can even die. This is called fault tolerance in reliability engineering. It is actually a simple idea borrowed from nature. The question is: how to build a u-system that is reliable as a whole from un-reliable and un-safe u-elements under uncertain situations?

The above u-things related definitions and discussions are the base for depicting our ubisafe vision and presenting some ideas to achieve the ubisafe computing environment. But before that, let us first give an overview of existing representative computing techniques as well as their trends and novel features in the next section. These techniques appear somewhat disparate but actually share many things in common, although they are called by different names and proposed and studied by different communities or groups.

3   Computing Trends and Profound Novel Features

Safe/safety related computing is not new and has been studied in various computer and computer-based systems for decades. It is related to many technical aspects such as reliability, security, fault tolerance, survivable computing, dependable computing and so on. Some non-technical aspects covering social and human factors have also been studied.

Trusted/trustworthy computing (TC) [14] recently garnered great attention and is intending to build a unified framework or general computing paradigm to cover or integrate various safety related aspects including security, privacy, reliability, risk, reputation, and so on. The United States Department of Defense has defined that a trusted system or component is one that can break the security policy. In fact, as discussed in the last section, a trusted u-object may be the most dangerous source to result in very serious or fatal security problem in a u-environment, in case the trusted u-object is not really reliable.

Trust is indeed very important and greatly expected especially in cooperation among hardware, software, services, etc. In our life experience, trust is only one of the key elements in cooperative processes. The cooperation is just one relationship between entities in the real world. Actually there are many other relationships, such as loosely coupled, mutual use, non-cooperation, competition, fight, and so on. No matter what relationships exist, what users often desire is that they can get things done satisfactorily and safely.

It is a fact that computers and networks have permeated more places and areas in the real world and our life. Thus, the computing environments and features are changing continuously. The computing technology has to accordingly evolve to fit the new environments and features. To predict the next possible computing evolutionary direction or stage must be, therefore, to first identify fundamental changes of computing environment and then find out basic features brought due to the trends of ubiquitous/pervasive computing. In terms of safety impacts, the following three profound features are considered the most essential.

A. Unobtrusive computers attached/embedded/blended to real objects/ environments

The computing systems (the u-systems) are developing in two extreme directions. One is to become bigger, so that the whole world can be covered. The other is to become smaller, so that ordinary u-persons are even not aware of their existence in surroundings. Talking about the latter, nowadays various kinds of computing chips/devices for information acquisition, storage, processing and communication, have become so small that they can be attached/embedded/blended (AEB) to real physical objects and environments. Such AEB computers are often unobtrusive and even invisible. These computers are parts of real object (artifacts, instruments, goods, etc.) to enhance their usages with adding some kinds of information functions. Due to the small size and power consumption restriction, an AEB computer may have low CPU speed with very limited ROM/RAM and short communication distance. Thus, one AEB computer may be functioned only in a single simple or very limited task, and many of the AEB computers can be interconnected via networks and organized together to complete a large u-complex or high-level u-system. These u-systems will eventually be pervasive in real physical environments of the world. In this sense, the AEB computers are true u-objects, and they are making u-systems truly ubiquitous.

Perhaps the first of the most fundamental factors related to safe/ubisafe in terms of the ubiquity or pervasiveness of the unobtrusive computers is from *physical characteristic oriented* aspects since the u-objects (the AEB computers) would be in environments that may be open, changed, or leading to worse conditions, etc. Let us take some examples. (1) Suppose the working conditions of some u-objects are not good (such as being outside and suffering sunshine, rain and so on), the u-objects may sometimes not work normally or even fail with a high probability. How to quickly detect the anomaly/failure and then take proper actions to make the whole u-system and/or associated u-persons still safe? The hardware redundancy is one of the fault tolerant approaches to improve system reliability. The point is: What is a suitable redundant method to put these various u-objects together, and form a well-organized or even self-organized reliable u-system? (2) Suppose the u-objects are in some open space (indoor or outdoor) in which some people harboring malicious intent can also enter. They may possibly communicate with the u-objects, move/steal/damage them, or put some bad-intent u-objects in the same u-environment. How to guarantee that the system is working correctly/safely/reliably as well as serving true user privacy under such unavoidable malicious behaviors? (3) Generally, the strength of a cryptographic algorithm is related to its complexity, which needs more computations. Due to physical restrictions of size and energy, the computational and communicational resources of AEB computers are often very limited, and thus it is unfeasible to adopt very complex security schemes and protocols. The problem is how to use the limited computing resources to provide enough security/safety protection in a barely controllable u-environment?

B. Diverse users covering all (ubiquitous) people with different features/demands

Computers and their corresponding environments were originally designed for experts, later extended to technical people and now to ordinary people who posses or can gain certain knowledge about computer usages. One of the profound changes for AEB computers is that they are integrated into real things to form u-objects to serve various u-persons including very young children and even babies who have no computer related knowledge at all. That is, the u-persons are to be eventually extended to all people including babies, school children, aged people, disabled persons, men and women who have different professions, etc. However, the usages of AEB computers will be totally different from the conventional ones such as PCs, and the u-objects will be used by u-persons consciously or unconsciously. A person, whether he/she likes or dislikes, may not be able to escape completely from with the presence of computers since the u-objects are becoming ubiquitous in the real ambient environments surrounding us.

Perhaps the second most fundamental factor related to safe/ubisafe in terms of the ubiquity of various users is from *human characteristic oriented* aspects. It has been realized that a very large proportion of safety incidents in IT related systems is caused by human mistakes or incorrect usages. An example is the recently publicized incident where a stock staff's mistaken data input led to huge money loss. The incorrect usages would become very common in a u-environment since some kinds of u-persons may have no computer knowledge at all, no intention to follow the pre-defined usage instructions, no awareness of possible dangers approaching, no ability to deal with occurring dangers, and so on. In addition, whether a circumstance is safe or not is relative, varied, and greatly dependent upon the associated people's situations and backgrounds such as ages, states, needs, etc. How to generally describe the complex scenarios of safety and correctly judge concrete safe/unsafe situations is really hard due to the relative and varied safety demands of diverse humans and their characteristics.

C. Life-like systems, i.e., smart/intelligent u-things from small to large scales

Most traditional computers such as conventional PCs and PDAs, although with many functions, are relatively *passive*. They often wait for the users' inputs, take some actions, and send outputs to the users. They usually have no information about users' physical situations and social statuses as well as ambient states. In contrast, the u-systems are becoming relatively *active* by sensing users and/or physical environments and possibly taking some autonomous actions according to the sensed information. Such active character is an outcome of the following three features of the u-systems: (1) computers are too small to be visible when they are attached/embedded/blended in u-objects; (2) too many computers exist to be interact-able simultaneously by a human user; (3) computer systems are too complex to be managed by human users especially for non-technical people. It is expected that the active u-objects may possess some *smart* behaviors, such as context-aware, reactive, proactive, adaptive, automated, autonomic, organic, sentient, perceptual, cognitive, thinking, or intelligent. The u-systems with the above behaviors seem becoming *life-like* systems. A large scale u-systems may include many small scale u-elements and other u-objects, all of which may form various kinds of relationships, passive or active, positive or negative, loosely or tightly, static or dynamic, locally or globally, etc.

Perhaps the third most fundamental factor related to safe/ubisafe in terms of the ubiquity of active/smart u-systems is from *life-like system characteristic oriented* aspects. Being life-like, a u-system should be able to sense necessary information, *i.e.*, so-called contexts. However, the sensed contexts are usually some approximations to states of the real environment surrounding a u-system because the real world is constantly changing, intrinsically uncertain, and infinitely rich. Therefore, the contextual information acquired may not be sufficient and precise enough to characterize a real environment. Due to the incomplete and uncertain contexts, it would be not rare for u-systems to have misjudgments and incorrect decisions, which may probably result in un-safety of their users (other u-objects or u-persons). It is also expected that u-systems can somehow understand their users' needs. The question is how much can be expected to correctly and promptly know the users' true needs? Detecting users' physical states and activities is one thing, while knowing users' needs is a much harder task. When a u-system involves many associated u-objects and u-persons, an event occurring in one u-object may generate a sequence of cascaded events or consequences to others. How to know if a small local event initiated by something will make other things or even the whole system unsafe?

It can be seen from the above that AEB computers and networks based u-systems have to face many fundamental and hard issues that are novel but crucial to build ubiquitous safe computing environments to offer ubiquitous safe services to all people, at all places, at all times, and under all situations. These call for radically re-thinking safety related computing, and natural emergence of ubisafe computing.

4   Ubisafe Vision Related to Ubiquitous Safety

One of main purposes of ubisafe computing is to provide a unified solution for solving various safety problems related to all kinds of u-objects. In the last section, we discussed three fundamental safety-related factors and some new unsafe sources faced by tiny u-objects, by u-systems built from these tiny u-objects, by global u-systems, by life-like systems, and so on. There will be infinitely many issues if we consider the safety problems faced by all kinds of u-objects. Thus, instead of talking about specific u-objects, we talk about the safety problem using a general language in this section.

First of all, the ultimate goal of ubisafe computing is to build a u-environment in which any u-person, an ordinary user, a programmer, a system manager, or others, can get satisfactory services safely anytime and anywhere in any situations. Other non-human u-objects should also be safe in order to guarantee the safety of u-persons. However, as will be discussed latter, some u-objects should be in un-safe states/positions so as to provide a safe environment to guarantee the safety of u-persons. Ideally, we should provide a u-environment in which all *u-persons* are *absolutely safe*. From the definition of Section 2, a u-person is absolutely safe if it is not directly related to any negative u-objects. That is, all kinds of attacks or risks are (should be) invisible to an absolutely safe u-person. When all u-objects in a u-environment are both non-negative and reliable (thus trustable), there will be no risks and attacks. This kind of u-environment is *an extremely ideal vision for ubisafe.*

However, in practice, some of the u-objects are neither non-negative nor reliable. Most u-persons are non-negative but not reliable. A non-negative u-person can also "attack" other u-objects and make trouble due to their mistakes (although he/she is a good person, and does not intend to hurt others). The risks/attacks may come from negative u-persons or u-objects; they can also come from a u-person him/herself. Thus, to guarantee the absolute safety of all u-persons, we must have a specialized u-systems to detect, prevent, and avoid the risks/attacks. For these u-systems, the risks/attacks should be visible, observable, predictable, and counter-able. Thus, *a modified vision for ubisafe* is as follows. The goal is to build some anti-risk/attack u-systems in the u-environment that are so powerful that any u-person can be isolated from risks/attacks from outside; and all kinds of risks/attacks from a u-person him/herself can be predicted and prevented. In this u-environment, all u-persons can receive guaranteed safe services anytime, anywhere, and do not have to think about the safety problem at all.

This poses another question: shall we trust the anti-risk/attack u-systems completely? The answer unfortunately is NO. In fact, no system (existing one or to be developed) can predicate and detect all kinds of risks/attacks produced by many different u-objects. The most powerful computer systems employed in some of the largest banks cannot even predict some trivial mistakes made by some users. Although an anti risk/attack u-system may make mistakes with a low probability, the cost or consequence as the result of the mistake might be very high or serious. Thus, to make a safe u-environment, it is not a good idea to make just a few giant anti-risk/attack u-systems. It might be better to distribute the risks to many u-objects. In this case, it is inevitable that some of the u-objects related to a u-person are not absolutely safe. If so, neither will the u-person be absolutely safe. Thus, instead of requiring absolute safety, we should build a u-environment in which all u-persons are relatively safe, *i.e.*, getting requested safety level of service. *This is a more practical vision for ubisafe.*

To make all u-persons in a u-environment relatively safe, it is necessary to embed some small-scale risk/attack detection/warning u-systems into the u-objects that are connected or related to each u-person. These small-scale u-systems serve as some of kind of firewalls, and they are not powerful enough to make all kinds of risks/attacks invisible, but should at least be able to detect the risks/attacks. Proper actions can be taken by more powerful u-systems whenever necessary. Note that it is impossible and not necessary to guarantee the safety of all u-objects. If we want to guarantee the safety of u-persons, some u-objects must be un-safe. That is, in order to isolate u-persons from attacks, some u-objects must receive the attacks, and they may face dangers all the time.

In the above discussion we highlighted some vision for ubisafe in terms of safety. The most practical one is to guarantee the relative safety of all u-persons in the u-environment. So far we have not considered the specific risks or attacks faced by a u-person. To make the discussion more concrete, we present some scenarios.

In most cases a u-person is an ordinary user. Let us take a scenario in which a u-system is a health-care system, the u-person is a patient with, say heart disease. In a ubisafe u-environment, the u-system should monitor the u-person anytime and anywhere, so that whenever his/her condition changes, proper advice/instruction/action can be provided. Here, the risk mainly comes from the u-person himself (even if there is no attack from other u-objects). What we meant by ubisafe computing is to provide an infrastructure in which the u-person can get high quality safety service anytime and anywhere. That is, the related u-system should be available anytime and anywhere and it should not stop working anytime.

A similar scenario is the kids-care system. Here, the u-persons are young kids, say less than 10 years old. The risks may come from the kids themselves due to inappropriate actions (*e.g.* trying to jump down from a high place or go across a road with heavy traffic); or come from negative u-persons (*e.g.* people who want to kidnap the kids). The u-system should be able to monitor the kids anytime anywhere, and take proper actions or give proper instructions to protect the kids.

Another simpler scenario is the case when the u-system is a home computer, and the u-person is a human user. There are many possible risks and attacks. The person may play Internet game for too long, and get tired or sick; the personal information might be observed by some other u-objects through spy-ware; the password of his bank account might be stolen by some fishing email; and so on. Ubisafe computing should provide some way to protect the u-persons as well as their privacy/properties.

Besides the above scenarios, there are many situations in which various safety-related problems are important and fatal. Imagining that the safety-critical systems, such as the traffic systems, the flight control systems, the power plant, the financial system, and so on, are all controlled by computers, what will happen if some of them are attacked by some negative u-objects? What will happen if the attack comes from the mistakes of a positive u-person? As described in the last section, since the u-objects are becoming smaller in one extreme, and the u-systems are becoming larger in another, it is becoming difficult to have everything under control.

5 Ubisafe Computing Issues and Challenges

Now let us talk about some technical issues related to ubisafe computing, mainly from safety aspects. In fact, the most important thing is to detect the risk/attack. In the case of heart disease, we can understand the change of the patient's condition using some sensors, and the sensor outputs can be obtained via wired or wireless communications. This is relatively easy. In the case of kids-care, however, this is very difficult. How can we know a kid is going to jump from a high place? In the case of home computer, how can we know the user is too tired and should rest? Some risks look trivial but they are actually very hard to detect by computing machines. Some artificial intelligent (AI) and soft computing techniques are useful, but it seems inadequate to solve these kinds of challenging problems related to real daily life.

Another challenge is that, how can we detect new risks/attacks? A simple example is to detect a virus and kill it from the computer. Usually, we can remember all virus patterns, and can detect a virus through pattern matching. However, this method cannot prevent new viruses from infecting our computers. Thus, before killing the virus, our computers must be infected first. One approach to solve this problem is to learn from the immune system of our bodies. The basic idea is to produce some small risks or weak attacks, and distribute them to all u-objects. These risks/attacks serve as the vaccine and the u-objects, especially the anti risk/attack u-systems can learn from them and improve their immune system. The questions are: How to produce the vaccines and how to improve the immune system? These questions are related to artificial evolution (AE) computation, or biological computing in general.

To offer ubiquitous services, it is necessary to acquire contextual information ubiquitously from the ambient and surroundings, both in physical and cyber worlds. As mentioned in Section 3, the AEB computers can serve both as data collectors and processors. However, since they are not so capable, we must have some mechanism to integrate the information. There can be two approaches. First, we can just transmit the results (after some limited pre-processing) of many AEB computers to a relatively large-scale host computer, and ask the host computer to make the final decision. As mentioned before, this kind of centralized, giant-system approach can have serious safety problems. The second approach is a distributed approach, in which all AEB computers are used to construct a network, and this network can make decisions directly. To allow quick decisions and reactions, the AEB computer network should be decomposable, so that each part (or any part) can be autonomous, and can make decisions based on local information. This is a self-symmetric network, in which each part (any part) is again a complete system that can make decisions. Results obtained from cellular automaton (CA) might be helpful to build up such a network. Further, since many nodes (a node is an AEB computers or a collection of AEB computers) of the network may provide incorrect results (due to limited processing capability) or may not provide any information at all (due to some kind of failures), the network should be able to make decisions based on incomplete and ambiguous information.

In practice, the network considered above can be a hybrid of many different computers. The construction of this kind of heterogeneous and asynchronous systems might be easy (just put some kind of computer somewhere in the u-environment); their control, management, and maintenance can be a very hard task. This is another challenge for ubisafe computing. The point is, even if each node or each sub-network may change during the lifetime of the network, the network as a whole should be safe, and should be able to provide high quality services to all its users. These issues are also addressed in security computing, non-stop computing, persistence computing, autonomic computing, organic computing, amorphous computing, and so on.

There are lots of challenges to create such expected ubisafe environments. Many new issues and hard challenges are basically from the three essential ubicomp/percomp features: unobtrusive AEB computers, diverse people and life-like u-things. The most fundamental and urgent research is to study all possible unsafe sources of various u-objects from the three aspects of physical, human and life characteristics. The safety related issues become harder when the above three aspects are interwoven with the diversity and complexity of the real world. Ubisafe, or "you-be-safe" or "all-be-safe", is ideal. How about the two fighting sides in a military battle? Here ubisafe becomes "you be unsafe, I am safe". Most people in the world are good but bad persons are not few and they can also use the ubisafe technologies/ environments to do bad things. It is absolutely necessary to study how to prevent malicious uses of the ubisafe technologies to do bad/criminal acts "safely". It would not be enough to only rely on engineering technologies to fully guarantee all safety in the ubiquitous world, which is certainly needed to combine social forces including law, regulation, ethics, and so on, but these are beyond our engineering research.

6 Concluding Remarks

In this paper, we have tried to present the vision for ubisafe computing mainly from safety aspects, although it is very difficult to do so due to both novelty and complexity of the ubisafe concept. Through the discussions presented in this paper, we should at least agree with the following points. First, a unified theory or methodology is needed for systematically solving a variety of conventional and new safety problems faced by different u-objects. Second, the safety guarantee (although relatively) should be offered to all (non-negative) u-persons no matter what the age, sex, race, profession, culture, preference and so on. Third, the study of ubisafe computing itself may motivate some revolutionary progresses in computing technology. We hope that in the not far future, all persons can become (non-negative) u-persons, and all of them can fully enjoy the u-environment provided by ubisafe computing – without talking about the safety problem any more. This is similar to invisible computers that disappear from human eyes as dreamed by Mark Weiser. We are working on the ubiquitous satisfaction aspect of ubisafe vision, which would be more challenging.

Acknowledgements. Dr. Ismail K. Ibrahim and Dr. Thomas Grill were involved in our early discussions on the ubisafe computing vision which the authors greatly appreciate. We would also like to thank Dr. Frank Hsu, Dr. Zhong Chen, Dr. Bernady Apduhan, Dr. Joseph Landman, and Dr. Qing Li for the helpful discussions on ubisafe concepts, terms, problems, issues, etc.

References

1. Weiser, M.: The Computer for the Twenty-First Century. Scientific American, September (1991) 94-104
2. Satyanarayanan, M.: Pervasive Computing: Vision and Challenges. IEEE Personal Communications, August (2001) 10-17
3. The European Union Report on AmI: Scenarios for Ambient Intelligence in 2010. ftp://ftp.cordis.lu/pub/ist/docs/istagscenarios2010.pdf (2001)
4. Shchilit, B.N., Adams, N., Want, R.: Context Aware Computing Applications. Proc. of Workshop on Mobile Computing, Systems and Applications, CA, December (1994)
5. Yau, S., Karim, F., Wang Y., Wang B., Gupta, S.K.S.: Reconfigurable Context-Sensitive Middleware for Pervasive Computing. IEEE Pervasive Computing, 1(3) (2002) 33-40
6. Addlesee, M., Curwen, R.W., Hodges, S., Newman, J., Steggles, P., Ward, A., Hopper, A.: Implementing a Sentient Computing System, IEEE Computer. Vol. 34, No. 8 (2001) 50-56
7. Tennenhouse, D.L.: Proactive Computing. Communications of ACM, 43(5) (2000) 43-50
8. Kephart, J.O., Chess, D.M.: The Vision of Autonomic Computing. IEEE Computer, Vol. 36, No. 1, January (2003) 41-50
9. Abelson, H., Allen, D., Coore, D., Hanson, C., Rauch, E., Sussman, G.H., Weiss, R.: Amorphous Computing. Communications of the ACM 43, No. 5 (2000) 74-82
10. Mamei, M., Zambonelli, F.: Spray Computers: Frontiers of Self-organization for Pervasive Computing. 3rd Italian Workshop From Objects to Agents, September (2003)
11. Müller-Schloer, C.: Organic Computing – On the Feasibility of Controlled Emergence. Proceedings of CODES + ISSS, ACM Press, September (2004) 2-5
12. Cheng, J.: Persistent Computing Systems as Continuously Available, Reliable, and Secure Systems. Proceedings of 1st International Conference on Availability, Reliability and Security, IEEE Computer Society Press, April (2006) 631-638
13. Ma, J.: Smart u-Things – Challenging Real World Complexity. IPSJ Symposium Series, Vol. 2005, No. 19 (2005) 146-150
14. Mundie, C., de Vries P., Haynes, P., Corwine, M.: Trustworthy Computing. http://www.microsoft.com/mscorp/twc/twc_whitepaper.mspx (2002)

Source Authentication of Media Streaming
Based on Chains of Iso-hash Clusters⋆

Zhitang Li, Weidong Wang, Yejiang Zhang, and Weiming Li

College of Computer Science and Technology
Huazhong University of Science and Technology, Wuhan, 430074, China
{leeying, wangwd}@hust.edu.cn

Abstract. We propose an efficient multicast source authentication protocol called Chains of Iso-hash Clusters scheme (**CIC**), which shows more lossy resistibility, less communication cost, less average delay at receivers. The **CIC** scheme is based on combination of single Chain scheme and Hash Tree Chains scheme, and integrates the advantages of both. In this scheme, stream is firstly divided into blocks with n packets, and each block consists of m clusters, everyone of which contains a tree of packets. All clusters are chained together. Through **CIC**, packets of one cluster can be authenticated by any packet of the previous cluster. Compared to other multicast authentication protocols, the proposed scheme has the following advantages: 1) dramatically improves the resistance to burst packets loss, 2) low computation and communication overhead, 3) imposes low delay on the sender side and no delay on the receiver side, assuming no loss occurs.

1 Introduction

Data confidentiality, authenticity, integrity, and non-repudiation are basic concerns of securing data delivery over an insecure network, such as the Internet [1][2]. Our concerns are data authenticity, integrity and non-repudiation for delay-sensitive packet flows, particularly flows transferred on application-level multicast. To assure non-repudiation of a multicast stream origin, flows should be signed.

In multicast communication, two types of communication exist: pre-recorded and real-time data. In pre-recorded data, the content is known in advance, such as films. On the other hand, for real-time data, the content is produced in real-time, such as financial stock quotes. In the present paper, an effective scheme for authenticating pre-recorded data applications is proposed which overcomes burst loss and long-run loss with a low communication overhead.

Current digital signature mechanisms are very computationally expensive. Therefore, it is not practical to sign each packet of the multicast stream. Some proposals amortize signature over several packets for providing multicast authentication [3]. However, these signature amortization schemes don't focus on resisting packet loss, especially on resisting burst loss.

⋆ This work is supported by National Science Foundation of China under grant No.605731120.

L.T. Yang et al. (Eds.): ATC 2006, LNCS 4158, pp. 398–407, 2006.

For multicast, packets loss can not be avoided, due to that TCP/IP is based on best-effort service. Some solutions proposed introduce redundancy in the authentication information, in a way that even if some packets are lost, the required authentication information can be recovered in order to verify received packets' authenticity [2][4][5][7][8][9][10]. But the proposals are inapplicable for P2P media streaming.

In application-level multicast system, a stream is exchanged by lots of peers over an insecure overlay network. The vicious peers should be detected and restricted. So peers must forward only "good" data to other peers. In P2P topology, verification latency at receivers and verification probability are key factors which affect scalability of multicast system. We pay more attention to the following three requirements: loss tolerance, less average latency at receivers, less communication overhead. We highlight that authenticity of every packet must be verified, which will be transferred to other peers.

We propose a novel scheme called Chains of Iso-hash Clusters scheme (**CIC**), which is based on combination of single Chain scheme and Hash Tree Chains scheme. Delay at receiver side can be decreased using signature tree technology and communication overhead can be decreased due to signature chain technology. Compared to other multicast authentication protocols, the proposed scheme has the following advantages: 1) dramatically improves the resistance to burst packets loss, 2) low computation and communication overhead, 3) imposes low delay on the sender side and no delay on the receiver side, assuming no loss occurs.

In the next section, we give a brief overview of the previous work about multicast message authentication. The basic solution for our approach, along with the detailed authentication/verification procedure, is given in Section 3. In Section 4, we discuss the authentication probability and average latency of our scheme using two different loss models. In Section 5, we evaluate the performance of our technique, comparing it with three previous proposed schemes. Finally, the paper is concluded in the last section.

2   Related Work

Multicast authentication is an active area of research, and researchers have suggested many schemes. Early work about amortizing signature over several packets was done by Gennaro and Rohatgi [3]. The stream is divided into blocks of m packets and a chain of hashes is used to link each packet one by one. The hash of the last packet is signed. Each receiver must buffer all of m packets and the signature packet, then checks the signature of the sender and uses the chain of hashes to authenticate subsequent packets. Although this approach solves the computation and communication overhead problem, it has a major drawback that, in case of any packet loss, the authentication chain is broken and subsequent packets cannot be authenticated.

Efficient multi-chained stream signature (EMSS), which was proposed by Perrig et al. [4][7], is an extension of Gennaro and Rohatgi's stream signing technique

[3]. The basic idea is that multiple hashes with each packet are sent to tolerate packet loss. Other similar proposals were proposed in [8][9]. EMSS stores same number of hashes in packets (besides the tail of chains), while augmented chain [8] is combination of hash chains scheme and hash list scheme. The latter achieves higher verification probabilities compared to EMSS (with the same communication overhead) at the cost of increased delay on the sender side. Piggybacking scheme [9], is specifically designed to resist multiple bursts within a block. In the scheme, n packets are partitioned into r equal-sized priority classes, and hence each class is of size $z = n/r$. It is assumed that the packets in the highest priority class are spaced evenly throughout the block, so that, two consecutive packets of the highest priority class are located exactly r packets apart. By constructing hash chains in the special manner, packet P_i can tolerate x_i bursts of size at most $b_i = k_i * r$. Our scheme is also similar to these multi-hash chains schemes, but more efficiently to resist packets loss.

Wong and Lam [2] proposed another solution to solve the problem of packet loss. In their proposal, the stream is divided into blocks of m packets and a tree of hashes of degree 2 is constructed. The hashes of the m packets correspond to the leaves of the tree and only the root of the tree needs to be signed. Each parent corresponds to the hash of its children. Since each packet carries the information required for its authentication, any packet loss will not affect the ability of the receiver to authenticate packets arrived after the loss. On the other hand, this solution suffers from a high communication overhead, since it requires the appending of log_2^m hashes to each packet. We benefit from this option to resist bursty packets loss and to reduce authentication delay at receivers.

SAIDA [10] was proposed by Jung et al., which is to encode the hash values list and the signatures with Rabin's Information Dispersal Algorithm (IDA) to construct an authentication scheme that amortizes a single signature operation over multiple packets. This strategy is especially efficient in terms of space overhead, because just the essential elements needed for authentication (i.e, one hash per packet and one signature per group of packets) are used in conjunction with an erasure code that is space optimal. The scheme efficiently solves the problem about signature information's reliable transmissions, which is other schemes' weakness. But SAIDA increases total delay on the sender side and on receiver side.

3   Proposed Solution

3.1   CIC (Chains of Iso-hash Clusters)

We focus on a probabilistic model of packet loss within the network. According to several studies [6], packet loss on the Internet is often bursty in nature. We propose a novel way to process burst loss.

The following steps describe the authentication procedure in detail:

1) Let $||$ denote concatenation. A stream of packets is first divided into blocks. We denote a stream as $B = B_1||B_2||\ldots$, and B_i is a block which includes n

packets (i.e, $B_i = M_{(i-1)n}||\cdots||M_{in-1}$). The same operations are performed on every group, so we will only focus on the first group.

2) We divide each block into strips, we call the strips clusters, whose size is powers of 2. We denote $B = (C_1, C_2, \ldots, C_m)$, $m = n/c$, $c = 2^k$, $k \in (1, 2, \ldots, \log_2^n)$, and C_i includes c packets(i.e., $C_i = (M_1^{(i)}, M_2^{(i)}, \ldots, M_c^{(i)})$). As shown in Fig. 1, same cluster's packets are evenly distributed over whole block.

3) We denote $D^{(i)}$ as digest of hashes of cluster C_i. We first compute $D^{(m)}$, then compute other $D^{(i)}$ with sequence of $(D^{(m-1)}, D^{(m-2)}, \ldots, D^{(1)})$. As shown in Fig. 1, the steps to compute $D^{(i)}$ follow below($k = 3, c = 8$):

a) $D_j^{(i)} = \begin{cases} h(M_j^{(i)}) & i = m \\ h(M_j^{(i)}||D^{(i+1)}) & i < m \end{cases}$

b) $D_{1-2}^{(i)} = h(D_1^{(i)}||D_2^{(i)}); D_{3-4}^{(i)} = h(D_3^{(i)}||D_4^{(i)}); \cdots$

c) $D_{1-4}^{(i)} = h(D_{1-2}^{(i)}||D_{3-4}^{(i)}); D_{5-8}^{(i)} = h(D_{5-6}^{(i)}||D_{7-8}^{(i)})$

d) $D^{(i)} = D_{1-8}^{(i)} = h(D_{1-4}^{(i)}||D_{5-8}^{(i)});$

4) As shown in Fig. 1, for every block, C_1 is the first cluster, and C_m is the last cluster. $D^{(1)}$ is signed by an asymmetric-key signature scheme using the sender's private key.

5) Each packet needs to carry 1+k hashes, one is for $D^{(i+1)}$ while other k is for siblings' digests. For example, $P_5^{(i)}$ includes following sequence: $M_5^{(i)}$, $D^{(i+1)}$, $D_6^{(i)}$, $D_{7-8}^{(i)}$, $D_{1-4}^{(i)}$.

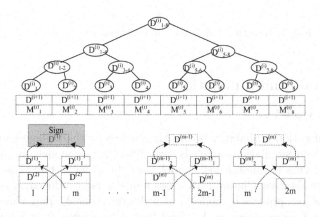

Fig. 1. Up:Constructing Digest of Cluster i($D^{(i)}$) with c=8. Down:Constructing Chains of Hash Clusters with c=2.

We assume that signature information is received, $D^{(1)}$ can be decoded, and authentications of packets belong to C_1 can be immediately verified. Each packet of C_1 carries $D^{(2)}$, so we get trusted $D^{(2)}$, and so on. A Hash Buffer (HB) for $D^{(i)}$ is introduced to our implement due to convenience of verification. On receiving a packet, 3 steps of verification will be employed are stated below (assume $P_5^{(i)}$ is received):

a) Compute $D'^{(i)} = h(D_{1-4}^{(i)}||h(h(h(h(M_5^{(i)}||D^{(i+1)})||D_6^{(i)})||D_{7-8}^{(i)}));$

b) Check if $D'^{(i)} = D^{(i)}$ in *HB*. If it is true, the received packet is authenticated.

c) If $D^{(i+1)}$ does not exist in *HB*, get $D^{(i+1)}$ from the packet and add it to *HB*.

3.2   Resisting Loss

In a scheme constructed as in Sections 3.1, these are two parameters associated with each packet $P_j^{(i)}$: the max size of bursts that $P_j^{(i)}$ can tolerate(b), and long-run loss rate(p). As shown in Fig. 2, $c=2$, $n=2m$, $b=n-n/c=m$. Even if continuing m packets, assuming from 2 to m+1, the remained m packets (1, m+2,...,2m) can be verified. For any loss model, including multi-burst loss model, if n is large enough, only long-run loss rate is our concern.

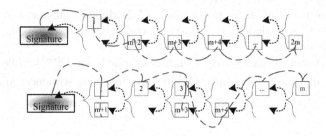

Fig. 2. Resisting bursty loss and random loss (n=2m,c=2)

4   Analysis and Simulations

4.1   Loss Model

The authentication probability is directly affected by the loss model used in the analysis. In our simulations analysis, two different loss models are used to test our scheme. One is random loss model, and the other is burst loss model. In [10], a 2-state Markov Chain (2-MC) loss model was introduced. It is defined as follows: The loss process is modeled as a discrete-time Markov chain with two states-0 and 1-representing no loss and loss, respectively. It is defined by four transition probabilities (i.e. p_{00}, p_{11}, p_{01}, and p_{10}). The stationary probabilities (the long-run proportion of transitions in a given state) are denoted as π_0 and $\pi_1 = 1 - \pi_0$. The expected burst-loss length , and probability of loss q can be expressed using the four parameters of the Markov chain. The four transition probabilities can be expressed using β, π_0 and π_1 as follows:

$$p_{10} = 1/\beta, p_{01} = \pi_1/(\beta\pi_0), p_{11} = 1 - 1/(\beta), p_{00} = 1 - \pi_1/(\beta\pi_0).$$

As burst loss model, the 2-MC loss model is uesd in our simulations. We call the 2-MC loss model as MC for convenience.

4.2   Verification Probability

We denote $P_j^{(i)}$ as packet j of C_i. If $P_j^{(i)}$ is received without authentication, then none packet of $C_{(i-1)}$ is received or $C_{(i-1)}$ cannot be authenticated. Only if all packets of one cluster lose, the chains of iso-hash clusters will break. So **CIC** is similar to single chain of hashes. There are two basic differences comparing with single chain of hashes:

1) Probability of $D^{(i)}$ loss is very low, which is p^c.

2) Length of chains is n/c. For single chain of hashes, the average probability that P_i is received and authenticated is:

$$P_r = 1 - \frac{\sum_{i=0}^{n-1} p(1-p)^i(n-1-i)(1-p)}{n(1-p)} = 1 - \frac{\sum_{i=0}^{n-1} p(1-p)^i(n-1-i)}{n}.$$
(1)

For **CIC** scheme, the probability is:

$$P_r = 1 - \frac{\sum_{i=0}^{n/c-1} p^c(1-p^c)^i(n/c-1-i)}{n/c}.$$
(2)

Because $p^c \geq 0$, $1 \geq 1 - p^c \geq 0$, we can get:

$$P_r \geq 1 - p^c \frac{\sum_{i=0}^{n/c-1}(n/c-1-i)}{n/c} = 1 - \frac{1}{2}(\frac{n}{c}-1)p^c.$$
(3)

Substitute 2^k for c in (3),

$$P_r \geq 1 - \frac{1}{2}(\frac{n}{2^k}-1)p^{2^k}.$$
(4)

When $k = \log_2^n$, $P_r = 1$, **CIC** is equivalent to Hash Tree; when k=0, $P_r \geq= 1 - \frac{1}{2}(n-1)p$, **CIC** is equivalent to single hash chain. With k increasing, P_r is not sensitive with n. For example, when $k=4$, $p=0.20$, $P_r > 0.99$, we can get $n < 48,000,000,000$.

According to (4), Table 1 lists some parameters when P_r is more than 0.99.

Instead of computing the probability precisely, we wrote a program to perform simulations. Our simulation (with 5000 samples simulating different loss rate, 0.005-0.64) runs on 3 case: k=1,2,3, with random model and MC model. The following simulation parameters were used:

1) Block size (n): 128 packets

2) Average length of burst loss (β): 8 packets (for MC model)

We also computed analytical result according to (2). As shown in Fig. 3(**Left**), the empirical results (random loss model) are similar to computed results. Moreover, the verification probability running on MC model is higher than the result running on random model.

In Fig. 3(**Right**), we show the verification probability (i.e., the fraction of verifiable packets) on different burst length (from 0.625 to 12.625) with c=4,

Table 1. Appropriate parameters ($n = 128, Pr > 0.99$)

Number of hashes per packet	Degree(c)	n/c	Loss rate(p)
1	1	128	≤ 0.00016
2	2	64	≤ 0.02
3	4	32	≤ 0.16
4	8	16	≤ 0.43

p=0.2, MC model. It is apparent in the figure that the verification probabilities increase gradually with β increasing. So our scheme has high capability for resisting burst loss.

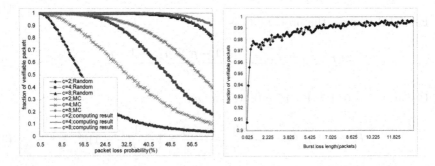

Fig. 3. Left: Comparing computed result with empirical. **Right:**Verification probabilities with increasing bursty loss.

4.3 Delay Analysis

In our scheme, delay at sender is n, and delay at receiver is 0, assuming no loss occurs. In case of loss, delay will be variable. Let la (average latency) denote the variable. Two factors affect la, which are n and k. la is larger while n increases and k decreases. To reduce la, just replace n with $n/2$.

5 Performance Evaluation

Compared with other multi-chain schemes, **CIC** is more effective to authenticate other packets. In other multi-chain schemes, one hash value can verify only one packet. In our scheme, as shown in Table 1, one packet that carries 4 hashes can verify 8 packets.

In our comparison, we only consider the schemes that amortize a signature over multiple packets in general. This class of schemes is more space efficient than other approaches. We compare our solution with three other previously proposed schemes-Authentication tree, EMSS, and SAIDA. In order to conduct the comparison, the following general assumptions are considered:

- the stream to be authenticated is divided into blocks of n packets,
- in order to provide authentication, one signature is needed for each block,
- hash size (h) is 16 bytes and h_n is the number of hashes per data packet,
- signature size(s) is 128 bytes.

The comparison will be undertaken according to the following criteria:

Sender delay: delay on the sender side (in number of data packets) before the first packet in the block is transmitted.

Receiver delay: delay on the receiver side (in number of data packets) before verification of the first packet in the block is possible.

Average latency: average latency of all received packets on the receiver side (in number of data packets) before the packets is verified.

Computation overhead: number of hashes and signatures computed by the sender per block.

Communication overhead (bytes): size of the authentication information required for each packet.

Verification probability: number of verifiable packets of the entire stream divided by the total number of received packets of the stream.

Max length of burst loss: max length of burst loss (in number of data packets) can be resisted.

Table 2 summarizes the four authentication schemes based on the performance criteria explained above. Its values were obtained based on the general assumptions explained above and the following assumptions: Communication overhead of the authentication tree is obtained for a binary tree. For EMSS, b is average number of hashes per data packet. For SAIDA, n is the number of encoded pieces, and m is the minimum number needed for decoding. For **CIC**, c is the degree of a hash cluster, where $c = 2^k$, $k \in (0, 1, \ldots)$.

Table 2. Comparison between Authentication tree, EMSS, SAIDA, and the proposed scheme (**CIC**)

	Tree	EMSS	SAIDA	CIC
Sender delay	n	0	n	n
Receiver delay	0	n	[m,n]	[0,n-n/c]
Average latency at receiver (no loss occurs)	0	$\frac{n-1}{2}$	$\frac{m(m-1)}{2n}$	0
Average latency at receiver (in case of loss)	0	variable	variable	variable
Computation overhead	2n-1, 1	n+1, 1	n+1,1	$\frac{n}{c}(2c-1)$,1
Communication overhead	$s + h\log_2^n$, -	$s + h$, $h_n h$	$\frac{hn+s}{n}$ $\frac{n}{m}$, -	$s + h\log_2^c$, $h(\log_2^c +1)$
Verification probability	1.0	variable	variable	variable
Max length of burst loss can be resisted	any	variable	n-m	n-$\frac{n}{c}$

The authentication tree technique has the favorable property of guaranteeing the verification of every received packet, but at the cost of a larger communication overhead-an overhead on the order of several hundred bytes would be required for practical block sizes. The authentication tree technique can also be converted to a probabilistic method by simply inserting the block signature in a subset of the packets instead of all the packets within the block. Even with this variation, the authentication tree method requires a larger communication overhead compared to other schemes, because each packet must include all path hash values needed to compute the authentication tree.

Fig. 4(*Left*) shows the change in verification probability as the communication overhead is kept constant, and the packet loss probability is increased. The following parameters were used:

General parameters: $n=128$; $\beta = 8$ (for MC loss model). Parameters for EMSS: number of hashes in signature packet: 5; $h_n = 3, 4$. Parameters for **CIC**: number of hashes in signature packet: 1; $h_n = 3, 4$. Parameters for SAIDA: $m = 42, 31$.

Curves for EMSS drop steeply to unacceptable levels, when the loss rate is increased. In contrast, the curves for **CIC** and SAIDA drop much more moderately. With same hashes per data packet, it shows that verification probability for our scheme is much higher than EMSS, but is lower than SAIDA.

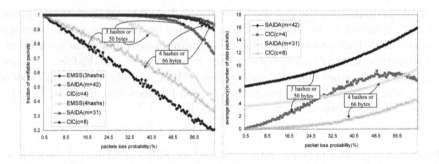

Fig. 4. Left: Verification probability with increasing loss. **Right:** Average latency with increasing loss.

As shown in Table 2, average latency in our scheme is zero, assuming no packet loss occurs. Fig. 4(*Right*) shows the change in average latency (in number of data packets) while the packet loss probability is increased. This depicts that average latency for our scheme is much lower than SAIDA even if the packet loss probability is very high.Our scheme can dramatically reduce average latency on receiver side.

6   Conclusions

In this paper, the problem of securing multicast communication is discussed. Many solutions proposed to solve the multicast authentication problem can be classed as hash tree, hash chain(s), and hash list. Hash tree scheme has the lowest delay on receiver side and the highest verification probability while hash chain scheme and hash list scheme have lower communication overhead. Our proposed **CIC** scheme is based on combination of single Chain scheme and Hash Tree Chains scheme. It integrates the advantages of both.

Mass simulation demonstrates that **CIC** is an efficient authentication method that is highly robust against packet loss, especially against burst loss. With the same amount of communication overhead, it achieves higher verification probability than other hash chain authentication schemes, and least average delay at receivers than other probabilistic authentication schemes.

Table 2 suggests that there is no single scheme that is superior in all aspects. Depending on the delay, computation, and communication overhead requirements, different schemes are appropriate for different applications. Our scheme is more applicable to source authentication in peer-to-peer media streaming.

References

1. T. Ballardie, "Scalable Multicast Key Distribution, RFC 1949," May 1996.
2. C. K. Wong and S. S. Lam, "Digital signatures for flows and multicasts," IEEE/ACM Transactions on Networking, vol. 7, pp. 502-513, 1999.
3. R. Gennaro and P. Rohatgi, "How to sign digital streams," Advances in Cryptology (CRYPTO '97), Aug. 1997, pp. 180-197
4. A. Perrig, R. Canetti, J. D. Tygar and D. Song, "Efficient authentication and signing of multicast streams over lossy channels," IEEE Symposium on Security and Privacy, pp. 56-73, May 2000.
5. A. Pannetrat and R. Molva, "Efficient multicast packet authentication," Proceeding of 10th Annual Network and Distributed System Security Symposium, February 2003-Symposium, 2003.
6. V. Paxson. "End-to-End Internet Packet Dynamics," IEEE/ACM Transactions on Networking 7 (1999), pp 277-292.
7. R. C. A. Perrig, D. Song, and D. Tygar., " Effcient and secure source authentication for multicast.," presented at proceedings Network and Distributed System Security Symposium, (NDSS '01), San Diego, CA, Feb., 2001.
8. P. Golle. and N. Modadugu., "Authenticating Streamed Data in the Presence of Random Packet Loss," presented at NDSS'01: The Network and Distributed System Security Symposium, 2001.
9. S. Miner and J. Staddon, "Graph-based authentication of digital streams," IEEE Symposium on Security and Privacy, May 2001, pp 232-246.
10. P. Jung Min, E. K. P. Chong, and H. J. Siegel, "Efficient multicast packet authentication using signature amortization," Proceedings of the IEEE Computer Society Symposium on Research in Security and Privacy, 2002, p227-240

Self-certified Mutual Authentication and Key Exchange Protocol for Roaming Services

Xiaowen Chu[1], Yixin Jiang[2], Chuang Lin[2], and Fujun Feng[2]

[1] Department of Computer Science, Hong Kong Baptist University
Hong Kong, P.R. China
chxw@comp.hkbu.edu.hk
[2] Department of Computer Science and Technology, Tsinghua University
Beijing, 100084, P.R. China
{yxjiang, clin, fjfeng}@csnet1.cs.tsinghua.edu.cn

Abstract. In this paper, based on self-certified mechanism, we propose a novel mutual authentication and key exchange protocol for roaming services in the global mobility network. The main new features included in the proposed protocol are (1) identity anonymity, which protects location privacy of mobile users in the roaming network environment; (2) one-time session key renewal, which frequently updates the session key for mobile users and hence reduces the risk of using a compromised session key to communicate with the visited network. The performance analysis shows that the computational complexity of our protocol is low and suitable to be used on mobile equipments.

Keywords: Self-certified, authentication, roaming services.

1 Introduction

The widely deployment of Global mobility network (GLOMONET) [1] increases the possibility of illegal access from malicious intruders. Several authentication protocols for global roaming service have been developed for GLOMONET. Suzuki et al. developed an authentication protocol for roaming service [1]. They introduced a challenge/response interactive authentication mechanism with a symmetric cryptosystem to construct their authentication protocol. Buttyan et al. pointed out that there are several drawbacks of Suzuki's authentication protocol vulnerable for attacking, and further proposed a modified protocol to eliminate these drawbacks and made it resistant against the presented attacks [2]. Subsequently, Hwang et al. [3] introduced a new mechanism, named self-encryption, to simplify Buttyan's protocol.

There is no support of identity anonymity in Hwang's scheme, however. The security of the long-term shared key K_{MH} between the mobile user M and his home network H could be compromised, since the shared key K_{MH} is calculated as $K_{MH} = f(ID_M)$, where ID_M is the identity of user M, and f is a secure one-way function. This limitation may permit some attacks once the user identity is illegally obtained by intercepting the exchanged messages, and then the advantage of self-encryption mechanism is counteracted. Moreover, the disclosure of user identity will allow

L.T. Yang et al. (Eds.): ATC 2006, LNCS 4158, pp. 408–417, 2006.

unauthorized entities to track the user's moving history and current location. The identity anonymity is one of the important properties that should be considered in roaming service environment.

Generally, a secure protocol design for roaming services requires the following properties, as pointed out in [5]: (1) Prevention of fraud by assuring that the mobile user and network entity are authentic; (2) Assuring mutual agreement and the freshness of session key; (3) Prevention of replaying attack; (4) Privacy of information about mobile user's locations during the communication, i.e., to provide an identity anonymity mechanism. Additionally, since the protocols are partially implemented on the mobile devices, there are two more factors to be considered. First, the low computational power of mobile devices makes unfeasible the security protocols which require very heavy computations [6]. Second, the low bandwidth and high error rate in wireless networks result that the security protocols should be designed to minimize the message size and also the number of exchanged messages.

In this paper, aiming at enhancing the security of existing authentication protocols for roaming service in GLOMONET environment, we propose a mutual authentication and key exchange protocol. Our scheme is based on self-certified scheme [8]. We present two mechanisms for roaming service, which are identity anonymity and one-time session key renewal. The *identity anonymity* property prevents the disclosure of mobile users' real identities and protects their privacy in the roaming environment. The *one-time session key renewal* can assure the mutual authentication and the freshness of session key. It provides a way for a mobile user to update his session key with visited network frequently, and therefore, reduces the risk of using a compromised session key to communicate with visited networks. Note that although we increase such security features, the computational complexity of our protocol is not high.

The rest of paper is organized as follows. In section 2, the basic self-certified scheme is briefly reviewed. In section 3, we propose our new authentication and key exchange protocol for roaming service. In section 4, we give the security analysis. In Section 5, the performance comparisons between previous roaming protocols and our proposed protocol are investigated. Finally, we conclude our work in Section 6.

2 Basic Self-certified Scheme

Self-certified scheme combines the advantages of certificate-based and identity-based public key cryptosystems, and also provides a mechanism for authenticating a user's public key [8-10]. We briefly introduce a simple self-certified scheme in this section.

First, the Trusted Third Party (TTP) chooses a modulus n as the product of two numbers p and q where $p = 2p'+1$, $q = 2q'+1$, p' and q' are primes. TTP generates a base element $g \neq 1$ of order $r = p' \cdot q'$, and then chooses a large integer $u < r$. Let $t \in Z_u^*$ be an element of Z_u^* of order u. A one-way function f will output positive integers less than p' and q'. The TTP makes g, u, f, and n public, and keeps r secret. Then p and q are discarded. Next, any user U_i can register with TTP by performing the following steps:

Step 1) User U_i chooses a random $x_i \in \{2,3,\ldots,u-1\}$ as his secret key, computes $y_i = g^{x_i} \pmod{n}$ as his public key and sends y to the TTP.

Step 2) The TTP prepares a string I_i associated with the personal information (Name, Address, etc.) of U_i, computes $w_i = y_i^{f(I_i)^{-1}} \pmod{n}$ as a witness for user U_i, and sends message $\{I_i, w_i\}$ to U_i.

Step 3) User U_i verifies I_i and witness w_i by checking whether the equation $y_i = w_i^{I_i} \pmod{n}$ holds.

Regarding to the security strength of self-certified scheme, Saeednia [7] claimed that forging a valid witness w_i for user U_i is equivalent to breaking an instance of RSA cryptosystem.

Suppose that users U_i and U_j intend to exchange a secret key used for secure communications. To achieve this, they can perform the following protocol based on the well-known Diffie-Hellman key distribution system.

Step 1) U_i send $\{w_i \| I_i\}$ to U_j, where $w_i = y_i^{f(I_i)^{-1}} \pmod{n}$ is a witness for U_i.

Step 2) U_j send $\{w_j \| I_j\}$ to U_i, where $w_j = y_j^{f(I_j)^{-1}} \pmod{n}$ is a witness for U_j.

Step 3) U_i can compute the secret key shared with U_j as $k = w_j^{f(I_j) \cdot x_i} \pmod{n}$.

Step 4) U_j can compute the secret key shared with U_i as $k = w_i^{f(I_j) \cdot x_j} \pmod{n}$.

There are two weaknesses in the basic self-certified key exchange scheme. One is that the secret session key exchanged in this protocol is invariant. The second is that the witness w_i computed by TTP is not self-certified. This defect makes is possible for a cheating user to have the chance of getting a forged self-certified witness.

3 The Proposed Protocol for Roaming Services

The security of our scheme is based on the intractability of the problem of discrete logarithm problem (DLP) [11]. Given a large prime p, a generator over Z_n, and $y = g^x \pmod{n}$, it is computationally infeasible to get x.

Our proposed protocol is based on the above Self-Certified scheme. It includes two phases: (Phase I) Mutual authentication protocol; (Phase II) Session key renewal protocol. A summary of notations used in this paper is shown in Table 1.

In Phase I, the visited network V authenticates a roaming user M through M's home network H. The key idea is to regard H as a temporary TTP for roaming services. When user M roams into a visited network V, both of them will initialize a registration procedure with H, where V acts as an access agent for M. If M and V have successfully registered with H, each of them will obtain a witness from H respectively; and then the trust relation between M and V can be established. Afterwards, M can directly establish or negotiate the session key with V without accessing H.

In phase II, the user M can establish or renew a session key with V. Then, M can directly visit V and V can provide responding services for M. Here we also introduce a novel mechanism called "one-time session key renewal" to assure the mutual authentication and the freshness of session key.

Table 1. Notations

M	mobile user
H	the home network
V	the visited network
T	the timestamp
ID_M	the identity of mobile user M
TID_M	the temporary identity of mobile user M
$\oplus$	bitwise XOR operation
$\parallel$	concatenation operation
$f(\cdot)$	A one-way function used for self-certified scheme
$h(\cdot)$	a one-way hash function used for key renewal protocol
$E_k(\cdot)$	symmetric encryption with key k (e.g. DES, AES)
$D_k(\cdot)$	symmetric decryption with key k (e.g. DES, AES)

3.1 Mutual Authentication Protocol (MAP)

The aim of MAP protocol is to provide a mechanism for user M and V to authenticate mutually and then establish a trusted relation between them.

Our MAK protocol for roaming services is shown in Fig. 1. Compared with the previous roaming protocols, we mainly introduce a new feature, *identity anonymity*, which can efficiently prevent unauthorized entities from tracing the mobile user's roaming history and his current location. Our solution for identity anonymity is to replace the real identity ID_M of a mobile user M with his temporary identity TID_M.

Suppose $y_M = g^{r_M} \pmod{n}$ and $y_V = g^{r_V} \pmod{n}$, where random numbers r_M and r_V are generated by user M and V respectively. Let I_M and I_V be two strings associated with the information (Name, Address, etc.) of M and V respectively. In addition, let w_M and w_V be the witness of M and V, which are calculated by H as:

$$w_M = ((y_M \oplus I_M)^{f(I_M)^{-1}}) \bmod (n) \tag{1}$$

$$w_V = ((y_V \oplus I_V)^{f(I_V)^{-1}}) \bmod (n) \tag{2}$$

In Fig. 1, the temporary identity TID_M is generated as follows: First, M calculates key K_{MH} as $K_{MH} = (PK_H)^{r_M}$, where $PK_H = g^{SK_H}$ is the public key of H which is known by M in advance (SK_H is the secret key of H). Second, the temporary identity TID_M is calculated as follows:

$$TID_M = E_{K_{MH}} (g^{r_M} \oplus ID_M) \qquad (3)$$

We will show that H can recover the real identity of M, i.e., ID_M, based on TID_M.

> Message 1. $M \rightarrow V$: y_M, ID_H, TID_M
>
> Message 2. $V \rightarrow H$: $y_M, y_V, E_{K_{VH}} (y_V \| ID_V \| TID_M \| T_V)$
>
> Message 3. $H \rightarrow V$: $E_{K_{VH}} (w_V \| I_V), E_{K_{MH}} (w_M \| I_M \| ID_V)$
>
> Message 4. $V \rightarrow M$: $E_{K_{MH}} (w_M \| I_M \| ID_V)$

Fig. 1. Mutual Authentication and Key Exchange Protocol for Roaming Services

Now, let us describe our proposed MAP protocol in detail according to the message exchange order as follows:

Step 1) The mobile user M does the followings: (1) Generates a random $r_M \in Z_u^* \setminus \{1\}$ and computes $y_M = g^{r_M}$; (2) Computes the shared key K_{MH} by $K_{MH} = (PK_H)^{r_M}$ and uses it to compute $TID_M = E_{K_{MH}} (g^{r_M} \oplus ID_M)$; (3) Sends y_M, ID_H, and TID_M to V.

Step 2) The visited network V chooses a random $r_V \in Z_u^* \setminus \{1\}$, computes $y_V = g^{r_V}$, and sends message $\{y_M, y_V, E_{K_{VH}} (y_V \| ID_V \| TID_M \| T_V)\}$ to H. T_V is a timestamp. We assume K_{VH} is the shared key between V and H.

Step 3) H first decrypts $E_{K_{VH}} (y_V \| ID_V \| TID_M \| t_V)$. If the timestamp T_V is reasonable and the decrypted value y_V^* is equal to the clear-text y_V, H computes the shared key K_{MH} by $K_{MH} = y_M^{SK_H}$. Notice that, $y_M^{SK_H} = (g^{r_M})^{SK_H} = (g^{SK_H})^{r_M} = (PK_H)^{r_M} (mod\, n)$. Then H decrypts $TID_M = E_{K_{MH}} (g^{r_M} \oplus ID_M)$ with K_{MH}. Therefore H can get the real identity of user M by computing the following formula:

$$ID_M = D_{K_{MH}} (TID_M) \oplus g^{r_M} . \qquad (4)$$

Afterwards, H can verify the authenticity of ID_M. If it is legal, H does the following: (1) Prepares two strings I_M and I_V associated with the information (Name, Address, etc.) of user M and V, respectively; (2) Computes the witness w_M and w_V for M and V according to Eq.(1) and (2). Then, H sends $E_{K_{VH}} (w_V \| I_V)$ and $E_{K_{MH}} (w_M \| I_M \| ID_V)$ to V.

Step 4) V decrypts $E_{K_{VH}} (w_V \| I_V)$, then verifies witness w_V and I_V by checking whether the following equation holds:

$$y_V = ((w_V)^{f(I_V)} mod(n) \oplus I_V) . \qquad (5)$$

If true, then V successfully registers with H and it believes that M is an authorized user of H. Subsequently, V forwards $E_{K_{MH}}(w_M \parallel I_M \parallel ID_V)$ to M.

Step 5)   Similarly, M decrypts $E_{K_{MH}}(w_M \parallel I_M \parallel ID_V)$ and verifies I_M and witness w_M
by checking

$$y_M = ((w_M)^{f(I_M)} \bmod(n) \oplus I_M) . \tag{6}$$

If true, M successfully registers with H and he believes that the trust relation
between M and V has been established with the help of home network H.

3.2   One-Time Session Key Renewal Protocol (SKRP)

The main functions in phase II are to establish or renew a session key between M and
V. As compared with traditional roaming protocols, we introduce a novel mechanism
called "one-time session key renewal". This new feature allows mobile user M to
establish or renew his session key frequently and reduces the risk that he uses a compromised session key to communicate with V.

Suppose that a mobile user M requires renewing his session key K_{MV} with V for
the ith time period. He can obtain the new session key after he has exchanged the two
messages shown in Fig. 2 with V.

Message 1. $M \rightarrow V$: w_M, I_M, g^{t_M}

Message 2. $V \rightarrow M$: w_V, I_V, g^{t_V}

Fig. 2. One-time Session Key Renewal Protocol

In Fig. 2, random numbers $t_M, t_V \in Z_u^*$ denote two different elements of Z_u^* of order u. The session key K_{MV} can be calculated respectively by user M and V, respectively. For mobile user M, the session key can be computed as

$$y_V = (w_V^{f(I_V)} \bmod(n)) \oplus I_V , \tag{7}$$

$$K_M = y_V^{t_M} \cdot (g^{t_V})^{r_M} = g^{r_V t_M + r_M t_V} \bmod(n) , \tag{8}$$

$$K_{MV} = h(K_M) . \tag{9}$$

For V, the session key is acquired similarly:

$$y_M = (w_M^{f(I_M)} \bmod(n)) \oplus I_M , \tag{10}$$

$$K_V = y_M^{t_V} \cdot (g^{t_M})^{r_V} = g^{r_V t_M + r_M t_V} \bmod(n) , \tag{11}$$

$$K_{MV} = h(K_V) . \tag{12}$$

Evidently, the session keys calculated by M and V are the same, owing to:

$$h(K_M) = h(g^{r_V t_M + r_M t_V} \bmod(n)) = h(K_V) \tag{13}$$

where h is a hash function. Key confirmation is done implicitly during the session.
Moreover, this protocol can yield a different key for each session renewal.

The security of the key exchange is especially enhanced by using this approach, since every session key is used for only once. Moreover, as compared with the previous protocols, the number of message exchanges is decreased to only two.

4 Security Analysis

The security requirements for mobile communication have been introduced in Section 1. Here we give an analysis of whether these requirements can be satisfied.

4.1 Identity Anonymity and Intractability Analysis

As shown in Fig. 1, the real identity ID_M of mobile user M is replaced with his temporary identity TID_M, which is computed as $TID_M = E_{K_{MH}}(g^{r_M} \oplus ID_M)$, where $K_{MH} = (PK_H)^{r_M}$. Since only home network H knows its own secret key SK_H, nobody else can calculate the shared key K_{MH} as $K_{MH} = (g^{r_M})^{SK_H}$. Hence, only H can decrypt TID_M with key K_{MH} and obtain the real identity ID_M by computing $ID_M = D_{K_{MH}}(TID_M) \oplus g^{r_M}$. Since an illegal tracker cannot obtain the shared key K_{MH}, it is impossible for him to extract the real identity ID_M from TID_M and then trace the location of a mobile target user.

The identity untraceability is assured by two measures: (1) When user M roams in different visited networks, TID_M is different in each session due to the different random r_M; (2) The shared key $K_{MH} = (PK_H)^{r_M}$ is one-time-use so that there is no direct relationship between these shared keys. The change of random r_M guarantees the freshness of TID_M and the shared key in different roaming domains.

4.2 Prevention of Relaying Attacking

In this section, we analyze the *relaying attacks* in session key renewal protocol (Fig. 2). Consider the case that an adversary pretends to act as M and tries to exchange a secret key with V such that V intends to share the secret key with M. The adversary can randomly choose an integer $\alpha \in Z_u^*$; then he sets $r_M^* = \alpha \cdot f(I_M)$ as a fake secret key for M and replace M's original public key y_M with $y_M^* = g^{r_M^*} \bmod(n)$. However, the adversary cannot compute a valid witness w_M^* for M, because the original witness $w_M = ((y_M \oplus I_M)^{f(I_M)^{-1}}) \bmod(n)$ for user M is self-certified. Therefore although the adversary can intercept the message $\{w_M, I_M, g^{r_M}\}$, he still cannot forge the correct message $\{w_M^*, I_M, g^{r_M}\}$ which satisfies the following relation $w_M^* = ((y_M^* \oplus I_M)^{f(I_M)^{-1}}) \bmod(n)$. So it can be seen that the proposed protocol is able to resist such replaying attacks. Similarly, an adversary that impersonates V also cannot obtain the same secret key with mobile user M.

4.3 Mutual Agreement and the Freshness of Session Key

In our scheme, the mutual key agreement mechanism is evident. Consider such mechanism in SKRP protocol. The new session key K_{MV} is obtained with the mutual agreement mechanism. The reason is that according to Eqs. (8) and (9) we can derive key K_{MV} as $K_{MV} = h(g^{r_V t_M + r_M t_V} \mod(n))$, where the two random t_M and t_V are respectively determined by M and V independently. In addition, the two numbers, r_M and r_V, are also randomly selected by M and V, respectively.

Finally, the freshness of session key is evidently assured, since the exchanged Message 1 and 2 in SKRP protocol safeguard the freshness of the two numbers t_M and t_V, which are randomly selected by M and V, respectively (See Fig. 2).

4.4 Prevention of Fraud

Firstly, our MAP scheme can efficiently prevent an intruder from impersonating attacks, since our scheme provides secure mutual authentication mechanisms between mobile user M and V, M and H, or V and H. Consider the following impersonation attack scenarios in MAP Protocol (See Fig. 1).

Case 1) An intruder has no way to impersonate H to cheat V, since he does not possess the long-term secret key K_{VH}. Hence it is impossible for an intruder to generate the response $E_{K_{VH}}(w_V \parallel I_V \parallel g^{r_M})$ to V.

Case 2) V has no way to impersonate H to cheat M. Since the shared key K_{MH} is unknown to V, and V cannot generate $E_{K_{MH}}(w_M \parallel I_M \parallel ID_V \parallel g^{r_M} \parallel g^{r_V})$ where w_M contains y_M generated by user M.

Case 3) An intruder also has no way to impersonate M since he cannot know the real identity of M. If the intruder uses a phony identity ID_M', the corresponding spurious temporal identity PID_M' can be identified by H, since H can obtain the ID_M' by computing $ID_M' = D_{K_{MV}'}(TID_M') \oplus g^{r_M}$ and then H can detect the spurious identity ID_M'. Moreover, the real identity is secret in our scheme. Hence nobody except the user himself and his H can know his real identity.

Similarly, we can also consider the impersonation attack scenarios in SKRP Protocol (Fig. 2) as follows.

Case 1) An adversary has no way to impersonate M to cheat V. Since it is impossible for an adversary to obtain the secret r_M unless he can resolve the problem of computing discrete logarithm modulo a large composite. Hence, the adversary can not pretend to act as user M to share or obtain the same session key K_{MV} with the visited network V, even though any adversary can easily compute an authenticated pair (w_M, I_M) for user M satisfying the following equation $y_M = g^{r_M} = (w_M^{f(I_M)} \oplus I_M) \mod(n)$.

Case 2) Owing to the same mechanism, an adversary also has no way to impersonate V to cheat mobile user M.

Compared with the basic self-certified scheme, we only replace the witness $w_M = ((y_M \oplus I_M)^{f(I_M)^{-1}}) \bmod(n)$ with the original $w_M = y_M^{f(I_M)^{-1}} \bmod(n)$. Our improvement provides a self-certified mechanism to prevent a cheating user from having a chance to get forged self-certified witness, while it only requires one more XOR operation than the original step.

5 Complexity Analysis

In this section, we compare the algorithm complexity of our protocol with that of previous protocols. The results are shown in Table 2 and 3, for Phase I and Phase II respectively. We mainly compare the following metrics: number of hash operation, symmetric encryption/decryption, and exponential operation in different protocols. Moreover, the number of transmissions (message exchanges) is also compared. Since ASPeCT [4] protocol cannot provide session key renewal mechanism, we only compare with Hwang et al.'s protocol in Table 3.

According to Table 2 and 3, it can be generally concluded that though the identity anonymity capability, session key renewal mechanism, and distributed security management scheme are introduced into our schemes for roaming service, the complexity of our protocols is still less than or equal to Hwang et al.'s protocol, and the computation requirement for mobile device is quite low.

Table 2. Performance Comparison (Phase I)

Comparison Item		Protocol in [3]	ASPeCT [4]	Our Protocol
Exponential operation	M	N/A	2	1+2Pre.
Hash operation	M	1 (Step 1)	1	1 (step 1)
Symmetric Encryption	M	1 (step 1 or 5)	2	1 (step 1)
Symmetric Decryption	M	1 (step 5)	N/A	1 (step 5)
Transmissions	$M \leftrightarrow V$	3	3	2
Anonymity		No	No	Yes
Session Key Renewal		Yes	No	Yes

Note: M: Mobile; V: Visited Network; Pre: Pre-computation exponentiation operation

Table 3. Performance Comparison (Phase II)

Comparison Item		Protocol in [3]	Our Protocol
Exponential operation	M	N/A	1+2Pre
Symmetric Encryption	M	1	N/A
Symmetric Decryption	M	1	N/A
Transmissions	$M \leftrightarrow V$	3	2
Anonymity		N/A	Yes

6 Conclusions

In this paper, we propose a new mutual authentication and key exchange protocol for roaming service in GLOMONET. With the goal of enhancing the security and further simplifying previous protocols for roaming service, we introduce two new mechanisms in our protocols: identity anonymity and one-time session key renewal mechanism. For anonymity, we generate the temporary identity by encrypting the real identity with the shared key. For one-time session key renewal, we update the session key by utilizing a modified self-certified scheme based on the Diffie-Hellman system. The performance comparisons between our protocol and previous roaming protocols show that, although we provide such new security mechanisms, the complexity of our protocol is still not higher than previous protocols.

Acknowledgement

This relative work was supported in part by Grant RGC/HKBU210605, Hong Kong; the NSFC under contracts No.60573144, 60218003, 60429202, and 90412012; the Projects of Development Plan of the State High Technology Research under contract No. 2003CB314804; and Intel IXA University Research Plan.

References

[1] S. Suzuki and K. Nakada. "An Authentication Technique Based on Distributed Security Management for the Global Mobility Network." IEEE J. on Selected Areas in Comm., Vol.15, Issue:8, pp.1606-1617, 1997.

[2] L. Buttyan, C. Gbaguidi, et al. "Extensions to an Authentication Technique Proposed for the Global Mobility Network." IEEE Trans. on Comm., Vol.48, Issue:3, pp.373-376, 2000.

[3] K.-F. Hwang and C.-C. Chang. "A Self-Encryption Mechanism for Authentication of Roaming and Teleconference Services." IEEE Trans. on Wireless Comm., Vol. 2, Issue:2, pp.400-407, 2003.

[4] G. Horn and B. Preneel. "Authentication and Payment in Future Mobile Systems." Proc. of the 5th European Symposium on Research in Computer Security, LNCS, Vol.1485, pp.277-293, 1998.

[5] S. Patel. "Weakness of North American Wireless Authentication Protocol," IEEE Personal Comm., Vol.4, pp.40-44, 1997.

[6] D. S. Wong and A. H. Chan. "Mutual Authentication and Key Exchange for Low Power Wireless Communications." Proc. of IEEE MILCOM 2001, Vol.1, pp.39-43, 2001.

[7] S.-L. Ng and C. Mitchell. "Comments on mutual authentication and key exchange protocols for low power wireless communications." IEEE Comm. Letters, Vol.8, Issue:4, pp.262 – 263, 2004.

[8] S. Saeednia. "Identity-Based and Self-Certified Key Exchange Protocols." In Proc. of the Second Australian Conference on Information Security and Privacy, pp.303-313, 1997.

[9] S. Saeednia. "A Note on Girault's Self-certified Model." Information Processing Letters, Elsiver, Vol 86. Issue:6, pp.323-327, 2003.

[10] T.-C. Wu, Y.-S. Chang, and T.-Y. Lin. "Improvement of Saeedni's Self-Certified Key Exchange Protocols." Electronics Letters, Vol.34, Issue:11, pp.1094 – 1095, 1998.

[11] L. Adelman and K. McCurley. "Open Problems in Number Theoretic Complexity." Proc. of the 1994 Algorithmic Number Theory Symposium, Springer-verlag, pp291-322, 1994.

Remote Authentication with Forward Security

Zhenchuan Chai, Zhenfu Cao*, and Rongxing Lu

Department of Computer Science and Engineering, Shanghai Jiaotong University,
1954 Huashan Road, Shanghai 200030, P.R. China
zcchai@gmail.com , zfcao@cs.sjtu.edu.cn

Abstract. Password authentication has been accepted as an easy-to-use solution in network environment to protect unauthorized access to a remote server. Although many schemes have been proposed, none of them can achieve survivability in case of compromise of a server. Once a server's secret key is leaked, the system is totally broken, and all the legally registered users have to be rejected for security reason, which is the most undesirable tragedy in business applications. In this paper, we propose a remote authentication scheme with forward security to reduce the potential damages caused by key exposure problem in authentication schemes. In our scheme, an intruder can not masquerade as an legal user registered at previous periods even if he has obtained server's secret keys.

1 Introduction

Password authentication is one of the most popular methods to guarantee that resources provided by remote servers could only be accessed by legal users. Since the needs for authentication grow tremendously, password authentication has found numerous applications in many areas such as computer networks, wireless networks, remote login, operation systems, and database management systems [1]. Over the past few years, considerable research efforts [1,2,3,4,5,6,7,8,9,10, 11,12,13,14,15,16,17,18,19,20,21,22,23,24] have been made to minimize the time and storage requirements of the authentication protocols, as well as to maximize their robustness in the face of various attacks [4,6,8,9,16,18,20,21,22,24,25], such as stolen-verifier attack [25], replay attack, and impersonation attack. However, few scheme has survivability in case of compromise of a server. Once the server's secret key is leaked, the whole system collapses, and all the registered users have to be rejected for security reason, which is the most undesirable tragedy in business applications. This paper addresses the above issue and proposes a password remote authentication scheme with forward security, which guarantees that even if an intruder has obtained a system secret key, he can not masquerade as a previous registered user.

1.1 Key Exposure Problem

In traditional authentication schemes, a user first registers himself at a remote server by submitting his identity ID and a password PW to the server, and

---

* Corresponding author.

L.T. Yang et al. (Eds.): ATC 2006, LNCS 4158, pp. 418–427, 2006.

the server will store ID and PW pair in local database for later authentication with the registered user. It has been pointed out that such approach suffers from complex maintenance of a growing password table and the risk of stolen verifier attack [1,25]. So, numerous schemes have been proposed to remove the password table from the server, where the server stores only a secret key. When a new user submits his ID and PW, the server will compute a user-dependent information from ID and PW using the secret key, and then store the information into a smart card. The smart card is issued to the user.

The security of these schemes depends heavily on the assumption that the secret key of the server is not exposed. Thereby, many solutions have been proposed to minimize the chance of key exposure, such as threshold authentication [27,28]. But those solutions which minimize the risk of key exposure do not guarantee the secret key will never be leaked [29]. Once the key is obtained by an intruder, the intruder could impersonate any user. And a more severe consequence is that all the previously registered users have to be rejected during the system recovery and have to re-register as new users after the system is restored. Such consequence of key exposure is a real disaster in business applications.

1.2   Forward Security

To address key exposure problem, forward security was put forward to reduce the potential damage caused by key leakage [31]. Forward security was first proposed in key agreement protocol to ensure that past session key could not be learned even if an intruder had obtained two parties' long term private keys [30]. And a signature scheme is called forward secure if an intruder who has learned the private key of a victim singer could not forge a signature of past periods [31,32]. In this paper, we introduce forward security into authentication schemes, where an intruder can not impersonate any previous registered users or register himself as an old user, even if he obtains the current system key.

Forward-security is often achieved by key evolution. The idea of key evolution [33] is illustrated in Fig.1. In a forward-secure scheme, the time during which a remote server is supposed to be functional is divided into T periods. And during these periods, the server holds an evolving secret key SK_i $(i = 0, \cdots, T)$ with other information fixed. The secret key of current period is computed from the secret key of last period, using an one-way function $f()$, so the leakage of current key does not lead to exposure of previous keys.

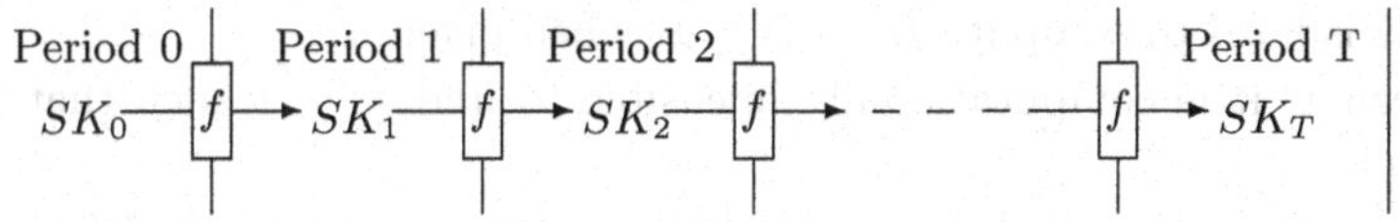

Period 0 | Period 1 | Period 2 | Period T
$SK_0 \boxed{f} \rightarrow SK_1 \boxed{f} \rightarrow SK_2 \boxed{f} \rightarrow - - - - \boxed{f} \rightarrow SK_T$

Fig. 1. Key evolving scheme

1.3 Related Work

In 1981, Lamport [14] proposed the first well-known password authentication scheme. The scheme uses a password table at the server end to achieve user authentication. Therefore, Lamport's scheme suffers from the risk of stolen-verifier attack [25] and the high cost of protecting and maintaining the password table. To overcome the weakness, Hwang and Li [13] proposed a new smart card based remote user authentication scheme in 2000, in which the remote system only keeps a secret key and doesn't need to maintain password tables. However, in their scheme, users can not freely choose their passwords, but receive strong cryptography keys returned by the server. These keys are too difficult for people to remember. Therefore, schemes that alow user to choose their own passwords are most desirable. In 1999, Yang and Shieh [19] presented a timestamp-based password authentication scheme that allows users to freely choose their passwords. And examples of such user-friendly schemes are those in [7], [23]. However, all these schemes don't possess the property of forward security.

Up to now, the only authentication scheme aimed to address the key exposure is proposed by Awasthi and Lal [2] in 2003. However, their scheme is pointed out incorrect since the server can not validating a given equation [37,38].

In this paper, we propose a remote password authentication scheme with forward security. Our scheme does not need password table at the server side and allows user to choose their own passwords. The rest of paper is organized as follows. In Section 2, we give a brief review of some basic concepts and tools used in our scheme. In Section 3, we present our concrete scheme. Then we discuss the scheme's security in Section 4. A conclusion is drawn in Section 5.

2 Preliminary

In this section, we recall some basic concepts and tools used in our scheme.

2.1 One-Way Hash Function

An one-way hash function H is said to be secure, if the following properties are satisfied [34]:

- Given x, it is easy to compute $H(x) = y$, while inverting $H()$ is hard, that is, it is hard to compute $H^{-1}(y) = x$, when given y.
- Given x, it is computationally infeasible to find $x' \neq x$ such that $H(x') = H(x)$.
- It is computationally infeasible to find any two pair x and x' such that $x' \neq x$ and $H(x') = H(x)$.

Note that if the output of $H()$ is sufficient long, then, given x, it is computationally infeasible to find x', such that $H(x') = aH(x)$ with an integer a.

2.2   RSA Problem

Let p and q be two large prime numbers, satisfying $p = 2p' + 1$ and $q = 2q' + 1$, with p', q' themselves primes. Then a RSA modulus is computed as $N = p \times q$.

The RSA problem is the following [35]: given a randomly generated RSA modulus N, a random $A \in Z_N^*$, an exponent a, to find $g \in Z_N^*$ such that $A = g^a \bmod N$.

It is assumed that it is computational infeasible to solve RSA problem.

2.3   Guillou-Quisquater's Practical Zero-Knowledge Protocol

We recall Guillou-Quisquater's practical zero-knowledge protocol (GQ protocol) [36] to provide intuition for our construction.

In GQ protocol, to prove the knowledge of a v-th root A of J over RSA modulus N, i.e, $J = A^v \bmod N$, a prover (P) will interact with verifier (V) as follows:

1. P randomly selects $r \in Z_N^*$, computes $T = r^v \bmod N$, then sends T to V.
2. V returns P a random challenge integer d.
3. P computes and sends $t = r(1/A)^d \bmod N$.
4. V checks whether $T = J^d t^v \bmod N$ holds.

The above interactive scheme could be readily converted to non interactive (signature) scheme by letting the challenge b be a hash value of some designated information, such as identity, time stamp.

3   Forward Secure Remote Authentication Scheme

In this section, we start by presenting our new forward secure remote authentication scheme, then show how to change user's password without re-registration.

3.1   The Proposed Scheme

The scheme is composed of five phases: set up phase, key evolution phase, registration phase, login phase and authentication phase. Our scheme uses the key-evolving technique to obtain forward security, and the whole server-valid time is divided into $T + 1$ periods, starting from period 0 to period T. Server S initiates at period 0 in set up phase, generating some system parameter and secret key (g_0, s_0), where the subscript 0 denote period 0. In key evolution phase, S updates the secret key without changing system parameters. In registration phase, S will issue a smart card to new user U. In login phase, a request message will be generated by smart card of user U, and be sent to S. Then the request message will be validated by S in authentication phase.

In our scheme, we use three distinct collision free one-way hash functions $H(.), h_1(.), h_2(.)$ for illustration purpose. Indeed, these hash functions could be implemented using MD5 or SHA-1.

The details are described below.

Set up: Taking in the number of total periods T at period 0, remote server S prepares system parameters as follows:

1. generate two large prime p and q, such that $p = 2p' + 1$, and $q = 2q' + 1$, where p', q' are also two large primes, compute $N = p \times q$.
2. randomly select $g_0 \in Z_N^*$, satisfying g_0 is a primitive element in both $GF(p)$ and $GF(q)$.
3. compute $s_0 = g_0^{\prod_{j=1}^T H(j)} \bmod N$ and $V = 1/g_0^{\prod_{j=0}^T H(j)} \bmod N$, then discard p, q. Note, here $s_0^{H(0)} = 1/V \bmod N$.

After set up phase, server S holds system parameter $< N, V, T, H(), h_1(), h_2() >$, and maintains master key (g_0, s_0).

Key Evolution: At the end of period $j(j = 0, \cdots, T)$, S updates the master key as follows:

If $j = T$, then S gives a warning that it has reached the maximum period number. Otherwise S computes the new master key of period $j + 1$ as

$$g_{j+1} = g_j^{H(j)}(\bmod N), \quad s_{j+1} = g_{j+1}^{\prod_{k=j+2}^T H(k)}(\bmod N),$$

then discards (g_j, s_j).

It is worth pointing out that, since $g_j = g_{j-1}^{H(j-1)} = \dots = g_0^{\prod_{k=0}^{j-1} H(k)}$, then:

$$
\begin{aligned}
s_j^{H(j)} &= g_j^{H(j) \cdot \prod_{k=j+1}^T H(k)} \\
&= g_0^{\prod_{k=0}^{j-1} H(k) \cdot H(j) \cdot \prod_{k=j+1}^T H(k)} \\
&= g_0^{\prod_{k=0}^T H(k)} = 1/V(\bmod N)
\end{aligned}
\tag{1}
$$

Registration Phase: When a new user U submits his identity ID and a password PW to the remote server for registration at period j $(0 \le j \le T)$, the remote server first checks the validity of ID and then computes user-dependent information as follows, see Fig. 2:

1. randomly select $z \in Z_N^*$, and compute $Z = 1/z^{H(j)} \bmod N$.
2. compute $Y = z s_j^{h_1(ID,Z,j)} \bmod N$ and $Y' = Y - h_2(PW) \bmod N$.

Then, server S stores the parameters $(Y', Z, j, N, T, H(j), h_1(.), h_2(.))$ to a smart card. Finally, S issues the smart card to the user U via a secure channel.

Login Phase: When U wants to login to the remote server, he attaches his smart card to the login device and keys in his ID and PW. Then, the smart card will perform as follows, see Fig.3:

1. select a random number $r \in Z_N^*$, and compute $R = r^{H(j)} \bmod N$.
2. pick up the current date and time t of the login device, and compute

$$\sigma = h_1(ID, R, Z, j, t)$$

$$C = r(Y' + h_2(PW))^\sigma = r(z s_j^{h_1(ID,Z,j)})^\sigma \bmod N \tag{2}$$

3. send the request message $M = (C, \sigma, Z, j, t, ID)$ to the remote server.

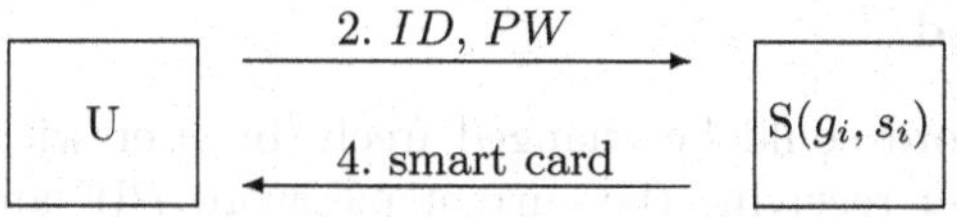

$$2.\ ID,\ PW$$

U

$$S(g_i, s_i)$$

4. smart card

1. Choose ID, PW

3. $Z = 1/z^{H(j)} \bmod N$,
$Y' = zs_j^{h_1(ID,Z,j)} - h_2(PW)$,
$(Y', Z, j, N, T, H(j), h_1(.), h_2(.))$
$\rightarrow$smart card

Fig. 2. Registration phase at period j

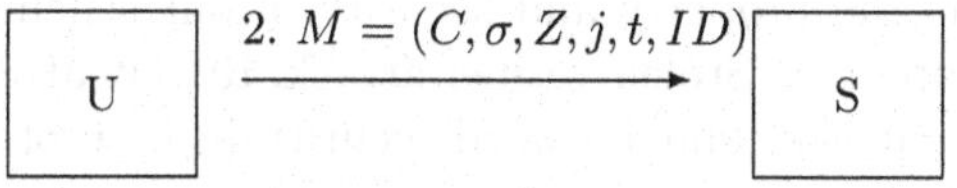

$$2.\ M = (C, \sigma, Z, j, t, ID)$$

U

S

1. $R = r^{H(j)} \bmod N$,
$\sigma = h_1(ID, R, Z, j, t)$,
$C = r(Y' + h_2(PW))^\sigma$
$\quad = r(zs_j^{h_1(ID,Z,j)})^\sigma$

3. $R' = C^{H(j)}(ZV^{h_1(ID,Z,j)})^\sigma \bmod N$,
verify $\sigma \overset{?}{=} h_1(ID, R', Z, j, t)$,

Fig. 3. Login and authentication phase

Authentication Phase: Suppose that the remote server receives the request message M at t', where t' is the current date and time of the system. Then the following operations are performed to facilitate the authentication:

1. check the validity of identity ID, if the format is incorrect, the login request will be rejected;
2. check the time interval between t and t', if $(t' - t) \geq \Delta t$, where Δt is the expected legal time interval for transmission delay, the remote server will reject the login request;
3. compute $R' = C^{H(j)}(ZV^{h_1(ID,Z,j)})^\sigma \bmod N$
4. check $\sigma = h_1(ID, R', Z, j, t)$. If it does hold, the remote server will accept the login request. Otherwise, the request will be rejected.

The correctness could easily be checked:

$$
\begin{aligned}
R' &= C^{H(j)}(ZV^{h_1(ID,Z,j)})^\sigma \\
&\overset{equation(2)}{=} (r(zs_j^{h_1(ID,Z,j)})^\sigma)^{H(j)}(ZV^{h_1(ID,Z,j)})^\sigma \\
&= r^{H(j)}(z^{H(j)}s_j^{H(j)h_1(ID,Z,j)})^\sigma(ZV^{h_1(ID,Z,j)})^\sigma \\
&\overset{equation(1)}{=} R(\frac{1}{ZV^{h_1(ID,Z,j)}})^\sigma(ZV^{h_1(ID,Z,j)})^\sigma = R
\end{aligned}
$$

therefore $\sigma = h_1(ID, R, Z, j, t) = h_1(ID, R', Z, j, t)$.

3.2   Changing Password

In our scheme, the password could be changed freely by user without registration again. That is, after receiving the current password PW and the new password PW^*, the login terminal will first confirm the validity of PW (e.g. by interacting with $\mathcal{S}$), if PW is valid, then the login terminal replaces $Y'(= zs_j^{h_1(ID,Z,j)} - h_2(PW))$ with $Y' + h_2(PW) - h_2(PW^*)$, otherwise, the changing password request is rejected.

4   Discussion

In this section, we examine the property and security of our scheme in terms of the following security properties: Stolen-verifier attack, Replay attack, Guessing attacks, Impersonation attack, and Forward-security in case of server key exposure.

- **Stolen-verifier attack:** Traditional authentication schemes maintain a verification table at the server side to store all the registered users' passwords. Therefore, an intruder can impersonate a legal user by stealing the user's ID and PW from the verification table. However, such attack does not work in our scheme, since there is no password or verification table stored in servers.
- **Replay attack:** Our scheme can defeat replay attack. The messages transmitted over the network in our scheme can not be intercepted for reuse, because of the involvement of time stamp. And the server could check the freshness of a received message by testing whether the transmission time is within legal transmission delay $\triangle t$.
- **Guessing attacks:** In general, guessing attack could be mounted online or offline [26]. In online attacks, the attacker may enumerate all possible passwords to log into a remote server. When an attacker has got a victim user's smart card, he may generate a trial request message with a guessed password PW^*. However, such trial-and-error method could be detected by the server. The server may lock the account for a few minutes after detecting a consecutive number of login failures, which may prevent the attacker from checking sufficiently many passwords in a reasonable time. Therefore, our scheme resist online guessing attacks.

  Unfortunately, our scheme only resists weak off line guessing attacks, but not resist strong off line guessing attacks. In weak off line attack, the attacker may manager to learn the secret information stored in a victim user's smart card, including $(Y' = zs_j^{h_1(ID,Z,j)} - h_2(PW), Z, j, N, T, H(j))$. And he may continue to compute $Y'' = Y' + h_2(PW^*)$, however, without knowing value V, which is stored in remote server, he can not further validate Y'', thus can not determine the validity of PW^*. In strong off line attack, the attacker may additionally eavesdrop a request message, including $(C = r(zs_j^{h_1(ID,Z,j)})^\sigma, \sigma)$, and thus can determine the validity of PW^* by checking $\sigma \stackrel{?}{=} h_1(ID, C^{H(j)}(Y''^{H(j)})^\sigma, Z, j, t) \bmod N$.

In order to resist strong off line guessing attacks, tamp-proof smart cards are required in our scheme.

- **Impersonation attack:** No one can impersonate a legal user to login the remote server in our scheme. In our scheme, an attacker may have already possessed a registered user's secret information, such as $(zs_j^{h_1(ID,Z,j)}, Z, ID, j)$. However, because of the hardness of RSA problem, it is computationally infeasible for the attacker to calculate server's secret key s_j if the RSA modulus N is long enough ($|N| > 1024$ bit). And without s_j, it is hard for the attacker to forge a new registered information on any ID^* other than ID. Indeed, the security of our scheme is closely related to that of Guillou-Quisquater's zero-knowledge of $h(j)$-th root protocol. So our scheme can resist impersonation attack.

- **Forward-security:** Suppose that an intruder breaks into a remote server at periods $j + 1$ and obtains system secret key (g_{j+1}, s_{j+1}). Now he wants to masquerade as a previously registered user of periods j. As we have discussed, the intruder has to calculate a secret key of periods j, namely s_j, to masquerade as such a user. Recall that $g_{j+1} = g_j^{H(j)} \bmod N$, it is infeasible to calculate g_j from g_{j+1}, which prevents the intruder from computing s_j directly. Another way to learn s_j is to check whether there exists an integer a, such that $H(j + 1) = aH(j)$. If so, $s_j = s_{j+1}^a \bmod N$ since $s_j^{H(j)} = s_{j+1}^{H(j+1)} = s_{j+1}^{aH(j)} = V \bmod N$. However, the probability that $H(j + 1)$ is a multiple of $H(j)$ is neglectable if the output length of hash function $H()$ is long enough. Therefore, the intruder can not obtain any secret key of past periods, and can not masquerade as an old user. Our scheme possesses the property of forward security.

5   Conclusion

In this paper, we analyze the key exposure problem in authentication schemes, and propose a concrete password authentication scheme with forward security.

In our scheme, an intruder could not able to masquerade as a registered user of past periods even if he has obtained current secret key of server. Moreover, our scheme does not require password table stored in a remote server, and allows user to choose and change their own passwords.

Acknowledgement

This work was supported in part by the National Natural Science Foundation of China for Distinguished Young Scholars under Grant No. 60225007, the National Research Fund for the Doctoral Program of Higher Education of China under Grant No. 20020248024, and the Science and Technology Research Project of Shanghai under Grant No. 04DZ07067, and the Special Research Funds of Huawei.

References

1. Liao,I.E., Lee,C.C., Hwang,M.S.: A password authentication scheme over insecure networks. J. Comput. System Sci. 2005.
2. Awasthi,A.K., Lal,S.: A remote user authentication scheme using smart cards with forward secrecy. IEEE Trans. Consum. Electron. Vol. 49 (4)(2003)1246 - 1248
3. Chang,Y.F., Chang,C.C.: A secure and efficient strong-password authentication protocol. ACM SIGOPS Operating Systems Review. Vol. 38(3)(2004)79-90
4. Chan,C.K., Cheng,L.M.: Cryptanalysis of a remote user authentication scheme using smart cards. IEEE Trans. Consum. Electron. 46 (4)(2000) 992 - 993
5. Chien,H.Y., Chen,C.H.: A remote authentication scheme preserving user anonymity. In: Proceedings of the 19th International Conference on Advanced Information Networking and Applications - AINA 2005. 245 - 248
6. Chan,C.C., Hwang,K.F.: Some forgery attacks on a remote user authentication scheme using smart cards. Informatics. Vol. 14 (3)(2003) 289 - 294
7. Chien,H.Y., Jan,J., Tseng,Y.: An efficient and practical solution to remote authentication: smart card. Computer Security. Vol. 21 (4)(2002) 372 - 375
8. Hsu,C.L.: Security of Chien et al.'s remote user authentication scheme using smart cards. Computer Standards and Inerfaces. Vol. 26(3)(2004) 167-169
9. Lee,S.W., Kim,H.S., Yoo,K.Y.: Improvement of Chien et al.'s remote user authentication scheme using smart cards. Computer Standards and Inerfaces. Vol. 27 (2005)181-183
10. Chang,C.C., Wu,T.C.: Remote password authentication with smart cards,IEE Proceddings-E.Vol. 138 (3)(1993)165 - 168
11. Das,M.L., Saxena,A., Gulati,V.P.: A dynamic ID-based remote user authentication scheme. IEEE Trans. Consum. Electron. Vol. 50 (2)(2004)629 - 631
12. Hwang,M.S., Lee,C.C., Tang,Y.L.: A simple remote user authentication scheme. Math.Comput.Model. Vol. 36(2002) 103-107
13. Hwang,M.S., Li,L.H.: A new remote user authentication scheme using smart cards. IEEE Trans. Consum. Electron. Vol. 46 (1)(2000)28 - 30
14. Lamport,L.: Password authentication with insecure communication. Communication of ACM Vol. 24 (11)(1981) 770 -772
15. Lu,R.X., Cao,Z.F.: Efficient remote user authentication scheme using smart card. Computer Networks. Vol. 49(4) (2005) 535-540
16. Leung,K.C., Cheng,L.M., Fong,A.S., Chan,C.K.: Cryptanalysis of a modified remote user authentication scheme using smart cards. IEEE Trans. Consum. Electron. Vol. 49 (4)(2003) 1243-1245
17. Sun,H.M.: An efficient remote user authentication scheme using smart cards. IEEE Trans. Consum. Electron. Vol. 46 (4)(2000) 958 - 961
18. Shen,J.J., Lin,C.W., Hwang,M.S.: A modified remote user authentication scheme using smart cards. IEEE Trans. Consum. Electron. Vol. 49 (2)(2003) 414 - 416
19. Yang,W.H., Shieh,S.P.: Password authentication schemes with smart card. Computer Security. Vol. 18 (8)(1999) 727 - 733
20. Chan,C.K., Cheng,L.M.: Cryptanalysis of timestamp-based password authenticatin scheme. Computers & Security. Vol. 21(1)(2002)74-76
21. Fan,L., Li,J.H., Zhu,H.W.: An enhancement of timestamp-based password authenticatin scheme. Computers & Security. Vol. 21(7)(2002)665-667
22. Shen,J.J., Lin,C.W., Hwang,M.S.: Security enhancement for the timestamp-based password authentication scheme using smart cards. Computers & Security. Vol. 22(7)(2003)591-595

23. Wu,S.T., Chieu,B.C.: A user friendly remote authentication scheme with smart cards. Computers & Security. Vol. 22(6)(2003)547-550
24. Yang,C.C., Wang,R.C.: Cryptanalysis of a user friendly remote authentication scheme with smart cards. Computers & Security. Vol. 23(2004)425-427
25. Chen,C.M., Ku,W.C.: Stolen-verifier attack on two new strong-password authentication protocal. IEICE Transactions on Communications. Vol. E85-B,(11)(2002)2519-2521
26. Kwon,T., Song,J.: Efficient and secure password-based authentication protocols against guessing atacks. Computer Communications. 21(1998)853-861.
27. MacKenzie,P., Shrimpton,T., Jakobsson,M.: Threshold password-authentication key exchange, CRYPTO 2002, LNCS, Vol. 2442. Berlin: Spring-Verlag. 385-400.
28. Raimonodo,M.D., Gennaro,R.: Provably secure threshold password authenticated key exchange. In: Eurocrypt 2003, LNCS, vol 2656, Springer-Verlag
29. Chai,Z.C., Cao,Z.F.: Factoring-Based Proxy Signature Schemes with Forward-Security. CIS 2004, Shanghai, Lecture Notes in Computer Science, Vol. 3314, (2004) 1034-1040
30. Gunther, C. G.: An Identity-based Key-exchange Protocol. Advances in Cryptology EUROCRYPT89, LNCS, Vol. 434,Berlin: Spring-Verlag,(1990) 29-37
31. Abdalla,M., Miner, S., et al.: Forward-secure Threshold Signature Scheme. RSA'01
32. Abdalla, M., Reyzin, L.: A New Forward-Secure Digital Signature Scheme. Asiacrypt 2000, Lecture Notes in Computer Science
33. Bellare, M., Miner, S.: A forward-secure digital signature scheme. Advances in Cryptology Crypto'99 Proceedings, Lecture Notes in Computer Science, Vol.1666, Wiener, M. ed., Springer-Verlag 1999
34. Damgard,I.: A design principle for hash functions. in: Advances in Cryptology, CRYPTO 89, LNCS, Vol.435 (1989) 416-427
35. Rivest,R.L., Shamir,A., Adleman, L.: A method for obtaining digital signatures and public-key cryptosystems. Communications of the ACM. Vol.21(2)(1978) 120-126
36. Guillou,L., Quisquater,J.: A practical zero-knowledge protocol fitted to security microprocessor minimizing both transmisson and memory. Eurocrypt 88, LNCS, Vol. 330, springer-verlag, (1988) 123-128
37. Lee,S.W., Kim,H.S., Yoo,K.Y.: Comment on a remote user authentication scheme using smart cards with forward secrecy . IEEE Tran. on Consumer Electronics. Vol 50(2)(2004) 576-577
38. Kumar,M.: Some remarks on a remote user authentication scheme using smart cards with forward secrecy. IEEE Tran. on Consumer Electronics. Vol. 50(2)(2004) 615-618

A Parallel GNFS Algorithm with the Biorthogonal Block Lanczos Method for Integer Factorization

Laurence T. Yang[1,2], Li Xu, Man Lin, and John Quinn

[1] Department of Computer Science and Engineering
Jiangsu Polytechnic University
Changzhou, Jiangsu Province, 213164, P.R. China
[2] Department of Computer Science
St. Francis Xavier University
Antigonish, Nova Scotia, B2G 2W5, Canada
{lyang, x2002uwf, mlin, jquinn}@stfx.ca

Abstract. Currently, RSA is a very popular, widely used and secure public key cryptosystem, but the security of the RSA cryptosystem is based on the difficulty of factoring large integers. The General Number Field Sieve (GNFS) algorithm is the best known method for factoring large integers over 110 digits. Our previous work on the parallel GNFS algorithm, which integrated the Montgomery's block Lanczos algorithm to solve the large and sparse linear systems over GF(2), has one major disadvantage, namely the input has to be symmetric (we have to symmetrize the input for nonsymmetric case and this will shrink the rank).

In this paper, we successfully implement the parallel General Number Field Sieve (GNFS) algorithm and integrate with a new algorithm called the biorthogonal block Lanczos algorithm for solving large and sparse linear systems over GF(2). This new algorithm is based on the biothorgonal technique, can find more solutions or dependencies than Montgomery's block Lanczos method with less iterations. The detailed experimental results on a SUN cluster will be presented as well.

1 Introduction

Currently, Rivest-Shamir-Adleman (RSA) algorithm [16] is the most popular algorithm in public-key cryptosystem. It also has been widely used in the real-world applications such as: internet explorer, email systems, online banking, critical electronic transactions and many other places. The security of this algorithm mainly relies on the difficulty of factoring large integers. So far, many integer factorization algorithms have been developed such as: Trial division [18], Pollard's p-1 algorithm [14], Lenstra Elliptic Curve Factorization (ECM) [9], Quadratic Sieve (QS) [15] and General Number Field Sieve (GNFS) [1,2,3,11] algorithm.

Although GNFS algorithm is the fastest integer factoring algorithm over 110 digits so far, it still takes a long time to factor large integers. In order to reduce

L.T. Yang et al. (Eds.): ATC 2006, LNCS 4158, pp. 428–438, 2006.

the execution time, one natural solution is to distribute jobs to parallel computers. The GNFS algorithm contains several time consuming steps. The most time
consuming one is the sieving part which is used to generate enough relations.
This step is very suitable for parallelization because the relation generations are
independent. Another possible step is, in GNFS, the Montgomery's block Lanczos algorithm [12]. It is used to solve large and sparse linear systems over GF(2)
generated by the GNFS algorithm. This block Lanczos algorithm has two drawbacks: 1. The input of this algorithm is restricted to a symmetric matrix. For
the nonsymmetric inputs, we have to make them symmetric first by multiplying
the coefficient matrix A with A^T. However over GF(2), the rank of the product
$A^T A$ is, in general, much less than that of A. Thus, when applied to find elements of the nullspace of A, the Montgomery's block Lanczos method may find
many spurious vectors. 2. It will break down for some case. The biorthogonal
block Lanczos [5] has overcome the first drawback and can find more solutions
or dependencies than Montgomery's block Lanczos method with less iterations.
In this paper we have successfully implemented the biorthogonal block Lanczos
algorithm and integrated together with the GNFS algorithm.

The rest of this paper is organized as follows: First we briefly describe the
original GNFS algorithm in section 2. Then we present two block Lanczos algorithms, namely the Montgomery's block Lanczos algorithm [12] and the biorthogonal block Lanczos algorithm [5] in section 3 and 4 respectively. Section 5 shows
the detailed implementation and corresponding parallel performance results.

2   The GNFS Algorithm

The General Number Field Sieve (GNFS) algorithm [2,3,11] is derived from the
number fields sieve (NFS) algorithm, developed by Lenstra et al [10]. It is the
fastest known algorithm for integer factorization. The idea of GNFS is from the
congruence of squares algorithm [8].

Suppose we want to factor an integer n where n has two prime factors p and
q. Let's assume we have two integers s and r, such that s^2 and r^2 are perfect
squares and satisfy the constraint $s^2 \equiv r^2 (mod\ n)$. Since $n = pq$, the following
conditions must hold [2]:

$$pq|\,(s^2\text{-}r^2)\ \Rightarrow pq|\,(s\text{-}r)(s\text{+}r)$$
$$\Rightarrow p|\,(s\text{-}r)(s\text{+}r)\ and\ q|\,(s\text{-}r)(s\text{+}r).$$

We know that, if $c|ab$ and $gcd(b,c) = 1$, then $c|a$. So p, q, r and s must satisfy
$p|(s\text{-}r)$ or $p|(s\text{+}r)$ and $q|(s\text{-}r)$ or $q|(s\text{+}r)$. Based on this, it can be proved that
we can find factors of n by computing the greatest common divisor $gcd(n,(s\text{+}r))$
and $gcd(n,(s\text{-}r))$ with the possibility of $2/3$ (see [2]).

Therefore, the essence of GNFS algorithm is based on the idea of the factoring
n by computing the $gcd(n,\ s\text{+}r)$ and $gcd(n,\ s\text{-}r)$. There are six major steps [11]:

1. Selecting parameters: Choose an integer $m \in Z$ and a polynomial f which
   satisfy $f(m) \equiv 0\ (mod\ n)$.

Table 1. The composite number n and the results after integer factorization

Name	Number
tst100$_{30}$	727563736353655223147641208603 = 743774339337499●978204944528897
F7$_{39}$	680564733841876926926749214863536422914 = 570468920068512905472●59649589127497217
tst150$_{45}$	79935628258069264412799144371299175399045096969 = 32823111293257851893153●2435345861758349730367
Briggs$_{51}$	556158012756522140970101270050308458769458529626977 = 1236405128000120870775846228354119184397●449818591141
tst200$_{61}$	1241445153765162090376032461564730757085137334450817128010073 = 11271920071376973729239511669799●11013608559180526498134069115187
tst250$_{76}$	3675041894739039405533259197211548846143110109152323761665377505538520830273 = 6911985578081562539099797454222489432●5316911983139663491615282437374262651

2. Defining three factor bases: rational factor base R, algebraic factor base A and quadratic character base Q.
3. Sieving: Generate enough pairs (a,b) (relations) to build a linear dependence.
4. Processing relations: Filter out useful pairs (a,b) that were found from sieving.
5. Building up a large and sparse linear system over GF(2) and solve it.
6. Squaring root, use the results from the previous step to generate two perfect squares, then factor n.

3   Montgomery's Block Lanczos Algorithm

In 1995, Montgomery proposed an algorithm for solving linear systems over GF(2) named Montgomery's block Lanczos algorithm [12]. This block Lanczos algorithm is a variant of standard Lancozs method [6,7]. Both Lanczos algorithms are used to solve linear systems. In the standard Lanczos algorithm, suppose we have a symmetric matrix $A \in \mathbb{R}^{n \times n}$. Based on the notations used in [12], the algorithm can be described as follows:

$$w_0 = b,$$

$$w_i = Aw_{i-1} - \sum_{j=0}^{i-1} \frac{w_j^T A^2 w_{i-1}}{w_j^T A w_j}. \tag{1}$$

The iteration will stop when $w_i = 0$. $\{w_0, w_1, \ldots w_{i-1}\}$ are basis of $span\{b, Ab, A^2 b, \ldots\}$ with the properties:

$$\forall 0 \le i < m, \quad w_i^T A w_i \ne 0, \tag{2}$$

$$\forall 0 \le i < j < m, \quad w_i^T A w_j = w_j^T A w_i = 0. \tag{3}$$

The solution x can be computed as follows:

$$x = \sum_{j=0}^{m-1} \frac{w_j^T b}{w_j^T A w_j} w_j. \tag{4}$$

Furthermore the iteration of w_i can be simplified as follows:

$$w_i = A w_{i-1} - \frac{(A w_{i-1})^T (A w_{i-1})}{w_{i-1}^T (A w_{i-1})} w_{i-1} - \frac{(A w_{i-2})^T (A w_{i-1})}{w_{i-2}^T (A w_{i-2})} w_{i-2}. \tag{5}$$

The time complexity of the Standard Lanczos algorithm is $O(dn^2)+O(n^2)$, d is the average nonzero entries per row or column.

The Montgomery's block Lanczos algorithm is an extension of the Standard Lanczos algorithm by applying it over GF(2). There are some good properties on GF(2), for example, we can apply matrix to N vectors at a time (N is the length of computer word) and we can also apply bitwise operations. Instead of using vectors for iteration, we using subspace instead. First we generate subspace:

$$\begin{aligned} \mathcal{W}_i \quad & is \ A-invertible, \\ \mathcal{W}_j^T A \mathcal{W}_i = \{0\}, & \ \{i \neq j\}, \\ A\mathcal{W} \subseteq \mathcal{W}, \quad & \mathcal{W} = \mathcal{W}_0 + \mathcal{W}_1 + \ldots + \mathcal{W}_{m-1}. \end{aligned} \tag{6}$$

Then we define x to be:

$$x = \sum_{j=0}^{m-1} W_j (W_j^T A W_j)^{-1} W_j^T b, \tag{7}$$

where W is a basis of $\mathcal{W}$. The iteration in the standard Lanczos algorithm will be changed to:

$$\begin{aligned} W_i &= V_i S_i, \\ V_{i+1} &= A W_i S_i^T + V_i - \sum_{j=0}^{i} W_j C_{i+1,j} \quad (i \geq 0), \\ \mathcal{W}_i &= \langle W_i \rangle, \end{aligned} \tag{8}$$

in which

$$C_{i+1,j} = (W_j^T A W_j)^{-1} W_j^T A (A W_i S_i^T + V_i). \tag{9}$$

This iteration will stop when $V_i^T A V_i = 0$ where $i = m$. The iteration can also be simplified as follows:

$$V_{i+1} = A V_i S_i S_i^T + V_i D_{i+1} + V_{i-1} E_{i+1} + V_{i-2} F_{i+1}.$$

where $D_{i+1}, E_{i+1}, F_{i+1}$ can be computed:

$D_{i+1} = I_N - W_i^{inv}(V_i^T A^2 V_i S_i S_i^T + V_i^T A V_i)$,

$E_{i+1} = -W_{i-1}^{inv} V_i^T A V_i S_i S_i^T$,

$F_{i+1} = -W_{i-2}^{inv}(I_N - V_{i-1}^T A V_{i-1} W_{i-1}^{inv})(V_{i-1}^T A^2 V_{i-1} S_{i-1} S_{i-1}^T + V_{i-1}^T A V_{i-1}) S_i S_i^T$.

S_i is an $N \times N_i$ projection matrix (N is the length of computer word and $N_i < N$). We can reduce the iteration time from $O(n^2)$ to $O(n^2/N)$ (n is the matrix's row or column size) using the block Lanczos algorithm.

4   Biorthogonal Block Lanczos Algorithm

The Biorthogonal block Lanczos algorithm is from standard biorthogonal scalar Lancozs algorithm. The idea of standard biorthogonal scalar Lancozs algorithm is proposed by Lanczos [7]. Like the symmetric case we described in section 3, first we choose two vector u_0 and v_0 from $\mathbb{K}^n$ form two basis $\{u_0,...u_{m-1}\}$ and $\{v_0,...v_{m-1}\}$, and the following conditions must be held [5]:

$$\forall 0 \le i < m \qquad u_i^T A v_i \neq 0,$$
$$\forall 0 \le i < j < m \quad u_i^T A v_j = u_j^T A v_i = 0. \tag{10}$$

Then the solution will be:

$$x = \sum_{i=0}^{m-1} \frac{u_i^T b}{u_i^T A v_i} v_i. \tag{11}$$

With the condition (10), now we are ready to give the new iterations:

$$u_{i+1} := A^T u_i - \sum_{k=0}^{i} \frac{(A^T u_i)^T A v_k}{u_k^T A v_k} u_k,$$

$$v_{i+1} := A v_i - \sum_{k=0}^{i} \frac{(A^T u_k)^T A v_i}{u_k^T A v_k} v_k. \tag{12}$$

Proposition 1. If $u_0,....,u_i$ and $v_0,....,v_i$ are defined in (12), then $u_i^T A^2 v_k = u_k^T A^2 v_i = 0$ for all $0 \le k < i-1$ [5].

According to the Proposition 1, all the projections will be vanished except the last two, the iterations are simplified to follows:

$$u_{i+1} := A^T u_i - \frac{(A^T u_i)^T A v_i}{u_i^T A v_i} u_i - \frac{(A^T u_i)^T A v_{i-1}}{u_{i-1}^T A v_{i-1}} u_{i-1}, \tag{13}$$

$$v_{i+1} := A v_i - \frac{(A^T u_i)^T A v_i}{u_i^T A v_i} v_i - \frac{(A^T u_{i-1})^T A v_i}{u_{i-1}^T A v_{i-1}} v_{i-1}. \tag{14}$$

Instead of using scalars in real fields, now we extend this standard biorthogonal scalar Lancozs algorithm to our problem over GF(2). The input of this algorithm can be either symmetric or nonsymmetric. Montgomery's block Lanczos algorithm only takes a symmetric matrix as the input. For the nonsymmetric matrix, some preconditioning must be performanced first, such as $A^T A$. Generally speaking, The rank of $A^T A$ is much less than the rank of A, Thus, when applied to find elements of the nullspace of A, the Montgomery's block Lanczos method may find many spurious vectors, then lose some solutions accordingly.

The procedure of biothogonal block Lanczos algorithm are: first we choose u_0, $v_0 \in \mathbb{K}^{n \times N}$ randomly and uniformly. (here u and v are block vector). Then we compute u_1, $u_1,...u_{m-1}$ and v_1, $v_1,...v_{m-1}$. Two matrices ξ_i and ω_i are also computed by the columns of u_i and v_i.

The following conditions must be hold through the whole algorithm:

1. $K(A^T, u_0) = \bigoplus_{i=0}^{m-1} \langle \xi_i \rangle$.
2. $K(A, v_0) = \bigoplus_{i=0}^{m-1} \langle \omega_i \rangle$.
3. for all $0 \leq i < m$, $\xi_i^T A \omega_i$ is invertible.
4. for all $0 \leq i$, $j < m$ with $i \neq j$, $\xi_j^T A v_i = u_i^T A \omega_j = 0$.

Assuming all the conditions are held, we can give the biorthogonal Block Lanczos iterations. Let ξ_i and ω_i be two projection matrices and define by $\xi_i = u_i s_i$ and $\omega_i = v_i t_i$.

The iterations for u_{i+1}, v_{i+1} are:

$$u_{i+1} := A^T \xi_i s_i^T + u_i - \sum_{k=0}^{i} \xi_k (\omega_k^T A \xi_k)^{-1} \omega_k^T A^T (A^T \xi_i s_i^T + u_i), \qquad (15)$$

$$v_{i+1} := A \omega_i t_i^T + v_i - \sum_{k=0}^{i} \omega_k (\xi_k^T A \omega_k)^{-1} \xi_k^T A (A \omega_i t_i^T + v_i). \qquad (16)$$

We also want to simply the iterations like what we did in standard biorthogonal scalar Lanczos algorithm. In every iteration, we pick out as many columns as possible from the previous iteration results u_i, v_i then project them into the Krylov basis [5].

We also have: when $0 \leq k < i < m$,

$$
\begin{aligned}
\xi_k^T A^2 \omega_i &= s_k^T s_k \xi_k^T A^2 \omega_i \\
&= s_k^T (A^T \xi_k s_k^T)^T A \omega_i \\
&= s_k^T \left(u_{k+1} - u_k + \sum_{j=0}^{k} \xi_j (\omega_j^T A \xi_j)^{-1} \omega_j^T A^T (A^T \xi_k s_k^T + u_k)\right)^T A \omega_i \\
&= s_k^T u_{k+1}^T A \omega_i - s_k^T u_k^T A \omega_i \\
&= s_k^T u_{k+1}^T A \omega_i. \qquad (17)
\end{aligned}
$$

So $\xi_k^T A^2 \omega_i$ can be simplify to $s_k^T u_{k+1}^T A \omega_i$, and similarly, we can simplify $\omega_k^T (A^T)^2 \xi_i$ to $t_k^T v_{k+1}^T A^T \xi_i$. This tells us that for some $j < i$, if all the columns of u_{k+1} have been chosen and projected into $\xi_{k+1},...\xi_j$, this term will be vanished which means $u_{k+1}^T A\omega_i = 0$.

5   Implementation Details

As we mentioned before, the most time consuming part in GNFS is the sieving part. This part has already been parallelized in our previous work [19,20]. Another part in GNFS program can be improved is to solve the large and sparse linear systems over GF(2) by biorthogonal block Lanczos algorithm, instead of using the Montgomery's block Lanczos algorithm which only takes symmetric input. With the new algorithm, we would not lose any solutions. Our parallel code is built on the sequential source GNFS code from Monico [11].

5.1   Parallel Sieving

The sieving step in sequential GNFS is very suitable for parallel. The purpose of sieving is to find enough (a,b) pairs. The way we do sieving is: fixing b, let a change from $-N$ to N (N is a integer, usually larger than 500), then we check each (a,b) pair whether it smooth over factor bases. The sieving for next b can not start until the previous sieving is finished. After we got enough relations from the sieving step, we start building a linear system over GF(2). This linear system's coefficient could be either symmetric or nonsymmetric, both can be solved by the biorthogonal block Lanczos algorithm.

In parallel, we use several processors do sieving simultaneously, each slave node takes a small range of b, then send results back to master node. The detailed parallel sieving implementation can be found in [19,20].

5.2   Hardware and Programming Environment

The whole implementation uses two software packages, the sequential GNFS code from C. Monico [11] (Written in ANSI C) and sequential biorthogonal block Lanczos code from Hovinen [5] (Written in C++). For parallel implementation, MPICH1 (Message Passing Interface) [17] library is used. In order to do arbitrary precision arithmetic, the GMP 4.x is also used [4]. We use GUN compiler to compile whole program and MPICH1 [13] for our MPI library. The version of MPICH1 is 1.2.5.2. The cluster we use is a Sun cluster from University of New Brunswick Canada whose system configurations is:

- Model: Sun Microsystems V60.
- Architecture: x86 cluster.
- Processor count: 164.
- Master node: 3 GB registered DDR-266 ECC SDRAM.
- Slave node: 2 to 3 GB registered DDR-266 ECC SDRAM.

In the program, Each slave node only communicates with the master node. Fig. 1 shows the flow chart of our parallel program.

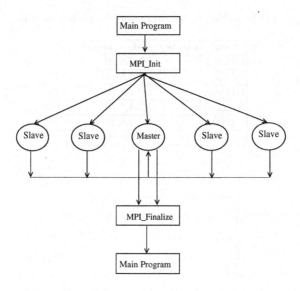

Fig. 1. Each processors do the sieving at the same time, and all the slave nodes send the result back to master node

6   Performance Evaluation

We have six test cases, each test case have a different size of n, all are listed in Table 1.

The sieving time increases when the size of n increases. Table 2 shows the average sieving time for each n with one processor. Table 3 shows the number of processors we use for each test case. Fig. 2 and Fig. 3 show the total execution time for each test case in seconds.

The total sieve time for test case: tst100, F7, tst150, Briggs and tst200 are presented in Fig. 4. Fig. 5 gives the total execution time, sieve time, speed-up and parallel efficiency with different processor numbers for test case tst250. Fig. 6 gives the speed-up and parallel efficiency for each test case with different processor numbers.

Table 2. Average sieving time for each n

name	number of sieve	average sieve time(s)
$tst100_{30}$	1	35.6
$F7_{39}$	1	28.8
$tst150_{45}$	5	50.6
$Briggs_{51}$	3	85.67
$tst200_{61}$	7	560.6
$tst250_{76}$	7	4757.91

Table 3. Number of processors for each test case

name	number of slave processors
$tst100_{30}$	1,2,4,8,16
$F7_{39}$	1,2,4,8,16
$tst150_{45}$	1,2,4,8,16
$Briggs_{51}$	1,2,4,8,16
$tst200_{61}$	1,2,4,8,16
$tst250_{76}$	1,2,4,8,16

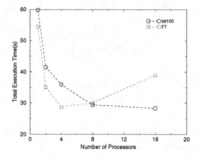

Fig. 2. Execution time for tst100 and F7

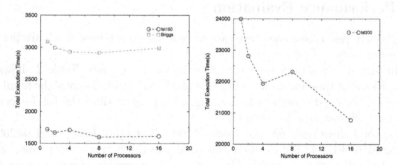

Fig. 3. Execution time for tst150, Briggs and tst200

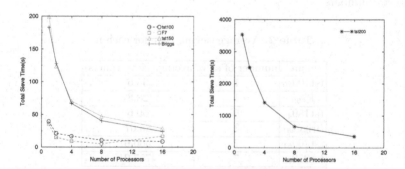

Fig. 4. Sieve time for tst100, F7, tst150, Briggs and tst200

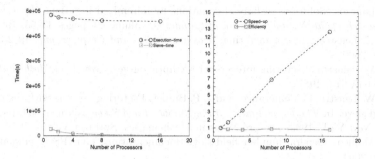

Fig. 5. Total execution time, sieve time, speedup and efficiency for test case tst250

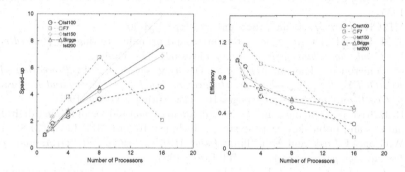

Fig. 6. Speedups and parallel efficiency

Acknowledgements

We would like to thank C. Monico of Texas Tech University and B. Hovinen of University of Waterloo. Our work is based on their sequential source codes. They also helped us with some technical problems through emails. Dr. Silva from IBM advised us many good ideas for our parallel program.

References

1. M. E. Briggs. An introduction to the general number field sieve. Master's thesis, Virginia Polytechnic Institute and State University, 1998.
2. M. Case. A beginner's guide to the general number field sieve. Oregon State University, ECE575 Data Security and Cryptography Project, 2003.
3. J. Dreibellbis. Implementing the general number field sieve. pages 5–14, June 2003.
4. T. Granlund. *The GNU Multiple Precision Arithmetic Library.* TMG Datakonsult, Boston, MA, USA, 2.0.2 edition, June 1996.
5. B. Hovinen. Blocked lanczos-style algorithms over small finite fields. Master Thesis of Mathematics, University of Waterloo, Canada, 2004.
6. C. Lanczos. An iteration method for the solution of the eigenvalue problem of linear differential and integral operators. In *Journal of Research of the National Bureau of Standards*, volume 45, pages 255–282, 1950.

7. C. Lanczos. Solutions of linread equations by minimized iterations. In *Journal of Research of the National Bureau of Standards*, volume 49, pages 33–53, 1952.
8. A. K. Lenstra. Integer factoring. *Designs, Codes and Cryptography*, 19(2-3):101–128, 2000.
9. H. W. Lenstra. Factoring integers with elliptic curves. *Annals of Mathematics(2)*, 126:649–673, 1987.
10. H. W. Lenstra, C. Pomerance, and J. P. Buhler. Factoring integers with the number field sieve. In *The Development of the Number Field Sieve*, volume 1554, pages 50–94, New York, 1993. Lecture Notes in Mathematics, Springer-Verlag.
11. C. Monico. General number field sieve documentation. GGNFS Documentation, Nov 2004.
12. P. L. Montgomery. A block lanczos algorithm for finding dependencies over gf(2). In *Proceeding of the EUROCRYPT '95*, volume 921 of *LNCS*, pages 106–120. Springer, 1995.
13. MPICH. http://www-unix.mcs.anl.gov/mpi/mpich/.
14. J. M. Pollard. Theorems on factorization and primality testing. In *Proceedings of the Cambridge Philosophical Society*, pages 521–528, 1974.
15. C. Pomerance. The quadratic sieve factoring algorithm. In *Proceeding of the EUROCRYPT 84 Workshop on Advances in Cryptology: Theory and Applications of Cryptographic Techniques*, pages 169–182. Springer-Verlag, 1985.
16. R. L. Rivest, A. Shamir, and L. M. Adelman. A method for obtaining digital signatures and public-key cryptosystems. Technical Report MIT/LCS/TM-82, 1977.
17. W.Gropp, E.Lusk, and A.Skjellum. *Using MPI: portable parallel programming with the message-passing interface*. MIT Press, 1994.
18. M. C. Wunderlich and J. L. Selfridge. A design for a number theory package with an optimized trial division routine. *Communications of ACM*, 17(5):272–276, 1974.
19. L. Xu, L. T. Yang, and M. Lin. Parallel general number field sieve method for integer factorization. In *Proceedings of the 2005 International Conference on Parallel and Distributed Processing Techniques and Applications (PDPTA-05)*, pages 1017–1023, Las Vegas, USA, June 2005.
20. L. T. Yang, L. Xu, and M. Lin. Integer factorization by a parallel gnfs algorithm for public key cryptosystem. In *Proceddings of the 2005 International Conference on Embedded Software and Systems (ICESS-05)*, pages 683–695, Xian, China, December 2005.

An Access-Control Policy Based on Sharing Resource Management for a Multi-domains Environment

Hong Zhu[1], Sujuan Duan[1], Fan Hong[1], and Kevin Lü[2]

[1] Huazhong University of Science and Technology, Wuhan, Hubei, 430074, P.R. China
[2] BBS, Room76, Tin Building, Brunel University, Uxbridge, UK UB8 3PH

Abstract. This paper proposed an access control policy based on sharing resource management for a multi-domain environment, where multi-domains have coalesced to achieving a common goal and furthermore a root organization domain is trusted by the multi-domains. Role association is defined and used which set up the foundation for our approach. Each domain unifies the management of shared resources via role associations. A new sharing security domain is established, which is based on the extended hierarchy of roles in the root organization domain. The formation rules of the roles and the way of construction of the roles hierarchy in sharing security domain are also introduced. The role association conflicting issues and rules for role maintenance are also analyzed. Our approaches have enhanced the security measures of shared resources and resolved the problems of the domain crossing and covert promotion which exist in other approaches.

1 Introduction

With the rapid proliferation of the Internet and the Intranet, complicated isomerism features appeared in the distributed computer systems, which issue a rigid challenge of security in distributed systems. As the main features of distributed systems are distribution, autonomic and open, there is an urgent need for providing a new access-control strategy as traditional technologies cannot deal with new problems.

A number of previous work has been in the decentralized, independent and autonomous multi-domains environment. Kapadia presented a secure interoperability model I_RBAC2000[6] for multi-domains based the principle of *Dynamic Role Translation*. Although it resolves the interoperation problems between two domains where their structures are equivalent to each other, but it has problems when the number of domains increases. It would cause the *domain crossing* and *covert promotion* problems, by which a subject could cross the boundary of domains and return to its initial domain with a higher privilege than its initial role so as to promote its privileges covertly. Although I_RBAC2000 use certificates appending the initial domain information for subjects to prevent these two problems, it still needs cooperation of all domains participating in the interoperation, otherwise the two problems can't be resolved. Inspired by the idea of ARBAC97 [9], Al-Muhtadi proposed the AIRBAC2000 model [4] and resolved the management problem for the roles among domains after transformations. But the two problems mentioned above still exist. Mohamed Shehab [7] presented a *secure role mapping* technique between

L.T. Yang et al. (Eds.): ATC 2006, LNCS 4158, pp. 439–448, 2006.
© Springer-Verlag Berlin Heidelberg 2006

two domains. It attached a user's access path to the user's access requests. The administrator of the domain, in which the user belongs to, updates the user's path and forwards the request to the target domain. The administrator of the target domain extracts the user's path, checks the path's authenticity and evaluates the user's request. If the user passes the *check* and the *evaluation*, the user acquires a role in target domain. The *secure role mapping* technique is suitable to such an environment where there are less domains participating in interoperations, because the administrators of the domains should responsible for *request evaluation, path verification* and *update*. The workload of administrators would be increased when the number of the domains is large. Joon S. Park and Keith P. Costello et al presented a composite Role-Based Access Control (RBAC) approach [5], by separating the organizational and system role structures and then by providing the mapping between them. It still uses the role mapping technique among domains. Basit Shafiq and James B.D. Joshi proposed a policy integration framework for merging heterogeneous RBAC policies of multiple domains into a global access control policy [1]. They proposed an integer programming (IP)-based approach to resolve the conflicts that may arise among the RBAC policies among individual domains. However, it makes a trade-off between seeking interoperability and preserving autonomy. Vijayalakshmi Atluri et al proposed a coalition-based access control policies [10] over the shared resources for dynamic coalition environment. It consists of multiple levels: *coalition, role, and user-object layer*. They used a *coalition policy translation protocol* as the policy to percolate to the coalition level. It is suitable for dynamic, ad-hoc formations of information sharing systems for coalition domains that share objects based on object attributes and credential attributes. Freudenthal proposed a distributed dRBAC model [3] for dynamic coalition environments. It uses role authorization and monitor to implement dynamic coalitions. The work in [3] and [10] is suitable for the environment in which the status of all the domains participating in coalition is equal. Actually, there exists an application in which multi-domains have coalesced to achieving a common goal and furthermore a root organization domain is trusted by the multi-domains. This scenario appears in many places, such as the systems for government, military and large corporations. For example, many large companies have their subsidiary companies in different areas. And every subsidiary company has its own domain. When some employees' posts in subsidiary companies need to be changed within the company, or when the domains for some subsidiary companies collaborate to complete a project or a task and the director of the project is the parent company, the parent company will manage the variation of the employee's posts or the schedule of the project or task. At this time, the domains for the subsidiary company need to open their local resources and at the same time keep their original security policies. The domain for the parent company becomes the root organization domain which is trusted by domains for subsidiary company. The solutions for this scenario on sharing resource management have not been addressed in above work.

This paper focuses on the problem of access-control policy for the multi-domains environment; our efforts can be summarized as follows.

(1) An access-control policy based on shared resources management is proposed. Every coalition domain submits some of their shared resources and roles to root organization domain. Based on the role hierarchy and the extensions of the root

organization domain, a new sharing security domain is established via role associations.

(2) The formation rules of roles and the way of construction of the roles hierarchy in sharing security domain are proposed. The role association conflicting issues and rules for role maintenance are also analyzed.

The rest of this paper is organized as follows: Section 2 describes the secure domain based on RBAC. Section 3 presents the access-control policy via role association. Section 4 analyzes the security and presents summaries.

2 The Description of the Secure Domain Based on RBAC

2.1 Basic Hypotheses

(1) *A root organization domain* is trusted by all of other coalition domains. The status of other domains participating in coalition is equal. The coalition domains cannot interoperate each other while they interoperate with the root organization domain. Each domain including root organization domain is autonomous.

(2) Every domain uses the RBAC model as in [8] to manage the roles and defines its roles and a role hierarchy. In the distributed environment, the privileges and assignments of privileges-roles are local autonomous, but not global.

(3) All of the domains provide the security for network transmission and the data encryption to ensure the confidentiality and integrity.

2.2 The Description of the Secure Domain

There are n domains in the coalition environment and they are $D'=\{D_1,...,D_n\}$. We call them *secure domains*.

The ith($i \in$ N) RBAC *secure domain* is a *seven-tuple*: $\prod_i = (U_i, R_i, P_i, M_i, UA_i, PA_i, RH_i)$. The meanings of these seven components are:

(1) The user set in domain D_i is U_i.

(2) The role set in domain D_i is R_i.

(3) The resource set in domain D_i is M_i.

(4) The privilege set in domain D_i is P_i.

(5) $UA_i \subseteq U_i \times R_i$ is a many-to-many relationship from a user set U_i to a role set R_i in domain D_i. UA_i is the assignment relationship of the users and roles. For any user $u \in U_i$ and a role $r \in R_i$, if $(u, r) \in UA_i$, then user u has privileges of role r.

(6) $PA_i \subseteq P_i \times R_i$ is a many-to-many relationship from a privilege set P_i to a role set R_i in domain D_i. PA_i is the assignment relationship of the privileges and roles. For any privilege $p \in P_i$ and role $r \in R_i$, if $(p, r) \in PA_i$, then role r has privilege p.

(7) $RH_i \subseteq R_i \times R_i$ is a role hierarchy relationship in domain D_i, which is an partial-order relationship in R_i, and denoted by $\geq$. For any $r_1, r_2 \in R_i$, $r_1 \geq r_2$(i.e. r_1 dominates r_2 in domain D_i), if and only if the following two conditions are satisfied:

(I) For any $p \in P_i$, if $(p, r_2) \in PA_i$, then $(p, r_1) \in PA_i$;

(II) For any $u \in U_i$, if $(u, r_1) \in UA_i$, then $(u, r_2) \in UA_i$.

Definition 1. *The role-role graph in domain D_i*. *The role-role graph in domain D_i is a directed graph $G_i=(V_i, E_i)$. Every vertex in V_i is a role in R_i. For any two roles r_1, $r_2 \in R_i$, if $r_2 \geq r_1$ and if there does not exist a role r_3 such that $r_2 \geq r_3 \geq r_1$, then there exists a directed edge from vertex r_2 to r_1 in E_i. We call r_2 is the parent of r_1 and r_1 is child of r_2. And the role hierarchy of r_2 is higher than that of r_1 in role-role graph.*

Definition 2. *Assume n is the number of domains participating in coalition. **The coalition domain set is*** $CD = \{D_i \mid D_i = (U_i, R_i, P_i, M_i, UA_i, PA_i, RH_i), i \in \{1,2,...,n\}\}$.

Assume the *root organization domain* is $D_0=(U_0, R_0, P_0, M_0, UA_0, PA_0, RH_0)$. Our work on constructing a sharing secure domain is based on it.

3   The description of Access-Control Policy

3.1   The Role Association

When we discuss the concept of *role association*, a secure domain $D= (U, R, P, M, UA, PA, RH)$ denotes a domain, which is different from D_i.

Definition 3. *The equivalent role association*. *Assume there are a domain D_i in coalition domain set CD and a secure domain D. The role r_{ik} and role r_l belong to D_i and D respectively. In order to make the role r_{ik} in domain D_i has privileges to access the shared resource accessed by r_l in D and let them have same privileges in D, we create a relationship between two roles. The relationship is called equivalent role association, and is denoted by $\{r_{ik}, r_l\}$.*

Fig.1 shows an example of an *equivalent role association* between r_l and r_{ik}. There are two arrows on the dashed line between r_l and r_{ik} in the role-role graph in Fig.1. The role r_{ik} can be added to the role set R in domain D and make $r_l=r_{ik}$ after an equivalent role association is created.

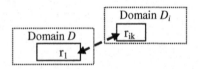   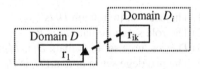

Fig. 1. The equivalent role association   **Fig. 2.** The downwards role association

Definition 4. *The minimal role association*. *For $\forall D_i \in CD$, if $r \in R_i$ and there exists a minimal role Guest$\in D$, the equivalent role association $\{r, Guest\}$ is called minimal role association.*

Obviously, the minimal role association is an equivalent role association between r in Domain D_i and the *Guest* role in R. Then the role in D_i can obtain the privileges of minimal role *Guest* in a secure domain D via the minimal role association. This type of role association is simple. However, it cannot satisfy the requirement of opening more shared resource among domains and it is not flexible enough.

Definition 5. *Downwards role association*. *Assume D_i is a domain in a coalition domain set CD and D is a secure domain. The role r_{ik} and role r_l belong to D_i and D respectively. In order to make the role r_{ik} in the domain D_i has the privilege to access the shared resource accessed by r_l in D and let the role hierarchy of r_{ik} is higher than that of r_l in D, we create a relationship from r_{ik} to r_l. We call this relationship as downwards role association, and it is denoted by (r_{ik}, r_l).*

Fig.2 illustrates an example of downwards role association. After the downwards role association is created, role r_{ik} can be added into the role set R in domain D such that $r_{ik} \geq r_l$. The downwards role association is illustrated by single arrow on the dashed line from r_{ik} to r_l in the role-role graph.

Assume $r_{ik} \in R_i$, according to the semantic of r_{ik}, in secure domain D we cannot create a suitable role association. We have two methods for this scenario. The first, there are two roles r_a and r_b in domain D and r_b is the parent of r_a. If the privileges of r_{ik} needed are higher than that of r_a and lower than that of r_b, we create a new role r_m in D such that $r_b \geq r_m \geq r_a$ and r_m has the same privileges with r_{ik}, and then create an equivalent role association between r_{ik} and r_m. The second, we split the role r_a into two roles; the one is r_m which has the same privileges with r_{ik}, and then create an equivalent role association between r_m and r_{ik}.

Definition 6. *The mediacy role association*. *Assume there are two roles r_1, $r_2 \in R$ in a domain D and r_1 is parent of r_2. We create a new role r_m in D, such that $r_1 \geq r_m \geq r_2$ and the privileges of r_m are equal to privileges of r_{ik}, and then we create an equivalent role association between r_{ik} and r_m. We call it mediacy role association.*

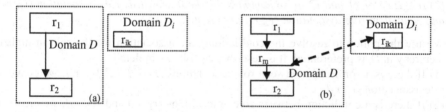

Fig. 3. The example of mediacy role association

Fig.3(a) shows a role-role graph before role association is created. According to the semantic of the role and the requirement of shared resource, we can create r_m whose privilege is equal to that of r_{ik}. Then we create an equivalent role association between r_{ik} and r_m. Fig. 3(b) is an example of *mediacy equivalent role associations*.

Definition 7. *The ramify role association*. *Assume there are two roles r_1, $r_2 \in R$ in domain D, and $r_1 \geq r_2$. We split role r_1 into r_1 and r_{12} and keep $r_1 \geq r_2$, such that $r_{12} \geq r_2$ and $r_1 \neq r_{12}$ and the privileges of r_{12} are equal to privileges of r_{ik}. Then we can create the role association between r_{ik} and r_{12} and call it ramify role association.*

Fig.4 illustrates an example of ramify equivalent role association between r_{ik} and r_{12} after r_1 is split into role r_1 and r_{12}. The new roles, which are produced when we create medicay and ramify role association, are visible to other domains after we create new role associations between domain D and other domains.

It is not difficult to image the scenario in which one of the role associations conflicts with another one. Fig.5 shows an example. After we create an equivalent role association $\{r_1, r_{i3}\}, \{r_{i1}, r_2\}$, the vertex r_1 and r_{i3} will be combined into one vertex in domain D, r_2 and r_{i1} will also combine into another vertex. Now in the domain D, vertex r_1 and r_{i3} will become the parent of vertex r_2 and r_{i1}. But in domain D_i, r_{i1} is parent of r_{i3}. If we still keep the partial-order relationship $r_{i1} \geq r_{i3}$ in domain D, the role association confliction occurred. For example, it is enigmatical for role *manager* in a subsidiary company to acquire a role in the parent company which is lower than the role acquired by the role *staff* in the subsidiary company via another role association.

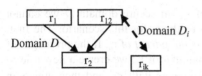

Domain D

Domain D_i

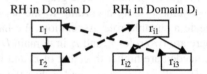

RH in Domain D   RH$_i$ in Domain D$_i$

Fig. 4. Example of ramify role association   **Fig. 5.** Example of confliction of role association

Definition 8. *The confliction of role associations.* *Assume roles r_1, $r_2 \in R_i$ are roles in a domain D_i, the roles r_3, $r_4 \in R$ are roles in a secure domain D and $r_3 \geq r_4$. If one of the following conditions is true, then following two pairs of role associations are conflicted with each other.*

(1) If $r_2 \geq r_1$, or r1 and r2 are incomparable, the equivalent role association $\{r_1, r_3\}$ and $\{r_2, r_4\}$ are created.

(2) If $r_2 \geq r_1$, or r1 and r2 are incomparable, the downwards role association (r_1, r_3) and equivalent role association $\{r_2, r_4\}$ are created.

We use the policy to resolve the conflictions: the association for the role in higher hierarchy in D_i is preferential. It is described as follows in detail:
(1) If there is a confliction between role associations $\{r_1, r_3\}$ and $\{r_2, r_4\}$, we create a role association $\{r_1, r_3\}$.
(2) If there is a confliction between role associations (r_1, r_3) and $\{r_2, r_4\}$, we create a role association (r_1, r_3).

3.2 Definition of Sharing Secure Domain

Definition 9. *Sharing secure domain.* *Assume that there is a coalition domain set $CD = \{D_i | D_i = (U_i, R_i, P_i, M_i, UA_i, PA_i, RH_i), i \in \{1,2,...,n\}\}$, and a root organization domain D_0 is trusted by coalition domains in CD. The sharing secure domain is D= (U, R, P, M, UA, PA, RH) whose components are described as follows.*

(1) $M = M_{1p} \cup ... \cup M_{ip} \cup ... \cup M_{np} \cup M_{0p}$, $M_{ip} \subseteq M_i$, i.e. some resources in sharing secure domain come from coalition domains, $i \in \{1, 2, ..., n\}$;

(2) $R = R_{1p} \cup R_{2p} \cup ... \cup R_{np} \cup R_{0p}$, $R_{ip} \subseteq R_i$ $i \in \{1, 2, ..., n\}$;

(3) $U = U_{1p} \cup U_{2p} \cup ... \cup U_{np} \cup U_{0p}$, $U_{ip} \subseteq U_i$, and $U_{ip} = \{u | \exists r_k \in R_{ip}$, such that $(u, r_k) \in UA_i\}$, i.e. some users in the sharing secure domain come from coalition domains;

(4) P is a set of privileges, which comes from the privileges of sharing resources in coalition domains. UA is the assignments of users to roles. PA is the assignments of privileges to roles. The set of role hierarchy is $RH \subseteq R \times R$.

We construct the sharing secure domain based on the root organization domain. We integrate the resources and privileges from coalition domains, and create new roles or role associations to form a new global sharing roles hierarchical relationship RH.

(5) The procedures for construction of role hierarchical relationships are as follows:

(I) If the resources accessed by a role r_l in a domain D is shared by a role r_{ik} in a domain D_i and an equivalent role association $\{r_{ik}, r_l\}$ is created between role r_{ik} and r_l, then r_l and r_{ik} are the same roles, i.e. the two vertexes are superposition in a role-role graph of RH.

(II) If the resources accessed by a role r_l in a domain D is shared by a role r_{ik} in a domain D_i and a downwards role association (r_{ik}, r_l) is created from the role r_{ik} to the role r_l, and then r_l is child role of r_{ik} in a role-role graph of RH.

(III) If the relationship of two roles in domain D_i is parent-child, then their relationship will be kept in domain D, i.e. for $\forall r_m \in R$ (or after r_m is added into R), if r_{ik}, $r_m \in R_i(r_{ik} \geq r_m)$, and there does not exist role r_{ij} in domain D_i such that $r_{ik} \geq r_{ij} \geq r_m$, then if r_{ik} is added into R in domain D, then $(r_{ik}, r_m) \in RH$, i.e. there exists an directed edge from r_{ik} to r_m in role-role graph of domain D.

(IV) The mediacy, ramify, and minimal role associations which can be converted into corresponding equivalent role associations, their process is the same as (I).

3.3 The Construction of Role Hierarchical Relationships in a Sharing Secure Domain

(1) The expanded rule
If a sharing secure domain D does not have minimal role *Guest*, then we expend $R' = R \cup \{Guest\}$, such that $\forall r \in R'$, $r \geq Guest$. Namely, we add a minimal role *Guest* for sharing secure domain D if it does not have minimal role.

(2) The specific rule
We can specify a role association between the role in sharing secure domain and the role in coalition domains. We have following sub-rules.

(I) We can create an equivalent role association such that r_{ik} in D_i is equivalent to some shared role r_l in sharing secure domain, then r_{ik} and r_l will be superposition in D.

(II) We can create a downwards role association such that r_{ik} is parent of role r_l in D.

(III) We can create a minimal role association such that r_{ik} is equivalent to the minimal role *Guest* in D.

(IV) We can create a mediacy role association such that r_{ik} is equivalent to a role r_m newly created.

(V) We can create a ramify role association such that r_{ik} is equivalent to a role r_m newly split.

(VI) The $(x, y)_{NT}$ and $\{x, y\}_{NT}$ denote untransferable downwards and equivalent role association respectively. We explain the untransferabe property of role association as: when we create RH, for downwards role association $(r_{ik}, r_l)_{NT}$, r_{ik} will be added into R and r_{ik} is parent of r_l; for equivalent role association $\{r_{ik}, r_l\}_{NT}$, r_{ik} will be added into R and let $r_{ik} = r_l$; for any minimal, mediacy and ramify role association, they can be converted to corresponding equivalent role association. But for $\forall r_{il} \in R_i$, if $r_{il} \geq r_{ik}$, r_{il} cannot be added into R for all of the untransferable role associations.

In Fig.6, domain D_1, D_2, ..., D_n make up of coalition environment, and a root organization domain D_0 is trusted by them. The role hierarchies in coalition domains are RH_0, RH_1, RH_2, ..., RH_n. The arrow in real line from x to y in a domain indicates that x is parent of y. These domains have coalesced to achieving a common goal and need to open local resources and at the same time keep their original security policy. Domain D_1, D_2, ..., D_n submit their shared resource and privileges to D_0. Then we create a new role hierarchy based on original role hierarchy in D_0. Some of the users in coalition domains also share the resources of roles in D_0. Then a sharing secure domain D is constructed (in Fig.6, assume that D_0 doesn't open its role, and the sharing secure domain D illustrated in dashed line frame).

We create three role associations in Fig. 6 to form a sharing secure domain D. Role r_{02} in domain D_0 permits the role r_{12} share its resource and create the equivalent role association $\{r_{12}, r_{02}\}_{NT}$. That indicate the role r_{11} who is parent of r_{12} cannot have privileges of r_{02} even if r_{12} is added into D_0. The roles are added into root organization domain via role associations and then sharing secure domain is formed.

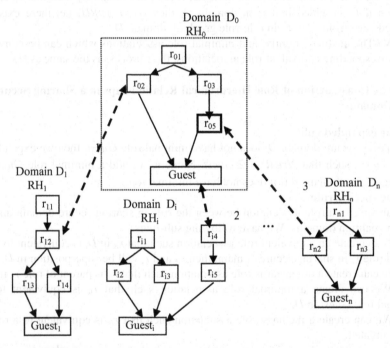

Fig. 6. Construction of role hierarchy in sharing secure domain

(3) Partial specific rule
The partial specific rule can create transferable role association and keep the partial-order relationship of roles in D. Therefore, the roles on which no specific role associations are created can be added into the set of roles in sharing secure domain by transferability of role association.

(I) If r_{il} is a role in domain D_i, for any role $r_2 \in R$, we create an equivalent role association $\{r_{il}, r_2\}$, then r_{il} will be added into R and such that $r_{il} = r_2$. At the same time, for $\forall y \in R_i$, if $y \geq r_{il}$, y will also be added into R and kept $y \geq r_2$ in R.

(II) If r_{il} is a role in domain D_i, for any role $r_2 \in R$, we create a downwards role association (r_{il}, r_2), then r_{il} will be added into R such that r_{il} is parent of r_2. At the same time, for $\forall y \in R_i$, if $y \geq r_{il}$, y will also be added into R and kept $y \geq r_2$ in R.

(III) The minimal, mediacy and ramify role association can be converted to corresponding equivalent role association and can be processed like (I).

For the downwards role association (r_{n2}, r_{05}) in Fig.6, because the privileges of role r_{n2} is inherited by its ancestor, all the shared resource accessed by r_{05} can be accessed by ancestor of r_{n2}. Then we can add r_{n1} into sharing secure domain impliedly and keep their original role hierarchical relationship. That is the transferability of role association.

3.4 The Deletion of Roles

If we delete role r_{ik} in $D_i = (U_i, R_i, P_i, M_i, UA_i, PA_i, RH_i)$, we should inform sharing secure domain to maintain its roles. For the role $r_{ik} \in R$ in domain $D = (U, R, P, M, UA, PA, RH)$, we use following rules to add or delete role associations between roles in sharing secure domain D and roles in coalition domain.

(1) If $\exists r_m \in R$ in domain D such that $r_m = r_{ik}$ and $r_m \notin R_j (j \in \{1, 2, \dots, n\})$, i.e. r_m is not in coalition domains, then r_{ik} is added into R by an equivalent role association when the sharing secure domain is constructed. So far as role r_{ik} is deleted from R, for $\forall r \in R_i$ and $r \notin R$, if $r \geq r_{ik}$ and there does not exist $y \in R_i$, such that $r \geq y \geq r_{ik}$ in R_i, then we create an equivalent role association $\{r, r_m\}$ and add r into R, let $r = r_m$ in R. Namely, we can delete role association between r_{ik} and $r_m (r_m \in R$ and $r_{ik} = r_m)$ and add a series of new equivalent role associations between the parent of r_{ik} and r_m.

(2) If $\exists r_m \in R$ in domain D such that $r_{ik} \geq r_m$ and $r_m \notin R_j (j \in \{1, 2, \dots, n\})$, i.e. r_m is not in coalition domains, and at the same time there does not exist $x \in R$ such that $r_{ik} \geq x \geq r_m$, then r_{ik} is added into R by downwards role association when the sharing secure domain is constructed. So far as role r_{ik} is deleted from R, for $\forall r \in R_i$ and $r \notin R$, if $r \geq r_{ik}$ and there does not exist $y \in R_i$, such that $r \geq y \geq r_{ik}$ in R_i, then we create a downwards role association (r, r_m) and let r is parent of r_m in R. Namely, we delete downwards role association between r_{ik} and $r_m (r_m \in R$ and $r_{ik} = r_m)$ and add a series of new downwards role associations between the parent of r_{ik} and r_m.

(3) If $\exists r_m \in R$ in domain D and r_m is created when a mediacy and ramify role association are created, we delete r_m after all the role associations on it are deleted.

(4) If it is not the case in (1) and (2), then the role is added into R because of the transferability of the role association. We only delete r_{ik} in R and adjust the role hierarchy because of deletion.

4 Summaries

An access-control policy based on shared resources management for multi-domains environment is proposed. It is suitable for the application environment where multi-domains have coalesced to achieving a common goal and furthermore a root organization domain is trusted by the multi-domains. The features of the policy can be summarized as follows:

(1) The centralized management of the sharing resource enhances the security measures amongst multi-domains. Because a new sharing secure domain is created to manage the shared resource, there only exists interoperation between sharing secure domain and coalition domains. Our policy doesn't change the security measures in coalition domains and keeps the original partial-order relationship of role hierarchy in sharing secure domain. Thus the autonomous property and security of coalition domains is kept. Compared with other models, our policy avoids the problem of domain crossing and covert promotion. And the workload of administrators in coalition domains is alleviative.

(2) The policy is very flexible because it does not compulsively require all of the roles in coalition domains should share the resource in sharing secure domain. It also doesn't require the role associations must be transferable or untransferable, and doesn't require which type of role associations must be created.

References

1. Basit, S., James, B.D., Joshi, M., Elisa, B., and Arif, G.: Secure Interoperation in a Multi-domain Environment Employing RBAC Policies, IEEE Transactions on knowledge and data engineering, vol.17, No.11, Nov. 2005.
2. Franco, A., Fabio, F., Enrico, N., Maurizio, T.: a Layered IT Infrastructure for Secure Interoperability in Personal Data Registry Digital Government Services. In Proceedings of the 14th International Workshop on Research Issues on Data Engineering: Web Services for E-Commerce and E-Government Applications (RIDE'04). 2004:95 - 102.
3. Freudenthal, E., Pesin, T., Port, L., Keenan, E. et al: dRBAC: Distributed Role-based Access Control for Dynamic Coalition Environments. In: Edward, K.(eds.): Proceedings of the 22nd IEEE International Conference on Distributed Computing Systems (ICDCS). Vienna, Austria. Los Alamitos, CA, USA: IEEE Computer Society, 2002: 411-420.
4. Jalal, A., Apu, K., Roy, C., Dennis, M.:The A - IRBAC2000 Model: Administrative Interoperable Role-Base Access Control. ACM Transactions on Informatin and Systems Security, 2001, 3(2): 173 - 182.
5. Joon S. Park, Keith, P. C., Teresa, M. N., Josh, A. D.: A composite rbac approach for large, complex organizations. ACM Symposium on Access Control Models and Technologies, 2004: 163-172.
6. Kapadia, A., Muhtadi, J.A., Campbell, R.H. et al:IRBAC 2000: Secure Interoperability Using Dynamic Role Translation. In Proceedings of The 1st International Conference on Internet Computing (IC 2000), Las Vegas, Nevada, Jun. 2000: 231-238.
7. Mohamed, S., Elisa, B., Arif, G.:SERAT : SEcure role mApping technique for decentralized secure interoperability, in Proceedings of the tenth ACM symposium on Access control models and technologies. Jun. 2005: 159-167.
8. Ravi, S., Edward, C., Hal, F., et al: Role-Based Access Control Models. IEEE Computer, 1996, 29(2): 38-47.
9. Ravi, S., Venkata, B., and Qamar, M.: The ARBAC97 Model for Role-Based Administration of Roles. ACM Transactions on Information and System Security, Feb.1999, 2(1): 105-135.
10. Vijayalakshmi, A., Janice, W.: Automatic Enforcement of Access Control Policies Among Dynamic Coalitions. ICDCIT (2004): 369-378.

Efficient Signcryption Without Random Oracles*

Qianhong Wu[1], Yi Mu[1], Willy Susilo[1], and Fangguo Zhang[2]

[1] Center for Information Security Research
School of Information Technology and Computer Science
University of Wollongong, Wollongong NSW 2522, Australia
{qhw, wsusilo, ymu}@uow.edu.au
[2] Department of Electronics and Communication Engineering
Sun Yat-sen University, Guangzhou 510275, P.R. China
isszhfg@mail.sysu.edu.cn

Abstract. Signcryption is an asymmetric cryptographic method that simultaneously provides confidentiality and authenticity at a lower computational and communication overhead. A number of signcryption schemes have been proposed in the literature, but they are only proven to be secure in the random oracle model. In this paper, under rational computational assumptions, we propose a signcryption scheme from pairings that is proven secure *without* random oracles. The scheme is also efficient and comparable to the state-of-the-art signcryption schemes from pairings that is secure in the random oracle model.

1 Introduction

One of the most important applications of cryptography is to build a trusted computing environment by providing confidentiality and authenticity. Usually, these properties are achieved by independent cryptographic primitives such as public key encryption and signature. However, in many applications, both security services are required. A simple combination is usually an inefficient solution. Moveover, such a simple combination may potentially be insecure.

To address such issues, a separate primitive, named signcryption, has been introduced by Zheng in [19]. The original motivation is to achieve a tailored, more efficient solution than a simple composition. Most of these initial work on signcryption are lacking of formal definition and analysis. In [1,9], the formal definitions of signcryption were independently presented. Subsequently, a number of signcryption schemes (e.g. [7,15,11,16,17]) have been proven secure in the random oracle models introduced in [8].

Although the random oracle methodology leads to the construction of efficient and provably secure schemes, it has received a lot of criticism, that the proofs in the random oracle model are *not* proofs. They are simply a design validation methodology capable of spotting defective or erroneous designs when they fail

* This work is supported by ARC Discovery Grant DP0557493 and the National Natural Science Foundation of China (No. 60403007).

[2,3,10,13]. Hence, due to the importance of signcryption, it is essential to have signcryption schemes that are secure in the standard model.

We also note that it is possible to construct a signcryption scheme in the standard model by combining signature schemes with the Cramer-Shoup encryption schemes [12] by using one of the suitable generic composition methods considered by An, Dodis and Rabin in [1]. In fact, another generic construction suggested by Malone-Lee [14] does not make use of random oracles. However, such generic constructions mainly concentrate on a secure combination of encryptions and signatures and hence, such generic constructions are usually not more efficient than a simple combination of the underlying signature and encryption schemes.

Following the original work due to Zheng's signcryption scheme [19], we investigate special effort into designing a more efficient solution than a mere composition of signature and encryption. The main contribution of this paper is an efficient signcryption scheme from pairings. Our construction is based on variants of the Boneh-Boyen signature [4] and the ElGamal encryption. Under the q-Strong Diffie-Hellman (q-SDH) assumption and a candidate Double Decision Diffie-Hellman (DDDH) assumption, the confidentiality and authenticity of the signcryption scheme are proven *without* using random oracles. For performance evaluation, compared to the underlying original ElGamal cryptosystem, the scheme requires only 2 more modular exponentiations in the sender side and 3 more modular exponentiations plus a pairing computation in the receiver side. The ciphertext is about 2 times of that of the original ElGamal cryptosystem. The performance is comparable to the state-of-the-art signcryption scheme from pairings in the random oracle model.

2   Security Definitions

We review the security definitions of signcryption in [1] with a slight extension. In [1], the user's key to produce signature can also be used to receive and decrypt ciphertext. In the following, we distinguish the key to signcrypt messages from the key to de-signcrypt ciphertext.

Definition 1. *A signcryption scheme SC consists of four algorithms: SC = ($Gen_S(\cdot)$, $Gen_R(\cdot)$, $SigEnc(\cdot)$, $VerDec(\cdot)$):*

- *$(SK_S, PK_S) \leftarrow Gen_S(1^\lambda)$ is a polynomially probabilistic time (PPT) algorithm which, on input a security parameter λ, outputs the sender's private/public key pair (SK_S, PK_S).*
- *$(SK_R, PK_R) \leftarrow Gen_R(1^\lambda)$ is PPT algorithm which, on input a security parameter λ, outputs the receiver's private/public key pair (SK_R, PK_R).*
- *$\sigma \leftarrow SigEnc(m, SK_S, PK_R)$ is a PPT algorithm which, on input a message m from the associated message space M, the sender's private key SK_S and the receiver's public key PK_R, outputs a signcryption ciphertext σ.*
- *$m/ \perp \leftarrow VerDec(\sigma, SK_R, PK_S)$ is a polynomial-time deterministic algorithm which, on input a signcryption ciphertext σ, the receiver's private key SK_R and the sender's public key PK_S, outputs $m \in M$ or $\perp$, where $\perp$ indicates that the message was not encrypted or signed properly.*

Definition 2. (Correctness.) *For any* $m \in M$, $(SK_S, PK_S) \leftarrow \text{Gen}_S(1^\lambda)$, $(SK_R, PK_R) \leftarrow \text{Gen}_R(1^\lambda)$, $m = \text{VerDec}(\text{SigEnc}(m, SK_S, PK_R), SK_R, PK_S)$ *holds.*

Definition 3. *(Confidentiality.)* *An SC scheme is semantically secure against chosen ciphertext outsider attack (SC-IND-CCA) if any PPT adversary $\mathcal{A}$ has a negligible advantage in the following game with the challenger $\mathcal{CH}$:*

1. $\mathcal{CH}$ *runs* $\text{Gen}_S(1^\lambda)$ *and* $\text{Gen}_R(1^\lambda)$ *to generate the sender and the receiver's private/public key pair (SK_S, PK_S) and (SK_R, PK_R), respectively. SK_S and SK_R are kept secret while PK_S and PK_R are given to adversary $\mathcal{A}$.*
2. *In the first stage, $\mathcal{A}$ makes adaptive queries to the following oracles:*
   - *Signcryption oracle: $\mathcal{A}$ prepares a message $m \in M$, and queries $\mathcal{CH}$ for the result of $SigEnc(m, SK_S, PK_R)$.*
   - *De-signcryption oracle: $\mathcal{A}$ provides a signcryption ciphertext σ and queries for the result of $VerDec(\sigma, SK_R, PK_S)$.*
3. *$\mathcal{A}$ chooses $m_0, m_1 \in M$ and sends them to $\mathcal{CH}$. $\mathcal{CH}$ flips a coin $b \leftarrow \{0, 1\}$. It computes and sends $\sigma^* \leftarrow SigEnc(m_b, SK_S, PK_R)$ to $\mathcal{A}$.*
4. *$\mathcal{A}$ makes a number of new queries as in the first stage with the restriction that it cannot query the de-signcryption oracle with σ^*.*
5. *At the end of the game, $\mathcal{A}$ outputs a bit b' and wins if $b' = b$.*

The advantage of $\mathcal{A}$ is defined as $Adv^{IND-CCA}(\mathcal{A}) = Pr[b' = b] - \frac{1}{2}$, and the probability that $b' = b$ is called the probability that $\mathcal{A}$ wins the game.

Definition 4. *(Unforgeability.)* *An SC scheme is said to be existentially unforgeable against chosen-message outsider attack (SC-EUF-CMA) if any PPT forger $\mathcal{F}$ has a negligible advantage in the following game with $\mathcal{CH}$. (1) This step is the same as Step 1 of the SC-IND-CCA game. (2) This step is the same as Step 2 of the SC-IND-CCA game. (3) $\mathcal{F}$ produces a signcryption ciphertext σ' and wins the game if $VerDec(\sigma', SK_R, PK_S) \in M$, where σ' is not the output of the signcryption oracle. The advantage of $\mathcal{F}$ is defined as $Adv^{EUF-CMA}(\mathcal{F}) = Pr[VerDec(\sigma', sk_R, pk_S) \in M]$. It is called the probability that $\mathcal{F}$ wins the game.*

3 Mathematical Aspects

3.1 Bilinear Pairings

In recent years, the bilinear pairings have been found in various applications in cryptography. We adopt the notations from [5,6], and briefly review the necessary facts about bilinear pairings as follows. Let `PairingGen` be an algorithm that, on input a security parameter 1^λ, outputs $\Upsilon = (p, \mathbb{G}_1, \mathbb{G}_2, \mathbb{G}_T, g_1, g_2, e)$, where $\mathbb{G}_1 = \langle g_1 \rangle$ and $\mathbb{G}_2 = \langle g_2 \rangle$ have the same prime order p, and $e : \mathbb{G}_1 \times \mathbb{G}_2 \to \mathbb{G}_3$ is an efficient non-degenerate bilinear map such that $e(g_1, g_2) \neq 1$ and for all $h_1 \in \mathbb{G}_1, h_2 \in \mathbb{G}_2$ and $u, v \in \mathbb{Z}$, $e(h_1^u, h_2^v) = e(h_1, h_2)^{uv}$.

3.2   Computational Assumptions

Let $\Upsilon = (p, \mathbb{G}_1, \mathbb{G}_2, \mathbb{G}_T, g_1, g_2, e) \leftarrow \texttt{PairingGen}$ where $2p+1$ and $(p-1)/2$ are both primes. Let the binary length of the element in $\mathbb{G}_1$ be ℓ_1 and $\mathbb{G}_3$ a cyclic group of prime order p', where $p' > 2^{2\ell_1} > p^2$. Assume that there exists an efficient encoding method $\pi : \mathbb{G}_1 \to \mathbb{Z}_{p'}$ but we do not require that the decoding procedure is efficient. For instance, we can simply set $\mathbb{G}_3$ as any finite cyclic group of prime order $p' > 2^{2\ell_1} > p^2$ such that the discrete logarithm is difficult in $\mathbb{G}_3$. In this case, the binary representation of an element in $\mathbb{G}_1$ can be naturally viewed as the binary representation of certain element in $\mathbb{Z}_{p'}^*$. Accordingly, for the generator g_1 of $\mathbb{G}_1$, if we view $g_1 \neq 1 \in \mathbb{Z}_{p'}^*$ as an element of $\mathbb{Z}_{p'}^*$, it is also a generator of $\mathbb{Z}_{p'}^*$ since $1 < g_1 < p'$ and p' is prime. Without confusion, we denote $g_3^{\pi(g_1^a)}$ by $g_3^{g_1^a}$ for simplicity and so on.

In [4], Boneh and Boyen presented the q-Strong Diffie-Hellman (q-SDH) assumption to prove the security of their short signature. In their assumption, the attacker is given $g_2^{x^i}$, $g_1^{x^i}$ for $i = 1, \cdots, q$. The attacker is required to output a pair $(c, g_1^{1/x+c})$. In this paper, we slightly extend the q-Strong Diffie-Hellman problem by additionally providing q-Strong Diffie-Hellman problem attacker $h_1^{x^i}$ for $i = 1, \cdots, q$, where h_1 is an independent generator of $\mathbb{G}_1$. Meanwhile, the attacker is required to additionally output $h_1^{1/x+c}$.

Definition 5. *(**Extended** q-**SDH** **Assumption**) The extended q-Strong Diffie-Hellman assumption in $(\mathbb{G}_1, \mathbb{G}_2)$ states that for any PPT algorithm $\mathcal{A}$,*

$$
\Pr \left[x \leftarrow \mathbb{Z}_p^* \,\middle|\, (c, g_1^{1/x+c}, h_1^{1/x+c}) = \mathcal{A} \begin{pmatrix} g_1, g_1^x, g_1^{x^2}, \cdots, g_i^{x^q} \\ h_1, h_1^x, h_1^{x^2}, \cdots, h_1^{x^q} \\ g_2, g_2^x, g_2^{x^2}, \cdots, g_2^{x^q} \end{pmatrix} \right] \leq \varepsilon.
$$

Clearly, the above extended version of q-SDH Assumption is slightly weaker than the original q-SDH Assumption: By simulating the input of the above extended q-SDH Assumption and running the according attacker, we can also solve the original q-SDH Assumption. We also require a security assumption related to the standard DDH assumption. But it is potentially weaker than the DDH assumption.

Definition 6. *(**DDDH Assumption**) The Double Decision Diffie-Hellman assumption in $(\mathbb{G}_1, \mathbb{G}_2, \mathbb{G}_3)$ states that for any PPT algorithm $\mathcal{A}$,*

$$
\left| \Pr \left[\begin{matrix} a, b \leftarrow \mathbb{Z}_p^*, c_1 \leftarrow \mathbb{Z}_{p'}^*, \\ c_0 = g_1^{ab}, \rho \leftarrow \{0,1\} \end{matrix} \,\middle|\, \rho' = \mathcal{A}(g_1, g_2, g_3, g_1^a, g_1^b, g_2^{a^{-1}}, g_3^{c_\rho}) \wedge \rho' = \rho \right] - \frac{1}{2} \right| \leq \varepsilon.
$$

Clearly, as g_1^{ab} can be calculated out by a CDH adversary, an CDH adversary can be efficiently converted into a DDDH adversary. On the other hand, as g_1^{ab} is masked in the discrete logarithm form $g_3^{g_1^{ab}}$, a DDH oracle cannot be used to solve the DDDH problem efficiently for a proper group $\mathbb{G}_3$. Hence, it is possible to define a group $\mathbb{G}_3$ such that the DDH problem in $\mathbb{G}_2$ and/or $\mathbb{G}_1$ is easy while the DDDH problem in $(\mathbb{G}_1, \mathbb{G}_2, \mathbb{G}_3)$ is difficult.

4 Proposed Signcryption Without Random Oracles

4.1 The Scheme

Let $\Upsilon = (p, \mathbb{G}_1, \mathbb{G}_2, \mathbb{G}_T, g_1, g_2, e) \leftarrow \texttt{PairingGen}$ where $2p+1$ and $(p-1)/2$ are both primes. Assume that the binary length of the element in $\mathbb{G}_1$ is ℓ_1. $\mathbb{G}_3$ is a cyclic group generated by g_3 with prime order p', where $p' > 2^{2\ell_1} > p^2$. The discrete logarithm problem in $\mathbb{G}_3$ is assumed difficult. We remind the reader that if necessary, the binary representation of the element in $\mathbb{G}_1$ will be viewed as the binary representation of the element in $\mathbb{Z}_{p'}^*$ as specified in the previous section.

Receiver's Key Generation: $s, z \leftarrow \mathbb{Z}_p^*$, $h_1 = g_1^s$, $w = g_1^z$. The receiver's public key is (h_1, w). Its secret key is (s, z).

Sender's Key Generation: $x, y \leftarrow \mathbb{Z}_p^*$, $u = g_2^x \in \mathbb{G}_2$, $v = g_2^y \in \mathbb{G}_2$. The sender's public key is (u, v). Its secret key is (x, y).

Signcryption: Given a message $m \in \mathbb{Z}_p^*$, choose a random $r \leftarrow \mathbb{Z}_p^*$ and compute $\sigma_1 = g_1^{1/x+my+r}, \sigma_2 = h_1^{1/x+my+r}, \sigma_3 = (m\|r) \oplus g_3^{w^{1/(x+my+r)}}$. When $x + my + r = 0 \bmod p$, try again with a different random r. The signcryption ciphertext is $(\sigma_1, \sigma_2, \sigma_3)$.

De-signcryption: Given secret key z and a signcryption ciphertext $(\sigma_1, \sigma_2, \sigma_3)$, compute $(m\|r) = \sigma_3 \oplus g_3^{\sigma_1^z}$. Verify that $e(\sigma_1, uv^m g_2^r) = e(g_1, g_2)$ and $\sigma_1^s = \sigma_2$. If both equations hold, output m; otherwise output $\perp$.

Note that $\mathbb{G}_1$ and $\mathbb{G}_2$ are in a symmetric status and the public keys of the sender and receiver are in the same shape. When the receiver wishes to send another signcypted message to the sender, they can simply exchange their role and the scheme still works.

4.2 Security Analysis

Now we consider the security of the scheme. The correctness of the scheme is obvious. Before proceeding to the confidentiality of the signcryption against adaptive active attackers, we consider a weak security notion of signcryption, namely the chosen-plaintext security. In this notion, the adversary has to distinguish signcryption ciphertexts of two messages without having any access to a signcryption or de-signcryption oracle. We show the original signcryption is semantically secure against a chosen-plaintext attacker. In the this case, the signcryption ciphertext is $(\sigma_1 = g_1^{1/x+my+r}, \sigma_2 = h_1^{1/x+my+r}, \sigma_3 = (m\|r) \oplus g_3^{w^{1/x+my+r}})$, where $m \in \mathbb{Z}_p^*$ is the plaintext and r is a random number in $\mathbb{Z}_p^*$. We prove the following claim by paying additional attention to the encrypted randomizer r.

Lemma 1. *The signcryption scheme is semantically secure against chosen plaintext attack under the DDDH assumption in $(\mathbb{G}_1, \mathbb{G}_2, \mathbb{G}_3)$.*

Proof. We show that an attacker $\mathcal{B}$ can break the DDDH assumption by running an signcryption distinguisher $\mathcal{A}$. Suppose that attacker $\mathcal{B}$ is challenged by a DDDH challenge $(g_1, g_2, g_3, g_1^{\alpha}, g_2^{\alpha^{-1}}, g_1^{\beta})$ and c_{ρ}, where $\rho \in \{0, 1\}$ is the bit that $\mathcal{B}$ is trying to compute, $\alpha, \beta \in \mathbb{Z}_p^*$, $c_0 = g_3^{g_1^{\alpha\beta}}$ and c_1 is random in $\mathbb{G}_3$. $\mathcal{B}$ provides $\mathcal{A}$ with public parameters g_1, g_2, g_3. Then $\mathcal{B}$ chooses random $\delta, \gamma, y \in \mathbb{Z}_p^*$ and runs $\mathcal{A}$ on input $PK_{\mathsf{S}} = (u = g_2^x = g_2^{\alpha^{-1}-\gamma}, v = g_2^y)$ and $PK_{\mathsf{R}} = (h_1 = g_1^\delta, w = g_1^\beta)$. Given the challenge plaintext pair $(m_0, m_1) \in \mathbb{Z}_p^* \times \mathbb{Z}_p^*$, $\mathcal{B}$ chooses a random bit $b \in \{0, 1\}$ and produces the challenge ciphertext $(\sigma_1 = g_1^\alpha, \sigma_2 = \sigma_1^\delta, \sigma_3 = (m_b\|r) \oplus c_\rho)$, where α plays the role of $1/(x + m_b y + r)$ and $r = \gamma - m_b y$. Then $\mathcal{B}$ outputs 0 if and only if $\mathcal{A}$ outputs b. Note that $e(\sigma_1, uv^{m_b} g_2^r) = e(g_1^\alpha, g_2^{\alpha^{-1}-\gamma}(g_2^y)^{m_b} g_2^r) = e(g_1^\alpha, g_2^{\alpha^{-1}-\gamma+m_b y+r}) = e(g_1^\alpha, g_2^{\alpha^{-1}}) = e(g_1, g_2)$. Similarly, $e(\sigma_2, uv^{m_b} g_2^r) = e(h_1, g_2)$. The reduction works because $\rho = 0$ produces a perfect real attack simulation, while $\rho = 1$ produces a ciphertext independent of b.

Now prove the confidentiality of the signcryption defined in Definition 3.

Theorem 1. *(Confidentiality) If the DDDH assumption in $(\mathbb{G}_1, \mathbb{G}_2, \mathbb{G}_3)$ and the extended q-SDH assumption in $(\mathbb{G}_1, \mathbb{G}_2)$ hold, the signcryption scheme is semantically secure against chosen ciphertext attack.*

Proof. To prove the theorem, we will prove that under the extended q-SDH assumption, a chosen ciphertext adversary $\mathcal{A}$ interacting with a challenger $\mathcal{B}$ defined in the game of Definition 2 cannot do better than a chosen plaintext adversary. Hence, combined with Lemma 1, the scheme is secure in the active attack defined before.

Assume that $\mathcal{B}$ is challenged by a random instance of the extended q-SDH problem in $(\mathbb{G}_1, \mathbb{G}_2, \mathbb{G}_3)$. Given a tuple
$$(g_1, g_1^x, g_1^{x^2}, \cdots, g_1^{x^q}; h_1, h_1^x, h_1^{x^2}, \cdots, h_1^{x^q}; g_2, g_2^x, g_2^{x^2}, \cdots, g_2^{x^q})$$
for unknown $x \in_R \mathbb{Z}_p^*$, $\mathcal{B}$ is required to output a tuple $(\alpha, g_1^{1/x+\alpha}, h_1^{1/x+\alpha})$, where $\alpha \in \mathbb{Z}_p^*$, and g_1, h_1 are independent generators of $\mathbb{G}_1$ and g_2 generator of $\mathbb{G}_2$.

We assume that the signcryption queries $q_{SC} = q-1$ without lost of generality. $\mathcal{B}$ plays the role of the challenger in the SC-IND-CCA game and interacts with $\mathcal{A}$ as follows. The approach is similar to those in [4,18].

Preparation phase: $\mathcal{B}$ picks randomly $\alpha_1, \alpha_2, \cdots, \alpha_{q-1} \leftarrow \mathbb{Z}_p^*$. Let $f(y)$ be the polynomial $f(y) = \prod_{i=1}^{q-1}(y + \alpha_i)$. Expand $f(y) = \sum_{i=0}^{q-1} a_i y^i$ where $a_0, \cdots, a_{q-1} \in \mathbb{Z}_p$ are coefficients of the polynomial $f(y)$. Let $A_i = g_2^{x^i} \in \mathbb{G}_2, B_i = g_1^{x^i} \in \mathbb{G}_1, D_i = h_1^{x^i} \in \mathbb{G}_1$ for $i = 1, \cdots, q$. Compute:
$$h_2 = \prod_{i=0}^{q-1}(A_i)^{a_i} = g_2^{f(x)}, \quad u = \prod_{i=1}^{q}(A_i)^{a_{i-1}} = g_2^{xf(x)} = h_2^x.$$
Let $f_i(y) = f(y)/(y + \alpha_i) = \prod_{j=1, j\neq i}^{q-1}(y + \alpha_j)$. We expand it as $f_i(y) = \sum_{j=0}^{q-2} b_j y^j$. Compute for $i = 1, \cdots, q-1$:
$$\tilde{g}_1 = \prod_{i=0}^{q-1}(B_i)^{a_i} = g_1^{f(x)}, \quad S_i = \prod_{j=0}^{q-2}(B_j)^{b_j} = g_1^{f_i(x)} = \tilde{g}_1^{1/(x+\alpha_i)} \in \mathbb{G}_1.$$
$$\tilde{h}_1 = \prod_{i=0}^{q-1}(D_i)^{a_i} = h_1^{f(x)}, \quad s_i = \prod_{j=0}^{q-2}(D_j)^{b_j} = h_1^{f_i(x)} = \tilde{h}_1^{1/(x+\alpha_i)} \in \mathbb{G}_1.$$
Randomly select a generator h_3 of $\mathbb{G}_3$. $\mathcal{B}$ provides $\mathcal{A}$ with public parameters $(\mathbb{G}_1, \mathbb{G}_2, \mathbb{G}_T, \mathbb{G}_3, \tilde{g}_1, h_2, h_3, e, p)$.

Public key generation: $\mathcal{B}$ picks randomly $y \in \mathbb{Z}_p^*$. It sets the sender's public key $PK_{\mathsf{S}} = (u, v = h_2^y)$. $\mathcal{B}$ picks randomly $z_1, z_2 \in \mathbb{Z}_p^*$ and sets the receiver's public key $PK_R = (\tilde{h}_1, w = \tilde{g}_1^{z_1} \tilde{h}_1^{z_2})$. $\mathcal{B}$ provides $\mathcal{A}$ with the valid public keys PK_S and PK_R of the sender and the receiver, respectively.

Signcryption simulation: Assume that adversary $\mathcal{A}$ accesses signcryption oracle up to $q_{SC} = q - 1$ queries in an adaptive fashion. $\mathcal{B}$ maintains a list L-list of tuples (m_i, r_i, W_i) and a query counter t which is initially set to 0. Upon receiving a query for m, $\mathcal{B}$ responds as follows and increments t by one.

Check if $h_2^{-m} = u$. If so, $\mathcal{B}$ obtains the secret value in the challenge and can compute the pair $(\alpha, \tilde{g}_1^{1/(x+\alpha)}, \tilde{h}_1^{1/(x+\alpha)})$ for any $\alpha \in Z_p$. Hence, $\mathcal{B}$ can answer the extended q-SDH challenge and terminates the simulation. Otherwise, set $r_t = (\alpha_t - my) \in \mathbb{Z}_p^*$. If $r_t = 0$, $\mathcal{B}$ reports failure and aborts (In the $q - 1$ queries, at least one such bad event happens with probability at most $(q - 1)/p$ and negligible). Otherwise, $\mathcal{B}$ computes $\sigma_{1,t} = S_t, \sigma_{2,t} = s_t, \sigma_{3,t} = (m||r_t) \oplus h_3^{S_t^{z_1} s_t^{z_2}}$. This is a valid signcryption since the following de-signcryption checks hold:
$$e(\sigma_{1,t}, uv^m h_2^{r_t}) = e(S_t, h_2^x h_2^{my} h_2^{\alpha_t - my}) = e(\tilde{g}_1^{1/(x+\alpha_t)}, h_2^{x+\alpha_t}) = e(\tilde{g}_1, h_2),$$
$$e(\sigma_{2,t}, uv^m h_2^{r_t}) = e(s_t, h_2^x h_2^{my} h_2^{\alpha_t - my}) = e(\tilde{h}_1^{1/(x+\alpha_t)}, h_2^{x+\alpha_t}) = e(\tilde{h}_1, h_2).$$
If $\mathcal{B}$ does not stop, it adds the tuple $(m, r_t, v^m h_2^{r_t})$ to the L-list.

De-signcryption simulation: Given a signcryption ciphertext $(\sigma_1, \sigma_2, \sigma_3)$, compute $(m||r) = \sigma_3 \oplus h_3^{\sigma_1^{z_1} \sigma_2^{z_2}}$. Output m if both $e(\sigma_1, uv^m h_2^r) = e(\tilde{g}_1, h_2)$ and $e(\sigma_2, uv^m h_2^r) = e(\tilde{h}_1, h_2)$ hold; otherwise output $\perp$.

Challenge ciphertext: After a series of adaptive signcryption and de-signcryption queries, $\mathcal{A}$ provides $\mathcal{B}$ with two message $m_0, m_1 \in Z_p^*$ which have never been queried to the signcryption oracle. $\mathcal{B}$ randomly picks $b \in_R \{0, 1\}$ and computes $r = \alpha_{q-1} - m_b y, \sigma_1^* = S_{q-1}, \sigma_2^* = s_{q-1}, \sigma_3^* = (m_b||r) \oplus h_3^{S_{q-1}^{z_1} s_{q-1}^{z_2}}$. $\mathcal{B}$ sends $(\sigma_1^*, \sigma_2^*, \sigma_3^*)$ to $\mathcal{A}$ as the challenge signcryption ciphertext.

$\mathcal{A}$ is still allowed to access the signcryption and de-signcryption oracles if $t < q - 1$. But $\mathcal{A}$ cannot query $(\sigma_1^*, \sigma_2^*, \sigma_3^*)$ to the de-signcryption oracle. Finally, $\mathcal{A}$ outputs $b' \in \{0, 1\}$. We analyze the probability that $b = b'$ happens.

We here prove that, in the above game, for $\mathcal{A}$'s query $(\sigma_1, \sigma_2, \sigma_3)$ to the de-signcryption oracle, if $\mathcal{B}$ outputs m, then $(\sigma_1, \sigma_2, \sigma_3)$ is an output of the signcryption oracle except a negligible probability. Note that $(\sigma_1, \sigma_2, m, r)$ should satisfy that $e(\sigma_1, uv^m h_2^r) = e(\tilde{g}_1, h_2)$ and $e(\sigma_2, uv^m h_2^r) = e(\tilde{h}_1, h_2)$. Let $W = h_2^r v^m$. $\mathcal{B}$ searches the L-list and there are two cases:

Case 0: No tuple of the form $(\cdot, \cdot, W)$ appears in the L-list.
Case 1: The L-list contains at least one tuple (m_j, r_j, W).

Case 0 implies that $m = -x$ or $r + my = \alpha \notin \{\alpha_1, \cdots, \alpha_{q-1}\}$. Let the queries to the de-signcryption oracle be less than $q - 1$. During the game, $m = -x$ happens with probability at most $(q - 1)/p$ and negligible. As $e(\sigma_1, h_2^{x+r+my}) = e(\sigma_1, uh_2^r v^m) = e(\tilde{g}_1, h_2)$, we have $\sigma_1 = \tilde{g}_1^{1/(x+r+my)} = \tilde{g}_1^{1/(x+\alpha)} = g_1^{f(x)/(x+\alpha)}$. Let the polynomial $f(x) = \delta(x)(x + \alpha) + \gamma$, where $\delta(x) = \sum_{i=0}^{q-2} \delta_i x^i$ and $\gamma \neq 0 \in \mathbb{Z}_p$. We have $f(x)/(x + \alpha) = \gamma/(x + \alpha) + \sum_{i=0}^{q-2} \delta_i x^i$. Then we can compute $g_1^{1/x+\alpha} = (\sigma \prod_{i=0}^{q-1} (B_i)^{-\delta_i})^{1/\gamma}$. Similarly, we can compute $h_1^{1/x+\alpha} = (\sigma \prod_{i=0}^{q-1} (D_i)^{-\delta_i})^{1/\gamma}$. $(\alpha, g_1^{1/x+\alpha}, h_1^{1/x+\alpha})$ is a solution to the extended q-SDH problem. It happens with negligible probability under the extended q-SDH assumption. Hence, case 0 happens with negligible probability.

Case 1 implies that $r+my \in \{\alpha_1, \cdots, \alpha_{q-1}\}$. It follows that $r+my = r_i+ym_i$ for some $i \in \{1, \cdots, q-1\}$. Note that $m \neq m_i$ as m has never been queried by $\mathcal{A}$. It follows that $y = (r-r_i)/(m-m_i)$. Due to the discrete logarithm assumption (implied by the extended q-SDH assumption), it happens with probability at most $(q-1)/p$. Hence, case 1 happens with only negligible probability.

Hence, we conclude that for $\mathcal{A}$'s query $(\sigma_1, \sigma_2, \sigma_3)$ to the de-signcryption oracle, if $\mathcal{B}$ outputs m, then $(\sigma_1, \sigma_2, \sigma_3)$ is an output of the signcryption oracle except a negligible probability. That is, except a negligible probability, $\mathcal{A}$ cannot provide a valid ciphertext except the output of signcryption oracle. Hence, except the same probability, these queries contribute no information for $\mathcal{A}$ to answer the challenge signcryption ciphertext. Therefore, except this negligible probability, the probability for $\mathcal{A}$ to win this game is the same as that to win the semantical security game of the signcryption against the chosen plaintext attack. Under DDDH assumption, the latter probability is negligible. Hence, $\mathcal{A}$ wins the above game with negligible probability and the scheme is SC-IND-CCA secure.

Theorem 2. *(Unforgeability). Under the q-SDH assumption, the signcryption scheme is existentially unforgeable against chosen-message outsider attack.*

Proof. We prove that a chosen message adversary $\mathcal{A}$ interacting with a challenger $\mathcal{B}$ defined in the unforgeability game of Definition 4 can be run as a subroutine by $\mathcal{B}$ to break the q-SDH assumption. It is similar to the existentially unforgeability proof of the short signature in [4].

Assume that $\mathcal{B}$ is challenged by a random instance of the q-SDH problem in $(\mathbb{G}_1, \mathbb{G}_2)$. Given a tuple $(g_1, g_1^x, g_1^{x^2}, \cdots, g_1^{x^q}; g_2, g_2^x, g_2^{x^2}, \cdots, g_2^{x^q})$ for unknown $x \in_R \mathbb{Z}_p^*$, $\mathcal{B}$ is required to compute a tuple $(\alpha, g_1^{1/(x+\alpha)})$, where $\alpha \in \mathbb{Z}_p^*$, and g_1 is a generator of $\mathbb{G}_1$ and g_2 generator of $\mathbb{G}_2$.

Similar to the proof of Theorem 1, $\mathcal{B}$ picks randomly $\alpha_1, \alpha_2, \cdots, \alpha_{q-1} \leftarrow \mathbb{Z}_p^*$. Let $f(y) = \prod_{i=1}^{q-1}(y+\alpha_i)$, $A_i = g_2^{x^i} \in \mathbb{G}_2$, $B_i = g_1^{x^i} \in \mathbb{G}_1$ for $i = 1, \cdots, q$. $\mathcal{B}$ can compute $h_2 = g_2^{f(x)}$, $u = h_2^x$, $\tilde{g}_1 = g_1^{f(x)}$ and $S_i = \tilde{g}_1^{1/(x+\alpha_i)}$.

$\mathcal{B}$ randomly selects a generator h_3 of a proper finite cyclic group $\mathbb{G}_3$. $\mathcal{B}$ provides $\mathcal{A}$ with public parameters $(\mathbb{G}_1, \mathbb{G}_2, \mathbb{G}_T, \mathbb{G}_3, \tilde{g}_1, h_2, h_3, e, p)$, where $\mathbb{G}_1 = \langle \tilde{g}_1 \rangle$, $\mathbb{G}_2 = \langle h_2 \rangle$ and $\mathbb{G}_T$ have the same prime order p, and $e : \mathbb{G}_1 \times \mathbb{G}_2 \to \mathbb{G}_T$ is an efficient non-degenerate bilinear map.

$\mathcal{B}$ picks randomly $y \in \mathbb{Z}_p^*$. It sets the sender's public key $PK_{\mathsf{S}} = (u, v = h_2^y)$. $\mathcal{B}$ picks randomly $\delta, z \in \mathbb{Z}_p^*$ and sets the receiver's public key $PK_{\mathsf{R}} = (\tilde{h}_1 = \tilde{g}_1^\delta, w = \tilde{g}_1^z)$. $\mathcal{B}$ provides $\mathcal{A}$ with the valid public keys PK_{S} and PK_{R} of the sender and the receiver, respectively.

Whenever $\mathcal{A}$ requests a signcryption ciphertext with message m_i, $\mathcal{B}$ computes $\sigma_{1,t} = S_t, \sigma_{2,t} = S_t^\delta, \sigma_{3,t} = (m_i \| r_t) \oplus h_3^{S_t^z}$, where $r_t = (\alpha_t - my) \in \mathbb{Z}_p^*$. Clearly, this is a valid ciphertext on m_i since the corresponding de-signcryption checks hold. The simulation is successful except a negligible probability.

Assume that $\mathcal{A}$ made $q-1$ queries. Finally, $\mathcal{A}$ will output a valid signcryption ciphertext $(\sigma_1, \sigma_2, \sigma_3)$ on message m, where m has never been queried. Now $\mathcal{B}$ can de-signcrypt $(\sigma_1, \sigma_2, \sigma_3)$ and obtain (m, r). If $r + my \in \{\alpha_1, \cdots, \alpha_{q-1}\}$, it means that $y = (r - r_i)/(m - m_i)$. As the discrete logarithm problem (implied by the q-SDH assumption) is difficult, this bad event happens with probability negligible. Hence, $\alpha = r + my \notin \{\alpha_1, \cdots, \alpha_{q-1}\}$. Similar to Theorem 2, let the polynomial $f(x) = \delta(x)(x + \alpha) + \gamma$, where $\delta(x) = \sum_{i=0}^{q-2} \delta_i x^i$ and $\gamma \neq 0 \in \mathbb{Z}_p$. It follows that $f(x)/(x + \alpha) = \gamma/(x + \alpha) + \sum_{i=0}^{q-2} \delta_i x^i$. Then $\mathcal{B}$ can compute $g_1^{1/x+\alpha} = (\sigma \prod_{i=0}^{q-1} (B_i)^{-\delta_i})^{1/\gamma}$. Hence, $\mathcal{B}$ obtains a solution to the q-SDH problem. It contradicts to the q-SDH assumption.

4.3   Efficiency Comparison

We compare our scheme with the state-of-the-art signcryptions from pairings and assume the same pairings and security parameters are used.

Table 1. Comparison of the state-of-the-art signcryption schemes

	ciphertext length (bits)	signcryption	de-signcryption
[7]	$2\ell_1 + \ell$	4Exp + 1P	2Exp + 4P
[15]	$\ell_1 + 2\ell$	4Exp + 2P	2Exp + 4P
[11]	$2\ell_1 + \ell$	3Exp + 1P	1Exp + 3P
[16]	$\ell_1 + 2\ell$	2Exp	2Exp + 1P
Our scheme	$2\ell_1 + 2\ell$	4Exp	4Exp + 1P

In the above table, the ciphertext length does not include the bits to represent the sender's identity or public key. ℓ_1 is the binary length of the element in group $\mathbb{G}_1$. ℓ is the binary length of the message to be sent. Exp represents a exponentiation and P a pairing computation. There is a two-base exponentiation in the de-signcryption of our scheme. It requires slightly more computations than a single-base exponentiation. As the pairing computation is much more inefficient than the exponentiation in pairing-based cryptography, it is important to reduce the number of pairing computations. From the above table, our scheme is one of the most efficient schemes. Furthermore, our scheme is in the standard model while others are in the random oracle model.

5   Conclusions

In electronic transactions such as secure e-mails and electronic commerce, the confidentiality and authenticity are simultaneously required to enable a secure and trustable communication and computation environment. It is essential to integrate the services of traditional encryption and signature into the new primitive of signcryption for not only efficiency reason but also security reason. This paper presented a signcryption scheme from pairings that is secure in the standard model (without random oracles). The scheme is very efficient and comparable to the state-of-the-art signcryption scheme from pairings that is secure in the random oracle model.

References

1. J. H. An, Y. Dodis, and T. Rabin. On the security of joint signature and encryption. Eurocrypt'02, LNCS 2332, pp. 83-107. Springer-Verlag, 2002.
2. B. Barak. How to go beyond the black-box simuation barrier. In 42nd FOCS, pp. 106-115. IEEE Computer Soceity, 2001. Available at: http://www.wisdom.weizmann.ac.il/ boaz.
3. B. Barak, Y. Lindell, and S. P. Vadhan. Lower bounds for non-black-box zero knowledge. In FOCS'03, pp. 384-393. IEEE Computer Soceity, 2003.
4. D. Boneh and X. Boyen. Short signatures without random oracles. Eurocrypt'04, LNCS 3027, pp. 56-73. Springer-Verlag, 2004.
5. D. Boneh and M. Franklin. Identity-based encryption from the Weil pairing. Crypto'01, LNCS 2139, pp. 213-229. Springer-Verlag, 2001.
6. D. Boneh, B. Lynn, and H. Shacham. Short signatures from the Weil pairing. Asiacrypt'01, LNCS 2248, pp. 514-532. Springer-Verlag, 2001.
7. X. Boyen. Multipurpose identity-based signcryption: A swiss army knife for identity-based cryptography. Crypto'03, LNCS 2729, pp. 382-398. Springer-Verlag, 2003.
8. M. Bellare and P. Rogaway. Random oracles are practical: A paradigm for designing efficient protocols. 1st ACM Conference on Computer and Communications Security, pp. 62-73. ACM press, 1993.
9. J. Baek, R. Steinfeld, and Y. Zheng. Formal proofs for the security of signcryption. PKC'02, LNCS 2274, pp. 80-98. Springer-Verlag, 2002.
10. R. Canetti, O. Goldreich, and S. Halevi. The random oracle methodology, revisited. Journal of the ACM, Vol. 51, No. 4, pp.557-594, July 2004.
11. L. Chen and J. M. Lee, Improved identity-based signcryption. PKC'05, LNCS 3386, pp. 362-379. Springer-Verlag, 2005.
12. R. Cramer and V. Shoup. A practical public key cryptosystem provably secure against adaptive chosen ciphertext attack. Crypto'98, LNCS 1462. Springer-Verlag, 1998.
13. S. Goldwasser, and Y. T. Kalai. On the (in)security of the fiat-shamir paradigm. Proceedings of the 44th Annual IEEE Symposium on Foundations of Computer Science, pp. 102-113. IEEE press, 2003.
14. J. M. Lee. A General Construction for Simultaneous Siging and encrypting. Cryptography and Coding 2005, LNCS 3796, pp. 116-135. Springer-Verlag, 2005.
15. B. Libert and J. J. Quisquater. New identity-based signcryption schemes from pairings. In IEEE Information Theory Workshop 2003, pp. 155-158. IEEE press, 2003.
16. B. Libert, and J. Quisquater. Improved signcryption from q-Diffie-Hellman problems. SCN'04, LNCS 3352, pp. 220-234. Springer-Verlag, 2005.
17. J. M. Lee, W. Mao. Two birds one stone: Signcryption using RSA. CT-RSA'03, LNCS 2612, pp. 211-225. Springer-Verlag, 2003.
18. R. Zhang, J. Furukawa and H. Imai. Short signature and universal designated verifier signature without random oracles. ACNS 2005, LNCS 3531, pp. 483-498. Springer-Verlag, 2005.
19. Y. Zheng. Digital signcryption or how to achieve cost (signature & encryption) $\ll$ cost(signature) + cost(encryption). Crypto'97, LNCS 1294, pp. 165-179. Springer-Verlag, 1997.

Two Novel Packet Marking Schemes for IP Traceback

Hanping Hu[1], Yi Wang[2], Lingfei Wang[3], Wenxuan Guo,[4] and Mingyue Ding[5]

[1] Institute for Pattern Recognition and Artificial Intelligence, Huazhong University of Science and Technology, 1037 Luoyu Road, Wuhan 430074, P.R. China
hphu@mail.hust.edu.cn
[2] Institute for Pattern Recognition and Artificial Intelligence, Huazhong University of Science and Technology, 1037 Luoyu Road, Wuhan 430074, P.R. China
wangyier@263.net
[3] Institute for Pattern Recognition and Artificial Intelligence, Huazhong University of Science and Technology, 1037 Luoyu Road, Wuhan 430074, P.R. China
blueemotion@sohu.com
[4] Institute for Pattern Recognition and Artificial Intelligence, Huazhong University of Science and Technology, 1037 Luoyu Road, Wuhan 430074, P.R. China
guowenxuan2105@tom.com
[5] Institute for Pattern Recognition and Artificial Intelligence, Huazhong University of Science and Technology, 1037 Luoyu Road, Wuhan 430074, P.R. China
myding_2000@yahoo.com.hk

Abstract. Two novel packet marking schemes, the non-Repeated Varying-Probability Packet Marking (nRVPPM) and the Compressed non-Repeated Varying-Probability Packet Marking (CnRVPPM), are presented. To solve the repeated marking problem, we propose in the nRVPPM that one packet is marked by routers only one time with the probability which is varying with the distance the packet has traveled. Besides, the nRVPPM makes the victim receives the packets marked by each router with the same probability. Based on the nRVPPM, we bring forward the CnRVPPM by employing the redundancy brought about by the similarity of IP addresses. Our simulation studies show that the proposed schemes offer high precision and efficiency, and can dramatically reduce the number of packets required for the traceback.

1 Introduction

Distributed denial of service (DDoS) attack is one of the greatest threats to the Internet today. Unfortunately, Internet has not been equipped with proper defense mechanisms against DDoS attacks. IP traceback [1], the subject of this paper, has emerged as a promising solution to DDoS attack problem.

Savage et al. [2] proposed Probabilistic Packet Marking (PPM), which divides each router's IP address and redundancy information into several fragments and marks the IP packets with one of the fragments probabilistically. Once the victim gets enough marked packets, it can extract the marked fragments from IP packets and reconstruct the full path, even though the IP address of the attacker is spoofed. According to the coupon collecting problem [3], Tao Pen et al. [4] developed a technique to adjust the probability for routers to mark packets, for the purpose of reducing the number of packets needed by the victim to reconstruct the attack paths. These methods, however, do not solve the repeated marking problem.

L.T. Yang et al. (Eds.): ATC 2006, LNCS 4158, pp. 459–466, 2006.
© Springer-Verlag Berlin Heidelberg 2006

In this paper, we present a novel packet marking scheme, the non-Repeated Varying-Probability Packet Marking (nRVPPM). According to the nRVPPM, packets are marked only one time along the forwarding path, which solves the repeated marking problem. Routers mark a packet with the probability of 1/(33-i) (i denotes the distance the packet has traveled). In this way, the victim would receive the packets marked by each router with the same probability, which will be proved later. Then, on the basis of the nRVPPM, we employ the redundancy caused by the similarity of the IP addresses in a path to reduce the fragments of a sample node, thereby to decrease the packets required for IP traceback, and propose another scheme, the Compressed non-Repeated Varying-Probability Packet Marking (CnRVPPM), which is greatly improved in reducing the number of packets required for traceback. We evaluate the effectiveness of the proposed schemes through simulation studies. Our studies show that the proposed schemes offer high precision and efficiency, and dramatically reduce the number of packets required for the traceback process.

The rest of this paper is organized as follows: section 2 and Section 3 explain the nRVPPM and CnRVPPM respectively, Section 4 shows the experimental results of the two schemes, Section 5 gives the conclusions.

2 nRVPPM

We assume that there are d routers ($R_1, R_2, \ldots\ldots, R_d$) on the path from an attacker to the victim in a Denial of Service (DoS) scene. Router R_1 is the closest to the attacker and Router R_d is the closest to the victim. $P^R_i (1 \leq i \leq d)$ denotes the marking probability of router R_i, $P^V_i (1 \leq i \leq d)$ denotes the probability of the victim receiving the packets marked by router R_i. To avoid repeated packet marking problem, a router does not mark a packet which has been marked. Then we obtain the following equitation:

$$P^V_1 = P^R_1$$
$$P^V_2 = P^R_2(1 - P^R_1)$$

$$P^V_3 = P^R_3(1 - P^R_1)(1 - P^R_2)$$

$$\cdots\cdots$$

$$P^V_d = P^R_d \prod_{1 \leq i < d}(1 - P^R_i), (d > 1)$$

The ideal case for packet marking is to receive packets marked by each router with the same probability: $P^V_1 = P^V_2 = \ldots\ldots = P^V_i = \ldots\ldots$. Therefore, when the length of the path is d,

$$\frac{1}{d} = P^V_1 = P^R_1$$

$$\frac{1}{d} = P^V_2 = P^R_2(1 - P^R_1)$$

$$Y_d = P^V_3 = P^R_3(1 - P^R_1)(1 - P^R_2)$$

$$\cdots\cdots$$

$$Y_d = P^V_d = P^R_d \prod_{1 \le i < d}(1 - P^R_i), (d > 1)$$

We can summarize the marking probability formula for router R_i as:

$$P^R_i = Y_{(d+1-i)}, (i = 1, 2, \ldots\ldots, d).$$

From the formula above, it is clear that to implement this marking scheme, we have to know the length of the path d and the distance i from the attacker to the router R_i. However, before a packet arrives at its destination, the routers along the forwarding path are unaware of the exact length of the path d. According to the statistics of distances of the internet [5], the lengths of almost all network paths are smaller than 32. So we assume that the distance from the attacker to victim is 32 hops, namely $d = 32$.

For the distance i, we propose to use a marking field to record the number of hops than the packet has been traveled, and to tell the router its position in this forwarding path. The initial value for this field is 0 when a packet enters network at R_1. Each time the router receives a packet which is not marked, it extracts the distance i from the packet and marks the packet with probability $P_i = Y_{(33-i)}$. If the router decides not to mark this packet, it increases this value by 1 and forwards this packet. Once a packet is marked, the following routers can never make any changes to the marking field in the packet. It seems that the nRVPPM induces more computational overhead for the routers than the PPM[2] do, because they need to calculate the P_i for every unmarked packet that they receive. However, this is neglectable compared with the expense of the generation of pseudo numbers, which is used by all PPM schemes to simulate probabilities.

Usually, PPM schemes overload the 16-bit IP Identification field to store the traceback information, and then the marked packets can't be reassembled. So, the Fragment Offset field is useless. Then, in the nRVPPM, routers overwrite the Identification field, the Fragment Offset field and the reserve field in IP header with their IP information. But we must remember that: after having extracted the traceback information marked in the packets and before these packets are passed to the IP reassembly routine, we must set the reserve field and the Fragment Offset field back to zero.

We divide this 30-bit space into four marking fields, as shown in figure 1.

1. HASH (15 bits): this field stores the encoded 32-bit IP address, acting as the "identification" of a segment. The segments with same HASH field will be collected for reconstruction of the IP address. It should be noted that different IP addresses may have the same encoded HASH value.
2. SEGMENT (8 bits): this field keeps a part of an IP address. Several packets with different Segments but with the same HASH field can be used to reconstruct the encoded 32-bit IP address.
3. OFFSET (2 bits): this field indicates the offset of the segment in IP address.
4. DISTANCE (5 bits): this field shows the distance (in hops) from the attacker to the marking router.

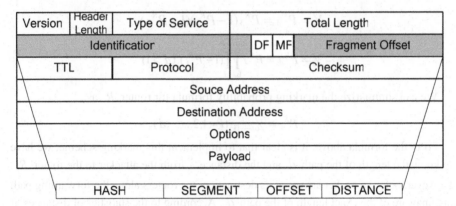

Fig. 1. IP packet format and marking fields

In the nRVPPM, an IP address is divided into four segments whose OFFSET values are 0,1,2,3 respectively. Each segment is stored in the SEGMENT field in a packet. The victim uses DISTANCE and HASH field to identify all segments belonging to the same IP address, and assemble them into many IP addresses according to their OFFSET values, then use HASH value to verify whether the reconstructed IP is correct.

3   CnRVPPM

In an autonomy area, adjacent routers may have similar IP addresses. For example, there may be two directly linked routers whose IP addresses are 1.2.3.4 and 1.2.3.127. This similarity of IP addresses is employed to reduce the number of segments required to reconstruct IP address, and eventually the number of packets for needed for IP traceback would be decreased. Note that routers can easily learn the IP addresses of their adjacent routers by various routing protocols.

Suppose two directly linked routers, R_{i-1} and R_i , their IP addresses are $Seg_3^{i-1}.Seg_2^{i-1}.Seg_1^{i-1}.Seg_0^{i-1}$ and $Seg_3^i.Seg_2^i.Seg_1^i.Seg_0^i$,respectively; and $Seg_3^{i-1} = Seg_3^i$. Therefore, with the knowledge of R_{i-1}'s IP address and $Seg_2^i, Seg_1^i, Seg_0^i$, we can reconstruct the IP address of R_i without knowing Seg_3^i.

The router R_1 can easily know that it is the first router on the path from the fact that the DISTANCE field equals to 0. Therefore, it must mark all the four segments of its IP address, while the following routers just need to mark some segments of their IP addresses. When the victim reconstructs the path and segments are not enough to reconstruct an IP address, it needs to extract the missing part from the preceding router's IP address. For example, in the case of a DDoS which has 2000 attack sources, when the victim only finds two segments of R_i's IP address, Seg_1^i, Seg_0^i, it needs to extract the other two parts Seg_3^i, Seg_2^i from those already reconstructed addresses whose corresponding distance fields are $i-1$, rebuild the addresses and validate them. It should be noted that the rebuilding process is carried out only 2000 times rather that 4,000,000 times, since the extracted two segments Seg_3^i, Seg_2^i are treated as a whole to reconstruct the address.

4 Simulation Results

To evaluate our schemes in real settings, we conduct experiments on simulated attacks with a real network topology database from CAIDA [6]. This topology database contains about fifty thousand different paths from a single source. In the experiments, we set this single source as the victim, and the paths in the topology database as the DDoS attack paths. We randomly select a number of paths from the database and simulate the routers that mark the packets along these paths. The marking is implemented randomly, too. In the end, we also simulate the victim which reconstructs the attack paths using the marked information from the collected packets. To obtain genuine results, for every datum in the figures we carried out many independent experiments and obtained the average result.

The platform for our experiment is: AthlonXP 1700+, 512M DDR266, Windows XP professional with sp2, JDK1.5.03, MySQL 4.1.12a. The simulation program is encoded in Java, and the MySQL database acts as the marked information base (MIB), which stores the traceback information marked in the packets collected by the victim.

The number of packets required for IP traceback in the nRVPPM is shown in figure 2.

Compared with uniform marking probability in [2], the nRVPPM can dramatically reduce the number of packets required for reconstructing the paths, especially the long ones.

We name the ratio of the number of packets required when using the nRVPPM to the number when the CnRVPPM is used for the same path the compression ratio of this

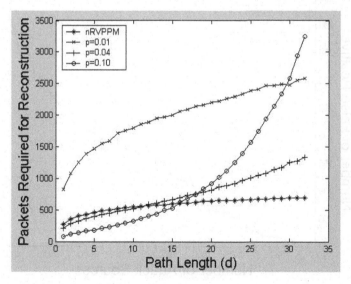

Fig. 2. The number of packets required to reconstruct the path using the nRVPPM and PPM [2] with different marking probabilities (p=0.01, p=0.04, p=0.10)

path. According to our statistic, the compression ratios for most paths in the database [6] are between 0.6 and 0.9, which suggests that the CnRVPPM can indeed reduce the number of packets required for IP traceback, as shown in figure 3. When combining the nRVPPM with CnRVPPM, we can further reduce the packets for IP traceback.

The nRVPPM offers very high precision, nearly zero false positive, but the CnRVPPM induces many errors during the reconstruction, as shown in figure 4.

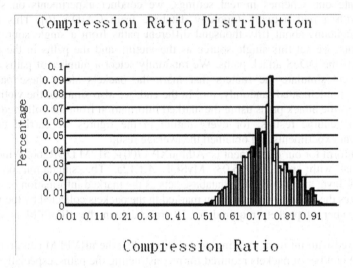

Fig. 3. The Compression Ratio

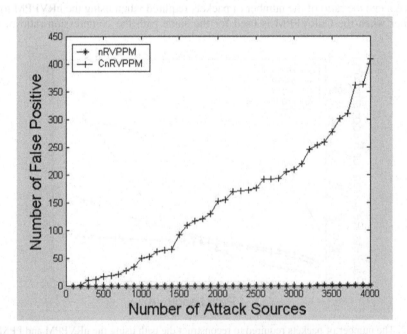

Fig. 4. The number of False Positives in the case of different number of attack sources

The reason is that according to the CnRVPPM, the victim needs to search all the packets marked by the preceding routers on all paths (no information marked about paths) to find out the missing part of an IP address if the IP address can not be reconstructed. Therefore, the CnRVPPM is much more time-consuming than the nRVPPM.

As shown in figure 5, when using the nRVPPM, the victim only needs 30 seconds to reconstruct all the necessary IP addresses for traceback under a major DDoS, which has 4000 attack sources. As for the CnRVPPM, however, 700 seconds are required to finish the same work.

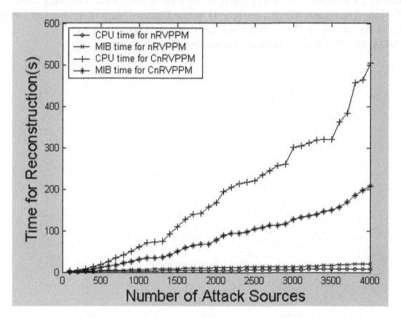

Fig. 5. The time (seconds) required by the nRVPPM and CnRVPPM with different numbers of attack sources

5 Conclusions

In this paper, we propose two novel and efficient packet marking schemes for IP traceback, the nRVPPM and CnRVPPM, which can evidently decrease the false positive errors. These schemes are very useful in identifying Distributed Denial of Service attack sources. The main advantages of employing the nRVPPM/CnRVPPM are that the repeated marking problem is eliminated and the number of packets needed by the victim for the traceback process is significantly reduced, which leads to faster and more scalable identification of attack sources. Simulation studies show that the proposed schemes are highly accurate and efficient for tracing DDoS attacks. Furthermore, We can get higher accuracy and efficiency using a combination of the nRVPPM and CnRVPPM.

References

1. Andrey Belenky, Nirwan Ansari, "On IP Traceback," IEEE Communications Magazine, July 2003
2. Stefan Savage, David Wetherall, Anna Karlin, Tom Anderson, "Practical Network Support for IP Traceback," Proceedings of the 2000 ACM SIGCOMM Conference, August 2000
3. Arnon Boneh, Micha Hofri, "The Coupon-collector Problem Revisited [J]," Commun. Statist. Stochastic Models, Vol.13, 1997
4. Tao Peng, Christopher Leckie, Kotagiri Ramamohanarao, "Adjusted Probabilistic Packet Marking for IP Traceback," Proceedings of Networking 2002, Pisa ,Italy, May 2002
5. Wolfgang Theilmann, Kurt Rothermel, "Dynamic Distance Maps of the Internet," Proceedings of the 2000 IEEE INFOCOM Conference, March 2000
6. CAIDA, http://www.caida.org/tools/measurement/skitter/index.xml

A Novel Rate Limit Algorithm Against Meek DDoS Attacks*

Yinan Jing, Xueping Wang, Xiaochun Xiao, and Gendu Zhang

School of Information Science & Engineering, Fudan University, Shanghai, China 200433
{jingyn, wangxp, xxiaochun, gdzhang}@fudan.edu.cn

Abstract. Distributed denial-of-service attack is one of major threats to Internet today. Rate limit algorithm with max-min fairness is an effective countermeasure to defeat flooding-style DDoS attacks under the assumption that attackers are more aggressive than legitimate users. However, under a "meek" DDoS attack where such an assumption is no longer valid, it will fail to protect legitimate traffic effectively. In order to improve the survival ratio of legitimate packets, an IP traceback based rate limit algorithm is proposed. Simulation results show that it could not only mitigate the DDoS attack effect, but also improve the throughput of legitimate traffic even under a meek attack.

1 Introduction

A denial-of-service (DoS) attack is characterized by an explicit attempt to prevent the legitimate use of a service. Distributed denial-of-service (DDoS) attacks can cause more damage by exploiting a group of zombie hosts. By sending a large number of spoofed requests, flooding-style DDoS attacks could overwhelm the victim's limited resources. Due to lack of a simple way to distinguish good requests from bad ones, it is extremely difficult to defend against these flooding-style attacks [1].

There are two fundamental reasons to make flooding DDoS attacks possible [2]. First, the victim's susceptibility to DDoS attacks depends on the security of the rest of the global Internet. Second, resources are always limited. These limit resources are common targets of flooding attacks. As we all known, if all machines on the Internet were secured correctly, then no hosts could be exploited to launch attacks. But it is unrealistic. So we deem that the key to defeat flooding-style attacks is to make sure that aggregate traffic will not overwhelm the resource bottleneck and improve the throughput of legitimate traffic as possible as we can. Rate limit is a most direct measure to reach this goal.

A good rate limit algorithm should have following three properties. (1) It should be able to control aggregate traffic destined for the victim under the limit of resource bottleneck. (2) Legitimate traffic should be passed to the victim as possible as we can. (3) The rate limiter should be deployed as close to attackers as possible. While near the victim, attack and legitimate traffic will aggregate together to be a very huge volume, normal routers could not distinguish attack traffic from legitimate traffic, and even neither afford so great traffic volume. In contrast, if performing rate limit closer to

---

* Supported by the National Natural Science Foundation of China under Grant No. 60373021.

L.T. Yang et al. (Eds.): ATC 2006, LNCS 4158, pp. 467–476, 2006.

attackers, it could regulate attack traffic ahead of time and avoid collateral damage on legitimate traffic.

Max-Min based rate limit algorithm proposed by Yau et al is an effective rate limit measure under the assumption that the attacker is much more *"aggressive"* than the legitimate user, i.e. the rate of one attacker is significantly higher than that of one legitimate user [5,6,7]. However, under a *"meek"* DDoS attack where aforementioned assumption is no longer true, it will cause collateral damage on legitimate traffic to a comparable extent as well as attack traffic.

In this paper, we propose an IP traceback based rate limit algorithm, which can not only mitigate the DDoS attack effect closer to attack source end, but also improve the throughput of legitimate traffic even under a meek attack.

2 Related Work

Since DDoS attacks came forth, many countermeasures have been proposed, such as IP traceback, rate limit, filtering and so on [3]. In this paper, due to space limitation, we only review the related work about the rate limit techniques.

Mahajan et al [4] viewed flooding-style attacks as congestion events, which are due to traffic aggregation. Local Aggregate-based Congestion Control (Local ACC) is a local mechanism for detecting and controlling high-bandwidth aggregates. Furthermore, a Pushback mechanism has been proposed to ask adjacent upstream routers to control an aggregate. However, because pushback starts resource sharing decision at the congestion point, legitimate traffics might be severely punished [7].

Yau et al [5,6,7] viewed DDoS attacks as a resource management problem and proposed a router throttle algorithm. This algorithm needs an assumption that attackers are significantly more aggressive than regular users [7]. But when this assumption does not hold, it will fail to protect legitimate traffic effectively.

Sung et al proposed to leverage the attack graph educed by IP traceback to preferentially filter out packets that are more likely to come from attackers [8]. AITF (Active Internet Traffic Filtering) [9] is a similar mechanism. It leverages recorded route information in place of IP traceback to block attack traffic. However, these two filtering techniques have not taken into account of fairness when allocating resources.

DefCOM [10] is a distributed cooperative DDoS defense system via an overlay to detect and stop attacks. DefCOM leverages classifier nodes near attack sources to distinguish attack packets from legitimate ones. However, if attack packets have no distinct signature, then classifier nodes will not work. Unfortunately, the flooding-style attack traffic produced by modern attack tools usually has no distinct characteristics at the attack source end.

3 Analysis on Max-Min Based Rate Limit Algorithm

The basic mechanism of Max-Min based rate limit algorithm is for a server under stress to install throttles at selected upstream routers to proactively regulate the contributing packet rates to more moderate levels before attack packets can aggregate to overwhelm the server [7]. And when allocating the server's capacity among the throttles, the level-k max-min fairness is complied with. To simplify analysis, we transform the adaptive throttle algorithm [7] into the algorithm 1 (Max-Min based rate limit algorithm). Table 1 lists related variables and their descriptions.

Table 1. Related variables in Max-Min based rate limit algorithm (Algorithm 1)

Variables	Description
C	max capacity of the victim's resource bottleneck
C_s	spare capacity which could be allocated
T	set of throttles
N	$|T|$, number of elements in set T
$Rate(i)$	rate of the flow passing through the throttle i to the victim, i.e. amount of resources desired by the throttle i
$Limit(i)$	amount of resources allocated to the throttle i (zero initially)

As algorithm 1 show, upon detecting an attack, the rate limit decision maker (i.e. the victim here) will allocate the limited resource among throttles according to their requirements with max-min fairness. The rate information of one throttle can be obtained by some packet flow monitor tools, such as Cisco's NetFlow [16].

Algorithm 1. **Max-Min based Rate Limit Algorithm**

```
Let C_s = C;
While( T ≠ Φ  AND  C_s > 0 )
    N = |T|;
    Share = C_s / N;
    For each i in T
      If( Rate(i) ≤ (Limit(i)+Share) )
          Limit(i) = Rate(i);
          C_s = C_s - Limit(i);
          T = T - {i};
      Else
          Limit(i) = Limit(i) + Share;
          C_s = C_s - Share;
      End If
    End For
End While
```

After algorithm 1 performed, the throttle i can drop the packets destined for the victim with a certain dropping probability (p), which can be obtained by the following equation (1). If *Limit* is more or equal to *Rate*, then p will be 0, i.e. it is unnecessary to drop any packets. Through probabilistic packet dropping, the throttle can restrain the rate below the rate limit.

$$p = \max(0, \ 1 - Limit / Rate) \tag{1}$$

Router throttling with max-min fairness is fair effective under the assumption that attackers are significantly more aggressive than legitimate users, because attackers could not occupy more resources even though they send more attack traffic. However, this assumption is not always valid. Some subtle attackers could "*dilute*" each of attack flows by recruiting more zombie hosts to launch a same volume of attack. For example, network worms provide chances for attackers to recruit more zombies in a shorter time. Related research has shown that nowadays network worms can infect all vulnerable hosts on Internet within several minutes [11]. And the DDoS attack using reflectors could also result in dilution [12]. In such a *"meek"* DDoS attack, each zombie behaves like a normal user. The experimental results in [7] have shown that max-min fairness may fail, and punish both attackers and legitimate users equally.

Next we give an example to illustrate the drawback of max-min fairness. Figure 1 shows a simple topology. We suppose that throttles have been installed on routers $R_1 \sim R_8$. Each router connects to a traffic generator (S_i) which sends packets to the victim (V). The limited resource of the victim is the bandwidth (1Mbps) of the bottleneck link between R_9 and V. If there is no special claim, in the rest of this paper the limited resource of the victim always means the bandwidth of the bottleneck link.

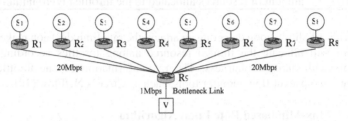

Fig. 1. A simple topology

When V is suffering from an attack, it will allocate the bottleneck link bandwidth among throttles according to the algorithm 1. Table 2 shows two different scenarios. In these two scenarios, each legitimate user sends 0.2Mbps traffic.

Table 2. User distribution in two scenarios

	User distribution	
	Attackers	Legitimate users
Scenario I	S_1, S_2	S_6, S_7, S_8
Scenario II	S_1, S_2, S_3, S_4, S_5	S_6, S_7, S_8

In scenario I, attackers whose individual rate is 1Mbps are more aggressive than legitimate users. Table 3 shows bandwidth allocation among 8 throttles according to algorithm 1. By Eq. (1), only throttles connected with attackers need to rate limit.

Table 3. Bandwidth allocation in scenario I

	R_1	R_2	R_3	R_4	R_5	R_6	R_7	R_8
Rate(i)	1	1	0	0	0	0.2	0.2	0.2
Limit(i)	0.2	0.2	0	0	0	0.2	0.2	0.2

In scenario II, the total attack traffics keep the same volume (2Mpbs) as that of scenario I. But the number of attacker increases to five, and each individual attack flow is diluted to 0.4Mbps, which is as *"meek"* as a legitimate flow. Table 4 shows the bandwidth allocation under such a meek attack. By Eq. (1), the legitimate users will also be penalized unreasonably. So under a meek DDoS attack, max-min fairness will fail to protect legitimate traffic and cause more collateral damage.

Table 4. Bandwidth allocation in scenario II

	R_1	R_2	R_3	R_4	R_5	R_6	R_7	R_8
Rate(i)	0.4	0.4	0.4	0.4	0.4	0.2	0.2	0.2
Limit(i)	0.125	0.125	0.125	0.125	0.125	0.125	0.125	0.125

The realistic topology is much more complex than that depicted in Fig. 1, but above-mentioned analysis results are enough to indicate max-min based rate limit algorithm can not work well under a meek DDoS attack. The reason is that it excessively emphasizes fairness but neglects the priorities of legitimate flows when allocating bandwidth. Hence, if we know the throttles through which only legitimate flows are passing, we could preferentially satisfy the bandwidth requirement of these throttles to avoid collateral damages because of max-min fairness.

4 IP Traceback Based Rate Limit Algorithm

IP traceback technique allows the victim to identify the sources of DoS or DDoS attacks even in the presence of IP spoofing. Although IP traceback itself could not mitigate DDoS attack effect, it can assist other countermeasures such as router throttle to distinguish legitimate traffics from attack traffics and to be deployed in the best places. Since DDoS attacks came forth, a number of approaches have been proposed for IP traceback, such as link testing, ICMP-based iTrace, probabilistic packet marking (PPM), and so on [13]. The detail of IP traceback process is out of the scope of this paper. Our focus is on how to use IP traceback results to improve the performance of rate limiting.

By leveraging one concrete IP traceback technique such as PPM, the victim could reconstruct a traffic tree rooted itself and identify the attack sub-tree. By utilizing traceback results, we could not only install throttles closer to attackers (i.e. at the leaf nodes of the traffic tree), but also identify those "*clean*" throttles that should preferentially obtain the bandwidth allocation. Algorithm 2 shows the IP traceback-based rate limit algorithm.

Algorithm 2. **IP Traceback based Rate Limit Algorithm**

```
Let  Cs = C;
For each i in T
    If( i.isPolluted == FALSE  AND  Cs > 0 )
        Limit(i) = Rate(i);
        Cs = Cs - Limit(i);


    T = T - {i};
    End If
End For
```

```
While( T ≠ Φ  AND  Cₛ > 0 )
    N = |T| ;
    Share = Cₛ / N;
    For each i in T
        If( Rate(i) ≤ (Limit(i)+Share) )
            Limit(i) = Rate(i);
            Cₛ = Cₛ - Limit(i);
            T = T - {i};
        Else
            Limit(i) = Limit(i) + Share;
            Cₛ = Cₛ - Share;
        End If
    End For
End While
```

As algorithm 2 shows, we add a variable *isPolluted* for each throttle to indicate whether there is attack traffic passing through it. If *isPolluted* equals to FALSE, it means that there is only legitimate traffic passing through it, i.e. all users connected to it are legitimate users. Hence, we preferentially allocate bandwidth to these clean throttles. After that, the remained bandwidth will be allocated to those *"polluted"* throttles still according to max-min fairness. By algorithm 2, we could protect legitimate traffics and avoid collateral damage caused by max-min fairness.

5 Simulation Results

We use following two performance metrics to evaluate the performance of the rate limit algorithm.

- *Aggregate Traffic Rate at Bottleneck Link*. This metric reflects whether the rate limit algorithm could regulate the victim's load within its limit.
- *Survival Ratio*. It is the percentage of legitimate packets received by the victim in all legitimate packets. This metric reflects the extent to which one rate limit algorithm causes collateral damage on legitimate packets. The higher is the survival ratio, the smaller collateral damage will be.

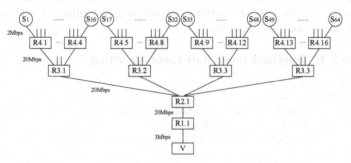

Fig. 2. Experimental topology from Pushback experiments [4]

Because max-min based rate limit algorithm has been compared with pushback approach in [7], we only compared algorithm 1 with 2 on survival ratio of legitimate packets. We implemented algorithm 1 and 2, and conducted experiments on NS-2 (Ver 2.27) [15]. Figure 2 shows the experimental topology, which is same as that of pushback approach [4].

As Fig. 2 depicts, there are four levels of routers. The links between four levels have 20 Mbps bandwidth. Each router at level 4 connects to four sources (S_i) with bandwidth 2Mbps. The victim (V) is connected with R1.1 by a 3Mbps bottleneck link. In the following experiments we only allocate 4/5 bandwidth (i.e. 2.4Mbps) of the bottleneck link, while the remainder is preserved for the possible new accessing users. Rate limit decision is made by a centralized control point, which may be a server deployed by ISP. In order to adapt to the dynamic changes, rate limit decision is refreshed every 2 seconds. This parameter can be tuned according to different application scenarios.

Table 5 lists parameters of 2 groups of experiments. Each group includes A and B experiments, in which different attack traffic patterns are used. ICBR (intermittent CBR) pattern means each attacker independently chooses a random interval to intermittently send a double rate of CBR traffic. For a long run, the average rate of ICBR is similar to that of CBR. The ICBR pattern is mainly used to simulate the fluctuating rate attack [3]. In each experimental scenario, there are 10 legitimate users who send 0.2Mbps of UDP CBR traffic individually. All users including attackers and legitimate users begin to send packets at an independent random time between 0 and 4 seconds. Suppose an attack is detected at 3rd second and then rate limit takes effect.

Table 5. Parameters of two groups of experiments

Exp ID	Parameters		Attack traffic pattern
	User distribution		
	Attackers	Legitimate users	
E1.A	4 users from S_1 every 3	10 users from S_{17} every 3	1Mbps CBR
E1.B	4 users from S_1 every 3	10 users from S_{17} every 3	2Mbps ICBR
E2.A	16 users from S_1 every 1	10 users from S_{33} every 1	0.25Mbps CBR
E2.B	16 users from S_1 every 1	10 users from S_{33} every 1	0.5Mbps ICBR

For each experiment, there are a, b two figures to show results. Figure (a) includes three curves: (1) solid line "Aggregate Traffic" represents theoretic aggregate traffic rate arriving at the bottleneck link, (2) "No Rate Limit" denotes aggregate traffic arriving at the bottleneck link with no rate limit mechanism, (3) "With Rate Limit" denotes the aggregate traffic rate at the bottleneck link with IP traceback based rate limit mechanism. Figure (b) also includes three curves, which respectively demonstrate the survival ratio under three different cases: (1) "No Rate Limit", (2) "Max-Min" based rate limit. (3) "IP Traceback" based rate limit.

E1 scenario is intended to simulate a DDoS attack where a few aggressive attackers are sending attack traffic individually at 1Mbps rate on average, which is five times of legitimate users. These 4 attackers and 10 legitimate users are distributed sparsely and separately. Figure 3 and Figure 4 show simulation results of experiment E1.A and E1.B respectively. As Fig. 3(a) and Fig. 4(a) show, our algorithm can successfully regulate aggregate traffic under the limit of the bottleneck link no matter what the attack traffic pattern is. And Fig. 3(b) and Fig. 4(b) both show that the survival ratio of IP traceback based algorithm is higher than that of max-min based algorithm, reaching over 90%.

E2 scenario is intended to simulate a "meek" DDoS attack. While keeping the same total attack traffic volume (4Mbps) as previous scenario, the traffic rate of each attacker is diluted to 0.25Mbps on average. As table 5 shows, in E2 16 attackers and 10 legitimate users are distributed sparsely and separately. Figure 5 and Figure 6 show simulation results of experiment E2.A and E2.B respectively. As Fig. 5(a) and Fig. 6(a) show, under a meek attack our algorithm could still regulate traffics well. As Fig. 5(b) and Fig. 6(b) show, however, the survival ratio of max-min is very low, even lower than that of no rate limit (Fig. 5(b)). In contrast, the survival ratio with IP traceback is very high, reaching over 90%. So through these two experiments, we can see that under a meek attack the IP traceback based algorithm could not only regulate the traffic for the victim successfully, but also protect legitimate traffic more effectively than the max-min based rate limit algorithm.

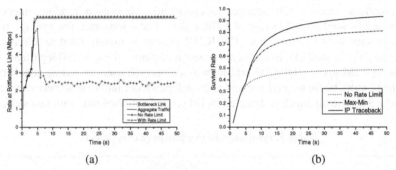

Fig. 3. A few sparsely distributed aggressive attackers send 1Mbps CBR attack traffics (E1.A)

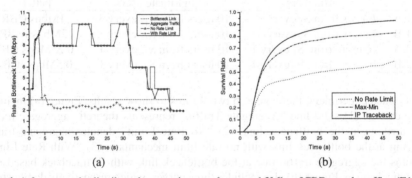

Fig. 4. A few sparsely distributed aggressive attackers send 2Mbps ICBR attack traffics (E1.B)

6   Discussion

6.1   Impact of the Underlying IP Traceback Scheme

Traceback speed and accuracy of the underlying IP traceback scheme has the direct impact on the performance of the IP traceback based rate limit algorithm. Fortunately, with the development of IP traceback technique, more and more schemes with higher speed and accuracy have come forth, such as the FIT (Fast Internet Traceback) scheme [14]. On the other hand, although IP traceback has not been deployed widely on Internet now, those partial deployment can still play an assistant part when rate limiting. Its usefulness will increase greatly along with the widespread deployment.

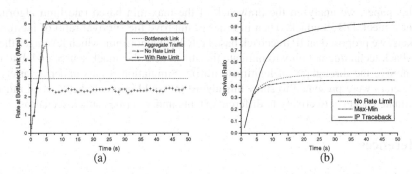

Fig. 5. Many sparsely distributed meek attackers send 0.25Mbps CBR attack traffics (E2.A)

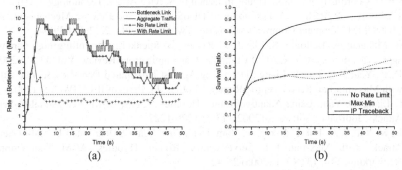

Fig. 6. Many sparsely distributed meek attackers send 0.5Mbps ICBR attack traffics (E2.B)

6.2 Control Policy of the Rate Limit Algorithm

In this paper, we adopted a centralized control policy, i.e. the rate limit decision making is delegated to a credible third party, such as ISP. Although it will bring extra management and communication costs, we believe these costs are controllable. For example, the third party need only monitor a few specific flows on demand of the victim, rather than monitor all flows whenever. The centralized policy has following two advantages. First, it could enhance the security of the rate limit decision-making process and throttle installation, because the third party is trustworthy. Second, it is easy to enable cross-domain rate limit by establishing trust relationships between trustworthy third parties in various domains, while it is challenging in [7].

6.3 Transformation of Other Limited Resources

Because the victim's resource bottleneck might be other forms, such as CPU, memory and so on, we have to transform these limited resources into bandwidth metric. Note that it is not necessary that transformation is perfectly precise, as long as the transformed quantity could equivalently reflect the processing capability of traffic.

7 Conclusion

In this paper, we analyzed the drawback of the max-min based rate limit algorithm under a meek DDoS attack. Then in order to improve the survival ratio of legitimate packets, we proposed an IP traceback based rate limit algorithm, which leverages the IP traceback technique not only to mitigate the attack near the attack source end, but also to improve the throughput of legitimate traffic. Simulation results under a variety of parameters were presented to show this algorithm could improve the survival ratio of legitimate packets effectively to different extents under various attack scenarios.

References

1. D Moore, G Voelker, S Savage.: Inferring Internet denial-of-service activity. In: 10th ACM USENIX Security Symposium, Washington USA (2002)
2. CERT Coordination Center. Trends in Denial of Service Attack Technology. (2001)
3. J. Mirkovic, P. Reiher.: A Taxonomy of DDoS Attacks and Defense Mechanisms. ACM SIGCOMM Computer Communications Review, Vol. 34, No. 2, (2004) 39-54
4. R. Mahajan, S. Bellovin, S. Floyd, V. Paxson, S. Shenker.: Controlling high bandwidth aggregates in the network. ACM Computer Communications Review, Vol. 32(3), (2002)
5. D. K. Yau, J. C. Lui, F. Liang.: Defending Against Distributed Denial-of-Service Attacks with Max-min Fair Server-centric Router Throttles. In: Proc. of IEEE IWQoS, (2002)
6. F. Liang, D. Yau.: Using Adaptive Router Throttles Against Distributed Denial-of-Service Attacks. Journal of Software, (2002), 13(7):1220-1227
7. D. K. Yau, J. C. Lui, F. Liang, Y. Yam. Defending Against Distributed Denial-of-Service Attacks with Max-min Fair Server-centric Router Throttles. ACM Transaction on Networking, Vol. 13, No. 1 (2005) 29-42
8. M. Sung, J. Xu.: IP traceback-based intelligent packet filtering: A novel technique for defending against Internet DDoS attacks. In: Proc of 10th IEEE ICNP, France (2002)
9. K. Argyraki, D. Cheriton. Active Internet Traffic Filtering: Real-Time Response to Denial-of-Service Attacks. In: USENIX 2005 (2005)
10. J. Mirkovic, M. Robinson, P. Reiher, G. Oikonomou.: Distributed Defense against DDOS Attacks. University of Delaware CIS Department Tech Report CIS-TR-2005-02 (2005)
11. David Moore, et al.: Internet Quarantine: Requirements for Containing Self-Propagating Code. In: IEEE INFOCOM 2003, (2003)
12. V. Paxson. An analysis of using reflectors for distributed denial-of-service attacks. Computer Communication Review 31(3), July (2001)
13. A. Belenky, N. Ansari.: On IP traceback. IEEE Communications Magazine, (2003), 41(7): 142-153
14. A Yaar, A Perrig, D Song.: FIT: Fast Internet Traceback. In: INFOCOM 2005 (2005)
15. Network Simulator 2. http://www.isi.edu/nsnam/ns, 2004-07-10
16. Cisco. Cisco IOS NetFlow Overview. http://www.cisco.com/univercd/cc/td/doc/ product/ software/ios124/124cg/hnf_c/nfb_ov.htm, (2005)

Resistance Analysis to Intruders' Evasion of a Novel Algorithm to Detect Stepping-Stone

Yongzhong Zhang[1], Jianhua Yang[2], and Chunming Ye[1]

[1] College of Management, the University of Shanghai for Science and Technology
516 Jungong Rd, Shanghai, 200093 China
{yzhang, ychunming}@shtvu.edu.cn
[2] Department of Computer Science, University of Houston
4800 Calhoun Rd. Houston, TX, 77204 USA
jhyang@cs.uh.edu

Abstract. Most intruders used to make use of stepping-stones to launch their attacks for safety reason. Some of them even evade stepping-stone detection by conducting manipulations. Most of the approaches proposed to detect stepping-stone are vulnerable in detecting intruders' evasion, such as time perturbation, and chaff perturbation. In this paper, we propose a new algorithm to detect stepping-stone by comparing the self and cross packet matching rates of a session. The analysis and simulation results show that this algorithm detects not only stepping-stone without misdetection, but also intruder's evasion with less limitation. It can resist to intruders' time perturbation completely, as well as chaff perturbation.

1 Introduction

Most intruders usually use stepping-stones [1] to attack other computers, hosts or networks indirectly. The main purpose of using stepping-stones is to make them safe and avoid being detected. There are many methods proposed to detect stepping-stone in the past ten years. The first one is thumbprint [2] which is proposed by Staniford-Chen in 1995. Its main idea is to compare the thumbprints of two connections to see if they are close enough. Thumbprint is the summary of the contents flowing in a connection during a period of time. The major problem of this method is that it does not work for encrypted sessions, which are used often in recent years.

In 2000, there are two methods proposed to detect stepping-stone no matter a session is encrypted or not. One is proposed by Zhang [1] and another one is proposed by Yoda [3]. Zhang's main idea is to compare the ON and OFF time between two connections. If the two connections are in a same chain, the ON and OFF time between the two connections should be almost the same or very close, otherwise they should be different. Yoda's main idea is to compute the deviation between two connections to determine if they are in a same chain. If the deviation is very small, the chance that the two connections are in a same chain is very big, otherwise it is not. Both ON, OFF time and deviation have a fatal problem that is they are very easy to be manipulated. That means an intruder can maneuver a connection to make whatever ON, OFF or deviation are different from that of another connection even if the two connections might be in a same chain, and thus evade detection.

L.T. Yang et al. (Eds.): ATC 2006, LNCS 4158, pp. 477–486, 2006.
© Springer-Verlag Berlin Heidelberg 2006

Wang [4] and Peng [5] proposed watermark-based methods to detect stepping-stone. Even if these two methods have better performance in detecting intruders' evasion than the above two, but they still have some problems. First they are active methods, the watermark needs to be injected into an incoming connection and decoded from an outgoing connection. The computation cost is a problem, further-more, there is no guarantee if the watermark embedded is affected by intruders' manipulation even though the author claimed that the computation cost is low and there is a low chance that the watermark can be affected. Another problem of the method in [5] is that the chaff packets must obey Poisson distribution. The fact is that an intruder can conduct chaff perturbation by inserting meaningless packets into a connection with any way he/she wants, not necessary to be Poisson distribution.

Donoho [6] proved by using Wavelet theory that a stepping-stone can be detected even if the session are jittered by implementing time or chaff perturbation as long as sufficient packets are observed. The problems of this method are 1) it did not show us how sufficient it is; 2) the analysis on chaff perturbation is still based on the assumption that the chaff must obey Poisson distribution. Blum [7] continued Donoho's work and proposed the number of send packets is observed necessarily in order to obtain given confidence. His method does not need to assume that chaff must obey Poisson distribution. Blum's method can detect time perturbation well, but for detecting chaff perturbation, its resistibility is low. According to Theory 7 in [7], chaff perturbation can be detected by the method in [7] as long as no more than x packets inserted in every $8(x+1)^2$ packets. It indicates that for every 200 packets in a session, an intruder only needed to insert more than 4 packets, his detection system would be bypassed. Blum's method is very weak in detecting intruder's chaff evasion.

In this paper, we propose a novel algorithm, which is called round-trip time (RTT) based algorithm (RTT-Algorithm), to detect stepping-stone. With the RTT-Algorithm, all the send and echo packets of each connection are matched first and their matching-rates are computed. Then we compare the matching-rates between an incoming connection and an outgoing connection to see if they are close enough to determine if the two connections are in a same chain. The advantage of this method is that it can not only detect stepping-stone, but also detect intruders' evasion. Whatever a session is chaffed or time perturbed, even though the matching-rate for each connection might be changed, but the difference of the matching-rates between two connections in a same chain should be very small. Moreover, this method does not care what kind of distribution the chaff is; it can be any distribution. The simulation result showed that this method can resist to time perturbation completely, as well as chaff perturbation to a high degree, which is much better than Blum's approach.

The RTT-Algorithm was motivated by the ideas proposed in papers [8], [9], [10], [11]; these methods can be used to detect stepping-stone, as well as stepping-stone intrusion. Actually they are mainly focusing on detecting intrusion. RTT-Algorithm is mainly used to detect stepping-stone. So we do not want to go further about the ideas in papers [8], [9], [10], [11]. But there is one thing we must mention is that being used as a stepping-stone does not equal to an intrusion. The methods proposed in detecting stepping-stone always have false alarms when they are applied to detecting intrusion. The packet matching algorithm used in this paper is the one proposed in paper [12], which is a clustering, standard deviation based packet matching algorithm.

The rest of this paper is arranged as following. In Section 2, problem statement is given, and some concepts are defined in this section. Section 3 presents the RTT-Algorithm to detect intrusion and evasion. In Section 4, we discuss the resistibility of this algorithm to intruders' time perturbation. And in Section 5, we further discuss the resistibility to chaff perturbation. Finally, in Section 6, the whole work is summarized, and future work is presented.

2   Problem Statement

A network intruder may compromise some hosts h_1, h_2, ..., h_n , called stepping-stones, to invade any other host h_{n+1}, which is assumed the victim site, from host h_0. For any two hosts h_i and h_{i+1}, the flow $h_i \rightarrow h_{i+1}$ is called one connection, which is an outgoing connection of host h_i, as well as an incoming connection of host h_{i+1}. The sequence of connections $h_0 \rightarrow h_1 \rightarrow ... \rightarrow h_i \rightarrow h_{i+1} \rightarrow ... \rightarrow h_{n+1}$ is called a connection chain, or a chain. Each connection of a host, no matter it is an incoming connection or an outgoing connection, must have two streams: request stream and response stream. Request stream is composed of Sends (defined below), and response stream is composed of Echoes (defined below). We use symbol $C_i^{(1)}$ to represent the ith incoming connection of host h_i, where the superscript is used to distinguish an incoming connection or an outgoing connection. Similarly, symbol $C_i^{(2)}$ can be used to represent the ith outgoing connection of host h_i. Symbol $S_i^{(k)}$ is used to represent the request stream of the ith connection of host h_i, where $k=1$ represents incoming connection, and $k=2$ represents outgoing connection. Similarly, symbol $E_i^{(k)}$ is used to represent the response stream of the ith connection. Fig.1 shows all of them and their relations, where solid arrow represents request stream and dash arrow represents response stream. In this paper, we only focus on TCP Send and Echo packets, which are defined as the following,

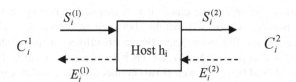

Fig. 1. Demonstration of connections and streams of a host

Send: A TCP packet is defined as a Send if it propagates downstream and has either both flags 'Push (P)' and 'Acknowledgement (A)' or only flag 'P' [13];

Echo: A TCP packet is defined as an Echo if it propagates upstream and has either both flags 'Push (P)' and 'Acknowledgement (A)' or flag only 'P'.

Each host might have more incoming connections, as well as more outgoing connections. To detect if a host is used as a stepping-stone is to determine if an incoming connection and an outgoing connection of the host are in a same chain. As Fig.1 shows that if we can determine $C_i^{(1)}$ and $C_i^{(2)}$ are in a same connection chain, then host h_i is used as a stepping-stone. Therefore, the statement of detecting stepping-stone becomes the statement of determining if there is one incoming and outgoing connection pair in a same chain; this pair is called a stepping-stone pair, otherwise it is called a normal pair.

At a same period of time, we collect all the Sends and Echoes in each connection, then we have streams $S_i^{(1)}, S_i^{(2)}, E_i^{(1)}$, and $E_i^{(2)}$. We suppose that in the ith incoming connection n Sends, m Echoes are captured, then in the ith outgoing connection n Sends and m Echoes are supposed to be captured if we assume there is no packet drop, combination, insertion, and generation. If the connections are not manipulated, the simplest way to determine if the incoming and outgoing connections are in a same chain is to check if the elements of $S_i^{(1)}$, and $S_i^{(2)}$ have the same or close timestamps, or the same number of elements [7]. However, under time and chaff perturbation, this way does not work obviously. In order to detect intruder's evasion, we propose the RTT-Algorithm in the following section.

3   RTT-Algorithm

3.1   The Basic Idea

Given the request stream of the ith incoming connection $S_i^{(1)} = \{s_1, s_2, ..., s_n\}$, and the response stream of the ith outgoing connection of host h_i, $E_i^{(2)} = \{e_1, e_2, ..., e_m\}$, correspondingly, we capture the same request packets stream $S_i^{(2)}$ as $S_i^{(1)}$ at the outgoing connection, and the same response packets stream $E_i^{(1)}$ as $E_i^{(2)}$ at the incoming connection if the two connections are in a same chain because we have assumed that there is no packet drop, combination, insertion, and generation.

If we match the packets between $S_i^{(1)}$ and $E_i^{(1)}$, and the packets between $S_i^{(2)}$ and $E_i^{(2)}$, ideally, the number of the matches between them should be the same if the two connections are in a same chain; it is called self matching. However, it does not mean if the numbers of the self matches between an incoming connection and an outgoing connection are the same, then two connections are in a same chain. The reason is that if we collect n Sends for each connection, ideally, the number of matched packets should be n. So even if two connections are not in a same chain, but it is still possible they have the same number of matches.

To reduce the false positive errors, we take a different way to correlate the ith incoming connection and one outgoing connection. We match $S_i^{(1)}$ and $E_i^{(1)}$ of the ith incoming connection, and denote the number of matches $N_i^{(1)}$, as well as matching $S_i^{(2)}$ and $E_i^{(2)}$ of the ith outgoing connection, the number of matches is denoted as $N_i^{(2)}$. In addition, we also match the packets between $S_i^{(1)}$ and $E_i^{(2)}$, as well as matching the packets between $S_i^{(2)}$ and $E_i^{(1)}$, and denoted them as $N_i^{(1,2)}$ and $N_i^{(2,1)}$, respectively; it is called cross matching. Now we compare the four numbers $N_i^{(1)}, N_i^{(2)}, N_i^{(2,1)}$, and $N_i^{(1,2)}$, if the two connections are in a stepping-stone pair, then ideally they are equal each other, and vice versa. For a normal pair, even though it is still possible that the above relations are satisfied, but the probability is very small. The false positive error to detect stepping-stone could be decreased as low as zero by checking self and cross packet matching together.

3.2 RTT-Algorithm

Based on the idea we have discussed, we propose the RTT-Algorithm to find a stepping-stone pair between all the incoming connections and all the outgoing connections of a host. We assume there are n Sends captured, and $0 < \varepsilon < 1$.

RTT-Algorithm ($S_i^{(1)}, E_i^{(1)}, S_i^{(2)}, E_i^{(2)}, \varepsilon$):

1. Call the matching algorithm in [12] between $S_i^{(1)}$ and $E_i^{(1)}$, $S_i^{(1)}$ and $E_i^{(2)}$, $S_i^{(2)}$ and $E_i^{(1)}$, $S_i^{(2)}$ and $E_i^{(2)}$, and get the number of matches $N_i^{(1)}, N_i^{(1,2)}, N_i^{(2,1)}$, and $N_i^{(2)}$, respectively;

2. Computing the ratios: $r_{11} = N_i^{(1)} / n, r_{12} = N_i^{(1,2)} / n, r_{21} = N_i^{(2,1)} / n, r_{22} = N_i^{(2,2)} / n$;

3. Compare the ratios among $r_{11}, r_{12}, r_{21}, r_{22}$ to see if the following inequalities are satisfied,

$$\frac{|r_{11} - r_{12}|}{|r_{11} + r_{12}|/2} < \varepsilon, \frac{|r_{11} - r_{21}|}{|r_{11} + r_{21}|/2} < \varepsilon, \frac{|r_{11} - r_{22}|}{|r_{11} + r_{22}|/2} < \varepsilon$$

$$\frac{|r_{12} - r_{21}|}{|r_{12} + r_{21}|/2} < \varepsilon, \frac{|r_{12} - r_{22}|}{|r_{12} + r_{22}|/2} < \varepsilon$$

$$\frac{|r_{21} - r_{22}|}{|r_{21} + r_{22}|/2} < \varepsilon$$

4. If all the inequalities in Step 3 are satisfied, then output stepping-stone pair and exit; otherwise continue to check other connections until no one is left.

End

The computation cost of this algorithm is dominated by the computations in Step 1 which is used to match Sends and Echoes. Paper [12] points out that the time complexity of the efficient clustering algorithm is $O(nm^2)$, where n is the number of Sends, and m is the number of Echoes. We assume that we have p incoming connections and q outgoing connections at a host, in the worst case, the time complexity of detecting stepping-stone is $4 * O(nm^2) * p * q \approx O(pqnm^2)$.

3.3 Experimental Verification

In this section we evaluate the performance of the RTT-Algorithm through experimental result. We set up four connection chains which passed through Acl08, which is a local host under control. We did the experiments hundreds of times under different situations, each time it can give us the expected results. Here we show a typical one. We monitored all the four incoming connections $C_1^{(1)}, C_2^{(1)}, C_3^{(1)}$, and $C_4^{(1)}$, as well as the four outgoing connections $C_1^{(2)}, C_2^{(2)}, C_3^{(2)}$, and $C_4^{(2)}$, and captured all the

Sends and Echoes of each connection in the same period of time. The number of Sends and Echoes of each connection are (1140, 1351), (890, 1043), (991, 1256), and (741, 975), respectively. Here the first element of each pair represents the numbers of send packets of each incoming and outgoing connection, and the second element represents the echo packets number.

Table 1. The results of the RTT-Algorithm for the four chains

Outgoing / Incoming	$C_1^{(2)}$	$C_2^{(2)}$	$C_3^{(2)}$	$C_4^{(2)}$
$C_1^{(1)}$	$r_{11}=0.951$ $r_{22}=0.951$ $r_{12}=0.951$ $r_{21}=0.951$	$r_{11}=0.951$ $r_{22}=0.937$ $r_{12}=0.011$ $r_{21}=0.063$	$r_{11}=0.951$ $r_{22}=0.891$ $r_{12}=0.001$ $r_{21}=0.002$	$r_{11}=0.951$ $r_{22}=0.922$ $r_{12}=0.000$ $r_{21}=0.006$
$C_2^{(1)}$	$r_{11}=0.937$ $r_{22}=0.951$ $r_{12}=0.001$ $r_{21}=0.032$	$r_{11}=0.937$ $r_{22}=0.937$ $r_{12}=0.937$ $r_{21}=0.937$	$r_{11}=0.937$ $r_{22}=0.891$ $r_{12}=0.007$ $r_{21}=0.000$	$r_{11}=0.937$ $r_{22}=0.922$ $r_{12}=0.002$ $r_{21}=0.063$
$C_3^{(1)}$	$r_{11}=0.891$ $r_{22}=0.951$ $r_{12}=0.007$ $r_{21}=0.012$	$r_{11}=0.891$ $r_{22}=0.937$ $r_{12}=0.004$ $r_{21}=0.000$	$r_{11}=0.891$ $r_{22}=0.891$ $r_{12}=0.892$ $r_{21}=0.891$	$r_{11}=0.891$ $r_{22}=0.922$ $r_{12}=0.051$ $r_{21}=0.023$
$C_4^{(1)}$	$r_{11}=0.923$ $r_{22}=0.951$ $r_{12}=0.092$ $r_{21}=0.001$	$r_{11}=0.923$ $r_{22}=0.937$ $r_{12}=0.000$ $r_{21}=0.000$	$r_{11}=0.923$ $r_{22}=0.891$ $r_{12}=0.004$ $r_{21}=0.000$	$r_{11}=0.923$ $r_{22}=0.922$ $r_{12}=0.923$ $r_{21}=0.922$

Table 1 shows the computation result by applying the RTT-Algorithm. This result is exactly the same as what we expect: $C_1^{(1)}$ and $C_1^{(2)}$ are in one chain, and so are $C_2^{(1)}$ and $C_2^{(2)}$, $C_3^{(1)}$ and $C_3^{(2)}$, $C_4^{(1)}$ and $C_4^{(2)}$. From the result of this table, we also know that only comparing the matches in each connection will not uniquely identify the stepping-stone pair, which might introduce false alarms. But by taking the cross matches into consideration, false positive rate is decreased largely. This result is under an assumption that the sessions are not manipulated. Most intruders like to conduct time and chaff perturbation to evade stepping-stone detection. In Section 4, and 5, we discuss the resistance of the RTT-Algorithm to intruders' evasion.

4   Resistance to Time Perturbation

We have proposed the RTT-Algorithm to detect stepping-stone by comparing the self matches and the cross matches between incoming and outgoing connections. The experimental results showed that it works perfect without any perturbation on the session. How does it work under perturbation? In this section, we center on analyzing the performance of the RTT-Algorithm under time perturbation.

An intruder could manipulate an interactive TCP session at any host along the chain, even conduct manipulation concurrently. To simplify our analysis, we assume that an intruder can only manipulate a session on any one host of the session. Based on the effects of manipulation to packet matching, there could be three places along a chain, they are as Fig.2 shows: one is the place before a monitor point (MP) where our detecting program resides (including the incoming connections of the MP); second one is at the outgoing connections of the MP; and the third place is at any host after h_i, but before the victim host.

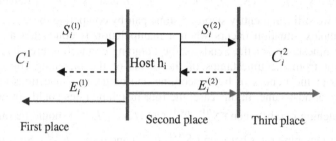

Fig. 2. An intruder's possible manipulation positions

If an intruder conducted time perturbation at any host of the first place, it would not affect the performance of the RTT-Algorithm to detect stepping-stone. The main reason is that it would not affect the packet matching rate, even the packet matching. Assume that a manipulation occurs at host h_j ($j<i$) which is before host h_i, the intruder can delay each send packet with time Δ_i ($1 \leq i \leq n$) in the outgoing connection of h_j with any way he wants. When this perturbation propagates to host h_i, it affects the timestamps of Sends and Echoes of incoming connection at the same time with the same quantity. And thus it does not affect the RTT of each Send. We draw the same conclusion for the outgoing connection of the host h_i. If the two connections are in a same chain, the self matches and cross matches remain the same no matter where the perturbation is conducted within the range of the first place.

However, if a time perturbation is performed at any host of the third place, the packet matching is affected, and thus affects the packet matching rate. But it does not affect the performance of the RTT-Algorithm to detect stepping-stone because the self matching rate and cross matching rate still keep the same under the time perturbation. This kind of time perturbation can only affect the timestamps of echo packets of incoming and outgoing connections of the host h_i. The following equations (1) and equations (2) represent the timestamps of Sends and Echoes of h_i before and after time manipulation is performed, respectively.

$$S_i^{(1)} = \left\{ s_1^{(1)}, s_2^{(1)}, ..., s_n^{(1)} \right\}, \quad S_i^{(2)} = \left\{ s_1^{(2)}, s_2^{(2)}, ..., s_n^{(2)} \right\}$$
$$E_i^{(1)} = \left\{ e_1^{(1)}, e_2^{(1)}, ..., e_m^{(1)} \right\}, \quad E_i^{(2)} = \left\{ e_1^{(2)}, e_2^{(2)}, ..., e_m^{(2)} \right\} \tag{1}$$

$$S_i'^{(1)} = \left\{ s_1^{(1)}, s_2^{(1)}, ..., s_n^{(1)} \right\}, \quad S_i'^{(2)} = \left\{ s_1^{(2)}, s_2^{(2)}, ..., s_n^{(2)} \right\}$$
$$E_i'^{(1)} = \left\{ e_1^{(1)} + \Delta_1, e_2^{(1)} + \Delta_2, ..., e_m^{(1)} + \Delta_m \right\}, \tag{2}$$
$$E_i'^{(2)} = \left\{ e_1^{(2)} + \Delta_1, e_2^{(2)} + \Delta_2, ..., e_m^{(2)} + \Delta_m \right\}$$

The two equations show that after time perturbation, the RTTs are changed because the timestamp of each Echo is changed. It means that we will not get the self matching rate and cross matching rate which are the same as ones unperturbed because we use clustering method to match the Sends and Echoes, some gaps that represents the real RTTs might not involved into the RTT cluster. But the matching rates among ($S_i'^{(1)}, E_i'^{(1)}$), ($S_i'^{(1)}, E_i'^{(2)}$), ($S_i'^{(2)}, E_i'^{(1)}$), and ($S_i'^{(2)}, E_i'^{(2)}$) remain the same ideally. So we still can identify stepping-stone pair by comparing these rates.

The complex situation occurs when a manipulation is conducted at the second place. The timestamps of the Sends of the outgoing connection are changed, which are different from the timestamps of the Sends of the incoming connection. The timestamps of the Echoes of both incoming and outgoing connections are affected, but they are almost same. In this case, the four matching rates could not be the same. But the matching rate between ($S_i'^{(1)}, E_i'^{(1)}$) and ($S_i'^{(1)}, E_i'^{(2)}$) should be same, as well as the other matching rates between ($S_i'^{(2)}, E_i'^{(1)}$) and ($S_i'^{(2)}, E_i'^{(2)}$). So sometimes we do not need to check all the matching rates, just need to check one side self and cross matching rates to detect stepping-stone. Our conclusion is the RTT-Algorithm can detect time perturbation completely.

5 Resistance to Chaff Perturbation

Another attack used by an intruder is chaff perturbation which means an intruder could manipulate an outgoing connection by inserting some meaningless packets into the original Send sequence with purpose of evading stepping-stone detection system. It is possible that an intruder could manipulate the hosts of a session concurrently. To simplify our analysis, we assume that an intruder can conduct his chaff manipulation at only one host of a session. Chaff cannot be echoed because they must be removed before reaching the destination host. Based on the places to conduct chaff and remove them, there are four cases: 1) inserting and removing chaff either before the MP or after the MP; 2) inserting chaff before the MP and removing them after the MP; 3) inserting chaff before the MP and removing them at the outgoing connection of the MP; 4) inserting chaff at an outgoing connection of the MP and removing them at any host after the MP.

In case 1, chaff perturbation does not affect the RTT-Algorithm at all because the packet matching including self matching and cross matching at the MP is not affected. In case 2, chaff perturbation affects the packet matching and matching rate, but does not affect the RTT-Algorithm to detect stepping-stone. If chaffs are inserted before the MP and removed after the MP, then there are some meaningless packets in both $S_i^{(1)}$ and $S_i^{(2)}$; these packets are not matched ideally because chaffs are not echoed. If the gap between chaff and an echo is within the RTTs range, it is possible this chaff is matched. This chaff appears at both $S_i^{(1)}$ and $S_i^{(2)}$, even if the packet matching is affected, but the matching rates keep same among ($S_i^{(1)}, E_i^{(1)}$), ($S_i^{(1)}, E_i^{(2)}$), ($S_i^{(2)}, E_i^{(1)}$), and ($S_i^{(2)}, E_i^{(2)}$).

In case 3, the chaff perturbation affects the packet matching at incoming connection of the MP, but it does not affect the packet matching at an outgoing connection of the MP. Thus we can still apply the RTT-Algorithm to detect stepping-stone. Chaffs are inserted before the MP, but are removed exactly at outgoing connection of the MP. This results in $S_i^{(1)}$ and $S_i^{(2)}$ having different contents and thus the four matching rates cannot remain the same. The contents in $E_i^{(1)}$ are the same as the contents in $E_i^{(2)}$, so the matching rate between $S_i^{(1)}$ and $E_i^{(1)}$ is the same as that between $S_i^{(1)}$ and $E_i^{(2)}$. Similarly, the matching rate between $S_i^{(2)}$ and $E_i^{(1)}$ is the same as that between $S_i^{(2)}$ and $E_i^{(2)}$. So in this situation, the RTT-Algorithm can still detect stepping-stone.

The analysis of case 4 is similar to case 3. Our conclusion is that the RTT-Algorithm can detect intruders' chaff evasion. Comparing to Peng's method [5], this algorithm does not care the distribution of chaff packets; comparing to Blum's method [7], there is no limitation on the number of inserted packets.

6 Conclusions and Future Work

In this paper, we have proposed the RTT-Algorithm to detect stepping-stone, as well as analysis the resistance of this algorithm to intruders' time and chaff perturbation. The main idea of this algorithm to detect evasion is that even though send packets can be easily manipulated, but the self and cross matching rate cannot be changed easily if two connections are in a same chain. Our conclusion is that the RTT-Algorithm can not only detect stepping-stone efficiently, but also resist to intruders' evasion completely.

It might have been bewared that we did not take a situation into consideration that an intruder could manipulate a session at more hosts concurrently. And we assume that only send packet stream can be manipulated, rather than both send and echo streams. In fact, intruders can manipulate both of them. If we took all the above situations into consideration, the RTT-Algorithm would not work well. In the future, one work is to modify this algorithm to make it meet all the challenges. Even though there are some deficits of the RTT-Algorithm, but at least this algorithm makes intruders manipulate a session harder than before.

References

[1] Yin Zhang, Vern Paxson: Detecting Stepping-Stones. Proceedings of the 9th USENIX Security Symposium, Denver, CO, August (2000) 67-81.
[2] S. Staniford-Chen, L. Todd Heberlein: Holding Intruders Accountable on the Internet. Proc. IEEE Symposium on Security and Privacy, Oakland, CA, August (1995) 39-49.

[3] K. Yoda, H. Etoh: Finding Connection Chain for Tracing Intruders. Proc. 6th European Symposium on Research in Computer Security (LNCS 1985), Toulouse, France, September (2000) 31-42.

[4] X. Wang, D.S. Reeves: Robust Correlation of Encrypted Attack Traffic Through Stepping-Stones by Manipulation of Interpacket Delays. Proceedings of the 10th ACM Conference on Computer and Communications Security (CCS 2003), Washington DC, Oct (2003).

[5] P. Peng, P. Ning, D. S. Reeves and X. Y. Wang: Active Timing-Based Correlation of Perturbed Traffic Flows with Chaff Packets. Proceedings of the 2nd International Workshop on Security in Distributed Computing Systems (SDCS-2005), Columbus OH, June (2005).

[6] D. L. Donoho (ed.): Detecting Pairs of Jittered Interactive Streams by Exploiting Maximum Tolerable Delay. Proceedings of International Symposium on Recent Advances in Intrusion Detection, Zurich, Switzerland, September (2002) 45-59.

[7] A. Blum, D. Song, And S. Venkataraman: Detection of Interactive Stepping-Stones: Algorithms and Confidence Bounds. Proceedings of International Symposium on Recent Advance in Intrusion Detection (RAID), Sophia Antipolis, France, September (2004) 20-35.

[8] Kwong H. Yung: Detecting Long Connecting Chains of Interactive Terminal Sessions. Proceedings of International Symposium on Recent Advance in Intrusion Detection (RAID), Zurich, Switzerland, October (2002) 1-16.

[9] J. Yang, S-H S. Huang: A Real-Time Algorithm to Detect Long Connection Chains of Interactive Terminal Sessions. Proceedings of 3rd International Conference on Information Security (Infosecu'04), Shanghai, China, November (2004) 198-203.

[10] J. Yang, S-H S. Huang: Matching TCP Packets and Its Application to the Detection of Long Connection Chains. Proceedings of 19th IEEE International Conference on Advanced Information Networking and Applications (AINA'05), Taipei, Taiwan, March (2005) 1005-1010.

[11] J. Yang, S.H. S. Huang: Characterizing and Estimating Network Fluctuation for Detecting Interactive Stepping-Stone Intrusion. The proceedings of 3rd International Conference on Communication, Network and Information Security, Phoenix, Arizona, November (2005) 70-75.

[12] J. Yang, Y. Zhang: Probabilistic Proof of an Algorithm to Compute TCP Packet Round-Trip Time for Intrusion Detection. Lecture Notes in Computer Science (LNCS) by Springer-Verlag, Vol. 3989, (2006) 18-32.

[13] University of Southern California: Transmission Control Protocol. RFC 793, September (1981).

A New ID-Based Broadcast Encryption Scheme

Chen Yang, Xiangguo Cheng, Wenping Ma, and Xinmei Wang

Ministry of Education Key Lab. of Computer Networks and Information Security,
Xidian University, Xi'an 710071, China
yfych@eyou.com, chengxgo@sina.com, wp_ma@hotmail.com,
xmwang@xidian.edu.cn

Abstract. This paper presents a new efficient identity-based broadcast encryption scheme using bilinear mapping. Both private-key storage for one authorized user (only two group elements) and communication transmission bandwidth (three group elements) in our scheme are of constant size regardless of the number of colluders. In terms of efficiency and security, our scheme is very efficient with lower encryption and decryption computational cost and more secure against k number of colluders by introducing self-enforcing protection strategy.

1 Introduction

Broadcast encryption is a mechanism that allows a data provider to securely distribute data contents to authorized users. In a broadcast encryption scheme, the data provider or the broadcast center encrypts the messages and broadcasts them to some subset S of authorized users who are listening on a broadcast channel. Any authorized user in S can decrypt the encrypted broadcast using his private key. However, even if all users outside of S collude they cannot obtain any information about the messages of the broadcast. Broadcast encryption plays a very important role in pay-TV, online database, and DVD content protection, *etc*. Since it was first proposed in [1] and formally defined and researched in [2], broadcast encryption has become a key topic in cryptography and got extensively studied in the literatures [3-5].

Key management is a critical issue in broadcast encryption system. As we may encounter the special case where some authorized users may leak their private keys to someone else or even collude to create new decryption keys to construct a pirate decoder, and the resulting pirate decoder allows non-subscribers to extract the digital content. A number of techniques have been suggested or are currently employed to make pirate either inconvenient or traceable. Dwork[6] introduced the concept of self-enforcing protection strategy which would efficiently deter one authorized user from leaking his private key and contributing to a pirate decoder by relating his decryption key to his personal sensitive information (*e.g.* credit card number, signature key in public key infrastructure). And to simplify the key management in broadcast encryption system and to eliminate the need for directories and certificates, retyping, many identity-based broadcast encryption schemes were proposed using bilinear mapping [7, 8]. However, both proposed schemes cannot realize key self-enforcing protection, and the communication transmission bandwidth of [7] is linearly dependent of the user size. In this paper, we present a new efficient ID-based

L.T. Yang et al. (Eds.): ATC 2006, LNCS 4158, pp. 487–492, 2006.
© Springer-Verlag Berlin Heidelberg 2006

broadcast encryption scheme in which both the private keys and communication transmission bandwidth are independent of the number of the users in the system. The proposed scheme makes pirate more inconvenient and is more secure against k number of colluders by introducing self-enforcing protection strategy.

The rest of the paper is organized as follows. Section 2 recalls the background concepts of bilinear mapping and some mathematical problems. Our proposed ID-based encryption broadcast scheme is presented in section 3. In section 4, we give the security and performance analysis of the scheme. The last section is the conclusion of our paper.

2 Preliminary

In this section, we briefly review the basic concepts of bilinear mappings and some related mathematical problems with the security of our proposed scheme.

2.1 Bilinear Mapping

Let G_1 and G_2 be two multiplicative cyclic groups with the same large prime order q, and g is a generator of G_1. We assume that the discrete logarithm problems in both G_1 and G_2 are hard. A cryptographic bilinear mapping e is defined as $e : G_1 \times G_1 \rightarrow G_2$ with the following properties:

1. Bilinearity: $\forall\, P, Q \in G_1$ and $\forall\, a, b \in Z_q$, we have $e(P^a, Q^b) = e(P, Q)^{ab}$
2. Non-degeneracy: for any point $P \in G_1$, $e(P, Q) = 1$ for all $Q \in G_1$ iff $P = O$.
3. Computability: there exists an efficient algorithm to compute $e(P, Q)$ for any $P, Q \in G_1$.

Admissible bilinear mapping can be constructed from Weil or Tate pairings associated with super-singular elliptic curves or Abelian varieties.

2.2 Mathematical Problems

Let G be a bilinear group of prime order q and g be a generator of G_1. We define the *Extended Bilinear Diffie-Hellman Inversion* (k-BDHI) assumption and k-CAA problem as follows.

Definition 1: Extended Bilinear Diffie-Hellman Inversion problem (k-BDHI)

Given $(g, g^t, g^{t^2}, \cdots, g^{t^{k-1}}) \in (G_1^*)^k$, compute $e(g, g)^{\frac{1}{t}} \in G_2^*$.

Definition 2: k-BDHI Assumption

Given $(g, g^t, g^{t^2}, \cdots, g^{t^{k-1}}) \in (G_1^*)^k$, no probabilistic polynomial time algorithms exist that can efficiently compute $e(g, g)^{\frac{1}{t}} \in G_2^*$ with non-negligible probability under the assumption that solving elliptic curve discrete logarithm problems is NP hard.

Definition 3: k-CAA (collusion attack algorithm with k traitors)

An algorithm that computes $g^{\frac{1}{x+yv_0H(ID_0)}}$ from $g^{\frac{1}{x+yv_1H(ID_1)}}, g^{\frac{1}{x+yv_2H(ID_2)}}, \cdots, g^{\frac{1}{x+yv_kH(ID_k)}}$,

where $g^{\frac{1}{x+yv_iH(ID_i)}}$, $i = 1, 2, \cdots, k$ are different from each other.

3 New ID-Based Broadcast Encryption Scheme

3.1 ID-Based Public Key Infrastructure

ID-based public infrastructure involves a trusted Key Generation Center (KGC) and users. The basic operations consist of *Setup* and *Private Key Extraction.*

Setup: KGC runs BDH parameters generator[9] to generate two groups G_1 and G_2 of prime order q and a bilinear mapping $e : G_1 \times G_1 \rightarrow G_2$, chooses two random elements $x, y \in Z_q^*$ and a secret generator g_2 of G_1 as his secret master keys and defines a cryptographic hash function: $H : \{0,1\}^* \rightarrow G_1$.

Private Key Extraction: User i submits his identity information ID_i and $v_i \in Z_q^*$ to KGC, where v_i is his secret information (*e.g.* credit card number or password) or randomly chosen as his secret signature and encryption key in Public Key Infrastructure. KGC computes $K_i = g_2^{y/(x+yv_iH(ID_i))} \in G_1$ and sends (v_i, K_i) to user i as his private keys. KGC stores (G_1, G_2, q, e, H) as public system parameters and (x, y, g_2) as system private keys.

3.2 Our Proposed Scheme

In this section, we describe a new ID-based broadcast encryption scheme. Assume there are $n+1$ participants in our proposed scheme: a data provider and n users. We denote the identity number of users are ID_i, $i = 1, 2, \cdots, n$, respectively, and assume the data provider can obtain both public system parameters and system private keys from ID-based PKI. The data provider also selects a conventional symmetric encryption function $E(\cdot, \cdot)$ (*e.g.* AES), $D(\cdot, \cdot)$ the corresponding decryption function, to encrypt the data contents with a session key. If the data provider wants to broadcast the digital content m to the authorized users, he does as follows:

Encryption: The data provider randomly chooses a generator g_1 of G_1 and a random number $r \in Z_q^*$, and computes $X = g_1^{xr}$ and $Y = g_1^{yr}$. He also randomly selects a session key $s \in Z_q^*$ and computes the controlling header H as follows:

$$H = (X, Y, se(g_1, g_2)^r)$$

Encrypt the digital content m using $E(\cdot,\cdot)$ with session key s:

$$C = E(s,m)$$

And broadcast (H,C).

Decryption: After having received (H,C), user i firstly decrypts m using his private keys (v_i, K_i) and decrypts m from C as follows:

$$s = se(g_1,g_2)^r / e(K, X(Y)^{v_i H(ID_i)})$$
$$m = D(s,C).$$

Secure subsequent broadcasts can be achieved with different session key s when encrypting different digital contents.

4 Analysis of Proposed Scheme

4.1 Security Analysis

We will firstly show that our scheme is collusion-free for any coalition of non-authorized users. In our proposed scheme, if one wants to compute s, he should get $e(g_1,g_2)^r$. However, as g_1 and g_2 are both kept secret in the scheme, so it is impossible for the non-authorized users to compute $e(g_1,g_2)^r$ from the broadcast information and further get the session key s.

For coalition of authorized users to collude a pair of decryption keys, we have the following theorem.

Theorem 1: Under the (k-BDHI) assumption, no k-CAA (collusion attack algorithm with k traitors) exists, *i.e.* no coalition of at most k traitors can collude out a pair of decryption keys.

Proof. Assume k-CAA exists, and $(g, g^t, g^{t^2}, \cdots, g^{t^{k-1}}) \in (G_1^*)^k$ is given. As $v_i \in Z_q^*$ is used as the secret signature and encryption key of user i in Public Key Infrastructure, user i would not like to leak $v_i \in Z_q^*$ in contribution to the construction of a pirate decoder. By implementing self-enforcing protection strategy in [8], our scheme will be more secure against collusion attack. Here we take into account the rare case where all k users in the coalition of pirate will leak their secret keys, so the colluders can compute $g_2^{\frac{1}{x+yv_1 H(ID_1)}}, g_2^{\frac{1}{x+yv_2 H(ID_2)}}, \cdots, g_2^{\frac{1}{x+yv_k H(ID_k)}}$. Denote $H'(ID_i) = yv_i H(ID_i)$, $i = 1, 2, \cdots, k$ where $H'(ID_i)$ is different each other. Set $x = t - H'(ID_0)$, and Let

$$g_2 = g^{\prod_{i=1}^{k}(x+H'(ID_i))}$$

By substitution, we will have the followings:

$$g_2^{\frac{1}{x+H'(ID_j)}} = g^{\prod_{\substack{i=1\\i\neq j}}^{k}(x+H'(ID_i))} = g^{\prod_{\substack{i=1\\i\neq j}}^{k}(t-H'(ID_0)+H'(ID_i))} \qquad , j = 1, 2, \cdots, k$$

In each equation, the power of g is a polynomial of degree $k-1$ in the variable t.

As k-CAA exists, we get $g_2^{\frac{1}{x+H'(ID_0)}}$, and further we can compute

$$g_2^{\frac{1}{x+H'(ID_0)}} = g_2^{\frac{1}{t}} = g^{\frac{1}{t}\prod_{i=1}^{k}(x+H'(ID_i))} = g^{\sum_{i=-1}^{k}a_i t^i}$$

As $(g, g^t, g^{t^2}, \cdots, g^{t^{k-1}}) \in (G_1^*)^k$ are given, and $H'(ID_i), i = 0,1,2,\cdots,k$ are different from each other, we will easily compute a_i in at most $O(k^2)$ of time, and $a_{-1} \neq 0$. By computation, we have

$$g^{\frac{1}{t}} = (g_2^{\frac{1}{x+H'(ID_0)}} / g^{\sum_{i=0}^{k}a_i t^i})^{a_{-1}^{-1}}.$$

And we can compute

$$e(g,g)^{\frac{1}{t}} = e(g, g^{\frac{1}{t}}).$$

Thus the k-BDHI problem is solvable. □

4.2 Efficiency Analysis

In terms of efficiency, we note that the controlling header size is only three group elements. The main computational cost of encryption for the data provider includes three exponential computations in G_1 and one paring computation. However, by selecting the same g_1 and pre-computing $e(g_1, g_2)$, we need not do the paring computation any more. The main decryption cost requires only one exponential computation in G_1 and one pairing computation, if the computational cost of multiplication and division in G_1, compared to paring computation or exponential computation, is negligible.

5 Conclusion

We describe a new efficient ID-based broadcast encryption scheme of which the security is based on k-BDHI assumption. By introducing self-enforcing protection strategy, the resulting scheme is even more secure against k number of colluders and needs smaller transmission size than the previous ID-based broadcast encryption scheme presented in [6]. An interesting open problem is how to construct efficient Black-box traitor tracing schemes using our proposed ID-based broadcast encryption scheme.

Acknowledgment

The authors would like to thank anonymous referees for useful comments. This research is partially supported by "Program for New Century Excellent Talents in

University" and the Natural Science Foundation of China under Grants No.60373104 and No.90604009.

References

1. Berkovits, S.: How to Broadcast a Secret. Advances in Eurocrypt'91. Lecture Notes in Computer Science, Vol. 574. Springer-Verlag, Berlin Heidelberg New York (1991) 536-541.
2. Fiat, A., Naor, M.: Broadcast Encryption. In Proc. of Crypto'93. Lecture Notes in Computer Science, Vol. 773. Springer-Verlag, Berlin Heidelberg New York (1994) 480-491.
3. Stinson, D.R., Wei, R.: Key Preassigned Traceability Scheme for Broadcast Encryption. In Proc. of SAC'98. Lecture Notes in Computer Science, Vol. 1556. Springer-Verlag, Berlin Heidelberg New York (1998) 144-156.
4. Halevi, D., Shamir, A.: The LSD broadcast encryption Scheme. In Proc. of Crypto'02. Lecture Notes in Computer Science, Vol. 2442. Springer-Verlag, Berlin Heidelberg New York (2002) 47-60.
5. D'Arco, P., Stinson, D. R.: Fault Tolerant and Distributed Broadcast Encryption. In Proc. of CT-RSA 2003. Lecture Notes in Computer Science, Vol. 2612. Springer-Verlag, Berlin Heidelberg New York (2003) 263-280.
6. Dwork, C., Lotspiech, J., Naor, M.: Digital Signets: Self-Enforcing Protection of Digital Content. Proceedings of the 28th Symposium on the Theory of Computation, 1996. 489–498.
7. Du, X., Wang, Y., Ge, J., Wang, Y.M.: An ID-based broadcast encryption for key distribution. IEEE Transactions on broadcasting, 2005, 51(2):264-266.
8. Mu, Y., Susilo1, W., Lin, Y.X.: Identity-Based Broadcasting. INDOcrypto'03. Lecture Notes in Computer Science, Vol. 2904. Springer-Verlag, Berlin Heidelberg New York (2003) 177–190.
9. Boneh D., Lynn B. and Shacham H.: Short signatures from the Weil pairing. In Proc. of Asiacrypt'01. Lecture Notes in Computer Science, Vol. 2248. Springer-Verlag, Berlin Heidelberg New York (2001) 514--532.

Automated Abduction for Computer Forensics

Andrei Doncescu[1] and Katsumi Inoue[2]

[1] LAAS-CNRS UPR 8001, Avenue du Colonel Roche,
31007 Toulouse, France
andrei.doncescu@laas.fr
http://www.laas.fr
[2] National Institute of Informatics, 2-1-2 Hitotsubashi, Chiyoda-ku
Tokyo 101-8430, Japan
ki@nii.ac.jp
http://www.nii.ac.jp

Abstract. This paper describes a diagnostic system designed to aid an investigator to determine how a computer intrusion was accomplished. This wants to be a decision support by figuring out how a hacker created an unauthorized computer account. The diagnostic of this system is based on automated abduction. Abduction is inference that begins with data describing some state and produces an explanation of the data. Since abduction is ampliative and plausible reasoning may not be correct. The plausibility of an explication depends on how much better it is than the alternatives, how good it is independent of the alternatives, how reliable the data is. Therefore, abduction is nonmonotonic. To solve the problem of intrusion we consider the relationship between abduction, default logic and circumscription.

1 Introduction

The Artificial Intelligence offers today an alternative to intrusion detection problems. Basically, the expert systems contains rules for intrusion detection. They face difficulties in acquiring and representing knowledge. In this paper we present and describe an abductif reasoning approach to intrusion detection. An intrusion is an unauthorized access or usage of the resources of a computer system. Within a distributed system two types of intrusion could be find out: external which can be detected by auditing login records and internal intrusion detected by resources access attempt. The expert systems provide alarms by attaching meaning to situations and appropriate responses to the perceived security threats. Examples of intrusion detection detection expert system include MIDAS, NADIR and USTAT. The objective of our research is a decision support system for computer diagnosis. Diagnosis is the process of deducing the most likely mechanism that caused an observed condition. Discovering how a hacker created an unauthorized computer account is an example of diagnosis. Diagnosis is a type of abduction.

L.T. Yang et al. (Eds.): ATC 2006, LNCS 4158, pp. 493–499, 2006.

2   Knowledge Expertise in Databases

The emerging field of data mining and knowledge discovery in databases has recently attracted significant attention. It is an area that deals with automatic or semi-automatic ways to discover significant, valid, novel, potentially useful, and ultimately understandable patterns in massive data sets (or in short, data mining attempts to extract knowledge from data). Data mining builds on techniques from several disciplines including machine learning, statistics, pattern recognition, databases, knowledge representation, visualisation and graphics, optimisation, computational mathematics, and the theory of algorithms. The emergence of the field is triggered by the fact that while more and more data becomes available in corporate and private databases and on the internet our resources to interpret and extract information from available data remains relatively constant. Few people or businesses today (at least in the industrialised part of the world) suffer from lack of access to data, but rather from an overload of it. It has therefore become essential to find efficient ways to automatically analyze and extract useful information from these large data sets. The ease of understanding as well as the expressive power of the pattern language is a strong motivation for the use of ILP for expertise in databases.

2.1   Inductive Logic Programming

Inductive Logic Programming (ILP) is the part of machine learning where the underlying model is described in term of first-order logic. We briefly outline here the standard definitions and notations. Given a first-order language L with a set of variables Var, we build the set of terms Term, atoms Atom and formulas as usual. The set of ground terms is the Herbrand universe H and the set of ground atoms or facts is the Herbrand base B. A literal l is just an atom a (positive literal) or its negation $\tilde{a}$ (negative literal). A substitution s is an application from Var to Term with inductive extension to Atom. We denote $Subst$ the set of ground substitutions. A clause is a finite disjunction of literals and a Horn clause is a clause with at most one positive literal. A Herbrand interpretation I is just a subset of B : I is the set of true ground atomic formulas and its complementary denotes the set of false ground atomic formulas. We can now proceed with the notion of logical consequence. Given A an atomic formula, I, $s \vdash A$ means that s(A) belongs to I. As usual, the extension to general formulas F uses compositionality. $I \vdash F$ means : $\forall s, I, s \vdash F$ we say I is a model of $F \vdash F$ means : $\forall I, I \vdash F$. $F \vdash G$ means that all models of F are models of G.

Stated in the general context of first-order logic, the task of induction is to find a set of formulas H such that: $B \cup H \vdash E$ given a background theory B and a set of observations E (training set), where E, B and H here denote sets of clauses. In this paper, E is always given as positive examples, but negative examples can also be introduced as well. A set of formulas is here, as usual, considered as the conjunction of its elements. Of course, one may add two natural restrictions : $(B \vdash E)$ since, in such a case, H would not be necessary to explain E. $(B \cup H \vdash \perp)$: this means $B \cup H$ is a consistent theory.

ILP machine

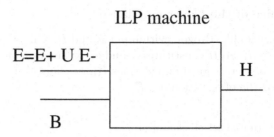

Fig. 1. The principle of ILP Machine

In the setting of relational databases, inductive logic programming (ILP) is often restricted to Horn clauses and function-free formulas, E is just a set of ground facts. The main reason of this restriction is due to easiness for handling such formulas. An extension to non-Horn clauses in B, E, and H is, however, useful in many applications. For example, indefinite statements can be represented by disjunctions with more than one positive literals, and integrity constraints are usually represented as clauses with only negative literals. A clause-form example is also useful to represent causality. The inductive machinery developed by [2] can handle all such extended classes. There are two other remarks on the logic for induction. The distinction between B and E is a matter of taste. In fact, some induction problems which often be seen in data mining do not distinguish between B and E, and extracts rules merely from the whole knowledge base. However, the distinction is important from practical viewpoints (Inoue and Saito 2004). When we already have our current knowledge B and then a new observation E is obtained to update B, this E should be assimilated into our knowledge in a way that E should change the current theory B into the augmented theory $B \cup H$ such that $B \cup H \vdash E$ holds. In this case, background knowledge is intrinsic to knowledge evolution. We cannot realize continuous and incremental learning if we merely treat examples without any prior knowledge. When we investigate induction deeper, some subtlities appear according to the properties of induction (e.g., whether the closed-world assumption is applied or Mathematical logic has always been a powerful representation tool for declarative knowledge and Logic Programming is a way to consider mathematical logic as a programming language. A set of first order formulae restricted to a clausal form, constitutes a logic program and as such, becomes executable by using standard mechanisms of theorem proving field, namely unification and resolution. The data and their properties, i.e. the observations, are represented as a finite set of logical facts E. E could generally been discomposed into the positive examples E^+ and the negative ones E^-. In case of background knowledge, it is described as a set of Horn clauses B. This background knowledge is supposed to be insufficient to explain the positive observations and the logical translation of this fact is : $B \not\models E^+$ but there is no contradiction with the negative knowledge: $B \cup E^- \not\models \bot$. S.

2.2   The Choice of the Covering Clause

An ILP machinery [6] like Progol , with input E and B, will output a program H such that $B \cup H \models E$. So H constitutes a kind of explanation of our observations E. Expressed as a set of logical implications (Horn clauses) $c \rightarrow o$, c becomes a possible cause for the observation $o \in E$.

Initialize : $E' = E$ (initial set of examples)
$\qquad\qquad H = \emptyset$ (initial hypothesis)
While $E' \neq \emptyset$ do
$\qquad$ Choose $e \in E'$
$\qquad$ Compute a covering clause C for e
$\qquad H = H \cup \{C\}$
$\qquad$ Compute $Cov = \{e' \mid e' \in E, B \cup H \models e'\}$
$\qquad E' = E' \setminus Cov$
End while

Fig. 2. General Progol scheme

The main point we want to update is the choice of the relevant clause C for a given training example e. Let us precise here how this clause is chosen.

It is clear that there is an infinite number of clauses covering e, and so Progol need to restrict the search in this set. The idea is thus to compute a clause C_e such that if C covers e, then necessarily $C \models C_e$. Since, in theory, C_e could have an infinite cardinality, Progol restricts the construction of C_e using mode declarations and some other settings (like number of resolution inferences allowed, etc...). Mode declarations imply that some variables are considered as input variables and other ones as output variables : this is a standard way to restrict the search tree for a Prolog interpreter.

At last, when we have a suitable C_e, it suffices to search for clauses C which θ-subsume C_e since this is a particular case which validates $C \models C_e$. Thus, Progol begins to build a finite set of θ-subsuming clauses, $C_1, \ldots, C_n$. For each of these clauses, Progol computes a natural number $f(C_i)$ which expresses the *quality* of C_i : this number measures in some sense how well the clause explains the examples and is combined with some compression requirement. Given a clause C_i extracted to cover e, we have :

$$f(C_i) = p(C_i) - (c(C_i) + h(C_i) + n(C_i))$$

where :

- $p(C_i) = \#(\{e \mid e \in E, B \cup \{C_i\} \models e\})$ i.e. the number of covered examples
- $n(C_i) = \#(\{e \mid e \in E, B \cup \{C_i\} \cup \{e\} \models \bot\})$ i.e. the number of incorrectly covered examples
- $c(C_i)$ is the length of the body of the clause C_i
- $h(C_i)$ is the minimal number of atoms of the body of C_e we have to add to the body of C_i to insure output variables have been instantiated.

The evaluation of $h(C_i)$ is done by static analysis of C_e. Then, Progol chooses a clause $C = C_{i_0} \equiv \arg \max_{C_i} f(C_i)$ (i.e. such that $f(C_{i_0}) = max\{f(C_j) \mid j \in [1, n]\}$). We may notice that, in the formula computing the number $f(C_i)$ for a given clause C_i covering e, there is no distinction between the covered positive examples. So $p(C_i)$ is just the number of covered positive examples. The same computation is valuable for the computation of $n(C_i)$ and so success and failure could be considered as equally weighted.

To abbreviate, we shall denote $Progol(B, E, f)$ the output program P currently given by the Progol machine with input B as background knowledge, E as sample set and using function f to chose the relevant clauses.

It is important to note that a logic program is inherently non deterministic since a predicate is generally defined with a set of distinct clauses. In the field of classification, it is known that this approach, minimizing the error rate over the sample set (here we have zero default on the sample set) does not always guaranty the best result for the whole concept C. Nevertheless, as far as we know, no alternative induction principle is used for ILP.

2.3 Inverting Entailment for Abduction

Abduction is one of the three fundamental modes of reasoning characterized by Pierce, the other being deduction and induction. Therefore, according to Pierce abduction is "the only kind of reasoning which supplies new ideas, the only kind which is , in this sense synthetic". An important issue involved in abduction is the problem of hypothesis selection : what is the best explanation, and how can we select it from a number of possible explanation which satisfy some rules. So what is an explanation ? Explanation give causes; to explain something is to assert its cause. But more of that we want the "best" explanation which means the true one. To figure out the criteria one of the possibilities is the traditional maxim of Occam's razor, which adopt the simple hypothesis. Abduction is elegantly characterized by consequence finding as follows. Let $E_1, E_2, ..., E_n$ be a finite number of observations. We want to explain the observations the observation the $E = E_1 \wedge ... \wedge E_n$ from an abductive theory (B, Γ). Then, $H = H_1 \wedge ... \wedge H_k$ is an abductive explanation of E from (B, Γ) if :

$$1. B \wedge (H_1 \wedge ... \wedge H_k) \models E_1 \wedge ... \wedge E_n \tag{1}$$

$$2. B \wedge (H = H_1 \wedge ... \wedge H_k) \text{ is consistent} \tag{2}$$

$$3. H_i \in \Gamma \tag{3}$$

An explanation H of E is minimal if no proper sub-conjunction H' of H satisfies $B \wedge H' \models E$.

3 A System for Diagnosis of Computer Intrusions

An intrusion scenario is a sequence of commands that results in an unauthorized access. Acquiring information about these scenarios is not an easy task.

The key aspect of any reasoning system is the domain representation. In our case the domain description defines a list of predicates that define the state representation. These predicates are used for situation, action, and problem descriptions. We define : R1 R2 Router, h1 h2 unix-host, A B C - Network and the predicate "connected".

$$connected(h1, A)$$
$$connected(R2, C)$$

Another kind of predicates is represented by action grouping the commands in the operating system. We have defined the next actions:

$$ACCESS()$$
$$DUPLICATE()$$
$$CREATE()$$
$$EXECUTION()$$

Hypothesis generation is the most important part of automated diagnosis. The problem is specified by the user based on an unauthorized access to particular resources. We implemented in our hypothesis generation system based on ILP machine the capability to make assumption about attacker formulated in the given examples. The final step of our diagnosis is to match log entries from ILP hypothesis to records from the victim system. Current intrusion detection knowledge is neither easily created nor update. In general background knowledge is non-intuitive and requires the skills of system administrator and security analyst to define scenario and key events that are threats to the security of the target system.

The main problems that need to be addressed when applying ILP techniques to extract useful knowledge from such databases are the following:

1. Efficiency - When a large number of examples and background predicates are available, most current ILP systems have problems with efficiency. Methods are needed for restricting and efficiently exploring the search space.
2. Noise - Most current ILP methods have only limited abilities to handle noise, and this is a significant problem for knowledge discovery in real world databases, as it is not to be expected that useful hypotheses are consistent with all training data.
3. Continuos-valued attributes - Continuous-valued attributes are used frequently in many real world databases, which requires that the applied ILP methods should be able to efficiently and effectively handle such attributes.

In learning there is a constant interaction between the creation and the recognition of concepts. Therefore in the feature work we will develop a hybrid intrusion model by combining ILP with Fuzzy Logic.

4   Conclusion

In this paper, we proposed an architecture which can deal with intranet et internet communications by performing speculative computation in problem solving. This approach is useful in practice in intrusion analysis where the traffic changes over the time. The goal of this methodology is to obtain a model of intrusion, which can be used in a supervisory system for condition monitoring. The main problem with model-based diagnosis is its computational complexity. To make this approach practical it is necessary to make a number assumptions about the domain.The complexity of this model imposes the co-operation of data mining techniques along with the expert knowledge. Therefore the problem of relevance of information imposes the retrieval and selection among the hypothesis.

References

1. G. Antoniou, A.P. Courtenay, J. Ernts and M.A. Williams, A system for computing Proceeding of Jelia '96, Lecture Notes in Artificial Intelligence, Vol. 1126 (Springer, 1996) pp. 237-250.
2. L. Breiman. Bagging predictors. In *Machine Learning*, number 26, pages 123–140, 1996.
3. C.L. Blake and C.J. Merz. UCI repository of machine learning databases, 1998. http://www.ics.uci.edu/~mlearn/MLRepository.html.
4. T. Bylander, D. Allemang, M. C. Tanner, J. R. Josephson. The computational complexity of abduction. *Artificial Intelligence*, 49:25-60,1991.
5. P. Domingo and M. Pazzani. On the optimality of the simple bayesian classifier under zero-one loss. *Machine Learning*, 29,103-130, 1998.
6. S. Muggleton. Inverse entailement and Progol. *New Gen. Comput.*,13:245-2,1998.
7. S. Muggleton and John Firth. CProgol4.4: a tutorial introduction. Report of Departement of Computer Science, University of York.
8. S. Muggleton. Stochastic logic Programs. *Advances in Inductive Logic Programming* IOS Press/Ohmsha, 1995.

A Framework for Specifying and Managing Security Requirements in Collaborative Systems

Stephen S. Yau and Zhaoji Chen

Department of Computer Science and Engineering
Arizona State University
Tempe, AZ 85287-8809, USA
{yau, zhaoji.chen}@asu.edu

Abstract. Although security has been recognized as an increasingly important and critical issue for software system development, most security requirements are poorly specified: ambiguous, misleading, inconsistent among various parts, and lacking sufficient details. In this paper, a framework for specifying unambiguous, interoperable security requirements and detecting conflict and undesirable emergent properties in collaborative systems is presented. The framework includes a core ontology representing hierarchical security requirements, an ontology-based security requirement specification process, a set of security requirement refining rules, an algorithm for automatic security requirement refinement and an analysis algorithm to detect inconsistent security requirements. In this paper, the specification and refinement of security requirements are emphasized.

Keywords: Software security, security specification, hierarchical security requirements, framework, collaborative systems, ontology, requirement refinement algorithms

1 Introduction

Software development is traditionally driven by satisfying functional requirements: what the system must do. However, non-functional requirements, such as security, performance, and interoperability, are often as important as functional requirements. Today, people increasingly rely on information systems, which often consist of software systems running on many interconnected computers with various capabilities, such as servers, desktops, laptops, cell phones and PDAs [1]. The pervasive connectivity has not only enhanced our ability to quickly exchange information and share computation resources, but also increased the chances for attackers to launch malicious attacks on information systems. With the growing concerns over system availability, data integrity and privacy, security has become an increasingly critical issue for most software systems [2, 3].

It is well recognized that requirement engineering is both important and economical to successful software development. The later the security is addressed in the development cycle, the costlier it becomes [4]. To build secure software, accurate and consistent security requirements must be specified. Despite its importance, little research has been done on integrating security in software development. Security requirements are usually generated in an ad-hoc manner, and the specified requirements may have the following undesirable properties [3]:

L.T. Yang et al. (Eds.): ATC 2006, LNCS 4158, pp. 500–510, 2006.
© Springer-Verlag Berlin Heidelberg 2006

- *Ambiguous*: Requirements are specified in natural languages, which are usually vague and difficult to validate.
- *Misleading*: Two collaborating developers may use different terms for the same meaning or use the same term for different meanings.
- *Inconsistent*: To address different functional requirements, different developers may generate contradictory security requirements.
- *Lacking of sufficient detail information*: Some security requirements stay at very high level and lack sufficient information for them to be enforced or evaluated.

Most efforts in non-functional requirements have focused on well-specified requirements like real-time or usability, and security issues are likely left for maintenance in the infamous *penetrate and patch* manner [5]. Because various security requirements may be related, the method chosen to address a security requirement may impact other security requirements. Increasing complexity and extensibility of software, as well as dynamic operational environments, make it difficult to generate well-specified security requirements.

Although there have been several approaches to generating security requirements specification and refinement, so far no approaches can provide unambiguous semantics, automated or semi-automated refinement, and situation-awareness simultaneously. Several *product-oriented* approaches have tried to formally address non-functional requirements by quantifying them [6] and evaluating a system to what degrees it meets its requirements. However, quantitative approaches may not be suitable for addressing security requirements. For example, the possible risk of a programming bug in the core module, which can cause to a system, is much greater than that caused by the same bug in a peripheral module. A *process-oriented* approach [2] specifies security requirements as goals and refines them to specific sub-goals based on design knowledge captured. The correlation rules address how one goal may affect some other goals. This approach can adopt an agent-oriented requirements modeling paradigm to capture social relations among different entities and actors in a system as intentional dependency [7]. Both approaches cannot handle operational environment changes, where conflicting or harmonious goal interactions may change or actors may change from allies to enemies. An *aspect-oriented* approach based on UML [8] can encapsulate solutions to satisfy certain non-functional requirements as aspects, which can be integrated with a primary model based on predefined composition directives. Composed system module can be analyzed to detect any conflict or inconsistency among various aspect models and the primary model. This approach reduces the complexity of requirement engineering and facilitates fast system evolution. However, it does not address qualitative requirements and is difficult to handle large complicated systems, especially when it involves multi-party collaboration because it requires a name-match during composition. Other UML extensions [9] tried to accommodate access control in UML, but they have focused only on static design model, which is close to implementation, not security requirements.

To fully incorporate security concerns in software development, new approaches are needed to systematically address security requirement specification and management. In this paper, we present a framework to facilitate parties in large-scale collaborative systems to specify unambiguous, interoperable security requirements for software development. It can detect and remove all four undesirable emergent properties mentioned before and be used as an add-on component for other trust management frameworks [10, 11].

2 Overview of Our Approach

Our framework consists of the following five major components as shown in *Figure 1*:

C1) A core ontology for representing hierarchical security requirements.

C2) An ontology-based security requirement specification process for formally specifying security requirements based on C1).

C3) A set of security requirement refining rules and an algorithm to decompose and organize the specified security requirements into application-specific tasks according to a given operating environment.

C4) A feedback agent that records user feedbacks if the generated result is different from what the user wants, and uses this knowledge in future refining process.

C5) Inconsistency checking algorithms.

It is noted that C2 will unambiguously specify security requirements of collaborating parties based on C1 and its extensions. The refining process carried out based on C3 can establish interoperable security requirements by unifying the use of certain terminologies among multiple parties, and take care of underspecified security requirements by decomposing them into application specific subtasks with more domain knowledge and operational information. Since refinement results are automatically generated based on predefined refining rules, they may not be exactly what the users want. C4 records user feedback about the generated results and update refining rules accordingly. After the refining process, C5 will be used to detect possible contradictions or inconsistencies in requirements. If a developer wants to use a commercial off-the-shelf (*COTS*) module, the security requirements for the candidate module will be treated same as the new modules, except their implementations which are already completed.

The major innovations in our approach are the use of the

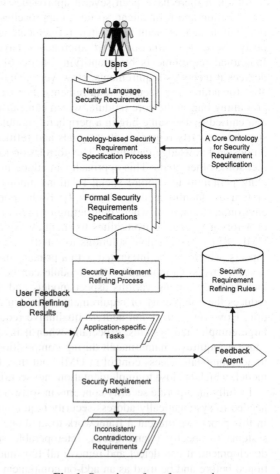

Fig. 1. Overview of our framework

core ontology and the security requirements refining rules. Our framework provides the following support:

- Semantic interoperation support: A core ontology and its extensions serve as a common base of understanding, which can help multiple collaborative parties to establish unambiguous, easy-to-understand security requirement specification.
- Requirements management support: The specified security requirements should be easy to trace, refine, reuse and prioritize.

In the following sections, we will provide detailed discussions on these components and an example to illustrate the use of our framework.

3 Security Requirement Specification

An ontology is in general a description of concepts and their relationships [12]. Because it is infeasible to list all the security concerns of possible applications in our framework, based on some common system security evaluation criteria, such as those in the "Orange Book" [13], we can only incorporate common high-level security concerns and their relations into an ontology. This ontology, which serves as a *core component* of our framework and can be extended by developers to address more application-specific security requirements, is referred as the core ontology of our framework.

The generic classes in the core ontology shown in Figure 2 are defined as follows:

- *anything* is the top of the class hierarchy for security requirement specification. It does not have any real meaning, but serves as a root class for other classes.
- *entity* is a generic security entity class which is derived from *anything*.
- *actor* is a class derived from *entity* to represent active entities within a system that carry out actions to achieve certain goals.
- *resource* is a class derived from *entity* to represent system components that need to be protected.
- *attribute* is a class derived from *anything* to describe those named values.
- *situation* is a class derived from *attribute* to identify a situation ex-

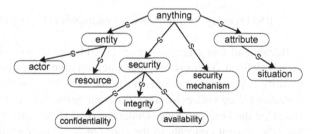

Fig. 2. The core ontology

pression used in security requirement specifications. The value of a situation expression is determined by situation-aware processors [14].
- *securityMechanism* is a class specifies which security mechanism should be used.
- *security* is a generic class derived from *anything* to address security concerns, which can further be divided into *confidentiality*, *integrity* and *availability*.

A security requirement is essentially a goal about adding some security properties to certain parts of a system. These goals, often specified in a natural language, are usually ambiguous. This problem is exacerbated when multiple parties are involved, where different uses of the same term may create confusing statements. Based on the core ontology, a security requirement $\mathcal{R}$ in our framework is specified as a quadtuple:

$$\mathcal{R} = (E, P, M, S), \quad\quad\quad (1)$$

where $E \in$ *entity*, $P \in$ *security feature*, $M \in$ *securityMechanism*, and $S \in$ *situation*. The quadtuple is interpreted as follows: security requirement $\mathcal{R}$ implies that entity E has security property P by using security mechanism M under situation S. M can be omitted when users do not care about which security mechanism the system adopts. S can be omitted if property P applies to all situations. For example, $\mathcal{R}_1 =$ (*account_no, confidentiality, encryption, __*) means that account numbers stored in a system should always be encrypted to ensure confidentiality. If a project is intended to use some plug-in *COTS* modules since the *COTS* modules are usually developed for some other purposes, even if they can satisfy the new functional requirements needed by the project, the *COTS* modules may not meet the security requirements of the project. Hence, the security requirements of the candidate *COTS* modules should also be specified and analyzed in the framework. Our approach to specifying security policies is summarized as follows:

RS1) Describe security requirements in a natural language.
RS2) Generate an ontology for the specified security requirements based on the core ontology as follows:
   2.1) Determine what kinds of situations we need to consider in RS1).
   2.2) Specify entities and create corresponding subclasses of `entity` in RS1).
   2.3) Specify security properties and security mechanisms in RS1), and generate subclasses for each of `security` and `securityMechanism`.
RS3) Specify requirements as quadtuples (1) using the results generated in RS2).

Because all four elements are specified based on our core ontology, each element is clearly defined. There is only one interpretation for a quadtuple, and thus a specified security requirement can only have one unambiguous meaning. However, confusing statements may still exist since different parties can derive and use their own terms based on the core ontology. Underspecified statements may also exist if a user only uses the general concepts in the core ontology, instead of extending them to express more detailed application-specific information. These two problems are taken care of by security requirement refinement which will be discussed in Section 4.

4   Security Requirements Refinement

In this section, we will discuss components C3 and C4 and the process of using them to refine security requirements. The security requirement refining rules specify how security requirements can be transformed. In our framework, there are three types of refining rules: *substitution*, *decomposition* and *combination*.

The *substitution* rules are used to provide interoperability among parties. In large collaborative systems with multiple developers involved, these developers may specify the same security requirement using different terms, or they may interpret one term with different meanings. Arranging meetings with all parties involved and specifying requirements together is one way to solve this problem. However, this approach is costly, inefficient, and sometimes infeasible. In our framework, we address this problem using the core ontology and its user-defined extensions. We assume that each team has its well-defined terminologies that all developers in the team will follow. Instead of getting all developers in all teams to work together, each team can work independently and specify its security requirements. Before the framework integrates all security requirements together, the common understanding of different teams on various terminologies can be established by a group with a representative from each team. This common understanding is defined as *substitution* rules and our framework will automatically apply these rules during security requirement integration among different parties. A *substitution* rule specifies that if the two terms T and T' have the same meaning, and for any two security requirements $\mathcal{R}_1$ and $\mathcal{R}_2$, if the only difference is one uses T and the other uses T', we can substitute $\mathcal{R}_1$ with $\mathcal{R}_2$, vice versa. If T and T' appear to be entities, the *substitution* rule is expressed as follows:

$$\mathcal{R}_1: (T, P, M, S) \rightarrow \mathcal{R}_2: (T', P, M, S). \tag{2}$$

Similar rules can be specified for security properties, security mechanisms or situations.

The *decomposition* rules decompose general, high level security requirements into more specific individual tasks. Security requirements specified by various developers vary in levels of detail. Some stay at very high level, like "Accesses to the account should be controlled". Some include great details like "Access to the account can only be granted to those people listed in the access control list during normal business hours". This phenomenon sometimes is referred as *local heroes* [5], which means the specification relies heavily on individual expertise. This means that if a developer knows the area well, he is likely to put down more detailed and complete specifications. Comparing the above two requirements, the second requirement is much easier to implement, test and evaluate. But, not everyone in a development team is a local hero. Thus, from time to time, we have to deal with underspecified security requirements. In our framework, we summarize the expertise from those *local heroes* into *decomposition* rules. Based on these rules, a general, underspecified security requirement will be automatically refined by adding application-specific constraints or decomposing it into several individual sub-goals. A decomposition rule is specified as follows:

$$\mathcal{R}_0:(E_0, P_0, M_0, S_0) \rightarrow \mathcal{R}_1:(E_1, P_1, M_1, S_1) \wedge \mathcal{R}_2: (E_2, P_2, M_2, S_2), \tag{3}$$

which means requirement $\mathcal{R}_0$ can be satisfied by satisfying both $\mathcal{R}_1$ and $\mathcal{R}_2$.

The *combination* rules are used to reorganize individual tasks generated by *decomposition* rules. In a collaborative system, security requirements specified by different users may be interrelated. After applying decomposition rules, we may have several individual requirements concerning the entity with the same E. Although they may not be exactly the same, it is still helpful if we can combine all interrelated security requirements and address them together. When $E_1 = E_2 = E$, since $\mathcal{R}_1$ and $\mathcal{R}_2$ both concern with entity E, the combination of $\mathcal{R}_1$ and $\mathcal{R}_2$ can be carried out by combining the security mechanisms used, or by satisfying both security properties required in $\mathcal{R}_1$ and $\mathcal{R}_2$. If $\mathcal{R}_1$ and $\mathcal{R}_2$ require the same entity to use the same security mechanism under the same situation to satisfy two different security properties, the combined result should require the entity to satisfy both properties P_1 and P_2. In this case, a combination rule can be specified as follows:

$$\mathcal{R}_1{:}(E_1, P_1, M_1, S_1) \wedge \mathcal{R}_2{:}(E_2, P_2, M_2, S_2) \wedge (E_1 = E_2) \wedge (M_1 = M_2) \wedge (S_1 = S_2) \tag{4}$$
$$\rightarrow \mathcal{R'}{:}(E_1, P', M_1, S_1), \quad P' = P_1 \wedge P_2.$$

Similar rules can be specified for security mechanisms or applicable situations.

For a large, distributed collaborative system, we can have hundreds of these refining rules. The number of specified security requirements for such a large system can also be very large, and hence manually applying each suitable refining rule to the specified security requirements will not be feasible. Thus, we develop the following algorithm to automatically applying suitable refining rules:

```
Initialization:
Store all refining rules in a database table T_R,
Store each security requirement R_j in a list L_R, n is
the number of nodes, and L_R[i] is the i^th node in L_R.


Refinement process:
int count, head = 0, tail = n-1;
  while ( head ≠ tail){
    count = 0;
    for(int: i from head to tail){
        while(found L_R[i]→ R_i' in T_R)
        L_R[i] = R_i';
        if(found L_R[i]→ R_i1 ∧ R_i2 in T_R){
        delete L_R[i] from L_R;
        append R_i1 and R_i2 to the end of L_R;
        count ++;}
    }
    head = tail+1 - count;
    tail = tail + 2*count-1;
  }
  for (int:i from 0 to tail)
  for (int:j from i to tail)
    if((L_R[i]∧L_R[j]→R_k)or(L_R[j]∧L_R[i]→R_k) in T_R){
        delete L_R[i] and L_R[j] from L_R;
        append R_k to the end of L_R;
        tail --;
    }
```

After the refinement, a *feedback* agent will record user feedback on the generated results and update refining rules so that future refining results can be closer to what users expect. For example, one refining rule R_1 states that security requirement $\mathcal{R}_1$: (E_1, P_1, M_1, S_1) should be decomposed into $\mathcal{R}_2$ and $\mathcal{R}_3$. But, there is a specific situation

S_1', which is a special case in situation S_1 and has not been carefully examined in R_1. For situation S_1', users want $\mathcal{R}_1$ to be decomposed to $\mathcal{R}_2$' and $\mathcal{R}_3$'. Based on this user feedback, a new refining rule R_2 shown in (5) specifically addressing S_1' can be added to the repository:

$$(E_1, P_1, M_1, S_1') \rightarrow (E_2, P_2, M_2, S_2') \wedge (E_3, P_3, M_3, S_3'). \tag{5}$$

5 An Example

To show how to use our framework for specifying and refining security requirements, let us consider an example of collaborative software development project for a credit card management system. This system is being developed by two teams: $Team_A$ and $Team_B$. It is desirable to use a *COTS* module developed by *CompanyC* in the project.

$Team_A$ is responsible for developing the *POS* purchase authorization module, and it has specified one security requirement: the credit card numbers must always be encrypted during communication between the *POS* machine and the central server.

$Team_B$ is responsible for developing the online account management module and it has specified two security requirements. The first requirement is that the account information must not be stored in plain text for confidentiality reason under any circumstances. The second requirement is that when a cardholder first registers, he must choose a password more than 6 characters long with at least one letter and one number.

The *COTS* module that developers want to reuse was developed to allow cardholders to access their accounts by phone. The only security requirement is that the system must ask the caller to enter his/her password before releasing any account information.

Following the three steps in Section 3, we have

RS1) Security requirements have already been described in natural languages as given above.

RS2) Generate the ontology from RS1) as follows:

2.1) Determine the situations we need to consider
- S_{A1}(pos_comm) :: *situation*: S_{A1} specifies situation when a *POS* machine is communicating with the server.
- S_{B2}(pass_requirement1) :: *situation*: password requirement for S_{B2}.
- S_{C1}(pass_requirement2) :: *situation*: password requirement for S_{C1}.

2.2) Specify the entities in the requirements by corresponding subclasses of the entity class. There are two entities in this example. Hence, we have
- *account_info[account_no, other_info]* :: *resource*.
- *creditcard_no* :: *resource*,

2.3) Specify the security features we need to address and the security mechanisms we want to adopt. In this example, we have
- *encryption* :: *securityMechanism*: the encryption class
- *authentication* :: *securityMechanism*: the authentication class
- *password* :: *authentication*: authentication can be done through password

RS3) Specify the requirements as quadtuples (1) as follows:
- $\mathcal{R}_{A1}$: (*creditcard_no, confidentiality, encryption, S_{A1}*)
- $\mathcal{R}_{B1}$: (*account_info, confidentiality, encryption, __*)
- $\mathcal{R}_{B2}$: (*account_info, integrity, password, S_{B2}*)
- $\mathcal{R}_{C1}$: (*account_info, integrity, password, S_{C1}*)

Then, the refining process is carried out according to the algorithm in Section 4:

Initialization: Store all refining rules in T_R. First, when the system is for a credit card company, the "account number" is the same as the "credit card number". We also know that the account information is stored as the account number plus other information. Thus, in this example, we have the following rules:

$$(creditcard\_no, P, M, S) \rightarrow (account\_no, P, M, S); \tag{R1}$$

$$(account\_info, P, M, \_\_) \rightarrow (account\_no, P, M, \_\_) \wedge (other\_info, P, M, \_\_); \tag{R2}$$

$$(E, P, M, S_1) \wedge (E, P, M, S_2) \rightarrow (E, P, M, S'), \quad S' = S_1 \wedge S_2. \tag{R3}$$

Store all four security requirements specified in RS3) in a list $L_{\mathcal{R}}$. Thus we have: n =4 and $L_{\mathcal{R}}[0] = \mathcal{R}_{A1}$, $L_{\mathcal{R}}[1] = \mathcal{R}_{B1}$, $L_{\mathcal{R}}[2] = \mathcal{R}_{B2}$, $L_{\mathcal{R}}[3] = \mathcal{R}_{C1}$.

Refinement process: Automatically apply suitable refining rules to specified security requirements. At the beginning, head=0, tail=3. We enter the while loop, go over all four security requirements in $L_{\mathcal{R}}$, search and apply suitable substitution and decomposition rules. For the first round, $L_{\mathcal{R}}[0] = \mathcal{R}_{A1}$ matches R1, and $L_{\mathcal{R}}[1] = \mathcal{R}_{B1}$ matches R2. Thus, we have

$$\mathcal{R}_{A1} \rightarrow \mathcal{R}_{A1}': (account\_no, confidentiality, encryption, S_{A1}). \tag{6}$$

$$\mathcal{R}_{B1} \rightarrow \mathcal{R}_{B1}': (account\_no, confidentiality, encryption, \_) \wedge$$
$$\mathcal{R}_{B1}'': (other\_info, confidentiality, encryption, \_). \tag{7}$$

We have the following operations: $L_{\mathcal{R}}[0] = \mathcal{R}_{A1}'$; delete $\mathcal{R}_{B1}$; add $\mathcal{R}_{B1}'$ and $\mathcal{R}_{B1}''$ to $L_{\mathcal{R}}$ as $L_{\mathcal{R}}[3]$ and $L_{\mathcal{R}}[4]$; count++, so now count =1. In the second round, the while loop only starts at the newly added requirements: $\mathcal{R}_{B1}'$ and $\mathcal{R}_{B1}''$. But, none of them matches any *substitution* or *decomposition* rule in T_R, the while loop stops.

Now, $L_{\mathcal{R}}$ has: $L_{\mathcal{R}}[0] = \mathcal{R}_{A1}'$, $L_{\mathcal{R}}[1] = \mathcal{R}_{B2}$, $L_{\mathcal{R}}[2] = \mathcal{R}_{C1}$, $L_{\mathcal{R}}[3] = \mathcal{R}_{B1}'$, and $L_{\mathcal{R}}[4] = \mathcal{R}_{B1}''$. We begin to traverse $L_{\mathcal{R}}$ again to apply suitable *combination* rules. When $L_{\mathcal{R}}[0] = \mathcal{R}_{A1}'$ and $L_{\mathcal{R}}[3] = \mathcal{R}_{B1}'$, $L_{\mathcal{R}}[0] \wedge L_{\mathcal{R}}[3]$ matches (R3), we have:

$$\mathcal{R}_{A1}' \wedge \mathcal{R}_{B1}' \rightarrow \mathcal{R}_1: (account\_no, confidentiality, encryption, S_1), S_1 = S_{A1} \vee \_$$

and the following operations: delete $\mathcal{R}_{A1}'$ and $\mathcal{R}_{B1}'$; add $\mathcal{R}_1$ to $L_{\mathcal{R}}$. When $L_{\mathcal{R}}[1] = \mathcal{R}_{B2}$ and $L_{\mathcal{R}}[2] = \mathcal{R}_{C1}$, $L_{\mathcal{R}}[1] \wedge L_{\mathcal{R}}[2]$ matches (R3), based on RS3) we have:

$$\mathcal{R}_{B2} \wedge \mathcal{R}_{C1} \rightarrow \mathcal{R}_2: (account\_info, integrity, password, S_2), S_2 = S_{B2} \wedge S_{C1}$$

and the following operations: delete $\mathcal{R}_{B3}$ and $\mathcal{R}_{C1}$; add $\mathcal{R}_2$ to $L_{\mathcal{R}}$.

Note that for $\mathcal{R}_1$, $S_1 = S_{A1} \vee_- = S_{A1}$, and it is a satisfiable situation. But for $\mathcal{R}_2$, S_{C1} requires users to enter password from a phone, which implies it can only be numbers. But S_{B2} requires a password to have at least one letter. Thus, $S_2 = S_{B2} \wedge S_{C1} = \varnothing$, which means this situation can never happen. This indicates there could be a conflict. No further refinement rules could be applied and the refining process is completed.

6 Conclusion and Future Work

In this paper, we have presented a framework for security requirement specification and management for collaborative systems. Our approach to specifying security requirements is easy to follow, and developers can easily adopt our approach without much effort. Our refining process is automatic. But because the complexity of this process is $O(n^2)$, where n is the number of security requirements generated in RS3), this process may take a long time to complete when n is very large. The processing time may be reduced by sorting and rearranging the security requirement list to decrease the number of iterations in the algorithm. We will complete the security requirement analysis for inconsistency detection in the framework by considering the class hierarchy among entities, security mechanisms being adopted and possible effects of satisfying each security requirement as well as under what situations these effects will occur. In addition to formalizing these correlation effects and performing system analysis, we will also focus on developing algorithms for the feedback agent.

Acknowledgment

This work is supported in part by the US Department of Defense/Office of Naval Research under the Multidisciplinary Research Program of the University Research Initiative, Contract No. N00014-04-1-0723. We would like to thank Yisheng Yao of Arizona State University for many helpful suggestions and discussions.

References

1. M. Howard and D. LeBlanc, *Writing Secure Code*, Microsoft Press, 2001.
2. L. Chung, "Dealing with Security Requirements during the Development of Information Systems", *Proc. 5th Int'l Conf. On Advanced Information System Engineering*, 1993, pp. 234-251.
3. N. R. Mead and T. Stehney, "Security Quality Requirements Engineering (SQUARE) Methodology", *Proc. Workshop on Software engineering for Secure Systems*, 2005, pp. 1-7.
4. K. S. Hoo, A. W. Sudbury, and A. R. Jaquith, "Tangible ROI Through Secure Software Engineering", *Secure Business Quarterly*, vol.1(2), 2001. available at: http://www. sbq. com/sbq/ rosi/ sbq_rosi_software_engineering.pdf
5. J. Viega and G. McGraw, Building Secure Software: *How to Avoid Security Problems the Right Way*, Addison-Wesley, 2001.
6. S. E. Keller, L. G. Kahn and R. B. Panara, "Specifying software quality requirements with metrics", *Tutorial: System and Software Requirements Engineering, R. H. Thayer and M. Dorfman, Editors*, IEEE Computer Society Press, 1990, pp. 145-163,

7. L. Liu, E. Yu and J. Mylopoulos, "Analyzing Security Requirements as Relationships Among Strategic Actors", *E-Proc. 2nd Symp. on Requirements Engineering for Information Security (SREIS'02)*, 2002. available at: http://www.sreis.org/old/2002/ finalpaper9. pdf.
8. R. France, I. Ray, G. Georg and S. Ghosh, "Aspect-oriented Approach to Early Design Modeling", *IEE Proc. Software*, vol.151 (4), 2004, pp.173-185.
9. T. Lodderstedt, D.A. Basin, and J. Doser, "SecureUML: A UML-Based Modeling Language for Model-Driven Security," *Proc. 5th Int'l Conf. On Unified Modeling Language*, 2002, pp.426-441.
10. S. S. Yau, Y. Yao, Z. Chen and L. Zhu, "An Adaptable Security Framework for Service-based Systems", *Proc. 10th IEEE Int'l Workshop on Object-oriented Real-time Dependable Systems (WORDS2005)*, 2005, pp.28-35.
11. S. S. Yau, D. Huang, H. Gong and Y. Yao, "Support for Situation-Awareness in Trustworthy Ubiquitous Computing Application Software", *Jour. Software Practice and Experience*, 2006, available at: http://www3.interscience.wiley.com/cgi-bin/fulltext/112600143/ PDFSTART
12. T. R. Gruber. A translation approach to portable ontologies. *Knowledge Acquisition*, vol.5(2), 1993, pp.199-220.
13. U.S. Department of Defense, "Trusted Computer Systems Evaluation Criteria", DOD 5200.28-STD, Dec. 1985, available at: http://csrc.nist.gov/secpubs/rainbow/std001.txt
14. S. S. Yau, Y. Wang, D. Huang and H. P. In, "Situation-aware Contract Specification Language for Middleware for Ubiquitous Computing," *Proc. 9th IEEE Workshop on Future Trends of Distributed Computing Systems*, 2003, pp. 93-99.

System Architecture and Economic Value-Chain Models for Healthcare Privacy and Security Control in Large-Scale Wireless Sensor Networks

Won Jay Song[1], Im Sook Ha[2], and Mun Kee Choi[2]

[1] Department of Computer Science, University of Virginia, VA 22904-4740, USA
[2] School of IT Business, Information and Communications University, 305-732, Korea
wjsong@cs.virginia.edu

Abstract. In this paper, we have designed and modeled the ubiquitous RFID healthcare system architecture and framework workflow, which are described by six classified core players or subsystems, and have also analyzed by an economic value-chain model. They consist of the patient and wearable ECG sensor, network service, healthcare service, emergency service, and PKI service providers. To enhance the security level control for the patient's medical privacy, individual private and public keys should be stored on smart cards. All the patient and service providers in the proposed security control architecture should have suitable secure private and public keys to access medical data and diagnosis results with RFID/GPS tracking information for emergency service. By enforcing the requirements of necessary keys among the patient and service providers, the patient's ECG data can be protected and effectively controlled over the open medical directory service. Consequently, the proposed architecture for ubiquitous RFID healthcare system using the smart card terminal is appropriate to build up medical privacy policies in future ubiquitous sensor networking and home networking environments. In addition, we have analyzed an economic value-chain model based on the proposed architecture consisting of RFID, GPS, PDA, ECG sensor, and smart card systems in large-scale wireless sensor networks and have also derived customer needs in the proposed service architecture using the value-chain model. Therefore, we also conclude that the business and technology issues for the service providers should exist in the networks.

1 Introduction

Recently, electronic healthcare systems have extended to ubiquitous healthcare systems such as personal home networking healthcare. They enable medical professionals to remotely make real-time monitoring, early diagnosis, and treatment for potential risky disease, and to provide the medical diagnosis and consulting results to the patient via wired/wireless communication channels. In addition to new ubiquitous medical equipments for patients (e.g., wearable healthcare sensor systems), smart home/sensor networks, radio frequency identification (RFID), public-key infrastructure (PKI), and Grid computing technology for large-scale physiologic and electrocardiogram (ECG) signal analysis have been studied and developed [1]-[8].

In spite of all the research and development in ubiquitous healthcare systems for a variety of applications, the system should still have to address both access control and

L.T. Yang et al. (Eds.): ATC 2006, LNCS 4158, pp. 511–520, 2006.
© Springer-Verlag Berlin Heidelberg 2006

privacy protection issues for the patient's individual medical data. These problems are serious when unauthorized persons or groups trying to monitor and access to the systems, remotely and stealthily. The problem can be complicated since it is possible to collect the patient's medical data from a wide variety of ubiquitous sensor nodes and to track an individual patient's location in ubiquitous networking world. To address those issues systematically, advanced study of privacy and security control architecture is critical. We have designed and modeled an architecture based on RFID and smart card technologies for ubiquitous healthcare in wireless sensor networks. Our novel architecture can effectively protect personal medical data and diagnosis results [4],[9]-[11].

Additionally, a need for an efficient method of storing personalized medical data, while providing security, reliability and portability, has arisen for ubiquitous RFID healthcare system in large-scale wireless sensor networks. The current PC-based smart card terminal should not only be designed to interface with smart cards and to control the retrieval or storage of data on the card but should also consist of several hardware components [12]. The microprocessor, memory, and the other hardware components needed for data encryption are embedded in the IC chip of the smart card. Therefore, smart cards are usually used in the area of wireless sensor networks. There is a need for smart card terminal-based systems with technical specifications for specific IC card operations [13],[14].

Finally, most research for new system architectures has only focused on technical aspects. In this paper, however, we have described not only the technical approach but also performed economic evaluation of the architecture using a value chain model. The value chain is a systematic approach to examining the development of competitive advantage and it was introduced by M.E.Porter [16]. The chain consists of a series of activities that create and build value. Moreover, it serves a useful analytical tool of emerging new system or service, particularly under rapidly changing telecommunications environments [17]. Thus, this paper describes that a value chain of the healthcare system and core players of each stage exist for value creation of RFID wearable sensor healthcare systems.

2   Architectural Design Process

2.1   Ubiquitous RFID Healthcare System

In the proposed security control architecture for ubiquitous healthcare system, we use radio frequency identification (RFID) tag, wearable electrocardiogram (ECG) sensor, smart card, Grid computing, PhysioNet, wired/wireless networks, and public-key infrastructure (PKI) technologies. The system architecture and framework are described by six classified core players or subsystems as shown in Figure 1.

They consist of the patient (PAT) and wearable ECG sensor provider (WSP), network service provider (NSP) with encrypted medical database and Grid computing, healthcare service provider (HSP) with PhysioNet database, emergency service provider (ESP), and PKI service provider (PSP) with certificate and directory databases. The individual private and public keys should be stored on the smart card and be used to enhance security level control for the patient's medical privacy.

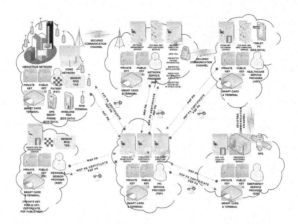

Fig. 1. The schematic diagram consisting of six core player or subsystems with their individual components and functions at privacy and security control architecture for ubiquitous RFID healthcare system

The WSP supplies its wearable ECG sensor system with RFID tag to the PAT, whose tag has unique identification information for the wearable sensor node. In order to protect the patient's privacy, all of the providers only recognize and use the tag information, instead of directly accessing to the patient's personal data. In addition, unique RFID tag information can be also used to track a patient in wearable RFID sensor system for emergency service by the ESP under ubiquitous RFID terminal network environments.

All individual public keys with correspondence to each private key should be stored on the PKI key server at the PSP. To verify the unique identification of each player or subsystem, the certificate of each public key should be issued by using the private key of the PSP and be stored on the PKI directory server. Then, both the certificates and the public key with correspondence to the private key of the PSP should be in service to all of the patient and providers via wired/wireless secure communication channels.

2.2   Security Features of Healthcare Smart Card

Digital Signature. A smart card can carry all the data needed to generate the holder's digital signature in sensor networks. The main components are encryption and decryption keys (private/public key pair) and a signed digital certificate. Digital signatures use a method of encryption and decryption known as 'asymmetric.' This method uses two keys, one to encrypt and the other to decrypt. If a message is encrypted using one key, it can only be decrypted using the other. These key pairs need not both be secret.

In 'public-key encryption' systems, one key is private, the users, and the other is the public domain. Note that in these cases, key distribution is trivial since the private key is never conveyed to anyone and the public key is available to everyone. An electronic signature cannot be forged. It is a computed digest of some text that is encrypted and sent with the text message. A digital signature ensures that the document originated with the person signing it and that it was not tampered with after the signature was applied.

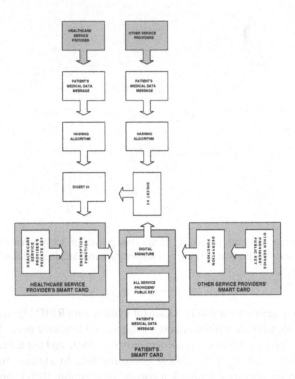

Fig. 2. The first processing sequence required to generate a digital signature for authentication purposes in ubiquitous RFID healthcare systems

Smart Card Authentication. As shown in Figure 2, you have to have access to that public key. Not only do you need that access, but you also need to be sure that the public key you obtain really is the public key for the person in question. One way to verify the validity of a public key is to sign it with yet another key, whose public key you know to be valid. Thus, it belongs to a trusted third party and a patient's smart card. This is the 'signed' digital certificate [15].

Public-Key Infrastructure. A Public-Key Infrastructure (PKI) is a collection of services that enables the use of public-key encryption techniques. The functions of a PKI include creating digital certificates, storing public keys, and tracking expiration dates of certificates. A public key obtained through a PKI is trustworthy. By managing these keys and certificates, an organization, such as the National Health Service (NHS), establishes and maintains a trustworthy networking environment. The existence of a PKI is therefore a critical factor in the use of the HPC in the NHS.

As commonly used, a digital certificate contains: (1) an expiration date, (2) the name of the certifying authority that issued the certificate, (3) a serial number, (4) the digital signature of the certificate issuer and the Certification Authority (CA), (5) the identity of the registered holder, and (6) the holder's public key. Using smart cards in conjunction with a PKI implies that the CA issues the card with certificates and key pairs already

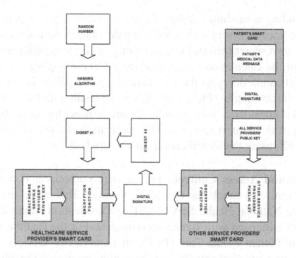

Fig. 3. The second processing sequence required to generate a digital signature for authentication purposes in ubiquitous RFID healthcare systems

written on it. This would apply both to the healthcare professional card and the patient's data card. Signed public keys are stored in a public directory. In the NHS, this would be the managed directory service [15].

2.3   Functions of Healthcare Smart Card

Login Process.   The Healthcare Professional Card (HPC) is the core of the login process, which involves verification of the user and authentication of the HPC. Authentication is the process that identifies and validates either the principal(s) involved in a transaction, or the origin of a message. We assume for the sake of illustration that the HPC holder wishes to use a healthcare application. We also assume that the application is a client/server system with a wireless PDA acting as the user terminal and that it is fitted with a smart card terminal.

The first part of the login process will comprise the user inserting the HPC into the terminal. The application will request the HPC to generate the holder's digital signature. At the same time, the application will request the user to enter identification details. This will enable the application to verify that the user is the authorized holder of the HPC and that the card is genuine, and then start the session. The user identification might include the use of a Personal Identification Number (PIN) or password. This method has often been dismissed as 'weak' security and easily compromised. However, this is not necessarily the case, and the weaknesses often lie in sending clear text to the authentication server [15].

Request and Response Procedures.   The authentication process performed by the application is achieved using a request and response procedure employing the cryptographic algorithm recorded on the HPC. To authenticate the HPC, the system requests the card by sending a random number. Figure 2 shows the first part of the request process. i.e., the 'message' sent to the card being the random number. The card uses this number and its own secret (private) key as input to its cryptographic algorithm [15].

The output of the calculation is then transmitted to the application as a digital signature. The application decrypts the signature using the public key obtained through the Public-Key Infrastructure (PKI). It compares the result with the original. If the two match, the card is considered to be genuine. Figure 3 shows the authentication process, the second part of the request-response. The application obtains the public key for the user from the PKI, using the identification details supplied.

Authentication and Access Control. For security purposes it is necessary for the healthcare application to check that the card is genuine. This means that the card must be issued by the National Health Service (NHS) Certification Authority (CA) for the holder's GP and initialized with signed security data. For the Healthcare Professional Card (HPC) and Patient's Data Card (PDC) interaction, two services are required as the PDC has to prove its authenticity and the healthcare professional has to prove access rights [15]. When proving access rights, an authentication procedure has to be performed. If after successful authentication a read or update command is performed on a smart card file, the application has to verify that the respective security condition described in the security attributes of this PDC file is fulfilled. Access rights can be expressed in terms of either individual professionals or identifiable groups, or both. The problems with the application can therefore be complicated by the need to recognize the HPC holder as a member of an access group [15].

The PDC authentication procedure assumes that the professional has already logged into the healthcare application using an HPC. The patient holds a healthcare smart card, which is plugged into the auxiliary card terminal. The PDC is authenticated by the challenge-response method. This entails the professional entering the patient's NHS number at the user terminal.

Authentication proves that the PDC belongs to the NHS number supplied and was created by an authorized professional. When the application reads data from the card, it checks that the professional currently in session has the right to access that data. If not, the application will inform the professional that access has been denied, but provide an override facility for emergency purposes. If the professional makes a decision that affects the card's data, the application will check that the professional has the right to amend the data. If the professional is not authorized, an emergency override facility will be offered [15]. Any data written will have the professional's digital signature attached. Referring to Figure 2, the 'message' represents the data to be written to the card. The digital signature is a function of the data written. Therefore any later unauthorized attempt to alter the data written will result in the digital signature not matching the data.

3   Architectural Integration Process

In the proposed architecture combined with wearable and wireless sensor network environments, the patient's ECG signals should be automatically measured and periodically stored on the internal flash memory of the wearable ECG sensor system. The stored

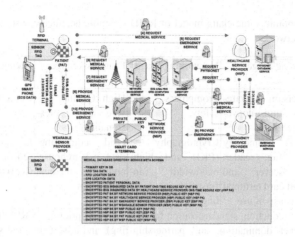

Fig. 4. The schematic diagram consisting of five core player or subsystems without public-key service provider

medical raw data will be transferred to the patient's or medical professional's wireless PDA with a 2-way double-type smart card terminal or GPS smart phone. For the data transfer, near-field wireless communications such as the Bluetooth wireless technology is used. The transferred data should be encrypted by using the patient's one-time secure key at the handheld devices.

As illustrated in Figure 4, all the data in wearable ECG sensors as well as analyzed data in Grid computing with PhysioNet should be encrypted by using an individually generated one-time secure key with expire-time by the PAT's and HSP's private keys, respectively. Additionally, the issued one-time secure keys are also encrypted by using public keys of the patient and pre-approved service providers. These encrypted medical data and encrypted secure keys will be also transferred to the network service provider via secured communication channels in wired/wireless networks. The encrypted data and keys with unique RFID tag information should be stored on the secured database directory of network service provider. The database meta-schema has decrypted and encrypted fields, that are used to make access control among the patient and providers.

4   Economic Value-Chain Modeling Process

The value chain is the full range of activities that are required to bring a product from its conception to its end use. This consists of activities such as design, production, marketing, distribution, and support to the final consumer [16]. In the value chain of ubiquitous system, however, subsystems of the existing value chains are regrouped in response to major function of system's players. Table 1 shows the reconfigured value chain. The reconfiguration value chain of the system consists of four parts; sensing, networking, diagnosis, and acting stages. Each stage has its own customer demands, technical issue, and business issue [18]. The proposed six classified core players in large-scale wireless sensor networks should match with four stages in value chain corresponding to common function.

Table 1. The economic value-chain model of RFID wearable healthcare systems in large-scale wireless sensor networks

Value Chain	Sensing Stage	Networking Stage	Diagnosis Stage	Acting Stage
Customer Needs	Precision aware-ness and conve-nience	Promptness and safety	High Quality ser-vice and profes-sionalism	Quick response
Technical Issues	RFID technology (e.g. tag, reader, and server) and smart card terminal with easy of use	Cryptography (PKI) and high-bandwidth in-frastructure for huge data handling	Grid computing, data warehouse, and medical equipment	Location based sensor and sensing (RFID/GPS)
Business Issues	Cost reduction, standardization for the market domination, and partnership between network provider and PKI service provider		Service pricing, CRM (data min-ing), and advertising and subscription model	
Player	Patient and wear-able ECG	Network service provider and PKI service provider	Healthcare service provider	Emergency service provider

Sensing Stage. In the sensing stage, it is essential to have a precise awareness and convenient sensing technology. Through the ubiquitous RFID/GPS technology, the patients can be diagnosed in any place at any time so that the importance character-istics of this stage is sensor and sensing technology such as wearable ECG sensor. Additionally patients can feel comfortable to attach senor without any trouble. The technology issues are RFID technology in terms of weight and easy of use (e.g., tag, reader, and server). The main player of sensing stage is patient and wearable ECG sensor.

Networking Stage. The following stage is networking. Privacy and security are crit-ical for the customer, especially in this stage. Network service provider provides wireless sensor networks, and PKI service provider supports high-level encryption and decryption algorithm for the protection of patients' medical data. Thus, the two players carry out important technical issues. Moreover, high-bandwidth infrastruc-ture for huge data handling is also essential.

Diagnosis Stage. The third stage is a diagnosis stage. The correct and high-quality diagnosis service of a medical specialist is major customer needs based on the collected patients' medical data. The major technical issue of this stage is grid computing technology. It also provides the ability to perform computations on large medical data sets and to accomplish more computations at once with accuracy. From the accumulating patient's medical data, healthcare service provider analyzes the symptom and prescribes the medicine or treatment.

Acting Stage. Finally, last stage is an acting stage which is the reaction and control of hospital or pharmacy for the diagnosed patients. Emergency service provider (ESP) can be a core player of this stage. When any alerts from the diagnosis is announced, the ESP can track him through location-based system and then it gives expediency and bring the patients to the proper hospital or organization within a short time. The technology issue of this stage is location-based sensor and sensing, for example, RFID and GPS.

The former two stages (sensing and networking) are based on the technology. To have comparative advantage in those business cost reduction, standardization for the market domination, and partnership between network provider and PKI service provider are necessary. The latter two stages (diagnosis and acting) are for the service from hospital or pharmacy. ESP can be a good business model for these stages. What we have to consider in terms of business is service pricing, customer relation management (CRM), advertising, and subscription model.

5 Conclusion

In the proposed privacy and security control architecture for ubiquitous RFID healthcare systems in large-scale wireless sensor networks, all of the patient and providers need suitable secure private and public keys in order to access to ECG medical raw data and diagnosis results with RFID and GPS tracking information for emergency service. By enforcing the requirements of necessary keys among the patient and providers, the patient's ECG data can be protected and effectively controlled over the open medical directory service of network service providers. Consequently, the proposed architecture for ubiquitous RFID healthcare system is appropriate to build up medical privacy policies. The architecture can provide a new business model to wired/wireless network service providers. In the future, the system architecture workflow and protocols will be modeled and verified using Petri nets.

The new emerging system and service have only been considered customer requirements analysis, systems design, integration, implementation, and verification passing over economic aspects. However, this paper analyzes not only the verification of proposed system architecture in technical aspect but also evaluating economic value creation through developing an economic value-chain model. The value chain model developed in this paper is also reconfigured in response to common function of classified six players. The reconfiguration value chain of the system describes four activities: the (1)sensing, (2)networking, (3)diagnosis, and (4)acting stages. The results show that sensing stage contains patient and wearable ECG sensor, the networking stage has network service provider and PKI service provider, the diagnosis stage has healthcare service provider, and the acting stage contains emergency service provider. In addition, it should be proposed technical and business issues for four service providers. Therefore, this new value-chain should be contributed to a better understanding of RFID wearable healthcare system in large-scale wireless sensor networks and economic implications for each player. It will be expanded by examining six players considering the evolution of networks

Acknowledgement. This research work has been supported in part by the Korea Research Foundation Grant (KRF-2005-M01-2005-000-10434-0) and the Information Technology Research Center program supervised by the Institute of Information Technology Assessment in Republic of Korea.

References

1. W.J.Song, S.H.Son, M.K.Choi, and M.H.Kang, "Privacy and Security Control Architecture for Ubiquitous RFID Healthcare System in Wireless Sensor Networks," *Proceedings in the IEEE ICCE 2006*, January 2006.
2. S.S.Choi, W.J.Song, M.K.Choi, and S.H.Son, "Ubiquitous RFID Healthcare Systems Analysis on PhysioNet Grid Portal Services Using Petri Nets," *Proceedings in the IEEE ICICS 2005*, December 2005.
3. G.B.Moody, R.G.Mark, and A.L.Goldberger, "PhysioNet: A Web-Based Resource for the Study of Physiologic Signals," *IEEE Engineering in Medicine and Biology*, vol.20, no.3, pp.70-75, May/June 2001.
4. K.Finkenzeller, *RFID Handbook*, 2nd Edition, Wiley & Sons, April 2003.
5. D.S.Nam, C.H.Youn, B.H.Lee, G.Clifford, and J.Healey, "QoS-Constrained Resource Allocation for a Grid-Based Multiple Source Electrocardiogram Application," *Lecture Notes in Computer Science*, vol.3043, pp.352-359, 2004.
6. G.Eysenbach, "What is e-healthcare?" *Journal of Medical Internet Research*, vol.3, no.2, 2001.
7. J.Marconi, "E-Health: Navigating the Internet for Health Information Healthcare," *Advocacy White Paper*, Healthcare Information and Management Systems Society, May 2002.
8. J.Joseph and C.Fellenstein, *Grid Computing*, Prentice Hall, 2004.
9. H.Chan and A.Perrig, "Security and Privacy in Sensor Networks," *IEEE Computer*, vo.36, no.10, pp103-105, October 2003.
10. C.H.Fancher, "In Your Pocket: Smartcards," *IEEE Spectrum*, vol.34, no.2, pp.47-53, February 1997.
11. R.W.Baldwin and C.V.Chang, "Locking the e-safe," *IEEE Spectrum*, vol.34, no.2, pp.40-46, February 1997.
12. W.Rankl and W.Effing, *Smart Card Handbook*, 2nd Edition, New York, John Wiley & Sons, 2000.
13. ISO/IEC 7816-1:1998, *Identification Cards – Integrated Circuit(s) Cards with Contacts - Part 1: Physical Characteristics*, International Organization for Standardization, 1998.
14. W.J.Song, W.H.Kim, B.G.Kim, B.H.Ahn, M.K.Choi, and M.H.Kang, "Smart Card Terminal Systems Using ISO/IEC 7816-3 Interface and 8051 Microprocessor Based on the System-on-Chip," *Lecture Notes in Computer Science*, vol.2860, pp.364-371, November 2003.
15. NHS, *NHS IT Standards Handbook*, National Health Service (NHS) Information Authority, June 2001.
16. M.E.Porter, *Competitive Strategy: Techniques for Analyzing Industries and Competitors*, New York: Free Press, 1980.
17. P.Olla and N.V.Patel, "A Value Chain Model for Mobile Data Service Providers," *Telecommunications Policy*, vol.26, no.9-10, pp.551-571, 2002.
18. Y.H.Lee, H.W.Kim, Y.J.Kim, and H.Sohn, "A New Conceptual Framework for Designing Ubiquitous Business Model," *IE Interfaces*, vol.19, no.1, pp.9-18, March 2006.

On Email Spamming Under the Shadow of Large Scale Use of Identity-Based Encryption

Christian Veigner and Chunming Rong

University of Stavanger, Box 8002, 4068 Stavanger, Norway
christian.veigner@uis.no, chunming.rong@uis.no

Abstract. In 1984 Adi Shamir requested a solution for a novel public-key encryption scheme, called identity-based encryption (IBE). The original motivation for IBE was to help the deployment of a public-key infrastructure. The idea of an IBE scheme is that the public key can be any arbitrary string, for example, an email address, a name or a role. An IBE scheme does not need to download certificates to authenticate public keys as in a public-key infrastructure (PKI). A public key in an identity-based cryptosystem is simply the receiver's identity, e.g. an email address. As often, when new technology occurs, the focus is on the functionality of the technology and not on its security. In this paper we briefly review about identity-based encryption and decryption. Later on we show that IBE schemes used for secure emailing render spamming far easier for spammers compared to if a PKI certificate approach is used.

1 Introduction

Recently, identity-based cryptography, i.e. identity-based encryption (IBE) and identity-based signatures (IBS), has been a popular topic of research in several research communities around the globe. Especially since Boneh and Franklin suggested the first practical and efficient identity-based encryption scheme from the Weil pairing on elliptic curves [4]. This solution came after several not-fully satisfactory proposals [2, 3].

Some previous solutions required users not to collude, others that the Private Key Generator (PKG) spent a long time for each private key generation request. Some solutions even required tamper resistant hardware.

It is fair to say that, until now, constructing a usable IBE system has been an open problem. In the same paper Boneh and Franklin also showed how an IBE scheme immediately could be converted into a signature scheme. Use of IBE was now suggested by different research communities for many different purposes [5,6,7,8]. In [10] and [11] we analyze the possibilities of using IBE for symmetric key agreement in Wireless Sensor Networks (WSN).

Use of IBE for email content encryption has also been suggested. Voltage [9] offers secure business communication via email and instant massaging with end-to-end content level encryption through their SecureMail implementation. Their solution offers the first secure email solution that makes secure ad-hoc business communication as easy as traditional, non-encrypted messaging. The use of IBE in email systems opens a number of business opportunities not possible before; for example, external broker communication can now be conducted securely via email in a natural ad-hoc fashion.

L.T. Yang et al. (Eds.): ATC 2006, LNCS 4158, pp. 521–530, 2006.
© Springer-Verlag Berlin Heidelberg 2006

Due to security concerns regarding privacy when sending emails, an ever increasing number of users apply encryption to their email content. The difficulties of symmetric keys scalability has lead to a world-wide acceptance of asymmetric cryptography for realizing privacy in such schemes. Nowadays, the award winning identity-based encryption (IBE) scheme designed by Boneh and Franklin [4] is considered applicable in almost every cryptographic area. As mentioned, Voltage [9] has implemented an IBE-suite for secure emailing. However due to certain properties of IBE, we fear that spammers now get an advantage in compare to when emails are encrypted using a PKI like scheme.

Spam, also referred to as unsolicited email, is often offensive and illegal. ISPs are strongly against it because it consumes the ISP's resources due to its vast volumes and angers the ISP's customers. Most spam mails are meant to promote a product or service. However, very few of these emails will include a valid *from:* address, so tracing their origin can be challenging.

In IBE there is no need for sender Alice to obtain receiver Bob's public-key certificate. When Bob receives an encrypted email, he contacts a third party called Private Key Generator (PKG). Bob obtains his private key by authenticating himself to the PKG, in the same way he would authenticate himself to a CA in a PKI scheme. Bob can then read his email. Note that unlike the existing secure email infrastructure, Alice can send encrypted emails to Bob even when Bob has not yet set up his public-key certificate.

The rest of this paper is organized as follows. Section 2 introduces some available solutions on how to prevent spam when encryption is not applied. Section 3 introduces symmetric an asymmetric cryptography used in email solutions. Section 4 describes basic ideas and properties of identity-based encryption. In section 5, we give a brief intro on how IBE may be used for securing emails. Section 6 touch upon viruses, followed by section 7 which concludes this paper.

2 Preventing Email-Spam and Viruses in Unencrypted Emails

Generally, there are two different angles of incidence for a spammer to dispatch unsolicited emails. Originally, spammers used their own servers to generate and send spam and thereby devised techniques to avoid being blacklisted. Today, spammers often rely on virus writers and hackers to provide a constant supply of servers to hide their identity and generate huge volumes of mail. We will show that protection against both of these techniques is already available.

2.1 Filtering Incoming Emails

Several companies offer email-filtering technology to customers, e.g. [14,15,16]. In the case of a customer using Securence's email filtering technology, SecurenceMail [14]; whenever an email is sent to the customer's mail server the email is initially redirected to Securence through its MX record. MX record is short for *mail exchange record*, an entry in a domain name database that identifies the mail server responsible for handling emails for that domain name. The MX record points to an array of servers that runs in Securence's data center in Minneapolis and Milwaukee, figure 1.

Before an email can be forwarded by Securence, a series of steps must occur to ensure "clean" delivery. This is known as filtering. According to Securence, 99% of all spam mails are detected by their filtering technology.

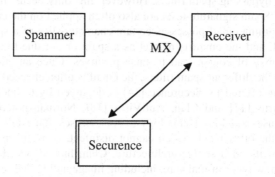

Fig. 1. Filtering emails

2.2 Filtering Emails from Hijacked Servers

In the case of hijacked computers, the owner of such systems, often organizations with high speed Internet connections and high processing power, may in fact protect themselves from being used for sending unsolicited emails. This can be achieved due to Frontbridge's technology. Frontbridge [15] provides technology for this as shown in figure 2. Emails are filtered for spam and viruses at Frontbridge's Global Data Center Network (GDCN) before they are forwarded to the receiving mail server.

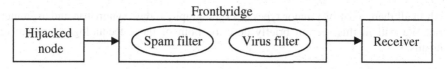

Fig. 2. Frontbridge's filtering technology

Utilizing both of these schemes for filtering emails, the receiver will not notice any additional processing load. However, the hijacked node in figure 2 is exposed of an additional load generating and/or sending these unsolicited emails. Such emails should be detected by Frontbridge, but still, the hijacked node suffers additional processing and transmission costs. As this is another problem, we will not discuss it any further in this paper.

2.3 Filtering Techniques

Often, filtering-processes filter spam, viruses, worms, junk mail, malicious content and attachments before reaching the end user. To detect spam, the message subject, sender, content of the email and attachments are checked for signs to determine whether the email actually is a spam mail.

Blacklisting of source IP addresses are in most cases checked once the email enters the filtering technology. Once the IP source has been authenticated, whitelist filtering is often applied. All emails from IP addresses on this whitelist are delivered directly to the recipient, bypassing spam filters. However, this only occurs if the source is not on the blacklist. Spam signature-tests are also often applied on the email to determine whether the incoming email possesses certain characteristics of a spam email. A rating is generated, and the email is market as a spam or not due to a threshold value. This approach may of course lead to false positives. Once an email has gone unmarked through the different spam filters, the email is often checked for viruses.

Virus filtering offered by Securence [14] is deployed by technology provided by Norman AntiVirus [17] and Clam AntiVirus [18]. Norman not only disinfects an email, but also uses Sandbox technology to spot viruses that don't yet have a signature. Clam, on the other hand, which cannot disinfect, is useful in searching for viruses because of its open source architecture. Clam has advanced mechanisms that protect against new types of malware, including image and HTML exploits, as well as phishing attacks. By providing these two anti-virus technologies with a number of anti-spam filtering techniques Securence delivers a powerful email filtering solution.

Apart from the mentioned technologies in section 2.1 and section 2.2, there are several other proposals on how to prevent spam. Such proposals include use of tokens [19], challenge-response schemes [20], pre-challenge schemes [21], graylisting [22], domain-based email authentication [23] and encapsulation of policy in email addresses [24]. Password-based systems [25] and micropayment systems [26] have also been proposed.

3 Securing Emails

All in all there exist two major types of cryptography today, symmetric and asymmetric. We will in this section briefly describe both of these technologies applied on emails.

3.1 Symmetric Cryptography

Starting in the 1970s, symmetric cryptosystems have been widely adopted both in military and academic communities as well as in the commercial market segment. An example of this is the Data Encryption Standard (DES) system [12] which is still a vital component of many cryptographic protocols. DES and its descendant, Advanced Encryption Standard (AES) [13] are examples of symmetric block ciphers which are used in symmetric cryptosystems.

Implementing such a cryptosystem for the Internet however, calls for a distribution scheme for distributing session keys shared by the sender and receiver of emails.

Such schemes have a major shortcoming when applied for securing email systems; it is not a very scalable solution when incorporated in an email application ranging outside a small group of users. Schemes that used the server approach for authenticating one of the parties to the other one quickly rendered the server overloaded as the amount of email users increased. Also, if the server is down, session-key distribution is impossible.

3.2 Asymmetric Cryptography

While a symmetric-key cryptosystem could have been used for an email system containing limited number of users, the 1990s Internet boom, and hence email use, would render it useless. Now schemes that didn't require online servers for broking session keys to all users were suggested.

These schemes are often referred to as asymmetric or public-key infrastructure (PKI) systems. In a PKI system there exist a pair of keys for each user, one is private and the other one is public. The public key is signed by a Certificate Authority (CA) and kept in a verifiable certificate. The certificate may be kept at the node which the public key belongs to or in a directory server. After validating the certificate against a revocation list and validating the signature of the CA on the certificate, the email-sending node extracts the public key belonging to the receiving node. The email is now encrypted with this key and sent to the destination node. On reception, the receiver decrypts the email with its private key.

Using a PKI system to encrypt emails, it is believed that the spam problem would be history. This is partly due to the difficulties of locating certificates and hence public keys. It is believed that the net gain for a spammer would be less than the effort needed to manage sending the unsolicited emails. In reality however, it is believed that a global PKI would collapse under the administrative weight of certificates, revocation lists, and cross-certification problems. Certificates are not easily located due to the lack of standard directories that publishes these certificates. The CA must also be online, and the client must validate the received certificate, and match the certificate policy with the client's own policy requirements. This can be very time consuming. The size of the revocation lists may also become a problem as the client must check against them for deprecated certificates. Additionally, a global PKI would render political challenges. Would all the countries in the Middle East trust a root PKI CA located in the USA and vice versa?

As we see, there are lots of challenges both in the symmetric as well as in the asymmetric cryptography approach. Hence, separately, neither of these solutions gives life to a perfectly working and secure email scheme. New approaches are needed to solve the confidentiality and integrity problems of current email applications.

4   Identity-Based Encryption

In this section, we briefly review the identity-based encryption (IBE). Later on we will describe its use in securing email solutions.

4.1   Basic of IBE

The concept of identity-based cryptography was first proposed in 1984 by Adi Shamir [1]. In his paper, Shamir presented a new model of asymmetric cryptography in which the public key of any user is a characteristic that uniquely identifies the user's identity, like an email address. In such a scheme there are four algorithms: (1) **setup** generates global system parameters and a master-key, (2) **extract** uses the master-key to generate the private key corresponding to an arbitrary public key string $ID \in \{0, 1\}^*$

(3) encrypt encrypts messages using the public key ID, and (4) decrypt decrypts messages using the corresponding private key.

The distinguishing characteristic of identity-based encryption is the ability to use any string as a public key. The functions that compose a generic IBE are thus specified as follows.

Setup: takes a security parameter t_s and returns t_g (system parameters) and *master-key*. The system parameters include a description of a finite message space M, and a description of a finite ciphertext space C. Intuitively, the system parameters will be publicly known, while the *master-key* will be known only to the Private Key Generator (PKG).

Extract: takes as input t_g, *master-key*, and an arbitrary $ID \in \{0, 1\}^*$, and returns a private key K. Here ID is an arbitrary string that will be used as a public key, and K is the corresponding private decryption key. The Extract algorithm extracts a private key from the given public key.

Encrypt: takes as input t_g, ID, and $m \in M$. It returns a ciphertext $c \in C$.

Decrypt: takes as input t_g, $c \in C$, and a private key K. It return $m \in M$. These algorithms must satisfy the standard consistency constraint, namely when K is the private key generated by algorithm Extract when it is given ID as the public key, then $\forall\ m \in M$: Decrypt(t_g, c, K) = m where c = Encrypt(t_g, ID, c).

5 Identity-Based Encryption on Emails

Shamir's original motivation for identity-based encryption [1] was to simplify certificate management in email systems. When Alice sends an email to Bob at bob@company.com she simply encrypts her message using the public key string "bob@company.com". There is no need for Alice to obtain Bob's public-key certificate. When Bob receives the encrypted mail he contacts a third party, which we call the Private Key Generator (PKG). Bob authenticates himself to the PKG in the same way he would authenticate himself to a Certificate Authority (CA) and obtains his private key from the PKG. Bob can then read his email.

Based on the new public-key cryptography using a commonly known identifier as the user's public key, Voltage [9] has implemented a software agent called Secure-Mail. By utilizing the Boneh and Franklin IBE scheme, SecureMail can be used with existing email solutions and enable users to transparently send and receive their emails securely. The system eliminates the need for individual per-user certificates and the requirement to connect to a third-party server to verify these certificates before initiating secure emailing. Their solution is considered highly scalable because it eliminates the need for an additional infrastructure. Third-party CAs are not required and no information needs to be pre-shared. Using IBE for securing emails, the mails may even be encrypted or decrypted offline. Voltage's solution for email applications using IBE gives users the opportunities to conduct business securely from anywhere in the world. Voltage's SecureMail makes ad hoc business communication as easy as traditional non-encrypted emailing [9].

Though this seams very promising, our general concern regarding the use of IBE for securing emails is that a spammer more easily can manage to get hold of valid public keys. These keys can then be used for end-to-end email content encryption. Now, only the node associated with the public key, i.e. the email address, is able to decrypt the email. Hence no filtering services may be utilized before the mail is received at the destination node. This might be dangerous due to viruses and most bothering and time consuming due to spam. Of course such a scheme may also be used as a Denial of Service attack (DoS) as the recipient uses resources decrypting the received emails. Received emails should then subsequently be filtered for spam and viruses by the receiving node.

Note that unlike the existing secure email infrastructure, Alice can send encrypted emails to Bob even if Bob has not yet set up his public-key certificate; hence, it is even easier for Alice to get hold of potential victims. Also note that key escrow is inherent in identity-based email systems; the PKG knows Bob's private key. This might also compromise the security.

As mentioned in the abstract, a large-scale enrollment of IBE for securing emails on the Internet substantially increase the amount of spam possible for a spammer to send out during a given period of time compared to if a PKI solution is chosen.

The work required by a spammer is far less compared to if an ordinary PKI scheme is chosen. The spammer may simply use automated processes to generate random public keys once in possession of an organization's email format. To succeed, the only thing the spammer must do is to encrypt the unsolicited emails using the victims email addresses.

5.1 Hijacking

For unencrypted unsolicited emails from hijacked nodes, the standard Frontbridge solution manages the filtering very well [15]. For IBE encrypted ones however, the emails received at Frontbridge's network fails to be checked for spam and viruses due to the already existing IBE encryption. Therefore we recommend such emails to be dropped and hence not forwarded by Frontbridge to the intended recipient.

This solution should be easy to integrate in Frontbridge's scheme. Hence, the hijacking way of sending unsolicited emails should be problematic for the spammer, that is, whenever the hijacked node is secured by technology provided by e.g. Frontbridge. As an organization now can protect itself from being used by a spammer for sending unsolicited encrypted emails, the spammer now has to do all the work by itself.

Even though not fully described in this paper, Frontbridge provides IBE encryption from Frontbridge's network to the receiving node.

5.2 Securing Emails Using IBE and Its Associated Disadvantages

There are as we see it mainly two disadvantages with the IBE solution when it comes to spamming. The first disadvantage is that a spammer may easily discover valid public keys (email addresses), or even use automated processes generating lots of public keys based on the knowledge of an organization's email format. Though easy discovery of public keys is the main selling point of IBE schemes applied on emailing, we see it from the spammer's perspective as a huge opportunity for pumping out vast volumes of unsolicited emails. Thereby the spammer manages to send more spam compared to if a PKI-like solution is chosen. This is partly due to the difficulties of locating certificates containing valid public keys.

The other disadvantage, which is an even greater concern, is the processing now required at the spam-receiving node. Once an IBE encrypted email is received, decryption is needed before the content may be checked for spam and viruses. Compared to currently used email solutions where usually no encryption is applied and filtering often is done by a third party, this may be used to launch a DoS attack on the receiving node. Compared to a PKI solution, the work required by the spammer is far less. The work required by the destination node is comparable to what is required in a PKI solution. As often when new technology occurs, the focus is on the benefits compared to existing technologies. However, IBE as we see it is more vulnerable to DoS attacks, spamming and the associated virus diffusion.

5.3 Spam Directly from the Spamming Node

As we have analysed the server-hijacking phenomenon of doing spamming, both for encrypted as well as unencrypted emails, we are left with the unresolved problem of IBE spamming directly from the spamming node. Currently this is an open problem. Due to the IBE encryption employed by companies like Frontbridge, it would not be easy for the attacked node to know whether the incoming IBE encrypted email is sent directly from a node (e.g. a spammer) or through a filter provided by a third party filtering out spam and viruses as in [15]. So far, we have not succeeded in discovering a proper countermeasure to this form of spamming attacks.

One countermeasure would of course be to make the receiving node decrypt all incoming emails. This could be done in a sandbox to avoid possible infections from viruses. Decrypted emails could then be redirected to a service provider as Securence which supplies filtering technology as described in chapter 2. However, if the content of an email is to be secure, the decrypted email has to be encrypted once again, e.g. by a key shared by the destination node and Securence. The email may then be transmitted to Securence for filtering. Securence has to decrypt the email, filter it, and then encrypt it with the shared key. The email can then be sent back to the destination node which once again has to decrypt the incoming email. Now the email content can be read by the receiving node without the danger of being spammed or attacked by viruses from the originator of the email.

Though this is a possible solution, the required processing in this solution is immense, and hence not a good solution to the problem. Seen from a spammer's point of view, DoS attacks are in this scheme highly encouraged.

6   Viruses

A serious security risk today is the propagation of malicious executables through email attachments. This results in the need to filter out or block emails containing attachment types that can be used to carry viruses. Good anti-virus products include email filters that do this automatically. Due to the end-to-end encryption property, use of either PKI or IBE will make this filtering process useless if not done on the intended destination node.

Though this is a general problem when applying end-to-end encryption, we fear that the use of IBE may also become a tool for launching DoS attacks.

7 Conclusion

As often when new technology occurs, the focus is on the functionality of the technology and not on its security. In this paper we study some of the currently available technologies that provide spam and virus filtering on emails [14,15]. We also study the effect of applying IBE [1] on emails and the associated ease for a spammer to increase the amount of spam sent on the Internet.

Essentially, we have two main concerns about the use of IBE applied on emails. First, a spammer more easily manages to get hold of valid public keys to destination nodes. Second, denial of service attacks may be launched more successfully at a victim node due to the processing required to decrypt incoming emails. Filtering of spam and viruses also has to be done locally by the email-receiving node.

As Voltage [9] already provides confidentiality and integrity on emails based on the new IBE technology, we fear that this is purely business motivated. The technology should be studied at a micro level and analyzed for security breaches before it is applied on securing email applications. Such use of new, so called secure technology has been pushed several times before, often with limited success. Extensive research regarding the actual security properties of new technology should be conducted before the technology is being deployed.

However, use of new technology in free and/or commercial products may also be the path to success eventually. By using such technology in such products, security experts and hackers will often try to tear the product apart in their search for security breaches.

References

1. A. Shamir, "Identity-based cryptography and signature schemes", *Advances in Cryptology*, CRYPTO'84, *Lecture Notes in Computer Science*, vol. 196, pp. 47-53, 1985.
2. U. Feige, A. Fiat, and A. Shamir, "Zero-knowledge proofs of identity", *J. Cryptology*, vol. 1, pp. 77-94, 1988.
3. A. Fiat and A. Shamir, "How to prove yourself: practical solutions to identification and signature problems", In *Proceedings of CRYPTO'86*, pp. 186-194, 1986.
4. D. Boneh and M. Franklin, "Identity-based encryption from the Weil pairing", in *Advances in Cryptology*, CRYPTO 2001, *Lecture Notes in Computer Science*, vol. 2139, pp. 213-229,2001.
5. X. Boyen, "Multipurpose Identity-based signcryption, a Swiss army knife for identity-based cryptography", in *Proceedings of the 23rd Interna. Conf. On Advances in Cryptology, Lecture Notes in Computer Science, vol.* 2729, pp. 383-399, 2003.
6. L. Chen and C. Kudla, "Identity-based authenticated key agreement protocols from pairings", *Cryptology ePrint Archive*, Report 2002/184, http://eprint.iacr.org/2002/184, 2002.
7. B. Lynn, "Authenticated identity-based encryption", *Cryptology ePrint Archive*, Report 2002/072, http://eprint.iacr.org/2002/072, 2002.

8. B. R. Waters, "Efficient Identity-Based Encryption Without Random Oracles", *Cryptology ePrint Archive*, Report 2004/180, http://eprint.iacr.org/2004/180, 2004.
9. Voltage security, E-mail Security – The IBE Advantage, 2004.
10. C. Veigner and C. Rong, "Identity-Based Key Agreement and Encryption for Wireless Sensor Networks", in preprint.
11. C. Veigner and C. Rong, "Simulating Identity-Based Key Agreement For Wireless Sensor Networks", in preprint.
12. Data Encryption Standard (DES), FIPS 46-2, http://www.itl.nist.gov/fipspubs/fip46-2.htm
13. Advanced Encryption Standard (AES), FIPS 197, http://csrc.nist.gov/CryptoToolkit/aes/
14. Securence, www.securence.com
15. Frontbridge, www.forntbridge.com
16. MX Logic, www.mxlogic.com
17. Norman, www.norman.com
18. Clam Antivirus, www.clamav.net, www.clamwin.com
19. R. Schlegel, S. Vaudenay, "Enforcing Email Addresses Privacy Using Tokens", In *Information Security and Cryptology LNCS 3822, First SKLOIS Conference (CISC 2005)*, pp. 91-100, Springer-Verlag, December 2005.
20. SpamArrest, www.spamarrest.com
21. R. Roman, J. Zhou, J Lopez, "Protection against Spam using Pre-Challenges", In Security and Privacy in the Age of Ubiquitous Computing IFIP TC11, 20th International Information Security Conference (Sec'05), pp. 281-294, Springer-Verlag, May 2005.
22. E. Harris, "The Next Step in the Spam Control War: Graylisting" www.graylisting.org/articles/whitepaper.shtml, 2003.
23. M. Delany, Domain-based Email Authentication Using Public-Keys Advertised in the DNS (DomainKeys). IETF Draft, 2005.
24. J. Ioannidis, Fighting Spam by Encapsulating Policy in Email Addresses, *Symposium on Network and Distributed Systems Security (NDSS 2003)*, February 2003.
25. L. F. Cranor, B. A. LaMacchia, "SPAM!", *Communications of the ACM*, 41(8) pp. 74-83, August 1998.
26. M. Abadi, A. Birrell, M. Burrows, F. Dabek, and T. Wobber. "Bankable Postage for Network Services", *8th Asian Computing Science Conference*, December 2003.

Zero-Knowledge Proof of Generalized Compact Knapsacks (or A Novel Identification/Signature Scheme)*

Bo Qin[1,2,3], Qianhong Wu[2], Willy Susilo[2], Yi Mu[2], and Yumin Wang[1]

[1] National Key Laboratory of Integrated Service Networks
Xidian University, Xi'an City 710071, P.R. China
ymwang@xidian.edu.cn
[2] Center for Information Security Research
School of Information Technology and Computer Science
University of Wollongong,Wollongong NSW 2522, Australia
{qhw, wsusilo, ymu}@uow.edu.au
[3] Department of Mathematics, School of Science
Xi'an University of Technology, Xi'an City 710048, P.R. China
qinboo@xaut.edu.cn

Abstract. At FOCS 2002, a new generalized compact Knapsacks problem is introduced. It is shown that solving the generalized compact Knapsack problem on the average is at least as hard as the worst-case instance of various approximation problems over cyclic lattices. It is left as an open problem to construct a zero-knowledge proof of generalized compact Knapsack problem. In this paper, by investigating a new notion of one-way ensemble pair, we propose a generic construction of identification and achieve a signature with the Fiat-Shamir transformation. Following our generic construction, we implement a concrete scheme based on the *random* generalized compact Knapsack problem. Our scheme also implies the *first* efficient zero-knowledge proof of the generalized compact Knapsacks problem and results in a positive solution to the open problem at FOCS 2002.

1 Introduction

Entity authenticity and message integrity are essential to prevent impersonal attacks and malicious message modifications in communication and ubiquitous computation. The general problem we address is the classical problem of interactive entity authentication. It is known such interactive authentication can be converted into non-interactive authentication and digital signatures secure in the random oracle model with the Fiat-Shamir transformation [3]. For the files such as important business contracts, government documents, international

---

* This work is supported by ARC Discovery Grant DP0557493, the National Natural Science Foundation of China (No. 60403007) and the Project Foundation of Xi'an University of Technology in China (No. 108-210508).

L.T. Yang et al. (Eds.): ATC 2006, LNCS 4158, pp. 531–540, 2006.

conventions and so on, their signatures are required to keep valid for a long time (maybe tens to hundreds of years). The signatures of such files have to be not only immune to attackers at present but also (at least, plausibly) secure against more powerful adversaries in the future.

Most of the cryptographic primitives in use are based on factorization or discrete logarithm. However, it is risky to base the security of all the systems on merely two difficult problems. In fact, it has been shown that these two problems are tractable under the quantum computation model [18]. In 2001, Vandersypen *et al.* [20] implemented Shor's algorithm on a 7-qubit quantum computer. Physicists predict that within the next 15 to 20 years there will be quantum computers that are sufficiently large to implement Shor's ideas for breaking cryptographic schemes used in practice.

Although Shor's result demonstrates the positive side of the power of the quantum computation model [18], other results indicate its limitation. Bennett *et al.* show that relative to an oracle chosen uniformly at random with probability 1, class NP cannot be solved in the computation model in time $O(2^{n/2})$ [2]. Although this result does not rule out the possibility that NP$\subset$BQP, many researchers consider that it is hard to find a probabilistic polynomial-time algorithm to solve an NP-hard problem even in the quantum computation model. Hence, the NP-hard problems will be important to construct identification/signature schemes with a longer-term validity.

The attempt to create a zero-knowledge identification or signature scheme based on NP-hard problem is not new, for example PKP by Shamir [17], CLE by Stern [19] and PPP by Pointcheval [11]. Another well-known difficult problem is the Knapsack problem. The decisional version of Knapsack problem is NP-complete problem and the computational version is NP-hard [5]. It has been widely researched in applying it to construct public-key encryption systems ([7,9,10,15,16]). However, most of the attempts except the scheme in [10] which requires to solve discrete logarithms to generate the public key, fail due to some undesirable features introduced into the Knapsack vector. In fact, almost all the known constructions are obtained by disguising the special (easy) instances of the subset-sum problem as random instances. The attacks to Knapsack-based cryptosystems can be classified into two broad categories: (i) attacks targeted to specific public key cryptosystems that try to exploit the special structure resulting from the embedding of a decryption trapdoor (e.g., [16]) and (ii) attacks to generic Knapsack instances that can be applied regardless of the existence of trapdoor(e.g.,[6]).

It is important to realize that the second class of attacks dismisses most Knapsack cryptographic functions as practical alternatives to number theory based functions, not on the grounds of their inherent insecurity, but simply because of the large key sizes required to avoid heuristics attacks. In fact, there is theoretical evidence [1,14] that subset-sum can indeed be a good source of computational hardness, at least from an asymptotic point of view. Recently, Knapsack-like cryptographic functions have started attracting again considerable attention (e.g.[13]) after Ajar's discovery [1] that the generalized Knapsack problem over the additive group $\mathbb{Z}_p^n$ of n-dimensional vectors is provably hard to solve on the average based on a worst-case intractability assumption about certain lattice approximation problems for which no polynomial time solution is known.

In [8], a new class of generalized compact Knapsacks was introduced which are both very efficient and provably hard to solve in a strong sense similar to Ajar's function [1]. The generalized compact Knapsack function are conceivably hard to invert in a very strong sense. In particular, it has been proved that, the inverse of the generalized Knapsack function is at least as hard to invert on the average (even with non-negligible probability) as the worst-case instance of various lattice problems.

In this paper, we investigate further efforts in constructions of zero-knowledge identification and signature schemes based on NP-hard problems. The main contributions include the following two aspects.

- *The notion of closed one-way ensemble pairs.* We formalize the notion of closed one-way ensemble pairs which are similar to but different from one-way function. Using this notion, we propose a new construction of identification and obtain a signature with the Fiat-Shamir transformation. Under an intractability assumption related to one-way ensemble pairs, we prove that there is no interactive strategy for the Verifier communicating with the Prover, to extract any information whatsoever on the prover's secret.

- *Identification/signature schemes based on random instances of generalized compact Knapsack problems.* In contrary to the often weak trapdoor Knapsacks used in the past for encryption, we implement concrete identification and signature schemes based on the infeasibility of *random* instances of Micromania's generalized compact Knapsacks [8]. To break our identification scheme, an adversary has to solve random instances of the generalized compact Knapsack problem, which means a breakthrough in complexity theory, and hence it is impossible. Our scheme also implies the *first* zero-knowledge proof of a solution of a random generalized compact Knapsack instance and gives a positive solution to the open problem of constructing a zero-knowledge proof of generalized compact Knapsack problems in [8].

2   Preliminaries

In this section, we provide the notations throughout this report and review the definitions of identification schemes, digital signatures and the Fiat-shammer transform [3,4]. In the following, we are more interested in 3-round identification scheme, which is referred as canonical identification scheme.

Definition 1. (Canonical Identification Scheme.) *A canonical identification is a 3-round identification scheme for an NP-complete language $\mathcal{L}$, in which the first message $\xi = \mathcal{P}_{sk,pk}(r)$ is sent by the prover $\mathcal{P}$, the second message η is sent by the verifier $\mathcal{C}$ and consists of $\mathcal{C}$'s random coins, and the third message $\zeta = \mathcal{P}_{sk,pk}(\xi, \eta, r)$ is sent by the prover $\mathcal{P}$. The scheme meets the following properties:*

- *Soundness: For all PPT algorithms $\mathcal{P}'$, $Pr[(\mathcal{P}'(sk'); r)(pk) = 1] < \varepsilon(k)$, where $sk' \neq sk$.*
- *Zero-knowledge: There exists a PPT simulator Sim which, on input vk, outputs (ξ', η', ζ') computationally indistinguishable from (ξ, η, ζ) for any PPT distinguisher.*

Definition 2. (Digital Signature Scheme.) *A signature $\mathcal{S}$ is a polynomial time triple $\mathcal{S} = (\mathcal{G}, S, V)$: $(sk, vk) \leftarrow \mathcal{G}(1^k)$ A probabilistic algorithm that inputs security parameter k and outputs private signing keys sk and public verification keys vk. $\sigma \leftarrow S(m, sk)$ An (probabilistic) algorithm that inputs message m and private signing key sk and outputs signature σ.$1/0 \leftarrow V(m, \sigma, vk)$ A deterministic algorithm that inputs message m, signature σ, and public verification key vk and outputs either 1 or 0 that represents* **accept** *or* **reject**, *respectively. A signature scheme $\mathcal{S}$ is* **complete** *if, for any $(sk, vk) \leftarrow G(1^k)$ and any message m, it holds that $V(m, \mathcal{S}(m, sk), vk) = 1$. A signature scheme $\mathcal{S}$ is* **unforgeable** *if for every PPT forger family $\mathcal{F} = \{\mathcal{F}_k\}_{k \in \mathbb{N}}$, with oracle access to $\mathcal{S}$, the probability that, on input a uniformly chosen key $vk \leftarrow \mathcal{G}(1^k)$, $\mathcal{F}_k$ outputs a pair (m_0, σ_0) such that $V(m_0, \sigma_0, vk) = 1$ and such that m_0 was not sent by $\mathcal{F}_k$ as an oracle query to $\mathcal{S}$, is negligible in k, where the probability is over vk and over the randomness of the oracle $\mathcal{S}$.*

Definition 3. (The Fiat-Shamir Transform.) *Given any canonical identification scheme $(\mathcal{G}, \mathcal{P}, \mathcal{C})$ and any function ensemble $\mathcal{H} = \{\mathcal{H}_k\}_{k \in \mathbb{N}}$, the Fiat-Shamir transform transforms $(\mathcal{G}, \mathcal{P}, \mathcal{C})$ and $\mathcal{H}$ into a signature $(\mathcal{G}_\mathcal{H}, \mathcal{S}_\mathcal{H}, \mathcal{V}_\mathcal{H})$ defined as follows.*

- *The key generation algorithm $\mathcal{G}_\mathcal{H}$, on input 1^k: (1) Emulates algorithm $\mathcal{G}$ on input 1^k to generate $(sk, vk) \leftarrow \mathcal{G}(1^k)$. (2) Choose at random a function $h \in \mathcal{H}_k$. Outputs sk as the signing key and $vk = (pk, h)$ as the verification key.*
- *The signing algorithm $\mathcal{S}_\mathcal{H}$, on input a signing key sk, a corresponding verification key $vk = (pk, h)$, and a message m: (1)Tosses coins r for $\mathcal{S}$. (2)Computes $\xi = \mathcal{S}_{(sk, pk)}(r)$. (3)Computes $\eta = h(\xi, m)$. (4)Computes $\zeta = \mathcal{S}_{(sk, pk)}(\xi, \eta, r)$. (5)Outputs (ξ, η, ζ) as a signature of m.*
- *The verification algorithm $\mathcal{V}_\mathcal{H}$, on input a verification key $vk = (pk, h)$, a message m, and a triplet (ξ, η, ζ) (which is supposedly a signature of m), accepted if and only if both of the following conditions hold: (1) $h(\xi, m) = \eta$. (2)$(\xi, \eta, \zeta) \in View(\mathcal{C}(pk))$*

In [12], Pointcheval and Stern proved the following result.

Lemma 1. *In the random oracle model, the Fiat-Shamir transformation transforms a secure canonical identification scheme into a secure signature scheme.*

3   General Constructions

3.1   Assumptions

It is known that there are several ways to construct signature schemes based on the assumption of a one-way function. However, the constructions based on such a general assumption are inefficient in practice. In the following we require that the difficulty problems have some special properties. The following definitions capture such properties.

Definition 4. *Let Γ be the set of all maps $\{0,1\}^k \rightarrow \{0,1\}^k$. A subset $\mathbb{F} \subset \Gamma$ is a one-way ensemble of (Θ, Ω), where $\Theta, \Omega \subset \{0,1\}^k$, if for random $x \in \Theta$ and $y \in \Omega$, there exists no PPT algorithm to find a polynomial-time map $f \in \mathbb{F}$ such that $f(x) = y$ or to prove that there exists no such a map in $\mathbb{F}$.*

Example of one-way ensembles: Let us consider the well-known graph isomorphism problem. Although it is unknown whether it is NP-complete and some researchers conjecture that it is not NP-complete, there is no evidence to show that it can be solved efficiently even by quantum computers. Here, we show how to achieve a one-way ensemble from graph isomorphism problem. Let $\mathbb{G}$ be a set of properly selected k-vertex graphs such that graph isomorphism problem is difficult. Let Π be the set of all the permutations on $\mathbb{G}$. Then Π is a one-way ensemble of $(\mathbb{G}, \mathbb{G})$ as for two random elements $G, H \in \mathbb{G}$, there is no efficient algorithm to find a map π in Π such that $H = \pi(G)$.

Similar to the one-way function, the one-way ensemble dually demonstrates the hardness of difficult problems. However, there are subtle difference between these two notions. The latter is a family of functions while the former is only one function. In the case of one-way ensemble, the difficult problem is to determine a function f in the ensemble for given string y in the image set and a string x in the pre-image set such that $f(x) = y$, i.e., x and y are known. In the context of one-way function, the difficult problem is to determine a string x in the pre-image set for a given string y in the image set such that $f(x) = y$, i.e., f and y are known. We should notice that *a function f in a one-way ensemble should be efficient but it is not necessary to be one-way.* For instance, in the above example of one-way ensemble from graph isomorphism problem, any function f in the one-way ensemble Π is not one-way: Given H and $f \in \Pi$, it is efficient to find G such that $H = f(G)$.

For the goal of construction of secure signatures, we require the one-way ensemble has some additional prosperity.

Definition 5. *Let $\mathbb{F}_0$ and $\mathbb{F}_1$ be one-way ensembles of (Θ, Ω) and (Ω, Φ) respectively. $(\mathbb{F}_0, \mathbb{F}_1)$ is a closed one-way ensemble pair, if $\mathbb{F}_2 = \{f_1 \circ f_0 | f_0 \in \mathbb{F}_0, f_1 \in \mathbb{F}_1\}$ is a one-way ensemble of (Θ, Φ) or it is infeasible to find $f_0 \in \mathbb{F}_0, f_1 \in \mathbb{F}_1$ such that $f_2 = f_1 \circ f_0$, where $f_1 \circ f_0$ is the compound of functions f_1 and f_0. If $\Theta = \Omega = \Phi$ and $\mathbb{F}_0 = \mathbb{F}_1 = \mathbb{F}_2 = \mathbb{F}$, $\mathbb{F}$ is called a self-closed one-way ensemble.*

Consider the above example of one-way ensemble from graph isomorphism problem. Let $\Theta = \Omega = \Phi = \mathbb{G}$ and $\mathbb{F}_0 = \mathbb{F}_1 = \Pi$. Then $\mathbb{F}_2 = \{f_1 \circ f_0 | f_0 \in \mathbb{F}_0, f_1 \in \mathbb{F}_1\} = \Pi$ is a one-way ensemble of (Θ, Φ). Hence, $(\mathbb{F}_0, \mathbb{F}_1)$ is a closed one-way ensemble pair. Moreover, as $\mathbb{F}_0 = \mathbb{F}_1 = \mathbb{F}_2 = \Pi$, Π is a self-closed one-way ensemble.

One-way ensemble pairs are essential for our construction of secure and efficient identification and signature schemes. Hence, we require the following assumption.

Assumption 1. *There exist one-way ensemble pairs.*

3.2   Identification Scheme Based on One-Way Ensemble Pairs

Let $(\mathbb{F}_0, \mathbb{F}_1)$ be a closed one-way ensemble pair of (Θ, Ω) as defined in the above section. $\alpha \leftarrow \Theta$ is a public parameter. Randomly select $f \leftarrow \mathbb{F}_0$. $\beta := f(\alpha)$ is the public key which represents the identity of the prover and f is its private key. To prove its identity, the prover $\mathcal{P}$ and the verifier $\mathcal{V}$ run the following protocol.

1. $\mathcal{P}$ randomly selects $g \leftarrow \mathbb{F}_1$ and sends $\gamma := g(\beta)$ to $\mathcal{V}$.
2. $\mathcal{V}$ sends $c \leftarrow \{0,1\}$ to $\mathcal{P}$.
3. If $c_i = 0$, $\mathcal{P}$ sets $\tau := g$; else $\mathcal{P}$ sets $\tau := g \circ f$. $\mathcal{P}$ sends τ to $\mathcal{V}$.
4. If $c_i = 0$, $\mathcal{V}$ checks that $\tau \in \mathbb{F}_1$ and $\tau(\beta) = \gamma$; else $\mathcal{V}$ checks that $\tau \in \mathbb{F}_2$ and $\tau(\alpha) = \gamma$. If the check does not hold, $\mathcal{V}$ aborts the protocol.
5. $\mathcal{P}$ and $\mathcal{V}$ repeat the above protocol t times.

Obviously, if the prover knows f, it can successfully complete the above protocol. For impersonation attack, we have the following result.

Theorem 1. *If the probability of the challenge $c = 1/0$ is $1/2$, then the probability of success impersonation is 2^{-t}.*

Proof. It is natural to assume that the attacker does not know the private signing key S. Since the attacker is required to commit to g in advance and the probability of the challenge $c = 1/0$ is $1/2$, in order to answer τ accepted by $\mathcal{V}$, the attacker has to guess the challenge c' and has two strategies: (1) If $c_i' = 0$, select $g \in \mathbb{F}_1$ and compute $g(\beta) = \gamma$; (2) If $c_i' = 1$, select $g \in \mathbb{F}_1 \circ \mathbb{F}_0$ and compute $g(\alpha) = \gamma$.

If $c = 0$ and the forger uses the first strategy, then the check will succeed; else if the attacker uses the second strategy, then the i-th check will fail. Hence, in this case, to make the check succeed, the attacker have to compute a function $g' \in \mathbb{F}_1$ such that $g'(\alpha) = \gamma = g(\beta)$ to replace g. However, since $\mathbb{F}_1$ is a one-way ensemble, it cannot find such a function g'.

If $c = 1$ and the attacker uses the second strategy, then the check will succeed; else if the attacker uses the first strategy, then the check will fail. Hence, in this case, to make the check succeed, the attacker has to compute a function $g' \in \mathbb{F}_1 \circ \mathbb{F}_0$ such that $g'(\beta) = \gamma = g(\alpha)$ to replace g. However, since $\mathbb{F}_1 \circ \mathbb{F}_0$ is still a one-way ensemble, it cannot find such a function g'.

Let the attacker choose the first strategy with probability P. Then it chooses the second strategy with probability with $1 - P$. Hence, in each round, the attacker will succeed with probability $1/2 \times P + 1/2 \times (1 - P) = 1/2$. After t rounds, the probability of success impersonation is 2^{-t}.

Theorem 2. *The above protocol is a zero-knowledge proof.*

Proof. To prove that the protocol is a zero-knowledge proof, we need to construct a simulator Sim: (1) Sim tosses a fair coin and gets $c' \in \{0,1\}$. (2) If $c_i = 0$, Sim randomly selects $\tau' \in \mathbb{F}_1$ and computes $\tau'(\beta) = \gamma'$; else Sim randomly selects $\tau' \in \mathbb{F}_2$ and computes $\tau'(\alpha) = \gamma'$. (3) Sim outputs (γ', c', τ') as its simulated transcripts. Clearly, the simulated transcripts (γ', c', τ') is indistinguishable from the real output (γ, c, τ) of $(\mathcal{P}, \mathcal{C})$. Hence, the claim follows.

3.3 Signature Using Closed One-Way Ensemble Pairs

In this section, we provide a signature using closed one-way ensemble pairs with the Fiat-Shamir transformation.

Public system parameters: t is security parameter. $H : \{0,1\}^* \to \{0,1\}^t$ is a secure cryptographic hash function. $(\mathbb{F}_0, \mathbb{F}_1)$ is a closed one-way ensemble pair of (Θ, Ω) as defined in the above section. $\alpha \leftarrow \Theta$ is a public parameter.
Generation of signing/verification key: Randomly select $f \leftarrow \mathbb{F}_0$. $\beta := f(\alpha)$ is a public verification key and f is a private signing key.
Signing procedure: For a message m,

1. $g_1 \leftarrow \mathbb{F}_1, g_2 \leftarrow \mathbb{F}_1, \cdots, g_t \leftarrow \mathbb{F}_1$.
2. $\gamma_1 := g_1(\beta), \gamma_2 := g_2(\beta), \cdots, \gamma_t := g_t(\beta)$.
3. $c = (c_1, c_2, \cdots, c_t) := H(m||\alpha||\beta||\gamma_1||\gamma_2||\cdots||\gamma_t)$, where $c_i \in \{0,1\}$ for $i = 1, 2, \cdots, t$.
4. For $i = 1, 2, \cdots, t$, $f_i := \begin{cases} g_i & \text{if } c_i = 0 \\ g_i \circ f & \text{if } c_i = 1 \end{cases}$.
5. Output $(\gamma_1, \gamma_2, \cdots, \gamma_t; f_1, f_2, \cdots, f_t)$ as the resulting signature on m.

Verification procedure: Given verification key β, message m, and its signature $(\gamma_1, \gamma_2, \cdots, \gamma_t; f_1, f_2, \cdots, f_t)$,

1. $c = (c_1, c_2, \cdots, c_t) := H(m||\alpha||\beta||\gamma_1||\gamma_2||\cdots||\gamma_t)$;
2. For $i = 1, 2, \cdots, t$, if $c_i = 0$, check $f_i \in \mathbb{F}_1$ and $f_i(\beta) = \gamma_i$; else if $c_i = 1$, check $f_i \in \mathbb{F}_2 = \mathbb{F}_1 \circ \mathbb{F}_0$ and $f_i(\alpha) = \gamma_i$.
3. Output *accept* if and only if all the checks succeed.

From Lemma 1 and Theorem 1 and 2, we have the following result.

Corollary 1. *The above signature is unforgeable in the random oracle model.*

4 Implementations Based on Generalized Compact Knapsack Problem

In this section, we implement the above identification and signatures based on the generalized compact Knapsack problem following the signature formula using closed one-way ensemble pairs in Section 3.

4.1 Generalized Compact Knapsack Problem

Here, we review the generalized compact Knapsack problem in [8]. It has been proven NP-hard and there is no efficient algorithm to solve it on the average.

Definition 6. *For any ring $\mathbb{R}$, subset $\mathbb{S} \subset \mathbb{R}$ and integer $\ell \geq 1$, $\boldsymbol{a} \leftarrow \mathbb{R}^\ell$, $\boldsymbol{x} \leftarrow \mathbb{S}^\ell$, $y = \sum_{i=1}^{\ell} x_i a_i$, a PPT adversary $\mathcal{A}$ of the generalized Knapsack problem is required to output $\boldsymbol{x} \in \mathbb{S}^\ell$. Formally,*
$$\boldsymbol{x} \leftarrow \mathcal{A}(\mathbb{R}, \mathbb{S} \subset \mathbb{R}, \ell \in \mathbb{Z}, \boldsymbol{a} \in \mathbb{R}^\ell, y = \textstyle\sum_{i=1}^{\ell} x_i a_i \in \mathbb{R}).$$

In [8], the ring is set as $\mathbb{R} = (\mathbb{F}^n_{p(n)}, +, \otimes)$ of n-dimensional vectors over the finite field $\mathbb{F}_{p(n)}$ with $p(n) = n^{O(1)}$ elements, with the usual vector addition operation and *convolution* product $\otimes$. For brevity, $\mathbb{R} = (\mathbb{F}^n_{p(n)}, +, \otimes)$ is simply denoted as $\mathbb{F}^n_{p(n)}$. Here the notation $\mathbb{F}^n_p$ is used instead of $\mathbb{Z}^n_p$ to emphasize that $\mathbb{F}^n_p$ is the ring of vectors with the convolution product operation, rather than the componentwise multiplication of the product ring $\mathbb{Z}^n_p$. $\mathbb{S}$ is the set $\mathbb{S} = \mathbb{D}^n \subset \mathbb{F}^n_p$ of vectors with entries in an appropriately selected subset of $\mathbb{F}_p$.

4.2   Proposed Identification Scheme Based on Generalized Compact Knapsack Problem

Following the general construction of identification scheme using closed one-way pairs, we propose an identification scheme based on the generalized compact knapsack problem.

Public system parameters: $t, \ell, n \in \mathbb{Z}$ are secure parameters; Randomly select $\mathbb{R} = (\mathbb{F}^n_{p(n)}, +, \otimes)$ where p is a prime. Appropriately select sets $\mathbb{S}_1, \mathbb{S}_2 \subset \mathbb{R}$. $\mathbb{S}_3 = \{\theta | \theta = \sum_{i=1}^{\ell} x_i y_i \wedge \boldsymbol{x} \in \mathbb{S}_1^{\ell} \wedge \boldsymbol{y} \in \mathbb{S}_2^{\ell}\} \subset \mathbb{R}$. Randomly select $\boldsymbol{\alpha} \leftarrow \mathbb{R}^{\ell}$. $H(\cdot) : \{0,1\}^* \rightarrow \{0,1\}^t$ is a cryptographic hash function.
Public/private key generation: $\boldsymbol{S} \leftarrow \mathbb{M}_{\ell,\ell}(\mathbb{S}_1)$, where $\mathbb{M}_{\ell,\ell}(\mathbb{S}_1)$ denotes the nonsingular matrices of order $n \times n$ over $\mathbb{R}$ but its entities are limited in $\mathbb{S}_1 \subset \mathbb{R}$. Compute $\boldsymbol{\beta} = (\beta_1, \cdots, \beta_{\ell}) := (a_1, \cdots, a_{\ell})\boldsymbol{S}$, and $(\alpha_1, \cdots, \alpha_{\ell})\boldsymbol{S}$ is the multiplication of a vector and a matrix over $\mathbb{R}$. Public verification key is $\boldsymbol{\beta}$ and private signing key is $\boldsymbol{S}$.
Identification protocol: The prover $\mathcal{P}$ and the verifier $\mathcal{V}$ do as follows.

1. $\mathcal{P}$ randomly selects $\boldsymbol{X} = (x_1, x_2, \cdots, x_{\ell}) \leftarrow \mathbb{S}_2^{\ell}$;
2. $\mathcal{P}$ sends $w := \boldsymbol{\beta}\boldsymbol{X}^T$ to $\mathcal{V}$, where $\boldsymbol{X}^T$ is the transposition of $\boldsymbol{X}$;
3. $\mathcal{V}$ sends $c \leftarrow \{0,1\}$ to $\mathcal{P}$;
4. If $c = 0$, $\mathcal{P}$ sets $\boldsymbol{f} = (f_1, \cdots, f_n) := \boldsymbol{X}$; else if $c = 1$, $\mathcal{P}$ sets $\boldsymbol{f} = (f_1, \cdots, f_n) := \boldsymbol{X}\boldsymbol{S}^T$. $\mathcal{P}$ sends $\boldsymbol{f}$ to $\mathcal{V}$.
5. For $i = 1, 2, \cdots, \ell$, if $c = 0$, $\mathcal{V}$ checks that $\boldsymbol{\beta}\boldsymbol{f}^T = (\beta_1, \cdots, \beta_{\ell})(f_1, \cdots, f_{\ell})^T = w$ and $f_i \in \mathbb{S}_2$; else if $c = 1$, $\mathcal{V}$ checks that $\boldsymbol{\alpha}\boldsymbol{f}^T = (\alpha_1, \cdots, \alpha_n)(f_1, \cdots, f_n)^T = w$ and $f_i \in \mathbb{S}_3$. If the check does not hold, $\mathcal{V}$ aborts the protocol.
6. $\mathcal{P}$ and $\mathcal{V}$ repeat the above protocol t times.

Theorem 3. *If the probability the challenge $c = 1/0$ is $1/2$, then the probability of success impersonation in the identification scheme based on the generalized compact knapsack problem is 2^{-t}. The above protocol is a zero-knowledge proof*

Proof. Similar to Theorem 1 and 2.

4.3   Proposed Signature Scheme Based on Generalized Compact Knapsack Problem

Consider the same setting as the identification protocol. The signing procedure and verification procedure are as follows.

[**Signature procedure.**] For a message $m \in \{0,1\}^*$,

1. For $i = 1, 2, \cdots, \ell$ and $j = 1, 2, \cdots, t$, $X = (x_{i,j}) \leftarrow \mathbb{M}_{\ell,t}(\mathbb{S}_2)$. Let $X_j = (x_{1,j}, x_{2,j}, \cdots, x_{\ell,j}) \in \mathbb{S}_2^\ell$;
2. $(w_1, \cdots, w_t) := \beta X$;
3. $c = (c_1, \cdots, c_t) := H(m||\alpha||\beta||w_1|| \cdots ||w_t)$;
4. For $j = 1, 2, \cdots, t$, if $c_j = 0$, then $f_j = (f_{1,j}, \cdots, f_{n,j}) := X_j$; else if $c_j = 1$, then $f_j = (f_{1,j}, \cdots, f_{n,j}) := X_j S^T$.
5. The resulting signature on m is $(w_1, \cdots, w_t; f_1, \cdots, f_t)$.

[**Verification procedure.**] Give public verification key β, message m and its signature $(w_1, \cdots, w_t; f_1, \cdots, f_t)$, Let $c = (c_1, \cdots, c_t) := H(m||\alpha||\beta||w_1|| \cdots ||w_t)$. For $j = 1, 2, \cdots, t$, if $c_j = 0$, check $\beta f_j^T = (\beta_1, \cdots, \beta_\ell)(f_{1,j}, \cdots, f_{\ell,j})^T = w_j$ $f_j \in \mathbb{S}_2^\ell$; else if $c_j = 1$, check $\alpha f_j^T = (\alpha_1, \cdots, \alpha_n)(f_{1,j}, \cdots, f_{n,j})^T = w_j$ $f_j \in \mathbb{S}_3^\ell$. Output *accept* if and only if all the checks hold.

From the signing procedure, if $c_i = 0$, $\beta f_j^T = (\beta_1, \cdots, \beta_\ell)(f_{1,j}, \cdots, f_{\ell,j})^T$ $= w_j$ and $f_j \in \mathbb{S}_2^\ell$; else if $c_i = 1$, $\alpha f_j^T = (\alpha_1, \cdots, \alpha_\ell)S(x_{1,j}, x_{2,j}, \cdots, x_{\ell,j})^T$ $= (\beta_1, \cdots, \beta_\ell)(f_{1,j}, \cdots, f_{\ell,j})^T = w_j$ and $f_j \in \mathbb{S}_3^\ell$. All the checks hold. Therefore, the signature will be accepted and the scheme is correct.

From Lemma 1 and Theorem 4, we have the following result.

Corollary 2. *If the generalized compact Knapsack problem is intractable, the above signature is secure in the random oracle model.*

5   Conclusion

In this paper, we introduced the notion of the closed one-way ensemble and proposed a general construction of identification and signature schemes. At FOCS 2002, the generalized compact Knapsack problem was shown at least as hard as the *worst-case* instance of various approximation problems over cyclic lattices. Then we implemented them with *random* instances of the generalized compact Knapsack problem. Our scheme also implies the *first* zero-knowledge proof of a solution of a random generalized compact Knapsack instance and gives a positive solution to the open problem of constructing a zero-knowledge proof of generalized compact Knapsack problems.

References

1. M. Ajtai, Generating hard instances of lattice problem, Proceedings 28th Annual ACM Symposium on Theory of Computing, 1996, pp. 99-108, 1996.
2. C. H. Bennett, E. Bernstein, G. Brassard, and U. Vazirani, Strengths and weaknesses of quantum computing. SIAM J.Comput.26 ,5, pp.1510 -1523., 1997.
3. A. Fiat and A. Shamir. How to prove yourself: Practical solutions to identification and signature problems. Crypto'86, LNCS 263, pp. 186-194, Springer-Verlag, 1986.

4. S. Goldwasser and Y. Tauman Kalai. On the (In)security of the Fiat-Shamir Paradigm. FOCS'03, pp. 102-113. IEEE press, 2003.
5. R. M. Karp. Reducibility among combinatorial problems. In R. E. Miller and J. W. Thatcher, editors, Complexity of computer computation, pp. 85-103. Plenum, 1972.
6. J. C. Lagarias and A. M. Odlyzko. Solving low-density subset sum problems. Journal of the ACM, 32(1):229-246, Jan. 1985.
7. R. C. Merkle and M. E. Hellman. Hiding information and signatures in trapdoor Knapsacks. IEEE Transactions on Information Theory, Vol. 24, No. 5, pp. 525-530, 1978.
8. D. Micciancio. Generalized compact knapsaks, cyclic lattices, and efficient one-way functions from worst-case complexity assumptions. FOCS'02, pp. 356-365. IEEE Computer Society, 2002.
9. A. M. Odlyzko, The Rise and Fall of Knapsack Cryptosystems, Cryptology and Computational Number Theory, Am. Math. Soc., Proc. Symp. Appl. Math., Vol. 42, pp. 75-88, 1990.
10. T. Okamoto, K. Tanaka, and S. Uchiyama, Quantum Public-Key Cryptosystems, Crypto'00, LNCS 1880, pp.147-165. Springer-Verlag 2000.
11. D. Pointcheval: A new Identification Scheme Based on the Perceptrons Problem. Eurocrypt'95, LNCS 921, pp.319-328. Springer-Verlag, 1995.
12. D. Pointcheval, J. Stern. Security Arguments for Digital Signatures and Blind Signatures. J. Cryptology, Vol. 13, pp. 361-396, 2000.
13. Q. Wu, X. Chen, C. Wang, Y. Wang. Shared-Key Signature and Its Application to Anonymous Authentication in Ad Hoc Group. ISC'04, LNCS 3225, pp.330-341. Springer-Verlag, 2004.
14. O. Regev. New lattice based cryptographic constructions. ACM-STOC'03, pp. 407-426. ACM Press, 2003.
15. A. Shamir, A Fast Signature Scheme. MIT/LCS/TM-107, MIT Laboratory for Computer Science, 1978.
16. A. Shamir, A Polynomial-Time Algorithm for Breaking the Basic Merkle-Hellman Cryptosystem. IEEE Transactions on Information Theory, Vol. IT-30, pp. 699-704, 1984.
17. A. Shamir. An efficient Identification Scheme Based on Permuted Kernels. Crypto'89, LNCS 435, pp.606-609. Springer- Verlag.
18. P. W. Shor. Polynomial-time algorithm for prime factorization and discretelogarithms on a quantum computer. SIAM Journal of Computing, 26:1484-1509,1997.
19. J. Stern. Designing identification schemes with keys of short size. Crypto'94, LNCS 839, pp.164-73. Springer-Verlag, 1994.
20. L. M. K. Vandersypen, M. Steffen, G. Breyta, C. S. Yannoni, M. H. Sherwood, and I. L. Chuang. Experimental realization of shor's quantum factoring algorithm using nuclear magnetic resonance, Nature 414 (2001), 883-887.

A Real-Time and Reliable Approach to Detecting Traffic Variations at Abnormally High and Low Rates

Ming Li[1], Shengquan Wang[2], and Wei Zhao[2]

[1] School of Information Science & Technology, East China Normal University,
Shanghai 200062, P.R. China
mli@ee.ecnu.edu.cn, ming_lihk@yahoo.com
[2] Department of Computer Science, Texas A&M University, College Station,
TX 77843-1112, USA
{swang, wzhao}@cs.tamu.edu

Abstract. Abnormal variations of traffic are conventionally considered to occur under the condition that traffic rate is abnormally high in the cases, such as traffic congestions or traffic under distributed denial-of-service (DDOS) flood attacks. Various methods in detecting traffic variations at abnormally high rate have been reported. We note that a recent paper by Kuzmanovic and Knightly, which explains a type of DDOS attacks that may result in abnormally low traffic rate. Such a type of abnormal variations of traffic, therefore, can easily evade from detection systems based on abnormally high traffic rate. This paper presents a real-time and reliable detection approach to detect traffic variations at both abnormally high and low rates. The formulas in terms of detection probabilities, miss probabilities, classification criterion, and detection thresholds are proposed.

Keywords: Anomaly detection, real-time detection, reliable detection, traffic constraint.

1 Introduction

Detecting abnormal variations of traffic time series (traffic for short) in a network is important for both network operators and end users since traffic's abnormal variations caused by either malicious activities (e.g., DDOS flood attacks [1]) or unintentional ones (e.g., normal traffic jam [2]) may impact a network or an end user. Abnormal variations of traffic imply that statistical patterns of traffic differ significantly from normal ones [3], [4], [5], [6], [7], [8], [9], [10], where traffic models play a role.

As known, there are two categories in traffic modeling [11]. One is statistical modeling (e.g., long-range dependent (LRD) processes), see e.g. [12], [13], [14]. The other bounded modeling (i.e., deterministic modeling), which has particular applications to modeling traffic when its statistical properties are unknown, see e.g. [6], [15], [16]. We note that statistical models like LRD processes are usually for traffic in the aggregate case but there is lack of evidence to use them to characterize statistical patterns of real traffic at connection level or on a class-by-class basis in the DiffServ domain. As a matter of fact, finding statistical patterns of traffic at connection level or on a class-by-class basis remains challenging. To overcome

L.T. Yang et al. (Eds.): ATC 2006, LNCS 4158, pp. 541–550, 2006.
© Springer-Verlag Berlin Heidelberg 2006

difficulties in describing traffic at connection level or on a class-by-class basis, bounded modeling is used. As known, recent developments of networking exhibit that there exists an increased interest in DiffServ [16], [17], [18], [19]. DiffServ allows us to identify abnormality of traffic of interest on the class basis instead of detecting abnormality of traffic at all connections. Therefore, this research uses bounded modeling such that the present results are not only valid in the case of aggregate traffic but traffic in the DiffServ domain at connection level.

There are two crucial criteria for detection system design. One is reliable detection and the other real-time detection. By reliable detection, from a view of statistical detection, we mean that signs of abnormal variations of traffic can be detected according to given detection probabilities and given miss probabilities. By real-time detection, from the point of view of real-time systems, we mean that signs of abnormal variations of traffic can be detected at connection level. Our work [4] provided a general mechanism for reliable detection of abnormal variations of traffic but they do not run at connection time. Another work [20] proposed a reliable detection at connection level but it only considered traffic variations at abnormally high rate.

It is known that abnormal variations of traffic are conventionally considered to be caused by abnormally high traffic rate as can be seen from [1], [2], [3]. However, it is worth noting that a recent paper exhibits that abnormal variations of traffic may also appear when traffic rate is abnormally low, e.g., a type of DDOS attacks at abnormally low-rate traffic, see [21] for details.

The literature regarding detection of traffic variations at abnormally high rate is rich, see e.g. [4], [5], [6], [8], [9], [10], but the approach to identifying traffic variations at both abnormally high and low rates is rarely seen, to the best of our knowledge. For this reason, we substantially develop [20] to present a reliable and real-time approach to detecting traffic variations at both abnormally high rate and low rate. A key skill used in this paper, methodologically, is to extend deterministically upper and lower bounds of traffic to statistically upper and lower bounds so that we can achieve two statistical thresholds for that anomaly detection purpose.

In the following, Section 2 proposes statistically upper and lower bounds of traffic. Section 3 presents the results in detection probabilities, miss probabilities, detection thresholds, and classification criterion. Section 4 is discussions. Finally, Section 5 concludes the paper.

2 Maximum and Minimum Traffic Constraint Functions and Their Statistical Bounds

From a view of quality-of-service (QoS), service strategies in the Internet have two distinct categories: the Integrated Service [22] and the DiffServ [23]. The latter's architecture aims at providing differentiated QoS within the Internet at a manageable complexity. According to DiffServ, packets from different flows are marked at the DiffServ domain ingress as belonging to a number of different QoS classes, each one receiving a differentiated delivery service within the network.

As for DiffServ, two different approaches have been developed: relative DiffServ and absolute DiffServ. The former aims at providing differentiated performance to the different aggregates, without taking into account explicit per-flow guarantees [24]. The latter aims at providing end-to-end absolute performance guarantees to single flows, without the need of per-flow state in the core [16]. Taking into account real-time applications that must rely on absolute DiffServ so as to have guaranteed QoS, this research aims at providing an approach that is not only usable in absolute static-priority scheduling networks with DiffServ, where static-priority means that a priority is statically fixed and the same for any packet in a flow but also utilized by detecting abnormal variations of traffic in the aggregate case. In the following sections, we only consider arrival traffic at input ports of monitored sites.

In what follows, we first give the deterministic maximum and minimum traffic constraint functions. Then, we derive corresponding statistical bounds.

Definition 1. [15]: Let $x(t)$ be the instantaneous rate of arrival traffic at time t. Then, the amount of traffic generated in the interval $[0, t]$ is upper bounded by

$$\int_0^t x(u)du = y(t) \le \sigma + \rho t,$$

where σ and ρ are constants and $t > 0$. This property is written as $x \sim (\sigma, \rho)$. □

The finite quantity in the above expression may be neglected for sufficiently large interval, e.g., $(t - 0) \to \infty$. Thus, ρ implies the long-term average rate. Suppose time interval is infinitesimal. Then, σ relates to the burst size. Thus, (σ, ρ) characterizes a bound feature of $x(t)$ for any length of time interval. Denote $I = t$. Then, $\sigma + \rho t \triangleq F(I)$.

Definition 2 (Maximum traffic constraint function). [16]: Let $y(t)$ be arrival traffic function. If $y(t+I) - y(t) \le F(I)$ for $t > 0$ and $I > 0$, $F(I)$ is called maximum traffic constraint function of $y(t)$. It can be rewritten by

$$F(I) = \max_{t \ge 0}[y(t+I) - y(t)] \text{ for } I > 0. □$$

Similarly, we define the minimum traffic constraint function of $y(t)$ as follows.

Definition 3 (Minimum traffic constraint function). [6]: Let $y(t)$ be arrival traffic function. Then, the minimum traffic constraint function $f(I)$ of $y(t)$ means

$$f(I) = \min_{t \ge 0}[y(t+I) - y(t)] \text{ for } I > 0. □$$

Definitions 2-3 say the increment of $y(t)$ is upper-bounded by $F(I)$ but lower-bounded by $f(I)$. The following extends them to those in the DiffServ domain.

Definition 4. Let $y_{p,j,k}^i(t)$ be all flows of class i with priority p going through server k from input link j. Let $F_{p,j,k}^i(I)$ be the maximum traffic constraint function of $y_{p,j,k}^i(t)$. Then, $F_{p,j,k}^i(I) = \max_{t \ge 0}[y_{p,j,k}^i(t+I) - y_{p,j,k}^i(t)]$ for $I > 0$. Similarly, $f_{p,j,k}^i(I) = \min_{t \ge 0}[y_{p,j,k}^i(t+I) - y_{p,j,k}^i(t)]$ is the minimum traffic constraint function of $y_{p,j,k}^i(t)$. □

It is noted that $F_{p,j,k}^i(I)$ and $f_{p,j,k}^i(I)$ are in the sense of bounded modeling. We extend them to be statistical bounds as follows.

Observe maximum/minimum traffic constraint function in the interval $[(n-1)I,\ nI]$, $n = 1, 2, ..., N$. In each interval, denote maximum and minimum traffic constraint functions by $F_{p,j,k}^i(I,\ n)$ and $f_{p,j,k}^i(I,\ n)$, respectively. In the following, we first derive out the randomized $F_{p,j,k}^i(I,\ n)$ and then $f_{p,j,k}^i(I,\ n)$.

Usually, $F_{p,j,k}^i(I,\ n) \neq F_{p,j,k}^i(I,\ q)$ for $n \neq q$. Therefore, $F_{p,j,k}^i(I,\ n)$ is a random variable over the index n. Now, divide the interval $[(n-1)I,\ nI]$ into M non-overlapped segments. Each segment is of L length. For the mth segment, we compute the mean $E[F_{p,j,k}^i(I,\ n)]_m$ $(m = 1, 2, ..., M)$, where E is the mean operator. Again, $E[F_{p,j,k}^i(I,\ n)]_l \neq E[F_{p,j,k}^i(I,\ n)]_m$ for $l \neq m$. Thus, $E[F_{p,j,k}^i(I,\ n)]_m$ is also a random variable. According to statistics, if $M \geq 10$, $E[F_{p,j,k}^i(I,\ n)]_m$ quite accurately follows Gaussian distribution regardless of the distribution of the original variable y, [4], [5], [25]. In the case of $M \geq 10$, therefore, we have

$$E[F_{p,j,k}^i(I,\ n)]_m \sim \frac{1}{\sqrt{2\pi}\sigma_F}\exp[-\frac{\{E[F_{p,j,k}^i(I,\ n)]_m - F_\mu(M)\}^2}{2\sigma_F^2}], \tag{1}$$

where σ_F^2 is the variance of $E[F_{p,j,k}^i(I,\ n)]_m$ and $F_\mu(M)$ is its mean.

Similarly, we have

$$E[f_{p,j,k}^i(I,\ n)]_m \sim \frac{1}{\sqrt{2\pi}\sigma_f}\exp[-\frac{\{E[f_{p,j,k}^i(I,\ n)]_m - f_\mu(M)\}^2}{2\sigma_f^2}], \tag{2}$$

where σ_f^2 is the variance of $E[f_{p,j,k}^i(I,\ n)]_m$ and $f_\mu(M)$ is its mean.

Using probability expressions, we have

$$\text{Prob}\left[z_{1-\alpha_1/2} < \frac{F_\mu(M) - E[F_{p,j,k}^i(I,\ n)]_m}{\sigma_F\sqrt{M}} \leq z_{\alpha_1/2}\right] = 1 - \alpha_1, \tag{3}$$

where $(1 - \alpha_1)$ is called confidence coefficient. Let $C_F(M,\ \alpha_1)$ be the confidence interval with $(1 - \alpha_1)$ confidence coefficient. Then,

$$C_F(M,\ \alpha_1) = \left[F_\mu(M) - \frac{\sigma_F z_{\alpha_1/2}}{\sqrt{M}},\ F_\mu(M) + \frac{\sigma_F z_{\alpha_1/2}}{\sqrt{M}}\right]. \tag{4}$$

From (4), we have a statistically upper bound given by

$$B_F(M,\ \alpha_1) = F_\mu(M) + \frac{\sigma_F z_{\alpha_1/2}}{\sqrt{M}}. \tag{5}$$

Similarly, we have

$$\text{Pr ob}\left[z_{1-\alpha_2/2} < \frac{f_\mu(M) - E[f_{p,j,k}^i(I, n)]_m}{\sigma_f \sqrt{M}} \le z_{\alpha_2/2} \right] = 1 - \alpha_2. \tag{6}$$

Let $C_f(M, \alpha_2)$ be the confidence interval with $(1-\alpha_2)$ confidence coefficient. Then,

$$C_f(M, \alpha_2) = \left[f_\mu(M) - \frac{\sigma_f z_{\alpha_2/2}}{\sqrt{M}}, f_\mu(M) + \frac{\sigma_f z_{\alpha_2/2}}{\sqrt{M}} \right]. \tag{7}$$

From (7), we have a statistically lower bound given by

$$b_F(M, \alpha_2) = f_\mu(M) - \frac{\sigma_f z_{\alpha_2/2}}{\sqrt{M}}. \tag{8}$$

We note that Eq. (4) implies that $F_\mu(M)$ can be taken as a template of $E[F_{p,j,k}^i(I, n)]_m$. Similarly, (7) means $f_\mu(M)$ can be regarded as a template of $E[f_{p,j,k}^i(I, n)]_m$. In other words, we have $(1-\alpha_1)\%$ confidence to say that $E[F_{p,j,k}^i(I, n)]_m$ takes $F_\mu(M)$ as its approximation with the variation less than or equal to $\frac{\sigma_F z_{\alpha_1/2}}{\sqrt{M}}$. Similarly, we have $(1-\alpha_2)\%$ confidence to regard $f_\mu(M)$ as the approximation of $E[f_{p,j,k}^i(I, n)]_m$ with the variation less than or equal to $\frac{\sigma_f z_{\alpha_2/2}}{\sqrt{M}}$.

In the above expressions, if computations are consistent for both (4) and (7), we have $\sigma_F^2 = \sigma_f^2$. In addition, $\alpha_1 = \alpha_2$ if the same confidence level is set for both.

3 Detection Probabilities

For simplicity, denote $\xi \triangleq E[F_{p,j,k}^i(I, n)]_m$ and $\eta \triangleq E[f_{p,j,k}^i(I, n)]_m$. Then,

$$\text{Pr ob}[\xi > B_F(M, \alpha_1)] = \frac{\alpha_1}{2}. \tag{9}$$

On the other hand,

$$\text{Pr ob}\left[\eta < b_f(M, \alpha_2)\right] = \frac{\alpha_2}{2}. \tag{10}$$

Therefore, we have two thresholds for detecting traffic variations at abnormally high rate and abnormally low rate as follows.

$$V_h = B_F(M, \alpha_1), \tag{11}$$

$$V_l = b_F(M, \alpha_2).$$ (12)

Taking into account the terms used in radar systems [26], we explain two terms as follows. Correctly recognizing an abnormal sign means *detection* and failing to recognize it *miss*. According to the meaning of these two terms, we give the detection probabilities as well as miss probabilities by the following theorems.

Theorem 1 (Detection probability for traffic at abnormally high rate). [20]: Let P_{det-h} and P_{miss-h} be detection probability and miss probability for traffic at abnormally high rate, respectively. Then,

$$P_{det-h} = P\{V_h < \xi < \infty\} = (1 - \alpha_1 / 2),$$ (13)

$$P_{miss-h} = P\{-\infty < \xi < V_h\} = \alpha_1 / 2.$$ (14)

Proof: The probability of $\xi \in C_F(M, \alpha_1)$ is $(1 - \alpha_1)$. Hence, the probability of $\xi \leq V_h$ is $(1 - \alpha_1 / 2)$. Therefore, according to the meaning of *detection* mentioned above, $\xi > V_l$ exhibits a sign of abnormality of traffic at high rate with $(1 - \alpha_1 / 2)$ probability. Thus, (13) holds. Since detection probability plus miss one equals 1, (14) yields.   □

Similarly, we have

Theorem 2 (Detection probability for traffic at abnormally low rate). Let P_{det-l} and P_{miss-l} be detection probability and miss probability for traffic at abnormally low rate, respectively. Then,

$$P_{det-l} = P\{-\infty < \eta < V_l\} = (1 - \alpha_2 / 2),$$ (15)

$$P_{miss-l} = P\{V_l < \eta < \infty\} = \alpha_2 / 2.$$ (16)

Proof is straightforward from Theorem 1.   □

From Theorems 1~2, we can achieve the following statistical classification criterion for given detection probabilities by setting the values of α_1 and α_2.

Corollary (Classification): Let $y^i_{p, j, k}(t)$ be arrival traffic of class i with priority p going through server k from input link j at a monitored site. Then,

$$y^i_{p, j, k}(t) \in N \text{ if } \xi \leq V_h \text{ and } \eta \geq V_l,$$ (17)

where N implies normal set of traffic flow, and

$$y^i_{p, j, k}(t) \in A \text{ if } \xi > V_h \text{ or } \eta < V_l,$$ (18)

where A implies abnormal set. The proof is straightforward from Theorems 1~2.   □

The diagram of our detection is illustrated in Fig. 1 and the description about it is omitted.

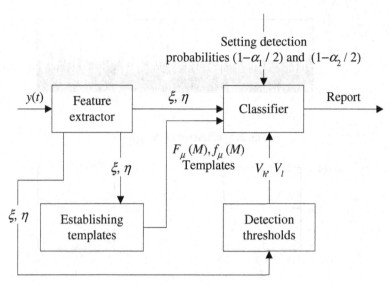

Fig. 1. Diagram of detection model

4 Discussions

In this section, we just use a Gaussian series synthesized by the method in [27] for showing the availability of the present approach. This does not lose the generality to discuss the availability on computations since statistical patterns of traffic at connection level on a class-by-class basis remain unknown.

Denote $y(i)$ synthesized series, indicating the number of bytes in the ith packet ($i = 0, 1, 2, \cdots$). Then, in the case of Transmission Control Protocol, we restrict the range of y by $40 \leq y \leq 1500$ (Bytes) (Fig. 2).

In Figs. 2~5, subscripts and superscripts of y and F are omitted for simplicity. According to Definition 2, we obtain $F(I, n)$ ($n, I = 1, 2, \ldots, 16$) as shown in Fig. 3, where only 4 plots are given due to the limited space. Figs. 4~5 indicate $\xi(n)$ and its histogram. From Fig. 5, we attain $\mu_\xi = 3,105$ and $\sigma_\xi = 344.402$. In the case of the computation precision being 4, we let $P_{det-h} = 1$, which yields the interval $[1,720, 4,467]$ and the threshold $V_h = 4,467$. The procedure to obtain V_l is similar to that of V_h and we omit it due to the limited space.

Let T_m and T_c be the time for recording data and computations in dada processing, respectively. Suppose we record a packet per 10 micro-second. Then, $T_m = 10^{-5}Q$, where Q is the number of data points involved in computations for making a decision. In the above case, $Q = 16 \times 16 = 256$. Thus, $T_m = 2.56$ ms. One the other hand, T_c for a series of 256 length on an average Pentium IV PC is negligible in comparison with T_m. So, the total time for getting both V_h and V_l is about $T_m = 2.56$ ms. This will be reduced if more powerful machine is used. Since the connection setup is typically on the order of several seconds [28], we see that the time for a detection decision based on the present approach is short enough to meet real-time requirements in practice.

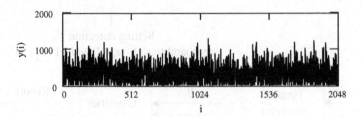

Fig. 2. Synthesized FGN series

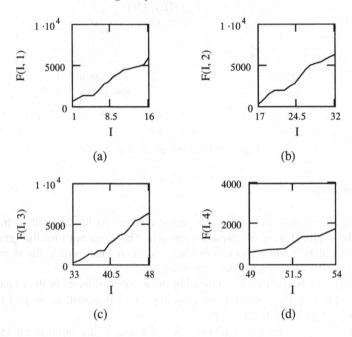

(a)

(b)

(c)

(d)

Fig. 3. Illustrations of traffic regulators

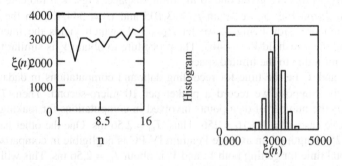

Fig. 4. The sample mean ξ **Fig. 5.** Histogram of ξ

5 Conclusions

We have derived statistically upper and lower bounds of traffic in the DiffServ domain as well as traffic in the aggregate case if i only implies one class, p just represents one priority, and j simply stands for all input links. We have derived formulas to compute detection probabilities and miss probabilities. A statistical classification criterion has been presented. Based on these, we have proposed a real-time and reliable approach for detecting traffic variations at both abnormally high and low rates. The present approach suggests that signs of traffic variations at both abnormally high and low rates can be identified according to predetermined detection probabilities and miss probabilities. The identification can be done at early stage that abnormal traffic variations occur not only because detection is at connection level but because the computation time for a detection decision is short enough as can be seen from the descriptions in the above section.

Acknowledgements

We show many thanks to anonymous referees' comments on this paper. This work was supported in part by the National Natural Science foundation of China (NSFC) under the project grant number 60573125, by the National Science Foundation under Contracts 0081761, 0324988, 0329181, by the Defense Advanced Research Projects Agency under Contract F30602-99-1-0531, and by Texas A&M University under its Telecommunication and Information Task Force Program. Any opinions, findings, conclusions, and/or recommendations expressed in this material, either expressed or implied, are those of the authors and do not necessarily reflect the views of the sponsors listed above.

References

[1] Garber, L.: Denial-of-Service Attacks Rip the Internet. Computer 33 (2000) 12-17
[2] Floyd, S., Jacobson, V.: Random Early Detection Gateways for Congestion Avoidance. IEEE/ACM T. Networking 1 (1993) 397–413
[3] Mahajan, R., Bellovin, S., Floyd, S., Ioannidis, J., Paxson, V., Shenker, S.: Controlling High Bandwidth Aggregates in the Network. Computer Communication Review 32 (2002)
[4] Li, M., An Approach to Reliably Identifying Signs of DDOS Flood Attacks based on LRD Traffic Pattern Recognition. Computer & Security 23 (2004) 549-558
[5] Li, M.: Change Trend of Averaged Hurst Parameter of Traffic under DDOS Flood Attacks. Computers & Security 25 (2006) 213-220
[6] Bettati, R., Zhao, W., Teodor, D.: Real-Time Intrusion Detection and Suppression in ATM Networks. Proceedings of the 1st USENIX Workshop on Intrusion Detection and Network Monitoring (April 1999)
[7] Schultz, E.: Intrusion Prevention. Computer & Security 23 (2004) 265-266
[8] Sorensen, S.: Competitive Overview of Statistical Anomaly Detection. White Paper, Juniper Networks Inc., www.juniper.net (2004)

[9] Cho, S.-B., Park, H.-J.: Efficient Anomaly Detection by Modeling Privilege Flows Using Hidden Markov Model. Computer & Security 22 (2003) 45-55

[10] Mirkovic, J., Dietrich, S., Dittrich, D., Reiher, P.: Internet Denial of Service: Attack and Defense Mechanisms. Prentice Hall (2004)

[11] Michiel, H., Laevens, K.: Teletraffic Engineering in a Broad-Band Era. Proc. IEEE 85 (1997) 2007-2033

[12] Willinger, W., Paxson, V.: Where Mathematics Meets the Internet. Notices of the American Mathematical Society 45 (1998) 961-970

[13] Li, M., Lim, SC.: Modeling Network Traffic using Cauchy Correlation Model with Long-Range Dependence. Modern Physics Letters B 19 (2005) 829-840

[14] Li, M.: Modeling Autocorrelation Functions of Long-Range Dependent Teletraffic Series based on Optimal Approximation in Hilbert Space-a Further Study. To appear, Applied Mathematical Modelling (2006)

[15] Cruz, L.: A Calculus for Network Delay, Part I: Network Elements in Isolation; Part II: Network Analysis. IEEE T. Inform. Theory 37 (1991) 114-131, 132-141

[16] Wang, S.-Q., Xuan, D., Bettati, R., Zhao, W.: Providing Absolute Differentiated Services for Real-Time Applications in Static-Priority Scheduling Networks. IEEE/ACM T. Networking 12 (2004) 326-339

[17] Carpenter B. E., Nichols, K.: Differentiated Services in the Internet. Proceedings of the IEEE 90 (2002) 1479-1494

[18] Carpenter B. E., Nichols, K.: Differentiated Services in the Internet. Proceedings of the IEEE 90 (2002) 1479-1494

[19] Minei, I.: MPLS DiffServ-Aware Traffic Engineering. White Paper, Juniper Networks Inc., www.juniper.net (2004)

[20] Li, M., Zhao, W.: A Statistical Model for Detecting Abnormality in Static-Priority Scheduling Networks with Differentiated Services. Springer LNAI (3802) (2005) 267-272

[21] Kuzmanovic, A., Knightly, E.: TCP-LP: Low-Priority Service via End-Point Congestion Control. To appear, IEEE/ACM T. Networking 14 (5) (2006)

[22] Braden, R., Clark, D., Shenker, S.: Integrated Service in the Internet Architecture: an Overview. IETF RFC1633 (1994)

[23] Blake, S., Black, D., Carlson, M., Davies, E., Wang, Z., Weiss, W.: An Architecture for Differentiated Service. IETF RFC2475 (1998)

[24] B. Choi, D. Xuan, C. Li, R. Bettati and W. Zhao, Scalable QoS Guaranteed Communication Services for Real-Time. IEEE Proceedings of ICDCS (2000)

[25] Bendat, J. S., Piersol, A. G.: Random Data: Analysis and Measurement Procedure. 2nd Edition, John Wiley & Sons (1991)

[26] Mahafza, B. R.: Introduction to Radar Analysis. CRC Press (1998)

[27] Li, M., Chi, C.-H.: A Correlation-based Computational Method for Simulating Long-Range Dependent Data. Journal of the Franklin Institute 340 (2003) 503-514

[28] Qiu, J., Knightly, E.: Measurement-Based Admission Control using Aggregate Traffic Envelopes. IEEE/ACM T. Networking 9 (2001) 199-210

A SCORM-Based Caching Strategy for Supporting Ubiquitous Learning Environment

Yun-Long Sie, Te-Hua Wang, Hsuan-Pu Chang, Shu-Nu Chang,
and Timothy K. Shih

Department of Computer Science and Information Engineering
Tamkang University, Taiwan, Republic of China
su1@mail.mine.tku.edu.tw

Abstract. With respect to the diverseness of learning devices and the different conditions of the internet connection availability, users might confront with some inevitable problems in traditional distance learning environment. The learning activities are always interfered while the network connection is failed. Furthermore, the learning contents become more and more miscellaneous with on-line multimedia presentations, and it is necessary for learners to wait for the learning resources to be downloaded from the remote learning server. In this paper, we propose a solution, called Caching Strategy, to solve those issues under the ubiquitous learning scope. According to some specific factors, we aim to provide the most needed learning resources for learners on the mobile learning devices even if the internet connection is not available intermittently. With our proposed methods, the waiting time of learning contents delivery can be reduced as well to smooth the learning activities online. In order to increase the efficiency of the strategy, we carefully examine some specific factors about the learning sequencing defined in the Sharable Content Object Reference Model (SCORM). After applying this strategy to distance learning system, the efficient ubiquitous learning will be easier to come true.

Keywords: Ubiquitous Learning, Distance Learning, SCORM, Caching, Agent.

1 Introduction

In the last decade, distance learning has shown its significant effects and won wide acceptance among people all over the world. People try to use many kinds of method to support teaching [1]. Due to the rapid improvement of hardware technologies and Internet services, it is more reasonable for users to learn with various learning devices in the distance learning environment nowadays. As the mobile devices are becoming more and more inexpensive, it is affordable for learners to use such devices to learn anytime anywhere, and the ubiquitous learning is expected to come true [2]. However, most mobile devices are in small size with limited storages capacities, and the internet connection is not always available while using the devices outdoors. Some online distance learning systems [3] may become paralyzed. Usability issues relating to the hardware and software had considerable impact on the learners' usage and satisfaction [4]. Even if a learner uses the computer with the internet connection at home, it is also

L.T. Yang et al. (Eds.): ATC 2006, LNCS 4158, pp. 551–560, 2006.
© Springer-Verlag Berlin Heidelberg 2006

inconvenient for him to wait for the learning contents to be downloaded from the remote server. This is because that large numbers of multimedia learning resources are used in the course [5] but the speed of network is not high enough to transmit them in real time.

In order to smooth the learning activities and to reduce the waiting time, users may need an auxiliary mechanism, such as an intelligent agent, to handle all the information while learning. Such kind of agents is able to prepare the necessary resources the users may need in advance. In this way, users can read the contents when the internet is disconnected and have not to wait a long time for the contents to be downloaded. In this paper, we demonstrated a specific solution based on SCORM (Sharable Content Object Reference Model), proposed by ADL [6], to solve the above mentioned issues in the ubiquitous learning environment. A set of factors are evaluated with our proposed Caching Strategy to forecast the learning resources that to be downloaded before the learning activities starting. In order to improve the accuracy of the caching strategy, we use the information about the learner and the devices, as well as the information defined in SCORM.

The remainder of this paper is organized as following. In section 2, we introduce some related works about SCORM. In section 3, the course caching system which runs with caching strategy is discussed. Some important factors which affect the caching strategy are also addressed in this section. Finally the conclusion and the future works are discussed in the section 4.

2 Related Works

SCORM is a well-known e-learning standard proposed by ADL in 1997 with the latest released version SCORM 2004. SCORM also introduces the learning sequencing for supervising the learners' learning behaviors and the corresponding learning records of the progresses. SCORM was widely used to assist the e-learning community in standardizing the best approaches to creating, storing, transferring and deploying learning content. In this paper, we put emphasis on the Sequencing and Navigation [7] in SCORM specification to facilitate our proposed caching strategy. The description about SCORM sequencing and navigation is illustrated in the following sections

In the definition of SCORM, course designers can use some sequencing rules to control and to record the behavior when learners are learning. These sequencing rules can be applied to a specific learning structure, called the cluster. The cluster includes a parent learning activity and its immediate children. The children can be a set of leaf learning activities which are the physical learning resources for delivering to learners, or can be another cluster. Generally, instructors can use SCORM-complaint authoring tools to specify the values and the attributes of the sequencing rules. Each cluster has its own sequencing rules to supervise the legitimate learning activities and behavior of a learner. In our proposed caching strategy, a cluster can be considered as the basic unit to be manipulated. Figure 1 illustrates an example of clusters defined in a SCORM-compliant course.

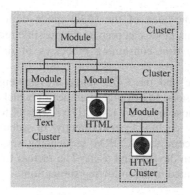

Fig. 1. An illustration of clusters within a course

Furthermore, in the sequencing definition model, there are many elements to describe and affect the learning behaviors of learners, such as Sequencing Control Modes for specifying the sequencing behavior, Limit Conditions for setting criteria of learning competence, Rollup Rules for gathering statuses from the child activities, etc. Within the sequencing control modes, we utilize three items as the primary rules to implement our proposed caching strategy, and they are: Sequencing Control Flow (Flow), Sequencing Control Choice (Choice), Sequencing Control Forward Only (Forward Only). If the value of Sequencing Control Flow in a cluster is true, learners can merely access the adjacent (i.e., the previous and the next) learning units in that cluster. If the value of Sequencing Control Choice is true, learners can choose any learning units which they want to read within that cluster. Finally, if the value of Sequencing Control Forward Only is set as true, learners can only read the next learning unit after accomplishing the current learning unit. With these concepts in mind, in the next section, we will introduce our proposed Caching Strategy which supports the efficient ubiquitous learning environment.

3 Course Caching System

The course caching system is an implementation of caching strategy. It can be applied to all available learning devices and the ubiquitous learning environment [8]. The system executes automatically as a Daemon program without any human control. The caching strategy includes two modes for dealing with different conditions of device and network requirements. One is called the VMM mode and another is called the COD mode. Due to the availability of the internet and the adopted learning device, the system will switch between these two modes to meet the needs of efficient ubiquitous learning. The idea of the VMM mode is similar to the concept of "Virtual Memory Management" in conventional operating systems. This mode can provide a virtual network environment for learners, and the learning activities, especially through the mobile learning devices, will not be suspended due to the intermittent network connection. Otherwise, the idea of the COD mode comes from the concept of "Caching of Disk", and this mode can prepare the possible required learning resources in advance to avoid the time-consuming processes of downloading the learning contents.

Both the VMM mode and the COD mode are implemented according to the forecast of learning behaviors. In this regard, to decide which parts of course contents should be cached is the most important issue. The results of forecast will influence the performance of the course caching system directly. In order to improve the accuracy of the forecast, we concern the SCORM sequencing setting and some available information collected from devices and users. The factors for forecast and the course caching system are illustrated in the following subsections.

3.1 Factors for Forecast

The caching strategy forecasts the user's action and pre-download the most needed parts of a course to the specific learning devices. This establishes the need for users to read the learning contents without either a permanent internet connection or waiting for a long time to download the courses. There are three types of data might be evaluated while the caching strategy is performed. The first one is about the course contents, and the second one is about the device characteristic. Eventually, the learning records of learners should be taken into account.

3.1.1 The Factors About Course

As mentioned in the previous sections, a set of factors are evaluated with our proposed Caching Strategy to forecast the learning resources that to be downloaded before the learning activities starting. Some of these possible factors can be derived from the essence of the course content. This kind of factors has strong relationship with SCORM sequencing, which is specified in each cluster. Note that, the basic unit to be downloaded or to be dropped in our proposed caching strategy is a cluster defined in SCORM specification. Each cluster has its own identifier and contains several learning resources. The size of a specific cluster totalizes the size of each physical learning resource within it. As a result, the size of a cluster can be considered as a factor for the forecast in caching strategy due to the limited storage capacity of the mobile learning devices.

The course caching system in the VMM mode prefers to download as many clusters as possible to increase the hit ratio when the learner chooses a lesson on the mobile learning device. The hit ratio can be calculated according to the availability of the chosen lesson on the mobile learning device at that time. The hit ratio will be increased if the chosen lesson has already been pre-downloaded to the mobile device; otherwise, it will be decreased if the chosen lesson needs to be downloaded from remote server to the mobile device. However, the course caching system in the COD mode prefers to download the biggest cluster first to reduce the waiting time when learner is reading online. The figure 2 shows the difference between these two modes.

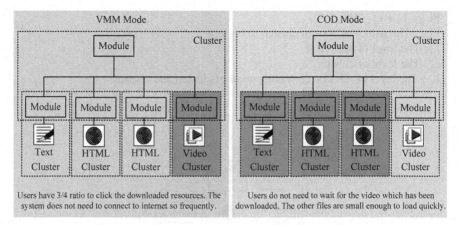

Fig. 2. One of the Factors for Forecast: The Size of a Cluster

In the SCORM sequencing control mode, the learner is allowed to read some parts of a course in a specific and relative order. The caching strategy can accurately forecast which parts of the course will be read first according to the setting of sequencing control mode. For example, the Sequencing Control Flow (Flow) allows users to read the next lesson or previous lesson linearly. Learners are not allowed to choose a lesson randomly and can not skip a lesson if they are unwilling to read it. With this information, the caching strategy can know that the next lesson and the previous lesson could be the most needed learning contents when user is reading a lesson. There are other attributes in sequencing control mode and the decisions of caching strategy are shown, respectively, in figure 3.

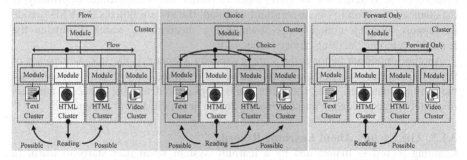

Fig. 3. One of the Factors for Forecast: The setting of Sequencing Control Mode. Note that, in the "Choice" case, the caching strategy needs other factors to determine which cluster is the most possible one.

In order to measure the relationship between two clusters, we quantify it with a simple value, called "path length." This factor can determine the relationship between two clusters is strong or weak. If a cluster has a stronger relationship with the current cluster, it might be more possible for learner to read after finishing the current learning activity. The path length is defined as the following algorithm, and figure 4 shows an example of the path length derivation.

$$PL_{ij} = L_i + L_j - 2*L_c \tag{1}$$

PL_{ij} : The path length from cluster$_i$ to cluster$_j$

L_i : The level of cluster$_i$

L_j : The level of cluster$_j$

L_c : The level of the first common parent of cluster$_i$ and cluster$_j$

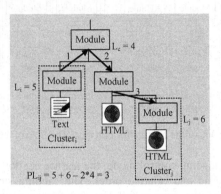

Fig. 4. One of the Factors for Forecast: Path Length

3.1.2 The Factors About Device

The second type of factors is about the characteristic of various learning devices. One of the most important factors is the capability of network connection. This factor determines which mode should be used in the course caching system. If the specific learning device is able to access the internet all the time with sustained connection capability, the system uses the COD mode to reduce the waiting time. Oppositely, if the connection capability is intermittent or failed, the system utilizes the VMM mode to support learning contents pre-downloading mechanism, which facilitates the learning on mobile learning devices especially.

Another important factor is the storage capacity. Generally, the storage capacity of the mobile devices which support the ubiquitous learning is insufficient to contain all the learning materials. Thus, the factor can be applied to determine either the numbers of clusters to be preloaded into the mobile device or the clusters to be replaced.

3.1.3 The Factors About Learning Record

Learning record is maintained by a learning system when user starts to learn. In another words, if the learner is not involved in the learning activities, the learning system will not keep the record for her. For this reason, the type of factors is only applied when the course caching system needs to replace some no longer used clusters with new downloaded clusters.

There are three factors regarding this type: reference count, last access time and downloading time. If a cluster is read frequently, it should be dropped later than the cluster which is seldom read. And if a cluster is read recently or is a new downloaded one, it is more important than the other clusters that have already existed in the learning device.

3.2 System Architecture

The course caching system is implemented with the caching strategy as above described. It contains the VMM and the COD mode. In the VMM mode, the course caching system will be triggered right after the learning device connected to the internet. With those pre-downloaded clusters, learners can continue reading in the off-line mode. If a learning device always connects to the internet, the course caching system runs in the COD mode in the background. By using the two modes appropriately and frequently, the system is able to provide the most suitable clusters for learners to reduce the waiting time in the ubiquitous learning environment.

Typically, the course caching system has two models to handle all the tasks, and they are the download management model and the replacement management model. The download management model is a function on the server side. It produces an efficient downloading order according the mentioned factors. The client just needs to download the learning contents from server followed by this specified order without any additional manipulations. The replacement management model is a function on the client side. This model determines which clusters should be dropped in order to load the new downloaded clusters. It also determines the proper time to request learning materials from server in the VMM mode or in the COD mode. Figure 5 illustrates the architecture of our proposed course caching system.

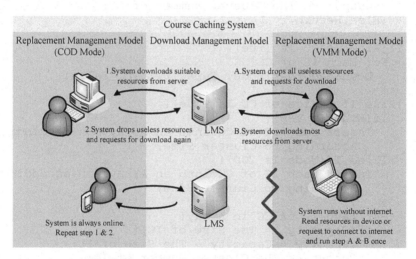

Fig. 5. The Architecture of Course Caching System

3.3 Download Management Model

The course caching system has a download management model on the server side to create the downloading order of clusters. It is the main function to affect the efficiency of the course caching system. With a proper order created by download management model, the client can avoid from the unnecessary downloading and replacement of the learning contents. The model uses some factors to forecast the possible user's learning behavior. The factors about course information are most important to the efficiency of the download management model. The download management model will first take into consideration the SCORM sequencing control mode in the beginning of the downloading process. If the "Flow" is set as true, the model will download the adjacent clusters first to the learning device. If the "Choice" is true, the model will find the cluster with the smallest path length to download. However, if there exist more than one cluster with the same path length, the download management model uses the size of clusters and the number of clusters to determine the downloading order. The following is the algorithm for caching strategy in the download management model.

```
Mode: VMM Mode or COD Mode
Capacity: The Available Capacity of Storage
CC: The Current Cluster
Flag: The Flag Displays That CC Has Been Downloaded
PC: The Parent Cluster of CC    IC: Immediate Children
Input: Mode, Capacity, CC, Flag
Output: The Order for Downloading Clusters from Server

Function DownloadOrder(Mode, Capacity, CC, Flag){
  If(Flag Is False){
    If(Capacity >= The Size of CC){
      Capacity = Capacity - The Size of CC;
      Output << The Cluster Number of CC;
    }Else Return;
  }
  If(Flow of CC Is True){
    For Each IC of CC{
      DownloadOrder(Mode, Capacity, IC, False);
    }
  }Else If(Choice of CC Is True){
    If(Mode Is VMM){
      Insert Each IC of CC into an Array Non-descending
        According to Cluster Size;
    }Else If(Mode Is COD){
      Insert Each IC of CC into an Array Non-ascending
        According to Cluster Size;
    }
    For Each IC of CC in Array{
      If(Capacity >= The Size of IC){
        Capacity = Capacity - The Size of IC;
        Output << The Cluster Number of IC;
      }
    }
    Sort Array According to Cluster Number;
    For Each IC of CC in Array{
      DownloadOrder(Mode, Capacity, IC, True);
    }
  }
  If(ForwardOnly of PC Is True){
    For Each IC of PC after CC{
      DownloadOrder(Mode, Capacity, IC, False);
    }
```

```
  }Else If(Flow of PC Is True){
    N = 1;
    While(There Still Have IC of PC){
      DownloadOrder(Mode, Capacity,
          The Nth IC after CC, False);
      DownloadOrder(Mode, Capacity,
          The Nth IC before CC, False);
      N = N + 1;
    }
  }
  DownloadOrder(Mode, Capacity, PC, False);
}
```

3.4 Replacement Management Model

The replacement management model is a function on the client side. It will drop some clusters automatically when the storage capacity of the learning device is reached and the new clusters are requested. In order to prevent dropping some clusters which might be necessary in the oncoming learning activities, it is important for this model to make a good decision. Furthermore, a good course caching system should not waste the resources of the internet too much. Accordingly the replacement management model can be considered as the kernel of the caching system to make it more efficient to access the internet. The algorithm of replacement management model is as below. In this algorithm, the model will drop the clusters with the maximum "distance" to the current cluster. The "distance" is the value derived from many factors, such as reference count, last access time, etc. For example, if a cluster is less possible be visited in the learning activities, the distance of the cluster is greater than other clusters.

```
Mode: VMM Mode or COD Mode
Capacity: The Available Capacity of Storage
CC: Current Cluster     RC: Removed Cluster
α : A Threshold Value
Input: Mode, Capacity, CC
Output: The Cluster Numbers Which have Been Dropped

Function Replacement(Mode, Capacity, CC){
  While(Capacity < α ){
    RC = The Clusterj Have the Max Distancei,j;
      // i: CC, j: Each Cluster in the Storage
    Remove RC from Storage;
    Capacity = Capacity + The Size of RC;
    Output << The Cluster Number of RC;
  }
  If(CC Has Been Downloaded){
    Download DownloadOrder(Mode, Capacity, CC, True);
  }Else{
    Download DownloadOrder(Mode, Capacity, CC, False);
  }
}
```

4 Conclusion

In this paper, we mainly focus on developing a course caching system, which facilitates the efficient ubiquitous learning environment based on SCORM. The system uses the VMM mode to simulate an environment as if the network connection is available. Users can learn anytime anywhere without concerning about the status of network. With respect to the miscellaneous learning resources, the COD mode is responsible for reducing the waiting time for the learning contents to be downloaded from the backend server.

Our works aim to explore a caching strategy which precisely forecasts the user's learning behavior and the most needed portions of learning contents in the specific learning devices, such as PDAs (Personal Digital Assistants), PCs, and even the smart phones. With utilizing the caching strategy, the goal of ubiquitous learning can be easier to achieve. Users are able to read the learning contents without either a permanent internet connection or waiting for a long time to download the courses to learn. Moreover, as the result of forecast is important for the whole system, we carefully examine some factors to be evaluated while the caching strategy is performed. Thus far, the caching system is integrated with our learning management system at (http://scorm.mine.tku.edu.tw). And some mobile devices are used for supporting the needs of ubiquitous learning.

References

[1] Herng-Yow Chen, Gin-Yi Chen, and Jen-Shin Hong (1999), "Design of a Web-based Synchronized Multimedia Lecture System for Distance Education" Proceedings of IEEE International Conference on Multimedia Computing and Systems (ICMCS1999)
[2] J. Waycott, and A. Kukulska-Hulme (2003), "Students' experiences with PDAs for reading course materials" Personal and Ubiquitous Computing Volume 7, Issue 1 (May 2003), ISSN:1617-4909
[3] Cerise Wuthrich, Gail Kalbfleisch, Terry Griffin, and Nelson Passos (2003), "ON-LINE INSTRUCTIONAL TESTING IN A MOBILE ENVIRONMENT" Proceedings of the Fourteenth Annual CCSC South Central Conference
[4] Dan Corlett, Mike Sharples, Tony Chan, and Susan Bull(2004), "A Mobile Learning Organiser for University Students" Proceedings of 2nd IEEE International Workshop on Wireless and Mobile Technologies in Education (WMTE'04)
[5] Peiya Liu, Liang H. Hsu, and Amit Chakraborty (2002), "Towards Automating the Generation of SCORM-Based Multimedia Product Training Manuals", Proceedings of 2002 IEEE International Conference Multimedia and Expo, 2002. (ICME'02)
[6] Advanced Distributed Learning (ADL) (2004), http://www.adlnet.org
[7] ADL (2004), SCORM Sequencing and Navigation Version 1.3, SCORM Book
[8] Hsuan-Pu Chang, Wen-Chih Chang, Yun-Long Sie, Nigel H. Lin, Chun-Hong Huang, Timothy K. Shih and Qun Jin (2005), "Ubiquitous Learning on Pocket SCORM", Proceedings of The Second International Symposium on Ubiquitous Intelligence and Smart Worlds (UISW2005)

FTCM: Fault-Tolerant Cluster Management for Cluster-Based DBMS[*]

Jae-Woo Chang and Young-Chang Kim

Dept. of Computer Engineering, Chonbuk National University
Chonju, Chonbuk 561-756, South Korea
{jwchang, yckim}@dblab.chonbuk.ac.kr

Abstract. In this paper, we design a fault-tolerant cluster management system for a cluster-based DBMS, called FTCM. To achieve it, FTCM manages the status of the nodes for a cluster-based DBMS as well as the status of the various DBMS instances at a given node. Using a graphical user interface (GUI), FTCM gives users a single virtual system image by showing the status of all of the nodes and resources for a cluster-based DBMS. In addition, we implement our FTCM by using Linux virtual server 0.81 as a load balancer and iBASE/Cluster as a cluster-based DBMS, under a cluster system with four server nodes. It is shown from our performance analysis that the sensing and recovery time of FTCM for the iBASE/Cluster is about 2 seconds while that of OCMS for Oracle DBMS is more than 20 seconds. Finally, we show that our FTCM can support nonstop service by performing its recovery procedure even in the case where all the nodes except one have failed.

1 Introduction

Being formed by connecting PCs and workstations using a high-speed network, a cluster system [1] is required to support 24 hours nonstop service for the Internet. Much research has been conducted regarding the use of cluster DBMS that can offer a mechanism to support high performance, high availability and high scalability [2]. They include Oracle 9i Real Application Server, Informix Extended Parallel Server and IBM DB2 Universal Database EEE. To manage the cluster DBMS efficiently, the following requirements for a cluster DBMS management tool can be considered. First, a cluster management tool should enable users to visualize a cluster system being composed of multiple nodes as a single virtual system image. Secondly, by using a graphical user interface (GUI), the cluster DBMS management tool should provide users with the status of all of the nodes in the system and all of the resources (i.e. CPU, memory, disk) at a given node. Thirdly, a load balancer is needed to make all the nodes perform effectively by evenly distributing the users' requests. Finally, a recovery procedure is needed to support a fault-tolerant system when one of its nodes has failed [3,4].

---

[*] This work is financially supported by the Ministry of Education and Human Resources Development (MOE), the Ministry of Commerce, Industry and Energy (MOCIE) and the Ministry of Labor (MOLAB) though the fostering project of the Lab of Excellency.

L.T. Yang et al. (Eds.): ATC 2006, LNCS 4158, pp. 561–570, 2006.

In this paper, we design and implement a fault-tolerant cluster management system for a cluster-based DBMS, called FTCM. To achieve it, FTCM manages the status of the nodes for a cluster-based DBMS as well as the status of the various DBMS instances at a given node. Using a graphical user interface (GUI), FTCM gives users a single virtual system image by showing the status of all of the nodes and resources for a cluster-based DBMS. In addition, we implement our FTCM by using Linux virtual server 0.81 as a load balancer and iBASE/Cluster as a cluster-based DBMS, under a cluster system with four server nodes. The remainder of this paper is organized as follows. The next section discusses related work on the existing cluster management systems. In section 3, we describe the design of our FTCM for a cluster-based DBMS and its graphical user interface. In section 4, we present the implementation and the performance analysis of our FTCM. Finally, we draw our conclusions in section 5.

2   Related Work

As related work, we introduce the typical cluster management systems, such as OCMS (Oracle Cluster Management System) [5] and SCMS (SMILE Cluster Management System) [6]. First of all, OCMS is a well known as a cluster management tool for the Oracle8i Parallel Server product on Linux. It provides cluster membership services, a global view of clusters, node monitoring and cluster reconfiguration. OCMS also consists of a watchdog daemon, node monitor and cluster manager. First, the watchdog daemon offers services to the cluster manager and to the node monitor. It makes use of the standard Linux watchdog timer to monitor selected system resources for the purpose of preventing database corruption. Secondly, the node monitor passes node-level cluster information to the cluster manager. It maintains a consistent view of the cluster and informs the cluster manager of the status of each of its local nodes. The node monitors also cooperates with the watchdog daemon to stop nodes which have an abnormally heavy load. Finally, the cluster manager passes instance-level cluster information to the Oracle instance. It maintains process-level status information for a cluster system. The cluster manager accepts the registration of Oracle instances to the cluster system and provides a consistent view of the Oracle instances. Next, SCMS was developed by Kasetsart university in Thailand as a cluster system management tool for Beowulf clusters. It consists of CMA (Control and Monitoring Agent), SMA(Systems Management Agent) and RMI(Resource Management Interface). First, the CMA runs on each node and collects system statistics continuously. The CMA reads system information through a layer called HAL(Hardware Abstraction Layer). Secondly, the system statistics are collected by a centralized resource management server called SMA. The SMA responds to user queries concerning the system status and sends some commands to the CMA. Finally, the RMI is provided as a set of APIs for system monitoring and logging applications. By using the RMI, the SCMS provides monitoring tool, configuration utilities and parallel Unix commands.

3 Design of FTCM

A cluster DBMS consists of multiple server nodes and uses a shared disk. All of the server nodes are connected to each other by means of a high-speed gigabit Ethernet, which is called cluster network. A master node receives a service request from clients through a service network and makes job assignment through the cluster network. Each server is connected to a shared disk by means of SAN (Storage Area Network) for data transmission. The Backup node serves as a new master node when it detects the failure of the master node and uses the cluster network for a fail-over mechanism. Figure 1 shows the overall architecture of a cluster DBMS which are needed to supports 24 hours nonstop database application services, e.g., map database provision.

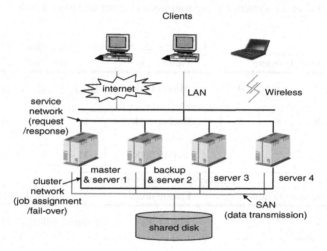

Fig. 1. Overall architecture of a cluster system for supporting a cluster-based DBMS

3.1 FTCM

We propose a fault-tolerant cluster management tool which can monitor the status of the nodes in a cluster DBMS as well as the status of the various DBMS instances at a given node. Based on the monitoring, our cluster DBMS management tool can provide an intelligent fail-over mechanism for dealing with multiple node failures in a cluster DBMS, thus making its fault-tolerance possible when combined with a load balancer. The cluster DBMS management tool consists of four components; probe, handler, CM (Cluster Manager) and NM (Node Manager). The probe monitors the status of the each node and generates events according to the status of the system. The handler stores the monitored information into a status table and performs a specific procedure for each type of event. The NM performs network communication with the CM at the master node. If the NM detects an error during the communication with the CM, the NM makes a connection with the backup node and transmits all of the available in-formation to it. If the NM does not receive a response from the CM during a defined interval, the NM considers that the CM has failed and makes a connection with a backup node. The CM, running on the master node, perceives the status of the net-works by sending a ping message to each node through both the cluster network and the service network. Based on the status of the networks, the CM manages all of the system resources and services. If the CM detects that the NM has encountered an error, it restarts the NM. If the CM detects an error, it generates an event and transmits it to the corresponding service handler, thus requesting it to perform its recovery procedure.

If the master node fails, our fault-tolerant cluster management tool terminates the master node, and then makes the backup node and one of server nodes be a new master and a new backup one, respectively. If the backup node fails, our management tool terminates the backup node and let one of server nodes be a new backup node. If a server node fails, our management tool just terminates the server node. Figure 2(a) shows the status of the system having four nodes before and after a node failure.

(M: master node, B: backup node, S: database server node)

Before node failure				Failure node	After node failure			
1	2	3	4	Master node	failure	M	B	S
M	B	S	S	Backup node	M	failure	B	S
				Server node	M	B	failure	S

(a) System having four nodes

Before node failure				Failure node	After node failure			
1	2	3	4	Master node	failure	failure	M	B
failure	M	B	S	Backup node	failure	M	failure	B
				Server node	failure	M	B	failure

(b) System having three nodes

Before node failure				Failure node	After node failure			
1	2	3	4	Master node	failure	failure	failure	M
failure	failure	M	B	Backup node	failure	failure	M	failure
				Server node	failure	failure	M	failure

(c) System having two nodes

Fig. 2. Status of the system before and after a node failure

At this time, we assume that the master node has failed, and then the second and the third node have been selected as a new master and a new backup one, respectively. Thus, if the new master node fails continuously, our fault-tolerant cluster management tool terminates the master node, and then assigns the backup node and the remaining database server node to the role of a new master and a new backup one, respectively. If the new backup node fails after the first node failure in Figure 2(a), our management tool terminates the backup node (the third one) and let the remaining database server node (the fourth one) be a new backup node. If a database server node fails after the fist node failure in Figure 2(a), our management tool just terminates the database server node (the fourth one). Figure 2(b) shows the status of the system having three nodes before and after a node failure. At this time, we also assume that the new master node has failed, and then the third and the fourth node have been selected as a new master and a new backup one, respectively. Thus, if the new master node fails con-tinuously, our fault-tolerant cluster management tool terminates the master node and just assigns the backup node to the role of a new master node. This is be-cause there is no running node. If the backup node fails after the first two nodes' fail-ures in Figure 2(b), our management tool just terminates the backup node (the fourth one) because there is no running database server node. Figure 2(c) shows the status of the system having two nodes before and after a node failure. The other cases can be dealt with similarly by our fault-tolerant cluster DBMS management tool. Conclu-sively, it is shown that our cluster management tool is fault-tolerant because it can work well even if one of nodes (database servers) survives in the system.

3.2 Recovery Procedures in the Case of Failures

The server nodes comprising a cluster system can be classified into the master node, the backup node, and the database server nodes. If there is no failure in both the ser-vice and the cluster network, the cluster system runs normally. If the ser-vice network fails, a server node can communicate with the other nodes, but it cannot receive user requests or return the results to the user. If the cluster network fails, a given server node cannot communicate with the others and so the master node cannot distribute user requests to any of the database server nodes. If neither the service nor the cluster network work, the situation is considered as node failure since the nodes cannot func-tion anymore. In order to recover the cluster system from the node failure, we provide an intelligent fail-over mechanism which can deal with multiple node failures in a cluster DBMS. The proposed fail-over mechanism is divided into two procedures; node failure detection and failure recovery. First, in order to detect the node failure, the CM and NM sends a ping message to each database server node in the cluster system and analyze the response of each server node. If it fails to receive any re-sponse from any of the database server nodes, it regards the situation as its node fail-ure or its cluster network failure. At that time, there can be an ambiguity as shown in the Figure 3. In the Figure 3(a), all of the database server nodes except the first one have failures (node failures or cluster network failures). In the Figure 3(b), only the first server node has a failure. However, both situations can never be distinguished because they have the same ping status. To solve this ambiguity, we propose an intel-ligent failure detection procedure which uses the history information of the ping status. Once, our cluster DBMS management tool detects a failure, it compares the current ping status with the past status. If two database server nodes have already failed due to their node failure or their cluster network failures, this situation can be considered as ' the failures of all the nodes except one. Otherwise, this situation can

be considered as a failure in only one node. In our intelligent failure detection procedure, it is assumed that more than one node (or cluster network) never fail at the same
time. This assump-tion is very realistic in a cluster DBMS environment.

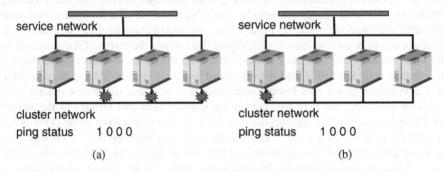

Fig. 3. Ambiguity between two failures

Master node failure. The master node of the cluster system manages the cluster
DBMS by distributing user requests to each server node. The master node sends a
ping message to each server node in the cluster system and detects the failure of a
node by analyzing the response of each server node. If the master node fails to receive
any response from any of the server nodes, it regards the situation as cluster network
failure. Meanwhile, when the backup node cannot communicate with the master node
using a ping message, it re-gards the situation as master node failure. To prevent this
situation, the backup node regularly checks for the failure of the master node by sending it a ping message peri-odically and itself becomes the new master node if the
master node fails.

Backup node failure. The backup node of the cluster system stores all of the information received from the CM and monitors the master node. If the master node fails,
the backup node becomes the new master node and it then selects one of the remaining server nodes as the new backup node. If the backup node fails, FTCM perceives
the failure and terminates the backup node. In addition, the backup node terminates
the active DB, Sysmon, NM and its backup CM. During this time, the master node
performs its recovery procedure, in order to remove the failed backup node from the
list of available server nodes and to select a new backup node from amongst these
remaining nodes.

DB server node failure. In the cluster system, the failure of a server node can cause
the failure of the entire cluster-based DBMS, because the cluster-based DBMS uses a
shared disk. Therefore, FTCM should perform a recovery procedure to preserve the
integrity of the data by preventing the failed server node from accessing any data.
First, if the service network fails, all of the server nodes should stop their transactions
and perform their recovery procedure, since they cannot return the results of any user
requests to the users. Sec-ondly, if the cluster network fails, all of the server nodes
should react in the same way as that described above, because they can neither receive
any user requests from the master node, nor communicate with any of the other server

nodes. Finally, if a server node fails, FTCM should remove this server node from the list of available nodes of the Linux virtual server and inform the other server nodes of the failure of this server node. During this time, the failed server node performs its recovery procedure to re-covers its transactions and terminate its database. The other server nodes should re-cover the data of the failed node.

3.3 User Interface of FTCM

We describe the convenient user interface of FTCM which presents both the status of the system information and the status of the DBMS information being monitored by the system probe at each server node. The system information consists of the CPU, memory, disk, network and node status. To present the status of the CPU and memory, we use the files /proc/meminfo and /proc/stat. We depict the status of the memory by showing the current usage rate of memory and the frequency of memory swapping. The left part of Figure 3 shows the user interface for the CPU and memory status part of the system information.

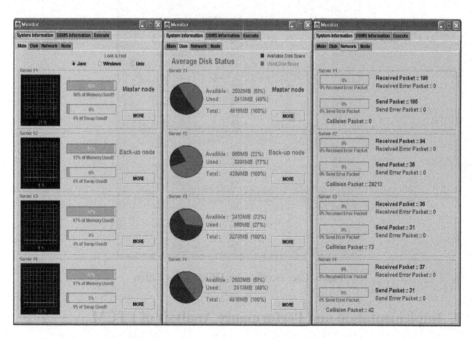

Fig. 4. User interface for system information

In this figure, we show that our cluster system consists of four server nodes and that the first node is the master node. In the master node, it is shown that the usage rate of CPU, memory and swap memory are 25%, 96% and 6%, respectively. To present the status of the disk, we use the file /proc/mounts. We depict the current used disk space, the available disk space, and the total mounted space. The central part of Figure 4 shows the user interface for the disk status part of the system information. In the master node, it is shown that the total mounted disk space, available disk space and current used space are 4916 Mbytes, 2502 Mbytes and 2413 Mbytes, respectively. For the status of the network, we make use of the file /proc/net/dev. We depict the network information such as the number of received packets, received error packets, sending packets, sending error packets. The right part of Figure 3 shows the user interface for the network status part of the system information. In the master node, it is shown that the number of packets received, error packets received, packets sent, and error packets sent are 198, 0, 185 and 0, respectively. Here ACTIVE denotes that the corresponding service is available, while INACTIVE denotes that the corresponding service program is not running on the server node. Figure 5 shows the user interface for the DBMS information. We can observe that there are multiple DBMS processes and node commit is running on the master node. The PID 959 process with S (Sleep) status makes use of 7% of the CPU.

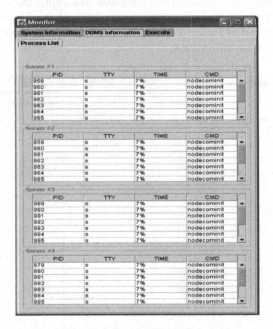

Fig. 5. User interface for DBMS information

4   Implementation and Performance Analysis of FTCM

In this section, we describe the implementation of our FTCM and the results of its testing. Table 1 describes our system implementation environment. We implement our FTCM by using Linux virtual server 0.81 [7] as a load balancer and iBASE/Cluster [8] as a cluster-based DBMS, under a cluster system having four server nodes, each of which is running on Redhat Linux 7.1 OS with its own iBASE/Cluster DBMS. In the normal situation, the service requests of users are transmitted to the master node. The Linux virtual server on the master node distributes the user request to one of the available server nodes according to its round-robin algorithm.

Table 1. System implementation environment

System	450 Mhz CPU/HDD 30GB/128MB Memory * 4
OS	Redhat Linux 7.1 (Kernel 2.4.5)
Compiler	gcc 2.96, make 3.79.1
Database	iBASE/Cluster
Load balancer	Linux virtual server 0.81

We conduct the performance analysis of our FTCM using iBASE/Cluster. We cannot directly compare the performance of FTCM with that of OCMS, because the latter is a cluster management system being dedicated to Oracle DBMS and does not support iBASE/Cluster's recovery procedure. According to the Oracle 9i Administrator's Reference [5], the sensing and recovery time of OCMS for Oracle DBMS is more than 20 seconds. Table 2 shows both the sensing time for the three types of node failures and the time required to perform the recovery procedure for each of them. It is shown from the result that OCMS is much worse than our FTCM because OCMS has to wait until Oracle instances are reconfigured. First, when the master node fails, the backup node becomes aware of the master node failure through the result of the ping message sent to the master node. We set the maximum response time for the ping message to 2 seconds. The time required for sensing the master node failure is 0.91 seconds and the time required for performing the recovery procedure is 0.78 seconds. Since the backup node is assumed to have the role of the master node, it resets its virtual IP and creates a thread to monitor the network status of the nodes in the cluster system. Secondly, when the backup node fails, the master node becomes aware of the failure and selects one of the available server nodes as the new backup node. The time required for sensing the backup node failure is 0.89 seconds and the time required for performing the recovery procedure is 0.51 seconds. The new backup node creates a thread to monitor the master node and periodically receives the information of the service status table of the master node. Finally, when the database server node fails, the master node perceives the failure and performs its recovery procedure. The time required for sensing the database server node failure is 0.81 seconds and the time required for performing the recovery procedure is 0.71 seconds. If the database server node fails, the master node removes the server node from the available server list, in order that user requests are no longer transmitted to the failed server node.

Table 2. Sensing time and recovery time for the three types of node failure

	Sensing time	Recovery time
Master node failure	0.91	0.78
Backup node failure	0.89	0.51
Database server node failure	0.81	0.71

Table 3 shows the major differences between FTCM and OCMS. First, the cluster manager of OCMS performs its task on each node and communicates each other through the private network. Assume that there are N server nodes, the total number of messages for communication in OCMS is (N-1)*N. However, our FTCM only needs 2N messages. That is to say, OCMS has more network overhead than FTCM. Secondly, OCMS uses a quorum partition to recognize the failure of other nodes. If the number of nodes is increased, more nodes attempt to read the quorum partition, thus resulting in the degradation of recovery performance. However, our FTCM keeps the history status information of every node to recognize failures. If a node detects multiple node failures based on the comparison between a current status and a history status, we consider it the failure of the detecting node since the multiple node failures are not assumed to occur at the same time. Because this scheme is not affected by the number of nodes, our FTCM is efficient than OCMS in terms of scalability.

Table 3. Differences between FTCM and OCMS

	FTCM	OCMS
Network Communication	Centralized	Distributed
Failure Detection	History status information	Quorum partition

5 Conclusions

In this paper, we described the design of a fault-tolerant cluster management system for a cluster-based DBMS, called FTCM. When such a failure occurs, FTCM performed its recovery procedure in order to provide normal service, regardless of the failure. Using a graphical user interface (GUI), FTCM enabled users to visualize a single virtual system image by providing them with the status of all of the nodes and resources. Finally, we implemented our FTCM by using Linux virtual server 0.81 as a load balancer and iBASE/Cluster as a cluster-based DBMS, under a cluster system with four server nodes. It is shown from our performance analysis that the sensing and recovery time of FTCM for the iBASE/Cluster is about 2 seconds while that of OCMS for Oracle DBMS is more than 20 seconds. Thus we can conclude that our FTCM can support nonstop service by performing its recovery procedure even in the case where all the nodes except one have failed.

References

1. Rajkumar Buyya, High Performance Cluster Computing, Vol. 1&2, Prentice Hall PTR, 1999.
2. J. Y. Choi and S. C. Whang, "Software Tool for Cluster," Communication of the Korea Information Science Society, Vol. 18, No 3. pp40~47, 2000.
3. G. F. Pfister, In Search of Clusters 2nd Edition, Prentice-Hall, 1998
4. Linux Clustering, http://dpnm.postech.ac.kr/cluster/index.htm
5. Oracle Corporation, "Oracle 9i Administrator's Reference Release2(9.2.0.1.0)," chapter F, Oracle Cluster Management Software, 2002.
6. P. Uthayopas, J. Maneesilp, and P. Ingongnam, "SCMS: An Integrated Cluster Management Tool for Beowulf Cluster System", Proceedings of the International Conference on Parallel and Distributed Proceeding Techniques and Applications, pp26-28, 2000.
7. Linux Virtual Server, http://www.linuxvirtualserver.org
8. H.-Y. Kim, K.-S. Jin, J. Kim, and M.-J. Kim, "iBASE/Cluster: Extending the BADA-IV for a Cluster Environment", Proceeding of the 18th Korea Information Processing Society Fall Conference, Vol. 9, No. 2, pp. 1769-1772, 2002.

Fault-Tolerant Scheduling Based on Periodic Tasks for Heterogeneous Systems

Wei Luo[1], Fumin Yang[1], Liping Pang[1], and Xiao Qin[2]

[1] School of Computer Science, HuaZhong University of Science and Technology,
Wuhan 430074, P.R. China
free_xingezi@163.com, yangfm@routon.com, lppang@hust.edu.cn
[2] Department of Computer Science, New Mexico Institute of Mining and Technology,
Socorro, New Mexico, 87801-4796, USA
xqin@cs.nmt.edu

Abstract. Most existing real-time fault-tolerant scheduling algorithms for heterogeneous distributed systems can achieve high reliability for non-preemptive and aperiodic tasks. However, the existing scheduling algorithms assume that status of each backup copy is either active or passive. To remedy this deficiency, we propose a novel reliability model tailored for preemptive periodic tasks. Next, we develop two real-time fault-tolerant algorithms (NRFTAHS and RDFTAHS) for heterogeneous distributed systems. NRFTAHS manages to assign tasks in a way to improve system schedulabilties, whereas RDFTAHS aims at boosting system reliability without adding extra hardware. Unlike the existing scheduling schemes, our algorithms consider backup copies in both active and passive forms. Therefore, our approaches are more flexible than the alternative ones. Finally, we quantitatively compare our schemes with two existing algorithms in terms of performability measured as a function of schedulability and reliability. Experiments results show that RDFTAHS substantially improves the overall performance over NRFTAH.

1 Introduction

With the development of high speed network and high performance computers, heterogeneous distributed systems have been widely applied for critical real-time systems, in which real-time and fault-tolerant abilities are two indispensable requirements.

To exploit high performances for real-time heterogeneous systems, much attention has been paid to real-time scheduling algorithms in context of heterogeneous systems. Ranaweer and Agrawal developed a scheduling scheme named SDTP for heterogeneous systems. Reliability costs was factored in some scheduling algorithms for tasks with precedence constrains [2][3]. Although schedulability is a main objective of these scheduling algorithms, the algorithms neither consider timing constraints nor support fault-tolerance. In addition, reliability models in these studies are geared to handle aperiodic, non-preemptive tasks.

Fault-tolerance, an inherent requirement of real-time systems, can be achieved in several approaches. One efficient fault tolerant technique, of course, is scheduling algorithms, among which the Primary-backup scheme plays an important role. In this approach, two versions of one task are scheduled on two different processors and an

L.T. Yang et al. (Eds.): ATC 2006, LNCS 4158, pp. 571–580, 2006.

acceptance test is used to check the correctness of schedules [4,5,6]. The three variants of this scheme include active backup copy[4], passive backup copy[5], and primary backup copy overlapping[6]. Generally speaking, backup copy is always preferred to be executed as passive backup copy, because it can take the advantages of *backup copy overloading* and *backup copy de-allocation* technique to improve schedulability[4,5]. Primary backup copy overlapping technique is a tradeoff technique between the other two and can exploit the advantages of both the other two approaches[6].

Both active backup copies and passive backup copies have been incorporated into the Rate-Monotonic First-Fit assignment algorithm to provide fault-tolerance[7]. This scheme overcomes the drawbacks of timing constraints on backup copies to some extends. However, this scheduling algorithm neither considers heterogeneous systems nor takes system reliability into account.

Qin *et. al.* extensively studied real-time fault-tolerant scheduling algorithms based on heterogeneous distributed systems[8,9,10]. However, theses algorithms assume that status of each backup copy is either active or passive. Moreover, they only consider non-preemptive and aperiodic tasks.

Although numerous algorithms have been developed with respect to real-time fault-tolerant scheduling for distributed systems, to the best of our knowledge no work has been done on reliability-driven real-time fault-tolerant scheduling tailored for periodic tasks for heterogeneous distributed systems. In this study, a novel reliability model for real-time periodic tasks is proposed by extending the conventional reliability model designed for aperiodic tasks. In our approach, the primary backup copy approach is leveraged to tolerate single processor failures. Furthermore, two real-time fault-tolerant algorithms are devised for heterogeneous distributed systems. The first algorithm named NRFTAHS aims at assigning tasks in a way to improve schedulabilty of system, while the second algorithm termed as RDFTAHS employs the reliability measure as a major objective for scheduling real-time tasks. To quantify the combined metric of schedulability and reliability, the *Performability* measure is introduced. Finally, simulation experiments were conducted to compare the two algorithms in several aspects. The experiments results indicate that RDFTAHS performs significantly better than NRFTAHS with respect to reliability with marginal degradation in schedulability and, therefore, RDFTAHS substantially improves the overall performance over NRFTAH.

The paper is organized as follows: In section 2, a system model and assumptions are presented. Section 3 proposes reliability model for periodic tasks. Two novel real-time fault-tolerant scheduling algorithms are outlined in Section 4. Simulation experiments and performance analysis are presented in section 5. Finally, Section 6 concludes the paper by summarizing the main contribution of this paper and commenting on future directions of this work.

2   Systems Model

Our paper considers a typical heterogeneous distributed systems consisting of a set of tasks and a set of processors which are characterized as follows.

- A set of processors

  $$\Omega = \{p_1, p_2, ..., p_M\}$$
  $$R = (\lambda_1, \lambda_2, ..., \lambda_M)$$

  Here, Ω is the processor set, p_i is the i-th processor and M is the total number of processor. All processors in the heterogeneous systems are connected by high-speed network. In this model, processor failures are assumed to be independent, and follow a Poison Process with a constant failure rate. R denotes the failure rates vector, wherein λ_i is the failure rate of p_i.

- A set of primary copy of real-time tasks

  $$\Gamma = \{\tau_1, \tau_2, \tau_3, ..., \tau_N\}$$
  $$\tau_i = (C_i, T_i) \quad (i = 1, 2, ..., N)$$

  Here, Γ is the set of tasks, τ_i is the i-th task, and N is the number of tasks which are periodic, independent and preemptive. C_i denotes an execution time vector: $C_i = [c(i,1), c(i,2),...,c(i,M)]$. Where $c(i, j)$ denotes the execution time of taskτ_i on processor p_j. T_i denotes the period of τ_i.

- A set of backup copy of real-time tasks

  $$B\Gamma = \{\beta_1, \beta_2, \beta_3, ..., \beta_N\}$$
  $$\beta_i = (D_i, T_i) \quad i = 1, 2, ..., N$$

  Here, $B\Gamma$ is the set of backup copy of real-time tasks Γ. β_i is the corresponding backup copy of τ_i. Hence, D_i is the execution time vector of β_i. In our mode, it is assumed that backup copy and primary copy of a task are completely identical, that is: $D_i = [c(i,1), c(i,2),...,c(i,M)]$. Correspondingly, T_i denotes the period of β_i.

  In our system model, as in [7], the backup copy has two statuses: *passive* backup-copy and *active* backup copy. When we assign a task, we assign its primary copy before assigning the backup copy. The status of backup copy is determined by the following:

$$Status(\beta_i) = \begin{cases} passive & T_i - R_{ij} > D_{ik} \\ active & T_i - R_{ij} \le D_{ik} \end{cases} \tag{1}$$

$$where \ P(\tau_i) = P_j \ and \ P(\beta_i) = P_k$$

Here, R_{ij} denotes the WCRT(worst case response time) of τ_i which is assigned to P_j. For ease of presentation, γ_i represents a primary copy or a backup copy, namely, $\gamma_i = \tau_i$ or β_i.

To concentrate on our concerned problems, we make the following assumptions about failure characteristic of the hardware:

1. Hardware provides fault isolation mechanism, that is a faulty processor cannot cause incorrect behaviors in a non-faulty processors;
2. Processors fail in a fail-stop manner, which means a processor is either operational or cease functioning;
3. The failure of a processor is detected by the remaining ones within the closest completion time of a task scheduled on the faulty processor.

3 Reliability Model Based on Periodic Tasks

In this section, we attempt to address the issue of reliability for periodic tasks in heterogeneous systems. In [2], reliability is defined as the probability that the system can run an entire task set successfully. Furthermore, the definition of reliability costs is proposed. However, the definition of reliability costs is based on aperiodic, non-preemptive tasks set which is not applicable for periodic, preemptive tasks set. Because, usually, the periodic tasks will run periodically and will not cease until we force it to or external events. To solve this issue, we firstly analyze the characteristics of periodic tasks and the failure characteristic of heterogeneous processors, and then a definition of reliability costs based on periodic, preemptive tasks set is investigated.

It is worth noting that not only the periodic tasks are periodic in nature, but also the behavior of real-time tasks set as whole is periodic. The hyperperiod H can be seen as the period of the tasks set. H is defined as the least common factor of periods of all tasks sets, namely, $H = \text{lcm}\{T_i | \tau_i \in \Gamma\}$).

It is also noted that the processor failures are assumed to be independent and follow a Poisson Process with a constant failure rate. Moreover, because the Poisson Process is a stable incremental process, the processors have equal fault probability during any equal time interval on the same processor. Thus, we can study the reliability of tasks set in a hyperperiod as the metric of reliability of the system.

To simplify our discussion without losing generality, we have the following assumptions:

1. If a processor fails when it is period, the failed processor will be replaced by a spare processor immediately. So, we do not consider it as a critical failure.
2. If a processor fails while the processor is working, we can use a spare processor and certain processor replacing mechanism(e.g., *FTRMFF-Replacing* presented in [7]) to recover the system to the non-faulty state after some time.

With the above two assumptions along with the single processor failure assumption, we can safely only consider the system reliability in fault-free scenario. Moreover, we only need to consider the effects of processors failure on tasks while processor is working. Therefore, we can redefine the system reliability based on periodic task set as the probability of system can run the entire task set in a hyperperiod while no critical failure occurs. Thus,

$$Reliability = \exp(-\sum_{k=1}^{M} (\sum_{P(\tau_i)=P_k} \lambda_k * C[i,k] * H\!\!\Big/_{T_i} + \sum_{P(\tau_i)=P_k}^{Status(\beta i)=active} \lambda_k * D[i,k] * H\!\!\Big/_{T_i})) \qquad (2)$$

$$= \exp(-H * \sum_{k=1}^{M} \lambda_k (\sum_{P(\tau i)=P_k} C[i,k]\!\!\Big/_{T_i} + \sum_{P(\tau i)=P_k}^{Status(\beta i)=active} D[i,k]\!\!\Big/_{T_i}))$$

According to the above definition of reliability, we can derive the definition of reliability costs based on our system model as.

Definition 1. When we assign both primary copy set Γ and backup copy set $B\Gamma$ of a set of real-time tasks on a set of heterogeneous processors Ω. The system Reliability-Costs is defined as follows:

$$Reliability\ Costs(\Gamma, B\Gamma, \Omega) = \sum_{k=1}^{M} \lambda_k \left(\sum_{P(\tau i)=P_k} C[i,k] \Big/ T_i + \sum_{P(\beta i)=P_k}^{Status(\beta i)=active} D[i,k] \Big/ T_i \right) \quad (3)$$

Clearly, in order to increase the reliability of system we have to reduce the reliability costs as much as possible. The first item in the parentheses of (2) denotes the unreliability contributed by primary copy on their corresponding processors, while the second item is due to the active backup copy. This inspires us that allocating primary copy and active backup copy with greater load to more reliable processors might be good heuristic to decrease the reliability costs. Moreover, it is highly desirable to make as many backup copies as possible to be executed as passive status. Because, on one hand, it can increase the system schedulability, and can decrease the reliability costs on the other hand.

4 Proposed Scheduling Algorithms

In this section, we propose two algorithms for scheduling periodic tasks set along with their corresponding backup copy on a heterogeneous distributed system. The objective of the first algorithm, NRFTAHS, is to maximize the schedulability of the system and does no take reliability into account. By contrast, the other one, RDFTAHS, tries to minimize the total reliability costs of the system while retaining the schedulability of the system.

As [7], before task copies are assigned, both primary copy and backup copy are ordered by increasing period to simplify our algorithm. Thus, tasks are assigned to processors following the order:

$$\tau_1, \beta_1, \tau_2, \beta_2, ..., \tau_N, \beta_N \quad (4)$$

4.1 NRFTAHS

The main objective of the NRFTAHS is to maximize the schedulability of the system. The gists of NRFTAHS are:

1. Try to assign primary copy to a processor on which the execution time is shortest.
2. Try to schedule backup copy as a passive copy whenever possible.
3. If a backup copy has to be scheduled as an active backup copy, the algorithm endeavors to assign backup copy to processor on which the execution time is minimal.

Before presenting our algorithm, an execution time order vector for each task is introduced.

Definition 2. Given a set of real-time tasks Γ and a set of processors Ω. An execution time order vector for each task τ_i is defined as exec_order(i) = $[et_{i1}, et_{i2}, ..., et_{iM}]$, where et_{ij} ($1 \leq j \leq M$) is the processor number. exec_order(i) is sorted in the order of non-decreasing execution time of τ_i on processor set Ω, namely:

$$\forall i \in [1, N], \forall j, k \in [1, M] : (j < k \rightarrow (C[i, et_{ij}] \leq C[i, et_{ik}]))$$

The algorithm NRFTAHS is described as follow:

Algorithm: NRFTAHS

1) Initialization: reorder primary and backup copies following decreasing RM priorities as (4); generate execution time vector Exec_order(i) of each task i;

2) **for** $i \leftarrow 1,2,..., N$ **do** /* allocating processor to both primary and backup copies of N tasks*/

3)   found_active ← FALSE;

4)   **for** $k \leftarrow 1, 2, ..., M$ **do**

5)   **for** $s \leftarrow 1, 2, ..., M$, $s \neq k$ **do**

   Step 5.1: Check the schedulability of τ_i and β_i on processor exec_orer[i, k] and exec_orer[i, k], respectively. Determine the status of β_i according to (1);

   Step 5.2: If both τ_i and β_i can successfully scheduled on processor exec_orer[i, k] and processor exec_orer[i, s] respectively, and status(β_i) = *passive*, then **go to** (2);

   Step 5.3: if both τ_i and β_i can successfully scheduled on processor exec_orer[i, k] and processor exec_orer[i, s] respectively, *status*(β_i) = *active* and found_active = FALSE, then found_active←TRUE, save the processor exec_orer[i, k], exec_orer[i, s] number to temporary variable;

6)   **end for**

7)   **end for**

8)   **if** (found_active = TRUE)

9)   Set P(τ_{ij}), P (β_i) to the processor recorded in step 5);

10)   **else**

11)   ret_value ← FAIL; **return** ret_value;

12)   **end if**

13)   **end for**

14) ret_value ← SUCCESS **return** ret_value;

4.2 RDFTAHS

RDFTAHS consider the heterogeneities of reliability costs, thereby improving the reliability of the system without extra hardware costs. The objective of RDFTAHS is to minimize the reliability costs. The gists of NRFTAHS are:

1. Try to assign primary copy to a processor on which the reliability cost is minimal.
2. Try to schedule backup copy as a passive copy whenever possible.
3. If a backup copy has to be scheduled as an active backup copy, the algorithm endeavors to assigned backup copy to processor on which the reliability costs is minimal.

Before presenting our algorithm, A reliability costs vector is defined.

Definition 3. Given a set of real-time tasks Γ, corresponding backup copy $B\Gamma$ and a set of processors Ω. A reliability costs vector of τ_i and β_i is defined as $RCV_i = [rcv_{i1}, ..., rcv_{iM}]$, where $rcv_{ij} = (rc_{ij}, \rho_{ij})$. rcv_{ij} is derived from vector C_i and Ω. Namely, $rc_{ij} = (C[i, \rho_{ij}]/T_i) \times \lambda \rho_{ij}$. Elements in RCV_i is sorted in order of non-decreasing reliability costs, namely:

$$\forall i \in [1, N], \forall j, k \in [1, M] : (j < k \rightarrow (rc_{ij} \leq rc_{ik}));$$

The algorithm RDFTAHS is described as follow:

Algorithm: RDFTAHS

1) Initialization: reorder primary and backup copies following decreasing RM priorities as (4);generate execution time vector exec_order(i) and reliability costs vector RCV_i for each task i;

2) *for* i $\leftarrow$ 1, 2, ...N *do*

3) found_active$\leftarrow$FALS, tmp_rc$\leftarrow$0 ;

4) *for* k $\leftarrow$ 1, 2, ...,M *do*

5) *for* s$\leftarrow$1, 2, ...M, s$\neq$k *do*

   Step 5.1: Assign primary copy τ_i to processor $RCV_i.\rho_{ik}$, which follows the order defined by reliability costs vector. Assign backup copy β_i to processor exec_order(i, s), which follows the order defined by execution time order vector; Status of β_i is determined by (1);

   Step 5.2: if both τ_i and β_i are schedulable, and status(β_i) = *passive*, then assignτ_i and β_i to processor $RCV_i.\rho_{ik}$ and Exec_order(i, s), respectively; *go to* (2);

   Step 5.3: if both τ_i and β_i are schedulable, and status (β_i) = *active*;

      Step 5.3.1: if found_active = FALSE, then calculate the reliability costs of β_i on processor exec_order(i, s), tmp_rc; found_active $\leftarrow$ TRUE ; save processor $RCV_i.\rho_{ik}$ and exec_order(i, s) to temporary variable.

      Step 5.3.2: if found_active = TRUE, and the reliability costs of β_i on processor exec_order(i, s) is smaller than tmp_rc, then set tmp_rc $\leftarrow$ reliability costs of β_i on processor exec_order(i, s); save processor $RCV_i.\rho_{ik}$ and exec_order(i, s) to temporary variable;

6) *end for*

7) *end for*

8) *if* (found_active = TRUE)

9)   Set P(τ_i) and P(β_i) with the processor number saved at Step 5.3; Set status(β_i) $\leftarrow$*active*;

10) *else* ret_value $\leftarrow$ FAIL; *return* ret_value;

12) *end if*

13) *end for*

14) ret_value $\leftarrow$ SUCCESS; *return* ret_value;

5 Performance Evaluation

In this section, a number of simulations are carried out to evaluate the two algorithms proposed in the paper and compare them in several aspects. Three performance metrics are used to capture there aspects of real-time fault-tolerant scheduling. The first metric is Reliability Costs, defined in (3); The second one is *Schedulability*, defined to be the minimal number of processors(MNP) required by a certain number of tasks. In order to comprehensively measure the performance of our algorithms, we introduce a new metric, *Performability*, defined to be the product of the *Schedulability* and Reliability Costs. Formally:

Performability(Γ, BΓ, Ω)=Schedulability$\times$ Reliability Costs(Γ, BΓ, Ω)

Here, *Schedulability* is the MNP of a set of primary copy Γ along with its corresponding backup copy set $B\Gamma$ scheduled by any algorithms proposed above. *Reliability Costs* is obtained by a scheduling Γ and $B\Gamma$ on MNP processors. Clearly, the smaller *Performability*, the better overall performances.

Our simulations are presented for large task sets with periodic tasks which are generated according to following parameters:

1) *Periods of tasks* (T_i)—a value generated randomly distributed in [0,500];
2) *Execution time of any task on any processor*$(C[i, j])$—a value taken from a random distribution in the interval $0 < C[i, j] \leqslant \alpha\, T_i$, parameter $\alpha = \max\limits_{i=1,\dots,N, j=1,\dots,M} C[i,j]/T_i$, which represents the maximum load occurring in the task set on all processors. Three values are chosen for α, namely, 0.2, 0.5, and 0.8.
3) *Size of any task set*(L)—a value selected from a specific set, namely, [200, 400, 600, 800, 1000].

Besides, for the heterogeneous systems, the failure rate(FR) for each processor is uniformly selected between the range 0.95 to $1.05*10^{-6}$/hour(10^{-4})[11].

5.1 Reliability

In this experiment, the Reliability Costs of the two algorithms are evaluated. Fig.1 displays the Reliability Costs obtained by two algorithms as a function of size of task set. The number of processor (*Processor_Num*) is in proportional to the size of task set. Formally:

$$Processor\_Num = (L*15)/200$$

From Fig.1, it is clear that all values of Reliability Costs increase as L increase, as expected. For fixed task set, Reliability Costs also increase as α increase. This is because the bigger L or α, the more computation time are needed; therefore, the Reliability Costs increase. Most importantly, it is observed that RDFTAHS performs better NRFTAHS, in terms of reliability costs.

5.2 Schedulability

Another important metric for real-time fault-tolerant scheduling algorithms is *Schedulability*. Here, the *Schedulability* is defined as the minimal number of processors(MNP) to which all tasks, together with their corresponding backup copy, can be scheduled to finish before their specific deadlines. Therefore, we devise an algorithm, called Find Minimal Number of Processors, to find the MNP of a give task set[13].

Fig.2 illustrates the simulation results. Actually, RDFTAHS requires only one more processor than NRFTAHS in most cases. This result indicates that NRFTAHS is a little inferior to RDFTAHS.

5.3 Performability

In order to compare the overall performance, the third experiment is carried out to compare the two algorithms in terms of *Performability*.

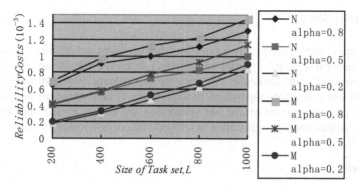

Fig. 1. Comparison of the Reliability Costs between NRFTAHS and RDFTAHS.

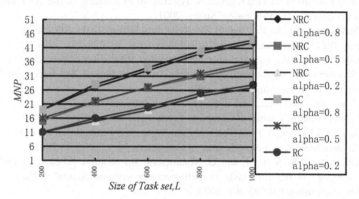

Fig. 2. Comparison of the MNP between NRFTAHS and RDFTAHS.

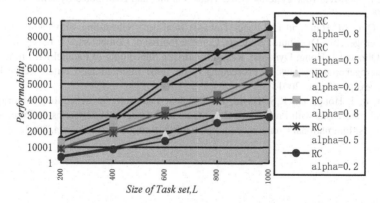

Fig. 3. Comparison of the *Performability* between NRFTAHS and RDFTAHS

Fig.3. reveals the Performability as a function of the size of task set. The number of processors used for each task set is MNP obtained in the previous experiment. As can be observed, RDFTAHS outperforms NRFTAHS considerably.

6 Conclusions

In this paper, we developed two real-time fault-tolerant scheduling algorithms for heterogeneous distributed systems and conduct extensive simulations about them in several aspects.Future studies in this area are two folders. First, we intend to study more efficient scheduling algorithms in the context of heterogeneous distributed systems. Second, we plan to extend our scheduling algorithms by incorporating precedence constrains and communication heterogeneities in distributed systems.

References

1. S. Ranaweera, and D.P. Agrawal. Scheduling of Periodic Time Critical Applications for Pipelined Execution on Heterogeneous Systems. In Proceeding of the 2001 International Conference on Parallel Processing, Spain, 2001
2. S. Srinivasan, and N.K. Jha. Safety and Reliability Driven Tasks Allocation in distributed Systems. IEEE Trans. Parallel and distributed systems, 10: 238-251, 1999
3. A. Dogan, and F. Ozguner. Reliable matching and scheduling of precedence-constrained tasks in heterogeneous distributed computing. In Proceeding of 29th International Conference on Parallel Processing, Spain, 2001.
4. C.H. Yang, G. Deconinck, and W.H. Gui, Fault-tolerant scheduling for real-time embedded control systems. Journal of Computer Science and Technology, 19:191-202, 2004.
5. H. Liu, and S.M. Fei. A Fault-Tolerant Scheduling Algorithm Based on EDF for Distributed Control Systems. Chinese Journal of Computers, 14:1371-1378, 2003.
6. A.l. Omari R, A.K. Somani, and G. Manimaran. An adaptive scheme for fault-tolerant scheduling of soft real-time tasks in multiprocessor systems. Journal of Parallel and Distributed Computing, 65: 595-608, 2005.
7. A.A Bertossi, L V Mancini, and F. Rossini. Fault-tolerant rate-monotonic first-fit scheduling in hard-real-time systems. IEEE Trans. Parallel and Distributed Systems, 10: 934-945, 1999.
8. X. Qin, Z.F Han, and L.P Pang. Towards Real-time Scheduling with Fault-tolerance in Heterogeneous Distributed Systems. Chinese Journal of Computers, 25: 121-124, 2002.
9. X Qin, and J. Hong, Dynamic, Reliability-driven Scheduling of Parallel Real-time Jobs in Heterogeneous Systems. In Proceeding of the 2001 International Conference on Parallel Processing, Spain, 2001.
10. X.Qin, J. Hong, and R.S. David, An Efficient Fault-tolerant Scheduling Algorithm for Real-time Tasks with Precedence Constraints in Heterogeneous Systems. In Proceeding of the 31st International Conference on Parallel Processing (ICPP), Canada, 2002.

Active Fault-Tolerant System for Open Distributed Computing

Rodrigo Lanka, Kentaro Oda, and Takaichi Yoshida

Graduate School of Computer Science and Systems Engineering
Kyushu Institute of Technology, Fukuoka, Japan
{lanka@mickey.ai, oda@ci, takaichi@ai}.kyutech.ac.jp

Abstract. Computer systems are growing in complexity and sophistication as open distributed systems and new technologies are used to achieve higher reliability and performance. Open distributed systems are some of the most successful structures ever designed for the computer community together with their undisputed benefits for users. However, this structure has also introduced a few side-effects, most notably the unanticipated runtime events and reconfiguration burdens imposed by the environmental changes. In this paper, we design a model that exploits the knowledge of pre-fault behavior to predict the suspected environmental faults and failures. Further, it can analyse the current underlying environmental behavior, in terms of current faults and failures. Therefore, this model mainly provides proactive as well as real-time fault-tolerant approaches in order to address unanticipated events and unpredictable hazards in distributed systems. Therefore, providing active fault tolerance could have a major impact with the growing requirements to support autonomic computing to overcome their rapidly growing complexity and to enable their further growth.

1 Introduction

Open distributed systems are some of the most successful structures ever designed for the computer community together with their undisputed benefits for users. Its importance is further highlighted by the ever increasing usage of open distributed systems in many aspects of today's life. However, this structure has also introduced a few side-effects, most notably the unanticipated runtime events and reconfiguration burdens imposed by the environmental changes. A general problem of modern distributed systems is that their complexity is increasingly becoming the limiting factor in their further developments. Moreover, in open systems, we cannot predict all future configurations at the system design stage because available services, resources, protocols, network bandwidth and security policies could change with its runtime environment.

In distributed computing, to gain high system performance, a required level of reliability has to be maintained. Therefore, depending on the fluctuations of the environment and its unpredictability, providing required reliability also brings in the need for meeting a set of complex requirements. Moreover, the reliability of distributed systems mainly depends on both the failures (i.e. operating systems, software, network and etc) as well as the performance (i.e. CPU load average, network latency, bandwidth, memory usage and etc) of the environment.

L.T. Yang et al. (Eds.): ATC 2006, LNCS 4158, pp. 581–590, 2006.

This paper highlights three main contributions: Firstly, the Active Fault-Tolerant (AFT) model exploits the knowledge of pre-fault behavior to predict the suspected environmental faults and failures. This fault prediction reduces the unpredictable nature of the failures up to a certain limit. For instance, high message failure rate, high latency, insufficient memory, high CPU load average and etc will give some indications to faults and failures that can occur in future with high probability. Therefore, this model can provide proactive fault-tolerant approaches in order to address suspected events and hazards in distributed systems. In other words, it provides the required reliability by analyzing the environment and selects the optimal AFT replication strategy for the existing (or suspected) conditions even before the failures occur.

Secondly, however, we can not ignore the traditional real-time fault-tolerant approaches, as we can not predict each and every fault and failure in advance. The unanticipated failures that cannot be predicted ahead of time, can severely affect the reliability and performance of open distributed systems. Some examples of such situations are failures of operating systems, failures of hardware components, network breakdowns and power interruptions. Therefore, AFT model deals not only as an actuator for sensor faults, but also tolerates current failures in the underlying system.

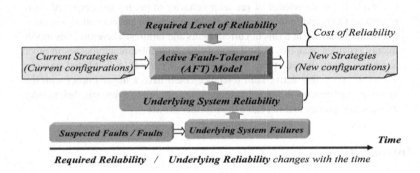

Fig. 1. The active fault-tolerant (AFT) model

Finally, the AFT model can cater the user required reliability which mainly depends on the degree of replication and the time required to reach the agreement among replicas. This reliability levels in the system may vary according to the decisions of users and its cost would be mainly depends on the environment as depicted in Figure 1. However, the user must consider the trade-off between the reliability degradation and the cost of gaining reliability (i.e. cost of reliability degradation due to a single replication protocol vs. dynamically transition overhead among multiple replication protocols).

The significance with the AFT model is that it uses information extracted from underlying system, replica members and clients to maintain both the reliability and performance of the system at its required level. Therefore, providing active fault tolerance could have a major impact with the demanding requirements to support autonomic computing to overcome their rapidly growing complexity and to enable their further developments. This pragmatic approach is a part of the Juice system which was developed by our research group and the new version of the Juice, Juice2.0 is been developed.

2   Approach of the Active Fault-Tolerant Model

The Active Fault-Tolerant (AFT) model is designed on the Juice object model, which comprises adaptability as one of the main features. It allows objects to change its behavior on the fly by replicating in a modular manner [1], [2]. Adaptation in this model is accomplished through reconfiguration of the object during its lifetime.

2.1   Proactive Approach

Proactive fault tolerance involves designing a mechanism that can forecast with some confidence to determine when and what kind of faults and failures can occur. For an example, if AFT predicted that a server had a high chance of failing within the next few minutes it could have taken necessary steps to avoid the failure. The proactive approach involves monitoring both the suspected and the current known faults of the underlying environment to trigger the AFT mechanisms in advance of the occurrence of the failure. For instance, the lost or delayed messages (timeout) are common in networked communication, and if occurs consecutively, such losses (faults) could cause system failures. It should be noted that the faults may not necessarily cause failures (unless the faulty part is used), but increases its probability.

Therefore, at this point, our aim is to employ available information about both the faults (suspected/current) and the suspected failures of the underlying system in order to provide the required reliability. AFT make use of the knowledge of faults and failures to notify potentially damaged areas of the system proactively. AFT does this in order to contain the tainted areas. Therefore, in proactive fault tolerance, there are two aspects. First, the ability to predict failures and second to tolerate the failures by using AFT strategies before they actually occur. These strategies (will be discussed in the next chapter) would enable the objects to change its respective behavior that fulfills the reliability requirements of the open distributed system.

2.2   Real-Time Approach

Though the proactive fault tolerant approach would gain some benefits than real-time fault tolerance, we identified that some failures might occur, so abruptly that AFT can not forecast them (i.e. network disconnections, power breakdowns, software crashes and etc). Therefore, it is not possible to ignore the real-time fault-tolerant approaches, as AFT can not predict each and every fault in advance. In contrast, the real-time approach involves monitoring of the current system failures and triggering the AFT mechanisms in order to maintain the required level of reliability dynamically. The real-time approach is therefore based on real-time decision-making and reconfiguring according to the current failures of the system, as it is not always possible to predict failures for every kind of faults. Therefore, under real-time fault tolerance, first AFT identifies current failures of the underlying system and then tolerates them by using its adaptation strategies accordingly.

3   AFT Strategies

The function of replication is a complex one as it includes the replication degree, the replica migration (placement), the replication protocol, the communication among the replicas and etc. Further, it is expected that open distributed systems maintain their reliability throughout its lifetime, even when it is frequently disturbed by the changes of the underlying environment. However, our argument is that it is still difficult to presume a single replication strategy to get the required level of reliability throughout the lifetime of an object. That is, because it is not practicable to provide one general-purpose replication strategy (to maintain reliability) that can be parameterized to accommodate all underlying environmental fluctuations. Furthermore, maintaining the degree of replication at constant level does not ensure a constant level of reliability as long as the underlying environment continues to change.

The AFT strategies can be classified as (a) Adjusting the degree of replication (b) Migration of current replicas and (c) Shifting into a suitable replication protocol adaptively. The key factor in strategy selection by AFT model is the trade-off between communication cost and reliability.

3.1   Adjusting the Degree of Replication

The optimal degree of replication can be achieved by the AFT model as it is able to adapt to the environment on the fly. According to the AFT policy, there are two aspects to why an object may change the degree of replication. On the one hand, an object will increase the degree of replication when a member is admitted to the group to increase the reliability (i.e. if AFT predicts that an object has a high probability of failing within the next few seconds or when the reliability of the underlying system goes down then the AFT creates a new replica and admits to the group to ensure the required reliability) or when one recovers from failure. On the other hand, it will decrease the degree of replication when an existing member leaves the group to reduce the reliability (this could occur when the group concerns about the additional communication costs incurred for unwanted reliability) or when an existing member fails.

3.2   Migration of Current Replicas

Replica placement is commonly employed by open distributed systems to improve the communication delay experienced by their clients. The reliability of a replicated object is significantly affected by not only the number of replicas it has but also their placement. Therefore, it appears that migrating of an object onto another member who is more reliable than the current member could also be a feasible strategy [3]. It means that migrating objects from heavily loaded processors onto relatively lightly loaded processors in order to meet the system requirements. Past researches also proposed some algorithms on dynamic replacement of objects and make the system more responsive to changes in the environment [4]. Moreover, other properties of members, such as available storage space, bandwidth, reliability of the server and etc are necessary to consider in replica placement. The prime concern of this strategy is to determine which nodes should host replicas considering the reliability and communication cost.

3.3   Shifting into a Suitable Replication Protocol Adaptively

Existing taxonomies of replication techniques take into account a broad spectrum of protocols, including those with both different levels of consistency, update frequency, communication and etc [5]. It is our conjecture that *the server architecture* and *the server interaction* are appropriate methods to classify the protocols into a spectrum (Figure 2).

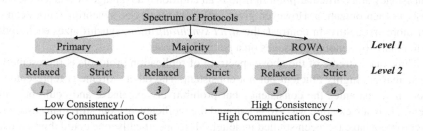

Fig. 2. Spectrum of replication protocols

Level 1 - The Server Architecture can be divided into three major protocols as *Primary copy, Majority quorums* and *Read-one Write-all (ROWA)* protocols.

The primary copy replication requires any update to the objects sent to the primary copy first. A message normally accesses a subset of all data items. When a data item is written, a write request is sent to the node that holds the primary copy. The updates are then propagated to other back-up sites asynchronously. Therefore, this extreme is more graceful when dealing with efficiency in terms of communication even when lots of write messages are available. However, primary copy approach has a single point of failure and elections problems.

In contrast, the other extreme is ROWA replication and it allows updates to be performed anywhere in the system. That is, updates can concurrently arrive at two different copies of the same data item and it is more graceful in situations, where it may be important that the information is replicated immediately. Conceivably sometimes, compared with the situation which requires the primary election procedures, ROWA approach is more graceful when dealing with failures since no election protocol is necessary to continue processing as the primary copy is needed.

A majority quorum system is defined as a set of sub sets of replicas, or quorums, with pair-wise non-empty intersections. The non-empty intersection property is crucial in that it allows any quorum to take decisions on behalf of the replica group and guarantee the overall consistency. In the majority quorum, read and write quorums must fulfill two constraints. That is twice the write quorum and both read and write quorums must be greater than the total replicas.

Other replication protocols revolve around theses protocols offering different configurations. Therefore, according to the requirements, we can accommodate more types of replication protocols (e.g. tree and grid) and pool them appropriately. A principle aspect of such selections is the trade-off between reliability and communication cost.

Level 2 - The Server Interaction can be divided into two synchronization methods as *relaxed synchronization* and *strict synchronization*. Message synchronization depends on both the network traffic generated by the replication algorithm and the overall communication overheads. Therefore, we consider two types of synchronizations according to the degree of communication.

The *relaxed synchronization*, synchronizes the replicas by sending a single message containing a set of updates within a given period of time. The ability to guarantee the consistency at a particular point in time is an additional advantage of relaxed (session-based) synchronization. However, given sufficient resources, synchronizations can occur more frequently. In contrast, the *strict synchronization*, synchronizes each update individually by sending messages on a per update basis.

Thus, one extreme of the above spectrum of replication protocols is represented by those that are highly efficient but not consistent. The other extreme is represented by those that guarantee the consistency but prohibitively expensive and could be inefficient. There are existing ways to get around the inefficiencies, but still, many aspects of the problem have not been studied in detail. More specifically, one could think of using quorum based strategies to achieve consistency across the cluster while still minimizing the overall cost in terms of performance penalties, communication overheads, and overall availability [6].

4   Design the AFT Model on the Juice Object

4.1   Internal Objects of the Juice Model

The Juice object [1], [2] is based on the adaptable object model. These objects are user-defined, first-class and adapt themselves to the changing execution environment and support network transparency and adaptation properties for open distributed environments. Adaptable Juice objects can reconfigure its internal objects at runtime according to the new configurations for the purpose of adapting to the changing execution environment. The adaptable Juice object consists of five internal objects as depicted in Figure 3.

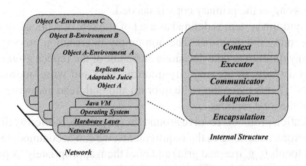

Fig. 3. The adaptable Juice Object model

4.2   Encapsulation of the AFT Model on Juice

The AFT model provides adaptation facilities for open distributed environments as this model is designed on the Juice object model (the internal structure of the model is illustrated in Figure 4). It can acquire adaptation as it inherits the properties of the Juice object model. Adaptation Handler (AH) and Underlying System Information Evaluator (USIE) reside within the adaptation object while Replication Handler (RH) and Client Member Information Evaluator (CMIE) reside within the communicator of the Juice object in such way that the communication cost can be minimized.

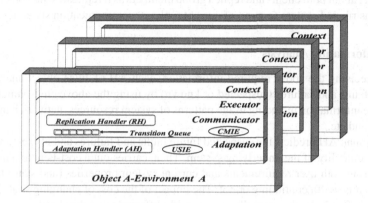

Fig. 4. Encapsulation of the AFT

5   AFT Framework

5.1   Collection of Information

The Underlying System Information Evaluator (USIE) runs on each replica (Juice object) of the replica group to collect the local resource information. The USIE collects the usage patterns of resources (i.e. available/used memory, effective network bandwidth, CPU load average and etc) and information of the underlying environmental failures (i.e. current failures of operating systems, network disconnections and etc) through **monitor objects**. To provide these two kinds of information to the USIE, each machine of the network holds a monitor object that seeks information from both the underlying virtual machine and operating system (Figure 5).

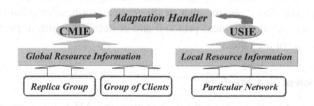

Fig. 5. Information flow of the AFT model

The Client Member Information Evaluator (CMIE) also handles both the current replica group member's information and the most recently connected client's information (i.e. message failure rate, response time, network latency and etc). This global resource information can be gathered from the **communicator** of the Juice model that communicates with all group members and clients. Therefore, USIE and CMIE are aware the situations of underlying environment, replica group and current clients and communicate this information to the Adaptation Handler (AH) which resides in the adaptation object of the Juice object model.

On the other hand, Replication Handler (RH) also provides the relevant information to the AH about both clients and replica group members as it replicates the objects across in the distributed system (e.g. no of current replicas, communication style and etc).

5.2   Information Analysis

After receiving the above required information, each AH of Juice object analyses the system faults and failures (suspected or known) by using the above environmental and resource information including usage patterns of system resources, network bandwidth, latency and etc.

After that, AH predicts the suspected future faults and failures and also estimates the current reliability of the underlying system. Then, carries out a cost-benefit analysis by considering both user requirements and current system properties (and state) to check whether it is worth continuing or not. The impact of the cost of changing strategies and the trade-offs need to be carefully studied with different reliability levels.

If it is worth to continue, AH analyses the underlying system and selects the best fit fault-tolerant strategy according to the AFT algorithm. This strategy suites the current environmental conditions and provides the required reliability for the system at the optimal cost. This information enables the AFT algorithm to decide how many replicas to create for each object (e.g. depends on message failure rate, CPU load average, system failure rate, network bandwidth and etc), where to place the replicas (e.g. depends on communication cost, CPU power and etc), and which replication protocol style to enforce for the replicated object (e.g. when need to change consistency levels, to eliminate unwanted cost for excess reliability and communication).

According to the environmental requirements, selecting the optimal replication protocol from the pool, should follow an agreement amongst all the adaptation handlers of the replica group. On the other hand, the selection of strategies could be done even according to the user requirements too. When the algorithm adopts the majority decision criterion to select the most optimal replication protocol, the members of the replica group take a vote, and if a majority agrees for switching into the new protocol, then they all switch together. Thus, one member of the replica group, selected at random, gathers the votes and decides the next protocol and switches the current protocol into the optimal on behalf of the others.

5.3   Execution of New Strategy

Finally, when a strategy is selected for execution, the AH notifies the RH to replace themselves with the new object according to the new strategy selected by itself (AH).

As an example, suppose when systems reliability goes down, then the model selects one strategy which suits system's reliability requirements.

The RH is the in charge of both enforcing the optimal strategy and maintaining information about all the clients associated with the replica group. The RH considers the network resources and the clients currently in the system, and enforces the strategy that needs to be executed. Finally, reconfigure the previous configurations according to the current one and the members then resume, pending and delivering messages according to the new communication protocol.

Each member compares whether the current system reliability satisfies with either system required or user required reliability level. However, it is difficult to estimate the total cost of the system, because each member of the replica group is affected by its local environmental changes. Therefore, while each member estimates its local cost by itself and the decision on total cost is made by all.

This model is based on component composition and addresses two levels of configuration: i.e. upper (Juice) and lower levels. The upper level handles the reconfigurations of the Juice object model components (i.e. communicator, adaptation object and etc) while the lower level reconfigures the objects that lie inside each Juice object model components (i.e. RH, AH and etc). One of the main advantages of this approach is that, because there are two separate configuration levels, it can help reconfiguring one level of components independently without any involvement of the other level. As a result of these two reconfigurable structures, this approach helps to perform its switching strategies without leading to any inconsistencies. Therefore, AFT infrastructure can enhance open distributed applications with novel capabilities of both proactive and real-time fault tolerance.

5.4 Communication Under New Strategy

The replication protocols which are based on group communication have the ability to enhance replication mechanisms by taking advantage of some of the properties of group communication primitives. Therefore, in this research we use an adaptable group communication model in order to keep the required consistency of the messages among the group members. Under the Juice model, the communicator is capable of selecting the optimal communication protocols from a meta-object (pool of all possible communication protocols), which are tailored to the specific strategies needed in each environmental situation [2]. Further, regarding the communication among the Juice replica group members, the message ordering algorithms can be changed and selected according to the type of replication protocol that can optimize the communication cost [7].

6 Concluding Remarks

This paper describes the design of the AFT model, which allows user to specify the quality of service required for replica groups in terms of reliability and performance. The AFT model that we have developed employs a combination of proactive and real-time fault-tolerant approaches in order to address suspected and unanticipated hazards in open distributed environments.

Proactive approach exploits the knowledge (i.e. underlying system states, replica group members and client's information) which gain from the two information evaluators namely USIE and CMIE to provide advance warning (or/and actions) for both suspected or known faults and failures. Further, it can significantly reduce failures by lowering the probability of having a fault in the system. Therefore, it reduces the number of faults and failures experienced at the user level. In contrast, the real-time approach is based on real-time decision-making and reconfiguring according to the current failures of the system as it is not always possible to predict failures for every kind of faults.

This adaptable model is based on three main strategies that can adopt according to the requirements of each adaptable object. Obviously, a single replication protocol cannot cope with all underlying environmental fluctuations that arise in an open distributed environment. The AFT model with its structure facilitates the required degree of reliability in the system and enables it to provide the optimal reliable service even when the underlying system changes prevail.

This paper has also identified the need for new replication protocol classification to deal with different environmental conditions and, thus lays a foundation for switching into an optimal protocol to build and maintain highly reliable and flexible systems.

The adaptable objects can maintain the user required reliability of the system whenever changes in the environment turn the working place to become hostile. AFT allows the system to reconfigure and execute under different situations of the underlying system. Therefore, unlike common replication protocols, our solution is tightly integrated with the underlying environmental changes.

References

1. Leonardo, J.C., Oda, K., and Yoshida, T.: An Adaptable Replication Scheme for Reliable Distributed Object-Oriented Computing, 17th International Conference on Advanced Information Networking and Applications, (2003)
2. Oda, K., Tazuneki, S., and Yoshida, T.: The Flying Object for an Open Distributed Environment, 15th International Conference on Information Networking, (2001)
3. Michal, S., Guillaume, P., and Maarten van S.: Latency-Driven Replica Placement, The International Symposium on Applications and the Internet, (2005)
4. Chen, Y., Katz, R. H., and Kubiatowicz, J. D.: Dynamic Replica Placement for Scalable Content Delivery, 1st International Workshop on Peer-to-Peer Systems, (2002)
5. Wiesmann, M., Pedone, F., Schiper, A., Kemme, B., and Alonso, G.: Understanding Replication in Databases and Distributed Systems, 20th International Conference on Distributed Computing Systems, (2000)
6. Jimenez-Peris, R., Patino-Martinez, M., Kemme, B., and G. Alonso.: How to Select a Replication Protocol According to Scalability, Availability, and Communication Overhead, 20th IEEE Symposium on Reliable Distributed Systems, (2001)
7. Yasutake, Y., Masuyama, Y., Oda, K., and Yoshida, T.: Clear Separation and Combination of Synchronization Constraint for Concurrent Object Oriented Programming, 17th International Conference on Advanced Information Networking and Applications, (2003)

A Time-Cognizant Dynamic Crash Recovery Scheme Suitable for Distributed Real-Time Main Memory Databases

Yingyuan Xiao[1], Yunsheng Liu[2], Xiangyang Chen[3], and Xiaofeng Liu[2]

[1] Department of Computer Science and Engineering, Tianjin University of Technology,
300191, Tianjin, P.R. China
xyyacad@tom.com
[2] Software College, Huazhong University of Science and Technology,
430074, Wuhan, Hubei, P.R. China
ysliu@mail.hust.edu.cn
[3] School of Computer Science and Engineering, Wuhan Institute of Technology,
430073,Wuhan, Hubei, P.R. China

Abstract. Rapid and efficient recovery in the event of site crash is very important for distributed real-time main memory database system. In this paper, the recovery correctness criteria of distributed real-time main memory databases are first given. Then, a time-cognizant dynamic crash recovery scheme (TCDCRS) based on log is presented. TCDCRS uses nonvolatile RAM as logging store and integrates the properties of partitioned logging, ephemeral logging and real-time logging in order to reduce the logging cost as possible during the normal running. During restart recovery after site crashes, a dynamic recovery method based on the classification recovery strategy, which supports concurrent of system services and recovery processing, is adopted to decrease the downtime to the most extent. Experiments and evaluations show that TCDCRS has better performances than traditional recovery schemes in two aspects: the missing deadlines ratio of transactions and the time of system denying services after crashes.

1 Introduction

A distributed real-time database system (DRTDBS) is defined as a distributed database system within which transactions and data have timing constraints. DRTDBSs usually adopt main memory database (MMDB) as their ground support. In an MMDB, "working copy" of database is placed in main memory and "secondary copy" of database on disks serving as backup. We define a DRTDBS integrating MMDB as distributed real-time main memory database system (DRTMMDBS).

The complexity of distributed environments together with volatility and vulnerability of main memory causes a larger possibility of failure in DRTMMDBSs than that in centralized disk resident database systems. At present, the studies of failure recovery for DRTMMDBSs are very scarce, and the existing related works focus on recovery processing for real-time database. To solve the problem of low efficiency of traditional sequential permanent logging, partitioned logging and ephemeral logging

L.T. Yang et al. (Eds.): ATC 2006, LNCS 4158, pp. 591–600, 2006.
© Springer-Verlag Berlin Heidelberg 2006

have been proposed respectively [1-3]. Partitioned logging stores log records according to transaction class (data class), so can avoid performance bottleneck caused by severe contention for single logging store partition. Ephemeral logging don't have to keep log records permanently. The advantage of ephemeral logging is log processing time after failures is reduced prominently. The techniques of accelerating recovery speed were given in [4, 5], but the techniques require stopping system services during the recovery processing after failures. Besides, shadow paging recovery scheme has been proposed [6]. This scheme doesn't require writing up log during the normal running of the system, but requires a large amount of main memory spaces.

This paper presents a time-cognizant dynamic crash recovery scheme (TCDCRS) suitable for DRTMMDBS.

2　Recovery Correctness Criteria

Definition 1. Temporal data object X is defined as the following 3-tuples:

$$<V(X), ST(X), VI(X)>$$

where $V(X)$ denotes the current state or value of X, $ST(X)$ is sampling time scale, i.e. the time of sampling the value of data object X, and $VI(X)$ is the period of validity of X.

Definition 2. A data object X is said to satisfy the temporal (external) consistency, iff $ST(X)+VI(X) \geq T_c$. Here, T_c denotes the current instant.

To aim at DRTMMDBSs, we give the following recovery correctness criteria.

Criterion 1. (Temporal data recovery criterion) $\forall X \in$ TDS, if $ST(X) +VI(X) \leq T_c$, UNDO and REDO recovery operations of aiming at X aren't necessary after failures, but recovering by sampling the corresponding object in real world. Here, TDS denotes the set of temporal data objects.

A DRTMMDBS interacts with the real world directly by triggering the activities, called control transactions that change the states of the real world.

We use A_T denote the activity triggered by a control transaction T, CA_T denote the compensatory or alternative transaction of T.

Criterion 2. (Real world state recovery criterion) If a control transaction T doesn't commit successfully and the same time A_T has happened, the real world states changed by A_T must be restored through executing CA_T.

Suppose a distributed real-time transaction $T=\{st_1, st_2, ... st_m\}$, where st_i $(1 \leq i \leq m)$ stands for a subtransaction of T executed at site i.

Criterion 3. (Distributed real-time transaction REDO recovery criterion) At the failure instant, if T has committed, at failure site i, REDO operations are required to confirm the effect of st_i exception to the following two conditions: 1) the values of data objects updated by st_i have been written into disk databases physically and 2) the data objects updated by st_i meet the condition: $ST(X) +VI(X) \leq T_c$

Criterion 4. (Distributed real-time transaction UNDO recovery criterion) At the failure instant, if T hasn't committed, for each st_i $(1 \leq i \leq m)$, at the corresponding site

UNDO operations are required to erase the effect of st_i exception to the following two conditions: 1) the values of data objects updated by st_i aren't written into disk databases physically and 2) the data objects updated by st_i meet the condition: $ST(X) + VI(X) \leq T_c$

3 Time-Cognizant Dynamic Crash Recovery Scheme

3.1 Logging Scheme of TCDCRS

The conventional recovery schemes adopt sequential permanent logging based on disks. Obviously, the logging scheme hasn't met the high performance requirements of DRTMMDBS. Therefore, we give the logging scheme based on nonvolatile RAM, which integrates the properties of partitioned logging, ephemeral logging and real-time logging, PERT-NVRAM for short.

3.1.1 Transaction Classification Based on PERT-NVRAM

PERT-NVRAM adopts the idea of logging partitions. Thus, the division of transaction classes decides the logging partitions in PERT-NVRAM. In the following text, transactions are classified according to the requirement of logging partitions.

In the following definitions, ST denotes the set of possible transactions in a DRTMMDBS; DS(ST) denotes the set of data objects accessed by the transactions belonging to ST; LS denotes the entire logging storage area; LS_i denotes a partition of LS and $Lr(T_i)$ denotes the log records belonging to transaction T_i.

Definition 3. Suppose $ST_1, ST_2 \subseteq ST$, if $ST_1 \cap ST_2 = \phi$, then ST_1 and ST_2 are said to be disjoint, notated by $ST_1 \perp ST_2$.

Definition 4. Suppose $B = \{ST_1, ST_2, ..., ST_n\}$, $ST_i \subseteq ST$ $(1 \leq i \leq n)$, if $\forall ST_i$, $ST_j \in B$ $(ST_i \perp ST_j)$, then B is said to be a disjoint set.

Definition 5. Let $B = \{ST_1, ST_2, ..., ST_n\}$ be a disjoint set, if $ST_1 \cup ST_2 \cup ... \cup ST_n = ST$, then B is said to be a division of ST, and ST_i $(1 \leq i \leq n)$ is said to be a transaction class.

Definition 6. Let $B = \{ST_1, ST_2, ..., ST_n\}$ be a division of ST, if $\forall ST_i$, $ST_j \in B$ $(DS(ST_i) \cap DS(ST_j) = \phi)$, then B is said to be an orthogonal division, notated by $B \equiv \perp_{division}$.

Definition 7. Suppose $L = \{LS_1, LS_2, ..., LS_n\}$, if the condition, $(\forall LS_i, LS_j \in L$ $(LS_i \cap LS_j = \phi)) \wedge (LS_1 \cup LS_2 \cup ... \cup LS_n) = LS$, is held, then L is said to be a division of LS.

Definition 8. Let $B = \{ST_1, ST_2, ..., ST_n\}$ be a division of ST, $L = \{LS_1, LS_2, ..., LS_n\}$ be a division of LS, $\forall ST_i \in B$, $LS_i \in L$, if the condition, $\forall T_i \in ST_i$ $(Lr(T_i) \in LS_i)$, is held, then L is said to be a division of LS relating to B, notated by $B \prec L$. Here, $Lr(T_i) \in LS_i$ denotes $Lr(T_i)$ is stored in LS_i.

In TCDCRS, the division of transaction classes requires considering the classification recovery strategy proposed in the following text to guarantee recovery correctness after failures. Therefore, the division of transaction classes suitable for TCDCRS must comply with the corresponding rule.

Rule 1 (transaction classification rule). To guarantee recovery correctness after failures, in TCDCRS, a division $\pi = \{ST_1, ST_2, ..., ST_n\}$ is required to meet the following conditions: $\exists \pi_1 = \{ST_{k1}, ST_{k2}, ..., ST_{kj}\} \subset \pi$ ($DS(\pi_1) \cap DS(\pi - \pi_1) = \phi$), i.e. $\{\pi_1, \pi_2\} \equiv \perp_{division}$, here $\pi_2 = \pi - \pi_1$.

If a division of ST meets rule 1, then it is said to be a qualified division. There exists the following theorem:

Theorem 1. If $\{\pi_1, \pi_2\} \equiv \perp_{division}$, $\{ST_{k1}, ST_{k2}, ..., ST_{kj}\}$ is a division of π_1 and $\{ST_{m1}, ST_{m2}, ..., ST_{mi}\}$ is a division of π_2, then $\{ST_{k1}, ST_{k2}, ..., ST_{kj}, ST_{m1}, ST_{m2}, ..., ST_{mi}\}$ is a qualified division.

Proof: Because of $\{\pi_1, \pi_2\} \equiv \perp_{division}$, according to rule 1, to prove the correctness of theorem 1 we only require proving the correctness of $\{ST_{k1}, ST_{k2}, ..., ST_{kj}, ST_{m1}, ST_{m2}, ..., ST_{mi}\}$ is a division of ST. Since $\{ST_{k1}, ST_{k2}, ..., ST_{kj}\}$ is a division of π_1, $\forall ST_{kp}, ST_{kq} \in \{ST_{k1}, ST_{k2}, ..., ST_{kj}\}(ST_{kp} \cap ST_{kq} = \phi)$ and $ST_{k1} \cup ST_{k2} \cup ... \cup ST_{kj} = \pi_1$. Similarly, because $\{ST_{m1}, ST_{m2}, ..., ST_{mi}\}$ is a division of π_2, $\forall ST_{mp}, ST_{mq} \in \{ST_{m1}, ST_{m2}, ..., ST_{mi}\}(ST_{mp} \cap ST_{mq} = \phi)$ and $ST_{m1} \cup ST_{m2} \cup ... \cup ST_{mi} = \pi_2$. Further, since $\{\pi_1, \pi_2\} \equiv \perp_{division}$, $\pi_1 \cup \pi_2 = ST$ and $\pi_1 \cap \pi_2 = \phi$; thus $ST_{k1} \cup ST_{k2} \cup ... \cup ST_{kj} \cup ST_{m1} \cup ST_{m2} \cup ... \cup ST_{mi} = ST$ and $\forall ST_{kp}, ST_{kq} \in \{ST_{k1}, ST_{k2}, ..., ST_{kj}, ST_{m1}, ST_{m2}, ..., ST_{mi}\}(ST_{kp} \cap ST_{kq} = \phi)$, i.e. $\{ST_{k1}, ST_{k2}, ..., ST_{kj}, ST_{m1}, ST_{m2}, ..., ST_{mi}\}$ is a division of ST. Therefore, $\{ST_{k1}, ST_{k2}, ..., ST_{kj}, ST_{m1}, ST_{m2}, ..., ST_{mi}\}$ is a qualified division.

According to theorem 1, we may easily construct a qualified division by means of the following method. First, we divide ST into two disjoint subsets: $ST_{>p} = \{T_i \mid Pr(T_i) > p, T_i \in ST\}$ and $ST_{<=p} = \{T_i \mid Pr(T_i) \le p, T_i \in ST\}$, where $Pr(T_i)$ denotes the priority of transaction T_i. Obviously, $\{ST_{<=p}, ST_{<=p}\}$ is a division of ST. Then, by means of adjusting the value of p, we guarantee the conditions, $DS(ST_{>p}) \cap DS(ST_{<=p}) = \phi$, is held, i.e. $\{ST_{>p}, ST_{<=p}\} \equiv \perp_{division}$. $DS(ST_{>p})$ accessed by the high priority transaction belonging to $ST_{>p}$ is said to be critical data class, and $DS(ST_{<=p})$ accessed by the low priority transaction belonging to $ST_{<=p}$ is said to be ordinary data class. Further, we divide $ST_{>p}$ into two (or multiple) subsets: $ST_{>p, >f} = \{T_i \mid Fr(T_i) > f, T_i \in ST_{>p}\}$ and $ST_{>p, <=f} = \{T_i \mid Fr(T_i) \le f, T_i \in ST_{>p}\}$, where $Fr(T_i)$ denotes the estimated execution frequency of T_i. Obviously, $\{ST_{>p, >f}, ST_{>p, <=f}\}$ is a division of $ST_{>p}$. Similarly, $ST_{<=p}$ is also divided into two (or multiple) subsets: $ST_{<=p, >f} = \{T_i \mid Fr(T_i) > f, T_i \in ST_{<=p}\}$ and $ST_{<=p, <=f} = \{T_i \mid Fr(T_i) \le f, T_i \in ST_{<=p}\}$. Obviously, $\{ST_{<=p, >f}, ST_{<=p, <=f}\}$ is a division of $ST_{<=p}$. Let $\sigma = \{ST_{>p, >f}, ST_{>p, <=f}, ST_{<=p, >f}, ST_{<=p, <=f}\}$, by means of theorem 1, σ is a qualified division.

3.1.2 Storage Media Organization Based on PERT-NVRAM

Storage media at each site consists of three tiers, i.e. disk storage, nonvolatile RAM and volatile main memory. Local disk resident database (LDDB), which acts as "secondary copy" of database, is stored on disks. Nonvolatile RAM serves as logging storage area and entire logging storage area is divided into four independent partitions (i.e. critical active logging partition, critical dull logging partition, ordinary active logging partition and ordinary dull logging partition, CALP, CDLP, OALP and ODLP for short, respectively) according to the qualified division σ. CALP, CDLP, OALP and ODLP are used for storing the corresponding log records of $ST_{>p,\,>f}$, $ST_{>p,\,\leq f}$, $ST_{\leq p,\,>f}$ and $ST_{\leq p,\,\leq f}$, respectively, i.e. $\{ST_{>p,\,>f}\,,\ ST_{>p,\,\leq f}\,,\ ST_{\leq p,\,>f}\,,\ ST_{\leq p,\,\leq f}\}$ $\prec \{CALP, CDLP, OALP, ODLP\}$. We call CALP and CDLP uniformly as critical logging partition, OALP and ODLP uniformly as ordinary logging partition. Local main memory database (LMDB) is placed in the volatile main memory, which is divided into two partitions, i.e. critical data partition and ordinary data partition which store critical data class and ordinary data class respectively.

3.1.3 The Types and Structure of Real-Time Log Record

In combination with the real-time commit protocol 1PRCP [7], we design five kinds of log record for PERT-NVRAM, namely Begin, Redo, Compensate, Ready and Commit. Figure 1 describes their structures.

Begin	P-TID	TID	B					
Redo	P-TID	TID	D	TS	BN	RID	AI	VTI
Compensate	P-TID	TID	CP	TS	CA			
Ready	P-TID	TID	R					
Commit	P-TID	TID	C	TS				

Fig. 1. Types and structures of real-time log record

In figure 1, P-TID denotes the identifier of a distributed transaction (global transaction) and is defined as follows: P-TID = (Cor-Adrr, SN), where Cor-Adrr stands for the network address of coordinator of the distributed transaction and SN denotes the serial number of the distributed transaction that is exclusive at the coordinator. TID denotes the identifier of a subtransaction of P-TID and is defined as (Adrr, SN), where Adrr stands for the network address of the site at which the subtransaction is executed and SN denotes the exclusive serial number of the subtransation. For a local transaction, P-TID is set as null. "B", "D", "CP", "R" and "C" are used for labeling the log record types of Begin, Redo, Compensate, Ready and Commit, respectively. TS denotes the logic timestamp when the Redo or Compensate or Commit log record are created, and here, we denote the logical timestamp at each site as a sequence number which starts at 0 and is incremented by 1 each time a new Redo or Compensate or Commit log record is written. RID stands for the identifier of the updated data object. BN denotes the logic number of the disk block that is the backup of the data page, which is in LMDB and contains the updated data object. AI denotes the after-image of the updated data object. VTI denotes the validity instant of the temporal data object, namely VTI = ST(X)+VI(X). For persistent data objects, VTI is set as infinite. CA denotes the compensating activity of the control transaction.

3.2 Local Checkpoint Scheme of TCDCRS

In TCDCRS, each site executes the local checkpointing process independently. During local checkpointing process, the updating of LMDB is written out to LDDB, some useless log records are deleted and the corresponding logging store area is freed. In TCDCRS, local checkpoint adopt fuzzy checkpointing schema, which allow the existence of active transaction during checkpointing process. In respect of the triggering mode of checkpoint, we don't adopt periodic triggering based on fixed time interval but deciding whether to trigger the local checkpoint or not according to the utilization rate of the logging storage area R_{LU}. Only if $R_{LU} > \alpha$, local checkpoint is triggered, where α is the threshold of R_{LU}, which can be adjusted dynamically according to the application requirements.

During the local checkpointing process, checkpointing log record is written into checkpointing logging partition, which resides in nonvolatile RAM. Checkpointing log record includes five fields: checkpointing bit field (CKB), critical transaction class recovery start timestamp (CTRST), ordinary transaction class recovery start timestamp (OTRST), checkpointing timestamp (CKT) and updating page field. CKB denotes whether this local checkpoint is completed successfully or not, and 1 stands for successful completion, while 0 represents crash happens during this local checkpointing process. CTRST denotes the minimal timestamp of critical transaction class that requires executing REDO recovery after a crash. OTRST denotes the minimal timestamp of ordinary transaction class that requires executing REDO recovery after a crash. CKT stands for the logic timestamp when this local checkpoint is triggered. Updating page field sets a bit for each page of LMDB to denote updating state of the data page, and 1 denotes the page is updated since last local checkpoint, while 0 denotes the page isn't updated yet. The local checkpointing procedure is described as follows:

Procedure *LocalCheckpoint()*
1: *CKB = 0, CKT = TCounter++;*
2: *Write data pages updated by committed transaction out to LDDB;*
3: *Set updating page field according to the updating state of data page;*
4: *Write the data pages whose updating bits are 1 out to LDDB;*
5: *Delete useless log records, i.e. the log records of aborted transactions or whose timestamp in Commit log records is not larger than CKT, and free the corresponding logging store spaces;*
6: *Get the minimal logging timestamp of critical transaction class, set the value of CTRST;*
7: *Get the minimal logging timestamp of ordinary transaction class, set the value of OTRST;*
8: *CKB = 1;*

In the above description and following recovery algorithm, *TCounter* denotes the counter of logic timestamp, which records the current value of logic timestamp.

3.3 Recovery Processing Based on the Classification Recovery Strategy

During recovery processing after a crash, first, LDDB is loaded into main memory to reconstruct LMDB, and then the recovery subsystem is responsible for restoring LMDB to recent consistent state. In order to improve the system performance, TCDSRS adopts the dynamic recovery method based on the classification recovery strategy. Our classification recovery strategy is based on PERT-NVRAM and its key characteristic is critical data class is first recovered, and then system services are brought back before ordinary data class is recovered. That is, our classification recovery supports the concurrent of system services and the recovery processing of ordinary data class. In combination with the real-time commit protocol 1PRCP, the recovery-processing algorithm based on our classification recovery strategy can guarantee failure atomicity of distributed real-time transactions.

In detail, the recovery-processing algorithm based on classification recovery strategy consists of the following steps:

(1) Reload critical data class into main memory to reconstruct LMDB.
(2) Recover critical data class to consistent state and eliminate the effects caused by uncommitted critical control transaction.
(3) Restore the system services of failure sites.
(4) Reload ordinary data class into LMDB.
(5) Recover ordinary data class to consistent state and eliminate the effects caused by uncommitted ordinary control transaction.

In the above steps, the realization algorithm of step (2) and step (5) is described as follows:

Procedure: CrashRecovery(char dc)
Input: dc denotes data class asking to be recovered, and dc="C" stands for critical data class, while dc="O" stands for ordinary data class.
1: *FT = TCounter;*
2: *if (dc="C") then*
3:   *RST = CTRST; scan critical logging partition (including CALP and CDLP) to look for all Compensate log reords $CPLog_{Ti}$, which satisfy the following conditions: the corresponding Commit log records $CommitLog_{Ti}$ don't exist, i.e. the corresponding transactions don't commit successfully, and the timestamp of $CPLog_{Ti}$ is smaller than FT. At the same time insert these $CPLog_{Ti}$ into compensating activity recovery list (CARL) in the order of their timestamp;*
4: *else*
5:   *RST = OTRST; scan ordinary logging partition (including OALP and ODLP) to look for all Compensate log reords $CPLog_{Ti}$, which satisfy the following conditions: the corresponding Commit log records $CommitLog_{Ti}$ don't exist, i.e. the corresponding transactions don't commit successfully, and the timestamp of $CPLog_{Ti}$ is smaller than FT. At the same time insert these $CPLog_{Ti}$ into CARL in the order of their timestamp;*

6: *Scan reversely CARL until the head of CARL and for each CPLog$_{Ti}$, execute the*
   corresponding compensating activity CPLog$_{Ti}$.CA;
7: **while** *(RST ≤ FT)*
8:   **if** *(dc="C")* **then**
9:     *Scan critical logging partition to look for the Redo log record RedoLog$_{Ti, k}$*
       whose timestamp is RST;
10. **else**
11:    *Scan ordinary logging partition to look for the Redo log record RedoLog$_{Ti, k}$*
       whose timestamp is RST;
12: **if** *(find the Redo log record RedoLog$_{Ti, k}$)* **then**
13:    **if** *(find the corresponding Commit log record CommitLog$_{Ti}$)* **then**
14:      **if** *(RedoLog$_{Ti, k}$.VTI > T$_c$)* **then**
15:        *REDO(RedoLog$_{Ti, k}$)*
16:        *RST ++; continue;*
17:      **else**
18:        *RST++;*
19:        *Triggeer the corresponding sample transaction to update overdue data;*
20:    **if** *(find the corresponding Ready log record ReadyLog$_{Ti}$)* **then**
21:      **if** *(receive Commit message)* **then**
22:        *REDO(RedoLog$_{Ti, k}$);*
23:        *Add CommitLog$_{Ti}$ to the corresponding logging partition;*
24:        *RST++;*
25:      **if** *(receive Abort message)* **then**
26:        *RST++;*
27:    **else**   *RST++;*
28: **else**   *RST++;*
29: **endwhile**

In the above algorithm, $RedoLog_{Ti, k}$ denotes the kth Redo log record of transaction T_i; the procedure, $REDO(RedoLog_{Ti, k})$, realizes the function, which restores the value of the data object whose RID is recorded in $RedoLog_{Ti, k}$ by using its AI (after-image); $RedoLog_{Ti, k}.VTI$ denotes the VTI of $RedoLog_{Ti, k}$; T_c denotes the current instant.

4 Performance Evaluation

The performance of a crash recovery schema is mainly decided by: 1) logging cost in system normal run time and 2) the time of system denying services after crashes. In this section, we first study how logging overheads affect the system run-time performance, and then test how the number of partitions affects the performance of PERT-NVRAM. Last, we evaluate the time of system denying services after a crash.

In our experiments, global main memory database (GMDB) consists of 50000 data pages and these data pages are equally allocated to five sites to form the corresponding LMDBs. Priority-assigning policy adopts Earliest Deadline First (EDF). The main performance metric used for evaluation is the ratio of transactions missing their deadlines, denoted as MDR. MDR is defined as follows: MDR = (Number of transactions missing their deadlines) / (Total number of transaction in the system). Main experiment parameters are presented in Table 1, where U[i, j] denotes a uniformly distributed random variable in the range [i, j].

Table 1. Experiment Parameters

Parameters	Value (unit)	Description
NS	5	Number of site of DRTMMDBS
S_{LMDB}	10000 (Page)	Size of LMDB at each site
R_{CD}	0.4	Ratio of critical data class in total data
R_{TD}	0.8	Ratio of temporal data in total data
NP	4	Number of logging storage partitions
SL	8 (MB)	Size of logging storage area (nonvolatile RAM) at each site
AET	0.4 (ms)	Average execution time per transaction operation
PU	0.4	Probability of a transaction operation to be update operation
Slack	U[2.0, 6.0]	Slack factor
NTO	U[4, 8]	Number of operations contained by a transaction
α	0.8	Threshold of the utilization rate of logging storage area

We compare PERT-NVRAM of TCDCRS with the other three kinds of logging schemes: Non-logging scheme (NLS), partitioned logging scheme based on disk (PLSD), sequential logging scheme base on disk (SLSD). NLS denotes there isn't the cost of transaction logging. Obviously, NLS can't meet the requirement of recovery processing. Here, NLS is regarded as the baseline of performance.

As shown in Figure 2, the experimental results show when arrival ratio of transaction enhances, MDR of all logging schemes increases, while PERT-NVRAM is closest to NLS and has got an distinct advantage over another two kinds of schemes. The number of logging partitions is an important factor, which influences the performance of PERT-NVRAM. Figure 3 shows how the number of logging partitions affects MDR in the case of fixed arrival rate of transaction (40 trans/sec.). As we can see, the system performance improves (i.e. MDR degrades) correspondingly with the increase of the number of logging partitions. However, when the number of logging partitions exceeds 8, further increment of logging partitions has not distinct influence on the performance. This is because the increment of number of logging partitions also causes the increment of recovery processing cost.

The downtime after a crash is another important metric measuring the performance of a recovery scheme. For a DRTMMDBS, The time of system denying services T_{down} mainly includes: 1) the time of loading data into main memory from LSDB, notated by T_1 and 2) the time of restoring LMDB to consistency state, notated by T_2. Due to the use of the classification recovery strategy, critical data class is first loaded and recovered, and then system services are restored before loading ordinary data class, so T_{down} of TCDCRS may be calculated approximately as follows: $T_{down} = T_1 + T_2 \approx S_{LMDB} \times R_{CD} \times T_{I/O} + (SL \times R_{CL} \times \alpha) \div S_{LR} \times T_{rp}$, where $T_{I/O}$ denotes the average time to perform one time disk access; R_{CL} denotes the ratio of critical logging partition in total used logging storage area; S_{LR} denotes the average size of a log record and T_{rp} denotes the average time of processing a log record. Because the ratio of critical data class in total data is usually small, TCDCRS can obviously decrease the downtime.

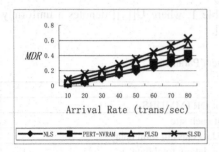
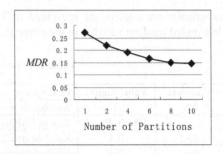

Fig. 2. Comparison of four logging schemes   **Fig. 3.** Influence of number of partitions

5 Conclusion

This paper presents a time-cognizant dynamic crash recovery scheme (TCDCRS) suitable for DRTMMDBSs on the basis of giving the recovery correctness criteria. TCDCRS adopts the real-time logging scheme integrating the characteristics of partitioned logging, ephemeral logging and uses nonvolatile RAM as logging storage area in order to reduce the logging cost as possible during the normal running. After a site crash, a dynamic recovery strategy based on classification recovery idea is adopted to decrease the downtime. Performance tests and evaluations show TCDCRS gets significant advantage over the traditional recovery schemes.

References

1. Sivasankaran, R.M., Stankovic, K., Stankovic, J., et al: Data placement, logging and recovery in real-time active database. In: International Workshop on Active and Real-time Database Systems, Jun. 1995
2. Lam, K.Y., Kuo, T.W.: Real-time database architecture and techniques. The first edition. Boston: Kluwer Academic Publishers, 2001
3. Agrawal, R., Jagadish, H.V.: Recovery algorithms for database machines with non-volatile memory. In Database Machines, Proceedings of Sixth International Workshop IWDM, Jun. 1989
4. Liu, P., Ammann, P., Jajodia, S.: Rewriting histories: Recovering from malicious transactions. Distributed and Parallel Databases, 2000, 8 (1): 7–40
5. Panda, B., Tripathy, S.: Data dependency based logging for defensive information warfare, Proceedings of the 2000 ACM symposium on Applied computing, 2000: 361-365
6. Shu, L.C., Sun, H.M., Kuo, T.W.: Shadowing-based crash recovery schemes for real-time database systems. Proceedings of the 11th Euromicro Conference on Real-time Systems, June 1999: 260-267
7. Xiao ying-yuan Liu yun-sheng, Deng hua-feng, et al: One-phase real-time commitment for distributed real-time transactions. Journal of Huazhong University of Science and Technology (Nature Science Edition), 2006, 34 (3): 1–4 (in Chinese)

An Efficient Fault-Tolerant Digital Signature Scheme Based on the Discrete Logarithm Problem

Iuon-Chang Lin[1] and Chin-Chen Chang[2]

[1] Department of Management Information Systems,
National Chung Hsing University, Taichung, Taiwan
iclin@nchu.edu.tw
[2] Department of Information Engineering and Computer Science,
Feng Chia University, Taichung, Taiwan
ccc@cs.ccu.edu.tw

Abstract. Data security and fault tolerance are two important issues in modern computer communications. This paper addresses the two problems simultaneously by providing an efficient fault-tolerant digital signature scheme. The proposed scheme can be used to verify the authorized sender and check the integrity of transmitted messages. Furthermore, in order to achieve fault tolerance, our scheme is able to detect the errors and then recover from that errors to correct ones by directly using the signature scheme. It does not require any extra mechanism, such as checkpoints, to achieve the property of fault tolerance. In particular, previous schemes have some security flaws while ours does not.

1 Introduction

So far, the techniques of digital signature and fault tolerance are usually developed separately. Most digital signature schemes do not consider the problem of fault tolerance and most fault tolerance methods are designed only for data transmission in a computer network. Therefore, the classical digital signature scheme requires extra mechanism, such as checkpoint, to achieve the property of fault tolerance. The overall overheads of combining the two issues are high.

In order to implement the two issues together to minimize the overall cost, recently, some digital signature schemes with fault tolerance have been proposed [4,7,9]. Xinmei Wang [7], in 1990, first proposed a signature scheme based on error correcting codes. Unfortunately, several literatures [1,6,8] have shown that Xinmei's scheme is insecure. In 1999, Zhang [9] proposed an RSA-based digital signature scheme with fault tolerance. The scheme provides the functions that can simultaneously deal with digital signatures, error detections, and error corrections. The main benefit of this scheme is that the total computational overheads for verifying the signature can be significantly reduced. However, Lee and Tsai [4], in 2003, showed that Zhang's scheme had a security flaw and then

L.T. Yang et al. (Eds.): ATC 2006, LNCS 4158, pp. 601–610, 2006.

proposed an improved version to overcome this security flaw. The improved version has the same advantages of Zhang's scheme. Besides, it is more efficient than Zhang's scheme. However, the scheme still has the same security flaw as Zhang's scheme, that is, a malicious user can easily construct a new message for an existing digital signature. This severely violates the principles of digital signature. A secure digital signature scheme, such as RSA [5] or ElGamal [2], must ensure that a digital signature for a message is computationally infeasible to forge it. Thus, digital signature can prevent the signer from denying that he/she did not sign it before.

In this paper, we shall propose an efficient and secure digital signature scheme with fault tolerance. Our proposed scheme is based on the discrete logarithm problem that is different from previous schemes that are based on error correcting codes and RSA cryptosystem. Our scheme can detect errors and then correct the found errors by using the constructed digital signature directly. It does not need to require any extra mechanism to do that. On the aspect of security, our scheme can fully satisfy the requirements of digital signature and eliminate the security flaws that occur in previous schemes. Therefore, our proposed scheme provides higher security.

2   Related Works

2.1   Overview of Zhang's Scheme

In the typical RSA cryptosystem [5], each user possesses two keys. One is the public key (e, N), and the other is the secret key d, where N is the product of two large primes p and q such that $N = p \times q$, and e and d must satisfy $d = e^{-1} \bmod (p-1)(q-1)$. Consider two users, A and B, will communicate with each other through a network. Let (e_A, N_A) and (e_B, N_B) be the public keys of users A and B, and also let d_A and d_B be their private keys, respectively. Here, $N_A \neq N_B$ and assume that the lengths of N_A and N_B are the same for the sake of simplicity.

Suppose that B wants to send a message M with its corresponding signature to A, and then A will verify the validity of the received message and signature. The following steps are executed by using Zhang's scheme [9].

1. B translates the message M into an $n \times m$ message matrix X, such that

$$X = \begin{bmatrix} x_{11} & x_{12} & \cdots & x_{1m} \\ x_{21} & x_{22} & \cdots & x_{2m} \\ \vdots & \vdots & \ddots & \vdots \\ x_{n1} & x_{n2} & \cdots & x_{nm} \end{bmatrix},$$

where the message block is smaller than N_A and N_B.

2. B constructs an $(n + 1) \times (m + 1)$ matrix X_h from a given $n \times m$ message matrix X, such that

$$
X_h = \begin{bmatrix}
x_{11} & x_{12} & \cdots & x_{1m} & X_1 \\
x_{21} & x_{22} & \cdots & x_{2m} & X_2 \\
\vdots & \vdots & \ddots & \vdots & \vdots \\
x_{n1} & x_{n2} & \cdots & x_{nm} & X_n \\
X^{(1)} & X^{(2)} & \cdots & X^{(m)} & h
\end{bmatrix},
$$

where

$$
X_i = \prod_{j=1}^{m} x_{ij} \bmod N_B, \; for \; i = 1 \; to \; n, \tag{1}
$$

$$
X^{(j)} = \prod_{i=1}^{n} x_{ij} \bmod N_B, \; for \; j = 1 \; to \; m, and \tag{2}
$$

$$
h = \prod_{j=1}^{m} (\prod_{i=1}^{n} x_{ij} \bmod N_B) \bmod N_B. \tag{3}
$$

3. B computes an $(n + 1) \times (m + 1)$ ciphered matrix C_h, such that

$$
C_h = \begin{bmatrix}
c_{11} & c_{12} & \cdots & c_{1m} & C_1 \\
c_{21} & c_{22} & \cdots & c_{2m} & C_2 \\
\vdots & \vdots & \ddots & \vdots & \vdots \\
c_{n1} & c_{n2} & \cdots & c_{nm} & C_n \\
C^{(1)} & C^{(2)} & \cdots & C^{(m)} & h_c
\end{bmatrix},
$$

where $c_{ij} = x_{ij}{}^{e_A} \bmod N_A$, $C_i = X_i{}^{e_A} \bmod N_A$, $C^{(j)} = X^{(j)e_A} \bmod N_A$, $h_c = h^{d_b} \bmod N_B$, for all $1 \le i \le n$ and $1 \le j \le m$.

4. Upon receiving the ciphered matrix C_h, A decrypts the ciphered messages c_{ij}'s and the ciphered check-sums by using A's private key d_A, and then checks the signature h_c by using B's public key e_B. The decrypted matrix X'_h is specified as

$$
X'_h = \begin{bmatrix}
x'_{11} & x'_{12} & \cdots & x'_{1m} & X'_1 \\
x'_{21} & x'_{22} & \cdots & x'_{2m} & X'_2 \\
\vdots & \vdots & \ddots & \vdots & \vdots \\
x'_{n1} & x'_{n2} & \cdots & x'_{nm} & X'_n \\
X^{(1)'} & X^{(2)'} & \cdots & X^{(m)'} & h'
\end{bmatrix},
$$

where $x'_{ij} = c_{ij}{}^{d_A} \bmod N_A$, $X'_i = C_i{}^{d_A} \bmod N_A$, $X^{(j)'} = C^{(j)d_A} \bmod N_A$, and $h' = h_c{}^{e_B} \bmod N_B$.

5. If the following verifications are positive, A will believe that the message was indeed sent by B and it was not be altered.

$$
X'_i = \prod_{j=1}^{m} x'_{ij} \bmod N_B, for \; i = 1 \; to \; n,
$$

$$X^{(j)'} = \prod_{i=1}^{n} x'_{ij} \bmod N_B, \text{ for } j = 1 \text{ to } m, \text{ and}$$

$$h' = (X'_1 \times X'_2 \times \cdots \times X'_n) \bmod N_B$$
$$= (X^{(1)'} \times X^{(2)'} \times \cdots \times X^{(m)'}) \bmod N_B.$$

Otherwise, from the given check-sums, A can detect that there is an error occurring in the decrypted message block x'_{kl} according to the following two equations:

$$X'_k \neq \prod_{j=1}^{m} x'_{kj} \bmod N_B, \text{ and} \tag{4}$$

$$X^{(l)'} \neq \prod_{i=1}^{n} x'_{il} \bmod N_B. \tag{5}$$

After detecting the error, A can correct the error by computing either one of the following equations:

$$x'_{kl} = X'_k \times (\prod_{j=1 \text{ to } m, j \neq l} x'_{kj})^{-1} \bmod N_B, \tag{6}$$

$$x'_{kl} = X^{(l)'} \times (\prod_{i=1 \text{ to } n, i \neq k} x'_{il})^{-1} \bmod N_B. \tag{7}$$

2.2   Overview of Lee and Tsai's Scheme

Recently, Lee and Tsai [4] pointed out that Zhang's scheme had a security flaw, that is, a malicious user can forge a valid signature for the other messages. We specify the security flaw as follows. Suppose that the forged message M^* for the existing signature h_c is

$$X_h^* = \begin{bmatrix} x_{11}^* & x_{12}^* & \cdots & x_{1m}^* & X_1^* \\ x_{21}^* & x_{22}^* & \cdots & x_{2m}^* & X_2^* \\ \vdots & \vdots & \ddots & \vdots & \vdots \\ x_{n1}^* & x_{n2}^* & \cdots & x_{nm}^* & X_n^* \\ X^{(1)*} & X^{(2)*} & \cdots & X^{(m)*} & h_c^* \end{bmatrix},$$

where $x_{11}^*, x_{12}^*, \cdots, x_{nm-1}^*$ are the new message blocks, $x_{nm}^* = (x_{11}^* \times x_{12}^* \times \cdots \times x_{nm-1}^*)^{-1} \times h \bmod N_B$, and $h_c^* = h_c$.

If the following equations hold, the receiver will believe that the signature h_c^* is valid for the message matrix X^*.

$$X_i^* = \prod_{j=1}^{m} x_{ij}^* \bmod N_B, \text{ for } 1 \le i \le n,$$

$$X^{(j)*} = \prod_{i=1}^{n} x_{ij}^* \bmod N_B, \text{ for } 1 \le j \le m, \text{ and}$$

$$h_c^{*e_B} = (X_1^* \times X_2^* \times \cdots \times X_n^*) \bmod N_B$$
$$= (X^{(1)*} \times X^{(2)*} \times \cdots \times X^{(n)*}) \bmod N_B.$$

In order to eliminate the security flaw in Zhang's scheme, Lee and Tsai also proposed an improved scheme [4] based on Zhang's scheme. In the improved version, the matrix X_h with its checksums is expanded as

$$X_h = \begin{bmatrix} x_{11} & x_{12} & \cdots & x_{1m} & X_1 & Y_1 \\ x_{21} & x_{22} & \cdots & x_{2m} & X_2 & Y_2 \\ \vdots & \vdots & \ddots & \vdots & \vdots & \vdots \\ x_{n1} & x_{n2} & \cdots & x_{nm} & X_n & Y_n \\ X^{(1)} & X^{(2)} & \cdots & X^{(m)} & Z_c \\ Y^{(1)} & Y^{(2)} & \cdots & Y^{(m)} \end{bmatrix},$$

where the parameters X_i and $X^{(j)}$ are the same as Zhang's scheme,

$$Y_i = \sum_{j=1}^{m} x_{ij} \bmod N_B, \text{ for } i = 1 \text{ to } n,$$

$$Y^{(j)} = \sum_{i=1}^{n} x_{ij} \bmod N_B, \text{ for } j = 1 \text{ to } m,$$

$$Z_c = (H(Y_1, \cdots, Y_n, Y^{(1)}, \cdots, Y^{(m)}, X_1, \cdots, X_n, X^{(1)}, \cdots, X^{(m)}))^{d_B} \bmod N_B,$$

and $H()$ is a public one-way hash function. Lee and Tsai mentioned that their improved scheme could solve the security flaw of Zhang's scheme. However, in fact, Lee and Tsai's scheme also had a security flaw that a malicious user can masquerade the legal signer to forge another message for the existing signature. For example, suppose that Z_c is a signature for the message matrix

$$X = \begin{bmatrix} a & b & c \\ b & c & a \\ c & a & b \end{bmatrix}.$$

We can find that a malicious user can easily permute the rows or the columns in a message matrix X to generate a different message matrix X', such that

$$X' = \begin{bmatrix} a & c & b \\ c & b & a \\ b & a & c \end{bmatrix},$$

which is corresponding to the same signature Z_c. This makes the digital signature schemes unreliable because a legal signer cannot prove that he/she did not sign the forged message matrix X'.

3   The Digital Signature Scheme with Fault Tolerance Based on the Discrete Logarithm Problem

Our scheme is developed from the concept of meta-ElGamal signature scheme [3] and the concept of Zhang's fault-tolerant signature scheme. In ElGamal digital signature scheme, a system first chooses a large prime p and a generator g, such that $g \in Z_p^*$ with order $p - 1$. Both p and g can be shared among a system of users. To generate a key pair, the signer A first chooses a random number x_A, $x_A \in Z_{p-1}$ and calculates $y_A = g^{x_A} \bmod p$. A keeps x_A secret and publishes y_A. Suppose that the signer Alice will send a message with her signature to the receiver Bob. Alice possesses a secret key x_A and a public key y_A. The proposed scheme can be divided into two procedures:

1. The signature generation procedure,
2. The fault tolerance and signature verification procedure.

The details of the two procedures are described as follows.

3.1   The Signature Generation Procedure

1. Alice first divides the transmitted message M into numerical 3×3 message matrices X_l's, such that

$$X_l = \begin{bmatrix} m_{11} & m_{12} & m_{13} \\ m_{21} & m_{22} & m_{23} \\ m_{31} & m_{32} & m_{33} \end{bmatrix},$$

where m_{ij}, $1 \leq i \leq 3$, $1 \leq j \leq 3$, is a message block and $m_{ij} \in Z_{p-1}$.
2. For each message matrix X_l, Alice calculates its signature and constructs an expand matrix D_l, such that

$$D_l = \begin{bmatrix} m_{11} & m_{12} & m_{13} & r_1 & s_1 & t_1 \\ m_{21} & m_{22} & m_{23} & r_2 & s_2 & t_2 \\ m_{31} & m_{32} & m_{33} & r_3 & s_3 & t_3 \\ r^{(1)} & r^{(2)} & r^{(3)} \\ s^{(1)} & s^{(2)} & s^{(3)} \\ t^{(1)} & t^{(2)} & t^{(3)} \end{bmatrix}.$$

The r_i, s_i, t_i, $r^{(j)}$, $s^{(j)}$, and $t^{(j)}$ can be calculated by using the following equations

$$r_i = g^{k_i} \bmod p, \tag{8}$$

$$t_i = \sum_{j=1}^{3} m_{ij} \bmod p - 1, \tag{9}$$

$$s_i = (H(m_{i1}) \cdot t_i - H(m_{i2}) \cdot x_A \cdot r_i)(H(m_{i3}) \cdot k_i)^{-1} \bmod p - 1, \tag{10}$$

$$r^{(j)} = g^{k_j} \bmod p, \tag{11}$$

$$t^{(j)} = \sum_{i=1}^{3} m_{ij} \bmod p - 1, \tag{12}$$

$$s^{(j)} = (H(m_{1j}) \cdot t^{(j)} - H(m_{2j}) \cdot x_A \cdot r^{(i)})(H(m_{3j}) \cdot k^{(j)})^{-1} \bmod p - 1, \tag{13}$$

where $H()$ is a public one-way hash function.

3.2 The Fault Tolerance and Signature Verification Procedure

1. Bob first detects errors by checking the equations

$$t_i = \sum_{j=1}^{3} m_{ij} \bmod p, \ and$$

$$t^{(j)} = \sum_{i=1}^{3} m_{ij} \bmod p.$$

If there is an error in m_{uv}, $1 \le u, v \le 3$, we must have that $t_u \ne \sum_{j=1}^{3} m_{uj}$ $mod \ p - 1$ and $t^{(v)} \ne \sum_{i=1}^{3} m_{iv} \ mod \ p - 1$. Therefore, the error could be easily detected.

2. After the error is detected in m_{uv}, it may be corrected by using either one of the following two equations

$$m_{uv} = t_u - \sum_{j \ne v} m_{uj} \bmod p, \tag{14}$$

$$m_{uv} = t^{(v)} - \sum_{i \ne u} m_{iv} \bmod p. \tag{15}$$

3. After correcting the errors, Bob has to verify the validity of the recovery and its corresponding signatures by checking whether

$$g^{t_i \cdot H(m_{i1})} = y_A{}^{r_i \cdot H(m_{i2})} \cdot r_i{}^{s_i \cdot H(m_{i3})} \bmod p, \tag{16}$$

$$g^{t^{(j)} \cdot H(m_{1j})} = y_A{}^{r^{(j)} \cdot H(m_{2j})} \cdot r^{(j)}{}^{s^{(j)} \cdot H(m_{3j})} \bmod p, \tag{17}$$

or not. If the above verifications are positive, Bob will believe that the contents of the recovered messages are valid. Otherwise, Bob can choose not to accept the receipted messages.

4 Discussions

4.1 Security Analysis

In this session, we will show that our signature scheme is secure and it does not have the same security flaw as Zhang's and Lee and Tsai's schemes.

Corollary 1: Without the secret key x, it is computational infeasible to derive a signature (r, s, t) for satisfying $g^{t \cdot H(m_1)} \equiv y^{r \cdot H(m_2)} \cdot r^{s \cdot H(m_3)}$ *mod* p, where (r, s, t) is the signature of the messages m_1, m_2, and m_3.

Proof: If the secret key x is known, then the parameter s can be easily gotten by computing $s \equiv (H(m_1) \cdot t - H(m_2) \cdot x \cdot r)(H(m_3) \cdot k)^{-1}$ *mod* $p-1$. Otherwise, we will just try to derive s from the congruence $g^{t \cdot H(m_1)} \equiv y^{r \cdot H(m_2)} \cdot r^{s \cdot H(m_3)}$ *mod* p. Here r and t can be generated arbitrarily, and g and y are publicly known. Therefore, we have that

$$r^{H(m_3) \cdot s} \equiv (g^{H(m_1) \cdot t})(y^{H(m_2) \cdot r})^{-1} \text{ mod } p. \tag{18}$$

Let $G = r^{H(m_3)}$ *mod* p and $D = (g^{H(m_1) \cdot t})(y^{H(m_2) \cdot r})^{-1}$ *mod* p, we can get $G^s \equiv D$ *mod* p from Equation 18. We can clearly find that if we want to derive s, we must compute the discrete logarithm of D to the base G in a finite field p, where p is a large prime. Since currently, there is no efficient method to solve the discrete logarithm problem, it is computational infeasible to derive s if the secret key x is unknown.

Corollary 2: If there is an existing signature (r, s, t) for the messages m_1, m_2, and m_3, it is infeasible to find the different messages $\tilde{m}_1$, $\tilde{m}_2$, $\tilde{m}_3$ whose signatures are the same as the existing signature (r, s, t).

Proof: Since (r, s, t) is the signature for the messages m_1, m_2, and m_3, we have that $H(m_1) \cdot t \equiv x \cdot r \cdot H(m_2) + k \cdot s \cdot H(m_3)$ mod $p - 1$ and $g^{t \cdot H(m_1)} \equiv y^{r \cdot H(m_2)} \cdot r^{s \cdot H(m_3)}$ *mod* p. If there exist three messages $\tilde{m}_1$, $\tilde{m}_2$, and $\tilde{m}_3$ that have the same signature as m_1, m_2, and m_3, such that $t = \tilde{m}_1 + \tilde{m}_2 + \tilde{m}_3$ mod p and $g^{t \cdot H(\tilde{m}_1)} \equiv y^{r \cdot H(\tilde{m}_2)} \cdot r^{s \cdot H(\tilde{m}_3)}$ *mod* p, where $\tilde{m}_1$, $\tilde{m}_2$, and $\tilde{m}_3$ are different from m_1, m_2, and m_3. From the equation $g^{t \cdot H(\tilde{m}_1)} \equiv y^{r \cdot H(\tilde{m}_2)} \cdot r^{s \cdot H(\tilde{m}_3)}$ *mod* p, we can find that if we want to find the three messages $\tilde{m}_1$, $\tilde{m}_2$, and $\tilde{m}_3$, we must solve the discrete logarithms. Therefore, it is difficult to find the three messages $\tilde{m}_1$, $\tilde{m}_2$, and $\tilde{m}_3$, that can satisfy $g^{t \cdot \tilde{m}_1} \equiv y^{r \cdot \tilde{m}_2} r^{s \cdot \tilde{m}_3}$ *mod* p.

4.2   Error Correctable Conditions

In the following, we will discuss the conditions in which an error is able to be corrected by using Equations 14 and 15. According to the step 1 of the

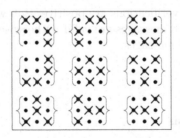

Fig. 1. The correctable conditions when there are four errors simultaneously occurring in a message matrix

fault tolerance and the signature verification procedure, we know that if an error occurs in m_{ij}, we must have that $t_i \neq m_{i1} + m_{i2} + m_{i3} \bmod p$, and $t^{(j)} \neq m_{1j} + m_{2j} + m_{3j} \bmod p$. If the rest of the messages m_{ik}'s, where $k = 1$ to 3 and $k \neq j$, in the ith row are correct, the fault message m_{ij} can be recovered by computing $m_{ij} = t_i - (\sum_{k=1 \ to \ 3, \ k \neq j} m_{ik}) \bmod p$. On the other hand, if the rest of the messages m_{kj}'s, where $k = 1$ to 3 and $k \neq i$, in the jth row are correct, the fault message m_{ij} also can be recovered by computing $m_{ij} = t^{(j)} - (\sum_{k=1 \ to \ 3, \ k \neq i} m_{kj}) \bmod p$.

Therefore, an error is correctable only when no other errors simultaneously occur in the same row i and the same column j. In our scheme, we can correct four errors in a message matrix X at most. Figure 1 illustrates the correctable conditions when four errors simultaneously occur in a message matrix. Therefore, all the four errors can be corrected by using the check-sums in either the row or the column direction.

Moreover, from Figure 1, we can find that some detected errors are not correct. For example, when six checksum equations do not hold, we can not correctly detect the true errors. Therefore, after correcting the errors, we have to verify the validity of recovery by using Equation 20 or 21.

4.3   Performance Evaluation

To simplify the measuring of performance, we assume that the main overhead in the signature generation is to compute the general signature equation $A \equiv x \cdot B + k \cdot C \bmod p - 1$ and the main overhead in the signature verification is to confirm the verification equation $g^A \equiv y^B \cdot r^C \bmod p$. For each 3×3 message matrix, the number of signature equation computations and verification equation computations required in our signature scheme are shown in Table 1. Furthermore, it also illustrates the message extending ration of generated signature to the original message. In our scheme, the generated signature is the same size as

Table 1. The overall overheads of our proposed scheme

Features	Our proposed scheme
# of signature equation computations	6
# of verification equation computations	6
message extending ratio	2

the signed messages, but we need sign each message in both the row and the column directions. Thus, the message extending ration is also 2.

5   Conclusions and Future Work

In this paper, we considered the problem of combining the concepts of digital signature and fault tolerance. Different from previous approaches, we presented a signature scheme with fault tolerance based on the problem of solving the discrete logarithm in a finite field. The capability of correcting the number of errors in our proposed scheme is four at most for each 3×3 message matrix. This scheme provides fault tolerance only when the errors occur in error correctable conditions. How to provide fault tolerance when an error occurs in the signature part is our future work.

References

1. M. Alabbadi and S. B. Wicker, "Security of Xinmei digital signature scheme," *Electronic Letters*, vol. 28, no. 9, pp. 890–891, 1992.
2. T. ElGamal, "A public-key cryptosystem and a signature scheme based on discrete logarithms," *IEEE Transactions on Information Theory*, vol. 31, no. 4, pp. 469–472, 1985.
3. P Horster, M. Michels, and H. Petersen, "Meta-message recovery and meta-blind signature schemes based on the discrete logarithm problem and their applications," *Lecture Notes in Computer Science-Advance in Cryptology: AsiaCrypt'94*, vol. 917, pp. 224–237, 1995.
4. N.Y. Lee and W.L. Tsai, "Efficient fault-tolerant scheme based on the RSA system," *IEE Proceedings-Computers & Digital Techniques*, vol. 150, no. 1, pp. 17–20, 2003.
5. R.L. Rivest, A.Shamir, and L.M. Adleman, "A method for obtaining digital signatures and public-key cryptosystems," *Communications of the ACM*, vol. 21, no. 2, pp. 120–126, Feb. 1978.
6. H. van Tilborg, "Cryptanalysis of the Xinmei digital signature scheme," *Electronic Letters*, vol. 28, no. 20, pp. 1935–1938, 1992.
7. W. Xinmei, "Digital signature scheme based on error-correcting codes," *Electronic Letters*, vol. 26, no. 13, pp. 898–899, 1990.
8. S. B. Xu, J. M. Doumen, and H. van Tilborg, "On the security of digital signature schemes based on error-correcting codes," *Designs, Codes and Cryptography*, vol. 28, no. 2, pp. 187–199, May 2003.
9. C.N. Zhang, "Integrated approach for fault tolerance and digital signature in RSA," *IEE Proceedings-Computers & Digital Techniques*, vol. 146, no. 3, pp. 151–159, 1999.

Author Index

Lecture Notes in Computer Science

For information about Vols. 1–4053

please contact your bookseller or Springer

Vol. 4098: F. Pfenning (Ed.), Term Rewriting and Applications. XIII, 415 pages. 2006.

Vol. 4097: X. Zhou, O. Sokolsky, L. Yan, E.-S. Jung, Z. Shao, Y. Mu, D.C. Lee, D. Kim, Y.-S. Jeong, C.-Z. Xu (Eds.), Emerging Directions in Embedded and Ubiquitous Computing. XXVII, 1034 pages. 2006.

Vol. 4096: E. Sha, S.-K. Han, C.-Z. Xu, M.H. Kim, L.T. Yang, B. Xiao (Eds.), Embedded and Ubiquitous Computing. XXIV, 1170 pages. 2006.

Vol. 4095: S. Nolfi, G. Baldassare, R. Calabretta, D. Marocco, D. Parisi, J.C. T. Hallam, O. Miglino, J.-A. Meyer (Eds.), From Animals to Animats 9. XV, 869 pages. 2006. (Sublibrary LNAI).

Vol. 4094: O. H. Ibarra, H.-C. Yen (Eds.), Implementation and Application of Automata. XIII, 291 pages. 2006.

Vol. 4093: X. Li, O.R. Zaïane, Z. Li (Eds.), Advanced Data Mining and Applications. XXI, 1110 pages. 2006. (Sublibrary LNAI).

Vol. 4092: J. Lang, F. Lin, J. Wang (Eds.), Knowledge Science, Engineering and Management. XV, 664 pages. 2006. (Sublibrary LNAI).

Vol. 4091: G.-Z. Yang, T. Jiang, D. Shen, L. Gu, J. Yang (Eds.), Medical Imaging and Augmented Reality. XIII, 399 pages. 2006.

Vol. 4090: S. Spaccapietra, K. Aberer, P. Cudré-Mauroux (Eds.), Journal on Data Semantics VI. XI, 211 pages. 2006.

Vol. 4089: W. Löwe, M. Südholt (Eds.), Software Composition. X, 339 pages. 2006.

Vol. 4088: Z.-Z. Shi, R. Sadananda (Eds.), Agent Computing and Multi-Agent Systems. XVII, 827 pages. 2006. (Sublibrary LNAI).

Vol. 4087: F. Schwenker, S. Marinai (Eds.), Artificial Neural Networks in Pattern Recognition. IX, 299 pages. 2006. (Sublibrary LNAI).

Vol. 4085: J. Misra, T. Nipkow, E. Sekerinski (Eds.), FM 2006: Formal Methods. XV, 620 pages. 2006.

Vol. 4084: M.A. Wimmer, H.J. Scholl, Å. Grönlund, K.V. Andersen (Eds.), Electronic Government. XV, 353 pages. 2006.

Vol. 4083: S. Fischer-Hübner, S. Furnell, C. Lambrinoudakis (Eds.), Trust and Privacy in Digital Business. XIII, 243 pages. 2006.

Vol. 4082: K. Bauknecht, B. Pröll, H. Werthner (Eds.), E-Commerce and Web Technologies. XIII, 243 pages. 2006.

Vol. 4081: A. M. Tjoa, J. Trujillo (Eds.), Data Warehousing and Knowledge Discovery. XVII, 578 pages. 2006.

Vol. 4080: S. Bressan, J. Küng, R. Wagner (Eds.), Database and Expert Systems Applications. XXI, 959 pages. 2006.

Vol. 4079: S. Etalle, M. Truszczyński (Eds.), Logic Programming. XIV, 474 pages. 2006.

Vol. 4077: M.-S. Kim, K. Shimada (Eds.), Geometric Modeling and Processing - GMP 2006. XVI, 696 pages. 2006.

Vol. 4076: F. Hess, S. Pauli, M. Pohst (Eds.), Algorithmic Number Theory. X, 599 pages. 2006.

Vol. 4075: U. Leser, F. Naumann, B. Eckman (Eds.), Data Integration in the Life Sciences. XI, 298 pages. 2006. (Sublibrary LNBI).

Vol. 4074: M. Burmester, A. Yasinsac (Eds.), Secure Mobile Ad-hoc Networks and Sensors. X, 193 pages. 2006.

Vol. 4073: A. Butz, B. Fisher, A. Krüger, P. Olivier (Eds.), Smart Graphics. XI, 263 pages. 2006.

Vol. 4072: M. Harders, G. Székely (Eds.), Biomedical Simulation. XI, 216 pages. 2006.

Vol. 4071: H. Sundaram, M. Naphade, J.R. Smith, Y. Rui (Eds.), Image and Video Retrieval. XII, 547 pages. 2006.

Vol. 4070: C. Priami, X. Hu, Y. Pan, T.Y. Lin (Eds.), Transactions on Computational Systems Biology V. IX, 129 pages. 2006. (Sublibrary LNBI).

Vol. 4069: F.J. Perales, R.B. Fisher (Eds.), Articulated Motion and Deformable Objects. XV, 526 pages. 2006.

Vol. 4068: H. Schärfe, P. Hitzler, P. Øhrstrøm (Eds.), Conceptual Structures: Inspiration and Application. XI, 455 pages. 2006. (Sublibrary LNAI).

Vol. 4067: D. Thomas (Ed.), ECOOP 2006 – Object-Oriented Programming. XIV, 527 pages. 2006.

Vol. 4066: A. Rensink, J. Warmer (Eds.), Model Driven Architecture – Foundations and Applications. XII, 392 pages. 2006.

Vol. 4065: P. Perner (Ed.), Advances in Data Mining. XI, 592 pages. 2006. (Sublibrary LNAI).

Vol. 4064: R. Büschkes, P. Laskov (Eds.), Detection of Intrusions and Malware & Vulnerability Assessment. X, 195 pages. 2006.

Vol. 4063: I. Gorton, G.T. Heineman, I. Crnkovic, H.W. Schmidt, J.A. Stafford, C.A. Szyperski, K. Wallnau (Eds.), Component-Based Software Engineering. XI, 394 pages. 2006.

Vol. 4062: G. Wang, J.F. Peters, A. Skowron, Y. Yao (Eds.), Rough Sets and Knowledge Technology. XX, 810 pages. 2006. (Sublibrary LNAI).

Vol. 4061: K. Miesenberger, J. Klaus, W. Zagler, A.I. Karshmer (Eds.), Computers Helping People with Special Needs. XXIX, 1356 pages. 2006.

Vol. 4060: K. Futatsugi, J.-P. Jouannaud, J. Meseguer (Eds.), Algebra, Meaning, and Computation. XXXVIII, 643 pages. 2006.

Vol. 4059: L. Arge, R. Freivalds (Eds.), Algorithm Theory – SWAT 2006. XII, 436 pages. 2006.

Vol. 4058: L.M. Batten, R. Safavi-Naini (Eds.), Information Security and Privacy. XII, 446 pages. 2006.

Vol. 4057: J.P.W. Pluim, B. Likar, F.A. Gerritsen (Eds.), Biomedical Image Registration. XII, 324 pages. 2006.

Vol. 4056: P. Flocchini, L. Gąsieniec (Eds.), Structural Information and Communication Complexity. X, 357 pages. 2006.

Vol. 4055: J. Lee, J. Shim, S.-g. Lee, C. Bussler, S. Shim (Eds.), Data Engineering Issues in E-Commerce and Services. IX, 290 pages. 2006.

Vol. 4054: A. Horváth, M. Telek (Eds.), Formal Methods and Stochastic Models for Performance Evaluation. VIII, 239 pages. 2006.